FREDERICK
THE GREAT

FREDERICK THE GREAT

King of Prussia

DAVID FRASER

FROMM INTERNATIONAL
NEW YORK

First Fromm International Edition, 2001

Copyright © 2000 David Fraser

Library of Congress Cataloging-in-Publication Data is available.

ISBN 0-88064-261-0

Manufactured in the United States of America.

Contents

CONTENTS

List of Illustrations

List of Maps

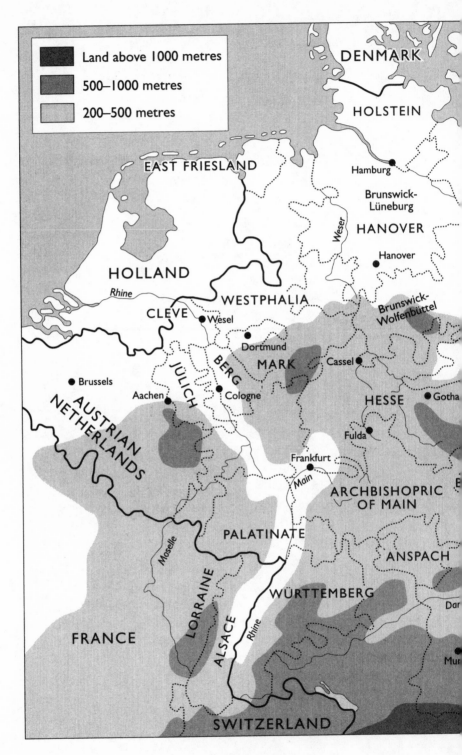

The Empire

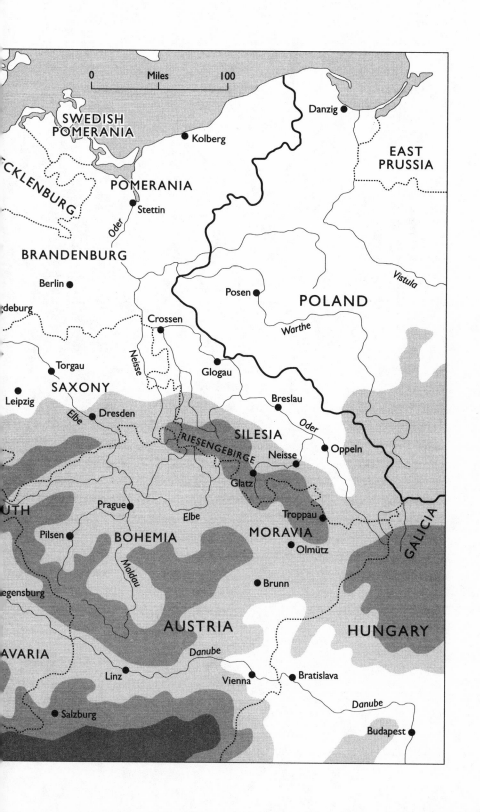

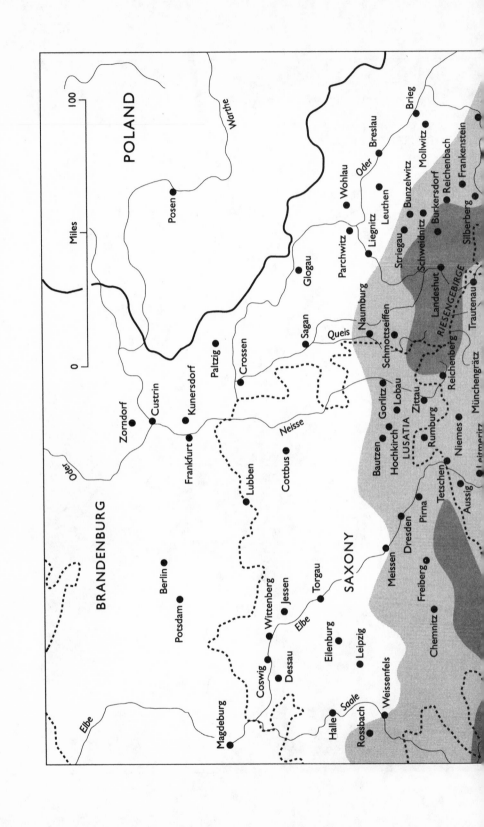

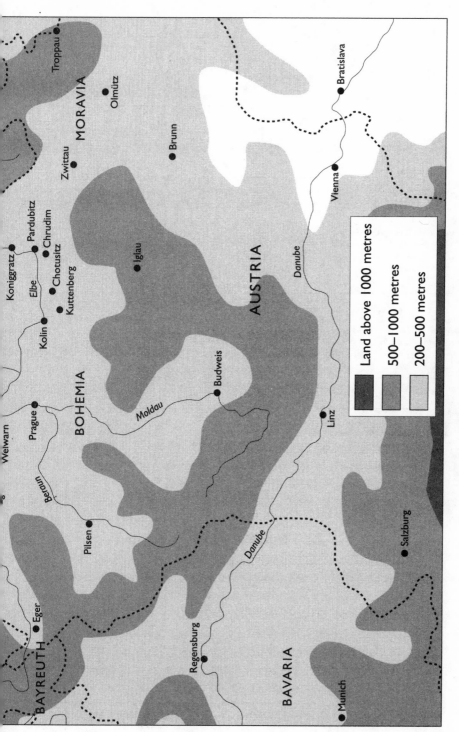

Area of Campaign

Ernst, Duke of Brunswick–Lüneburg (d. 1546)

Henry, Duke of Dannenberg (d. 1598)

Augustus

Anton Ulrich, Duke of Brunswick-Wolfenbüttel (d. 1714)

Ferdinand Albert, Duke of Brunswick-Bevern (d. 1687)

August Wilhelm (d. 1731)

Ludwig (d. 1735)

Elisabeth Christina m. Emperor Charles VI

Charlotte m. Tsarevich Alexis

Antoinette m. Frederick Albert, Duke of Brunswick-Bevern (succeeded to Wolfenbüttel)

Ernst Ferdinand, Duke of Bevern

Maria Theresa, Empress Queen m. Francis of Lorraine, later Emperor Francis I

Emperor Joseph

August Wilhelm, Duke of Bevern (Prussian Field Marshal)

Karl Wilhelm m. Charlotte of Prussia

Anton Ulrich m. Princess of Mecklenburg

Elisabeth Christina m. Frederick, Crown Prince, later King of Prussia

Ferdinand (Prussian Field Marshal)

Frederick Franz (k. 1758 at Hochkirch)

Louise m. August Wilhelm, Prince of Prussia

Albrecht (k. 1745 at Soor)

Juliana Maria m. Frederick, King of Denmark (second wife)

Karl Wilhelm (k. 1806 at Auerstadt) m. Augusta of Wales

Sophie Caroline m. Frederick of Bayreuth

Henry

Wilhelm (d. on campaign in Russian service)

Leopold

Elisabeth m. Frederick William of Prussia (divorced 1769)

Karl m. Frederica of Orange

George

Augustus

Augusta m. Frederick, Duke of Württemberg

Frederick William (k. 1815 at Quatre Bras)

Caroline m. George, Prince of Wales, later George IV of Great Britain

Wilhelmina, Margravine of Bayreuth

Frederick II, King of Prussia m. Elisabeth Christina of Brunswick

Frederica Louise, Margravine of Ansbach

Charlotte m. Karl Wilhelm of Brunswick-Wolfenbüttel

Sophia, Margravine of Brandenburg-Schwedt

Christian m. Margrave of Ansbach

Dorothea m. Frederick Eugen, Duke of Württemberg

Elisabeth Louise m. Ferdinand of Prussia

Philippa m. Frederick of Hesse-Cassel

Frederick m. (1) Augusta of Brunswick & (2) Charlotte of Wales

Ludwig

Eugen

Sophia m. Grand Duke Paul of Russia, later Tsar

Wilhelm

Ferdinand

The House of Brunswick

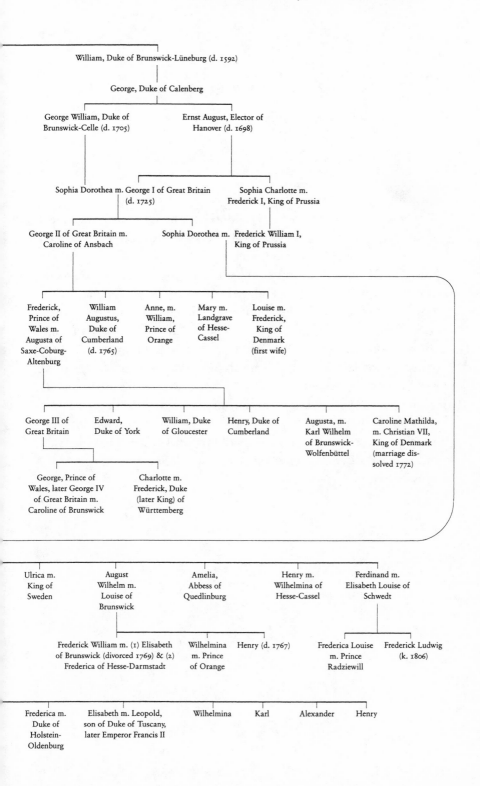

William, Duke of Brunswick-Lüneburg (d. 1592)

George, Duke of Calenberg

George William, Duke of Brunswick-Celle (d. 1705)

Ernst August, Elector of Hanover (d. 1698)

Sophia Dorothea m. George I of Great Britain (d. 1725)

Sophia Charlotte m. Frederick I, King of Prussia

George II of Great Britain m. Caroline of Ansbach

Sophia Dorothea m. Frederick William I, King of Prussia

Frederick, Prince of Wales m. Augusta of Saxe-Coburg-Altenburg

William Augustus, Duke of Cumberland (d. 1765)

Anne, m. William, Prince of Orange

Mary m. Landgrave of Hesse-Cassel

Louise m. Frederick, King of Denmark (first wife)

George III of Great Britain

Edward, Duke of York

William, Duke of Gloucester

Henry, Duke of Cumberland

Augusta, m. Karl Wilhelm of Brunswick-Wolfenbüttel

Caroline Mathilda, m. Christian VII, King of Denmark (marriage dissolved 1772)

George, Prince of Wales, later George IV of Great Britain m. Caroline of Brunswick

Charlotte m. Frederick, Duke (later King) of Württemberg

Ulrica m. King of Sweden

August Wilhelm m. Louise of Brunswick

Amelia, Abbess of Quedlinburg

Henry m. Wilhelmina of Hesse-Cassel

Ferdinand m. Elisabeth Louise of Schwedt

Frederick William m. (1) Elisabeth of Brunswick (divorced 1769) & (2) Frederica of Hesse-Darmstadt

Wilhelmina m. Prince of Orange

Henry (d. 1767)

Frederica Louise m. Prince Radziewill

Frederick Ludwig (k. 1806)

Frederica m. Duke of Holstein-Oldenburg

Elisabeth m. Leopold, son of Duke of Tuscany, later Emperor Francis II

Wilhelmina

Karl

Alexander

Henry

Acknowledgements

This book would not have been produced without the encouragement of my friend Stuart Proffitt, first at Messrs HarperCollins and later at Penguin Books. I am also grateful for the advice and expertise of Professor Dr Werner Knopp, Professor Piers Mackesy, Major-General Rex Whitworth and Prince Philipp of Württemberg. The maps were drawn by the Cartographic Unit of Southampton University under the direction of Mr Tim Aspden, whose skill and understanding I much appreciate. As always the staff of the London Library have been patient, knowledgeable and helpful. My wife has transposed to the word processor numerous editions, somehow interpreting my handwriting, shrewdly spotting inconsistencies and commenting vigorously both on the book and on its subject; as well as accompanying and driving me over many of the scenes of Frederick's life in Brandenburg and Saxony. My debt to her is beyond calculation.

PART I
1712-40

I

Education of a Prince

History has sometimes recorded a man or woman born to high position and responsibilities who happened also to be blessed with outstanding and appropriate personal qualities. Such coincidence was, in a more respectful age, generally regarded as natural – genetically probable and indicating, at the least, some sort of divine endorsement of hereditary arrangements. The mood of more recent times tends rather to cynicism – to look with as much disbelief as the evidence can bear on those whose talents and character allegedly matched their rank. The achievements were probably the doing of subordinates, we say; the doing of those whose place had been earned by performance (under whatever system) rather than derived from birth and blood. Or, we suggest with scepticism, the record may be sycophantic: wrong.

Yet there once lived a prince, an eldest son inheriting from a father, whose attributes of mind and taste were recognized throughout civilized Europe and beyond as placing him in a high rank among those now called intellectuals; a prince whose artistic sensibility and love of both music and literature coloured all stages of his eventful life; who composed and wrote with rare elegance; whose wit and intelligence were renowned. To these qualities and talents the same prince added an extraordinary and self-denying sense of duty, so that his entire life was devoted to the service of his people, particularly the poorest of them, working twice as hard and twice the hours of easier men, planning, writing, appraising, calculating for the common good. His actions were, beyond dispute, his own. His dedication was universally acknowledged, even by those who found fault with aspects of his policy; while his lack of ostentation – his selflessness and frugality – were a byword. He thought of himself, without affectation,

3

as a servant, owing to his subjects an example and a life of scrupulous probity. He had inherited – and wholly approved – a system of autocracy; but he regarded his authority entirely as a trust for his people.

In the arts of government he showed remarkable ability, carefully assessing the characteristics of his own and other peoples, investigating political economy and practising it, studying law and jurisprudence with an eye to far-reaching reforms (which he carried out) and always mindful of the condition of his treasury, a prime concern to him at all times, whether in peace or war; he remarked early that a ruler can do little unless his policy is underpinned by a robust and prosperous nation. He loved justice and was determined that it should be available to all, without fear or favour. He wished, he said, to be remembered as 'Le Roi des gueux', the king of the beggars.

Towards the opinions of all men he was sometimes mocking but almost invariably tolerant. In an age when bloody wars of religion were, at best, a recent memory he eloquently condemned prejudice and persecution. He spent a good deal of his time in philosophical exchanges with the best minds of his day, on the great questions of life and death, good and evil, freedom and compulsion, which agitated the intellects of Europe. Foreign affairs absorbed him; and in his dealings with other rulers he was as diplomatically adroit as he was witty and courteous so that even those resentful of his actions conceded his skilful mastery of international business.

Nor was this the most of it. He lived in an era when the heroic age of warrior princes had almost passed; but he, the last European of his kind, personally exercised in war after war the supreme military command he had inherited; and exercised it with such skill and won with his sword such renown that he was famous throughout the world by the age of thirty-three, and lived a further forty years acclaimed as the greatest soldier of his time. Despite his extensive gifts in and preference for the arts of peace, it was for war that he made such a singular mark on his country's history – a country which he found vulnerable and relatively insignificant in the European community but which he left formidable and, for a little while, secure.

Such a prince seemed – was – an extraordinary phenomenon, one to be remarked with dazzled admiration not only by his compatriots but by all, of any nation, who relished human talents and achievements. Yet Frederick II, King of Prussia, dedicated ruler, artistic patron, man of letters, lawgiver and commander, has more often than not been execrated as a villain who broke his word, was indifferent to human suffering and plunged Europe unnecessarily into war. One particular act at the beginning of his reign – one for which justifications could at least be argued, and one with plenty of precedents and subsequent examples – has been treated as marked by most particular infamy, 'an act of the blackest treachery'[1] surpassing or erasing all the brilliant and benevolent achievements of his kingship. Certainly he had many faults as well as extraordinary virtues; and certainly, like all positive characters, he did not lack critics in his own time – 'He is the completest tyrant God ever made for the scourge of an offending people,' wrote one British diplomat,[2] who served for only a few months as ambassador in Berlin, was violently prejudiced against the King and barely knew him. But posterity, especially although not only foreign posterity, has also often been harsh. 'A bad man with a bad heart,' Thomas Mann wrote in 1914,[3] and he has been described as possessing no principles,[4] as 'mischievous and dangerous, without moral code',[5] as a monster of callousness and duplicity. The paragon – and undoubtedly he was a paragon to many – has come to arouse in others not admiration and awe but fierce condemnation. The philosopher-prince has been turned into a brute.

To an extent, and inevitably, this derives from the course of history since Frederick's time, although opinion has not always followed national divisions. Frederick died in 1786, and for another century people beyond the borders of Prussia could and sometimes did look at the record of the great King with the sort of objective but not unmixed admiration bestowed on Alexander of Macedon, Julius Caesar, Charlemagne, Charles XII of Sweden – warrior leaders in their time, moulders of societies, makers of myth. There were always dissentients. Dr Johnson, surprisingly, misinterpreted Frederick's character and got most of his facts wrong in a piece written while the King was still alive. Macaulay, in a Whiggish denunciation, attributed to him virtually sole responsibility for the world-wide ferocities of the Seven Years War,[6] including those in India and North America between the adherents of Britain and France; while on the other side

Carlyle[7] indulged on his behalf some of his sonorous and fiercely Protestant tyrannophilia. But it was, ultimately, the tide of world events which had most effect on popular opinion, in opposite directions. After 1866, when Prussia took the leading place in a united and powerful Germany which became the German Empire four years later – a concept at variance with Frederick's own ideas and ambitions – it was inevitable that Frederick's achievements and character would be scrutinized in the prejudicial context of an increasingly divided Europe, and of three great wars associated with the name of Germany. The last two of these created such widespread misery, cruelty and suffering (not least for Frederick's own beloved Prussia) that Frederick and his legacy have been regarded by many as begetters of a malign virus.

This prejudice – which, at its most extreme, regards Frederick as some sort of spiritual progenitor of Adolf Hitler – is ignorant at essential points. Frederick was a man of the Enlightenment. He was as cultivated a ruler as ever came to power. His dearest ambitions were artistic and academic. Because he made himself the first soldier of his age he has appeared to some to betray the world of the mind and its sensibilities by the ferocity with which he embraced that of action; but this, too, is prejudice. Frederick went to war when he believed it necessitated by his duty to Prussia; and brought to it the same high and serious qualities he brought to every activity. Prejudice has too often clouded perceptions of one of the most extraordinary men ever to sit on a throne or command an army; one, furthermore, who came to manhood in frightful circumstances, circumstances which would plead for understanding had he subsequently become a criminal, a degenerate or a lunatic rather than, as happened, a genius.

Because his mother was a princess of Hanover, a daughter of George I, Elector of Hanover and King of England, there ran in Frederick's veins the blood of many of the royal houses of northern Europe as well as of Germany – Plantagenet, Tudor, Stuart, Orange-Nassau. In the male line, however, he was Hohenzollern.

The family of Hohenzollern descends from Frederick, Count of Zollern in Württemberg, southern Germany, who ruled from about 1145. Count Frederick, son and grandson of earlier Fredericks, a loyal supporter of the elected Hohenstaufen Emperor, married the daughter of the Burgrave of Nuremberg, whom he ultimately succeeded in right of his wife in about 1190. A later Frederick, after various complexities of descent and subdivisions of inheritance, became Margrave of Brandenburg* in 1411, disposing of his rights in Nuremberg. Thenceforth this branch of the Hohenzollerns would be identified with Brandenburg, whose ruler had already for two centuries been one of the Electors of the Emperor – German King and nominal suzerain of all or almost all the German lands.

The dignity of the Elector of Brandenburg, by a specific and (at the time) unusual provision, passed entire, in each generation, to the Elector's eldest son. The boundaries of the Electorate changed frequently with the vicissitudes of inheritance, warfare and debt. By the mid seventeenth century, when the Elector Frederick William, who would be known as 'The Great Elector', succeeded his father, his domains included Brandenburg itself (extending from the 'Old Mark' west of the middle Elbe to the 'New Mark' east of the lower Oder), the duchy of Cleve-Jülich on the Lower Rhine, the counties of Mark and Ravensburg in Westphalia, and the province of East Prussia. To these Eastern Pomerania was added soon afterwards.

Germany in the seventeenth century was ravaged by the wars which followed the Reformation. By the Peace of Augsburg in 1555 each German prince had decided the religion to be adopted in his realm. The Electors of Brandenburg had embraced Lutheran doctrines in the mid sixteenth century and had welcomed Huguenot and other refugees, many of whose descendants played distinguished parts in Prussian history. The Great Elector managed, however, to preserve neutrality in the final years of the Thirty Years War and to obtain the withdrawal of the Swedes (the great Protestant champion, Gustavus Adolphus of Sweden, had been his uncle) from most of his territory. By his dexterous conduct of international affairs and by the loyalty his wise rule and prudent financial management attracted domestically, the Great

---

* 'Margrave', originally a Margraf, or Count responsible for one of the marches or frontiers of Empire, was by this time a Sovereign Prince of the Empire – often with subordinate Margravates in his gift. Bayreuth and Ansbach were both, in origin, within the gift of the Margrave of Brandenburg; and both – also to be closely connected to Frederick through marriage to his sisters – were Hohenzollern.

Elector – our prince's great-grandfather – transformed the destiny of Brandenburg. He also reorganized the army of the Electorate, and made Brandenburg, small as it was, a significant military power. As a glorious denouement he drove the Swedes (who, as allies of Louis XIV of France, had returned to invade Pomerania) from his domains by the resounding victory of Fehrbellin in 1675.

Brandenburg, in political rather than geographic terms, soon became 'Prussia'. The duchy of Prussia – in recent times the province of East Prussia, itself earlier outside the Empire – was raised, with the Emperor's consent, into a kingdom in 1701, a kingdom which comprehended all the various lands, held under whatever title, of the Electors of Brandenburg in whom the kingly rank was vested. Degree and dignity mattered much in the curious republic of princes which the Empire represented and the precedence – including family precedence – which accompanied kingship was prized. The first king 'in' Prussia was Frederick I (Elector Frederick III of Brandenburg), son of the Great Elector. By the time of his inheritance Prussia, although small, was the most militarily formidable Protestant power in Germany. It was, however, a power whose territories were widely scattered, difficult to administer and to defend.

The son of Frederick I inherited from his father in 1713. This was Frederick William I of Prussia, born in 1688, a violent-tempered autocrat, in the words of his son 'a terrible man but a just man'. In one sense he was indeed a just man. He was an utterly honest and painstaking administrator. He lived a life of stern simplicity. He introduced in Prussia ideals of universal education and of universal obligation of service to the state. He was ruthless in the severity with which he handled the somewhat independent provincial nobility, in order to make them loyal servants of the crown. His financial arrangements were far-sighted and wise. A narrow and upright Calvinist rather than a Lutheran (although he rejected the Calvinist doctrine of predestination), his beliefs were rooted in the Old Testament and he, as much as any of his predecessors or successors, enforced a regime of absolute probity in the state's servants. The 'Prussian' ideals, at their best – discipline, frugality, integrity – owe much to Frederick William.

His love and chief concern was his army, and he set on Prussia the stamp of what would later be called militarism which came to be more associated with her than all the admirable principles which the King also inculcated. His youth had been passed amid tales of the savage battles, the marches, counter-marches and sieges of the War of Spanish Succession. He had been present in the Imperial forces at the battle of Malplaquet, Marlborough's and Eugen's bloody victory over the French in 1709, and the battle probably greatly affected the mind of the young Prince of Prussia, aged twenty-one. The casualties on both sides had been horrific – France lost over 12,000 men that day, while Marlborough and Eugen recorded casualties of 24,000 although they had won the fight. Such casualties on a European battlefield would not be seen again until Borodino nearly a century later: the dead, mutilated, stripped, lay thick on the ground for days. Frederick William lived his life as an enthusiast for military matters and was utterly convinced of their importance but he was certainly no enthusiast for war. Nor was he wholly a Philistine. He was fond of painting and found it therapeutic – like his son he suffered from gout. He loved music and did much to promote it, being particularly devoted to the works of Handel (he preferred wind instruments to others) and surprisingly indifferent to Telemann.[8]

But Frederick William was determined that Prussia, if it were to be secure, must have an army of outstanding quality. He thought his heritage vulnerable and reckoned that peace could only be assured by strength. Prussia might be relatively insignificant but its army must be excellently disciplined and drilled, a formidable nut to crack for any enemy seeking to take advantage of its small population and scattered territories. The army must be well-rooted in the population – Frederick William instituted a cantonal system for recruitment, so that each of his regiments had its recruiting district (the districts differed widely in size) and its responsibilities for registration, for maintaining lists of young men, organizing the periodic enrolments, recording the extensive rolls of exemptions for skilled artisans and so forth. Only about half of any registration were actually called up and after initial training the 'cantonist' served two months in the year with the colours, and went home for the balance, always liable to recall in emergency. For much of a peacetime year, therefore, the cost of a man's subsistence did not fall to the state. It was essential to leave sufficient able-bodied men to work the land, apart from those exempted, what a later age would call 'reserved occupations'; and the cantonal system could work to the disadvantage of the farming community, as when, for instance, the annual spring manoeuvres coincided with sheep-shearing.

Duration of service was elastic. The 'cantonists' were mixed in the ranks of the infantry* with longer-service regulars – a large minority – recruited from many different lands beside Prussia, men who, for whatever reason, preferred the idea of military service to life at home. But the system meant that each regiment had an immediate connection with a particular district and the soldiers – even if the individual's connection with that district was adoptive rather than bred – gained strength from family feeling, from local as well as general loyalty; while the King's government, by this system, decentralized much of the business of census and records on a military basis.

Frederick William shifted the seat of royal business from Berlin to the royal residence and private cabinet in Potsdam. He maintained a large military establishment for so small and basically poor a country as Prussia. When he died he bequeathed to his son an army of 90,000 men, some 4 per cent of the population, a vast proportion compared to other states. But he had always taken great trouble with the financial and administrative arrangements which should underpin the army in peace or in emergency, and his son realized what he owed to his father's management and in particular to the cantonal and regimental system. The realization would come to be rooted in long experience of war. '*Les cantons,*' Frederick wrote in 1768 when the army had been tested in years of campaigning, '*donnent de l'émulation à qui sera le plus brave et des amis ou parents qui combattent ensemble ne s'abandonnent pas facilement.*'†

Frederick William wrote, personally, the 'General Directory' for war, what might in today's terms be called the War Book, the exact measures demanded in emergency. He had inherited a kingdom still in essence feudal, a predominantly agricultural economy based on

---

* The cavalry were all-regular.

† Who will seem the most brave? Friends and relations who fight together don't lightly let each other down.

serfdom, the tying of the peasant to the land, with inherited obligations and restrictions; and to a marked extent he reformed its character, so that he left behind him something not unlike a modern, unitary state, served by a small bureaucracy of integrity and by an army second to none.

His approach to military matters, however, was that of a drill-sergeant rather than a commander-in-chief. He cared passionately for the appearance and regularity in close-order drill of his soldiers, but the care – admirable if measured – became obsessive. He formed a special Guards regiment of particularly tall men, sometimes bought or kidnapped from abroad if their dimensions made it desirable; all were over six foot ten inches, and some over eight foot. He loved the disciplines and atmosphere of the parade ground. He applied the same regularity to the recruitment and organization of his officer corps. The nobility – a large class, including all with relationships to the landowning or official élites – were to be the source of officers, and the King personally selected from the list of eligibles in each generation those who should be enrolled in the Cadet Corps in Berlin. The army was thus so closely identified not only with the crown but also with the nobility that it was reckoned in 1724 that hardly a noble family existed in Prussia without at least one son in the army; and so it remained. The King demanded from Prussian officers an absolute obedience and personal loyalty, but among themselves there was complete social as opposed to military equality. They formed a closed society, a caste.

Frederick William, therefore, worked with dedication to build the institutions of the state, according to his lights. In one sphere, however, he – 'a terrible man but a just man' – was more terrible than just. He was a dreadful parent.

He married, very young, Sophia Dorothea of Hanover, a daughter of that Elector of Hanover who became King George I of England and of that unhappy princess – his wife and first cousin, another Sophia Dorothea – whom George (himself brutal and unfaithful) discovered in a liaison with Count Königsmarck and, in revenge, kept imprisoned for thirty-two years until her death. Frederick William's wife bore him twelve children of whom Frederick, born in 1712 and baptized Karl Friedrich on 31 January of that year, was the eldest surviving son, two having died in infancy. Sophia Dorothea was an ambitious, cultivated woman, well-read and sophisticated. She had little in common with the tastes of her husband and she loved her eldest son; and he her. To the house of Hanover the Prussian court was rough and touched with barbarity.

Frederick William also loved his eldest son after his fashion – he took delight in him when he was very young, and had high hopes of his 'little Fritz'. But his fashion of love became terrible indeed.

The Europe into which Frederick was born had suffered from war through much of the preceding 100 years. In 1713 the Peace of Utrecht had marked the end of the War of Spanish Succession, a war in which the ambitions of the King of France had been decisively countered by allied forces, British and Dutch, serving under the Duke of Marlborough; and by the troops of the Empire led by Prince Eugen of Savoy. The Peace made a number of adjustments to the political map of Europe* but in spite of this war's cost in blood and treasure it did not radically alter the continental situation.

In the north Sweden was still suffering the wounds and scars of the 'Great Northern War' waged by the legendary Charles XII, a war at the end of which Sweden, once so dominant, would have lost most of its Baltic provinces to Russia. Internally divided and with a muddled constitutional settlement, Sweden would long be pulled between factions friendly to Russia or to France. She received from Denmark, however, in 1720 the province of Vorpommern–Pomerania west of the Oder; and thus had a foothold in Prussia.

In the west France remained by far the largest, the most populous and the most powerful unitary state. When Frederick was three years old the French King, Louis XIV, died. Splendid though many of his achievements had been, he left a kingdom plagued by unreformed and unpopular financial and administrative institutions, in appearance formidable but with a consequential canker at the heart. Culturally, however, France was pre-eminent. The court and manners of its Bourbon kings were imitated – on a smaller scale and often at crippling expense – by minor princes in many realms. It has been said of

---

* Incidentally separating the principality of Orange from Prussian authority. For his first year of life the infant Frederick was 'Prince of Orange'.

that time that all Europe thought in French, and the flowering of philosophy, literature and the arts which marked the reigns of Louis and his successor set the pace for much of European intellectual progress and artistic creation; and when Louis died this intellectual progress became strikingly more adventurous as the social and political immobility of the *ancien régime* was increasingly challenged in the aftermath of the Sun King's reign.

Beyond the Channel Britain, recently united as a kingdom, was perceived as a maritime power primarily interested in commerce and the accumulation of wealth, involved in continental affairs in time of war by periodic expeditions and, above all, by subsidies; but concerned to limit liability, yet also to dispute the power of France (a nation four times as populous) as in the recent war. This was materially to change in the coming decades. Britain would compete with France for maritime and commercial – and colonial – primacy on distant continents and oceans but, by the accession of the Elector of Hanover to the British throne in 1714, would also acquire a direct interest in the affairs of northern Germany, an interest which was often a tendentious factor in British politics, where British ministers and their supporters were frequently suspicious of any policy or expenditure which could seem to place on British taxpayers the onus for defending a German possession of a German-born sovereign. Also developing, however, was a strong and influential English philosophic tradition, with effects on many, particularly in northern Europe.

In the south-east of Europe the Ottoman Empire had been driven back into the Balkans in the 1680s by the campaigns of Prince Eugen. In the east Tsar Peter the Great had come to the throne in 1689, would reign until 1725 and was engaged in ruthlessly imposing some sort of modernizing revolution from above on the primitive savageries of Russia, inaugurating something like a western system of adminis-tration, importing more experts, including military experts, from abroad (there were a good many already in Russia), building a navy, creating a brilliant new capital; himself ceaselessly studying and learn-ing. Peter's chief concerns in foreign affairs – he was at war for a large part of his reign – were with the Swedes and the Turks. As for central Europe beyond his western borders, he believed strongly in maintaining an alliance with Austria. With the Empire.

But this Empire – the great central power in Europe, the Holy Roman Empire, the German Empire, as variously described according to epoch and context* – was a peculiar institution; and in a curious condition.

The Empire represented a noble idea, a historic aspiration, the secular unity of central European Christendom. In practice, even before being sundered by the Reformation, the Empire in Germany had always been a loose – generally a very loose – federation of principalities, each of which was more or less the personal fief of a ruling family, affected – like any estate – by the vicissitudes of marriage, financial dealing and inheritance. The concept of the nation-state, in the sense which became normal in the century which followed the French Revolution, did not exist. No map can do more than indicate the centres of gravity of principal patrimonies – like great estates but with outlying and separated farms – added to which were the 'free cities' of the Empire with statutory privileges, and the ecclesiastical principalities, inheritors of a medieval civilization where bishops and abbots had lay authority now surviving the Reformation. Frederick's sister was Abbess of Quedlinburg: the Duke of York was Bishop of Osnabrück. The Empire was a patchwork of territories whose rulers often had very different status, rights and dignities in different parts of their own domains – here Elector, here Imperial vassal, here king, and in some areas episcopal superior, where the Elector was a bishop. Regional traditions and sentiments, however, were strong – tribal, familial, cultural, local. People felt themselves to be Austrians, Saxons, Prussians, Bavarians.

Most also, however, felt themselves to be Germans: subjects of 'the Empire', subjects of this huge, amorphous conglomerate which for centuries had stood as some sort of unifying symbol for the numerous and widespread German peoples, dissimilar from each other though these were. The Empire was a changing and imprecise geographic unity but it represented – and thus the Emperor represented – the central European power balancing France in the west, as well as the defensive shield of Christendom against Islam in the east. As symbol of an aspiration – an earlier aspiration to Christian unity, a later

* Or, as best of all worlds, sometimes the 'Holy Roman Empire of the German Nation'.

aspiration to German unity – the Empire still existed. Its boundaries, at the time of Frederick's birth, lay in the north on the Baltic (except for the Swedish enclave) and the North Sea, only excluding the Dutch republics of the United Provinces: in the west on the Rhine, except where the 'Austrian Netherlands' extended the Empire to the English Channel; in the south and south-east on the Alps, and in the east on the Oder. The recently concluded war had been largely settled by the victories of the Empire, ally of Britain: and by the Imperial Prince Eugen.

The Empire as such, however, was now little more than a symbol – and an archaic symbol. Power in it was inevitably diffused, and as a player on the European stage it represented a shifting alliance rather than a polity, and was thus weak as an institution. Certain more or less ceremonial powers were in theory reserved to the Emperor. Lip service was paid. When Brandenburg-Prussia, for instance, was made into a kingdom in 1701 it was with the Emperor's assent: there was no other competent power and none was desired. But as more than a symbol – as an actual polity – the Empire had for so long been a loose and disunited confederation of independent princes that its coherence and effectiveness barely existed. There had been little real Imperial authority in Germany since the days of the Hohenstaufen Frederick Barbarossa in the mid twelfth century. For an organization to be strong, especially in the field of international policy, there has to be internal discipline and power of decision-making, binding on all parts. In the Empire there was little or none.

This incoherence had been fearfully demonstrated by the Thirty Years War which, although it had ended over sixty years before Frederick's birth, had marked the mind of every German. A war of religion between Catholic and Protestant princes, fought with merciless savagery, it had broadened to assume a dynastic rather than confessional character – had, indeed, largely lost its original motivation, however lamentable – and had seen the Catholic Bourbons of France (assisted in this by the Protestant Sweden of Gustavus Adolphus) ranged against the Catholic Habsburgs and those who followed them. The war had ended with the Peace of Westphalia in 1648, a peace of compromise and exhaustion. By it France had obtained Alsace. The Empire had lost territory to both France and Sweden but had bought a somewhat tenuous internal tranquillity, at least from religious turmoil, as the principle of *'cujus regio, ejus religio'* – that a man's domicile determined his religion in accordance with the principles of the Peace of Augsburg – was reaffirmed. The German states of the Empire, even more than before, felt and were regarded as independent of each other in every sense that mattered. Their rulers, although members of the Imperial Assembly, the 'Diet' at Frankfurt, were recognized as independent sovereigns, able to conclude treaties, and make war and peace. They had, however, suffered during that war the penalties of division as well as of weakness. French and Swedish armies had often marched across Germany without effective opposition. The Turks had taken advantage of European turmoil and by the end of the war had stood at the gates of Vienna.

Between the Peace of Westphalia and the birth of Frederick much had changed. The Turks had been driven back by the victories of Eugen. The War of Spanish Succession had deflated the ambitions of France. But within Germany, the Empire – despite recent successes in campaigns fought in its name – was as much a political fiction as it had been for centuries. It was not now united by religion, and in some cases the ruler held to a different religion from most of his subjects: Germany was a patchwork of opposing confessions, and even some of the historic episcopal dignities and abbacies had suffered a change of faith in the Thirty Years War. The Empire was not united by perception of a common enemy – the Electors of Cologne and Bavaria had taken the part of France in the recent war. It was not united by loyalty to a particular ruling house since the Imperial crown, at least in theory, was elective.

But in this last lay a considerable rub. The Habsburgs, Dukes of Austria, had occupied the Imperial throne since 1438, giving the Empire a continuity which was, or should have been, in welcome contrast to the chaos which had followed the end of the Hohenstaufen period. The rise of Habsburg power had been among the most striking developments of the sixteenth century; Austria was a large but not uniquely large territory in southern Germany. Yet there were periodic grumblings among the German princes at Habsburg attempts, as they saw it, to treat the Empire as if it were a hereditary kingdom, a Habsburg fief. On the contrary, they argued, it was an association of independent sovereigns, joined by general assent and electing a superior, with their independence (certainly since 1648) recognized as a legitimate fact of international life.

The Habsburgs may frequently have derived theoretic authority from their position as emperors but their actual power, like that of other princes, came from the extent of their lands, from their family inheritances, from the wealth in their treasury, from the number of subjects they could command. And in this there was an anomaly. A large part of the Habsburg possessions – increasingly, albeit inexactly, described as 'Austrian' possessions – lay beyond the boundaries of the Empire. Of these the largest and most significant was the kingdom of Hungary. Other parts of the Empire lay outside Germany altogether – the War of Spanish Succession had been ended at the Treaty of Utrecht by resignation of claims by the Habsburgs to the Spanish throne, and in return the Emperor had received – for the Empire – the 'Austrian' Netherlands; while Lombardy, Naples (the kingdom of the southern part of mainland Italy) and Sardinia had also been added. The Empire was not coterminous with Germany: it was not – although some wished it to be – a 'Greater German Reich' united by blood. Nor was it a unitary Habsburg possession. A Habsburg Emperor had resources – and commitments – far beyond Germany; and to German princes minded to regard the Empire as a proper focus for German loyalty it sometimes appeared that it was little more than an append-age, a grace-note, to the major theme of the inheritance of the house of Habsburg. The wide interests of the Habsburgs, particularly after the acquisition of Hungary and the extended involvement south-eastward along the Danube, became increasingly alien to what most German princes regarded as the interest of Germany, defined as the German lands of the Empire, the heartland.

As the eighteenth century passed this appearance would be increas-ingly offensive to the rulers of Prussia. Frederick William's instinct was one of loyalty to the Emperor, an instinct of near-feudal subordi-nation, to be *Kaisertreu*: but this instinct was at odds with the increas-ing sense of a state's identity – ultimately nationalism, an unknown concept – which the modern age was bringing in. Throughout Fred-erick's life the dominant issue, expressed in real rather than theoretic terms, would be whether Austria or Prussia should be the dominant power within Germany. It could be, and often was, given a theoretical dimension – any prince of the Empire at odds with Vienna was apt to proclaim himself a champion of the 'true' identity and ancient traditions of the Empire itself and Frederick was no exception, often with some justification. But the real issue was, in essence, a struggle between two states and two families. It would not be resolved for another century and a half. It had been looming ever since the time of the Great Elector, and it was to some extent divorced from the religious issue which had also polarized these two very dissimilar states. Austria, despite the far-flung and unconnected territories of its rulers and the multi-faith nature of their inhabitants, was southern, Catholic, Habsburg. Prussia was northern, in the main Protestant, Hohenzollern. The rivalry between the two might often be cloaked in the obscurities of the Imperial constitution and history but it was, in reality, primitive and direct.

The ambiguities between the role of Habsburg as elected Emperor (if he was) and Habsburg as inheritor of huge family possessions, both within and beyond the Empire, were at their sharpest if succession were or might be in dispute. In 1713, the year after Frederick's birth, the Emperor Charles VI, a weak and not very intelligent man who had succeeded his brother in 1711, was deeply concerned about the future of his possessions and composed a family document known as the Pragmatic Sanction. Charles had one daughter, Maria Theresa, and no son. The daughter was excluded from the succession to Austria by current interpretation of the ancient usages known as Salic Law; but the Sanction provided that she should, in default of a male heir, inherit all the Habsburg possessions whether within or beyond the Empire.

As well as contravening the Emperor's own father's wishes (he had expressly willed the Habsburg possessions, in default of a male heir, first to the daughters of his elder son, Joseph, whom Charles had succeeded), this questionable arrangement incidentally broke an entail. Joseph's two daughters had married; great care was taken in their marriage contracts to ensure that their claims were snuffed out, and they renounced them. Nevertheless for the Pragmatic Sanction to stand without forcible challenge it was necessary to seek wide international agreement. It was naturally argued that such a family deed might apply to family possessions but could not be regarded as effective in respect of territories which were the Emperor's only by election; and the identity of who was to wear the crown in Vienna and Budapest – and assert sovereignty on a very wide basis – was not a purely domestic matter.

The atmosphere, however, in the immediate aftermath of a long and expensive war, was favourable to the reaching of an accommodation. Charles VI, proceeding with offers of a number of '*douceurs*', obtained agreement from France (with a suggestion of reversion to France under certain circumstances of the duchy of Lorraine); from Britain (with an undertaking to suppress an East Indian trading company, the Ostend Company, which might compete with British interests in the east); from others. From the German princes of the Empire Charles, over a period, received pledges.

From Frederick William of Prussia he obtained endorsement of the Pragmatic Sanction with an important proviso. This was that the Emperor should look favourably on Hohenzollern claims to four particular duchies in Silesia. These duchies had been transferred by the Great Elector of Brandenburg to the Empire in return for the cession of different territory elsewhere; and this latter cession had been annulled by the then Emperor in the time of the Great Elector's son, Frederick I, in exchange for an Imperial promise of support in a distinct but family matter. In Prussian eyes the claims to the Silesian duchies were good – the terms of their transfer had been breached by Vienna, albeit with King Frederick I's feeble assent.* There was also, for Charles in dealing with Frederick William, a dispute over the territories of Jülich and Berg (capital, Düsseldorf) in the Rhineland in which the Emperor's good will for Prussian claims was sought, promised and later withdrawn. This breach of faith (as it appeared to Berlin) was exacerbated in 1737 when the Emperor, despite Prussian

---

* The disputes over the Silesian duchies went back even further, and, like many European territorial issues, were made for lawyers. One of the duchies – Liegnitz – had been conditionally willed by its Duke to the Electors of Brandenburg in 1537. This arrangement had been annulled in 1546 by Ferdinand I, Archduke of Austria and brother of Emperor Charles V, acting under what authority is unclear. Liegnitz, in 1675, over a century after these transactions, passed into Habsburg possession despite protests made at the time by the Great Elector.

claims, agreed that ultimate possession of these two Rhineland duchies could be subject to mediation.

Charles VI, however, was determined on the Pragmatic Sanction and somehow convinced himself that he had received the requisite international support. The process of negotiation and bargaining took many years. Of the German princes Bavaria and the Palatinate were never persuaded (the Elector of Bavaria had married one of Joseph's daughters, Charles VI's niece). Many others remained sceptical. Prince Eugen, who lived until 1736, was told by the Emperor that the rights of his daughter, Maria Theresa, would be guaranteed by the powers of Europe; the great soldier observed that the only guarantee worth having was an army of 200,000 men.

In Brandenburg Frederick William wished for a son who would be an image of himself. He had hoped for a boy, and then a young man, who would immerse himself in wholly practical matters and particularly the army; one who would in time give him friendship, brotherhood, comradeship, as he rather pathetically expressed it. He wished for a son who would wear the uniform of a Prussian officer with pride, one who would share his father's enthusiasm for hunting* and for boisterous masculine company; one who would, above all, eschew the sort of literary and intellectual tastes and refinements popularly associated with France. The King's ideas for the Crown Prince's education were, therefore, narrow and rigid. They were also extremely stupid. Frederick was, for instance, forbidden to learn Latin, as being dangerously impractical.

Any feminine influence on Frederick's upbringing ceased when he was seven. He had been in the care of a Huguenot governess, Madame de Rocoulles, who had also been governess to his father, and who was under the supervision of a senior lady-in-waiting to the Queen, Frau von Kameke. Thereafter for much of the year he was sent, as a child, to the lonely castle of Wüsterhausen a few miles south of Berlin with two senior officers, the sixty-five-year-old General Finck von Finckenstein and the younger, Swedish, Colonel Kalkstein,[9] as guar-

---

* In January 1729 Frederick William and his party killed over 3,000 wild boar in Pomerania and Brandenburg.

dians, discharging the strict and unimaginative orders of the King in a routine confined to prayer, Bible study, physical exercise, formal lessons in German, and eating within an exactly prescribed timetable drafted by Frederick William.

Frederick William then discovered that he had bred a young man who seemed at all points the opposite of himself, and the opposite of what, in his view, the throne of Prussia needed. The young Frederick, despite prohibitions, learned Latin secretly – and all the more enthusiastically, although never proficient. He showed, when not forced to conceal, a passion for literature and the arts. He wrote with taste, delicacy and increasingly elegant skill; and like most of cultured Europe at that time, he wrote and evidently thought in French. He wrote poetry prolifically although seldom with memorable felicity. He never spoke or wrote German with fluency or style and showed his distaste for the language. He detested hunting – 'to kill for pleasure is odious,' he wrote. He grew his curled hair long and dressed as exotically as possible. He loved music, composed and played the flute – well. Within the rigid constraints of his court life he managed, as he grew a little older, to incur debts. He seemed to go out of his way to infuriate his father. His personality as well as his tastes seemed to Frederick William perverse and inappropriate in one destined to rule Prussia.

Frederick William was not difficult to infuriate. He is thought to have suffered from porphyria and was in constant pain. He exploded into terrible violence, throwing plates at his wife, children and household officers at the slightest provocation. He beat his children savagely and often. The atmosphere at the Prussian court was one of fear, ferocity and hysteria. The King could be driven into paroxysms of rage by even a hint of rebellion or disobedience, and the non-conforming disposition of his eldest son was such as to take him to or over the brink of sanity and self-control. He was, too, suspicious of his son's morals, fearful that he might lapse into irreligion, watchful and unreasonable as Frederick grew up.

There was a formal visit by father and son to Dresden for four weeks in 1728, when Frederick was sixteen. Their host was the Elector of Saxony, Augustus 'the Strong'* of the ancient house of Wettin, a

* Also, at intervals, King of Poland.

prince of notoriously vigorous sexual habits whose wife, a Hohenzollern, had left him and had died in the year before the Prussian royal
visit. Frederick had never experienced anything like the liveliness and
extravagance of the Saxon court and wrote of it to his beloved sister,
Wilhelmina, in ecstatic terms. The effect of so brilliant a court with
its devotion to beauty and enjoyment was overwhelming, and made
an indelible mark on his aesthetic sensibilities. It also, perhaps, bred
a certain envious revulsion, in retrospect, at the extravagance he
witnessed and contributed to the sharpness of his comments on Saxony
and the Saxons which continued through much of his life. The effect
of Dresden may, therefore, have been mixed but he had never known
sheer enjoyment before, and was delighted when Augustus paid a
return visit to Berlin soon afterwards.

Then Frederick William learned that Augustus's mistress, the
delicious Countess Orczelska (who was also his illegitimate daughter),* had caught the eye of the sixteen-year-old Crown Prince of
Prussia and the hint of immorality, spiced with an incestuous connection, appalled him. Furthermore the little Orczelska also came to
Berlin on the return visit. Augustus may or may not have welcomed
this liaison (if it happened) but he probably, during the Dresden visit,
introduced the young Prince to at least one other and to the possible
delights of women. Back at Potsdam, when Frederick William heard
rumours about his son and the daughter of a music teacher he had
the girl, Dorothea Ritter, publicly whipped through the streets, in
front of both the town hall and her father's house, and then imprisoned
with a sentence of hard labour for life in Spandau. It is likely that her
only offence was to play the harpsichord for the Prince.† A new tutor,
Lieutenant-Colonel von Rochow, was appointed for the Crown Prince,
charged particularly to keep him from 'effeminate, lascivious, or
feminine occupations'.

Frederick William, therefore, was a devout Protestant, a disagree-

---

* Her son became Prince of Holstein – both son and grandson of Augustus. Orczelska,
daughter of Augustus by a French milliner in Warsaw, had been introduced to his
immediate circle by her lover, another son of Augustus and thus her half-brother!
Ultimately she married Holstein.
† It is agreeable to tell that when Frederick came to the throne he at once gave a pension
to the unfortunate girl.

able Puritan, a bullying tyrant and a most conscientious King. To all but his father Frederick was an attractive youth of middle height – he stood five feet, five inches – with a most intelligent face, brilliant dark-blue eyes, a musical voice on which everyone commented throughout life, an exceptionally sharp mind and a ready wit. 'He has,' wrote the French Ambassador, the Marquis de Valory, 'fine blue eyes, a little too prominent, which reflect his feelings and differ greatly according to circumstances.' A critic in this century has written of him that 'he loved no one and no one loved him'.[10] It was not true. When some companion, a tutor in his youth perhaps, could share a taste, respond to an enthusiasm, Frederick gave and received warm affection. Kindness aroused gratitude, and so it remained. He continued to write in later years, no longer suffering tyranny, to the few gentle spirits who had warmed his often frozen youth. There was Michael Fredersdorff, four years his senior and son of a state musician who joined the Crown Prince in 1739 as his senior valet, his *Erste Kammerdiener*, a tall, handsome man who became his wholly trusted man of business, 'one of the six friends I love best', as he wrote in 1741 before his first battle – his letters to Fredersdorff, examples of his execrable German, show the '*Kammerdiener*' responsible for virtually all personal administration.[11] There was his tutor, Duhan de Jandun, a small, dark-eyed Huguenot pastor whose father had been secretary to the Great Elector, and before that to the mighty Turenne – 'Adieu, dear Duhan [Duhan was dying], believe me, I love you with my whole heart'; Duhan had been sent into exile by Frederick William at a dark moment in the Crown Prince's life but he was always close to Frederick in spirit and affection. There was Charles-Etienne Jordan, another Huguenot who became Frederick's literary factotum – 'My quiet M. Jordan, my good, my benign, my peaceable, my most humane Jordan.' 'Do not grieve me by being ill,' he wrote to Jordan some years later in life, in 1746, when Jordan, too, was dying, 'Adieu, love me a little, try to comfort me by getting well,' and Frederick, now a great king, visited the dying man and stayed for an hour alone as often as he could.[12] Jordan was a man of culture and of principle who would frankly criticize if he did not admire; and 'It is not the King I love in him but the man,' he wrote. 'It is his qualities of mind and heart that attach me to him inviolably.' These letters, these reactions, do not indicate one without human feeling and the capacity for love.

It is also true that Frederick, throughout life, could show a distressingly heartless side when he formed a poor opinion of a man or woman. When a young brother-in-law, of whom he thought little, was killed in one of his battles he referred to it on the following day, in a letter to Fredersdorff, without the slightest delicacy: 'no great loss'. His lack of any attempt to pretend to a grief he did not feel could seem distressing. It was one part of the man. The other part was full of heart.

To Frederick William, however, Frederick's character was aberrant and his whole conduct an act of defiance. He had only to see his eldest son when an adolescent to lose his temper alarmingly. He thought Frederick cunning and opaque – 'What goes on in that head?' he would roar. Every subject, and especially every child of his, owed him absolute obedience and now his heir seemed a rebel. He greatly preferred his next son, August Wilhelm, his favourite. He yelled abuse at the Crown Prince before the whole court. He thrashed him freely in public with the cane he always carried and often used, including on one occasion in the presence of huge crowds assembled for a parade in honour of the Elector of Saxony at Mulberg in June 1730. He dragged him by the hair through the mud. He exposed him to ridicule on the military parades they attended together. He made clear his disgust with the future King of Prussia, and when Frederick pleaded for some understanding his father wrote to him that he was not prepared to tolerate an 'effeminate creature, with no manly inclinations',[13] who could neither ride nor shoot, was uncleanly in his person and wore his hair long.

Thus it seemed to Frederick William, ignorant of the fact that he was addressing a son who would spend longer in the saddle amidst shot and shell than any other German sovereign, and certainly than his father. But nobody could cross the King or challenge his rigid prejudices and it was unsurprising that at a certain point this persecution and the uncongenial atmosphere of the Prussian court drove Frederick to think of escape; to think of it, indeed, from about the time of the visit to Saxony in 1728 when he was sixteen. Frederick William watched the detail of everything. A prince brought up to fill every minute of every day with exercises and studies under the King's direct or indirect supervision was a prisoner and the only way to leave prison often appeared to be actual flight. There might, however, be another solution – a complete change of circumstances, an early marriage.

Frederick's mother, Queen Sophia Dorothea, was deeply ambitious for a project which became known as 'the English marriage', under which her eldest daughter, Wilhelmina, should be betrothed to her nephew, the heir of England, Frederick, son of the Prince of Wales, the future George II. The Queen first mooted the idea when her daughter was only fourteen, but more serious approaches were made two years later, in 1725. And there was a second and companion idea – that the Crown Prince of Prussia would at the same time be betrothed to the Princess Amelia of England, second daughter of the future George II. The 'English marriage' had become the 'double marriage'.[14] For a while the project lay dormant.

Then the King of England, George I, died in 1727 and Sophia Dorothea's ambitions revived. She was encouraged by her husband to write, tentatively, to her sister-in-law, the new Queen of England, Caroline of Ansbach. She was disappointed by the cool reception her ideas were apparently receiving in London, but she recognized that politics would complicate matrimonial plans. She took every opportunity, however, to promote her ideas and something of a 'Hanoverian party' formed at the Prussian court.

Frederick William (who loved his wife but who undoubtedly ruled the roost) was uncertain about these projects. Initially in favour of them, he was aware that the court of Vienna would probably look with disfavour on such a close association of Prussia with Hanover and England. He hoped that he would get renewed Imperial assistance in the Prussian claims on Jülich and Berg: and he was left in no doubt by his minister, the Pomeranian Count Grumbkow, that if he wished to please the Emperor Frederick William would not seek to marry his son to an English princess – or his daughter to the (now) Prince of Wales. An Imperial envoy, Field Marshal Baron von Seckendorff, had appeared at the Prussian court clearly briefed to work against the English marriage. Seckendorff was an old comrade-in-arms of Frederick William. Grumbkow was receiving payments from Vienna, where they hoped for an agreement (on a separate subject) with Berlin. These two, working together, soon obtained a considerable influence over the mind of Frederick William.

Nevertheless Frederick William wished not only to please the Emperor but – periodically – his own wife. Aware that the marriage projects were being discussed in London as well as (with disapproval) in Vienna, he told Sophia Dorothea to write to her brother of England and Hanover, George II, and ask for a firm proposal – or the reverse: for a yes or a no. It was autumn 1728 and on 28 December that year Frederick William, having received what he regarded as an equivocal response from London, concluded a treaty with Vienna. He was further irritated by certain border disputes with Hanover, and by a quarrel over the conduct of a recruiting party which at one moment almost threatened military operations between the two Electorates. He next ordered Sophia Dorothea to send something of an ultimatum to the Queen of England – the family transaction was being conducted between consorts – and this was sent on 1 February 1730.

During the past year young Frederick had built some hopes on the English marriage. He had seen and liked a portrait of the Princess Amelia and had covertly exchanged messages with her. He had recognized that another wild idea of his to escape by marriage – a proposal for the hand of the Archduchess Maria Theresa, heiress of Austria – would get nowhere. He loved his mother and respected her ambitions – both for himself and for his sister.

There was no explicit written response to Sophia Dorothea's 'ultimatum' but at the beginning of April 1730, a British envoy, Sir Charles Hotham, arrived in Berlin. Hotham, who had accepted the task with reluctance, had now been instructed to press for the 'double marriage'. As an additional, and somewhat peculiar, proposal the Princess Amelia, if she married the Crown Prince of Prussia, might be made George II's Viceroy of Hanover. Hotham's brief was to seek both marriages or none. He was also instructed to try to bring Frederick William back into a short-lived (and improbable) 'League of Hanover' between Britain, Prussia and France. His first audience with Frederick William was on 4 April.

Frederick William was perplexed. He thought that he had already agreed (although certainly not formally) to one marriage – Wilhelmina's. He knew very well that the betrothal of his heir to a daughter of England would displease Vienna, which he was anxious not to do. He was suspicious of people, especially people close to the Queen or to Hanover, who might seek to form a Crown Prince's party at court, potentially hostile to the sovereign. He said that Frederick was too young; Hotham reiterated his instructions – both marriages or none; and Frederick William said – and may have sincerely believed – that he was being pressed unreasonably and that Wilhelmina's betrothal had already been accepted. At a further audience in early July Hotham conceded a good deal. London would agree to the betrothal of the Prince of Wales to Wilhelmina if a date – even a distant date – could be agreed for the betrothal to the Princess Amelia of the Crown Prince of Prussia.

Frederick William reckoned he was being slighted – treated as if a supplicant. He said again that the Crown Prince was too young. Whenever he had tried to get straight answers from London earlier about these betrothals there had been equivocations; he had, for instance, been told that the British Parliament must be consulted. Now a pistol was being put at his head and his daughter's betrothal threatened. There was a certain human antipathy between the boorish Frederick William of Prussia and the small, dapper and somewhat vain George II of England. Frederick William's fundamental objection was, of course, political. Seckendorff and Grumbkow had done their work well. Hotham perfectly understood who had been working against him and produced to Frederick William at his last audience a letter showing Grumbkow's intrigue, which Frederick William rejected with somewhat discourteous comments. Hotham, offended, left Berlin on 12 July. The double marriage seemed doomed.

Frederick, desperate to escape the Prussian court, implored Hotham to take his good wishes to England. He had, earlier and indiscreetly, spoken to the Secretary of the British Legation, Guy Dickens (now Hotham's successor as senior representative), about a possible escape to England. He received, very properly, no encouragement, although Dickens was empowered to offer him some money in relief of his debts. Now the matrimonial route was closed and Frederick's mind again turned to physical flight. He had a number of friends among the young officers of Frederick William's Guards. Four of these had already agreed to help him and a wild plan had been made. It was now, at very short notice, to be put into effect.

Frederick was particularly attached to one of the royal pages, by name Peter von Keith, an attachment of which both his father and Wilhelmina disapproved; and he made a confidant of the young man, whose brother was an officer of the Guards. The Crown Prince was due to make a journey with his father to the western parts of the Prussian possessions and to pay a visit to his relations the Margrave and Margravine of Ansbach. It was secretly arranged that at a certain place and moment Frederick would slip away and ride for the French frontier. While the possibility of the English marriage had existed the plan had been shelved. Now it appeared urgent. It depended on the collusion of the page, Keith, and his brother as well as, importantly, another young officer, Hans Hermann von Katte, a dark and elegant young man, not handsome but intelligent and musical. Katte was to make some critical arrangements in Berlin.

The royal party set out, travelling by Heidelberg, Mannheim, Darmstadt, Frankfurt and aiming at the Prussian town of Wesel on the Rhine. They reached Bonn on 10 August and the escape attempt was planned to take place on the next lap of the journey. It was a desperate idea. Frederick was already an officer – he had been gazetted as a lieutenant-colonel in 1728 and had taken command of a regiment of two battalions, having been first commissioned at the age of under fourteen into the giant Potsdam Guards in 1725. He would be treated as a deserter and a traitor. The attempt would be regarded not only as treason but as black rejection of his father and the entire tradition of his house. And the consequences for any who had helped him would certainly be extreme.

The plot was detected and the page, Keith, confessed. Lieutenant Keith, his brother, escaped to England, where he was given a pension by George II and sent to Ireland for his personal safety.* All was betrayed to Frederick William when the royal party were boarding ship at Frankfurt to sail to the Main and the Rhine; and the King

---

* He returned to Berlin as a lieutenant-colonel soon after Frederick's accession, in December 1740.

confronted his son, cane in hand, and struck him until blood poured from his nose.

Frederick himself was placed in arrest, his sword was removed and – most awful of all – he was interrogated by his father. He was given a questionnaire of 185 loaded questions aimed at eliciting not only confession of guilt but implicit renunciation of his rights of succession. Frederick William's rage, on his return to Berlin, was vented on the rest of his family, who, he suspected (wrongly), had connived. He beat Wilhelmina severely, and roared that there could never again be any thought of matrimonial ties between his family and that of Britain – Britain which he was sure was at the heart of this dreadful, unnatural conspiracy. He naturally removed Frederick in disgrace from the colonelcy of a regiment, awarding it instead to his brother, August Wilhelm.

Frederick was escorted by General Buddenbrock to imprisonment in the fortress of Custrin on the Oder. He had answered the questionnaire with considerable subtlety and skill, saying that his life was being spent as a slave rather than as a prince.

A military court was convened – three in each rank of major-general, colonel, lieutenant-colonel, major and captain, all under the presidency of Lieutenant-General von der Schulenburg. In respect of Frederick the court's verdict was cautious. As 'officers and subjects' the members could only commit the Crown Prince to the King's mercy. Frederick was, in consequence, sentenced by his father to be confined indefinitely under the strictest of regimens, deprived of military rank, forbidden his uniform, restricted to certain religious and improving books, isolated from virtually all company. Some were surprised that the Crown Prince had not suffered death, but it was said that the Emperor (who received a full and immediate account of all from Seckendorff) was encouraged by Prince Eugen – a hero of Frederick William – to intercede, as did the courts of England, Russia and Sweden as well as a large number of the most distinguished men in the Prussian army itself. The Emperor was sympathetic – he later actually sent Frederick a small secret allowance, knowing how short he was kept. To the princes of Europe the thought of a Crown Prince being executed by his own father was horrifying, in spite of the terrible example set by Peter the Great, who had had the Tsarevich Alexis beaten to death.

The former governess-supervisor, Frau von Kameke, faced the King and asked him whether he wished to face his maker with the blood of his son on his hands. For whatever reason, good sense as well as mercy carried the day.

Only to a limited extent, however. Hans Hermann von Katte was brought before the same court at Custrin and sentenced to detention for life, although there were many votes for execution. The sentence needed confirmation by the King. Katte was a Prussian officer, bearer of a distinguished name, son of a general, grandson of a respected field marshal, von Alvensleben. Frederick William changed the sentence to death – beheading with the sword. He gave exact and detailed personal instructions for every aspect of the execution. The pleas of Katte's eminent father and grandfather achieved nothing.

At seven o'clock on the morning of 5 November 1730 Katte – whom Frederick probably loved and who showed unflinching loyalty to him – was brought into the courtyard of the fortress of Custrin. Frederick, by his father's order, was frogmarched to a window overlooking the courtyard at ground level. He shouted a plea for Katte's forgiveness and received a generous call – '*Monseigneur, n'en pensez pas, je vous prie*' – 'Don't give it a thought.' As Frederick would later describe it, 'the grenadiers held me to the window', where he saw his friend's young head struck off, the blood spurt. He fainted. The recollection of that November morning came back to him again and again throughout life.

2

Remusberg

Frederick's first resolve after the horror of Custrin was that he must in future keep his feelings entirely to himself. Frederick William had ordered a trusted Protestant pastor, Muller, to attend on his son immediately after the frightful day, instructed to seek Frederick's contrition. It was clear that if he were to live he must reach some sort of accommodation with his father. This would need pliancy. He therefore, a fortnight after Katte's execution, swore absolute obedience to the King. He went through the motions of sincere acceptance of Calvinist tenets of belief. He threw himself, abjectly, at his father's feet and craved forgiveness. Two days later he was sufficiently pardoned to be set to work while still undergoing a rigorous regime.

'Work' consisted of learning every detail of the domestic administration of the area round Custrin, of slaving at regulations and accounts, of riding out 'under instruction' to visit farms and enterprises, and of returning to the study of 'improving books' (list approved by Frederick William) in the evening, still under arrest. He attended sessions of the local War and Domains Board where he sat at a separate table (at a lower level – all details carefully ordered by the King) under the presidency of Christian von Manchow, a kind man, and the direction of a very learned civil servant, by name Christoph Hille. He was given a small allowance for his personal expenses, showing up meticulous accounts to his father and living always under the strict supervision of two monitoring chamberlains of the royal household. His letters to his father were models of filial devotion and so continued.

Frederick undoubtedly learned a great deal at this time about the Prussian system and although he had come by the experience as a punishment and in appalling circumstances he remained grateful for it. Frederick William had created War and Domains Boards which were modelled on a provincial scale on the General Directory in Berlin. At each level these boards were committees, where a principle of collegiality prevailed: they were the most important element in the Prussian machinery of government. It would be wrong to suppose the Prussian bureaucracy militarized, but a significant number of provincial councillors had served in the army, and a good many functionaries had been military clerks. Generals often became ministers. Frederick William had always insisted on total integrity; but the general ethos was extremely conservative, and the War and Domains Boards did not welcome innovation.

Frederick applied himself, too, to the study of the history of Brandenburg and of his family; and started writing, beginning what became a lifelong career with the pen. In his permitted excursions away from the fortress there were redeeming moments. He met, and fell youthfully in love with, the pretty young wife of the local military commander, Colonel von Wreech, at the Wreech house at Tamsel, always remembering her with wistful affection thereafter* and sending her flowery poems of devotion.

Meanwhile he would prepare himself. He was thinking deeply about government, about the duty of princes. Only three months after his incarceration began he started to draft his first political confession of faith. He was nineteen. The document, in the form of a letter to his gentlemen of the chamber, gave an extraordinarily accurate analysis of the foreign policy needs of Prussia. It could, indeed, be retrospectively regarded as something of a blueprint for conquest, or at least consolidation. He already appreciated the fundamental problems – and vulnerability – of his inheritance.

In August 1731 Frederick William visited Custrin and after a conversation in which Frederick showed the utmost abjectness the King relented enough to lighten the regime somewhat. Frederick might dine out twice a week and guests (no women) might be entertained by him. He was very, very bored. Then, in November 1731, a year after

---

* Louisa Eleanor, wife of Colonel Adolf Friedrich von Wreech, commander of the Cavalry Regiment 'Prince August Wilhelm'. In September 1732 she was noted as being pregnant and some stories imputed responsibility to Frederick, which he denied.

his initial disgrace, he was allowed temporary leave from fortress confinement to visit Berlin for the wedding of his elder sister, Wilhelmina, to the young heir of the Margrave of Bayreuth.

Frederick was fond of all his sisters but Wilhelmina was nearest to his heart for longest and he loved her dearly. They sometimes differed sharply and in her own memoirs she occasionally referred to his unexpected coldness – soon redeemed by a change to their old affections; but throughout life he corresponded with her, '*avec la plus parfaite tendresse, ma chère sœur*'. Wilhelmina died at the age of forty-nine when Frederick was forty-six and in the middle of the greatest war of his career. They had been companions of the schoolroom, happy in the childhood days before Frederick William conceived such apparent hatred for his son, happy in learning from their beloved governess, the Calvinist Mme de Rocoulles, and from the equally loved tutor Duhan de Jandun, who gave Frederick that devotion to French literature and poetry which lasted his entire life. The two children were pretty and alike in appearance. They had joined in the alarming childhood games of seeing how far they could tease and provoke their ferocious father before the skies fell in. Wilhelmina, like Frederick, had grown up in a climate of blows and anger although frequently told by her father that she was his favourite. And Wilhelmina had been his fellow-victim in the abortive project of the English marriage – the 'double marriage' and its aftermath. Wilhelmina had watched Frederick's recent treatment at their father's hands with understanding misery. Now she was marrying Bayreuth.

Wilhelmina had grown up with her mother's idea that she was destined for a grand marriage to the Prince of Wales. That had been frustrated – like her mother she detested Grumbkow and saw Austrian agents everywhere. Sophia Dorothea was unreconciled to the collapse of the English marriage and told her daughter that if she married elsewhere she could expect never to speak to her mother again.

Frederick William, however, reckoned that his daughter must marry, and soon. There was to be no Prince of Wales and he had therefore produced a small clutch of princes and ordered Wilhelmina, despite her mother, to choose one of them. The lot had fallen on Bayreuth; the wretched Princess could do nothing but obey her father, the more since acceptance of Bayreuth was made a condition of pardon for her beloved brother, Frederick – who himself, when able to give an opinion, deplored the Bayreuth match almost as much as his mother did. It was a bad marriage in material terms since the Bayreuths were particularly poor, and the Queen snubbed the young man on first meeting.

The Margrave, two years younger than his wife but soon to inherit, was to prove an unsatisfactory and inconstant husband; and Frederick was sympathetic to Wilhelmina over his infidelities although she often protested she was happy. But on the occasion of that visit by Frederick to Berlin something significant happened. The Prussian generals, assembled in the capital for the occasion, petitioned the King. On 27 November, headed by the famous 'Old Dessauer', Prince Leopold of Anhalt-Dessau, 'Old Moustache' – a man of immense prestige, a veteran of the siege of Namur in 1695, an implacable enemy, a faithful friend – they asked Frederick William to restore the Crown Prince to royal favour and to his position as a Prussian officer.

No doubt this *démarche* was prudently negotiated and timed with care: Frederick William was not a man to relish being taken by surprise or importuned by his officers, even by the Old Dessauer. But no doubt, too, the petition was welcome. Frederick William, beneath his brutality, longed somewhat pathetically for affection and he cannot have been unmoved by the alienation of his son, must surely have longed for rapprochement if it could be managed without apparent condonation of that son's behaviour. He assented. Frederick was reinstated as an officer. He was freed from fortress arrest and Custrin.

Once wearing uniform again, Frederick was soon raised to a position matching his royal status. On 4 April 1732 the King gave again to the Crown Prince the colonelcy of a regiment, the Goltz Regiment of Foot. This was no honorary distinction but meant actual ultimate responsibility for a regiment of two battalions, each commanded by a major, about 1,700 men. The Colonel was the 'proprietor' of the regiment (a Lieutenant-Colonel generally commanded on his behalf in the field or on parade) and his reputation was the regiment's. Even a general officer, if still 'chef' of a regiment, might place himself at its head. The tradition survived. In 1939 Colonel-General Werner von Fritsch, having been manoeuvred into resignation of his position as Commander-in-Chief of the army by scandalous Nazi intrigue and having retired with an honorary colonelcy, nevertheless accompanied 'his' regiment to Poland and fell to a sniper's bullet with them.

Frederick, although almost brought up on the barrack square, of course had much to learn. He was supervised (and reported on to the King) by older and more experienced officers. Nevertheless he himself was accountable, he was master of the little world of the regiment, and he was determined to be respected not as Crown Prince but as an efficient commander – although, being little more than a boy, he sometimes joined in the wilder escapades of the younger officers. But an efficient commander he certainly became; and soon military duty came congenially to him. Each April the regiment had to receive its annual intake of recruits, 'cantonists' from the regimental recruiting area – receive them, train them, absorb them into the ranks; and then parade as a regiment before the King in Berlin to demonstrate marching, drill, appearance. Frederick William, rightly, made these annual inspections occasions for rigorous judgement of each regiment in the Prussian army, occasions for praise or reprimand. Frederick was determined that his own regiment should excel; and it did.

The two battalions of the regiment were stationed at Nauen, twenty miles west of Berlin, and at Neuruppin, twenty-five miles north of Nauen. Frederick's regimental headquarters were with his 1st Battalion at Neuruppin. It was a landscape of lakes, sand, pines, a few miles from the historic battlefield of Fehrbellin. A fortnight after assuming command Frederick visited Potsdam 'to see the drill and find out if we are doing things properly here'.[1] His letters to his father contained plenty of regimental detail, congenial to the King. But his chief desire was for books and like-minded companions: and now that he was not forced to live as a prisoner or in close proximity to Frederick William he could follow his personal tastes and would soon do so very fully.

Frederick lived in a small house at Neuruppin. He made a garden there – he was always fascinated by gardens. With something like peace restored with Frederick William, at least superficially, with his own responsibilities to absorb him, with freedom to study, write and correspond, Frederick was about to begin perhaps the happiest period of his life, a period of discovery, friendship and the dawn of fulfilment.

There was only one cloud on the horizon: marriage. The Crown Prince had a duty to Prussia. He must marry.

Frederick was now conducting a long and intimate correspondence with his father's minister, Grumbkow. Grumbkow had been the prime agent in frustrating the English marriage, the double marriage, and thus destroying Frederick's earlier hopes. He was a corrupt intriguer and essentially disloyal. Nevertheless he was an intelligent, witty and perceptive man and he knew that since Frederick had survived it would be best to stand well with him. He had been admitted to see Frederick the day after Katte's execution and spoken helpful words. Frederick, for his part, needed a friend in his father's counsels and he recognized that he and the minister could serve each other. Although his letters to Grumbkow, like all his letters, were graceful, often flowery, seemingly affectionate, there was no inner feeling there – how could there be? – and Frederick openly rejoiced when Grumbkow, only fifteen years his senior, died at an early age.

Meanwhile Grumbkow's advice was shrewd and Frederick profited from it. He should, wrote Grumbkow, be frank in his dealings with his father, deferential, never facetious.[2] And since by now Frederick William was determined that the Crown Prince should marry, there were many exchanges about marriage. On this subject Frederick's rather immature admissions did not augur well – '*J'aime la sexe, mais d'un amour bien volage* [fickle],' he wrote, saying he wanted enjoyment and despised it afterwards. He reckoned, he told Grumbkow, that he was not cut out to be a good husband. He had a duty to marry but 'they want to make me a lover with blows and I've not got the temperament of a donkey'.

Frederick thought Grumbkow understood him and he probably did – more than Frederick imagined. Grumbkow sympathized with Frederick's determination not to be pushed into a marriage which repelled him. But Grumbkow had his own agenda. His stipend from Vienna was regular and there were definite views there about a bride for the Crown Prince of Prussia. The English-Hanoverian connection had been frustrated and now there must be a choice elsewhere.

Frederick William accepted that his son's choice of bride must be acceptable to the Emperor – anything else would at the present juncture be bad for Prussia. The choice, with the warm approval of her uncle, the Emperor, was eventually made of Princess Elizabeth Christina of Brunswick, eldest daughter of the Empress's sister, Antoinette, Duchess of Brunswick-Bevern.* Prince Eugen, dominant influence at the court of Vienna, told them that 'in all the circumstances' the Brunswick-Bevern marriage was the best idea,[3] and this influential view was soon communicated to Frederick William, who thereafter moved fast. The marriage took place on 12 June 1733, Frederick travelling to Brunswick for the occasion.

There was a ridiculous incident, inauspicious at the least, on the day before the wedding. There had just been a sudden change of policy in Vienna. The Emperor had decided, *pace* Prince Eugen, that, after all, an English marriage for the Crown Prince of Prussia might suit the Austrian book. It might buy British support for the Imperial nominee for the Polish throne, as well as further support for the Pragmatic Sanction. The King of England had been reconciled to the idea once again. Seckendorff, still accredited to Prussia, had therefore been instructed to try to persuade Frederick William, at the last minute, to cancel the Brunswick ceremony. To his credit Frederick William indignantly rejected the suggestion and the marriage went ahead.

'The Princess is not ugly,' Frederick William told his son, 'but she is not beautiful!' Elizabeth Christina was a quiet, unassuming girl, three years younger than Frederick, certainly not ugly, but without character. She was religious and kind but had been somewhat repressed in her own family circle. She blushed easily when spoken to.[4] Frederick's sisters found her unattractive and malodorous, and said so. She failed to win the sympathies of Wilhelmina — 'I have no love for the Princess, I feel repugnance,' the latter wrote. The Queen, predictably, thoroughly resented her and was disagreeable to her.

It is a wretched story and the light it throws on Frederick is

---

* The sisters were daughters of the Duke of Brunswick-Wolfenbüttel and Antoinette's husband, Brunswick-Bevern, succeeded his cousin and father-in-law as Brunswick-Wolfenbüttel in 1735. His eldest daughter married the Crown Prince of Prussia, his eldest son married Frederick's third sister, Charlotte of Prussia, and his second son — Anton Ulrich — married Anne, Duchess of Mecklenburg and nominated successor to the Empress of Russia. Their son, succeeding to Russia as a child, was deposed when the Tsarina Elizabeth seized the throne, and died after a life of miserable confinement.

unsympathetic, although he had been given little choice in the matter as his letters make very explicit. He made painfully clear that he felt aversion rather than attraction in his young bride's company – 'God be thanked it's all over!' he wrote to Wilhelmina after the wedding. The Princess shared no interests whatever with her young husband, although in the early days of their marriage she wrote of him with adoration and she always showed the greatest solicitude for him. He wrote of her with formal respect, even gratitude, but he said that his heart could not be dragooned and he was unable to pretend a love he could not feel. Dynastic unions were seldom accompanied by romantic feeling; it was to be expected that the hearts and desires of princes would move independently of the practical consideration which affected marriage. Frederick, however, was unsympathetic by nature to this sort of worldliness, although he soon came to recognize its inevitability. In his own case he found irksome a relationship built on nothing which can bind human beings to each other.

Some witnesses – by no means all – have referred to his insensitive behaviour to his wife.[5] His letters to her were cold and perfunctory – formal acknowledgements, two lines of good wishes for her health, a sentence or two about her debts, instructions on family observances. No expression of unforced affection can be found in his more than 100 letters to her during his reign. He never stayed with her at Schönhausen, the house north of Berlin presented to her by her father-in-law, Frederick William. He never invited her to Sans Souci, the palace he built at Potsdam where he felt most at home and which he loved. When he returned from seven years' absence at the wars his only comment about his wife was 'Madame is fatter!' As King and Queen they lived separate lives, although later, and especially after the Seven Years War, he often dined with her in company, including many others of her family, and he encouraged her to entertain at Charlottenburg, the most attractive Berlin palace. For her part the Queen never failed to attend the public celebrations of his victories, and often to inaugurate them. Very naturally she later became difficult to her household, subject to unpredictable swings of mood.

Frederick could enjoy the company and correspondence of a charming woman. He was not a misogynist. He found his sister-in-law, Elizabeth Christina's sister, later to be Queen Juliana Maria of Denmark and a woman of considerable character, excellent company. He exchanged animated letters with the lively and erudite Electress of Saxony – the Bavarian Maria Antonia, daughter of the Elector, a woman who shared Frederick's tastes for learning, literature and music and who paid two happy visits to Potsdam later in life. The Duchess of Gotha, befriended during the Seven Years War, he adored. But his Queen plays a shadowy and pathetic part in Frederick's story, and she bored her husband completely. Through life he loathed above all things to be bored.

The marriage was childless. It leads to discussion of Frederick's sexuality. Particularly after the beginning of the Seven Years War, when France was an enemy, the gossip in Paris made much of the King's alleged lack of masculinity – 'How can an impotent king make war?' French officers were alleged to ask. Dr Zimmermann, who attended him at the end of his life, referred, ambiguously, to the King 'through vehemence of his temperament weakening his body, when young, by misuse of the pleasures of love'.[6] Whether or not his marriage was consummated, the fact that he sired no children, that women played an insignificant part at his court, that he had a painfully obvious lack of interest in the Queen as a woman, that his name was not linked with famous mistresses like those of most other princes – these things, together with his unabashed aestheticism and the delicacy of his tastes (despite the occasional coarseness of his language), gave plausibility to his alleged impotence or homosexuality.

In some quarters this became an accepted feature of his repute. Although often proclaiming his admiration for the Stoics, he also voiced adherence to Epicurean ideals –

> J'aime tous ces plaisirs qu'un faux mystique blame,
> Ami des sentiments des Epicuréans,
> Je laisse la tristesse aux durs Stoiciens*

– he wrote in his *Poésies diverses* published in 1760, during the Seven Years War. He certainly loved beauty – beauty of sound, literature or form; and beauty of form might be human and either feminine or

---

* I love these pleasures that false mysticism reproves, a friend of Epicurean feelings, I leave gloom to the harsh Stoics.

masculine. It was remarked that Frederick admired and bought a superb statue of Antinous, the young exquisite adored by the Emperor Hadrian – a statue which had formerly belonged to Prince Eugen – and set it in a wooded grove at Sans Souci. It was also remarked, however, that he bought five nude pairs of lovers, male and gloriously female, painted by the Neapolitan Francesco Solimena, and hung them in the concert room there (his purchase of these, late in life, had added piquancy for him because he learned from his friend, the Marquis d'Argens, that the pictures had come from the Emperor's rooms in Vienna, where Maria Theresa – disapproving of their eroticism – had managed to remove them and put them on the market during a temporary absence of her son).*[7]

Imputations, however, were frequently made, despite the fact, reported by some, that in early days at Neuruppin Frederick had kept mistresses. Stories, some malicious, were put about – like all men and women of distinction Frederick never lacked enemies. One royal page, von der Marwitz, boasted that when a young man in the King's service the King's brother, Prince Henry, had made such a favourite of him that there was jealous anger between the royal brothers[8] – for Henry, too, was locked in a loveless marriage and stories were rife. And Frederick was known to caress, tickle, pinch the ear of some favoured page; particularly one like young von Pirch who was a rascal and made the King laugh. Frederick, among his considerable output of rather indifferent verse, included in his satires plenty of humorous *doubles entendres*, sometimes with a homosexual twist within the classical allusions. The same could be said of many major and minor poets and versifiers, from Byron to Gilbert. Voltaire, after they had quarrelled, wrote scandal about him, anonymously published in Paris and in London. Sir Charles Hanbury-Williams, an admittedly hostile

---

* They depicted Diana and Endymion, Acis and Galatea, Bacchus and Ariadne, Zephys and Flora, Venus and Adonis. Originally hung in his apartments at Vienna by the Emperor Joseph, they were taken down during redecoration, on Maria Theresa's orders, and bought at an attractive price by the dealer Gotzkowski, who did a good deal of buying for Frederick. Frederick at first rejected them – they were in Solimena's early manner, which he did not admire – but when the concert room was being furnished d'Argens persuaded him that the pictures would fit a wall: and the story of Maria Theresa's disapproval amused him.

witness, wrote of the Queen with pity: 'His unnatural tastes won't let him live with her,' as well as other bitter comments. It was suggested that Frederick favoured the pathic role in sodomy. But others, well placed to observe and frank with their pens, did not confirm the 'unnatural tastes' in any literal sense, perhaps – with better sense of proportion – seeing little beyond the varied inclinations of a cultivated sophisticate with a taste for bawdiness,* or, later, the fumblings of a lonely old man.

Frederick, when writing of the ideal education for a future King of Prussia, dealt with sex with the sort of cynicism which might be found in a nineteenth-century *grand bourgeois* in England, Germany or France. Having warned against 'evil companions' and 'debauchery' (but advised tolerance nevertheless), he likened his own views to those of Cato, who rejoiced when he saw a young Roman patrician leaving a brothel, because it indicated that he had not been dishonouring the wife of a Roman citizen. Lust fades with the years and is unimportant, Frederick wrote. More dangerous are strong attachments of the heart. He was always deeply aware of the influence (malign as he saw it) of the mistresses of Louis XV, such as Mme de Pompadour; or of Henry IV.

Nevertheless Frederick himself demonstrated 'strong attachments of the heart' – warm affection at least – towards favoured comrades-in-arms, or towards spirits who shared his intellectual and artistic tastes; and these were generally masculine. He preferred masculine company, although there is no report of any particular influences on Frederick deriving from a homosexual source; in any case Frederick was little influenced by his intimates, he held the initiative in friendships, he went his own way. The atmosphere of his court, however, the exaggeratedly affectionate terms used, the way Frederick was clearly captivated by such courtiers as the handsome Venetian Francesco Algarotti – all this was reckoned by some to imply homosexual orientation.

Certainly Frederick was fastidious; and he often spoke so vigorously against 'vice', 'immorality' – generally in the context of promiscuous

---

* G. B. Volz, editor of Frederick's voluminous correspondence, analysed all the 'sittlichen Anklagen' – moral accusations – he could discover, and found all unsubstantiated and most to be impossible; at least in any serious sense.

heterosexual behaviour – that it might argue a lack of balance, or 'normality'. Certainly, and sadly, he found his wife unattractive despite some rather unconvincing reports that in the early days of their marriage he boasted to some intimates of her physical charms and implied that she'd soon be pregnant,[9] as he was frankly advised would be desirable on every count – including by the Saxon Count von Manteuffel, a philosopher and loyal friend whom he admired* and who addressed Frederick on his marital relations with remarkable freedom.[10] Certainly, during that adolescent visit to Dresden with his father, he had become entangled with the Elector's mistress – at least according to Frederick William's suspicions – and since there were stories of his having contracted at that time an infection,† it might have put him off women.[11] There was enough trauma in his early days to give plausibility to any number of psychological problems. Later in his life a British Ambassador, not particularly close to the King in sympathy, observed cryptically that 'when he lays aside the monarch and indulges himself in every kind of debauchery he never suffers the instruments or partakers of these excesses to have the smallest influence over him'. Into which little or much might be read – Frederick was in general abstemious.[12]

All this is speculation. Despite his condemnation of promiscuity, furthermore, Frederick disliked intolerance. When, later in life, he heard of a maid of honour's pregnancy – 'Somebody takes a poor girl,' he wrote, 'in a moment of tenderness, says a lot of pretty things and gives her a child. Is that so dreadful? . . . get the poor girl away from court without a scandal!' What seems sure, however, is that women – and sexual relations of any kind – played a negligible part in his life and character; but that he was capable of feeling, expressing and receiving considerable love from the heart, whatever his physical inclinations or lack of them, is also sure.

Reconciliation with his father and reinstatement of position marked the beginning of a new and happy phase in Frederick's life. He was

---

* See Chapter 3.
† Or, according to another story, suffered from a bungled operation in the same area, cf. Zimmermann above. This version was discredited by witnesses who examined his body after death and found it completely normal in every region.

now the Crown Prince, colonel of a regiment, a married man. He must have an establishment. In 1733, the year of his marriage, Frederick William gave him the estate of Rheinsberg, fifteen miles north of his headquarters at Neuruppin, and he made it his home. His princess joined him there in August 1736 and a housewarming party was given that year after some alterations and delays; and their four years at Rheinsberg were those in which something like a companionable marriage seems to have been experienced, with visitors commenting on the charm of the Crown Princess and the delightful atmosphere.[13] The small baroque *Schloss*, attractively set with its lake in an amphitheatre of oak woods, became the centre of his life, the source of his voluminous correspondence, the place where he wrote his first books, where he began to amass in one of Rheinsberg's towers his own considerable library – nearly 4,000 volumes already, first lists made in Frederick's hand several years later and collections to be triplicated so that he could always be sure of having the same book at hand whether at Potsdam, Sans Souci or Charlottenburg. He loved the French language and wrote it with concision, elegance and beauty – he knew many of the works of Bossuet by heart and his own style was simple, musical and clear.

Frederick was already a thoughtful student of the European politics of his own day, and from Rheinsberg he continued his correspondence with Grumbkow about current affairs. 'I've just toured the whole of Prussia,' he wrote to him in October 1735. 'I've seen the good and the bare misery of the other side.' But most of his letters were concerned with foreign affairs and even earlier, in 1732, he had written in a letter to a 'Gentleman of his Household', Karl von Natzmer, a very bleak assessment of how he, the young Prince, saw the dangers to Prussia and their implications. Natzmer, a sympathetic character, had been one of Frederick's 'warders' at Custrin and admired him. 'A King of Prussia must take great care to maintain good relations with all his neighbours,' Frederick wrote to him, 'and since his lands cross Europe diagonally, cutting it in two, it follows that he must develop understanding (*garder intelligence*) with all kings, since he can be attacked from different directions. In this situation he would be deficient in imagination simply to let matters rest there. If one does not advance one retreats.'

For philosophy and political economy Frederick was insatiable. He also, from this time, immersed himself in the histories of the great masters of warfare, from Caesar to his own day. 'Meditate unceasingly on your profession and on the operations of great generals,' Eugen had advised him memorably. 'Read and reread the campaigns of the great Captains,' Napoleon would one day instruct aspiring commanders: and seventy years earlier Frederick had done exactly that. At Rheinsberg he felt happy and free. His mind at last could range. He gathered around him chosen friends – the Huguenot Jordan; Algarotti, a man of great intellect, taste and shrewdness although, Frederick ultimately concluded, very selfish; Dietrich von Keyserlingk, a brilliant linguist from Courland, who had earlier been one of his 'tutors'; de la Motte Fouqué, another Huguenot and the only soldier among them. He called his inner circle 'the Bayard Order', in which Frederick and eleven others took symbolic names; and he preserved the order as a sort of club of intimates well into his subsequent reign. Rheinsberg itself was given a code name, 'Remusberg', taken from a legend about the brother of Romulus and the origins of Rome. He referred often to *'la petite colonie de Remusberg'*. Keyserlingk was 'Cesarian', de la Motte Fouqué 'Chastity'; Ulrich von Suhm, the Saxon envoy, with whom Frederick enjoyed discussing philosophy, was 'Diaphanes'.

Informality ruled – what Frederick called 'none of that etiquette which kills pleasure'. There was animated conversation, with Frederick stretching the muscles of his mind, exploring the ideas and moods of the times, thinking, arguing, scribbling. And there was music most evenings; Frederick was now an excellent flute player. He took pleasure in assembling musicians and a choir at Rheinsberg, writing to the Prussian envoy in Venice, von der Schulenburg, with the casual brutality which was the other side of the century's elegance – 'Please try to get me a *castrato*, 14 or 15 years old, and with some musical experience. They are, I believe, obtainable from the Venice hospitals.'[14] He was a competent performer on the keyboard. He composed and improvised – he composed three symphonies, a cantata for soprano and alto, seventy or eighty solo flute pieces. In 1738 he secured the services of Carl Philipp Emanuel Bach, second son of Johann Sebastian, as harpsichordist and in due course accompanist of the royal chamber music. Bach used to accompany Frederick's flute solos and remained with him until leaving the King of Prussia in 1767.*

Philosophically the times, in Europe, were dominated by the French '*Encyclopédistes*' – by the 'Enlightenment': in Germany, the '*Aufklärung*'. But Frederick also enjoyed the writings of the English philosophers, of Hobbes, Locke, Bolingbroke – reasonable men, as he saw it, champions against obscurantism. He was highly entertained by Swift although he found some of his ideas outrageous; and he relished the wit and charm of Chesterfield.[15] He thought that England led the world in philosophy, France in literature. He might have added, but did not, Germany in music. From Voltaire he absorbed with enthusiasm ideas of religious scepticism and a great admiration for style – elegance and economy of language, wit. From the English he acquired – above all from Locke – a taste for judging truth solely by reasonable evidence. He did not wholly neglect the Germans, and when he became King persuaded Christian Wolff to return to Halle whence he had been ejected from his professorial position for irreligion by Frederick William. Frederick liked his rationalism, thought blasphemous by strict Calvinists. It was a period of intellectual ferment and battle, international, stimulating. The new wave of philosophic and literary fashion was hostile to traditional ideas, to institutional religion, to everything which did not derive from human reason – or from sincere human feeling. It was a fashion led above all by Voltaire.

Frederick, therefore, opened a correspondence with Voltaire and wrote during the same 'Remusberg' period to those he regarded as the intellectual élite of Europe – Fontenelle, Maupertuis, Rollin. 'The career of heroes is brilliant,' he wrote to Rollin in 1739, 'but it is stained with human blood. That of *savants* has less renown but leads equally to immortality!' His first letter to Voltaire was written on 8 August 1736 – 'At least may I hope one day to see him I have for so long admired from afar,' and more to the same effect[16] – 'Think of me as a somewhat sceptical philosopher and truly faithful friend. In God's name write to me as man to man and share my contempt for title . . .'

---

* His father, the great Johann Sebastian, visited Frederick at Potsdam in 1747, to the King's joy. Bach regarded it as the culmination of his career – he died in 1750.

François Marie Arouet de Voltaire was approaching forty at this time and was an inevitable object of Frederick's adoration. Like Frederick he was or had been a rebel against parental authority and the conventions of his youth. He had a brilliant and sarcastic mind and pen. He had already spent a good deal of life getting out of trouble into which his wit had led him, including two spells in the Bastille. He had superb facility with the French language and was a composer of verses – often libellous – of which the world talked. He was a successful playwright. His *Zaïre*, considered his best play, had been produced shortly before Frederick's arrival at Rheinsberg. It had been dedicated to an English merchant named Falkener; in cultural terms Europe was an international society and Voltaire, under a cloud at the French court, had spent almost three years in England from 1726 and been admired by the notables of English politics, society and letters – the Walpoles, Bolingbroke, Congreve, Pope; Europe, he wrote, is one great republic, divided into several states. He had then, despite returning to Paris with some sort of pardon, written an attack on French institutions which was published under the transparent guise of *Lettres philosophiques sur les Anglais*, a work which had been officially condemned in France and formally burned by the state hangman (the usual ceremony) in 1734.

Voltaire had left France for the comparative security of the independent duchy of Lorraine in 1735. He then settled with his mistress, the Marquise du Châtelet ('*La sublime Émilie*'), in her château at Cirey and lived there for many years. He was exactly the hero Frederick felt he needed – a brilliant intellect, a rebel against past conventions and in particular the conventions of religion. Here was a free spirit to encourage and perhaps endorse Frederick's own ideas; and one to help and criticize his own attempts at literary composition. His first letter to the great man continued with flowery expressions of appreciation, likening him to Corneille (to Voltaire's advantage) and describing him as encouraging the whole world towards morality, virtue and true glory, in poetic and irresistible terms. Frederick spread his flattery thickly – '*vos poésies . . . sont un cours de morale où l'on apprend à penser et à agir*'. This was most agreeable to Voltaire. He thought the letter peculiar but he had by now exhausted the patience and generosity of more than one exalted personage – including the Regent of France, the Duc d'Orléans, and the Duc de Richelieu. He had now apparently found what promised to be a most satisfactory substitute as patron – a young admirer, not without literary taste and ability, who would one day be a ruling sovereign with much to bestow. He had dedicated *Zaïre* to Falkener (who had entertained him in his house in Wandsworth in 1727, during the exile in England), but he later described the generous Falkener as '*un simple négociant*', a mere businessman, whereas now he might, clearly, seek permission to dedicate a new work to '*un espirit supérieur*', the Crown Prince of Prussia.

Prussia, Voltaire thought, might be northern, remote and painfully unlettered but it might yield a good deal. He sent back a long and fulsome tribute in verse to one whose wisdom and promise would, he wrote, certainly make him '*Le Salomon du Nord*'. Their first meeting would not take place for a further four years but the connection had now been made. Their exchanges seemed to compete in compliments. Frederick tried his own verses on Voltaire, to whom he was '*votre très parfaitement affectionné ami*'. They were, Voltaire replied courteously, '*dignes de leur auteur*' with much to the same effect. Prince and philosopher lamented to each other the ignorance, superstition and fanaticism of the world. Since Frederick himself could not visit Cirey, he sometimes sent messages by one of his circle, a sort of cultural ambassador with a letter of introduction. One such was von Keyserlingk, '*mon cher Cesarion*' (his name in the Bayard Order), who, 'despite the misfortune of coming from Courland', was likened to Plutarch and carried a gift, a portrait of Frederick, for Voltaire.

This was all most satisfying. Frederick was working on his first major book, the *Anti-Machiavel*, and to receive the comments of the premier sage of Europe was delightful. Voltaire wrote about correct rhyming, about emphasis and euphony – and spelling. There were exchanges about the natural sciences, about metaphysics, about the ancient philosophers. To learn from such a tutor was naturally gratifying to Frederick and despite the saccharine and artificiality there is much in the correspondence with Voltaire that is both interesting and charming. '*Ce n'est pas un homme qui fait le travail prodigieuse qu'on attribue à M. de Voltaire*,' Frederick wrote to him in February 1739, and continued that there was clearly at Cirey an academy of the world's élite – Newton, Corneille, Catullus, Thucydides. 'The work of the academy must be being published under the name of Voltaire.'

Frederick's first writings, including the *Anti-Machiavel*, were concerned with the duties of government, the philosophy which should inspire princes and lead to the happiness, prosperity and liberty of their people. His writings, their subjects and tenor (as well as the fact of his correspondence with Voltaire and others) became widely known among the '*philosophes*' of Europe. His reputation began to grow, as the 'philosopher-king' of some future, liberal, epoch. All Europe knew the character of King Frederick William of Prussia; the earlier sufferings of the Crown Prince were no secret. Now this thoughtful, sensitive, future sovereign of a potentially powerful north European state was showing attachment to modernity, to the ideas of the Enlightenment, and was becoming a gifted contributor to them. Voltaire wrote to him that 'A prince with such ideas can restore the golden age in his state', and Frederick not only wrote in general philosophic terms but kept the sage of Cirey *au courant* with the condition of Prussia. And as he learned more of the latter he began, in fact, to detect previously unrecognized merits in the rule of his fearsome parent, telling Voltaire that he 'found something heroic in the King's generosity and energy', although he was devastated by some of the misery he found. 'Unless the King opens the stores around New Year half the people will die of hunger!' he told Grumbkow in October 1735. The last two harvests had been bad.[17]

Frederick hoped, above all, to persuade Voltaire to visit him at Rheinsberg, where his portrait already occupied a place of honour. But his mind and writings at this time were not only focused on general subjects, political philosophy, the state of civilization, even the duty of princes. While he conducted his stimulating correspondence with the best minds in Europe, while he wrote indefatigably and hoped to perfect a literary ability which would attract the admiration of experts, he also worked conscientiously at the care of his regiment and at practical study of the profession of arms.

Frederick was already showing that extraordinary dedication to duty, that determination to understand every aspect of a problem or a task, which marked his entire life. He took great personal interest in the training of recruit intakes, the 'cantonists', and in all his later writings showed his concern – and expert understanding – for the military education of the young soldier. He appreciated how essential it was to coordinate mental alertness with mechanical skill – the latter necessary for the handling of the excellent flintlock musket, the former vital for the mastery of drill in an age where exact alignment could make the difference between a unit's effectiveness or the reverse; a body of men whose close order drill was perfect could, whether firing or assaulting, achieve a multiplied force effect, comparable to a machine. In this instruction – during which Frederick, immediately he became King, forbade physical blows except in extreme cases – he recognized that there needed to be a combination of absolute and instantaneous obedience with the inculcation of trust between comrades. Recruits were placed in the initial care of a senior, a trained soldier, who could teach by example and shared experience, as well as by order.

Frederick took as much trouble with the training of himself as of any. He studied most carefully the military experiences of his predecessors as rulers of Prussia, their achievements, their challenges, their failures – and the reasons for them. Not far from Rheinsberg and Neuruppin was the field of Fehrbellin, and Frederick conducted many battlefield tours there. He found an old man who remembered the battle and could describe it. At Neuruppin he exercised his regiment with great energy.

And he had already, albeit briefly, seen action, seen soldiers under fire. This had been at about the beginning of Frederick's 'Rheinsberg period', the happy interval between his restoration to his father's favour and that father's death. In 1733 Prussia was again for a short time at war and Prussian troops were in action. The quarrel, as often, was about the crown of Poland. The King of Poland had died (the crown was elective) and France was supporting the candidature of Louis XV's father-in-law – Stanislas Leszczynski: Stanislas had held the kingship earlier for a while and been deprived of it. The Emperor Charles VI, on the other hand, was supporting the claim of the Elector of Saxony, son of Augustus the Strong, Frederick's one-time host at Dresden. An Imperial army, under the veteran Prince Eugen, was confronting the French on the Rhine, since it appeared the issue was not to be settled by negotiation. Prussia, as a state of the Empire, had contributed a contingent of 10,000 men to Eugen's army. The French were besieging Phillipsburg.

In June 1734 Frederick William visited his troops at the front and sent the Crown Prince, rehabilitated in the previous year and now colonel of a regiment, ahead of him. Frederick, therefore, at the impressionable age of twenty-two, met Prince Eugen, the first soldier of the age, at Wiesenthal. He handed to him a message from his father in which Frederick William implored the Commander-in-Chief to teach his son all that he could. They appeared to have got on well. Eugen – rather unusually forthcoming – talked freely and gave advice which Frederick always later declared he had greatly valued. 'Read military history,' Eugen told him, 'and always keep the great objectives of a campaign in view.' Frederick, never backward, gave his own views on the condition of Europe. They talked about the art of war and about the present situation. In particular they talked about the Pragmatic Sanction, with Frederick declaring ignorance of what undertakings Frederick William had given; but assuring Eugen (an assurance to be kept confidential from his father) that he would, when King, keep his father's word.[18]

And Frederick was allowed to ride out with a reconnaissance party, saw French positions, experienced French artillery fire (apparently directed at him and his small party), saw French fire cause Prussian soldiers to begin to run and himself helped turn them back: and then coolly continued his absorbing conversation with Eugen, in the saddle as both were. That war was to continue, without much effect on the balance of European power, until November the following year, 1735, in which month, by a treaty signed in Vienna, hostilities were ended. Stanislas renounced the throne of Poland and was awarded the duchy of Lorraine, to revert to France on his death. And France recognized the Pragmatic Sanction.

But five days after Frederick's first sniff of powder Frederick William arrived in the camp. There he had a long talk with Eugen, his own admired former commander. In answer to the King's question Eugen said that Frederick, he could tell, would one day be not only a good soldier but a great general.[19]

3

The Challenge

The *Anti-Machiavel*, Frederick's first complete book, was finished in 1740. Voltaire had, in April 1739, warmly endorsed the idea and the title – '*Réfuter Machiavel est bien plus digne d'un prince.*' The book was a treatise on government, in one sense a work of idealistic political philosophy, in another a work of vigorous realism – a realism, sometimes disturbing, which was and would remain Frederick's dominant characteristic as writer, philosopher and ruler. Few men were less attracted by humbug. Frederick castigated Machiavelli as cynical to the point of immorality – 'This monster who desires to destroy humanity, Machiavelli's "Prince" is one of the most dangerous books in the world.' Frederick, however, somewhat caricatured Machiavelli's dismissal of the need for conventional morality in the necessary character of the ruler, in order to make his point.

In the *Anti-Machiavel* Frederick wrote that the ruler must, both in his public and personal conduct, above all be just. He must gain the assent, even the love, of the governed by a policy of even-handed justice. He must be tolerant of different shades of opinion, must oppose bigotry, suppress sectarian fervour and defend the moral liberty, the right to obey conscience, of all his peoples. These were early days and Frederick did not yet have any governmental responsibilities but he was to maintain a pretty high record in all this. He was, from the first, determined that Prussia should be a state in which the rule of law was respected and in which laws were equitable; equitable, and above all protective of the weak against the strong. Law and cultivated civilization must be the hallmarks of Prussia – a *Rechtstaat* as well as a *Kulturstaat*.

Frederick's later acts matched to an impressive degree his beliefs and

writings. He was high-minded and sincere; and the Prussians increasingly knew it. He also ceaselessly – even priggishly – emphasized the
ruler's identity as servant, 'The first servant of his people'. He stigmat-
ized the sort of ruler bent on self-aggrandizement, display: government
is not for the glory of the prince but for the honour, prosperity and safety
of his people. Frederick was being implicitly severe on such sovereigns
as Louis XIV. This aspect of the book, unsurprisingly, led Voltaire to
write that the welfare of the world demanded publication!

Through the generous sentiments of the *Anti-Machiavel* there ran,
however, a strain of cynicism about human nature which would
become stronger rather than milder with age. Frederick had experienced brutality. He had witnessed men's reactions to it. He had few
illusions and this increasingly made him distrustful despite his natural
propensity for affection and fellowship. If this was so in human
relations it had even more application to political affairs. In his
treatment of a prince's relations with other rulers scepticism and
mistrust are near the surface. He was already feeling sore about what
he had come to believe was the humiliation of his father – and of
Prussia – by 'princes devoid of honest principle' (he meant Austria).
The cynical realism – for to Frederick this was essentially realistic –
makes the title of the book often seem unfair to Niccolò Macchiavelli.

This is particularly so when Frederick discusses the matter of peace
and war. He would always reject charges of pure expediency and
opportunism but his language lends itself to a certain ambivalence.
He distinguishes three sorts of war. First, there is the most unarguably
just, the purely defensive war. Second, there is the 'war of interest'.
Rights are in dispute, the prince's cause is sound but he appreciates
that arguments have failed and that, in the interests of his people, the
matter can only be put to the test of battle – the alternative is the
surrender of their just requirements or their security. The third sort
of war, however, is the 'war of precaution': in other words the
pre-emptive strike. The prince – always mindful only of the people's
interest – decides that conflict is bound to come; there are issues
between states which make it inevitable, if not tomorrow then the
day after tomorrow. His enemies are probably already preparing it.
In these circumstances, convinced that war is a historic inevitability,
the prudent prince decides that it will be folly, a betrayal of the wisdom

he should bring to his trust, to await a rival's initiative. He has a moral right and duty to act. Nothing will prevent war *ultimately* happening and the prince should not forgo the advantages of offensive action at a time of his own choosing.

Macchiavelli could hardly improve on that and it is, of course, plain that Frederick had particular issues as well as general principles in mind. It would, however, be simplistic to regard him as preaching brazen opportunism. He is saying that while the world is as it is there will be occasions when the run of historical events is clearly going to make conflict ultimately unavoidable. The ruler, in anticipating such occasions, must be realistic. His people expect and deserve from him wisdom, courage, adroitness and decision; and realism. Frederick contends that the prince must be just in both his private and his public guise, but he is dismissive of illusions, of a starry-eyed approach to international affairs. Do not pretend, he is saying, that it is possible for the prince – responsible as he is for the safety and prosperity of many human beings, subjects, dependants – to act in the sphere of governmental decisions with the simple, straightforward openness and honest integrity a man can and should bring to his personal dealings, where only he and his family are at risk. In the world of politics a prince so naïve would be overwhelmed by predators and his innocence would be a betrayal of his people and his trust.

This can be called casuistry, but in this as in much Frederick was simply showing the clear-headedness to expound what others – then and now – would conceal behind a screen of pious platitude. He constantly reiterated his main point. The prince is the servant of his people; their interests and not his own aggrandizement or satisfaction must be his guiding star. This, to him, was the critical factor and distinguished him from many other rulers, although most would use the same language.

The concept of prince as people's champion in that age can be difficult to accept. The wars of religion were over: the wars of nationalism and ideology introduced by the French Revolution were yet to come. The wars of the eighteenth century appear, by contrast, familial, dynastic, remote from the true concerns of states and peoples. For Frederick, on the contrary, these limited struggles always represented some more profound conflict of interest which would ultimately affect the ordinary lives of men, although he sometimes wrote with very human sympathy of how distant from the sufferings of the wretched inhabitants must seem the grand quarrels which impelled armies to ravage their lands.

In Frederick's Germany there was indeed an undeclared background agenda behind the sort of disputes over crowns and successions which might provide some immediate *casus belli*; and this, increasingly, lay in the question of what 'Germany' was to mean, and who were to be the dominant players in the German lands. But in dealing with aspects of this question Frederick set out in his earliest writings some very definite moral and political principles. Before beginning the *Anti-Machiavel* in 1739 he had written (and shown to Voltaire) a treatise of more practical and particular relevance, entitled *Considérations sur l'état politique de l'Europe* – a title he used several times – a remarkable and prescient essay on European politics (he was twenty-six when he wrote it) which would not be published until after his death. Many of the reflections in it on the stark choices likely to confront a vulnerable Prussia had been expressed in his youthful 'Letter to Von Natzmer', and the ideas and principles he was already formulating would later find expression in his *First Political Testament*,[1] completed in 1752 but also unpublished until after his death; there would be a *Second Political Testament*,[2] written in 1768. These writings, whenever completed and whenever published, form a continuum. They were, of course, altered and modified as events in Europe moved on, but there are particular thoughts which appear in his earliest works as Crown Prince, and continue, fashioned and refashioned, throughout. Frederick attacked (in the *First Political Testament*) the 'cult of false glory': the 'instinct of aggression'. The people, he wrote, did not accept a ruler in order to increase *his* power but because they hoped he would be just, paternal, humane; above all, capable of protecting them against the attacks of others. He rejected what he called the 'ceaseless aggression' of great monarchies. He often and evidently had France in mind, despite his love and reverence for that country. Sometimes he had Austria in mind. He wrote, always, with sincerity; and always with a profound and often uneasy sense of the situation of Prussia and of the qualities necessary to rule her.

*

Prussia was divided. The Great Elector had made his mark on Europe and clearly his successors must ensure that it did not fade, but the fact remained that the King of Prussia's possessions were scattered and fragmented. If they were to be held safe the Hohenzollern territories needed to be consolidated into something like a defensible whole, or at least with secure communications between the various parts. The present situation, with Brandenburg divided from the isolated Rhineland duchies, with Pomerania divided from East Prussia by a wedge of Prussian Poland, spelled weakness and was in some respects historically unjust.

Prussia was strategically vulnerable. There were few naturally defensible boundaries. Defence against the Swedes naturally bulked large in Frederick's early thinking, and the Swedes still had a foothold in Pomerania little more than 100 miles north of Berlin. They could threaten Prussian communications with Mecklenburg and threaten Brandenburg itself. Were the western part of Pomerania in Prussian hands it could dispose of a threat and act as something of a buffer against Sweden. On the other flank the recovery of Prussian Poland would link Pomerania with East Prussia and control Polish access to the Baltic, a powerful asset. Without adjustments of this kind Prussia had inadequate strength in the north and north-east to offset her dangerous fragmentation in the west; fragmentation – and vulnerability. In the west was France, the greatest monarchy in Europe. And to the south, south-west and south-east were the various parts of the German Empire, directed (more or less) from Vienna and always potentially hostile to Prussia.

Prussia was poor. Her prosperity had been much restored by the Great Elector, she was well and economically administered, her finances were stable; but she was poorer than she might justly expect to be, despite the strict management of Frederick William; and her budget would always be under pressure. The land was in many parts unproductive. Industries and the raw materials for them existed, but in inadequate quantity. The population of Prussia was small. A few years later, in 1752, Frederick wrote that to be secure Prussia needed a population which would enable her to support an army of 180,000 – 44,000 more than at the time of writing, although by then she had grown significantly through Frederick's early acquisitions. Prussia needed to expand to live, and this was even more true in 1740. Lands meant men. Men meant armies. Armies meant security.

In all these connections the Silesian duchies claimed by the King of Prussia[3] – Liegnitz, Brieg, Jagerndorf, Wohlau – were important. Silesia was populous – about equally divided between Catholic and Protestant. Silesia was potentially rich; there were minerals (later to be a huge source of wealth), textiles, a flourishing linen industry. And Silesia had rebelled against Habsburg rule in the Thirty Years War. Silesia did not explicitly feature in Frederick's first writings but it had a prominent place in his mind as that mind matured during the years at Rheinsberg, and when he wrote the *Considérations* it is clear that he thought his father had been too accommodating towards the claims of Austria, despite his own soft words to Prince Eugen a few years previously.

He probably always thought so, and would soon be reinforced in that conclusion by Frederick William's own *Political Testament*, drafted while that fierce king thought he was dying, in 1722, when his son was ten years old and read by that son on his father's death. In this, Frederick William had written that his successors should never begin an unjust war *but must never relinquish what was justly theirs*: and Frederick was undoubtedly determined to act on this precept, albeit prudently. For the most part Frederick William's *Testament* was extensively reflected in Frederick's own writings. The King of Prussia should be economical, should keep a firm grip on the finances of the state. But, of equal importance to balance against this injunction, he should keep the army strong, and keep its control in his own hands. When he died in 1740 it could certainly be said of Frederick William that, whatever miseries he inflicted on his family, the Prussian treasury was in good trim and the Prussian army was a well-organized and formidable instrument with the best corps of officers in Europe.

In the governance of Prussia – and it was the theory and practice of government which dominated his early writings – Frederick also inherited moral injunctions from his father and despite his earlier alienation and his lifelong scepticism he was largely true to them. Of these one was towards personal morality; Frederick William was a narrow Puritan by conviction and his son, although of a wholly different temperament, certainly believed that the ruler must set an example to the ruled. Above all, however – and despite his own narrowness – Frederick William hoped to leave to Prussia a legacy of religious toleration: and in this Frederick undoubtedly believed. He certainly maintained toleration as a fundamental article of faith. His own religious opinions, like those of most people, probably developed over much of his life but they rarely drove him to intolerance.

After his death, when he had achieved heroic and legendary status, there was a natural tendency among some writers to ascribe to the great King of Prussia a piety of which there is only patchy evidence, but in his early days, the days when he aimed above all to be the 'Philosopher Prince', he was a free-thinker, a sceptic; and this continued at least until his middle years. It was said that he only attended divine service nine times in his entire reign. He wrote to Voltaire in June 1738 of 'the Christian fables, made sacred by their antiquity and by the credulity of man, puerile, absurd for people who reason logically'.[4] He derided Christian dogma, or most of it. A true child of the Enlightenment, he wrote of the education of a prince that 'he must know enough theology to recognize the Catholic cult as the most ridiculous of all'.[5] The implication was that the creed was a cult, and variations of it ridiculous in differing degrees. He gave few indications of trying to reach a doctrinal position through his own reason. Instead he was dismissive – 'I am neutral,' he wrote in 1752, 'between Rome and Geneva.' People of all religions should live peaceably together – Catholics, Calvinists, Lutherans, Jews. There were, of course, practical considerations to be taken into account if there was to be harmony in the state. They were factors in a ruler's calculations. The numbers of Jews should be limited because they injured the business of Christians and could arouse discord which a prince must pre-empt. For German Catholics Vienna and the house of Habsburg could hold more attraction, more affinity, than Berlin and the house of Hohenzollern. For German Protestants the reverse could apply. He looked at such things pragmatically, particularly when territorial questions were in play.

Frederick sometimes referred – particularly later in life, during the terrible war which dominated seven of his years – to 'the liberties of Germany', and to 'the Protestant cause' as two great, linked matters: but, in truth, Frederick was the champion of no cause and certainly no religious cause. He preferred, when it was possible, to find himself allied to France, the greatest Catholic monarchy, and culturally his spiritual home. He certainly always hoped, in combating the claims of Austria and the Catholic Habsburgs, to enrol Protestant support where he could find it. He knew how to beat the Protestant drum – with caution. But there was little sectarianism in his heart.

Nor was Frederick more personally intolerant than he was doctrinally. He was very strict in matters of honesty, integrity. In questions of matrimony he was broadminded to a degree which some found (and would now find) hard to accept. Marriage, he wrote, is basically a matter of civil contract; it should be dissolved simply if the two parties so agree. Excepting only incest of parent with child or brother with sister, marriage should be a màtter of free, individual choice: '*je permets avec indulgence qu'on se marie à sa fantaisie.*' This was the spirit he thought should prevail in Prussia. It was far from the Calvinist spirit of Frederick William.

Yet although he might be easy in matters of purely personal morality, and despite his affectation of Voltairean scepticism in theological questions, Frederick was not wholly indifferent. He was too intelligent to suppose that the whole of knowledge lay to hand, already grasped by man. He was too much a poet and an artist not to be affected by life's mysteries – and tragedies. He asserted belief in a Supreme Being: in effect he could have been described as a Deist, if no more. In August 1738 at Brunswick, persuaded by Prince Lippe-Buckeburg, he became a Freemason, a member of an early German lodge and consequently professing belief in God, however defined (he took little part in Freemasonry thereafter).* He was, perhaps inevitably, touched by Calvinist belief in predestination (rejected as a dogma by his father), in the sense that freedom of human will is an illusion, that we are all tiny and impotent compared to the remorseless workings of Fate, Providence, the Will of God, whatever it be called. The sorrows and joys of individuals could not have much significance but there must, perhaps, be something beyond the inadequate and often deplorable thoughts and actions of men. Certainly Frederick wrote[6] that all religions are based on more or less absurd fable, whose errors a

---

* Brunswick was prominent in German Freemasonry.

sensible man must immediately detect; but 'either God is wise', he also wrote (in a long letter to Voltaire about belief, in February 1738) 'or he does not exist ... and if not wise he is not God, but a Being without reason, a blind random of fortune, a self-contradictory association of attributes without objective reality . . .'[7] This was pretty confused, but in all these exchanges Frederick showed – it was an endearing characteristic – modesty about the validity of his views. He was not afraid to express theories, absurdities even, for the critical comment of others. He was a self-questioning undogmatic. He was, during the Rheinsberg period, introduced to the works of Christian Wolff, pupil of Leibnitz, who taught that belief in even ultimate truth could be attained through reason. Influential in this respect were two Saxons – counts von Suhm and von Manteuffel – in Berlin, of whom the former translated for Frederick Wolff's rather ponderous German into elegant French. Frederick always admired dependence on reason alone, as preached by the English School of John Locke. He remained throughout life a child of the Enlightenment.

And he always enjoyed discussing religious doctrine. He liked mocking certainties, attacking the defenders of dogma, seeing how far he could go in provoking. On the other hand he seems to have taken little note of the fact that probably the greatest of successors to Leibnitz and Wolff – Immanuel Kant – was teaching at Königsberg throughout the latter part of his reign; and Kant (who came greatly to admire Frederick) collided with orthodox Lutherans after Frederick's death, which would have bothered Frederick little. When Frederick met sincere belief, however, he tended to recognize it and desist. One of his generals, a devout Catholic, used to make the sign of the cross with his sword in battle, before attacking. Frederick noted it once, and referred to it with a smile. 'Sire,' was the response, 'don't meddle with such subjects. Provided I do my duty strictly and serve you with zeal, of what importance to you are my religious practices? And of what advantage to you is it to ridicule your most faithful servants?' Frederick was silent, and that was that.[8]

And the man who experienced for forty-five years so much of battle, bloodshed, danger, hardship and sudden death is unlikely to have endured it all with a sense of mere self-sufficiency whatever the iconoclastic theories of youth. His letters to his beloved sister,

Wilhelmina, protested confidence – whether wholly felt or not – that he would see her again in a better world. He sometimes seemed to understand, without specific spiritual association perhaps, the possibility of an inner peace, perhaps divinely bestowed and transcending the world's cares –

> Lorsque l'orage gronde,
> Le Sage dans son cœur garde une paix profonde,
> Et sans s'inquiéter d'un funeste avenir
> Il l'attend, sans le prévenir*

– he wrote in 1760, after disaster had struck him at the awful battle of Kunersdorf.[9] When he finally returned to Berlin after the seven years of war and a Te Deum was sung in the chapel of Charlottenburg, Frederick was seen to put his head in his hands with tears of gratitude flowing. And at Zorndorf, in August 1758, Frederick heard a melody played by one of his regiment's bands as they marched towards what would be one of his bloodiest fights. He asked its name and was told it was the tune of a Lutheran hymn – 'Ich bin, ja, Herr, in deiner Macht' – 'Yea, Lord, I am in thy keeping'. Frederick softly repeated the words to himself, much moved.

Frederick's Rheinsberg years as Crown Prince were immensely formative and the principal marks of the man showed. He evolved from personal experience those views on the education of a prince which he wrote with such force at various times. The prince must be made human, mild, clement. He must above all learn history; and he must be taught that of all failings in a ruler harshness is the worst. Some might one day think this out of character and unconvincing in the later Frederick but he reiterated it as a maxim as late as 1768.

Because he had wide interests, loved music, literature, philosophy – while devoting much of his mind to the arts of government, the duties and necessary skills of princes – Frederick was perceived as ambitious for a reputation as a universal man, a polymath. He was indeed a polymath and he probably at times 'played up' excessively

---

* When the storm roars, the wise man, inwardly at peace, awaits without distress the grim fate he can't avert.

to this, advertised too self-consciously his own versatility. It was a trait observed by, among others, the shrewd soldier diplomat Marquis de Valory, who spent eleven years as French Ambassador in Berlin from 1739 (and returned later). He knew Frederick well, first as Crown Prince and then as King. Valory took over duties as Ambassador from the popular Marquis de la Chétardie and at first Frederick found the change tedious – Valory, he wrote sharply to Voltaire in December that year, had the effect of reminding him every day how much his predecessor was missed.[10] He grumbled that Valory, an old soldier, somewhat prosy and extremely fat, conducted conversation as if his companion was some sort of enemy fortification to be carried; his military reminiscences were tiresome. Valory, nevertheless, saw Frederick clearly and on the whole sympathetically. The Crown Prince, Valory said, was a man of great intelligence – nobody had a more alert mind – but was apt to think few others possessed much. He talked well, with great vivacity and a certain impulsiveness but above all with wit, by which he set great store. His own tongue was extremely sharp and could be cruel. His personality was so strong it tended to be overwhelming, and although his wit could be highly entertaining and endearing it could sometimes offend. He talked not only well but a good deal, sometimes in his voluble enthusiasm contradicting himself; and, like many princes, he was less fond of listening. Valory remarked that he was excessively distrustful (perhaps natural for a French Ambassador to encounter) and there was no mistaking his imperious nature. He thought others were born to obey. Another French envoy, the Marquis de Beauvau, was less impressed than Valory with evidences of Frederick's good will. 'In his heart,' Beauvau wrote in December 1740, 'he detests France;[11] his real ambition would be to humiliate us.' This was too violent. In his heart Frederick never detested France.

Valory, however, was emphatic on two facets. Frederick had immense attraction, immense charm, and when he chose to exercise it could do so more effectively than any man – until he had achieved his aim, whatever it was. Then he was capable of turning off the tap of seduction with disconcerting abruptness. And – an enduring and central characteristic – he made up his own mind and kept to it. Procedural niceties meant nothing to him. When he was clear about the way ahead he acted. He was his own man, and he was resilient. The same resilience, the same independence of mind, was particularly noted years later by another Ambassador, the British Sir Andrew Mitchell, who (like Valory) knew Frederick over a very long period, being Ambassador for fifteen years including the worst years of war. Frederick made up his mind, Mitchell remarked, and acted with extraordinary resolution; but when he suffered a setback (and Mitchell would be the witness of many) he calmly devised something new. It is the distinguishing mark of the great field commander he became; and of the great sovereign, patient master of events.

Yet Frederick, in spite of the evolving sense of domination in his character, was at Rheinsberg still ready to learn from others; and he was particularly ready to learn in military matters. His inclinations at this time were primarily literary and artistic, and would remain so, but he was never in doubt about the role of a King of Prussia. His task must be to command the army if it took the field and his duty was to ensure that it was ready – and that he was himself prepared.

Frederick, therefore, read extensively about war. He enjoyed both recent and ancient history, relishing the lives of the Caesars and the scandalously informative writings of Suetonius in particular, but in his enormous library there was much on the history of campaigns; and in his own writings on military subjects Frederick would always illustrate his points with knowledgeable and perceptive examples from the past. At the practical level he was zealous and painstaking in the management of his regiment, so that the details of soldiering became second nature to him. And he picked the brains of others. He always treasured the memory of that one conversation with Prince Eugen, in the Low Countries. He had, at the same time, made a great friend of Prince Joseph Wenzel of Liechtenstein, a cultivated soldier sixteen years his senior and, like him, a connoisseur of the arts. He naturally found it easier to learn from those he recognized as by temperament congenial.

He also learned much from a very experienced officer in the Prussian service, Kurt Christoph von Schwerin, not only a veteran but a polished man of the world. Schwerin was already in his late fifties when Frederick's 'Rheinsberg period' began. He was a sophisticate, artistic as well as battle-hardened; but he was also a man who nourished the

Prussian virtues of self-discipline and austerity, starting his day with private prayer and setting a personal example to all. He had served in both the Dutch and Swedish armies before joining Frederick William. He was a firm but enlightened disciplinarian and his influence on Frederick was of great value. He would one day die in the field, a Marshal, as one of King Frederick's subordinates. When Frederick came to the throne, however, and during his first campaign in which Schwerin would play a leading part, the latter had not seen action for many years.

There were others. For the Crown Prince's interest and instruction, when opportunity arose, there was the conversation of Prince Leopold of Anhalt-Dessau, the Old Dessauer. The Old Dessauer, born in the year after Fehrbellin, veteran of campaigns against the French since 1695, comrade-in-arms of Prince Eugen, a field marshal since the year of Frederick's birth, was a dedicated military historian and writer. Frederick could learn much from reminiscence. He could learn from the written word. He could study and reflect. But from 1736 he desired above anything else the advice and companionship of one very different from the Old Dessauer.

The period from 1736 to 1740, the first four years of Frederick's correspondence with Voltaire, had been a happy period of mutual discovery, a honeymoon. Each saw the other through something of a golden haze. Frederick sent to Cirey pressing invitations but the philosopher found it impossible to accept them – not least, no doubt, because Frederick never included Mme du Châtelet in them although he sent graceful messages to her, while making clear it was Voltaire he wanted to see. Voltaire continued to write effusively, likening Frederick, '*le prince philosophe*', to Trajan as thinker, to Pliny as author, to the best of Frenchmen as a writer of French. He compared him to Marcus Aurelius. He was especially complimentary about the *Considérations*, which Frederick had sent for his comments. Then, at the end of May 1740, everything changed. King Frederick William died, in great pain, at Potsdam. Frederick was with him, having ridden from Rheinsberg and been greeted with unrestrained affection by the dying man.

Henceforth Frederick was sovereign, responsible ruler, slave to public affairs rather than amateur of philosophy and the arts. 'I thought I could joust with *l'aimable Voltaire*,' he wrote on 6 June 1740,[12] 'but now I must fence with *"le vieux Machiavel mitré"* [Cardinal Fleury].'* The enthusiastic correspondence continued, however, and Voltaire began a long and effusive verse sequence in a July letter,[13] '*Quoi! Vous êtes monarque et vous m'aimez encore!*' – no doubt with sincere relief.

His father's visits, the journeys and enterprises they had shared, had generally been disagreeable to Frederick. Although some sort of peace had existed between them after the first awful years which had culminated at Custrin, followed by a cautious reconciliation, there was a miserable lack of anything like affectionate ease, although some of Frederick's letters were sprightly, even gossipy. Frederick, having visited East Prussia in order to make a report to the King in 1735, went again, with Frederick William, in the summer of 1736. He paid a third visit, by himself, in July 1739 and, which was not only of fascinating interest but also very remunerative, he was given by his father the famous royal stud of Trakhenen, breeding-ground of noble horses. And Frederick, as he learned more of Prussia and of the army, had begun to appreciate the better side and undoubted achievements of the old tyrant. In a letter from East Prussia in 1739 he had told Voltaire about the remarkable results of his father's efforts in restoring a country ravaged by the plague, depopulated, impoverished. Frederick William had devoted enormous effort to a work of salvation and his son had been deeply and favourably impressed. And for his part Frederick William, although entirely out of sympathy with Frederick's personality and tastes, had nevertheless detected, somehow, the steel inside his son's skin. 'There stands one who will avenge me!' Frederick William once muttered, pointing at him as some particularly dismissive and patronizing attitude adopted towards Prussia in Vienna was being discussed, an attitude resented as much or more by Frederick as even by his father, and the King, although only in his forties, had indicated that with such a son he would die contented. The Emperor and his ministers had shown little gratitude for Prussian help in the recent war on the Rhine.

* Since 1726 principal minister of France.

And Frederick, whatever he had suffered, had cared more for his father's good opinion than for that of any other. Later in life he told of a recurrent dream; he was with the Austrian Marshal Daun, one of his opponents, and suddenly saw Frederick William before him. Then Frederick, in the dream, asked his father, 'Have I done well?' and received the simple reply, 'Yes'; then said to Frederick William, 'Your approval means more to me than the whole world.' There was probably much truth in the dream.[14]

His father's death, however, could not leave Frederick other than with a sense of liberation, although he wept with genuine feeling and his formal expressions were correct enough. He had fallen into a good deal of debt, through the expenses of Rheinsberg which outpaced his comparatively meagre income, and had been latterly kept afloat by secret subventions (immediately repaid on his accession) from his uncle George II of England. He now immediately took up residence at Charlottenburg and made some essential senior appointments in army and state. Schwerin was to be Commander-in-Chief. Count Heinrich von Podewils, Grumbkow's son-in-law, became First Minister: August Friedrich Eichel was made political secretary, 'Cabinet Secretary', an indefatigable worker always at his desk by 4 a.m., even before the King – and completely devoted to him. There were distinctions for some of the Rheinsberg circle. General von Katte, the wretched victim's father, was made a field marshal and a count.

Frederick at once began the immense personal correspondence which so marked his reign. Already in June he was writing in all directions: personal instructions to his envoys at foreign courts, to his own ministers in Berlin, to illustrious foreign statesmen such as Cardinal Fleury, to brother sovereigns abroad. To most he wrote in his easy, lucid French, naturally prefixing his letter according to the courtly and diplomatic usage of the day (Fleury was '*Monsieur mon Cousin*'); or with more familiarity when writing to his own officers – Colonel de Camas, in Paris, was '*Monsieur de Camas*' in a semi-formal instruction of 2 August 1740, but '*Mon cher Camas*' in a more expansive follow-up epistle written on the next day.[15] Camas's wife, whom Frederick adored, was a maternal figure to him and often addressed with protestations of undying love, until she died in 1766, as '*chère Maman*'. Camas, a gallant Huguenot, who had lost an arm in battle, was regarded as a somewhat undistinguished figure for so important an embassy as that to France; but Frederick knew him and reckoned him amenable to subtle instructions – he was to so talk in Paris as to spread anxiety about Frederick's proneness to precipitate action. It was widely realized that he knew Frederick well.

To the Foreign Ministry and particular officers on detached duty he tended to write in German – a German much criticized for grammatical inaccuracy and inelegance but probably often corrected by his admirable secretaries.* He signed his letters in French with 'Fédéric' (saying that to omit 'R' was more euphonious) and those in German with 'Friderich'; and whether in French or German he did not fail to acknowledge his correspondent's most recent letter or report with marked courtesy and generous expressions of gratitude – unless a rebuke was to be administered which would be harsh and unforgettable. His language to foreign princes and statesmen was, as is to be expected, a model of graceful good manners – but wholly devoid of ambiguity or equivocation.

To Voltaire, soon after his accession to the throne, he gave some details of his actions during his first three weeks as King. He had thought long about what he wanted to do immediately he was master of Prussia. He had, he wrote, inaugurated a new Academy, a College of Commerce and Manufactures. He intended to build up reserves of food and each Prussian province was to hold an eighteen-month reserve of grain. The army, 83,000 strong, was to be increased. Frederick was determined to end disproportionate military emphasis on outward appearance, important though it was in its place; he wrote later that if peace had lasted longer soldiers would no doubt have been ordered into rouge and beauty spots. Frederick William's regiment of 'Giant Grenadiers' was to be disbanded except for one battalion, but a new Household Cavalry 'Garde du Corps' was to be formed, as well as a new Foot Guards Regiment – with its 1st Battalion later increased by a 2nd and 3rd. Physical punishment for cadets of the Berlin Cadet Corps was to be banned (this was later reversed); and torture, in all processes of law, was abolished. There was to be abolition of press censorship and of public penance by unmarried mothers. Religious

* See Chapter 9.

freedom was guaranteed. Ceremonies associated with the sovereign were immediately curtailed – Frederick refused any formal coronation although he – personally or by deputy – received the customary homage from each province. And Voltaire, of course, must visit him.

The first meeting of the two took place at Cleve on 11 September 1740. Frederick was visiting Prussia's most westerly possession – there was a dispute being conducted not far away. The Bishop of Liège was arguing with Berlin about the barony of Herstal, just north of Liège city, to which he laid claim and where the inhabitants, in 1738, had attacked a Prussian recruiting party and received some episcopal support, although Frederick – and most authorities – reckoned that the Hohenzollern claim to the barony was good. Frederick, immediately he came to the throne, had sent a vigorous note to the Bishop ('*Mon Cousin*') and sent a Prussian general with troops to occupy Maseyck as a counterweight. It was the sort of situation, not unusual in Europe in the eighteenth century, where negotiation and bargain could probably bring a solution and Frederick was demanding (successfully) a large financial contribution – 180,000 thalers* – from the Bishop in return for the surrender of Prussian rights at Herstal and the evacuation of Maseyck. Meanwhile he visited Cleve to see how his general, von Borcke, was getting on.

The incident never came to bloodshed and it was improbable that it would, but it indicated a Prussian king ready to enforce or protect his rights where he thought them good. Nor did Frederick ever ignore the presentational side of policy. Noting in a letter to Podewils that 'the Prince Bishop of Liège has arranged publication of justificatory articles in the newspapers in Holland and Cologne', he instructed him to arrange some counter-balancing press releases, to put Frederick's side of the matter and to put it well: '*vous y devez employer une bonne plume*'![16] Meanwhile he prepared a camp at nearby Wesel and assembled a force there, ready to move at short notice into the disputed duchies of Jülich and Berg (a separate issue) if opportunity occurred.

Before these transactions, *en route* to Cleve via Bayreuth and a brief visit to Wilhelmina, Frederick decided to make a secret visit to Strasbourg, incognito. He travelled as 'Comte du Four' with one

---

* £30,000.

companion, Algarotti, as 'Count von Pfuhl'. There was nearly an awkward incident – in an inn an officer at the same table asked who Algarotti was. 'An Italian. From Italy,' Frederick answered, and the other took offence and reckoned this was an abrupt and discourteous response. Algarotti made peace, however, and, as Frederick said, 'a lot of champagne was drunk'. He also had to excuse himself from cards, saying he had promised a strict father never to play.[17] The Governor of Strasbourg, Marshal de Broglie, was somewhat embarrassed when he heard of the visit. Frederick then went on to Cleve. The detour was a long one – underestimated by the Prussian party as needing an extra three hours compared to a direct journey from Bayreuth – but Frederick travelled remarkable distances.

All this gave Frederick a chance to meet Voltaire, who travelled to Cleve. The meeting took place at the castle of Meuse, nearby. It went well; they were already firm – almost ecstatic – penfriends and Voltaire had been for some time commenting on drafts of the *Anti-Machiavel* with an estimable frankness familiar to many authors – 'I say with hardihood to Your Royal Highness that some of the chapters are rather long!' (He managed to get Frederick to shorten it by a quarter.)[18] Frederick was now more than ever determined not only to persuade the great man to visit him in Berlin, a visit which followed shortly afterwards, but one day to bring him firmly into the orbit of the Prussian court. There could, surely, be no greater intellectual ornament and no more vivid illustration of the new distinction of Prussia.

And the auguries seemed good. 'I have seen,' Voltaire wrote, 'one of the most amiable of men ... full of sweetness, complaisance, pleasantness: forgetting that he is a king as soon as he is with friends.' And he quoted to Frederick a citizen of Cleve who had (allegedly) asked him, 'Is it true that we have as a king one of the greatest geniuses of Europe, who, they say, has dared refute Machiavelli?'[19] Frederick may have begun to feel a certain scepticism but Voltaire, as Disraeli recommended of flattery to royalty, certainly laid it on with a trowel.

But before Voltaire could reach Berlin another event of more dramatic significance occurred. On 20 October 1740 the Emperor Charles VI died. One of his last acts, a fortnight before death, was to issue to Frederick a formal denunciation of his actions in respect of the Bishop of Liège, a denunciation which had no effect, then or later, except to hasten the Bishop's acceptance of the Prussian proposal. The Emperor's daughter, Maria Theresa, was now head of the house of Habsburg. 'This,' wrote Frederick with certainty and accuracy, 'is the signal for the complete transformation of the old political system.'[20]

Within days Frederick had given orders for the purchase of sufficient grain in Mecklenburg to supply the army in the field, had set in hand its transportation by barge and had held his first – and decisive – meeting with his minister, Podewils, and his trusted veteran commander, Schwerin. His mind was – had long been – made up. His war chest was adequately stocked with funds. The hour had come. '*Cette mort*,' Frederick wrote to Voltaire most unconvincingly, '*dérange toutes mes idées pacifiques.*' So far from being *dérangée*, his chief idea was perfectly clear. Silesia must be occupied. As of right, and if possible peacefully.

Podewils was cautious and anxious. He acknowledged the rights on the side of the house of Brandenburg but cited the solemn treaties Vienna would quote, whereby those rights – mistakenly – had been renounced for insignificant benefits elsewhere. To his demurrals Frederick finally, on 7 November, gave an answer which has been cited as evidence against him but which, by a different interpretation, shows his realism. The matter of rights, he told Podewils, was for the minister to work at and expound. The essential point was that the army was ready. Orders had already been given to the troops.[21] The cause was good, and 'If one has the position of advantage, must one not exploit it?' he had put as a (rhetorical) question to Podewils, on 1 November. '*Je suis prêt!*'

Frederick was always obsessed with secrecy and security of information. The march orders to the various detachments were accompanied or preceded by deliberately false details as to timing and destination – a deception measure. He gave route orders for two cavalry regiments, the Gessler and Buddenbrock regiments, which were to join the army subsequently, to two young officers, reporting to receive them; and he noted with approval how one of the two, Lieutenant Schach von Wittenau of the Buddenbrock, shuffled the pages of the order round so that if he were captured his captors could not make immediate sense of the paper, it would take them probably valuable time. Such details never escaped Frederick, who often incorporated them into standing orders thereafter.[22]

The Hohenzollern claim to the Silesian duchies was based on the various transactions whereby they had been transferred to the Empire by the Great Elector in return for concessions which, in the times of himself and his son, had allegedly been unilaterally revoked by Vienna. The Great Elector had himself envisaged the necessity for Prussia to occupy at least part of Silesia one day; and there was (in 1740) the further point that by the Pragmatic Sanction the Emperor might legitimately have bequeathed family possessions, but surely not those which were Imperial and by definition elective. Nor, surely, those subject to dispute – for it was firmly held in Berlin that Vienna had reneged on the Austrian part of the arrangement by which Austria had obtained all Silesia for the Empire. This was the legalistic issue and in an age when territorial claims between states differed little from litigation over family property between individuals the legalistic aspect was, of course, important; and, as in most legal disputes, more than one view could be taken. Frederick believed that his cause was good. He believed that by that part of the Pragmatic Sanction held by the Habsburgs to apply to Silesia the Emperor had acted *ultra vires*. He believed, furthermore, that the King of Prussia, his father, had only agreed to the Sanction in return for certain conditions – the cession of Jülich and Berg – which were still unsatisfied. For Frederick, Frederick William's agreement was void and on the Emperor's death the Silesian duchies should revert to the crown of Prussia.

But Frederick had motives beyond those of legalism and he was frank about them; and it is these motives, clearly expounded, which have led many to condemn him but which could rather be recognized as an accurate perception of the likely and perhaps inevitable course of European history. Silesia, Frederick wrote in a memorandum on 6 November, was the part of the Empire (as then constituted) to which Prussia had the strongest legitimate claim, and justice demanded maintenance of legitimate claim. But Silesia was a rich province, with control of the Upper Oder. Possession of that province would bring great benefits to Prussia, economically and strategically; and, above all, the various international factors were propitious. Others with Silesian ambitions – Saxony, Bavaria – were unlikely to move before

Prussia. England was at odds, and would probably shortly be at war, with France. France would welcome an Austrian setback. Russia would be deterred from action against Prussia by the hovering menace of Sweden (they would be at war within the year). As for Austria herself, she was never ready for war. Everything pointed to the need for rapid action. Frederick always believed in speed.

These were practical considerations, considerations of what would later be called *Realpolitik*, and when Podewils mentioned the treaties to which Austria would appeal Frederick brushed it aside – 'I have given orders to the regiments.' But Frederick was prepared to attempt negotiation as a supplementary means to his end. In a long memorandum on 29 October Podewils – supported by Schwerin – suggested a bargain with Vienna. Frederick should keep Silesia but would give up his claims to Jülich and Berg, would support Maria Theresa elsewhere and would back the candidature of her husband, Francis of Lorraine (they had married in 1738), to the elective Imperial throne. He might also offer as a *douceur* in return for agreement '*une couple de millions*'. Money. Money, Podewils and Schwerin argued, would speak loudest in Vienna. If none of this worked it might be necessary to try for the good will of Saxony and Bavaria, perhaps to obtain the good will of France. A deal might yet be done with the Habsburgs.[23] An ambassador, Count Gotter – a previous Prussian envoy to Austria – was sent to Vienna to try to transact something on these lines.

Frederick listened. For him the salient fact, the point he always made to his advisers, was that 'the army was ready' – ready, with its orders and with all preliminaries already accomplished. Europe watched. The British Government advised acceptance on Vienna, although when the British Ambassador, Dickens, tried to elicit a direct reply from Frederick about his intentions he was sharply snubbed.[24] Frederick knew that Maria Theresa was also threatened by claims from the Elector of Bavaria, who hoped for prizes in Bohemia and even for the duchy of Austria. She was also threatened by the distant menace of France, traditionally hostile and traditionally supportive of Bavaria; the French Government was torn in several directions and nervous about the character of the young King of Prussia but in the end the sentiment of bridling or scoring off Austria carried the day and a French 'defensive alliance' with Prussia was mooted. Prussian aspirations were not ill-based: and they were not unique.

The Austrians sent a very experienced old diplomatist, Marchese Botta d'Adorno, to Berlin to find out what he could of Frederick's intentions. To inquiries from other European powers about his attitude to the claims of Maria Theresa under the Pragmatic Sanction, Frederick sent careful and ambiguous replies. He was not hostile to her just claims. He was ready to support them – but some were not just and he had claims of his own. He avoided being too explicit – convinced that military action was about to become necessary, he had no intention of sacrificing the element of surprise. Diplomatic exchanges of that age were rich in expressions of courtly deception. Frederick's manoeuvres were not extraordinary. The Empire was always something of a lottery when successions were in play; but, unlike other players, the Prussian army was ready.

There was also a point of political psychology to be made. Prussia, Frederick reckoned, had too often been disregarded, treated as of little account, in recent years. If she was to have the place in Europe he believed should be hers, a noise should be made, a fanfare sounded. Assertion, drawn sword in hand, of Hohenzollern rights by the new young King of Prussia would sound that fanfare; and the world would pay attention. And not only Prussia but Frederick, too, needed this attention and needed it personally. He needed to prove himself, to make a mark, to show he could meet and defeat a challenge.

The world did indeed pay attention. Frederick's initiative, his manifest preparations, ultimately his actions, were predictably attacked by powers hostile or simply envious. To Maria Theresa, sincere and innocent in her reactions, he was an armed robber, using first menaces then weapons. He was, furthermore, a Protestant robber, and Silesia a largely Catholic province.

A high moral tone of criticism was and has been subsequently taken by many, with Frederick's policy described as shocking the conscience of Europe.[25] It is difficult to take these latter-day opinions too seriously – they smack of partiality rooted in the liberal sentiments of a later age, while contemporary censure must be judged by the lights of Frederick's own times. Frederick, aiming to occupy a Silesia which was closely akin to Prussia, could point if he chose to the remorseless moves by which France had extended her frontiers; to a British occupation of Gibraltar to the consternation of most of the inhabitants and without a shred of legitimacy. The reactions of other powers were largely composed of humbug, the invocation of double standards. It was the frequent practice of eighteenth-century princes – given a semblance of that legality which he certainly claimed in full – to act through self-interest seasoned with diplomacy; and diplomacy was and is still underpinned by strength of various kinds, relative to opposition, strength, moral, economic, military, psychological, presentational – the 'correlation of forces'. The difference between Frederick and his contemporary rivals was that he had the will-power, the resolution and the competence to act, and act fast. And, in his own somewhat chilling phrase, the army was ready.

Beyond the legalities, the bargaining, the calculation of short-term tactical possibilities and advantage, Frederick believed that there was an issue which might not yet receive much acceptance in the chancelleries of Europe but which mattered. Why, he could ask, should Austria and the house of Habsburg have the dominant voice in these matters? Silesians were not Austrians. They were divided in religion and there was no more natural affinity with Austria than with Prussia. Why should it be presumed that the inhabitants of the disputed Silesian duchies would be governed more justly and more happily from Vienna than from Berlin? Was not their own interest of importance? And Frederick would soon answer his own unspoken question by bringing considerable reforms to Silesia as well as greater efficiency of administration immediately Prussian possession of the province was confirmed; his reputation as a ruler grew in Silesia despite some initial difficulties with ecclesiastical governance – and it grew despite the disappointment of Silesian Protestants that he was entirely evenhanded and did not favour them as they had hoped. Beyond even this was a yet more fundamental question – why should Austria be accepted without cavil as the leading power in all Germany? Frederick often protested in letters that he would always defend the 'just rights' of 'the house of Austria' and this was not wholly dissimulation. But the emphasis was on *just* rights. He always claimed, for instance, to have respected the *spirit* of the Pragmatic Sanction; but some pretensions went beyond justice.

This was the crucial, underlying and unavoidable issue, whether openly recognized or not. Frederick William, in his own *Political Testament*, had written that he had always trodden carefully, to avoid the antagonism of Austria. Was this delicacy – or pusillanimity – to be an unalterable condition of German life? Austrian policy, speciously advertised as in the general German or Imperial interest, was more often in the simple interest of Austria. Yet in all these considerations Frederick was regarding the Silesian adventure as an essentially local matter, a piece of German business which would not necessarily embroil other powers. Europe, however, was in a combustible state. Any serious assault on Austrian authority would probably be seen by France and others as an opportunity. Any intervention by France would probably be seen as another opportunity – or a provocation – by Britain, where hostilities at sea between Britain and Spain were eagerly anticipated by some; and such hostilities were likely to involve France as Spain's ally. The young King of Prussia was striking a match and the powder train was long.

Frederick's special embassy to Maria Theresa achieved nothing. His written instruction to Count Gotter was signed on 8 December 1740, and before the Count had been received in Vienna the Prussian army was marching across the frontier. On 10 December Frederick made clear to the Austrian, Botta, exactly what was coming. The philosopher-prince had drawn his sword, and although he protested that his actions were peaceful, the first Silesian war had begun.

PART II
1740–50

4

The Mollwitz Grey

The Silesian wars, by Frederick's definition, were 'wars of interest'. Later they would also be what he called 'wars of precaution' – he knew that it would be a long time before his possession of Silesia was undisputed and when a challenge threatened he struck first. He condemned 'unjust' wars but he never wavered in his belief that his Silesian cause was just and legitimate; that the cause was sound in law. Like other princes of his day he regarded war as a regrettable but not an unacceptable expedient in such case. Unlike most of them he soon knew it at first hand. Wars, in the contemporary view, should not be waged *à outrance*, should not be aimed at total victory but at limited yet necessary advantages.

Before deciding to wage war a prince must have regard to the general European situation and to how his own state weighs in the scales: to the 'correlation of forces'. In 1740 Frederick reckoned this was favourable to Prussia. If matters dragged on and a *fait accompli* were not accepted, Prussia would undoubtedly need allies and his correspondence shows him putting his case in every direction – he knew that Prussia must outface Austria not only on the battlefield, if it came to that, but in the great marketplace of the chancelleries of Europe where rulers calculated and bargained for short- or long-term advantage. Frederick's 'weighting' in that market place would be immeasurably enhanced by material success; by the military occupation of Silesia. He hoped that it might be an almost bloodless operation – a peaceful and largely popular march of Prussian troops into neighbouring territories owing, whether they knew it or not, legitimate loyalty to Prussia.

Frederick, therefore, gave demonstrations of optimism, ostentati-

77

ously assuming that the world in general and Maria Theresa in particular would concede his case and lay aside resentment or hostility. This was to be no act of aggression against another state but simply the assertion of territorial rights which the Emperor's death had placed in Frederick's legitimate possession. 'My intention,' he wrote to his envoys Gotter and von Borcke in Vienna on 12 December, 'has never been to wage war on the Queen of Hungary and Bohemia'[1] – and he claimed that, on the contrary, he stood always ready to help her. He understood her anxieties about the French, about the Bavarians. But the situation in which Maria Theresa found herself surely implied that some sacrifices, somewhere, must be made – and were not Frederick's proposals sensible? These considerations, he told his representatives, must be put forcefully to the Austrians. His letter ended, however, on a different and harshly realistic note. He was leaving Potsdam to put himself at the head of 30,000 men for the Silesian enterprise and in four weeks would have a further 40,000 concentrated in the area of Berlin to support the operation *'contre tous ceux qui m'y voudraient traverser'*.[2] This was to be made absolutely clear to all. The one unambiguous factor in the situation was the Prussian army.

Frederick's policy towards the candidature for the Imperial throne, on the contrary, was anything but unambiguous. Gotter, in Vienna, was authorized to say that Prussia was prepared to support Maria Theresa's husband, Francis of Lorraine,* if other matters could be satisfactorily arranged: it did not appear likely that they could, and Frederick had no intention of offering his Electoral vote for nothing. Francis had met Frederick some years earlier when he had visited Berlin for Frederick's betrothal ceremonies. The two young princes – Francis was four years Frederick's senior – had made friends. Francis was a man of great charm. Stuart blood ran in his veins, as in Frederick's. Personal liking, however – let alone that consanguinity which connected most European princes – could not be allowed to affect policy beyond a certain limit; and few of the German princes were enamoured of the idea of the Duke of Lorraine as Emperor.

The limit, therefore, might be reached early. On the same day that

---

* Also Grand Duke of Tuscany; a grandson of 'Monsieur', of Orléans, brother of Louis XIV; and of 'Minette' of England, sister of Charles II.

Frederick wrote to Gotter and von Borcke with his hopeful – but, as he knew well, probably unrealistic – suggestions to Maria Theresa, he wrote an instruction to his minister-plenipotentiary at the Bavarian court in Munich, Joachim von Klinggraeffen. In this[3] he laid down as Klinggraeffen's chief task support of a vigorous policy by Bavaria to obtain the Austrian – the Imperial – succession for the Elector of Bavaria. Such a policy, he wrote, could only be encouraged covertly by Prussia *'avec tout de circonspection'* so that he did not appear openly to take the Bavarian part. He intended to keep his cards in his hand as long as possible. Such manoeuvres were and are not uncharacteristic of diplomacy, which has to be concerned with bargaining. Nor are they disreputable. But because Frederick in the field of foreign affairs, as in most things, was his own man, his own minister, negotiations and subterfuges which are the ordinary currency of international dealings – with inevitable periodic concealments – appear as very personal transactions, and sometimes very personal deceptions.

He did not evade this. It was part of his philosophy. The prince must do things for his people which the private man would never contemplate. Throughout his life Frederick was prepared to equivocate, to conceal his inner mind, to change his aim with circumstances. He was prepared to give assurances (generally worded with a subtlety which could protect him against later accusations) while knowing all the time that he might need to vary those assurances if the wind changed. He did not believe that the world of international politics had reached a point where a wise ruler, dedicated to his people's good, could neglect periodic and well-judged duplicity. There were, of course, limits. There are manners in duplicity as in everything. But duplicity involved the charge of bad faith – again, within limits.

The only plea to this is 'Guilty'. Frederick, throughout his long reign, was prepared to act with duplicity, was prepared to deceive. Indeed he often went to considerable pains to deceive. He believed that states, political associations – because of the competitive condition in which they are bound to exist – are in a state of undeclared war, a war which wise statesmen will manage to prevent turning into the sort of war in which men kill and are killed. In such an undeclared war deception and concealment are essential stratagems for success, even for survival. Periodic self-righteous disclaimers are simply additional stratagems. Personal morality (despite what Frederick wrote in his *Anti-Machiavel*) is a separate matter. The ruler, acting responsibly for his people, can only play the prince.

Meanwhile Frederick's letters were going in every direction to emphasize the just and reasonable basis of his actions and the limitations of his ambitions. He was particularly anxious to keep Russia quiet. The Tsarina Anna, to be succeeded briefly by her niece and that niece's unfortunate little child-Tsar, died within a few weeks of the Emperor Charles. Frederick's letters to his Ambassador in St Petersburg, Freiherr von Mardefeld, were explicit; and he was rewarded by a 'defensive alliance', agreed in January 1741, whose achievement owed a good deal to the work of General von Winterfeldt, a particular confidant of the King, sent for a short while on a special mission to the Russian court where he had family connections. In the matter of the Imperial Election Frederick could only write protestations, with sorrow at being misunderstood, to Francis of Lorraine. To Gotter he wrote on 26 December that 'the Duke of Lorraine appears intransigently hostile' to Frederick's ideas[4] but that the Ambassador should persevere, pointing to the advantages the house of Austria would gain by having Frederick's support and hinting that although he had claimed *all* Silesia he might moderate this to only a part of that province if it were possible to reach a 'sincere accommodation'.

Frederick had little expectation of success in this line of policy and kept up pressure elsewhere for support in the face of Vienna's angry defiance. The first months of 1741 were filled with kaleidoscopic shifts in the attitudes of the European powers. Frederick's diplomatic manoeuvres were ultimately rewarded with a certain success in the early summer, when France and Bavaria joined him in alliance against Austria, thus significantly widening the dimensions of the war. By then, however, he had fought his first battle.

Frederick had left Rheinsberg for Berlin on 2 December and had given instructions to Jordan to keep him informed of public opinion, of what people were saying. November had been marked not only by urgent military preparations but by the first visit of Voltaire to 'the most amiable of men'. Voltaire had stayed a week at Rheinsberg during which he was able to discuss and play the editor for the *Anti-Machiavel*.

The visit, although long-awaited and enjoyable to both, was slightly clouded by external circumstances as well as by Voltaire's comments on Frederick's book which, elegantly expressed though they undoubtedly were, Frederick accepted in the manner of most authors: that is, not very well. Voltaire had conveyed, too, Mme du Châtelet's irritation at her exclusion from the invitation, no doubt frequently vented on her lover. Frederick had written, on 2 August 1740, a brief and rather brisk letter in which he said that he would write to the lady since Voltaire seemed to wish it, but 'to speak frankly about her journey', he added, rather bravely, 'it is *you* I want to see, my friend . . .' *La divine Émilie* (their affectionate nickname for Mme du Châtelet) 'with all her divinity is only an accessory'.[5] Only an accessory! This cannot have made Voltaire's life easier.

Besides this, however, there was the imminent adventure in Silesia. Frederick was secretive but it was suspected in France from the moment of the Emperor's death that he had designs on Maria Theresa's possessions. His correspondence with Voltaire periodically bore signs of having been opened and read, signs which he always reported in his next letter, while carefully disclaiming particular allegations about responsibility – at least that would show the French ministers that his eyes were open. They, of course, were very aware of the relationship and its possible usefulness. Before Voltaire had set out for Prussia Cardinal Fleury, *le vieux Machiavel mitré*, had requested Voltaire (with a bribe) to find out what he could on this first, fortuitous visit to the philosopher-king in Berlin.

In this Voltaire was singularly unsuccessful but it is unlikely that Frederick did not form his suspicions about the interests of his distinguished guest. The other circumstance which somewhat marred the short visit was the matter of Voltaire's expenses, which Frederick had naturally undertaken to cover fully. He was taken aback by the size of the bill. He probably already felt some unease about the character of his adored master in philosophy when it came to financial matters. Frederick had generously agreed to provide a pension for the young Marquis du Châtelet (*la divine Émilie*'s son-in-law – her daughter married another du Châtelet). Within days of writing about the Emperor's death Frederick received a letter from Voltaire asking very precisely for the pension to be paid in two parts, for administrative reasons. Such exactitude from the '*demandeur*' may not have been tactful at that moment.[6] Their affectionate correspondence resumed, however, after Voltaire's departure. For some time much of it, on both sides, was in verse, a comparatively neutral medium.

The area of central Europe over which Frederick was to campaign for much of the next three decades is distinguished by several great rivers, lines of communication, strategic highways for military movement and replenishment. Most easterly is the Oder, running northward through the Moravian gap in the mountains east of Olmütz, marking the western border of Silesia until reaching the Baltic at Stettin. In the centre is the Elbe, western border of Brandenburg, chief waterway of Saxony, running northward through the Bohemian gap into Saxony and ultimately to the sea at Hamburg. Most southerly is the Danube, the highway of the Empire, running eastward through the Bavarian gap into Austria and thence into Hungary and along the frontier with the Ottomans until it reaches the Black Sea.

The country is marked by a considerable mountain range, the Riesengebirge, the 'Giant hills', which form a chain linking the Thuringian forests of central Germany with the Carpathians of Ruthenia and Transylvania. The gaps through these hills were always important to a campaigner; but the hills also often afforded shelter. Frederick was chiefly concerned with the western part of this mountain range, the frontier hills between Saxony and Bohemia, and those between Bohemia-Moravia and Silesia; with the course of the Oder and its tributary the Neisse; and with the Elbe.

Frederick embarked on the first campaign of a very long fighting career with the sense of adventurous excitement natural in a young man of twenty-nine, riding to war for the first time and riding to war at the head of his country's army. 'I am undertaking a war,' he told the officers of the Berlin garrison, 'in which I have no support but your courage, no source of help except my luck . . .' The sentiment was rash, imprudent and accurate. Having crossed the Oder and entered Silesia, he wrote to Podewils on 16 December: 'I have crossed the Rubicon, colours flying and drums beating – *enseignes déployés et tambours battant*'. He hoped, nevertheless, that Silesia could be occupied virtually without loss.

Frederick kept up his diplomatic correspondence from the field. He wrote to von Borcke in Vienna next day that he had high hopes of the influence the King of England might bring to bear. This was reasonable – Frederick had written two personal letters to his uncle, George II, explaining the rationale of his actions and arguing the importance of keeping Maria Theresa from any thoughts of an alliance with France. Britain was a traditional ally of Austria but Frederick had also suggested that there might be territorial gains for Hanover in Mecklenburg after a Prussian success, even though that success would be at Austrian expense. He hoped that British influence might help persuade the Habsburgs to accept his terms *sans délai ni perte*. It was not difficult to hint that were Frederick's policy instead to be one of cooperation with France (in default of British support) it could be uncomfortable for Britain at this juncture – Britain and France would probably soon be at war with each other again* and for the King of England (who unfortunately disliked his nephew of Prussia) Hanover was a *point d'appui*, easily threatened by the Prussian army if the diplomatic wind changed. Frederick knew well that British ministers, unlike their King, would regard any threat to Hanover, whether Prussian or French, with a certain equanimity; but he also knew that for Britain France was always the enemy and France's friends (among whom he hoped soon to be counted) were at best suspect, at worst hostile. Later in life Frederick found himself, as an ally of France, counselling an offensive against Hanover† – news or rumours of which did little to improve personal feeling with his uncle. Meanwhile, his letter to von Borcke continued, he was under pressure from 'several powers' to take a different line to that he had adopted. He was offering to support Maria Theresa, provided only that he got Silesia, and it would be good that London should press Vienna to agree his terms; which they did – unsuccessfully.

Frederick seldom lost sight of the proper aim of military operations – to secure a more favourable political situation after their successful culmination. Militarily he was wholly optimistic. He was proud of the army as it moved peacefully and with excellent discipline through

---

* They were.
† See Chapter 6.

Silesia, posting Frederick's 'Proclamation to the Silesians' on every church door, with its promise of the King of Prussia's protection of liberty, justice and freedom of religious observance to all. The Lutheran minority, disadvantaged under Habsburg rule, would have equal rights while the Catholic majority could enjoy every continuing privilege. He wrote to Wilhelmina that Breslau, the Silesian capital, would soon be his (he reached it on the last day of the year) and that perhaps, if the Austrians wanted war *à outrance*, the Prussians would soon be at the gates of Vienna. He had spent Christmas at Herrndorf, near Glogau on the Oder, and sent Podewils a two-page memorandum giving a summary[7] of the reasons which had led Prussia to occupy Silesia. He was writing from outside Breslau on 2 January 1741. So far there had been no fighting.

The Prussians had advanced in two parallel columns, widely separated. Frederick himself had moved down the valley of the Oder while to the westward Schwerin had swept the country on a march through the hills bordering north-east Bohemia and Moravia. Where Frederick found a place garrisoned by Austrian troops he left it covered, as at Glogau, and marched on. He was encouraged by the welcome the Prussians were receiving in Silesia, and at Breslau, on 3 January, he made a ceremonial entry, accompanied only by his life guards, having secured the agreement of the city authorities that they would not open the gates to the armies of Maria Theresa; Breslau was a 'free city' of the Empire with certain privileges. His immediate objective was Neisse, a fortified place sixty miles south-east of Breslau and the strongest fortress in Silesia.

Both wings of the Prussian army ultimately converged on Neisse, where they found an Austrian garrison prepared to resist. There could be no question of exposing the troops to methodical siege operations in the conditions of winter and after trying, without success, intimidation by a ferocious ten-day bombardment, Frederick decided to leave Neisse and other unsurrendered places masked and to return to Berlin, which he reached on 26 January. He had lost only twenty men in all. He had completed the entire operation in a few weeks. 'My good, my benign, my pacific, my humanest M. Jordan,' he wrote to that beloved mentor on 14 January, 'I announce to Thy Serenity the conquest of Silesia!' He had, as intended, occupied Silesia or most of it, and had marched through the province from one end to the other. He had few expectations, however, that the game was over and he expected that the next move would be made by the enemy when spring came. He was still writing – fruitlessly – to his envoys at Vienna emphasizing that he was ready to support Maria Theresa *contra mundum* if only the just claims of the Hohenzollerns were recognized.

Although Frederick was conducting his own foreign policy, was sending detailed instructions to his ambassadors, was writing letters to brother sovereigns, to Cardinal Fleury, to foreign ambassadors at his own court like Valory, he took trouble to keep Podewils and his government in Berlin fully informed, especially when he was away and in the field – and to exchange ideas with them so that, in the tangled web of eighteenth-century diplomacy, they were fully in his mind. Considering the laborious business of sending dispatches, particularly in winter, this took time, but it minimized confusion. His style was normally brief and, dependent on content, formal – '*Monsieur de Podewils*'; but sometimes light and frivolous after some stroke he wanted approved by Podewils, as on the last day of 1740 – '*Mon cher Charlatan*'! Frederick's letters were always individualistic – they carried the hallmarks of his personality. There is an endearing directness about them, even when they are unashamedly concerned with how to deceive. That was the game of kingship and Frederick had no intention of losing it. But he also meant to enjoy it.

At moments he was what could only be described as naughty. At the end of a letter full of affectionate protestations to George II of England on 30 January – and not much else, beyond telling him for effect how damnably the poor Protestant people of Silesia had been treated before he liberated them – he added a postscript: '*J'ai oublié! que j'ai conclu une alliance défensive avec La Russie!*' Not so much an afterthought, more a sting in the tail. And he enjoyed teasing Podewils, who was prone to timidity – '*Vainquons ces difficultés, nous triomphons!*' he wrote to him in March, commenting on the performance of various Prussian envoys overseas – '*Truchsess* [Hanover] *avance, Mardefeld* [St Petersburg] *va son chemin, Chambrier* [Paris] *fait à merveille, Klinggraeffen* [Munich] *est adoré! Ainsi, cara anima mia, non disperar!*'[8]

Although so far the Silesian operation was a triumphant procession rather than a matter of fighting, this was Frederick's first test in a demanding skill he was to show through life – the simultaneous conduct of a campaign, a domestic government and a very active diplomacy. As to the latter, he had no illusions about his fellow-sovereigns. Whatever their views, protestations or assurances they would, he knew, act with Maria Theresa against Prussia if they saw advantage in it – nor did he condemn this. He knew that the Elector of Bavaria, with ambitions for the Imperial crown and territorial hopes as well, could play the part, for Maria Theresa's benefit, of a champion against Prussia; but he also knew – had himself suggested to the Elector – that the time might be ripe to push Bavarian claims in the Empire and that the support of France would probably be forthcoming; as soon happened. He knew that the Elector of Saxony would act with duplicity, promising to help Maria Theresa but simultaneously seeking an alliance with Frederick. He was uncondemnatory. This was the way of the world.

In March 1741 Frederick learned that Maria Theresa had given birth to a son, who would one day be the Emperor Joseph. Meanwhile his diplomacy seemed to be yielding little. There was no disposition in Vienna to come to terms. The King of England was apparently negotiating some sort of treaty with Austria in which George II's Hanoverian mistrust of Prussia was somewhat ahead of the feelings of his English subjects, although Frederick continued to play what he supposed an effective card in that direction, namely British antipathy to France and British hopes of pre-empting a Franco-Prussian alliance. Saxony, as usual, was a dubious quantity, with hopes of territorial pickings from Prussia were Frederick to be worsted, but little power or inclination to do much about it. Most concerningly Russia, with whom Frederick reckoned to have made a temporarily satisfactory defensive alliance (that alliance mentioned to George II as a footnote in his January letter), was showing signs of contemplating an understanding with Maria Theresa. 'La trahison de la Russie est épouvantable,' Frederick noted to Podewils on 17 March.[9]

Two things, however, gave Frederick hope about Russia and both – with incalculable consequences but promising short-term alleviation – were to happen in 1741. In the summer Sweden, influenced by France, attacked Russia, making it unlikely that there would be

Russian resources available to help the Habsburgs. And in a *coup d'état* in November the daughter of Peter the Great, Elizabeth, seized the throne of the Tsars, ousting Frederick's nephew-in-law, the wretched little child Ivan, son of Anton Ulrich of Brunswick.* This latter development looked likely to keep Russia occupied for a while: in fact it produced one of the most implacable of Frederick's enemies. But all these events and prevailing moods – the intransigence of Vienna, the distant coldness of George II, the jealousy of the Elector of Saxony, the unpredictability of St Petersburg – seemed likely to impel Frederick towards friendship with France (to which his heart always strongly inclined) and, *faute de mieux*, with Bavaria as the rival claimant to the Imperial throne and thus a counterweight to Maria Theresa's husband as candidate. Frederick did not relish the idea of a much-strengthened Bavaria but if Maria Theresa continued obdurate he needed friends. And at the moment, with the winter of 1740/41 not yet over, his concern was with the Austrian army, which was now concentrating in Moravia under the command of Field Marshal Count Neipperg. The Austrian object, without doubt, was to drive him from Silesia. The 'fair province', occupied with so little difficulty or sacrifice, would now need defending.

Frederick needed to decide how far forward towards or beyond the Moravian and Bohemian borders he was prepared to deploy. The Prussian army was, of necessity, in winter quarters, widely dispersed. A cavalry screen of observation patrols was maintained forwards. The Austrian garrisons which had been left isolated and masked by the December invasion still for the most part remained, although the fortress of Glogau on the Oder had been taken in a surprise night attack by Prince Max Leopold of Anhalt-Dessau, a son of the 'Old Dessauer'. Frederick wished to keep his billeted troops and therefore his places of subsequent concentration well north of the frontier, with his patrol screen not too far from the area of the main body. His instinct, a sound one, was that if the enemy advanced the Prussians must be sufficiently clear of contact to have liberty of movement. Schwerin, experienced in war, disagreed. He said that, as spring came, the Prussians must deploy their screen sufficiently far south to cover

---

* See Chapter 2.

the grazing and arable country south of the Oder. He had his way.

Eighteenth-century campaigning was largely about resources. Battles were won by numbers and firepower and a won battle might settle a campaign, but to maintain a campaign at all there had to be communications – road and river: there had to be magazines, stockpiles of supplies, built up and sufficiently protected; there had to be, or often were, fortresses – secure places which could hold up an enemy and menace his own communications unless reduced by systematic and time-consuming siege, and fortresses needed adequate garrisons: and for mobility and transportation there had to be huge numbers of horses. Horses meant fodder and grazing. An army dispersed to live, concentrated to fight; and the simple fact of marching through a territory had little strategic significance unless the march produced a real shift in resources from one side to another.

Availability of grazing, therefore, was certainly an important factor, as Schwerin argued, but the Prussian deployment made for vulnerability. The Prussians were quartered on a wide frontage in southern Silesia, extending as far west as Schweidnitz (thirty miles south-west of Breslau) and reaching back to the Oder. Frederick learned at the beginning of April that Neipperg was marching north from Moravia with 16,000 men. He was presumably directing his troops towards Neisse, and the Austrian garrisoned town of Brieg, half-way between Neisse and Breslau. Frederick was visiting some of the cavalry detachments of the screen far away in the south-east, near Jagerndorf,* when he first received information of the Austrian moves. The Austrian main body (as it turned out) was already north of him, had already passed the western limits of the Prussian screen line and was moving towards Neisse, where the Austrian garrison was relieved by Neipperg on 5 April. Neipperg had taken the first tricks and Frederick could have exclaimed like Wellington of Napoleon on 15 June 1815, 'He has humbugged me, by God!' It was now a question of concentrating the Prussian army from dispersed billets, of forming it as an effective unified force, of finding where the enemy were, and of deciding what to do. For Frederick it was an inauspicious introduction to serious war.

---

* Fifty miles south-east of Neisse.

The weather was hard, the country snow-covered. Frederick continued his diplomatic business, writing a long letter to George II (copied to Podewils with a note of supplementary instructions) on 6 April. This, consistent with earlier exchanges, suggested '*une amitié très sincère*',[10] based on Frederick's retention of Lower Silesia, including Breslau, and on King George's readiness to persuade Maria Theresa to agree. Meanwhile Maria Theresa's general, Neipperg, was apparently marching to the relief of the Austrians at Brieg and Frederick, with the Prussians now assembled, moved in a north-westerly direction towards Ohlau on the Oder. If Neipperg established the Austrian army at Brieg and Neisse the Prussians would be cut off from communication with Lower Silesia. Frederick was marching towards what looked like becoming a battle – his first – and he felt the natural mix of exhilaration and uncertainty.[11] '*Mon cher Jordan*,' he wrote on 9 April, 'we're going to fight tomorrow . . . if Heaven prolongs my days I'll write to you and tell you about our victory. *Adieu, cher ami . . .*' He had received sufficient information to show him that the Austrians had concentrated on a two-mile front near the village of Mollwitz, their right to some extent protected by some woods and convergent streams, their left near the village of Grüningen.

It was 10 April. Visibility, because of the combination of sun and snow, was difficult. When still two miles distant from Mollwitz the Prussians deployed into battle formation opposite the enemy – two lines of infantry, 250 yards apart, with cavalry on both wings. It was a manoeuvre which necessitated a right-angled change of direction and a good deal of time. Frederick supposed, and later wrote (mistakenly), that the Prussians were outnumbered by at least 6,000 in infantry, and that the Austrians had three times the Prussian cavalry strength. In fact the Prussian infantry were numerically superior. Having deployed, the Prussian advance began at about 1.30 in the afternoon. The artillery advanced by bounds, batteries moving in succession from one fire position to another.

Mollwitz was Frederick's first serious experience of battle. It did nothing for his military reputation but the course of the day was instructive. The Austrians were attempting to deploy on a line roughly parallel to the Prussians, and the first dramatic event of the battle was a charge by the Austrian cavalry of their left wing which, in superior

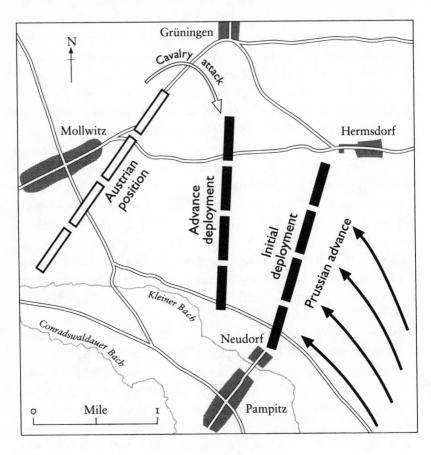

Mollwitz, 10 April 1741

numbers, struck the cavalry of the Prussian right flank and threw it into confusion. Soon the Prussian right flank cavalry were riding back in disorder into the ranks of the right-hand infantry battalions of the Prussian first line.

Frederick had placed himself with one of these and was soon carried by a confused mass of retreating and disorganized Prussian horsemen along the line of his own army. It seemed possible that that army would be rolled up by the enemy from right to left, or at the least cut in half, since a gap had now opened between the right-hand infantry battalions and the rest. Schwerin saw that some of the Prussian army was out of control. There was chaos on the right wing. He decided that the King should leave the field.

Frederick always showed fear of capture, of being exploited by his captors while unable to do his will, a puppet. He wrote more than once to Podewils to make clear that if he were ever taken prisoner his words and instructions were to be ignored. Now – with confusion all around him and the situation totally obscure – he accepted the counsel of the experienced Schwerin. Mounting a new horse, a strong grey, later named 'the Mollwitz grey', he took a few selected papers and galloped with his immediate aides to what he supposed would be the shelter of the walled town of Oppeln, many miles from the battlefield.

Oppeln, however, had already been occupied by a detachment of Austrian cavalry and on announcing themselves – '*Macht auf! Preussen!*' – Frederick's party were fired on. Frederick turned his horse and rode back towards Mollwitz, ultimately stopping at the village of Lowen, not far from where he had started. He was ignorant of the situation and he felt wretched, ashamed, a failure. He was near despair. And there were those who thought and said that the King of Prussia had deserted his army in the hour of crisis.

Only the unimaginative could fail to understand Frederick's misery at that moment. His courage was shown, through subsequent life, to be beyond question, but it had not yet been demonstrated. He had accepted the veteran Schwerin's urgings and had left the field during battle. Malicious tongues – especially in France – made much of the incident.[12] Legends accumulated. It was said that as he turned to gallop away from the field an Austrian horseman with raised sabre had grabbed his bridle and that Frederick had yelled, 'Let me go and I'll reward you,' that the Austrian had recognized him and, lowering his sabre, had shouted back, 'Right! After the war!' and had ultimately become a Prussian lieutenant-general. There was no word of truth in any of this, although the story appeared in print during Frederick's lifetime. But Frederick's escape from the carnage of Mollwitz, his loss of control – and thus of reputation – had derived from his inexperience and from the cocksureness of youth. He had been determined that he and he alone should command. He had earlier rejected suggestions that the Old Dessauer (who had been sceptical about the Silesian adventure) should accompany his suite, saying that the King of Prussia must not be seen to go to war with a tutor; now the absence of a tutor seemed most unfortunate. Frederick, as he often did, had ridden to war with some of his circle of intellectual cronies forming part of his staff. Maupertuis, for instance, the French mathematician and astronomer, a former officer in the army of Louis XIV, a Fellow of the Royal Society in London who had come to Berlin at Frederick's invitation (and later became President of Frederick's Academy of Sciences), was now in Frederick's suite; he was taken prisoner by the Austrians as Frederick rode away from Oppeln.*

There had been amateurish over-confidence in Frederick's behaviour. The philosopher-king had wanted to show companion philosophers that a king should also govern and command. He had failed to do so.

An early error of judgement may help the development of a major talent if it induces reflection and does not produce a general disaster. At Mollwitz Frederick was fortunate. The army had known nothing of his sudden departure. After Frederick had ridden off on that icy afternoon Schwerin had rallied the Prussian cavalry not yet destroyed and saved them. The day had been turned, however, by the Prussian infantry, infantry drilled to perfection by Frederick William and his regimental colonels (including Frederick himself). They had advanced in impeccable order 'like moving walls', the Austrians said, and had swept all before them. Frederick himself had very recently altered the

---

* Taken to Vienna, he was at once lionized by Viennese society and soon returned to Berlin in exchange for Cardinal von Sinzendorf, Archbishop of Breslau, who had been detained.

infantry drill so that regiments formed in three rather than four ranks to extend frontage and increase firepower, and although this was new the men had practised it endlessly and perfected it. It worked. The Austrian infantry line had been smashed into pieces by superior, disciplined firepower and the Austrian cavalry had been disinclined to face it. Losses were about even on both sides but by nightfall it was clear that the initial Austrian onslaught had achieved only local and temporary effect, the Prussians were masters of the field and Silesia was still in their hands. Frederick received Schwerin's report, telling the story, soon after he reached Lowen.

After battle, inquest. Two days later Frederick wrote to Podewils in Berlin.[13] Mollwitz had, in his mind, become a victory – his first, and in fact his least glorious. He wrote – as infrequently – in German. It had pleased God to bless Frederick's arms in such a way as to defeat an enemy army, 'at least 6,000 men stronger' and with almost three times the cavalry strength. Exaggeration after battle happens in every age and Frederick was writing with profound emotional relief. The truth was that the Prussian infantry, who had won as much of the day as could be described as a victory, probably outnumbered the Austrian infantry by about 6,000 rather than the other way round.

Frederick later called Mollwitz 'one of the most memorable days of the century'. This was perhaps comprehensible in that the great Habsburg Empire had noticeably failed to punish a constituent state and recover a possession. Mollwitz marked the beginning of a process which culminated a century and a quarter later on the field of Königgrätz. The horse which had carried Frederick on that stupendous ride through snow and darkness, the 'Mollwitz grey', lived into old age, wanting for nothing and occasionally ridden on parade by the King in the Potsdam Lustgarten, still recognizing the music of the Prussian marches and snorting when the colours passed until dying, aged forty, in 1762. Mollwitz, and all associated with it, became epic.

But Frederick admitted that he had been a complete novice at Mollwitz and to his credit resolved to learn its lessons, to put right what he supposed had gone wrong with the army and to take some lessons to his own heart. He blamed himself – rightly, although Schwerin must take some responsibility – for the excessive dispersion of the Prussians at the start of the campaign and for the consequent failure to concentrate until the enemy were already threatening communications between Prussia and Silesia. He blamed himself for failures of timely deployment when approaching the actual battlefield. And he could have blamed himself – and certainly profited from the lesson – for placing himself in so forward a position that the first Austrian cavalry attack swept him up and deprived him of the ability to command. As to the army, he reckoned that his cavalry were of poor quality with mediocre officers. The army had survived the battle with honour because of the high quality of the infantry.

There was a good deal in this, although Frederick was not immune from the frequent military failing of drawing too general a conclusion from an isolated occurrence. The Austrian cavalry – virtually the entire enemy cavalry force, under General Romer, who was killed in the battle – had outnumbered by two to one the Prussian cavalry of the right wing, had therefore attacked with overwhelming local superiority, had attacked when the Prussians were standing and vulnerable, and had enveloped their right. It was not necessarily correct to deduce Prussian qualitative inferiority. Frederick, nevertheless, reckoned that he had seen enough to cause him serious unease and after the battle he took the whole army into camp, north of Mollwitz, and set it to an intensive schedule of training, devised, ordered and supervised by himself. He rose, every day, long before dawn and was soon in the saddle on a ride of rigorous inspection. Despite his hours of misery Mollwitz had not destroyed his self-confidence and it had certainly not diminished the strength of his will.

The battle had not changed the basic strategic situation although it had demonstrated to the world the relative impotence of Austria, at least for a while, and those who hoped for prizes from Austria scented opportunity. Now from Bohemia and Moravia the Austrians looked northward towards a Silesia improperly, as they reckoned, occupied by the Prussian invader. Militarily, there was jockeying for position but no major encounter as the spring of 1741 turned to summer. There were periodic cavalry encounters. On 17 May Colonel von Ziethen – already forty-three and an officer who would play a key part in the improvement and development of the Prussian cavalry – with six squadrons of hussars surprised and beat a larger force of Austrian cavalry at Rothschloss; he was marked by Frederick as, exceptionally, a cavalryman whose ability he could trust and whose energy was impressive. At Neisse the Austrian garrison, undefeated, might one day act as a launchpad for wider adventures. Breslau still maintained its independence of the rival armies although twenty-five miles south-west of it, at Schweidnitz, Frederick created a large magazine and *place d'armes*.

Frederick pressed ahead with what he regarded as liberal and necessary reforms in Silesia itself. He took great trouble to be even-handed – the Protestant population soon resented this, as many had hoped for material advantage from the King's favour: the Archbishop of Breslau, Cardinal von Sinzendorf, was given the Black Eagle and made Vicar General of all Silesia – an appointment which the Vatican regarded as proper for the Pope rather than the King of Prussia to make, amid recriminations. His hold on the province was tenuous and he knew he would not be left in undisputed possession of it for long. Voltaire's congratulations had been composed in heroic couplets on 20 April and had likened Frederick, in the pantheon of victors, to Charles XII, Gustavus Adolphus, Turenne and Achilles! Frederick knew, however, that to retain Silesia he would need not gratifying historical comparisons but adroit diplomacy and military strength.

There had been delays in signing the earlier mooted defensive alliance between France and Prussia. The French had been uncertain; Mollwitz helped make up their minds. Then Frederick had hesitated, claiming that he was worried (as was justified) about the reactions of Britain and Russia. Marshal Belle-Isle, envoy of France, had then travelled to Breslau after Mollwitz, joining Valory there. Charles Louis Auguste Fouquet, Comte de Belle-Isle, was a grandson of the distinguished (and unfortunate) finance minister of Louis XIV, Nicolas Fouquet, builder of Vaux-le-Vicomte. He had made a most favourable impression on Frederick and had formed a high opinion of Prussian military system and of the King's mastery of detail. It was soon clear to Frederick that Maria Theresa had no intention of making peace or conceding anything: and the agreement was signed.

In consequence on 5 June 1741 France undertook to support Bavaria, in alliance with Prussia, in an offensive against Austria. Cardinal Fleury, virtual dictator of French foreign policy, was personally lukewarm but he was ninety years old, and younger men, including very much Belle-Isle, argued the ripeness of the moment. Austria was vulnerable, without allies, with a disputed Habsburg succession, an Imperial election pending, a depleted treasury and a vigorous Prussian enemy on her northern frontier. Austria's vulnerability was France's opportunity. There need be no official declaration of war – Bavaria provided the official front. France could simply support.

For Frederick this was a logical development and welcome. He was short of friends. The situation in Russia and Sweden was most uncertain. So was the attitude of Britain – Frederick had received the British Ambassador at Mollwitz in May and made clear that his minimum requirement for peace was Lower Silesia and Breslau, but he knew that his uncle, George II, distrusted him and had even tried to organize an alliance against him involving Saxony and Russia, as well as proposing an alliance with Austria. Hanover and Saxony could each hope to gain territory from a defeated Prussia.

To Britain Austria was still a traditional ally against a traditional enemy, France – a traditional ally led by a young and hard-pressed Queen in sad straits. There was, Frederick knew, little to hope for from London. The British Government would, certainly, explore his intentions and hope to bring about peace between Prussia and Austria because this would enable Austria to confront France more effectively, but Britain had no interest in the rights and disputes of Prussia and cared only for the discomfiture of France. When Podewils had suggested in May that there might yet be useful agreements to be won from London, Frederick told him that there was nothing to be expected from that quarter but *verbiage obscur*. For the moment the interests of France and Prussia were identical, he wrote on 21 May. He knew that this would be most unpopular in London but he saw no alternatives to an agreement which he made with the French at the beginning of June. To inquiries from the British Ambassador Podewils was instructed to say that the King was not disposed to fool about any longer (*pas d'humeur à se laisser amuser plus longtemps!*). If Austria were irreconcilable the only possible allies seemed to be France and France's protégé, Bavaria. Frederick wrote to Fleury on 30 May that he had just signed an alliance with the King, his master.[14]

Yet Frederick was to a degree uneasy. And Podewils, too, was uneasy. When the latter returned, in mid-June, to the point that it was unwise to antagonize England, Frederick told him sharply that he would suspect his minister of being hired by the British if he continued on that line, and received the dignified reply that Podewils believed both his reputation and his poverty argued for him. And the new alliance indicated further complications and commitments. France was now supporting the Elector of Bavaria's claim to the throne of Bohemia as well as his candidacy for the Imperial crown, and Frederick – who had also agreed to support the Bavarian candidacy, and had, indeed, suggested it – was unenthusiastic about a greatly expanded and strengthened Bavaria–Bohemia across his southern border. Under the new alliance he had agreed to surrender his claim to Jülich and Berg while his allies had agreed to recognize his Silesian rights. A Franco-Bavarian invasion of Austria would distract Vienna from what must inevitably one day come – a renewed counter-offensive to drive the Prussians from Silesia. So far it seemed a reasonable bargain.

But Frederick's uneasiness was deep-seated. He had no enthusiasm in the long term for a Franco-Bavarian triumph. It seemed impossible to do business with the Habsburgs on terms he would regard as acceptable, but Prussia could not live for ever in a state of declared or undeclared war with Austria. He was in possession, in so far as 'possession' had meaning, of most of Silesia and he regarded that as right and legitimate; and there was more, particularly the fortress of Neisse, which he reckoned should be his. But he knew that sooner or later he would probably need to draw his sword again to defend even what he held of Silesia, and it was clear to him that some ultimate accommodation with Austria, difficult though it might be, was a desirable object of policy. He had always indicated that were his claims in Silesia admitted (even in part) he was ready to support Maria Theresa in other directions – even to give his electoral vote to Francis of Lorraine. He had now switched the latter to support for Bavaria but he still felt that bridges should not absolutely be destroyed between Vienna and Berlin.

His ambivalence – and it never really disappeared – was increased by what he soon regarded as the lethargic military proceedings of his new allies, France and Bavaria. If the alliance was to be of use to

Frederick he wished for a vigorous campaigning effort, preferably up the valley of the Danube towards Vienna, and not into Bohemia as the Bavarians seemed to intend. He made that very clear in a personal letter to the Bavarian Elector on 26 July,[15] and he wrote with equal firmness to Fleury[16] that he had no intention of voting for the Elector of Bavaria in the Imperial election until that ruler acted – or before French troops entered Germany. Frederick's letters indicated clearly that he thought his allies lacked energy and a sense of urgency – two days after his first letter he wrote: 'if the Cardinal does not want to make war he ought to give up the alliance!' Considering that the agreement had only been made at the beginning of June, this was to show a grudging attitude to his allies and in turn raises the suspicion that Frederick wished to have reasons for reconsidering policy if it suited him. There are echoes of Stalin's brutal carpings at Anglo-American delays in an offensive against Germany in the Second World War – carpings which concealed an underlying hostility and divergence of political aim.

For the events of the latter months of 1741, the apparent *renversement des alliances*, the changes of attitude, have played a particularly large part in Frederick's reputation for duplicity. The facts are undisputed. Maria Theresa and her ministers found the situation near desperate. It seemed essential to try to detach one or more of her enemies from the hostile alliance. She tried to buy the neutrality of France with an offer to cede Luxembourg. She tried to buy Bavaria with some grants of Imperial lands and titles in Italy. And already, on 7 August, she had sent an offer, by the medium of the British Ambassador in Vienna, to cede to Prussia Imperial territory in Holland and pay 2 million *écus** if all Prussian troops withdrew from Silesia.

Frederick's response was swift and strong. He found the proposition both offensive and absurd. He had no pretensions in the Low Countries; his ambitions were confined to territories in Silesia which were his by right. So far the exchanges simply confirmed each party in a traditional position of intransigence. Frederick wrote to George II appealing to the Protestant faith to which both subscribed and presuming (with little conviction) that George would prefer him to keep

* £200,000.

rather than lose Silesia. He wrote on 4 September to his man in Munich, Count von Schmettau, saying that his loyalty to the Bavarian cause was undeviating, that he hoped to take Neisse in two weeks and presumed that a Franco-Bavarian attack towards Vienna would soon be undertaken?[17] To Voltaire he wrote at the same time that he supposed there would soon be more battles – 'It's a stupid business but one sometimes has to be mad in life!'[18]

This all seemed straightforward but other currents were flowing. Frederick was watching developments in Saxony very closely. The Elector of Saxony, King of Poland, Augustus III was a very different sort of man from his remarkable father, Augustus the Strong – he was vacillating and impressionable; and throughout his reign he was under the dominating influence of his chief minister, Count Brühl, a Protestant but one very hostile to Frederick. Saxony was too near Prussia for complacency. Bavaria was seeking accession of Saxony to the 'allied' – anti-Austrian – cause and Frederick was concerned at the sort of price which might be offered. In a letter to the French commander, Belle-Isle, on 16 September,[19] Frederick wrote that what he understood was being offered was, in his view, certainly too high. He had heard that Saxony was being offered Upper Silesia and Moravia; was that, Frederick inquired, really agreeable to the Elector of Bavaria? As the Franco-Bavarian army advanced eastward and Maria Theresa prepared for an enemy siege of Vienna, the Bavarians and Saxons continued with their plans to apportion Habsburg lands after the defeat of Habsburg armies, actually making an agreement on 19 September. Saxony was to get Moravia, Upper Silesia and part of Lower Austria. Bavaria was to get Upper Austria and Tirol. The Elector of Bavaria would be crowned King of Bohemia. The map of Germany was to be drastically redrawn.

And not in a way designed by Frederick. The anti-Austrian alliance seemed somewhat out of control.

Two developments now impinged. In June Maria Theresa, a princess of considerable spirit, had been crowned Queen of Hungary at Pressburg (Bratislava), where the dominant nobles of the Hungarian people had pledged their loyalty and undertaken to raise for her an army of 40,000 (of which about 20,000 were actually forthcoming). And Britain, once again, attempted to take a hand. The imminent downfall of the Habsburgs and the consequential increase in the power of France were, if they came about, most unpalatable in London; and the piece on the European chessboard which might be moved, but covertly moved, was the King of Prussia. George II disliked his nephew, Frederick. Hanover feared Brandenburg-Prussia. Theoretical concepts had been mooted whereby Frederick might be attacked by a combination of Hanover, Saxony, Britain, even Russia, and Prussian territories seized. To British ministers this seemed remote from the true interests of Britain. As to Austria, there was little disposition in the British Government to spend significant British treasure or British blood in the cause of Maria Theresa, however sympathetic some in England felt, but the spectre of France and France's proxies destroying the Empire and emerging dominant on the continent aroused sentiments which went back to Marlborough and Eugen; and to Louis XIV. King George might be obsessed with his Hanoverian possessions and the dangers from his Prussian relations – he had, indeed, made an agreement of neutrality with France, acting as Elector and without the endorsement of his British ministers, an agreement intended to preserve Hanover. As far as the wider war was concerned, Britain had pledged herself to neutrality in this confused continental struggle. Now the British Ambassador in Berlin, Lord Hyndford, informally opened the bidding again. Neutrality might need improved interpretation.

The British Ambassador in Vienna, Sir Thomas Robinson,* had already made those proposals to Frederick which had been so roughly rejected in August and Podewils was told by Frederick that any similar overtures by Hyndford should receive similar treatment. Nevertheless, on 25 September Colonel von Goltz, on Frederick's staff, made some suggestions to Hyndford. In all that followed Frederick used intermediaries, and Goltz was one.

Goltz wrote that perhaps arrangements might be devised by which Neipperg could withdraw into Moravia, unmolested, leaving the present military situation on the Moravian-Silesian border unchanged by major battle: at the same time there could be a sham investment

* Later, Lord Grantham. Frederick understood that he was deeply in love with Maria Theresa, a subject of mockery.

by the Prussians of Neisse and a capitulation by the Austrian garrison after an agreed period of fourteen days. The Austrians would have easement – a virtual armistice, albeit undeclared, on one front and ability to concentrate elsewhere against the French and Bavarians. In return for these covert arrangements Frederick would be given tacit agreement to his possession of Lower Silesia, but including both Breslau and the fortress of Neisse; and would give an undertaking to raise no taxes nor levy any impositions on Maria Theresa's present domains. The Prussian army would be formally in the field against the Austrians but would effectively do nothing and, with the coming change of season, go into winter quarters in Upper Silesia.

Goltz wrote that all must, naturally, be entirely secret. He took great trouble to deceive the French Ambassador, Valory, about Frederick's relations with Hyndford, actually telling him on 23 September that the King had indicated to Hyndford that his presence in the camp was no longer acceptable. In fact the King, his master,[20] now wished to convey his good will to Maria Theresa, Queen of Hungary, although certainly not proposing any formal agreement or cessation of hostilities. Goltz put it very frankly: Frederick 'wanted to stop making war but did not want to appear to have stopped!' This would give Frederick what he reckoned he wanted in the immediate situation. It would give him Silesia, at least for the time being. It would give relief to Maria Theresa and pre-empt that Franco-Bavarian triumph at her expense about which Frederick – although he had procured it or the beginning of it – felt strong reservations. An agreement – which, of course, betrayed Frederick's allies in fact and in spirit if not in formal words – was drafted by Hyndford, discussed with the Austrians through the British ambassadorial intermediaries, and considered at a secret meeting which took place on 9 October in the village of Klein Schnellendorf. The meeting was arranged by Hyndford and attended by both Frederick and Neipperg; the final paragraph of the resultant protocol enjoined absolute secrecy. Frederick, however, was careful to put his actual signature to nothing.

Frederick, very naturally, was concerned to keep all this from the French, the Bavarians and the Saxons. He was trafficking with the enemy. He went to considerable pains to deepen the deception, writing to Schmettau, his man at the Bavarian court, on 2 October[21] that the Franco-Bavarian advance up the Danube valley seemed deplorably slow. The Bavarian Elector, with his headquarters, was at Linz, which had fallen to the allies on 14 September; and Frederick simulated impatience. Precious time, he said, was being lost. He, Frederick, had been pressing the enemy '*autant qu'il a été possible*', but the Prussian army had been in the field for ten months and to continue too long without respite invited disaster. If the Bavarians delayed much longer Frederick would have no alternative but to take his men into winter quarters. He had supposed that by now a second French column would have appeared in Bohemia. Where was it? 'I have,' he wrote, 'up to now carried the whole burden on myself.' He was preparing the ground. On 7 October he wrote a more or less routine letter to Bavaria coordinating the movement of troops. On the 14th he wrote of threatening Neipperg's magazines in Moravia, although if Neipperg preceded ('*devançait*') the Prussians there Frederick would not attempt to follow[22] since the country was too defensible and the supply of a pursuing force too difficult. But in the seven days between these last two letters he had met Neipperg and Hyndford at Klein Schnellendorf; and had made his arrangements with the former.

The secret and temporary accommodation reached at Klein Schnellendorf suited Frederick. From his point of view the Habsburg power enthroned at Vienna should be weakened but not destroyed. The French and Bavarian alliance had been a necessary expedient at the time, in order to distract Austria and help save Prussia and Prussian possessions, but it must not become dominant and it had, for a while, played its part. Frederick's frequent protestations of support for the house of Austria have been dismissed as humbug but there was more to them than that. He had little regard for the Empire as such. He regarded it as largely an absurdity, an organization whose day had passed; but it provided a structured forum for the discussion, even the management, of German affairs, and as such it needed a head. That head should be a prince with sufficient resources of his own to provide leadership. The Habsburgs, whatever their double-dealings with Frederick William and his predecessors, could fill that bill as they had in the past – and fill it with Hohenzollern support provided that just Hohenzollern pretensions were recognized.

As to the immediate situation, the war, Frederick argued that he had not changed his fundamental position. Whatever the actions or inactivity of the troops – and this, in eighteenth-century warfare, had to depend on a large number of variables, including immediately available resources – Prussia was still at war with Austria. But the Prussian army had been in the field for some time and had suffered. Frederick had spent a good deal from his treasury. His Electoral vote would, if agreed conditions were satisfied, be given to the Elector of Bavaria; but Bavarian ambitions went further and there were limits to the energy with which Prussia should act, and Prussian blood be spilled to establish the house of Wittelsbach in Bohemia. He had made a covert and entirely practical agreement with the Austrian command which suited them both for the time being – such arrangements were not uncommon. The expedient was in the interest of Prussia and the Prussian people.

Neipperg and Frederick discharged their particular and immediate parts of the secret bargain. The Prussian army prepared to go into winter quarters. The demonstration was made against Neisse and the place capitulated as agreed, at the beginning of November 1741. Frederick received the formal homage of the free city of Breslau – in August he had managed to introduce Schwerin into the place by a bloodless subterfuge and a Prussian force was now in possession.

By late October, however, a few weeks after Klein Schnellendorf, it was clear that France and Bavaria were concerned at Frederick's military inactivity and at what it might or might not signify. Frederick emphasized – strictly true – that he had certainly not made peace with Maria Theresa. He reiterated that his engagements to Bavaria were solemn and indissoluble, but there were practical factors which limited what the Prussians could do. The French Ambassador to Frederick, Valory, expressed the anxieties of France and asked whether the King would consider a joint expedition with the French to invade Hanover? Frederick rejected the idea, carefully recounting all, for George II's benefit, to his Ambassador in Hanover on 18 October.[23]

There were, as ever, plentiful 'leaks' and most of them were deliberate and made for comprehensible political reasons. Besides keeping Hanover informed of such French approaches, Frederick told Cardinal Fleury all about approaches made by what he called *'l'artificielle et*

perfide cour de Vienne' through the British Ambassador, Hyndford.[24]
He had, he told the Cardinal, actually been asked by the British to
cooperate in the expulsion of Bavarian forces from Austria as well as
giving his Electoral vote to Francis of Lorraine! For this he would
have stood to receive much. Instead, he declared, he intended at the
right moment to march into Moravia, true to his allies, to help prevent
that expulsion. For good measure, he added to Fleury that the conduct
of the King of England was more suspicious with every day that
passed; and that the alliance with *'le Roi votre maître'* was the most
pleasing of his life. In a further and particularly effusive letter on 3
December he told Fleury that he felt a deep affinity with France and
an equal mistrust of Austria and England.[25]

The first letter to Fleury was written on 29 October. It is probable
that it was read by the immensely experienced eighty-eight-year-old
Cardinal with total absence of credulity. It was part of the elaborate
game of half-truth, untruth, dissimulation and occasional accuracy
which marked the diplomacy of eighteenth-century governments. To
Frederick this was the necessary game of power. If ends could be
achieved by it without bloodshed, fighting and destruction, so much
the better. It involved deception, of course, but it was a sort of war
and deception is a sinew of war. And in fact the sentiments in his
letter of 3 December happened to be largely true.

Another sinew of war was the actual possession not only of fortresses
but of territory. Billets for soldiers, forage for horses, a countryside
capable of producing some provisions – these things were vital, often
more vital than the actual operational benefits which could come from
the domination of key points, communications, roads and riverways.
Frederick had undertaken to the Austrians (his enemies) to go into
winter quarters after Neisse was his, and he also explained to the
French and Bavarians (his allies) that to go into winter quarters was
a necessity for his army after so long in the field. Some of these winter
quarters, he told the French commander, Belle-Isle, were in part
of Bohemia – about a fifth part, around Boleslav, Leitmeritz and
Königgrätz. Belle-Isle – and, no doubt, the Elector of Bavaria, who
hoped shortly to be crowned King of Bohemia – had been making
courteous inquiries about the deployment and intentions of the Prussian army.

Frederick's careful and limited undertakings at Klein Schnellendorf were not translated into a treaty with Austria. There was no peace formalized, and when Hyndford tried for this again on 30 November Frederick rejected the idea. He had hoped that a consequence of his secret agreement would be a certain relief for Maria Theresa's military position – it had looked uncertain whether she could hold Vienna itself and this relief was still only partial; on the same day that he rejected the proposal for some formal peace agreement he wrote to Belle-Isle to congratulate him on taking Prague four days earlier[26] and to tell him that Frederick was prepared to send twenty-five squadrons of Prussian cavalry to join the Franco-Bavarian forces and march on their left as far as the borders of Moravia. Frederick, whatever his friendly understandings with Neipperg, wanted strong Prussian representation in the forces of his nominal allies if they were to rampage through Bohemia. This marked another shift in position, a departure from the spirit of Klein Schnellendorf, but Frederick could see the possibility of a runaway Franco-Bavarian triumph at Austrian expense, with Prussia sidelined, a triumph which could nullify the influence Frederick hoped to have at whatever peace agreement ultimately ensued. Furthermore a Saxon army of 20,000 men had now joined the Bavarian forces. Most parties – his official enemy and his official allies – had now acquiesced in his possession of Silesia but such acquiescence could change; could, with other things, be bargained away.

The international market place at the peace would be crucially affected by the military situation at the time. Who would have what force where? Matters were moving rather fast and Frederick decided that it was time for Prussia, somehow, to take a more positive military hand in the game. Besides sending his detachment of cavalry to help the Franco-Bavarians in Bohemia he ordered Schwerin to move with a force southward out of Silesia and to take Olmütz, only fifty miles north-east of the Moravian capital, Brünn; and on 17 December Schwerin did so. These manoeuvres were inconsistent with Frederick's agreements with Neipperg, but – always resourceful – he invoked what he claimed was Austrian breach of the strict secrecy both parties had agreed at Klein Schnellendorf. As early as October Goltz had complained to Hyndford that in both Prague and Dresden people were aware of allegations about Frederick's dealings with Neipperg; and *'Le Roi en est dans une colère terrible!'*[27] He told Hyndford in the same letter that if the conditions of absolute secrecy about tentative agreements were not satisfied the King would feel bound to nothing.

In modern terms the Klein Schnellendorf agreements were 'deniable', and their discharge would depend on the degree of observance of confidentiality. Frederick reckoned he had cards in his hand to balance any accusations of bad faith in the aftermath of Klein Schnellendorf; and he knew that the Austrians had quietly revealed a good deal to the French and Bavarians, in order to apply pressure on him. He had, of course, always been vulnerable to this. He had made the agreements with his eyes open and they had had, as intended, a military effect. They had given him Neisse. They had given his army a little rest. And they appeared to have incommoded his allies, the Franco-Bavarian forces, remarkably little.

Perhaps too little. Frederick's allies were now considering a general advance on Vienna and he himself joined his army at Olmütz and proposed that this allied movement might take place from both north and north-east. In January Charles Albert of Bavaria was elected Emperor by unanimous vote. Austria was threatened from all directions. The influence of France was at a high point in Germany. But while Maria Theresa appealed to Frederick, invoking the secret Klein Schnellendorf understandings, the entire military situation started to change.

5

'A Most Imprudent Manoeuvre'

Frederick was not particularly energetic in promoting the idea of a major concentric allied advance on Vienna. He had signified readiness to take part. He recognized that he had leeway to make up in annulling his allies' suspicions of his dealings with the Austrians, but he was unwilling to risk his Prussians deep in Imperial territory for the (now legitimate) pretensions of Charles Albert of Bavaria. He was determined to safeguard at all times his communications with Silesia and its security – it was for Silesia, not for France, nor Bavaria, that he had drawn the sword. He established his Moravian headquarters at Seelowitz, near Brünn, and received yet more proposals for peace from Maria Theresa: and formulated some on his own account, including the possible cession not only of Silesia but of lands on the Upper Elbe in Bohemia – a cession which would make Bohemia virtually untenable for a power ruling in Vienna and which would certainly be unacceptable.

It had until very recently been doubtful which that power might be, and Frederick had been staking out claims in a shifting military situation. But now a remarkable transformation occurred, one which Frederick had certainly not foreseen. Having been the cautious and recently inactive witness of Austrian humiliation, humiliation possibly beyond a point he would welcome, he now watched an astounding Austrian recovery. The Austrians had one Franco-Bavarian enemy in Prague and another, Frederick, near Brünn. From both north and north-west Vienna was threatened, and the French and Bavarians were not far off, in the Danube valley. Then, with extraordinary speed, the Empire gathered together a renewed and re-inspired army, greatly reinforced from the eastern territories, from Hungary and

Croatia. In January 1742 an Austrian counter-offensive started. Two Austrian armies began moving west from the area of Vienna, and defeated the Bavarians at Scharding on 17 January.

Two days later Frederick travelled to Dresden, the Saxon capital, to confer with his allies. He had, only a few weeks earlier, been hedging his bets and strengthening the Prussian position against the eventuality of a complete Austrian collapse. Now the tables seemed to be turned. Frederick had, with mixed feelings, watched the near-triumph of France and Bavaria and now he was witnessing the triumphant resurgence of Austria. And that, too, was certainly not what he wanted. He found himself again enmeshed in coalition warfare in an unpromising military situation which, if it went wrong, could threaten the solid gains his earlier and original intervention had seemed to promise – the generally recognized accession of Silesia to Prussia.

A major Franco-Bavarian military success might have carried dangers for Frederick but he had reckoned he could modify these by being at the victors' table and being in possession of a good deal of the land he wanted; by the manoeuvres and movements of December his army was in some strength in Moravia. Now – because his allies had, in his view, made a mess of the campaign – he was threatened by their incompetence. He distrusted the Saxons. He professed to have a low opinion of the new French commander who had succeeded Belle-Isle – this was the Marshal de Broglie, with Belle-Isle serving as a subordinate. Broglie had been the Governor of Strasbourg when Frederick had made his indiscreet incognito visit before the war and some supposed that the incident had left resentment in Frederick's mind.[1]

Frederick now suggested that the Prussians should advance from Olmütz deeper into Moravia, in a south-westerly direction, taking Brünn if possible. He left the allied conference in Dresden with enhanced authority, in that it had been agreed that a large Saxon contingent and some French forces still in Bohemia should serve under his command, and he travelled via Prague to join his troops in Moravia. He had not disguised his wish to keep his Prussians out of a winter campaign in Bohemia if he could. He set up his court and his headquarters at Olmütz. 'The Devil, who has been leading me around, has now brought me to Olmütz,'[2] he wrote to Voltaire on 3 February

– he was reading and greatly enjoying Voltaire's book about Louis XIV – 'bad faith and duplicity are, unfortunately, the dominant characteristics of most men at the head of nations!' For some such sentiments simply demonstrate Frederick's boundless hypocrisy, but it is hard to believe that in writing to the man whose intellect he most admired he would indulge in trivial and gratuitous falsity of tone. Frederick did not believe that his own necessary twists and subterfuges in the game of diplomacy made him false.

The meeting at Dresden had produced little harmony despite the usual assurances of undeviating friendship; and five days later the Austrians had retaken Linz on their march westward. A great counter-offensive was under way. Ten thousand French had surrendered in Linz. Frederick cautiously strengthened his position in Moravia while, far to the west, the Austrians burst into Bavaria and on 12 February entered Munich. On the same day the Bavarian Elector, his capital now in enemy hands, was crowned Roman Emperor in Frankfurt.

Frederick's chief concern, very naturally, was for the security of his army in Moravia, for his defence of Silesia and for his communications with Prussia. He was now feeling that the alliance – French, Bavarian, Saxon, Prussian – was doing little for him and he frequently regretted its necessity. His mind was more and more turned towards peace, and his letters, particularly to Fleury, were full of it. He was sure Prussia needed peace. When Hyndford, on 1 February, indicated that he had further and helpful propositions to advance, Frederick did not rebuff him but simply suggested a short delay – he was far from Berlin, he said, and there were few indications that peace was uppermost in Maria Theresa's mind. Soon afterwards Frederick saw a letter which she had written to the States General of Holland, listing her grievances and complaints against her enemies – much of her anger was directed at the election, which had frustrated her ambition of setting her husband on the Imperial throne, but a good deal of it was directed at the conduct of the King of Prussia. Frederick wrote comments on the letter to his envoy at The Hague. He described Maria Theresa's accusations as untrue, injurious and obscure. He was, for instance, alleged to have twice made and then breached a peace agreement. If so, he wrote, why not produce this agreement?[3] It would be a novel way to manage international affairs to conclude hostilities without documents or formalities! The object of Maria Theresa's letters, he said, was simply to inflame his allies against him.

There was, of course, disingenuousness in this. It was true that he had signed nothing at Klein Schnellendorf, that his letters of esteem in all directions were no more than the usual courtesies of diplomatic life – even between formal enemies – and that a serious agreement of peace must have been marked by a formal signed document, not merely a protocol of provisional understanding initialled by one of the parties and nodded to by the others. There had been no peace treaty, the war had continued and Frederick had played, was playing, a continuing if reserved part in it. In so far as temporary agreements between military commanders went (and he had, of course, taken no formal cognizance of them), he had adhered to them. That was in the past. Nevertheless Frederick recognized that one of the impediments to peace between Austria and Prussia (as well as one of the impediments to wholehearted cooperation within the alliance opposed to Austria) was the reservation felt in many quarters – in Vienna, in Dresden, in Munich (or wherever the Elector now found himself, having been driven from his capital) or in Paris – about the reliability of the King of Prussia. And Frederick wanted peace.

Meanwhile Frederick had to go through the motions of continuing the war, disarming allied suspicions that he was lukewarm, that he was secretly actuated by the spirit of Klein Schnellendorf. In February he wrote to Belle-Isle (now a subordinate, but one trusted by Frederick) to say that some French operational moves were very necessary in order to distract the Austrians from marching in full force on himself. He wrote to the recently crowned Emperor on 20 February with plans for a campaign in the spring to drive the Austrians from the Upper Danube. He probably had little belief in these ideas (which involved the commitment of large French forces), and to write to the Emperor on the matter was little more than a matter of form – the Emperor, an exile from his own capital, commanded nothing. It was probably, however, one of those times when form mattered a good deal – Frederick was demonstrating himself as a scrupulous ally and a loyal prince of the Empire. More immediately and more practically Frederick wrote attempting to coordinate the movements and preparations of his troops in Moravia with his allies in Bohemia, around Iglau (between Prague and Brünn) and Neuhaus. He had seized a number of Austrian outposts, had led part of the Prussian army south from Olmütz to join strong Saxon forces and a smaller French corps; a total of more than 30,000 men under his command. His headquarters were at Znaim on the Thaya river, thirty miles south-east of Iglau. Meanwhile the Austrians were developing a movement northward towards Prague and into Moravia.

The Austrian offensive was led by Charles of Lorraine, Maria Theresa's brother-in-law,* who had taken over the command-in-chief from his brother and was considerably more efficient. Iglau had been retaken by the Austrians on 15 February and a French force had been withdrawn. Brünn had never fallen to the allies and Frederick, in March, ordered a movement of his troops in Moravia towards the Silesian border. He wrote in contemptuous terms of what he learned of Saxon conduct. They had, he understood, abandoned Iglau without orders – '*Ils ont une peur démesurée de l'ennemi!*'⁴ For what, he increasingly asked himself, was he fighting? He had spent a great deal of money, he had marched deep into Moravia to help the cause, and now he was in the process of marching out again. His allies were mismanaging military affairs. Nevertheless he still emphasized to his allied correspondents and brother sovereigns that any efforts to detach him from the Franco-Bavarian alliance would be in vain.

Some matters could change Frederick's normally courteous style and introduce asperity. 'I was astonished,' he wrote to the French Ambassador on 4 March,⁵ 'to learn that a man called Baron de Burnet has felt free to tell His Imperial Majesty that I am ready to lend six million florins to the States of Bohemia if His Imperial Majesty stands surety. I have never seen nor spoken to this man, I don't know him or who he is, and his impudence amazes me!' But more serious things were also irritating him at this time. A few weeks later he wrote that Belle-Isle (whom he generally admired) 'shows large armies on paper, plans of campaigns where he beats the enemy everywhere, but takes no account of what the *enemy* may do!' On 22 March he sent to Podewils his latest thoughts on a basis for peace. The letter was to act as an instruction in talking to Hyndford.⁶

*

* The brother of Maria Theresa's husband, Francis, he married her sister.

Frederick's thoughts went little beyond a reiteration of the position he had held from the start. His policy and aims had always been consistent. First, Lower Silesia – but including Breslau and Neisse – must be wholly ceded to Prussia, wholly independent of any fealty to the Empire or to Bohemia. The county of Glatz (the salient from Silesia south into Moravia, west of Neisse) with the areas of Königgrätz and Pardubitz on the bend of the Upper Elbe must also be ceded. Maria Theresa should give 'reasonable satisfaction' to Frederick's allies (this provided defence against charges of purely selfish policy); and should accept Frederick's mediation 'together with the maritime powers' in a general peace. The mention of the maritime powers should give a sop to Hanover, although by now Frederick was sure that France and Britain would not remain at peace for long. Until this 'general peace' were negotiated Frederick should also keep Upper Silesia in so far as not covered in the foregoing.

Frederick described these as the 'conditions of Seelowitz' (where he was installed ten miles south of Brünn, for three weeks from mid-March). If they were agreed he would completely withdraw his troops from Moravia. Podewils was to try this on Hyndford as intermediary and see how it went. 'If they're keen,' he wrote on 27 March,[7] 'we sell ourselves dear. If less so, be prepared to mix water with the wine!' He added that he would never agree peace if it meant overturning the outcome of the Imperial election (which would have signified a Habsburg triumph, albeit of negligible practical importance) or if it meant guaranteeing 'Maria Theresa's domains', which would mean depriving him of Silesia. As from the beginning, the crux was Silesia. He had set up a temporary commission to administer Silesia and then established two War and Domains Boards, on the Prussian model, at Glogau and Breslau. Ludwig Wilhelm von Münchow was appointed responsible minister, with very wide powers, and the – largely feudal – Silesian system was gradually brought to the Prussian model. Later, Frederick removed Silesia from the oversight of the Berlin General Directory altogether. Considering the complexities of a province divided in religion and with strong ecclesiastical authority and tradition, the Silesian administration proved effective and successful.

Having set out what he regarded as his basic requirements and some glosses upon them, Frederick followed this up on 31 March with two memoranda.[8] In these he considered two main courses of action. The first was to maintain the alliance with France: the second was to make peace with Austria – with 'the Queen of Hungary' as he always (and correctly) called Maria Theresa. In favour of the first course he stated, honestly although perhaps speciously, that he had no formal complaints of France. It was bad to break one's word without reason and France had not done that. If the present campaign ended well, Prussia would have 'the honour' (he presumably meant of an unbeaten army). France could not turn her back on German affairs at this juncture, could not indulge in a policy of what in another context would be called isolationism: there was too much turmoil, too much at stake. But Britain would never welcome peace between France and Austria, and were Frederick to cleave to the French alliance the implication was that he would generally find himself in opposition to British policy.

These were somewhat disjointed conclusions, which Frederick ended on a different, more ambitious and very particular note – no peace could last long, he wrote, unless Maria Theresa gave up Bohemia and Moravia. In the second memorandum, however, Frederick dealt with severely practical matters, and his conclusions were more anxious than ambitious. First, he cited indifferent French military support. He did not impute bad faith but he thought Franco-Bavarian efforts unimpressive, presumably since the taking of Prague. That was in the past – now he looked to the future. If Britain and Holland were to declare war on France and deploy forces in Flanders (as Frederick expected and as soon happened) France would withdraw troops from Germany and leave on Frederick the entire weight of the war. The Saxons were useless.

This was not chimerical. The British Government had indeed decided to play a more positive part in a war which was, from their point of view, a struggle against France in support of France's intransigent enemy, Austria. The British Prime Minister, Sir Robert Walpole, a man of peace, had resigned in February; the new Secretary of State, Lord Carteret, was keenly interested in European affairs and had proposed the deployment of about 16,000 men in the Netherlands. He had, Frederick wrote afterwards, 'sworn implacable hatred to everything which bore the name "French"'.[9] Carteret was no more interested in the fate of Silesia than any other British statesman, and – like his predecessors – tried (with a substantial subsidy) to persuade Maria Theresa to come to terms with Frederick. But the British hope was that these newly deployed troops could be combined with some hired troops from Hesse and with whatever Austria could contribute in the Netherlands; and that an allied army – against France with a contingent from Hanover – could thus be constituted (efforts to get some Dutch support met apathy at best, resistance at worst). Frederick was perfectly right to suppose that while these endeavours might distract the French to a degree they would not be decisive, and they could leave him bearing more of the burden of the war in central Europe – if that war were to continue. On the other hand, military success in the war, if that were achieved, would leave France the arbiter of Europe (he wrote 'of the world').

There were, however, other and countervailing factors which would work against French success and his own – he cited the military support Maria Theresa was now getting from her Hungarian kingdom. Under most combinations of circumstance, the continuance of the war threatened Prussia with intolerable burdens. The greatest limiting factor for both sides would probably be the financing of campaigns. The Austrian treasury, which had been weak from the start, was depleted; Maria Theresa was almost entirely dependent on British subsidies to keep her armies in the field. But the Prussian treasury too, despite Frederick's initial war chest, was seriously weakened.

Winter conditions would last until late April and the armies in Moravia – the Austrians who were advancing into it and the Prussians who were there already – could only exist by plunder, and plunder was arousing the desperate, famished resistance of the Moravian population. Both sides wanted peace, and humanity demanded it. Frederick, however, could not accept a peace which denied him his gains – legitimate, as he saw them, and sealed with blood. And Maria Theresa, having survived an appalling winter and seen the tide turn, would feel strong enough to base her own demands on restoration of her patrimony and on help in driving the French from Germany. Neither side was likely yet to concede anything to the other's position. It was depressingly clear to Frederick that at present the war must continue.

Diplomacy, therefore, would need to be complemented by battle. Were either of the contestants to win a decisive victory, bargaining positions would be wholly altered. The Prussian army was widely dispersed in northern Moravia, where its deployment, based on Olmütz, had effectively blockaded Brünn (still in enemy hands) and covered communication with Silesia. Now Frederick decided to march part of it round Brünn into Bohemia, to shift his centre of gravity somewhat to the west. He gave his reasons for this to his allies on 6 April, writing that the French and Saxons were much weaker in the field than he had been led to hope. His quarters were being beaten up by Austrian raiding parties. Security and logistics alike demanded redeployment, and also dictated the abandonment by Schwerin of Olmütz – Olmütz, later in the month, was occupied by the Austrians who had assembled unexpected strength in Moravia. He wrote that he planned to assemble, before the end of April, an allied army – 'allied' because it had been agreed at Dresden that all forces would serve under the Prussians; he put projected numbers, optimistically and unconvincingly, at 45,000 – in the neighbourhood of Pardubitz at the Elbe bend, south of Königgrätz, areas he hoped to win ultimately for Prussia.

Frederick supposed that, sooner or later, he would have to cooperate against those Austrian direct operations against the French around Prague which had started in February. This demanded a movement westward by himself. The Austrian concentration in Moravia in the first months of the year 1742 had surprised him. He had been forced to react to it and he wrote to the Emperor on 28 April that *'Je suis extrêmement mortifié'*.[10] He thus had the prospect of operations to his west, in the Prague area, and an Austrian concentration to his east, with Olmütz in enemy hands. On the most westerly front of all there were glimpses of light – Belle-Isle was to be restored by the French to command of the army in Bohemia, had already had one significant success and had ejected the Austrians from most of Bavaria.

By 10 May Frederick had – somewhat belatedly – appreciated the extent to which the enemy had reduced their forces in Bohemia, to his west, and built them up in Moravia to his east. Whatever was happening in Bavaria and the Danube valley, the local situation showed a large, concentrated Austrian army moving westward towards his eastern flank. His own forces, including allied troops, were still pretty widely dispersed and he gave orders to assemble them on 13 May, at Chrudim. Besides 15,000 of his Prussians, he had under his control about the same number of Saxons and nearly 3,000 French.

On 15 May 1742 Frederick began a march westward, in the general direction of Prague. He supposed that he needed to frustrate an enemy move against his allies in that area. He was mistaken. The objective of the enemy was Frederick's own army, and Charles of Lorraine was concentrating his forces from both Moravia in the east, and from the south, to deal Frederick an overwhelming blow from a southerly direction.

Frederick had divided his forces and was leading the advance element, about one third, having instructed the rest to follow next day, 16 May. The latter – in effect the main body – marched under the command of Prince Leopold Max of Anhalt-Dessau, eldest son of the Old Dessauer. Frederick, although unaware of it, was moving his whole army (dangerously divided into two parts) across the front of the enemy's main body; a most imprudent manoeuvre.

The main body of the Austrian army was concentrated south of a village called Chotusitz on the Bohemian-Moravian border, near Leopold Max's line of march. When Frederick at last appreciated this and recognized its significance – and the urgency it demanded – he realized that he must turn his own advanced detachment round, retrace his steps, march to rejoin Leopold Max and concentrate the army again in what were clearly most dangerous circumstances produced by his own lack of timely information and breach of fundamental principle. His troops were short of rations, overdue from depots at Königgrätz. He wrote late on 16 May to Leopold Max that because of the troops' exhaustion it was impossible to march towards him that day – bad consequence of an unsound plan – but he set out at five o'clock on the morning of the 17th and the two parts of the Prussian army, so unfortunately separated, were reunited in front of Chotusitz in the early daylight hours. Leopold Max met the King at 7.30 a.m. The Prince's troops were already in position and he was, inevitably, given command of the left wing of a hasty deployment, designed to meet the north-marching Austrians. The rest of the army

– that which had been Frederick's advanced detachment – were arriving piecemeal on the ground in a battleline which extended for three miles between the villages of Cirkwitz in the west and Sehuschitz in the east, with Chotusitz in the centre and a large stretch of water, 'the Cirkwitz pond', immediately east of the village of that name. They could see the Austrian masses to their south. Battle was clearly imminent. There was broken, wooded ground on both flanks and an open plateau with easy gradients in the centre. It was not a bad position on which to meet the enemy, but the battle was not of Frederick's designing.

The first act was an attack by the thirty-five cavalry squadrons of the Prussian right wing under the seventy-year-old General Buddenbrock against the left wing of the Austrian cavalry opposite them. Buddenbrock achieved initial success, outflanking the Austrian left, but was then counter-attacked most effectively by Austrian cavalry and infantry. By 9.30 a.m. the Prussians had been worsted, and at the same time a confused cavalry encounter in the centre of the field had been followed by a general mêlée, at the end of which the Prussians had abandoned Chotusitz after some fierce infantry fighting.

It was still only mid-morning. So far the Prussian infantry of the right wing had not been engaged – Frederick had held them uncommitted in a hollow behind the right centre of his line, immediately west of Chotusitz itself. At 10.30 this body of men, fourteen battalions, marched forward out of the hollow on to the plateau, formed to their left and opened long-range enfilade fire against the Austrian mass round Chotusitz.

The Austrians broke. By eleven o'clock that morning, 17 May, the battle of Chotusitz was over, a Prussian victory. Frederick had lost nearly 5,000 men. Enemy casualties were ultimately set at about 6,000, including a large number of prisoners.

Frederick felt elated after Chotusitz. He described it in a letter to the Old Dessauer as 'Eine complette victorie'.[11] It certainly could not be described, however, as the sort of victory wherein a great commander had seen events conform to his plan and his will. On the contrary, Frederick had acted on false assumptions about the intentions of the enemy, which he supposed focused on Prague. His intelligence had been defective and his appreciation faulty. He had,

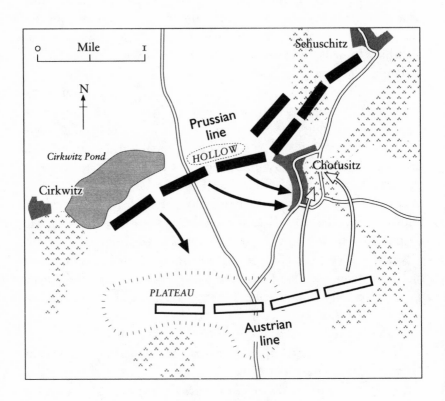

Chotusitz, 17 May 1742

in consequence, divided his army dangerously, adopted erroneous priorities and found himself drawn into a haphazard battle encounter not of his choosing. In it, as often happens, the day had been saved by the behaviour of particular troops and subordinate officers in one part of the field – in this case, as at Mollwitz, by the steadiness of the Prussian infantry, their drill, their disciplined firepower, their reliability. Frederick was not yet an experienced and authoritative commander. In time his army would come to trust him and rely upon him totally. At present he relied on them. He was learning.

But he knew he was learning. And with each stumble and error he recovered and stored in his mind a precept. 'He who divides his force will be beaten in detail,' he wrote in his *Instructions of the King of Prussia to his Officers* in 1745. The most enduring lessons are from one's own mistakes. After the battle Frederick decided that the army was in no condition to undertake a pursuit or exploit victory. There may have been a political reason also. 'I don't want to defeat them too badly,' he said at the time, and it was probably true, although the sentiment no doubt also derived from the realization that he had marched his men hard and unnecessarily exhausted them. He understood that the Austrians were assembling their forces both from the Danube valley and from the rest of Bohemia, and he moved his army into a defensible position near Kuttenberg south of Kolin. He presumed that the next enemy offensive would be aimed at driving the French back to Prague.

Frederick wanted peace, as he had done for some time. He hoped for movement on the diplomatic front. He had no desire to become further involved in this campaign, reckoning that for the time being the Prussians had done enough and lost enough. He was holding a strong position in Bohemia and his presence there, the threat it posed to Austria, was doing a good deal for the alliance. He had fought two battles, in neither of which had he been defeated. He had given up a good deal of Moravia but his communications with Silesia were, for the moment, unthreatened.

Frederick's letters to Podewils throughout April had been concerned with the possibilities of negotiation, a sequence only interrupted by the events of early May and the necessity to march west and fight another (inconclusive) battle for an alliance in which he had ceased to believe; ceased, that is, to believe in its value to Prussia. He had written on 26 April that Maria Theresa was in no condition to drive him from Silesia – or, indeed, Bohemia – so why not come to a reasonable arrangement? He hoped to use, once again, the good offices of the British Ambassador, Hyndford – although he kept the French sufficiently informed of his dealings with Hyndford to preserve something of his reputation as an ally. Indeed, on 14 May, just before Chotusitz, he told them that he had rejected most of Hyndford's proposals as unworthy and 'contrary to his way of thinking'! Britain appeared likely soon to support Maria Theresa openly, while France was asking for Frederick's help against a British force in the Rhineland. Militarily, Frederick's allies were lethargic. The war was more damnably expensive every day. There must be advantage for both sides in a peace of status quo, although it was unlikely Vienna would regard it as final.

But on 30 May Frederick wrote that Hyndford had 'done all that an honest man and a wise minister could'.[12] As at Klein Schnellendorf, Hyndford had brokered a deal between Maria Theresa and Frederick, although there was an essential difference between the two occasions. This time Frederick sent to Podewils an explicit instruction, dated 9 June from his camp at Kuttenberg, that the negotiation through Hyndford was to be put on a formal rather than a covert and deniable basis. Podewils, fully in Frederick's mind, was given all authority to treat.

As always Frederick prepared the diplomatic ground with a preliminary bombardment. On 13 June he wrote to Fleury[13] a letter of complaint about the inadequacy of de Broglie's operations, a failure which had prevented Frederick from doing as he had wished and marching towards Prague. He also – as frequently – grumbled bitterly about the behaviour of the Saxon ally. All this, he told Fleury, made for disagreeable news but he had concluded that peace of some sort was essential. He saw no alternative. Next day he sent to the opposing commander, Charles of Lorraine, a brief, courteous letter, to '*Monsieur mon cousin*'.[14] The second paragraph ran: '*J'ai donné ordre à l'armée de faire cesser toutes les hostilités, vous en ferez autant de votre part.*' Frederick, as he often wrote, preferred a partial, a 'particular', to a general peace. The ideal peace would give Prussia what she wanted and leave Austria at war with others. This, in effect, was what he now had. To Voltaire, at the same time, he sent a long poetic composition meditating on the impermanence of human glory. 'War,' he wrote, 'has made me more philosophic than ever.'[15]

The first Silesian war was over. Armistice turned into treaty. The Peace of Breslau, as it was called, was agreed in the Silesian capital in June 1742, with the formal treaty signed in Berlin in July. Frederick told his allies – had been carefully telling them for some time – that continuing war was too great a strain for Prussia. The treaty was soon followed by an agreement that Saxon forces should withdraw from Bohemia, and peace between Saxony and Austria was concluded at the end of the year. For Austria, however, supported by Britain, war went on. The French and the Bavarians were still in the field, although without Prussia. Thus it would remain for two years.

Under the Peace of Breslau Frederick's possession of Silesia was admitted, with certain exceptions. During the preliminaries there were quibblings over inessentials and titles – the Austrians had suggested Frederick be simply 'Ruling Duke of Lower Silesia', a proposal whose acceptability to the King Podewils queried. Frederick's reaction was brutally characteristic: '*Je me f— de titres pourvu que j'aie le pays!*' Prussian troops were to withdraw from those Austrian territories not formally ceded under the treaty. Frederick gave up his demands for the territories of Pardubitz and Königgrätz. He was, however, recognized as sovereign of the county of Glatz, that trapezium-shaped salient out of Silesia into and across the Moravian hills.

Frederick's conclusion of his 'particular peace' was naturally regarded with a good deal of disapproval by his allies, Bavaria and France. It has also been criticized for different reasons by some of his historian supporters. Considering the long struggle ahead, it has been argued that it would have been possible after Chotusitz to inflict a more serious defeat on the Austrians and gain greater strategic advantage.

This is hindsight. Chotusitz was not a decisive Prussian victory. Frederick by now knew his army and knew it needed peace and restoration. He was acutely aware of the state of his finances, which also needed restoration. Peace was, unfortunately, likely to be impermanent; he anticipated a new war in very few years if Maria Theresa were allowed to keep all Bohemia, and he had no illusions about her attitude to the Silesian question; but for a while peace was necessary for Prussia. His gains were real, although they would undoubtedly need defending again one day. Nothing final had been achieved but respite had been won.

As to his allies, some well-phrased letters pointing out his inviolable steadfastness in protecting their interests, as well as the burdens Prussia had borne for the common cause, would have to suffice. He mingled in his letters some delicate reminders (and some rather less delicate) of how disappointingly his allies themselves had sometimes behaved in the field. Only necessity and lack of actual means had forced him out of the war – 'one condemns nobody for having failed to do the impossible!' he wrote plaintively to Fleury on 18 June.[16] To Belle-Isle, two days later and pretty disingenuously (although in the ultimate event, accurately!), he described recent events as nothing but a 'cessation of operations',[17] rather than the sort of general armistice which had been mentioned. This was true, but when he wrote Frederick knew that a formal treaty would be signed within weeks. Belle-Isle described him as a betrayer and to most of the French he was – for a while – now branded as a faithless ally. Fleury wept.

Back in Potsdam, Frederick composed an ode – in some of its fourteen stanzas not far from a victory ode – for Voltaire's benefit,[18] and applied himself vigorously to the condition of the Prussian army. He knew it would not be inactive for long and he reckoned there was much to correct.

The Prussian army which in 1740 had invaded Silesia with a strength of 27,000 men had consisted of rather more than one third of the whole military establishment Frederick inherited from his father. That establishment had been composed of thirty-one infantry regiments, each of two battalions and with a regimental war establishment of 1,700: and of twenty-four cavalry regiments, each at about 850 horse. Of the cavalry thirteen regiments were heavy cavalry – breast-plated cuirassiers – and eleven were light cavalry or dragoons, expected to be capable also of infantry manoeuvres. There was to be one light infantry, *Jäger* unit, formed at company strength by Frederick himself in 1746.

Distinct from the main body of the cavalry there were nine squadrons of reconnaissance cavalry or 'hussars' on the Hungarian model renowned throughout Europe – a small force of 1,500 in total and of somewhat uneven quality. Frederick increased these after the Silesian wars to eight regiments, nearly 7,000 men, including the famous White, Black, Green, Red and Blue Hussars; hussars were armed with a short carbine as well as a curved sabre. The artillery arm he inherited had only one battalion – six companies, with a mix of twelve-pounders for heavier bombardment work and light guns, initially six-pounders, for support of the infantry. As with the cavalry Frederick planned change and expansion, although it would take a little time. He also built up the very small force of Engineers he had inherited and made a considerable study of field engineering as well as of fortification and fortress design – a study which would contribute much to the success of his campaigns.

In his writings Frederick often described Prussian military short-comings and particularly the shortcomings of the cavalry. He was insistent that he had inherited from Frederick William 'a bad cavalry' and he was determined to improve it. Early impressions are often deepest and Frederick's earliest picture of battle was of a shattered Prussian cavalry at Mollwitz. He wrote that the officers didn't know their jobs; that the troopers were afraid of their horses; and that the troops were seldom put through mounted exercises. Discipline, he said, was as necessary as for the infantry and training was more laborious because horsemanship was involved – a trooper was brave in proportion to his confidence in his mount. Cavalry was a costly arm and it was essential to see that money was wisely spent. Frederick changed the policy for horse purchase as well as for trooper selection. His father had liked huge men on massive horses. Frederick, on the contrary, decided that big horses were useless: just over fifteen hands – fifteen and three-quarters maximum, for heavy cavalry – must be the standard. Holstein or Prussian horses were to be preferred, although for the dragoons a proportion of Tartar horses was accept-able. Men need be no taller than five and a half feet.

Above all, Frederick ruled, the cavalry must be trained and exercised as arduously as the infantry. The individual trooper must receive thorough training – first on the parade ground, to teach him the essentials of soldiering and discipline; then in riding (initially without a saddle): and, at the same time, stable management. Frederick had been appalled during the recent campaign at how badly the horses were often cared for. Of course none of this was exactly new, and Prussia had many experienced cavalry commanders and horse masters. What was striking, however, was the immense thoroughness with which the King himself described, codified and often improved established practice.

But all this, essential though it was, was subordinate to Frederick's philosophy for the use of the cavalry arm. He had been disappointed – indeed shattered – by what he had seen at Mollwitz (rather little) and unimpressed by what he had seen at Chotusitz (a good deal more). Prussian success had been won by Prussian infantry. The enemy's cavalry had, on the whole, shown little better than his own and provided few lessons. And Frederick was determined to rectify this and to restore (as he saw it) cavalry to their proper place on the battlefield. He believed that heavy cavalry should be used to produce a *coordinated shock effect*.

This, in Frederick's view, meant that the sword, the cavalryman's primary weapon, must be used primarily for thrusting, in conjunction with his fellows on right and left, and that its impact must be heightened by a doctrine of increasing speed in the charge. Frederick therefore introduced the straight, double-edged sword, forty inches long, more effective than the curved sabre for what he had in mind; and what he had in mind was a mass of thrusting troopers, charging knee to knee. As for speed, Frederick William's cavalry had been trained to attack at a slow trot, followed by individual cut and thrust with curved sabres. Despite the conventional wisdom that greater speed led to loss of control, Frederick changed this. His initial orders were that the troops should quicken to a gallop when about thirty paces from the enemy, but after Chotusitz he increased this to 100 paces (and later to 200). He aimed to create a disciplined and controlled but formidable and alarming shock arm, and he believed that the quality of an army's cavalry set the pace of a campaign. If it was indifferent all would be sluggish and battles would be thought occasions to avoid rather than seek.

Frederick recognized, however, that the strength of the Prussian army lay at present with its infantry, and he had no doubt of the debt he owed to their drill and steadiness, to the Prussian infantrymen, in their coats of Prussian blue over white waistcoats, white breeches with black gaiters and boots, tricorn hats or grenadier mitres, those terrible 'moving walls' advancing on them remorselessly, in perfect order, to which the enemy had referred. He had, of course, most direct experience of infantry organization and training: his regiment at Neuruppin had been infantrymen. And in the infantry especially – not solely but especially – *esprit de corps* was vital. The soldier, he wrote much later, when his experience of war and troops was wide indeed, must have a *'meilleure opinion de son régiment que de toutes les troupes de l'univers!'*[19] As everywhere, however, discipline was the essential ingredient and severe punishment was necessary in cases of hesitation to obey – insubordination must receive no mercy. But there was another side to this, he wrote. The soldier would never do his duty if his officers were not competent to theirs, were not *'rangés à leur devoir'*.

The size of the individual infantryman was no longer important, Frederick wrote. Firepower had negated that factor. All that mattered was that a man should be strong enough to carry the requisite weight on the line of march and handle his weapon. But above all the infantry must be *numerically* sufficient. Frederick had lost a good many men on campaign both in his two battles and on skirmishes as well as from desertion – that perennial cause of leakage from eighteenth-century armies where many men were near-stateless volunteers of unreliable provenance. Frederick had also, of course, lost a good many men from sickness although his record of care was, by contemporary standards, good. He wrote that care for the sick and wounded, of both sides, must be a paramount concern of the commander – humanity and sense alike demanded a *'soin de père'* for men who risk their lives for their country, and great trouble must be taken to see that field hospitals were provisioned and stocks of disinfectant adequate. Numbers of effectives, nevertheless, had fallen, particularly in the infantry. Manpower would always be a problem. The ranks had been filled and casualties made good largely by drafts from the homeland although also from prisoners of war who, as often happened in the eighteenth century, could change their allegiance without too much difficulty. Frederick, however, had harsh words for commanders who found it expedient or easier to mix men from different regiments, men who did not know each other. Once formed and trained one should keep battalions together as such. Then, perfectly drilled, with high morale, the infantry unit would be a band of brothers, '*agile, adroite, mobile*'. 'I have never seen anything which compares for beauty,' wrote a French colonel to his King, Louis XV, 'with the Prussian troops on the march – their order, their discipline.'[20]

Battles were won by precision of movement and by firepower: and in both Frederick made changes. The basic infantry weapon was the musket, smooth bore, of ¾ inch calibre, about three and a half feet in length, loaded by an iron ramrod and fitted with a sword bayonet; it took about nine seconds to load and the rate of fire was five or six rounds in the minute. Under the system Frederick inherited (and no changes or experimentations had been possible under the eagle eye of Frederick William), infantry fire was by platoons. A battalion was organized in eight platoons. each of about 100 men at full strength – effectively a modern 'company'. Two platoons were usually grouped for tactical purposes under a captain. Fire by platoons, in theory, enabled continuous fire from part of a line to cover the somewhat protracted business of musket reloading; but it was difficult to control and attempts to create that control by laying down a platoon sequence of fire tended to complexity and ineffectiveness.

Frederick was less impressed than some of his contemporaries with the effectiveness of infantry firepower, in the current state of weapon development. He thought – the opinion only hardened somewhat later – that point-blank exchanges of infantry fire were intolerably expensive in men and seldom decided battles, while the contemporary inaccuracy and low velocity of the musket made long-range fire engagements of questionable value. Instead he had been impressed by the obvious *moral* effect of his infantry, particularly at Chotusitz. They had, it was true, engaged there at long range, but it was their presence, their formidable appearance, their obvious readiness to advance, remorseless, inexorable, which had, he was sure, really decided the day. The essence of the infantry must be perfect formation drill and a steady pace of advance. He ruled that a Prussian regiment must be formed up in three ranks, the men shoulder to shoulder, and should then advance towards the enemy, bayonets fixed, at a stately ninety paces to the minute, slowing to about seventy (equivalent, for instance, to a British ceremonial 'slow march') for the final stage before reaching the enemy line. Purposeful. Implacable. Faced with this no enemy would stand, and to make him break must be the object rather than to reduce his ranks by peppering it with musket fire at ineffective range. Platoon fire might see off cavalry, but for the infantry victory which every Prussian commander must seek the watchword must be to advance upon and close with the enemy. He wrote this in spite of what appears to have been the effect of Prussian enfilade fire at Chotusitz; but on that occasion the enemy – chiefly a confused mass of cavalry rather than infantry in line – had been disorganized and vulnerable. As to immediate logistic support, the first echelon consisted of one wagon per platoon in each regiment, and twelve bread wagons (in theory, six days' supply) per regiment as well as one 'surgeon's wagon'.

In developing the artillery arm Frederick, as in other armies and most ages, experimented with various weights and calibres, aiming at an ideal balance between weight of projectile, range of fire and mobility of the gun; and with varying success. He was faced for much of his life by a superior and evolving Austrian artillery and these were early days – there would come an hour when he would deploy artillery on a scale and with a skill which would not be matched on a European battlefield for forty years; but development took time. There was a great deal to be done in the field of weapons and ammunition manufacture and much of it would not be addressed until another war had been waged. In the artillery, as in other arms, Frederick applied his mind simultaneously to tactics, organization and technology: that is, to equipment.

Frederick introduced a new light gun, the three-pounder, as an infantry regimental gun. It weighed rather under 500 lb, was drawn by three horses and was intended by the King (against some opposition) as a close support weapon under regimental control, playing to some extent the same part as the German assault gun of later years. He had been impressed by the regimental guns he had already seen used but it was clear to him that they were too heavy, too slow and insufficiently mobile. For immediate tactical use in a fluid situation guns needed to be light. The new guns were in all regiments' hands by soon after the Peace of Breslau. He later experimented with several versions of a rather heavier gun, a six-pounder, also intended for close support work. Frederick's much heavier artillery pieces – twelve-pounders of varying marks – could be massed for operational effect, just as Napoleon would form 'grand batteries' to dominate a sector of the battlefield; and on at least one occasion he used high-angle howitzer fire to silence an enemy battery – gun neutralizing gun in a way novel for the eighteenth century. Both solid roundshot and canister shot – scattering small projectiles from a disintegrating canister – were used. Later in his life Frederick formed some brigades of horse artillery – six-pounders drawn by specially selected horses, trained to support the cavalry and move at something like cavalry speed. For his heavier artillery he relied a good deal, on campaign, on requisitioned farm horses.

In all arms of the Prussian service discipline was ferociously enforced. Frederick's instincts were humane. Many stories witness his kindness and consideration to individuals, of whatever rank, whether in uniform or out of it; and there was nothing affected about the paternal attitude he adopted and felt towards his soldiers, and which they recognized; nor was there anything false or contrived in the rough comradeship and jocularity he would share with them in camp or battle. When an under-officer in Bevern's regiment appeared utterly exhausted on the march to Kolin in June 1757 Frederick called out – 'What's wrong?'

'The march is too much for me.'

'How long have you served?'

'Forty-five years, beginning under the King, your father.'

'Right! If we get into winter quarters I'll pension you.'

'The worst disgrace possible,' was the reply. 'I'll live and die a soldier.' Frederick sent him a riding horse that evening, and in the winter of 1757 gave him a commission as the oldest lieutenant in a garrison regiment.[21] Most of the anecdotes of Frederick on campaign tell of the badinage he liked exchanging with the Prussian soldiers and they with him.[22] He was *Alter Fritz*. Nevertheless he believed – a rational belief – that the foundation of the army was discipline. Discipline meant precision and attention to appearance, it meant subordination and obedience. It demanded sanctions, punishments.

As in other armies casual blows were administered for trivial fail-ings. Capital offences meant death by hanging or firing squad. Short of the death penalty, the most feared formal punishment was the *Gassen laufen* – literally 'running down the lane' and often called 'running the gauntlet'. This – unless circumstances prescribed execution – was the usual award by court martial for desertion. Two ranks of soldiers, each of 100 men, were drawn up facing inwards to form a 'lane'. Each soldier was armed with a hazel switch. The condemned man, stripped to the waist, walked down the lane so that every man could strike him. He was forbidden to run, a ban enforced by a non-commissioned officer walking backwards in front of him with levelled carbine. At the end of the lane he turned about for a repeat performance until the sentence awarded of a given number of 'runs' was completed – desertion ranked twelve runs for the first offence. The maximum sentence permitted (thirty-six runs) was spread over three days.

In theory twelve runs implied the infliction of 2,400 strokes of a hazel switch on the bare back or shoulders in about twenty-five minutes, although it is probable that often fewer blows actually landed. It was a ferocious punishment, but must be compared to sentences awarded at that time, in, for instance, the British army, where up to 2,000 lashes* could be ordered, laid on by drummers relieved after every twenty-five strokes.

Discipline and punishment might be an inescapable albeit harsh part of military life. What most absorbed Frederick, however, was training. Much of his writing was devoted to training. He wrote that during a war – when it can easily be neglected because of the demands of operations – every opportunity must be taken to continue training. The training of the individual was fundamental. Field training was essential, and manoeuvres, the cooperation of different arms. But as vital was the training of commanders. Some of this might seem presumptuous in one whose own experience was still limited but Frederick's reading and reflection should never be underestimated and

---

* Exceptional. But several hundred were frequent. The maximum was set at 1,000 in 1807 – there had previously been no statutory limit; and the cat had nine tails.

he drew conclusions from it. He often assembled key officers for study days, staff rides and discussions. He believed strongly in developing, in so far as it can be developed, the *coup d'œil*, the ability to see the critical points in a piece of country and to use imagination in transposing it to possible tactical situations. 'Hunting can help!' he told his officers (although Frederick, personally, loathed blood sports of any kind). 'Travel and walking can help!'[23] 'Look at that ground,' he advised them, 'then suppose you have to attack it – it's an enemy post. How? Or defend it. How?' When walking or riding, he told them, 'do this all the time. And all the time estimate distance, judge it. Then measure it. Teach yourselves.' There is a reminiscence in another age and another army, of Lord Gort, famous VC, regimental officer, commander-in-chief of a British Expeditionary Force in a doomed campaign in 1940. 'How would you attack that hill?' Gort would suddenly bark at an officer. 'Don't think, tell me!' 'Don't think' – the story was told with a smile about the famously unintellectual Gort, but the practice was that of Frederick. And entirely sound, emphasizing the virtue of instinct and the need for instinct to be trained. Later in life, and when his own experience was great, he wrote that neglect of the training of generals and officers had lost many battles and there is little doubt that he wrote with feeling. Now that the war was over, in 1743, he inaugurated large-scale autumn manoeuvres of all arms, lasting several days, simulating various phases of battle and directed with unremitting energy by the King himself.

Frederick was thirty years old. He had been exactly two years on the throne. During those two years he had conducted a far-reaching campaign and acquired for Prussia a province, in his view legitimately hers, which would add greatly to her size and her prosperity. He had defied what he regarded as the illegitimate protests of the greatest power in central Europe and Silesia was his, provided he could hold it.

He cared passionately about Silesia – the 'fair province' with its exceptionally handsome people. He needed, all the time, to justify to himself and to history Prussia's acquisition. He gave one of his minis-ters particular responsibility for Silesian affairs and it was ultimately placed under a separate department, not under the General Directory. He rejoiced in the fact that in very few years a quarter of all Prussian state revenue would come from Silesia. He took immense interest in the development of the Silesian economy – one day, after Frederick's time, it would be one of the richest regions of Europe, particularly in mining and heavy industry. Meanwhile there was the linen industry which he encouraged in every way the state could. There was weaving. He introduced Merino sheep and helped Silesian agriculture.

Frederick, throughout life, was wholly autocratic in his political beliefs. He might pride himself upon being a child of the Enlightenment in philosophy and theology but he was a man of his time. Ideas of anything like democracy were anathema to him – absurdities, unreasonable. Nevertheless he was also the enemy of what he regarded as archaic and oppressive seigneurial rights, marks of unjust aristo-cratic governance; and he reckoned he found such in Silesia and set about removing them. To Frederick, the just prince, wise and even-handed, had as one of his principal duties the prevention of injustice by one class of his subjects to another. To some extent Silesia was transformed by Frederick, and very quickly.

He was always, however, very conscious that Silesia was internally divided on religious lines. His belief in religious toleration was sincere and he enforced it wherever he found the necessity and the opportunity. 'There must be no *over-vehement orations* against Papists – or vice versa!' he instructed the tutor of his nephew, the young Prince Frederick William, and the spirit of the order was characteristic. He realized that support for or opposition to him in Silesia often and naturally followed confessional lines but he genuinely aimed at even-handedness. He sometimes wrote (particularly to Protestant rulers whose good will he was courting) of the sad penalties he had found imposed by the Queen of Hungary on the poor Protestant people of the province, but he did not seek to exploit religious resentments for his own ends. He wished to be accepted by all and on the whole he was, although there were exceptions to the toleration of his governance. The county of Glatz was administered with some harshness by his Huguenot friend de la Motte Fouqué, and there was one instance in his reign of a priest, Fr Faulhaber, being hanged for refusing to break the seal of the confessional; it was alleged against Faulhaber that he had advised Catholic soldiers to desert the service of a Protestant prince, a charge he denied.[24]

Frederick had not yet established a reputation as one of the Great Captains, nor even as a distinguished field commander, whatever retrospective claims would be made. His strategic sense could be commended or criticized – in coalition warfare choices are usually hard, usually involve the balancing of difficult military and political factors. Frederick, by his own lights, had made defensible decisions for Prussia. At every point his criterion had been and would be the Prussian interest. He had faced the main Austrian army and been undefeated on two occasions. Battle, fought by the Prussian army, had significantly contributed to the allied cause. Battle had not forced Maria Theresa to make peace but it had prevented her from driving the Prussians from Silesia and had produced a reasonably promising correlation of forces for ensuing stages of the struggle, whether conducted in the military or diplomatic field. When he considered the campaign as a whole and his conduct between the two battles of Mollwitz and Chotusitz he could reflect that it had not been unsound to advance into Moravia. A major allied offensive towards Vienna after the fall of Prague had at one time seemed possible, in which case Prussia needed to be up with the hunt; while later a major Austrian offensive was actually threatening the French and the Bavarians and the Saxons, in which case Frederick could not avoid doing something to help. The 'something' involved moving into Moravia and incidentally giving depth to the defence of Silesia.

Throughout, Frederick would claim that his higher strategy had been essentially defensive. Sometimes, dependent on the pressures of alliance, that had demanded the operational offensive. Sometimes it might demand the pre-emptive offensive (as foreshadowed in the *Anti-Machiavel*). But the aim was to consolidate and to defend his gains, to protect the interests of the people over whom he had been set by destiny to rule. Including Silesians. As to bad faith with his allies of the moment – the most frequently levelled charge against Frederick – he was in his own curious way consistent. He was true to himself. The prince must conduct policy in a manner 'wise as serpents'. He must bring to his charge all the qualities he possesses, and all the intelligence; less than that is a betrayal of his people. If their interest demands (for instance) a temporary peace, he must secure it. If the reverse, he must comply with that too. Because men are as they are, and public events are as they are, he cannot do his duty by his people without frequent stratagem and deceit. Since international affairs are and should be conducted with courtesy, with desirable civility, with effusive compliments, these stratagems and deceits appear particularly duplicitous. They are, however, a necessary part of the duty laid upon the prince. Frederick defended every manoeuvre, every initiative, every realignment of policy, as dictated by his duty to Prussia.

Above all Frederick was very aware that the freedom and independence of his Prussian subjects depended on the Prussian army. His energy and initiative had earned for Prussia a new place in the Empire and in Europe. Prussia, in two years, had become a different sort of power. But he could have accomplished nothing without the army. It was they, and especially the disciplined 'moving walls' of the Prussian infantry, who had gained for the King of Prussia a new and alarming reputation among the states of Europe. He learned that the Austrian troops were cowed by the very presence of his Prussians and the word was satisfying. Only in such psychological ascendancy could Prussia hope to be safe. 'As to the future security of our new possessions,' he wrote to Podewils, 'I base it on a good and large army, a well-filled treasury, stout fortresses,' and, he added, 'a show of alliances, which impresses people!'[25]

As to whether and when that army would again need to take the field, Frederick later wrote that it was a capital error to trust a reconciled enemy: 'Distrust is the mother of security.' For the while Prussia was not fighting, but she was hardly at peace.

6

A Patchwork of Enemies

The remarkable woman with whom Frederick found himself engaged in ferocious war for much of his life was still only twenty-five years old. Maria Theresa was his wife's first cousin. Unlike Frederick, she was happily married and was to produce sixteen children. She loved her husband, Francis of Lorraine, whom she had married in 1736, and she had been bitterly disappointed when the Electors of the Empire had failed to offer him the Imperial crown. Maria Theresa, Archduchess of Austria, Queen of Hungary, to be crowned Queen of Bohemia in 1743 (a dignity usurped in the recent war by Charles Albert of Bavaria), had a profound sense of her duty to all her varied peoples and of the destiny of the house of Habsburg. She was intelligent, beautiful and had formidable personal magnetism. She was able, far more than most rulers, to arouse the loyal sympathies of the people, particularly in what were perceived as her misfortunes and persecutions at the hands of others. She had a famous sense of theatre. She could inspire. 'That woman's achievements,' wrote Frederick of her, 'are those of a great man.'

Like Frederick, Maria Theresa believed absolutely in the right and duty of a sovereign to rule absolutely – humanely, wisely, temperately and by securing maximum good will and consent; but absolutely. Like Frederick she was honest with herself – each was prepared to deceive others if duty demanded, but to fool oneself was absurd and self-defeating.

And, like Frederick, she was obsessed with Silesia.

Frederick had no illusions about the strength of Maria Theresa's will. He could refer to her in bitter terms – 'My most cruel enemy ... that creature I cannot name without my blood curdling, that

Medea . . .' This was highly complimentary, and later in life Frederick wrote with undisguised admiration – 'I must do her justice. Princesses like her are rare'.[1] Political circumstances had by then brought them warily closer, but from the earliest days Frederick recognized Maria Theresa as a magnificent, courageous and indomitable opponent, worthy of his respect as probably no other. Their interests, however, were incompatible unless one or the other accepted modification of claim; and it was unlikely that could be brought about except by military power. Maria Theresa, he knew, would never accept the loss of Silesia without bitter struggle. There would be many rounds to the contest. 'Of all powers,' he wrote in 1752, by which time another war had been fought over the same issue, 'Austria is the one to which we have given greatest offence. She will never forgive the loss of Silesia and portions of her authority in Germany.'[2]

Frederick, despite his congenital (and justified) mistrust, naturally longed for a time when he could regard Prussia as secure, at peace, her greater status recognized. His realism, however, compelled him to accept that such a condition was still remote. He was condemned to live with an ever-present threat of revenge and recovery. And, once again, Prussia now risked being isolated in Europe. He had accepted this, even courted it by the independence of his policy, but if war again looked likely it could be uncomfortable; and, sooner or later, Prussia would probably again need to fight. It was a question of when, and with what allies if any – and on what pretext. He recognized that his making peace had embittered his recent allies but he periodically reminded Fleury of how Austrian intransigence was likely equally to threaten French occupation of Lorraine and Prussian possession of Silesia. There were parallels and they might yet have common cause.

Fleury's interest had been in dealing a blow to Austrian prestige as Frederick had done. He was uninterested in territorial questions within Germany unless they affected the balance of power between Habsburgs and Bourbons.

The French were particularly embittered because their military situation was now difficult and dangerous. They had taken Prague in November 1741 but had then been trapped there by the turn in the military tide and the Austrian counter-offensive. Although Frederick's operations leading to Chotusitz had checked this, the French after the

Peace of Breslau were virtually besieged in the area of the Bohemian capital. Their numbers there were reduced to about 14,000, with Belle-Isle commanding, and what Frederick had described as his 'cessation of operations' in June 1742 had left them isolated and exposed. Belle-Isle's angry reactions were understandable. His army was in danger.

In August 1742 the Austrians demanded that in return for a grant of undisputed withdrawal from Bohemia the French should bind themselves to evacuate all parts of Germany they now occupied – a humbling condition, angrily refused. It showed, however, the extent to which their troops round Prague were now regarded by the enemy as hostages. Nevertheless a French relieving force under Marshal Maillebois was successful in marching towards Bohemia from north Germany and inducing the Austrians to redeploy to an extent away from the Prague area, although the garrison was still unrelieved. Frederick, watching from the sidelines, told Valory he was *charmé* by the Maillebois move and reiterated that he was on the French side; he was remote from *l'enthousiasme anglais*.[3] This must have been read sourly in Paris, and it is unremarkable that Frederick wrote on 27 August that, sadly, Cardinal Fleury still had suspicions about him.[4] He was, he said, surprised. France had nothing to fear from Prussia.

Before marching south the French army under Maillebois had been quartered in north Germany, in Westphalia. They had, in that position, effectively blocked any movement of Hanoverian troops to join the anti-French coalition of forces assembling in the Netherlands.* Now this impediment was removed, and on 24 August orders had been given to the contingent of troops from Hanover to march west and join their allies. The commander of the British forces was the Earl of Stair, and Stair hoped that if the various contributing allies could be brought to agree he might carry out some significant operation against the French – possibly an attempt on Dunkirk, possibly a move thereafter threatening Paris itself. This would need accomplishment before winter set in, but failing it there might be a move eastward against the French in Germany, not all of whom had marched with Maillebois. Such a move might be coordinated with a convergent move by the Austrians operating from Austria and Bohemia.

* See Chapter 5.

Something not wholly unlike this would happen in the following year, but in the autumn of 1742 there was considerable doubt in the British Government and in the British Hanoverian command as to what should be done and what part the various German states might play. In this peculiar and protracted conflict Britain was not – or not yet – at war with France, just as France, nominally supporting Bavaria, was not yet at war with Austria. The war was later named 'the War of the Austrian Succession' but had little to do with the Austrian succession, exactly defined. At one level it had to do, or was broadened to have to do, with the struggle of France for continental supremacy and the impending struggle of France with Britain for maritime supremacy. At another, and ultimately more far-reaching level, although it did not yet appear so, it was a struggle for the leadership and the very character of Germany.

It was, of course, good news for Britain that the King of Prussia, largely through the good offices of the British Ambassador, had made peace with Austria and thus abandoned the French side in practice, whatever his declarations. To what extent could his move be regarded as permanent and what other implications had it? Frederick's alleged remoteness from '*l'enthousiasme anglais*' was probably not unknown in London. Frederick spent the first weeks of September 1742 in Aachen, and visited Cleve in August *en route*. At Cleve he saw Count Otto von Podewils, nephew of his chief minister, who was Prussian envoy to the Low Countries and had just seen Lord Stair, British Commander-in-Chief. Stair, in the inevitable way of the day, was discharging a diplomatic as well as a military function: he was Ambassador and Plenipotentiary in The Hague as well as Commander-in-Chief. He was over seventy.

Podewils saw Frederick at the castle of Cleve on 28 August, at five o'clock in the morning. Frederick never pretended to enjoy early hours – his personal inclination was wholly against them. Nevertheless, winter or summer, he was always dressed and working by five or six o'clock; it was a matter of stern self-discipline and of using every possible minute. Podewils's subsequent report to Berlin conveys nothing surprising but gives a vivid, verbatim impression of Frederick's mind and manner.[5]

'I found His Majesty drinking coffee. "*He*, what had Stair to say? Has he got something new to suggest?"'

Podewils answered that Stair seemed more than ever set in his ideas, and Podewils had begun to despair of changing this. To Lord Stair, to every servant of the British Government, it was self-evident that any right-thinking German prince should unite with others against France and take early military action. To Frederick, France at least at the moment was an ally of last resort, sometimes of first resort, against Prussia's unrelenting enemy, Austria.

Frederick listened to Stair's 'ideas', for early military action. 'He must be mad! It's impossible that a sensible man can have such ideas!' Podewils said that in other matters Stair seemed to have good sense but on this matter he was a different man, regarding his own ideas as not only reasonable but actually practicable. Stair was arguing for a march by the German states, in alliance, towards the middle Rhine.

Frederick cross-examined.

'He actually thinks he'll be able to take Strasbourg, and so forth? Instantly?'

'He is entirely convinced of it, Sire.'

'How can he imagine that the Empire would agree to declare war on France? And even if they did *I* would never consent.'

Podewils explained that he had tried, without success, to persuade Lord Stair that his ideas were wholly unrealistic. But – 'He answered that I was talking of the Empire as if about China! He knew it better! He knew that all the German princes wanted war with France!'

Frederick intervened. Throughout the interview, Podewils reported, the King was walking up and down, pacing the room, in high good humour – '*la meilleure humeur du monde*'.

'If he talks like that again tell him that he's English and you're German and that you know better than him about the Empire! Tell him – tell him as if it's your own idea – that you can't understand why I'm taking the Queen of Hungary's part . . . try to make Lord Stair understand that the Emperor's* requirements are entirely reasonable . . .'

Later he shot different questions at Podewils. 'Tell me, and keep

---

* The Emperor, of course, was still the Elector of Bavaria, France's ally. But much of this was disingenuous. Frederick was hardly 'taking the Queen of Hungary's part'.

nothing back, do people in Holland believe I gave the Austrians a real beating at Chotusitz?'

Well-informed people did, Podewils replied tactfully, but the general public belittled the victory as far as possible. This was because of hatred of France and the strong prejudice in favour of Maria Theresa. If Frederick were to declare himself an enemy of France he would be as popular in Holland as any prince in Europe.

Frederick listened. 'No, I won't do that. Why do people hate France so much?'

'The memory of so many "*guerres sanglantes avec cette puissance*",' said Podewils. They talked then of Austrian attitudes, of British attitudes, of the recent movement of Maillebois's force from Westphalia to Bohemia. Frederick referred again to Stair and hoped that his Lordship would not be coming to Aachen.

Frederick was back in Potsdam by the middle of September and two months later he signed a defensive alliance with Britain under which each signatory guaranteed the European possessions of the other, undertaking to contribute troops – to a maximum of 10,000 – to enforce the guarantee if it came to it. This was of improbable use to Frederick if challenged by Austria, but it gave, for what it was worth, British sanction once again to his possession of Silesia and it helped George II in respect of Hanover. It was a disagreeable development for France.

The Austrian siege of Prague, not conducted with much rigour, was lifted in September and in December 1742 Belle-Isle marched westward with the fit residue, about 14,000, of the French army which had victoriously invaded Bohemia in the previous year. It was a brilliantly executed withdrawal and a most timely extrication in midwinter, but for France it was a humiliating end to an unsuccessful chapter. And for the French it was not hard to ascribe some of it to what they regarded as the twists and turns of Frederick.

The French side of the contest was in some disarray. The Emperor, the Elector of Bavaria, had been France's 'front man' in the war and he was now showing signs of natural disenchantment. His own Bavaria had been largely overrun by the Austrians although subsequently recovered by Belle-Isle, at least temporarily. He was without firmly held possessions and had little leverage in arguing his case against

Vienna. He had, he thought, received little from France. To France he was a broken reed, without influence, wealth or an army. In January 1743 Cardinal Fleury died, at the age of eighty-nine.

Looking forward for a while to the delights of peace – although well aware that these might be short-lived and would anyway involve a great deal of work and a good deal of austere economy – Frederick's mind turned with urgency to the desirability of another visit by Voltaire.

In the autumn of 1742 Frederick had invited Voltaire to meet him at Aachen, '*la capitale de Charlemagne*', and a brief visit may have taken place although illness, alleged by Voltaire to have brought deafness, had initially prevented it. Meanwhile letters from each to each were as devoted and complimentary as ever, as wittily irreverent about Christian doctrine, as adorned with verse and classical allusion. Frederick again happily sent his own compositions for comment to the one he called '*Votre Humanité*'. Peacetime, springtime, had been recovered.

Voltaire had been somewhat disturbed by the invasion of Silesia. Frederick as warrior – described by the King as 'a deserter from Apollo to Bellona' – was moving in a sphere where Voltaire could not follow and where he feared his own intellectual supremacy might be less powerfully evident. Voltaire, nevertheless, kept Frederick well-flattered: 'Mon Héros'; 'Mon Roi', 'Grand Apollon d'Allemagne', and so forth. He also kept Cardinal Fleury well-informed, sending him Frederick's letters from time to time, letters which can have done little beyond demonstrating to the Cardinal how intimate was Voltaire's friendship with the King of Prussia and, therefore, how significant a value should be placed on his services. It was hoped in Paris that Voltaire would be able to discover more of Frederick's mind and intentions than even the wiliest diplomat, and his relationship with the King was encouraged, regardless of the official French view of Voltaire himself. For his part Voltaire hoped for covert favours from the French Government.

His direct influence with Frederick was limited, however, when he moved beyond affectionate literary and philosophic exchanges. His own tragedy *Mahomet* was being read with fascination by Frederick, but he made the mistake – for it was already a mistake to presume on their relationship – of referring in a letter from Brussels of 2 October 1742[6] to the troubles of a certain Countess Waldstein. This lady, born Palffy, had tried to engage Voltaire's interest on behalf of a Baron Fürstenburg who was undergoing six months' fortress arrest at Prussian Wesel. Voltaire wrote a long letter, with verses describing the lady's beauty, and her grief –

> Je lui demandai pourquoi
> Ses beaux yeux versaient des larmes.
> Elle, d'un ton plein de charmes,
> Dit: 'C'est la faute du Roi'!*

– and continued facetiously, that he, Voltaire, had advised the Countess that either Fürstenburg should be liberated by an army of 100,000 or – more certainly – to appeal to 'ce premier roi de l'univers' who would recognize the supremacy of the 'belle commande' of Love.

Frederick's next letter[7] was full of historical reflections and some verses of his own. Of Countess Waldstein (he called her Walenstein) and Baron Fürstenburg, 'her so-called nephew', he wrote three curt lines; Frederick didn't know her, and Fürstenburg had behaved with insubordination. That was that. Voltaire's effusive appeal wholly failed to melt the heart of the King of Prussia, commander of the Prussian army. It was folly to suppose that it could. A few weeks later Voltaire made an equally impertinent attempt to get money (two and a half million florins) for the family of a colonel who had raised a regiment for the service of the United Provinces and had never been paid. Might not Frederick advance the money and collect the debt from the Dutch out of mortgages redeemed in Silesia?[8]

No answer.

Their literary exchanges continued, however, and flattery became ever richer. Voltaire likened Frederick particularly to Caesar, to Augustus, to the Antonines.[9] Frederick renewed his pleas that Voltaire should come to Potsdam – and in June 1743 was rewarded. Voltaire asked when it would be convenient to spend a few days 'auprès de mon

---

* I asked her why her beautiful eyes were shedding tears. She, in a charming manner, said, 'It is the fault of the King!'

héros';[10] and received Frederick's answer to the effect that France had failed to appreciate a great man to whom he, the King of Prussia, promised a satisfying establishment. Voltaire should leave France and come to Berlin.[11] At the end of August 1743 he arrived.

The year 1743 had seen the war continue in Germany, with Frederick warily watching from the sidelines; writing his courteous, often effusive letters to Louis XV, to Valory (still in Berlin), to George II, to his brother Electors, particularly the Palatine; writing his curt, uncompromising and entirely clear comments in the margins of Podewils's periodic reports on foreign affairs – '*Bon*', '*Oui*', '*Cela bon*'; emphasizing to his various envoys by personal letters how they must keep in touch with negotiations being conducted by third, fourth parties, to ensure that nothing was being concluded prejudicial to Prussian interests; always demanding detailed character assessments of foreign ministers: compiling his great unwritten bank of useful information about the personalities, the strengths, weaknesses, prejudices of the players in the European game.

From the Netherlands the British force under Stair had marched eastward in February 1743, had joined the Hanoverian contingent, and united with an Austrian force under the Duc d'Arenberg, with Frederick's old opponent, Neipperg, as his second-in-command. The whole army, named 'the Pragmatic Army', was under the command of the Elector of Hanover (George II) and in June it defeated a French army under Marshal de Noailles at Dettingen on the Main, east of Frankfurt. Frederick received the news at Rheinsberg *en route* to inspecting troops in Pomerania, and exploded! 'I won't hear the French named in my presence! I won't have their troops or their generals mentioned! Noailles beaten! And by whom? by men who understand *nothing* of deployment!' He had not anticipated this reverse and feared it might make more probable a grand alliance between Austria, Saxony, Russia and Denmark.[12]

Little attempt, however, was made to exploit victory and although by the end of the year French forces had largely withdrawn from German territory the battle had negligible immediate effect on the war situation – a war in which France was still not at war with Austria and Britain was not at war with anybody. Nor was Prussia; Frederick was able to keep his troops in their quarters and his cards on his hand. Each combatant was hoping to jockey other states into a combination against the opposition. Operations on the Main, however, had the effect of deterring France from reinforcing her troops in Bohemia and on the Danube; and in the game of manoeuvre being conducted in central Europe that year Austria might be said to be ahead on points.

Now Maria Theresa, strongly encouraged by the British Government, made an agreement with Charles Emmanuel, King of Sardinia. This pre-empted a similar agreement which he had been negotiating with France and culminated in the Treaty of Worms, a bargain struck in September 1743 by which each gained something. Maria Theresa gained Sardinian acceptance of the Pragmatic Sanction and Charles Emmanuel gained Habsburg territory in Italy. Each also ceded or undertook something – notably Charles Emmanuel, who agreed to provide 45,000 men to assist an Austrian army against the French in Italy in return for a British annual subsidy of £200,000. There were also provisions whereby Charles Albert of Bavaria, if persuaded to cede Bavaria to the Habsburgs, might be compensated in Italy. Frederick kept himself closely informed of these tortuous negotiations, hedged by conditions and full of contingency plans in certain circumstances if they arose. These manoeuvres were consistent with Britain's overarching aim; to organize the widest possible alliance against France, ostensibly under pretext of helping Maria Theresa whose hostility to France was taken as a fundamental assumption of policy.

Frederick was made anxious by these exchanges, some of which – those touching Bavaria in particular – were close to his own concerns. It was, he knew, one of the axioms of British policy that Prussia should be kept neutral but he was angered – ostensibly on behalf of the Emperor – at what looked like attempts by external powers to manage German affairs. He was also, reasonably, disturbed by references to endorsement of the Pragmatic Sanction without mention of the agreements he reckoned he had secured in respect of Silesia. He firmly rebutted any suggestion that he might contribute to an Imperial army against France – that, he wrote to Podewils in July, '*je ne ferai absolument point!*'[13] His views were diametrically opposed to this – he had no sympathy with the sort of arrangements which had produced the so-called Pragmatic Army. His mind was again turning towards the desirability, at some stage in the future, of renewed alliance between France and those German states (Prussia in the lead) prepared to drive Austrian forces from other parts of Germany; a combination against Austria pledged – explicitly or implicitly – to endorse his own possession of Silesia. Furthermore, in view of the way the Treaty of Worms had pushed to the sidelines Charles Albert of Bavaria – sitting impotently at Augsburg but still nominally Emperor – while discussing the future of his Electorate, such an alliance of German states with France, as envisaged by Frederick, might plausibly be described as acting in the name of the Empire. Periodic attempts by Maria Theresa to declare the last Imperial election invalid provoked him, less because he thought the Empire important than for what such attempts implied about the presumptions of Austria, understandable though these might be because of the ambitions of Maria Theresa for her husband.

Frederick's mind, however, was additionally exercised in 1743 by the situation in Russia. Since the day in 1741 when Elizabeth, daughter of Peter the Great, had been propelled to the Imperial throne by the Guards regiments, Frederick had been anxious for greater certainty on his eastern frontier. He had, in March 1743, concluded a defensive alliance with Russia. Neither party trusted the other and Frederick had increased reason for anxiety when, in August, the Empress Elizabeth brought to power a statesman, Bestuzhev, who was determined to reconcile Russia with Austria and Britain, in opposition to France: and, in all probability, to Prussia. Almost immediately Bestuzhev negotiated an end to the war with Sweden as well as major concessions of territory in Finland. Frederick saw the hand of Vienna in all this and in a letter to Podewils on 25 August referred to the '*revolution* in Russia, for thus I call it!'[14] He regarded Bestuzhev as '*vendu à l'Angleterre*'[15] and the Empress ultimately became his most intransigent enemy.

Nevertheless his letter to '*Madame ma Sœur*' in St Petersburg at the end of 1743 had as formidable a consequence as any. He recommended to the favour of Elizabeth the Princess of Anhalt-Zerbst and '*son aimable fille*'. Elizabeth was looking for a bride for her unprepossessing nephew and heir, Peter; and the young princess, about

'Frederick had high hopes of his little Fritz.' A portrait of the young Frederick (*c.* 1715–20), by Antoine Pesne

'Frederick William wished for a son who would share his father's enthusiasm for boisterous masculine company.' Frederick William in his *Tabakscollegium* with his cronies, *c.* 1737, by Georg Lisiewski

A visit to Dresden: 'Their host was the Elector of Saxony, Augustus the Strong, a prince of notoriously vigorous sexual habits.' Double portrait of Augustus II with Frederick William, *c.* 1720, by Louis de Silvestre

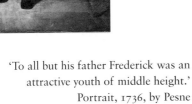

'To all but his father Frederick was an attractive youth of middle height.' Portrait, 1736, by Pesne

'Frederick was fond of all his sisters but Wilhelmina was nearest to his heart.' Portrait, *c.* 1740, by Pesne

'He met and fell youthfully in love with the pretty young wife of the local military commander, Colonel von Wreech.' Luise Eleonore von Wreech, 1737, by Pesne

'The choice, with the warm approval of the Emperor, was eventually made of Princess Elizabeth Christina of Brunswick.' Portrait, *c.* 1740, by Pesne

E X A M E N
DU PRINCE
D E
MACHIAVEL,
AVEC DES NOTES
Historiques & Politiques.

A LA HAYE,
Chez JEAN VAN DUREN,
M. D. CC. XLI.
Avec Privilége.

The *Anti-Machiavel*, a critique of the Florentine's *Prince*, was published in The Hague at about the time of Frederick's accession. Title page, 1739 edition

Count Heinrich von Podewils, 1731, by Pesne

'Maupertuis, French mathematician and astronomer, former officer in the Army of Louis XIV, Fellow of the Royal Society in London, later President of Frederick's Academy of Sciences, was now in Frederick's suite.' Engraving, *c.* 1740, by Johann Jakob Haid

à Schweinitz ce 16.

Mon cher Podewils. J'ai passé le Rubicon Enseignes Deployées et Tambour battant; Mes Troupes sont pleines de bonne Volonté Les officiers d'Ambition, et Nos generaux affamés de gloire, tout ira selon nos souhaits et j'ai lieu de presumer tout le bien possible de cette entreprise.

envoyé moi bulau, Caressé le beaucoup, et faite lui Voir Le propre interet de son Maitre, enfin, Usons de La Conaissance du Coeur humain faisons Agir en Notre faveur, L'interet, L'ambition, L'amour, La Gloire, et tout les ressorts qui peuvent emouvoir L'ame; ou je veu perir ou je Veux avoir l'honneur de Cette entreprise, mon Coeur me presage tout le bien du monde enfin un Certain instinc dont la Cause nous est inconüe me predit Du bonheur et de la fortune, et je ne ~~~~~~~~~~ paraitrai pas à berlin sans m'etre rendü digne du Sang dont je Suis issus et des braves Soldats que j'ai l'honneur de Comander. adieu je Vous recomande à la garde de Dieu. Frederic

'I have crossed the Rubicon,' he wrote to Podewils on 16 December 1740. A note in Frederick's hand

'The remarkable woman with whom Frederick found himself engaged in ferocious war for much of his life.' A portrait of the Empress-Queen, Maria Theresa, Archduchess of Austria, Queen of Hungary, 1744, by Martin Meytens

'Frederick was perfectly aware that Voltaire was keeping Paris informed of all that passed between them.' Portrait of Voltaire, *c*. 1736, after Maurice Quentin de La Tour

'Charles-Etienne Jordan – *Do not grieve me by being ill*, he wrote in 1746 when Jordan was dying. *Adieu, love me a little, try to comfort me by getting well.*' Undated portrait by Pesne

'James Keith, Russian field marshal, brilliant linguist, accomplished man of letters, would be one of Frederick's closest companions until his death in battle at the King's side.' Portrait by an anonymous artist after Pesne

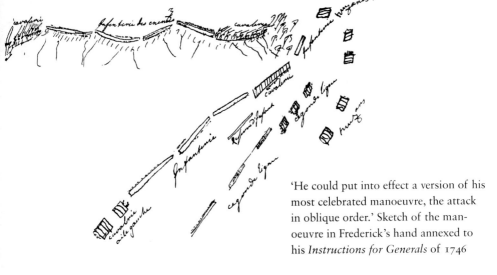

'He could put into effect a version of his most celebrated manoeuvre, the attack in oblique order.' Sketch of the manoeuvre in Frederick's hand annexed to his *Instructions for Generals* of 1746

MEMOIRES
POUR SERVIR
A L'HISTOIRE
DE LA MAISON
DE
BRANDEBOURG.

AU DONJON DU CHATEAU.

M. DCCLI.

'He wrote his history of the House of Brandenburg over a considerable period and often revised it.' Title page of the first edition, 1751

'Music continued to play an absorbing part in his life – he always loved composing.' *Solo for Flute*, a sheet from Frederick's pen

to visit Russia with her mother, was a candidate – Sophia Catherine of Anhalt-Zerbst. Later Frederick wrote again, advising the mother to hurry on with her journey. The Anhalt-Zerbsts, mother and daughter, arrived in Moscow early in the New Year; having spent some time in Berlin *en route*, where Sophia had been presented to, and had a long conversation with, the King. In Moscow, 'To the great astonishment of Europe,' Frederick recorded gleefully in his *Histoire de mon Temps*, they were well received by the Empress. Von Mardefeld, the Prussian Ambassador, had managed matters well: and nineteen years later Sophia became the Empress Catherine: the Great.[16]

On arrival in Berlin in August 1743 Voltaire paid his respects to the Queen Mother, who found him charming, and settled himself into the quarters provided for him. Since Frederick was generally either travelling or at Potsdam their correspondence sporadically continued, but was, of course, interrupted by a good many meetings. Frederick hoped to get Voltaire to accept a permanent post at his court, a court he wished to make a symposium of Europe's intellectual élite.

Voltaire took seriously – absurdly so – his duties as unofficial and covert emissary of France, part guest, part spy, part counsellor. He wrote to Frederick a long letter with various suggestions about international politics and relationships between states. The letter, with copious expressions of devotion to Frederick's interest, attempted to persuade him that his enemies were bent on another campaign of revenge for the loss of Silesia; in which case – 'Have you, Sire, any other ally but France?' Voltaire, with extraordinary naïvety in so sophisticated a man, ended by hoping that Frederick would give him some message which the French Government would find agreeable – he would be honoured to carry it.[17]

There had been, and there would soon be again, moments when Frederick's conclusions would coincide with this but he was certainly not inclined to think much of Voltaire's blandishments: he was very capable of making up his own mind about where his interest lay. He wrote his comments in the margin of Voltaire's letter in early September and they were unequivocal – 'I have nothing to fear and nothing to hope from France! If you like I'll compose a panegyric on Louis XV without a word of truth in it!' He said that if he, out of the blue, started writing his ideas to France about the European situation and balance of power, 'I should be ridiculous, and if you've got any sense you'll realize that!' Frederick added, disagreeably, that the only message he could with sincerity send to the French would be advice to conduct their affairs more intelligently than hitherto.

This was unlikely to be helpful to Voltaire and next day Frederick softened the snub (but only slightly) by explaining one or two serious criticisms of French policy. He ended this letter, however, with a plea to his guest to talk of poetry, not politics.[18] It was unsurprising that Frederick described Voltaire as 'of all men the least born for politics'. Nevertheless he offered to take the philosopher in his suite on a visit he planned to Wilhelmina at Bayreuth where the Margrave, delighted to play hostess to this distinguished party, had organized many entertainments. And in October 1743 he promised Voltaire a pension of 12,000 francs with a house and establishment of his choice. The offer was still on the table when Voltaire, that month, left Berlin. He hoped, despite the snubs, that Frederick would adopt a tone in his communications with Paris which would imply that Voltaire had played a part in making the King's attitude more francophile.

The hope was inevitably vain. Frederick was perfectly aware that Voltaire was keeping Paris informed of all that passed between them and was only interested in feathering his own nest. Frederick found implausible the attitudes Voltaire assumed of some sort of envoy – yet one without authority and one who declared that his suggestions, when made, were simply those of a private person and devoted friend. To Frederick diplomacy, the relations between states, were too serious for this kind of charade. The French Ambassador, Valory, was thoroughly irritated by these amateur initiatives. 'Deniable' initiatives by private individuals allegedly actuated by lofty motives are generally exercises in self-promotion and end in futility. So it was in this case.

Frederick had, anyway, already made up his mind about renewing warmer relations with France; and done so on his objective assessment of the developing situation rather than because of the ingenuous arguments of an amateur ambassador. Back at Cirey with Mme du Châtelet, Voltaire confined himself for a while almost entirely to verse. Any acceptance of Frederick's proposal for a long-term situation in

Berlin seemed remote, and Frederick ordered the furniture to be removed from the house he had assigned.

But although Voltaire's attempts at diplomacy and intrigue were in themselves nugatory, Frederick again had in his sights France as a partner. His cold references to France's recent errors of policy were sincere – he wrote in October a clear paper on what he thought the French, if sensible, should do – but he wrote as one hoping for the best for France and from France.[19] The French, he said, should somehow assemble a field army of 160,000 men in the new year. They should commit 70,000 under Noailles against the British, put 60,000 under Marshal de Coigny against the Austrians and deploy 30,000 in Flanders. At the end of March 1744, if not before, they should fall upon the communications of either the British or the Austrians and thoroughly alarm them.

This was a strategic plan which would strengthen France's position in Europe, but for an ambitious concept of this kind she would need allies. Only in Germany could she find them; and although Prussia could not openly help France without breaching the Peace of Breslau she could contribute to the 'support of the Empire'. The thing could be managed, provided there were French subsidies to a number of German rulers – disbursements which, with whatever plausibility, could be made in the Emperor's name. This would or could produce a force of 60,000 men within Germany itself, additional to the French armies. All of this could be done and Frederick could assist. All that would be required from France would be a guarantee to the King of Prussia of Silesia.

The paper was, of course, aimed at the French Government and Podewils, with Frederick's permission and 'under oath of confidentiality', showed it to Valory.[20] Frederick's instinct was that he would not be able to remain inactive for long. His resourceful enemy, Maria Theresa, was in the process of making an agreement – ostensibly defensive only – with Saxony. There was a tradition of friendship between Saxony and Russia, and Frederick sent a long pre-emptive instruction to his Ambassador in St Petersburg, von Mardefeld, on the last day of 1743, an instruction which ended with what in a modern brief might be headed 'Line to take'.[21] The line for von Mardefeld to take was to stress the unreliability and duplicity of the Saxon court, a court which had, by its recent dealings with Vienna, deceived the Russians, since the Russians had been assured by the Saxons that nothing of the kind would be done without consulting them.

Reproaches of this kind were not altogether convincing in Frederick's mouth, and he knew it. Nevertheless the signs were ominous. Austria – no doubt as unreconciled as ever despite the agreements secured at Breslau; Saxony; possibly Russia, in spite of Frederick's agreement of the preceding year; Britain, which had earlier tried to combine with Austria and Saxony against him, Britain, whose policy would undoubtedly be to try to ally Russia with the northern maritime powers, Britain, disappointed in the support of the German princes for a coalition against France, Britain, whose sovereign loathed him. Britain, Saxony, Russia, Austria. Frederick was again being edged by his own reading of the situation towards a French alliance, whatever the difficulties; and edged towards a point where he would again need to strike first or await the onslaught of a formidable combination. Silesia was not yet secure. Austria was untamed. Prussia was not yet safe.

On 17 February 1744 Frederick wrote an internal paper, to clear his own mind. He had been reflecting with a good deal of unease on the Treaty of Worms. He was depressed and anxious about the general European condition. France, on whom he would probably need greatly to rely, appeared incapable of making sensible appreciations of the situation. When he had made practical suggestions in October they had been coolly received. In the week before writing his paper he had learned that his man in Frankfurt, von Klinggraeffen, had been approached by the French representative, de Chavigny, with some 'strategic options', and Frederick had sent a scathing note,[22] making trenchant observations on the French proposals and referring to his earlier suggestions and their reception. The French were now, it appeared, mooting different ideas, alternatives. There might be an offensive in Flanders, combined with a defensive posture on the Rhine. There might, on the other hand, be a defensive posture in Flanders and an offensive beyond the Rhine, as far as Hanover. Nevertheless, Frederick wrote, France's preferred option seemed to be to induce a league of German princes (or some of them) to do France's work for it, while leaving the huge (330,000) French army inactive. Frederick wanted nothing to do with so half-hearted and ineffective a concept. He was prepared to support a sufficiently ambitious and concrete plan – provided, always, that France would support his own acquisitions, as undertaken in 1741.

The exchanges at Frankfurt were mere fencing. Frederick's mind was moving towards a French alliance sooner rather than later, provided it was on his terms, and provided that the strategic plan to give effect to such an alliance was a sound one. At the end of February he heard that de Chavigny had made some further concrete proposals – this time for a French advance under Belle-Isle towards Hanover – and he commented that this was not an idea to be dismissed out of hand although it might be better to shift the main line of advance towards Bohemia while simply threatening Hanover with the left wing.[23] Ten days earlier he had produced another strategic paper of his own.[24]

Frederick liked tabulating arguments, listing points for and against possible courses of action. In this paper, ostensibly giving his objections to the Treaty of Worms, he made his assumptions pretty clear from the title he gave the document: *Appréhensions des desseins pernicieux de la Reine de Hongrie et du Roi d'Angleterre*. The sequence of points which followed were to some extent disciplined by the provisions of the Treaty of Worms on which he was commenting. In effect, however, Frederick was producing a ragbag of resentments and fears, all feeding his powerful sense that Prussia was in danger and that the King's task was to consider alternatives and decide how to act. The document shows pretty clearly the state of Frederick's mind in the first months of 1744 and leaves little doubt of whither it was moving.

First, Frederick gave the background factors, as he saw them. The Austrians had assumed that the Peace of Breslau would cause a rupture between Frederick and his allies. They had therefore supposed him friendless and weak. Frederick had, in consequence, agreed too easily to cessions of territory, particularly high ground and hill passes in Upper Silesia, which he should have opposed. To the extent that this argument was valid it had surely reflected Frederick's sense *at the time* that the overall position of Prussia and its allies was weak and divided. It is difficult to imagine Frederick not driving a hard bargain, but it may have been so. His first point, therefore, was to suggest that he had been injured (albeit accepting the injury) at Breslau, and there was a wrong to right.

Then Frederick set out his complaints about the part played by Britain. The British ministers had wanted to keep him in a state of uncertainty and had exploited tensions between Hanover and Berlin. They had been keen to march troops into Germany in 1743, whereas Frederick had opposed it; this was a reference to Stair's campaign and Dettingen. Britain had, more troublingly, worked against Russian endorsement of the terms of the Treaty of Breslau.

Frederick wrote that the Treaty of Worms itself might be thought not to affect Prussia, since it was largely concerned with territorial horse-trading in Italy. On the contrary, he wrote, it affected him greatly. It would free Austrian troops from duties in Italy, and it was clear how those troops would next be used: in attempting to drive the Prussians from Silesia. As to Austria, she had formed an alliance with Saxony, which was of little importance; but she had also formed one with Denmark. What possible motive could Austria have in a treaty with Denmark? Only one. To oppose Prussia.

Frederick wrote that Maria Theresa was said not to be able to afford a war, so that his anxieties were baseless. This was a fallacy: Britain would subsidize her. The Austrians were proud. They cherished illusions. They thought Frederick weak and friendless and it was true that if the Imperial dignity reverted to Francis of Lorraine, as was the dearest wish of Maria Theresa, Prussia could have three-quarters of Europe ranged against her. This, of course, was to presume that the German states would in that case toe the Austrian line.

Most of this was familiar, the constant refrain of Frederick's life. Nor was it paranoid, although some of his assumptions were periodically pessimistic. It was absolutely true that Maria Theresa was as determined one day to regain Silesia as Frederick was to hold it. Each was perfectly and sincerely convinced of being in the right, and given the personalities involved that situation was likely to lead to conflict and again conflict. Silesia was written on his heart. His paper continued with listings of the possible courses of action and the risks attached to each.

The most important priority under the heading of 'Action' must be, he wrote inevitably and unarguably, to maintain a strong army and to have enough money. That accepted, there were options. Prussia might form a northern alliance, with Russia and Sweden; or she might again form an alliance with France. The last campaign had shown France to be, militarily, an unreliable ally and she was inevitably upset by the Peace of Breslau. Nevertheless her resentments against Prussia *might* be subordinated to the determination to humble Austria. This could not be taken as sure: Britain might support Maria Theresa in making offers to France of territories in Italy, perhaps might suggest restoring Bavaria to the Elector – offers which France might find it hard to resist.

But there might be different inducements for France. She might be attracted by the idea of a campaign in Bohemia 'in the name of the Empire' (Prussia could lead it) which might lead to the partition of Bohemia between the Empire and Prussia – even cutting in Saxony – after it had been decisively removed from the Habsburgs. The territorial consequences of such a campaign of German rulers against Austria could leave France with solid gains, and additional depth to the defence of France, on the line of the Rhine.

All this was a juggling with ideas and contingencies. If nothing like this happened, Frederick continued by asking himself, could he, alone, confront Maria Theresa – a Queen supported, as must be presumed, by the financial power of Britain? Only, he concluded, if Sweden could be involved and persuaded to attack Hanover. He was absolutely convinced, it is clear, that he would not be left unchallenged. It was a question of when, where and on what pretext. There were imponderables – he next wrote down the great conundrum 'What would happen if there were another revolution or violent and unpredicted change of government in Russia?' and decided that the best answer was to hope that there wouldn't be. Or not yet.

Much of this was disconnected and speculative. There was little tight logic in the sequence of thought and a certain relief can be sensed when Frederick, after several pages, reached the conclusions with which it is very likely that he started. The longer Prussia waited the stronger Austria would be (after the reliefs gained by the Treaty of Worms this was probably true). The most recent Prussian levies were inexperienced, but the army and the economy were restored and the underlying human quality second to none. The French had acknowledged weaknesses but if they became allies they would hardly need to be directly involved in a campaign in Bohemia, as considered by Frederick in his paper; although he would welcome it. British money was present everywhere. But at the end of his paper Frederick came back to the critical point, the point which never left him. In the present situation Prussia had no real security. It was necessary to distinguish, he wrote, between a '*sécurité momentanée*' and a '*sûreté réelle*'. Prussia was in a state of suspense. Austria could choose her place and time of attack; and would do so. War could be initiated against Prussia at any time, perhaps when no ally, no external circumstance, was available to distract the forces and attentions of Maria Theresa. If Prussia, rather than awaiting this disagreeable development, were to act first – preferably in the name of the Emperor, leader of the maximum number of German rulers against the pretensions of Vienna – she would be engaged in a war '*forcée pour prévenir les mauvais desseins de ses ennemis*'. Failing this, the situation would get worse, not better.

The paper's conclusion was unequivocal – the verbs and tenses assume a harder edge. '*Il faut couronner l'œuvre de la Silésie!*' This was the 'war of precaution' the *Anti-Machiavel* had defined. When Frederick next wrote to Paris he observed that during his recent campaign in Silesia Marshal Belle-Isle, his ally, had sent him a volume of the memoirs of the great Turenne. The book had been lost – would it be possible for Belle-Isle to send him another copy? It was significant for such as Belle-Isle that Frederick was refreshing his memory of the doings of Turenne, tireless campaigner against Austria. And Frederick spent a good deal of time in the next few months encouraging those of his fellow-princes in Germany who were not wholly committed to the pro-Austrian and anti-French camp – encouraging them to join a united effort against '*l'ambition démesurée*' of the Queen of Hungary.

Frederick developed his strategic thoughts into particular proposals at the end of March 1744,[25] listing them as 'reflections'. To carry out his project against Maria Theresa, which he had now convinced himself was the only prudent course, it was first essential to be on good terms with Russia. This might be difficult and it would be highly desirable to see Bestuzhev dismissed ('*culbuté*'). He developed this idea in the next few months, giving von Mardefeld in Moscow full powers to negotiate a defensive agreement of mutual assistance; and was particularly intent on this after hearing that the Russians had signed an agreement with Poland whose provisions were at first unknown to him.[26]

Frederick, therefore, was now determined to make war again on Austria; such a war was inevitable, he believed. He hoped to safeguard Prussia's eastern border by his exchanges with Russia. Above all, he hoped for the support of France. His strategic plan was to thrust into Bohemia from the west, from Saxony. For this he hoped for Saxon agreement – the move need not be regarded as threatening Saxony itself. At the same time French troops should march from the Moselle into Westphalia, thus isolating Hanover; and, with Saxony acquiescent, could then also move towards Bohemia.

If that were agreed as a strategic concept Frederick, in his March 'reflections', wrote that he, himself, could move in August 1744 – not before. Marching through Saxony into Bohemia he could take Prague; try to take Budweis, eighty miles south of Prague up the Moldau: and then turn his army north-west towards Pilsen while another Prussian corps took Olmütz in Moravia; the army would winter in Bohemia. A great deal of work was being done to strengthen the Silesian fortresses, covering the frontier and the course of the Oder. The Austrians would presumably respond to this invasion of Bohemia and Moravia by marching troops east from the Rhine front. They should be shadowed in this movement by an 'Imperial' army (composition not yet specified) which would reoccupy Bavaria in the name of the Emperor-Elector and advance along the Danube towards Linz. Dependent on the enemy's moves a main action might ensue near Pilsen. One good battle won, Frederick wrote, should settle the business. It was to be a short war and lead to a significant lift in the general situation.

All this was, of course, dependent on France's acceptance of his concept: and Frederick's own participation and initiatives were dependent on French acceptance not only of his strategic concept but of his claims – to Silesia, to the various territories he claimed in Bohemia along the Elbe: Pardubitz, Kolin, Chrudim. He set out his stall clearly in a letter of 30 March to his special envoy in Paris, Count von Rothenburg, listing every proposal and every condition.[27] All these exchanges, definite though they seemed, were preliminaries; Frederick, as often, gave a certain latitude to his ambassadors in matters of detail. There might be bargains struck in correspondence in the next few months. There might be negotiation over the ultimate lordship of some of the Bohemian territories with 'the Emperor' – who as yet had so little.[28] In the same way and at the same time Frederick bargained over the possible secularization of certain self-governing bishoprics – Paderborn, Fulda – and over the rights of certain independent Imperial cities. He knew how sensitive over their privileges the latter were, but his chief interest lay in the right to recruit soldiers from them. If he was to go to war for the security of Prussia he hoped to emerge from it with some solid advantages.

These ideas were tentative and exploratory. Frederick was resolved, but details would take time to clarify. He had few illusions about the difficulty of agreeing and coordinating strategy between future allies, some of whom might not participate at all. He hoped to be making clear his own conditions for action, and the messages he was getting from Paris gave reason for optimism about the French mood – although in that matter Frederick often emphasized that to be convinced of French support he would need deeds rather than assurances. As to the other German states, there would need to be much diplomacy and persuasion. What of Saxony? he had frequently to ask himself. What of many others? What, in particular, of Hesse?

Hesse-Cassel – Electoral Hesse – had a flourishing business in the provision of soldiers for hire by other states, a business inaugurated by the Elector-Landgrave Charles, who had died in 1730, and continued by his successor, Elector Frederick. The Elector of Hesse was now, through marriage, also the elected King of Sweden. Hesse itself was being effectively ruled by the Elector's brother, William, who ultimately succeeded him, but dynastic factors complicated Hesse's readiness to adhere to the 'Imperial' (in other words, anti-Austrian) cause now being organized by Frederick's persuasive pen.

There were other difficulties. Hesse's policy of providing troops for other rulers in return for money was economically driven but could not be wholly divorced from political consequences. An example of this was very much alive in 1744. Hesse had recently offered the British Government 6,000 men. The British army was small, an expeditionary force was still deployed in the Low Countries, and Britain now had need of troops at home. At the end of 1743 Louis XV had contemplated an invasion of England, in support of the Stuart dynasty whose princes were living in France and whose support lay in those factions in England and Scotland who detested the Whig settlement and revolution of 1688. French support for the anti-Hanoverian cause had often been mooted – it was a useful card in the long struggle between Britain and France – but never with the strength a successful military effort would demand. Nevertheless the possibility of a French invasion of Britain lived on through 1744 and 1745; and in 1745 (and with a new situation) 5,000 Hessians under Prince Frederick of Hesse would join the Duke of Cumberland's army in Scotland. Britain was, as ever, short of soldiers and a deal with Hesse was welcome although it might not need to be implemented.

If it were to be implemented, however, it would put Hesse in a difficult position and when Frederick heard of it he reacted vigorously, in the guise of organizer of the 'Imperial' alliance of German states. If this alliance were to take the field as Frederick hoped, and as was (in his view) in the general German interest, Hesse had obligations – engagements – to the Emperor. These engagements could not fail to be seriously prejudiced by the offer of troops to the British Government. If it came to the point Britain would undoubtedly take the offer up – Frederick had written emphatically on this point to the Elector's brother, Prince William – and not only would this place in question Hesse's important contribution of troops to the Imperial cause but it would also seriously endanger Hesse's treaty with France; a treaty from which she undoubtedly profited.[29] This issue – not of itself enormous, and to be satisfactorily resolved later – was characteristic of the problems of forming an 'Imperial' army where no central authority could impose decisions and where the component states of the Empire had effective autonomy in their external relations.

The situation may be compared to those in modern times where a 'European' policy towards some external threat or challenge is theoretically desirable and, in terms of resources, possible; but which may be impracticable because the will and machinery for united decision-making and executive action is missing. The outcome – disunity, indecision and inaction – may often be comparable to the problems at which Frederick often girded within the Empire. He knew that the only remedy lay in strong leadership by a particular state, and in ultimate strengthening of the processes of the Empire itself. Meanwhile he had little opinion of it as an institution although it provided a legalistic fiction which was on occasion useful. The Empire was too remote from the realities of executive power, which lay with sovereign states each too puny to be effective against or beside the power of Austria or the power of France. Thus it would remain for another century and a quarter; and it was this which necessitated increased size and power for Prussia.

Meanwhile the reliability of Hesse posed a question mark. Saxony was a problem of a different kind. Frederick had been scathing about the conduct of Saxon troops in the recent war in which they had been his allies. It would, however, be inconvenient if Saxony effectively allied itself with Austria – an Austro-Saxon defensive alliance existed* although Frederick did not believe it would greatly affect matters when it came to war. But Saxony's geographic position between Brandenburg and Bohemia meant that Frederick's plan of campaign (he was now sure there would be a campaign) could be upset and his programme disrupted if Saxony decided to be difficult. In May 1744 it looked as if she might be very difficult indeed – a more far-reaching agreement was signed between the Elector of Saxony and Maria Theresa which actually looked to the recovery of Silesia for the Habsburgs. Frederick was unsurprised. He knew now who were, for the moment, his friends and who his enemies but he hoped that if Prussian troops did minimum damage and behaved well during their march through Saxony under his grand design, and if that march were kept to as brief a period as possible, there might not be unmanageable consequences.

Nevertheless the Imperial forces under whose mantle of legitimacy Frederick had hoped to rally some of the German rulers in an anti-Austrian coalition with France now looked rather few. Bavaria, which could be regarded as a client of France; the Palatinate, perhaps; Hesse, unless her tedious obligation to Britain nullified her contribution; Prussia, inspiration and principal provider, must take the lead. As for the others, Hanover, of course, was firmly in the opposing camp in

---

* It had been signed in December 1743.

spite of having signed a defensive alliance with Prussia in November 1742 – Hanover, fief of the King of England, was second only to Austria within the German Empire as an enemy of France. It was a loose and unimpressive coalition. Frederick had stipulated that he could only move if others moved, principally France; and that not before August.

Frederick was, however, sure that movement there would be. He could not afford to appear too forward but he was confident that war would come and that he would not be alone. The pace of events began to quicken. In April 1744 France – at long last – declared war on Britain, Hanover and Austria. French troops under Maurice de Saxe – illegitimate son of the Elector Augustus the Strong of Saxony, Frederick's one-time host at Dresden and father of the present Elector – invaded the Austrian Netherlands. They were met by a force of Austrians, Dutch, Hanoverians and British. Within weeks the frontier fortresses were in Saxe's hands.

Frederick was told of the French declaration of war by the British Ambassador in Berlin, Hyndford – and sent him a personal note of acknowledgement. Hyndford – who had played a useful part more than once but whom Frederick disliked – referred to the defensive alliance concluded between Prussia and Britain in November 1742. Frederick replied with characteristic floweriness of phrase that nothing could exceed his readiness to honour such an obligation. There had indeed been a 'betrothal'. 'Were the realm of England and the possessions of the crown of England really to be attacked, really to be invaded,' he wrote, then he was, of course, ready to march, personally, at the head of an army of 30,000 men to the assistance of His Britannic Majesty. But the present situation seemed somewhat different. Might not recent British actions at sea and elsewhere be regarded as so insulting and hostile as to have forced France into war? And in that case were not the purely defensive arrangements made between Prussia and Britain wholly transformed?[30]

Frederick, of course, had assumed British hostility when making his move for the renewal of friendship with France. Hyndford – and Carteret – cannot have been greatly surprised by his reactions, and few things gave Frederick more enjoyment than the indulgence of a sardonic touch towards his uncle of England and Hanover, although he did his best to cultivate the friendship of the Prince of Wales. When telling his envoy in Paris, Baron Chambrier, of this exchange, Frederick pointed out that in making his near-facetious offer of leading an army to help King George he had not mentioned Hanover. He had referred to a 'betrothal' with Britain; but he supposed that a 'bride', represented by the King of Prussia at the head of 30,000 men on English soil, might be a most unwelcome addition to the family.[31] Thereafter Frederick kept his dealings with Hyndford more distant. Both sides knew that Frederick's relations with France would be decisive for British-Prussian friendship or its reverse; and in a further exchange in late May Frederick, writing through an official, left little doubt.[32] In London George II publicly turned his back on the Prussian Ambassador at a levée.

In most important directions Frederick's plans were maturing well. A formal treaty of alliance with France was being prepared and when Frederick wrote personally to Louis XV on 12 May[33] – a rare occurrence – he told him that this should unite the interests of France and Prussia for ever (an improbable aspiration). He also told him that he would always prefer France as an ally to any other power, and this was certainly true. Frederick kept his duty as a sovereign distinct from his feelings as a man as firmly as any prince in Europe but his heart would always uniquely respond to France. The treaty would give him genuine satisfaction, although he would rigorously scrutinize how the French carried out its provisions, how much they left on his own shoulders; and he would always be ready to excuse himself from its burdens if they threatened to be too much for Prussia. He expected that Austria, when attacked by Prussia under the 'grand design', would offer concessions to France and would hope to divide France from Prussia. Frederick hoped that he could count on Louis XV, 'fidèle allié', not to be taken in and to continue operations. His sensitivity was understandable.[34]

When Frederick looked north and east he saw Russian and Swedish relationships which seemed, for the while, unalarming. His next sister, Ulrica, was now engaged to the Crown Prince of Sweden.* He longed,

* Formerly Adolph Frederick of Holstein-Gottorp.

without much hope, for the removal of Bestuzhev from the Tsarina's counsels. The Princess of Anhalt-Zerbst seemed to have satisfied the Tsarina's hopes, to Frederick's credit and despite Bestuzhev's opposition to the marriage and (as Frederick heard) his incessant mischief-making and attempts to convince the Tsarina that Prussia had designs on Danzig. Furthermore the peace signed between Russia and Sweden in August 1743 had been very favourable to Russia. It was improbable that the Russians would disturb matters in the north by some inconvenient adventure on behalf of the Habsburgs. Frederick even hoped that Russian pressure – induced, perhaps, by French representations – might bring Saxony to some sort of acquiescence in Frederick's plans.[35]

Frederick, throughout this preparatory and planning phase, was careful to seek formal approval for his conditions from the 'Emperor'. The Emperor might now be a ruler in name only but one day he might be restored to the power which was his by election and he might be tempted or persuaded to disavow arrangements made under pressure of war or imminent war. On the justice of the war he referred vividly to the 'infinite rigour and cruelty' with which the Queen of Hungary had 'treated the hereditary possessions of the Emperor, intent on enslaving for ever German liberty!' Later (but before he marched) he wrote that for the German contingents arrayed against Austria (including the Prussian) it must not be forgotten that the war was a legitimate undertaking to restore to the Holy Roman Emperor his rightful possessions – a theme expanded in an ultimate *exposé des motifs* on 9 August.[36] In letters to Frankfurt in May (the Imperial seat of 'government' was at Frankfurt) Frederick had emphasized that he expected Imperial agreement to his ultimate possession of Austrian Upper Silesia as well as those Bohemian territories on the Elbe he had earlier claimed – Pardubitz, Königgrätz and so forth. This had not previously been spelled out, place by place. Now Frederick spelled it out.

Frederick now had most of the diplomatic pieces in position and could devote most of his thoughts to operational business. On 12 May he wrote an appreciation giving the various contingencies which might arise and the action each might require, a *Denkschrift*.[37] He then, for several weeks, took the waters at Bad Pyrmont while his treaty with

France was signed in Paris in June – he had negotiated it very personally and secretly. While at Bad Pyrmont he heard that the Prince of East Friesland had died. Frederick was his heir and sent two lines instantly to his own representative at Frankfurt, telling him to ensure that orders were given to Imperial troops to withdraw from the territory.[38] Prussian troops were soon moving in, marching from the Prussian Rhenish provinces. Additional territory meant additional recruits, and Ostfriesland yielded him a net 40,000 thalers* annually. Its possession also gave Prussia access to two seas, the Baltic and the North seas, and a good harbour at Emden. Occupation of the new territory was accomplished smoothly and peacefully and local administration was soon much simplified; and the number of local officials, Frederick noted with satisfaction, significantly reduced.

Frederick had always made clear that August was the first month in which he could take part in a campaign. He was not yet in a position to build up new stockpiles near the Bohemian-Saxon border and before August there would be inadequate forage for his horses in Bohemia. He had expanded the Prussian infantry by sixteen battalions (seven of them 'garrison battalions' of lower quality) and by twenty squadrons of light cavalry. New artillery pieces were still being produced and could not be in the hands of troops before August. He could, however, start his movements during that month and he told von Rothenburg in Paris (who was charged with the completion of the treaty) that by 1 September he hoped to have surrounded Prague with nearly 80,000 men, before the Archduke Charles could concentrate in that area.

Frederick's operational concept was simple. He intended to lead the main body of the Prussian army, 40,000 men under his personal command, through Saxony into Bohemia, having concentrated initially in the area of Berlin. A second group – 15,000 under Leopold Max of Anhalt-Dessau – would advance south up the river Neisse to the Bohemian frontier south of Zittau, cross the river and march south along the valley of the Iser towards Prague. Further east a third group – 16,000 under Schwerin – would advance from Silesia through the county of Glatz.

---

* The thaler was worth about one tenth of the pound sterling.

As to his French allies, Frederick had two requirements. The first was to distract Charles of Lorraine by sufficiently energetic operations and thus make difficult his march eastwards into Bohemia which the Prussian offensive would inevitably provoke. The French campaign – Saxe – in the Netherlands had gone well. On 9 July Frederick wrote an effusive letter to Louis XV, who had joined the French army there, congratulating him on French successes.[39] There was also, Frederick advised, a second requirement. There would be great merit in planning a French offensive towards Hanover; Maria Theresa was very dependent on British subsidies to Vienna.[40] With Charles of Lorraine entangled by a French army operating against his western flank, with a French threat to Hanover developing out of Westphalia and with the Prussian army dominating Bohemia and its capital, the situation confronting Maria Theresa would surely be most unwelcome. Both before and after operations began, Frederick was free with strategic and military advice to allies and his prestige was already sufficient to get it respectful attention.

Three days after his letter of congratulations to Louis XV, Frederick wrote in a very different key. He had just heard the news. Charles of Lorraine, at the head of an Austrian army, had taken the offensive. He was marching into Alsace[41] and had crossed the Rhine on the night of 30 June. There was an immediate threat to French forces in the Netherlands. From Alsace the Austrians might even march on Paris. They were moving into Lorraine – the Duke Stanislas, abdicated King of Poland and Louis XV's father-in-law, had fled from his capital at Luneville.

Frederick immediately adjusted his plans and advanced his planned timings somewhat, but he saw no reason why the grand design he had agreed with France and 'the Empire' should be set aside. He now told Louis that he would be on the march at the head of a Prussian army on 13 August 1744 and be at Prague by the end of that month. Exceeding the bounds of propriety, he implored Louis to place Belle-Isle at the head of the army which would, he hoped, drive Charles of Lorraine's Austrians back across the Rhine into Bavaria; and to place Saxe in command of another French force to march towards Hanover. In this immediate, dangerous, situation he counselled boldness. He invoked the names of Turenne and the Great Condé. He wrote to the

French commander in the Netherlands, Marshal de Noailles, in similar terms.[42] He feared that if the French failed to take offensive action across the Rhine the fragile anti-Austrian coalition of German principalities he had done so much to cobble together might succumb to fear at the latest Austrian military successes, and fall apart. Frederick might find himself leading his Prussians into Bohemia. Alone.

Frederick sent Count Schmettau, a field marshal, as a very senior liaison officer to the French court and briefed him personally and exactly. The French must be brought to realize, if they had not already, that Charles of Lorraine must not only be checked in his western advance but must be engaged so seriously that he could not easily turn to attack the Prussians in Bohemia where they soon would be.[43] There could be no doubt that the Austrian advance would soon stall, nor that when the Prussian offensive began Charles would turn and march east; and at that moment the French must *follow up vigorously*. This would also give 'Imperial troops' the opportunity to re-occupy Bavaria for the Elector-Emperor, but, more importantly, it would disrupt Austrian interference with Frederick's operation towards Prague.

On 15 August Frederick was writing from his army headquarters at Jessen, between Wittenberg and Schweidnitz: across the Saxon border. Five days later he wrote briefly to the King of Poland (the Elector of Saxony) explaining that he was engaged in leading the '*Troupes auxiliaires de Sa Majesté Impériale*', and that his only desire was to restore liberty and law throughout the Imperial domains. He wrote that he regretted any inconvenience to Saxony in the marches he had found necessary to make – he reckoned that all his troops would be clear of Saxon territory by 25 August, and he hoped the King of Poland would approve. He embroidered this a few weeks later by writing that he was trying to persuade the Emperor to look favourably on certain territorial adjustments to Saxony's advantage, as well as marriage between the Saxon and Bavarian royal houses!

Frederick was writing on 27 August from Lobositz in Bohemia, after a march of 150 miles and having crossed both the river Elbe and the Bohemian hills. By the beginning of September, as planned, he was outside Prague. The second Silesian war was under way.

7

The Taste of Victory

For France the campaign now beginning was simply a development in the long war she had been waging against Austria and Austria's allies, notably Britain: a war which would either further or reverse the French movement towards dominance of the European continent. For Britain it was the mirror image of this – a chapter in the struggle which dominated the eighteenth century against French hegemony, both within Europe and far beyond it. For Austria the campaign was part of her overall strategic defensive against France and her allies, a defensive whose outcome would be critical to the balance of power in Europe: it was also a strategic defensive which would crucially affect the future of the German Empire and the part played in it by Austria and the house of Habsburg. In this strategic defensive there had been and would be again operational offensives – most recently the Archduke Charles's advance in Alsace and Lorraine; but the aim of war, in Austrian eyes, was essentially defensive – to defend and consolidate Maria Theresa's possessions. This should include recovery of possessions previously lost: notably Silesia.

For the German princes of the Empire the campaign was one more stage in a long-running struggle for mastery – or at least hegemony – in the German lands between Austria and Prussia. Their concerns, complicated by various and sometimes irreconcilable individual agreements and undertakings, were with the placing and hedging of bets – investments. Only for Prussia was the war a matter of survival. Frederick was convinced – and it was a reasonable conviction despite the arguments which could be raised against – that the incorporation of Silesia into Prussia was legitimate, economically advantageous, beneficial for the Silesians themselves, and strategically necessary for

Prussian existence. He was also, again reasonably, convinced that he would not have been left for long unchallenged on this point by Vienna. Everything he learned of Austrian negotiations as well as the logic of the situation and his admiring estimate of Maria Theresa's character reinforced the conviction. These last two years since the Peace of Breslau had been an interlude, an armistice. Prussia must again fight. He had tried to muffle this conviction but he had always known, inwardly, that it would be so.

Encamped outside Prague, Frederick wrote to the French commanders, Belle-Isle and Noailles, at Metz, and to his representative, Schmettau, who was with them. He wrote tactfully. He was, so far, satisfied with the way things were going but he wanted to keep up pressure for maximum vigour from his French allies. Tact, however, gave way to sharpness when he wrote to his own envoys elsewhere. To Klinggraeffen, at Frankfurt, he wrote on 10 September 1744 that he would have expected Noailles to have made more effort to stop the Austrians recrossing the Rhine to the east bank as they had now done. It would, he said, have been easy to give them a hard time and an opportunity had been missed. To commanders in the 'Imperial army' he sent even harsher messages, saying that he could not understand why the Austrians were being handled so gently on their march eastward.[1] Frederick's grand design necessitated a mauling of the eastern withdrawing Austrians after their advance in Alsace had been checked. He had always, he thought, made this clear – it would weaken and distract Charles of Lorraine, be good for the Imperial army, and enable the Prussian offensive in Bohemia to proceed as it should. He was irritated when this essentially strategic advantage seemed to be placed in jeopardy by his allies' operational timidity.

Frederick was, however, concerned by a different matter as the French advanced into Germany. In a letter to Schmettau he advised particular caution in how the French handled such points as the status of free Imperial cities, like Ulm. Any breaches of well-known international conventions could arouse unnecessary hostility against France. This hostility would affect France's German allies, and was avoidable. These cautions and goadings – fussing is not too hard a word – indicate a Frederick not wholly confident in the wisdom and energy of his allies. Charles of Lorraine had, by mid-September, withdrawn from Alsace and was on the march towards Bohemia; and on the 16th Frederick could write to the Duke of Holstein-Beck, a Prussian field marshal, in command at Breslau – 'Prague is taken. We have 76,000 prisoners of war. Fire a gun salute from the ramparts, have Te Deums sung!'[2] It had been a comparatively simple business – thirty Prussian soldiers had been killed and sixty-six wounded, a small price for the huge tally of prisoners and the capital city of Bohemia. The Margrave Wilhelm of Brandenburg, a relative, had fallen at Frederick's side.

One week later Frederick learned that several corps of Saxon troops were on the march. It was possible that they might move north towards Hanover, threatened, as Frederick hoped it would be, by a French advance from Westphalia; but he thought it more likely that the Saxons were designed to join Charles of Lorraine, advancing towards Bohemia. It was clear, he reckoned, that the Saxons had now made their decision – to support Maria Theresa and Britain. They were in the enemy camp. This might, he believed, have been pre-empted had France acted more quickly.[3] Saxony had hesitated; more opportunism and less delay might have made up their minds for them in a different sense. As to any possible Saxon claims against Prussia arising from the Prussian army's march through Saxony, Frederick wrote curtly to his Foreign Affairs Minister that 'If the Saxons declare themselves against us, I pay *nothing! – Rien, comme de justice.*'[4] He soon established that a Saxon army of 20,000 men, including 6,000 cavalry, was marching to join Charles of Lorraine. He referred a good deal to Saxon perfidy but he cannot have been surprised.

Nevertheless Frederick had now to meet a much stronger force than that which Charles had led into Alsace. His calculations had been unjustifiably optimistic. The Austrians and Saxons together, unpressed by the French, were threatening his main body. It was important to him that the enemy should receive no further support from the north, from Hanover or from any Saxon forces which had been kept from Charles of Lorraine. There must, he wrote, be a diversion mounted, so that any troops contributed by Britain or Hanover to Maria Theresa's cause should be kept at arm's length. An 'Imperial' – or French – army should (as he had always recommended) march as soon as possible towards Hanover. He could help by assembling a Prussian corps near Magdeburg where they could threaten either Hanover or Saxony. Frederick's nightmare was of a combination of Saxons, Hanoverians and possibly British, ranging freely in north Germany; and perhaps of a hostile Russia across the eastern frontier, while he was wholly occupied with a main body of Austrians and Saxons in Bohemia. He thought he could deal with the latter threat provided the former were sufficiently occupied.

When dealing with Saxony Russia was always a factor, and at present Russia had agreements with both Saxony and Prussia. On 20 October 1744 Frederick wrote five long letters, all dealing in different degrees with the same problem – how to weaken the will and damage the reputation of the Saxon court. To von Mardefeld[5] he wrote that although it would obviously be desirable that Bestuzhev, the Grand Chancellor to the Tsarina, should be brought into sympathy with Prussia he understood very well how difficult this would be – his remarks about Bestuzhev had been vitriolic and were unlikely to be altogether secret, while the closeness of the relationship he now had with France must provide an obstacle; Franco-Russian relations were at present cool. Nevertheless, to disarm Russian hostility must be a strategic imperative, and Frederick sent messages of affectionate esteem to Bestuzhev. On the connection with France, he gave Mardefeld permission to let it be known – in confidence – that his policies were not impelled by any love of France; on the contrary, Prussia had acted entirely through a desire to help the Bavarian Emperor-Elector in the appalling situation created for him by the aggression of Austria. Frederick's objectives, he said – to support the Imperial dignity and the liberties of the German Empire – had, at the present juncture, made an alliance with France inevitable. Motive had been pure and lofty. It was to be hoped that the Tsarina could persuade the court of Saxony to withdraw the troops now deployed to help Maria Theresa. He sent a reminder of his own defensive agreement with Russia and hoped that the Saxon aggression would not force him to invoke it.

As for Britain (which had, Frederick knew, angled for Russian support), Frederick pointed out that he had assured King George that he would send him the help envisaged in British treaties with Prussia were his country actually attacked.* If Russia could oblige Prussia in the matter of Saxony she would not be betraying her friendship with Britain. To obtain a desired object Frederick seemed a juggler keeping many balls in the air.

Such dexterity has always increased Frederick's reputation for unreliability and double-dealing. In fact he pursued a consistent line. Believing, as he did, that the war was just, a pre-emptive war justified by circumstances, he had to use every device of diplomacy to prevent it going badly with him. He knew that the European powers were watching him and each other warily. His exchanges with his envoys were near-daily. He knew that in England the chief minister, Carteret, was suggesting the formation of an anti-Prussian alliance, to include Russia. He knew that the Saxons (the Saxon chief minister, Count Brühl, was as inveterate an opponent of Frederick as Frederick was of him) would like to deprive him of Silesia, of Magdeburg, of Halberstadt, of East Prussia, by negotiating a partition of his provinces with Austria, Hanover and Poland. He knew – it was his most immediate concern – that the French army, instead of cooperating in his own reiterated concept of strategy by pursuing Charles of Lorraine through Bavaria and into Bohemia with a concentrated thrust, were deploying significant forces to besiege Freiburg-im-Breisgau in Württemberg, a Habsburg possession with absolutely no strategic importance. He regarded his own policy as having been undeviating and sensible but he was now threatened with a concentration of enemies and the possibility of facing them virtually unsupported. It was understandable that he should try to arrange friendships where he could, regardless of the past and regardless of what malicious tongues would spread about his opinions. If Bestuzhev could be courted or bribed it was a duty to try. Others would be seeking the friendship of Russia. Of all the powers it seemed at that moment that the Tsarina might have the best chance (if she chose) of mediating a peace on terms acceptable to Frederick, whose minimum requirement – recognition of his rights in Silesia – was no threat to Russia. He had, he said, no desire to

---

* Not so fanciful as it may seem. In January a considerable fleet of French transports and escorts, with 7,000 men embarked under Marshal Saxe, had been ready for an expedition against England in support of Prince Charles Edward Stuart, who had just visited Versailles, and everyone knew how short of soldiers Britain was.

deliver Europe to French hegemony, any more than to Austrian. He was happy that Russia should know as much and should understand him. For good measure he sent a letter to the Princess of Anhalt-Zerbst, still in Moscow with her daughter, whose marriage Frederick had so assiduously promoted. 'Try to arrange, *Charmante Princesse*,' he wrote, 'that eyes are opened about Saxon treachery.'[6]

On 22 October the Saxon army joined Charles of Lorraine, who had reached Bavaria. Next day, taking part in a follow-up of the Austrians by French and Imperial forces which Frederick found dangerously leisurely, the Emperor-Elector re-entered his Bavarian capital, Munich. For a little, and Frederick knew well that it might not last, the tide had turned. Despite his agonizings and anxieties at this time, the dangers he envisaged, the fearful isolation which had haunted him, the Austrians were in trouble. They had been made to withdraw from their westward advance. The initiative was with their enemies. Bavaria had been reoccupied by the forces of, or allied to, its lawful sovereign. Prague was now in Prussian hands. If Vienna could be brought by the pressure of others to recognize the strategic situation there could be little reason, surely, for anybody to continue the war – there could be none for Prussia. The issue would have been settled, inexpensively and comparatively bloodlessly. In all his letters in the last months of 1744 Frederick was mooting the possibilities of peace. Peace would have been won by a forceful demonstration of his own, made on behalf of the Emperor and as an ally of France: made as an opponent of Austrian pretensions and ambitions. The favourable development of the situation had not been pre-empted or prevented by Russia; nor by Britain. Could matters not be declared over, at least for the time being? 'The King,' wrote his secretary to Podewils, in Berlin on 11 November, 'ardently desires to see peace restored this winter, at least in Germany.' There is no reason to doubt it. Frederick's own conditions were the same as ever: recognition of the Emperor (Maria Theresa was still objecting to the last Imperial election), restoration of the Emperor's domains, a reasonable bargain over certain disputed territories in Bohemia, and Upper Silesia to Prussia. These ambitions showed consistency rather than voracity. They would, in Frederick's view, represent a better balance of power in central Europe. They certainly showed a desire for peace rather than the lust for war and conquest sometimes ascribed to him. Reference to 'Upper' Silesia reflected his belief that there could no longer be argument over Lower Silesia.

But Austrian troubles were temporary and Frederick's hope that the Austrians would concede a strategic victory to their enemies was short-lived. His reading of the situation, of the correlation of forces, had been over-optimistic and he soon recognized that, as he had feared, French pressure on his enemies was proving inadequate to divert them from a considerable concentration against himself. He had hoped to fight a major action at some time after the capture of Prague but he was now outnumbered, or about to be. Others were watching him carefully. The Russians, through Mardefeld, were delicately inquiring whether the King of Prussia was contemplating an actual battle with Charles of Lorraine and Frederick retorted sharply that battles were not easy to force on an enemy in the broken territory of Bohemia. Whenever there had been skirmishes the Prussian troops had come off best, but logistics governed all and logistics could compel Frederick to withdraw, although if he did he would return in the following year.[7]

Circumstances were forcing circumspection on Frederick. When he had an opportunity for a major attack on the Austro-Saxon army at Marschewitz, twenty-five miles south of Prague and east of the Moldau, he deployed the army, reconsidered, and decided against battle; probably wisely. The second Silesian war was now going badly for Frederick. It had started well but the odds against him were becoming formidable. This had been predictable – he had needed more luck than he had had. He showed greatness of mind, however, in recognizing that his 'grand design' had failed and that new thinking was necessary. There could be no merit in sticking to preconceived notions or in failure to acknowledge reality. In early November, at the same time that he was writing urgently about peace to Podewils, he gave orders for the army to withdraw northward, to give up the advance in the Moldau valley and to leave Prague. By mid-November the army had been forced to retreat across the Bohemian frontier with a good deal of disorder, desperate for forage and supplies, and harried by the Hungarian and Croat light cavalry. The Prussians crossed the Elbe, withdrawing towards Silesia, on 9/10 November.

Frederick, contrary to his hopes of only a few weeks previously, had gained little beyond further embittering insights into the difficulties of coalition warfare. He had not lost a battle but he had lost a good many men, not least from disease. The balance of forces which had tilted to his disadvantage was to an extent a result of the Saxon intervention: but he had never anticipated good from Saxony and he had surely known that his own uninvited march through that country would not incline the court at Dresden in his favour. The logistic difficulties of campaign in Bohemia had been wholly predictable. The threat from Hanover, which had never materialized, had also been mentioned in his calculations from the beginning. Russia had made no move. His chief complaint – the undue leisureliness of the French operations and their negligible effect on Charles of Lorraine – might have some justification but cannot have been surprising – he had grumbled in a similar way in the previous war and there was little reason to suppose that either the developing situation or his words of exhortation would have a huge effect on the French commanders. And he had not manoeuvred (as he, himself, later admitted he could have done) to forestall the junction of the Saxons with the Austrians.

There is little sense, yet, of Frederick as a master of manoeuvre. Indeed the Austrians had called the tune and when Frederick considered the campaign, as he did frequently, he acknowledged the fact. The Austrians had jockeyed him out of a favourable situation, had made him march and countermarch with little threatening effect on themselves; had (with the Saxons) achieved superiority of force when and where it mattered; had compelled him to withdraw and kept him separate from the French. Austrian operations were directed by the elderly Field Marshal Traun (aged sixty-seven), and Frederick, at the end of his days as often before, paid tribute to Traun's skill and generalship. 'What a man!' he said. 'He was my master! He taught me the little I know! He corrected my faults!'[8] And when Frederick wrote a '*Relation de ma campagne 1744*' to Louis XV on 18 December he included passages of notable modesty. He was describing his uncertainty about what to do after taking Prague – 'I made two serious mistakes when I left Prague, which upset the entire campaign. I should not have moved so far from the place without making sure it was sufficiently provisioned . . .'

He had left an inadequate garrison of only six battalions and 300 horse and he blamed himself frankly for the arrangements. And his other mistake, acknowledged to Louis, was more serous – 'If we had marched to Pilsen we would have upset the junction of the Saxons with Prince Charles, taken the principal Austrian magazine and still covered Prague . . .'

Instead Frederick had marched south to Budweis and Tabor. In the first Silesian war the French had regarded their abandonment of these places as a grave error. Frederick had known it and been influenced. Wrongly.

Frederick thus wrote with candour about his mistakes. This was not a letter simply for posterity but one to a fellow-sovereign on whose alliance he was dependent for the whole enterprise. He had committed a mistake which recurs ceaselessly in military history. 'One imagines what one hopes for,' he wrote with honesty. He had 'made pictures' with inadequate evidence. His temperament was energetic and sanguine: he had failed to expect the worst while hoping for the best. Because the first Silesian war had opened with a battle he had presumed the pattern would be repeated, or that the speed of his own movements would sufficiently discomfort the enemy. None of this happened. Traun manoeuvred intelligently, frustrated Frederick's plans and soon achieved domination in northern Bohemia.

Frederick, like many commanders of many nationalities and generations, enjoyed writing accounts of his own campaigns. Voltaire flatteringly encouraged – 'It is for Caesar to write his commentaries!' Frederick's accounts well after the event in his *Histoire de mon Temps*, were less accurate and striking than in the often modest letters which followed when memory was immediate. His '*Relation*' to Louis XV contained justifications – and a vigorous denunciation of Saxony, ridiculing the terror of the Saxon ministers at the arrival of the Prussian army *en route* to Bohemia. The Saxons, he wrote, had been ready to produce all the help the Prussians could desire but had also made feeble and vainglorious attempts actually to deny passage to Frederick's troops. But when he came to the military operations themselves, to the difficulties of transportation and movement – particularly above the point to which the Elbe was navigable, at Leitmeritz – to his own errors and misgivings, he was frank and fair.

Frederick's withdrawal had been forced upon him by logistic difficulties, disease and enemy harassment but it had been timely. The
Austrians had, in early December, begun an offensive movement with
11,000 men into the county of Glatz, and from Glatz into Upper
Silesia. Frederick moved his headquarters to Schweidnitz, immediately
north of Glatz and south-west of Breslau. Matters were going ill
with him that winter in many directions. His dispatches were being
intercepted. He had reason to think that some of his ciphers had been
cracked – he wrote angrily to Schmettau about the latter's lack of
security, for which the King had rebuked him on a previous occasion.
It was an uncompromising reprimand and he followed it up with
another[9] in which he told Schmettau (now in Paris) to confine his
interventions with the French to those matters with which Frederick
had charged him. In the following week Schmettau was recalled.[10]

The turn of military events and Frederick's withdrawal into Silesia
provoked an example of a dilemma not unusual in eighteenth-century
warfare. To what extent was it ethical and legitimate to arouse the
inhabitants of an invaded territory against their ruler, even where his
rule was of questionable right? Frederick was naturally sensitive about
this since the sovereignty over Silesia was in such intractable dispute
between himself and Maria Theresa. Silesia, a province divided in
religion, had, by most accounts, been governed by him with equity
and to the satisfaction of most of its inhabitants. On the whole the
record is good. Now the Austrians were seeking to recover it by force
of arms – 'recover', by their lights, rather than 'conquer'. For the
ordinary Silesian authority and obedience posed painful problems.

With one of those curious twists produced by the habits of the age,
Frederick wrote on 19 December 1744 to George II of England, his
uncle – a prince with whom he was not formally at war but who, as
a strong partisan of Maria Theresa, was definitely in the opposing
camp.[11] Carteret had now given up office in London and Frederick
hoped for better relations and greater readiness for peace although
the chance was slender. Frederick told King George that a proclamation had been addressed by the Austrian court to the inhabitants of
Silesia exhorting them to renounce ('*soustraire*') Frederick's dominion.
Was this not deplorable? It was surely deplorable, as Britain must

agree, in practical terms, because he, Frederick, had assured religious liberty to the Protestant majority. But it was – again, as King George must agree – even more deplorable constitutionally for any power, in this case Austria, to try to agitate the inhabitants of another country against their legitimate sovereign, recognized as such by the international community, including Britain. There was a wider point at stake, even than legitimacy: the moral implications for any state of disturbing the internal order of another state simply because it was at war and because such disturbance might be strategically convenient. The encouragement or organization of 'resistance' movements exemplifies the same dilemma. At a later date than Frederick's, Wellington, with a sound moral sense and much experience, observed that if a people rise against their rulers and ask for help from an external enemy of those rulers it is reasonable to give it, as being requested and of self-evident strategic advantage; but that the people in question should not be encouraged to revolt – the responsibility is too great and the ability to save them from reprisal often too uncertain.

The year 1744, therefore, drew to an unpromising end for Frederick. His grand design had come to little. The French seemed to be doing little in Württemberg. Belle-Isle, the French commander whom Frederick most esteemed, had been taken prisoner by Hanoverian forces* in the Harz mountains when travelling to a conference, removing from the scene for a while a man whom Frederick, with reason, regarded as one of the most inveterate opponents of Austria as well as a skilful soldier. Frederick sent messages to Lord Harrington, now Secretary of State in London in succession to Carteret, expressing (with more confidence than he probably felt) optimistic views about his own military situation and reiterating his desire for an end to hostilities.[12]

The moment was not propitious. Frederick had always tried to preserve cordial relations with Holland, the 'United Provinces'. Keeping his envoy at The Hague informed, he had vigorously protested when he learned that France, his ally, planned an offensive into Holland and had actually suggested he might cooperate with a contribution

---

* He was kept prisoner a year in England, was confined for some of the time at Windsor and obtained the King's permission to rent Frogmore, at a rent of £600 per annum.

of troops. Yet in January 1745 Holland appeared leagued with his enemies.[13] Austria, Saxony, Holland and Britain signed, that month, a treaty of alliance unmistakably aimed at Prussia. Furthermore Russia might be drawn into this web – Frederick heard from St Petersburg of warlike preparations which seemed unjustified by the situation in northern Europe and which he ascribed, not unreasonably, to the influences of Saxony and of Britain. Saxony and Britain could be looking for Russian support with troops in a spring campaign against Prussia.[14] So much for the north. In southern Germany the Austrians had turned and were again threatening Munich, having effectively levered the Prussians out of Bohemia.

It is easy to remark that Frederick's misfortunes were of his own making. He need not have launched the second Silesian war at all. This is to neglect the sincerity and likely accuracy of his perception that he would, soon, have been attacked himself in his Silesian possessions. To Maria Theresa and to the more energetic of her ministers, Austria and the Habsburg dynasty were unsafe while the King of Prussia was left in occupation of any Silesian territories.

Then, on 20 January 1745, all changed. The Elector-Emperor, Charles VII of Bavaria, died.

Frederick at once began writing in all directions about the Imperial succession. It was clear to him that Maria Theresa, who could still hope to influence a majority of voters in the Imperial election, would work hard for the election at last of her husband, Francis of Lorraine. There might be ways in which the situation could develop favourably in terms of a general peace, a peace which, provided it satisfied his minimum requirements, Frederick would welcome. He wrote to his envoy in London, Andrie, asking what outcome to the Imperial election would be most welcome to the British – he, Frederick, wished only to help. In February he mooted, without much confidence, the idea of an agreement with Britain which would underwrite the principles of a peace with Maria Theresa.[15] To Munich he wrote of his attachment to the interests of the house of Bavaria (the late Emperor's son and heir, Max Joseph, was very young) but he learned that the prevailing sentiment in Bavaria now was to accede to Maria Theresa's wishes, a sentiment likely to be shared by a majority of German princes. To

Versailles he wrote that the Emperor's death had plunged everything into deep difficulty – it could not have happened at a moment '*plus mal à propos pour tous nos intérêts*'![16] Unless a French army supported the young Elector of Bavaria in his pretensions – if he had any pretensions – Bavaria would succumb to Maria Theresa's embrace. This seemed only too probable: meanwhile it was too early to assess with confidence how Vienna would react to the new development (beyond the certain candidature of Francis of Lorraine) or to make detailed preparations for a new campaign. These preparations must include restoration of a weakened Prussian army, for not only had there been much sickness but many men had deserted – a usual hazard in eighteenth-century armies, drawn as they were from numerous regions. Frederick was short of some 8,000 infantry on what he had calculated, and 700 horse. Morale was fragile. His treasury had been depleted. He knew what was wanted – in default of peace: a victorious battle.

It was, however, diplomatically important to put a brave face on the strategic situation – Prussia's military reputation still stood high and affected the minds of waverers among the powers, which meant almost all. At the end of February 1745 Frederick wrote to London that he was on the point of re-entering Bohemia. On 14 March, at Potsdam, he laid the foundation stone of the building which would become his beloved Sans Souci. Next day he left to join the army in Silesia and established court and military headquarters again at Breslau. It was only too likely that in the next campaign the initiative would lie with Austria and that Frederick, despite brave words about re-entering Bohemia, would find himself standing on the defensive against an Austrian invasion. The Austrians under Charles of Lorraine were concentrating at Olmütz in Moravia and Frederick reckoned that it would be best to let them advance from the border hills, deploy in Silesia, and expose themselves to what he still hoped would prove the superior skill and discipline of Prussian troops in open country.

Formally, France was only at war with Austria as supporting the rightful pretensions of the Emperor. Formally Prussia was only acting in the Emperor's name. But the Emperor was dead and everyone knew that Austria had firm views on who should be his successor, views which certainly differed from those of the previous (Bavarian) Emperor as well as from those acting in his name. The scenery, however, was being shifted, and on 22 April Bavaria made peace with Maria Theresa. The young Elector acknowledged the Pragmatic Sanction. Frederick learned that France, disgusted, was mooting the idea of trying to detach Saxony from the Austrian alliance and backing the Elector of Saxony, King of Poland, for the Imperial throne. 'Not while I have breath in my body!' Frederick wrote tartly,[17] although in February he, himself, had at least considered the idea as an alternative to an Austrian candidature and he did so again in July. It was now also made clear to him that he could not hope for a favourable peace through the mediation of Russia.

Formally, Prussia was at peace with Britain and Holland, although both had signed a compact with Austria and Saxony, Prussia's enemies. Frederick, indeed, was still trying to persuade Britain to adopt the role of honest broker in procuring a general settlement not unfavourable to Prussia; and although Saxony might appear an arch enemy, had given critical help to Austria in the last campaign and seemed ready to do so again while pursuing claims against Prussia arising from the march of the Prussian army through Saxon lands in the previous year, formally Prussia was at peace with Saxony. Amidst all the anxieties of war and business, however, Frederick's letters to Podewils in Berlin were as lightly teasing and delightful as ever. 'I've thrown my bonnet over the windmill,' he wrote on 29 April 1745. 'Adieu, dear Podewils, try to become as good a philosopher as you are a politician!' Podewils had been fussing and fretting over a possible Saxon invasion of Brandenburg and Frederick told him to relax – what mattered was to be always ready to leave this life with its preoccupations and possessions, goods, vanity and prestige.[18] 'Rest assured,' Frederick told him a fortnight later, 'I see the difficulties of my situation just as well, perhaps even more vividly than you do.' Frederick had the gift of combining chaff, soothing words and confidence in dangerous times. It was irresistible. Nevertheless he contemplated the moving of the government from Berlin to Magdeburg.

As Frederick conducted his unceasing correspondence and considered the state of his army after their tribulations in 1744 he might have envied had he been able to foresee the comparative simplicities of a later age with its definite distinctions between peace and war, its declarations, its unequivocal ruptures of diplomatic relations, its apparent certainties, genuine or assumed, of where national interest as well as international morality lay. For him, and, indeed, for his contemporaries, war and differing intensities of war were, as Clausewitz later expressed it, the continuation of politics using additional means.* And these additional means appeared imminent when, on 19 May, Frederick learned that the Austrians and Saxons, 60,000 strong, were marching north out of Moravia and Glatz towards Silesia. He gave orders to concentrate the Prussian army some miles north of Schweidnitz, forty miles from Breslau.

Far from Moravia and Silesia, as Frederick was told on 21 May, there was promising news. At Fontenoy, in the Low Countries (called Leuze, by Frederick, when referring to the engagement), the French, under Saxe, had defeated a force of Austrians, Dutch and British on 11 May. The British, too, would soon be compelled to move troops from the continent to deal with the Jacobite rising under Prince Charles Edward Stuart which began in the Highlands of Scotland that summer. 'A child,' Frederick wrote of Charles Edward, 'landed in Scotland without troops or support, forced the King to withdraw the British troops defending Flanders in order to support his shaken throne. France behaved wisely and owed her conquests in Flanders and Brabant to this diversion.'[19] The tide might be turning against Austria and her allies, and in central Europe Frederick had now concentrated an army approximately equal in numbers to the Austrian-Saxon enemy – 60,000, including 17,000 horse and fifty-four pieces of heavy artillery all under his personal command. He intended to wait until the enemy descended into the Silesian plain north of the Moravian hills, and to lure them to do so by deploying a force under General du Moulin from Schweidnitz which would withdraw before the Austrians when they appeared, giving the impression of a rearward movement towards Breslau. He spread disinformation – that the Prussians were nervous of being cut off from Breslau.

Every morning Frederick rode to a low range of hills near Striegau

---

* A much misunderstood as well as misquoted aphorism, Clausewitz's has been described as a pernicious doctrine, justifying war. On the contrary he was pointing to a *truth*, stated in moral and perceptive terms. If men go to war at all it is and must be for a political object – one kills or dies for a rational aim, not at random, or for fun.

from which he could see for many miles to the south, across a flat plain to the foothills of the border, past Hohenfriedeberg. His troops were bivouacked in a number of woods and hollows, largely (as he hoped) concealed from view until a late stage in an enemy advance. The Austrians would, he was sure, advance towards Breslau, first confronted and then enticed by du Moulin. On 2 June his regular morning reconnaissance was rewarded by the appearance of the leading enemy troops debouching from the Riesengebirge, the highest ground in central Europe, and he gave out preliminary orders. Next day, 3 June, his observation led him to deduce that the enemy main body would begin their advance later that day and, returning to his observation post in the afternoon, he saw eight columns of Austrians and Saxons marching forwards, to the audible sound of military music. This could be the victorious battle Prussia needed. It could be brought about next day. It might be followed by a long peace.

The battle of Hohenfriedeberg saved Silesia for Frederick.

Charles of Lorraine, in command of the Austrian-Saxon army, had deployed on a frontage of about four miles during the evening of 3 June, had descended from the hills and had marched across flat ground towards the small town of Striegau, extending his left wing some way towards a village, Pilgramshain. He had detached a number of grenadier companies to occupy some isolated high ground north-west of Striegau, points which could form a pivot for the advance of his own left wing or threaten in enfilade any counter-advance against it. The Austrian cavalry had orders to deploy on each flank of the battleline – on the right between the villages of Thomaswaldau and Halbendorf, on the left in front of Pilgramshain. The army spent the night in bivouac, ready for action on the following day.

Running south-west from Striegau, past another village called Gräben, was a stream, the Striegauerwasser. Frederick had a clear picture of where the enemy were, although he did not know that they had extended their left as far as Pilgramshain. He aimed to move in darkness, to cross the Striegauerwasser between Gräben and another village, Teichau, and then to march north until he could face left and move westward to envelop the enemy left flank. He could then put into effect a version of what became (under different and misleading names) his most celebrated manoeuvre, the attack in oblique order; to attack with concentrated strength one enemy wing while ignoring or engaging with less strength the rest of the enemy line. The main weight of attack, the *Schwerpunkt*, could then be reinforced from the comparatively inactive remainder and produce a preponderant mass which, having broken into the enemy line, could roll it up from the chosen flank. Frederick had not yet developed this tactical theory into an actual manoeuvre system as he subsequently did but its elements were all arranged in his mind.

The manoeuvre depended for success on good information about the enemy; and at Hohenfriedeberg this was defective. It also depended on an uninterrupted march to assault the chosen point, whereas at Hohenfriedeberg Frederick found his advance guard involved with unsuspected bodies of the enemy well before they had completed the approach march. The battle, therefore, does not give an example of Frederician tactical system and nor did Frederick so claim. Nevertheless elements of the famous 'oblique order' attack were there. He aimed not at a frontal attack but at an advance in echelon with the right leading so that the effect, supported by a concentration of the Prussian cavalry on the right flank, would be to break into the enemy left and enable Frederick to roll the enemy up from their left to their right; in this case from north to south.

Frederick gave out his final orders at two o'clock on the morning of 4 June. He had set the army on the move after returning from his reconnaissance on the previous afternoon and they had quitted their bivouac areas and been marching through the darkness since nightfall, about nine o'clock, 3 June. The main body was to march northward observing absolute silence, led by an advance guard. Having crossed the Striegauerwasser they were to form a battleline facing west, when the head was approaching Pilgramshain.

Frederick's first setback was to find the small hills north and west of Striegau occupied by Austrian detachments, so that the march of the advance guard – six battalions of infantry and twenty-eight squadrons of hussars, all under General du Moulin – was contested and interrupted. It was now unclear how far the main body could march before Frederick could face left and form his line. He sent a battery of guns forward to help du Moulin (whose situation was,

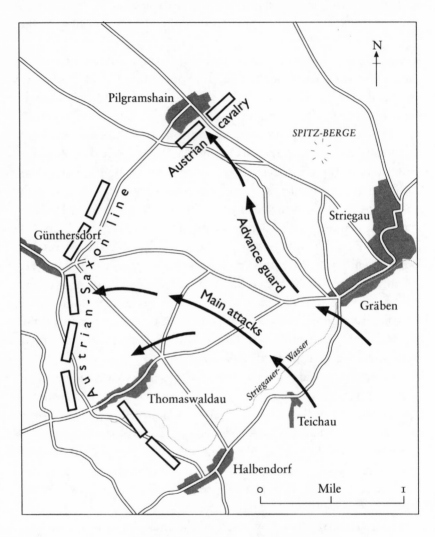

Hohenfriedeberg, 4 June 1745

naturally, obscure in every sense) and urged his main body to further efforts to hasten across the Striegauerwasser – bridged, but an obstacle to movement with the one bridge, at Teichau, soon to collapse. The infantry marched off the roads which were left clear for the artillery, but the ground was wet and progress was laborious and slow.

As often happens battle, when it came, bore little resemblance to the concepts of higher commanders. While the Prussians were struggling northward in the pale light just before dawn, Austrian and Saxon cavalry of their left wing were deploying south-east of Pilgrimshain under the Saxon Duke of Weissenfels. Frederick ordered the cavalry of his first line – twenty-six squadrons of cuirassiers – to move forward as fast as possible and soon these had joined du Moulin's hussars to engage Weissenfels's squadrons. Two miles to the south-east the Prussian infantry were still making what haste they could across the bridges south of Gräben. Frederick's enemies were now deploying into a line of battle with Saxons on the left, north and east of the village of Günthersdorf; with the Austrians extending south from Günthersdorf to Thomaswaldau and, on the extreme right, Halbendorf.

There could now be no hope of marching further north and seeking to envelop. In the north the cavalry of both armies were already engaged in ferocious hand-to-hand encounters with little possibility of control. In the centre, west of Gräben and having crossed the Striegauerwasser, the leading nine Prussian battalions, soon expanded by reinforcements on both their flanks to a force of twenty-one, were now deployed by Prince Leopold Max of Anhalt-Dessau and began to advance against the Saxons of the enemy left and centre who were still arriving on the ground. This was the same prince who had commanded the left wing at Chotusitz. He was good.

It was just after dawn. The Prussian infantry once again justified their reputation, marching straight towards the enemy and only halting to fire when at close range. Frederick's orders had been explicit: infantry to march sharply – *'mit starkern Schritt verrücken'* – and only opening platoon fire when 200 paces from the enemy.[20] He placed himself on rising ground in the centre of the field where there was a windmill, the Striegauer Windmühlerhohe. By seven o'clock on that morning of 4 June the Saxons had been defeated and the ground was thickly covered with their dead.

The Austrian battalions of the enemy right and centre were now deploying. Frederick, directing all available infantry to the sector between Günthersdorf and Thomaswaldau, was able to assemble a further eighteen battalions for an advance in line, an advance which, as he recorded grimly, 'was never easy'. His two brothers were with the army on the left wing – August Wilhelm, 'the Prince of Prussia', aged twenty-three, and the later extremely distinguished Henry, aged nineteen, to be one of the first soldiers of the age. Henry had already also been at Glogau, Mollwitz and Chotusitz. Frederick now made him a major-general.

By eight o'clock on the morning of 4 June the Austrians had been driven from the villages and were retreating in disorder. The cavalry of the Austrian right wing threatened, for a while, the cavalry of the Prussian left – which was at a temporary numerical disadvantage caused by the collapse of the bridge at Teichau; and a half-hour's savage cavalry battle took place between Thomaswaldau and Halbendorf between seven and eight o'clock. But Major-General von Ziethen – already a name to conjure with – had found a ford between Teichau and Gräben and passed enough squadrons across to complete the victory.

Meanwhile one of Frederick's regiments, the Bayreuth Dragoons, had been held in reserve, following up the infantry to a point south of Günthersdorf. From there they moved through the infantry battalions of the Prussian centre and attacked the Austrian first line. Bursting through it they charged the second line, taking 2,500 prisoners, sixty-seven colours and five pieces of artillery. 'What statues would not have been erected in Rome to these Caesars of the Bayreuth Regiment!' Frederick wrote exultantly to Podewils, ordering medals to be prepared in honour of the battle, although with '*inscriptions modestes et courtes*'.[21]

By nine o'clock in the morning everything was over. Frederick had his victory and he had earned it. Although the actual battle had run a different course from that planned, his concept had been sound. He had, rightly, been determined to wait until Charles of Lorraine had reached the plain from the foothills before seeking major battle. He had used darkness to conceal his army's approach march and had been able to strike his first blows while the enemy was still deploying.

When he realized that he had no hope of marching his main body as far north as his plan demanded, and that there would be a cavalry encounter battle on his right wing, he 'fed' that battle wisely and effectively. Thereafter he shifted his main point of attack from that earlier selected – or wholly assented in its shift on the initiatives of Anhalt-Dessau. To persist in a predetermined plan when the conditioning factors have changed is a defect, and Frederick is guiltless of it. He could see things as they are, and even in the darkness of Hohenfriedeberg he did so.

The climax was heroic. Troopers of the Bayreuth Dragoons, accompanied by the regiment's kettledrummers, ceremonially carried fifty captured colours and standards through the archway of the castle of Rohnstock, dipping them in homage as they passed the King, who had set up his headquarters there. On the debit side of the triumph Frederick had lost 900 dead, and further casualties of about 3,800. The Austrians and Saxons, however, had lost 13,800 men,* including over 3,000 dead.

Hohenfriedeberg was undeniably a victory. Frederick's dispatch may have been inexact in the detail of what happened in every quarter of the field; as Wellington observed, the history of a battle is rather like the history of a ball, with remarkably few people knowing much beyond their own immediate experiences. But Frederick's exultation – 'une des plus grandes actions qu'il y a eu'[22] – was certainly understandable. The losses of each side told their story, the speed with which the battle was decided was extraordinary and impressive, the Prussians were masters of the field. To Podewils Frederick wrote meekly, 'J'espère que vous serez content de moi!'[23] And when he heard that Voltaire intended to compose a poem about the triumph, he wrote to Rothenburg in Paris that he would prefer a copy of the latest revision of Voltaire's 'Pucelle', the satirical poem not openly published.[24]

Frederick has been criticized, not for the first or last time, for failure to exploit victory at Hohenfriedeberg, for allowing the beaten Austrians too easy a withdrawal and thus a recovery. It should have been, some said, what he himself had described as desirable – 'one good battle to finish the business'. Instead he moved the Prussian

* Initially put by Frederick at 25,000.

army forward across the hills into Bohemia and spent some time in that summer of 1745 marching and counter-marching; hoping to exhaust the enemy by threatening now here, now there; consuming forage and supplies thus denied to the enemy; and in the process perhaps exhausting his own army as much as the opposition. Criticisms of that kind sometimes neglect what is in the commander's mind, full as it is of hopes and speculations as well as appreciations and plans. Frederick, at that time, undoubtedly hoped for peace, and he hoped that operational frustration would bring the Austrians to the same mind.

A different sort of accusation has been made against Frederick at Hohenfriedeberg – that his orders to the cavalry were to give no quarter 'in the heat of the battle'. He denied this,[25] saying that his intentions were simply to order his cavalry not to be diverted from action and pursuit by the business of making prisoners. His critics have alleged, on the contrary, that on this occasion his policy was the murder of enemy soldiers who surrendered, contrary to the usages of war. The matter is uncertain, like many things in war and the records of war. Frederick's orders were generally humane in spirit. He explicitly emphasized care for the wounded, including the enemy wounded. It seems improbable that he departed from this at Hohenfriedeberg and the animus shown against him by many writers does not increase the probability. Stories of atrocity and war crime are generally best assessed with caution, not because examples do not abound in all armies and all wars, but because record and condemnation of them is often highly selective; and because the anger, fear, vengeful emotions, confusions, conditions and cruelties of the battlefield are hard to depict or understand with any justice in quieter times. It is true that there was in the Prussian army, as Frederick himself expressed it, '*Une haine non pareille contre les Saxons*';[26] and Frederick, in July, produced a *Manifesto* listing Saxon outrages in Silesia and citing the iniquity of Saxon aggression in support of Maria Theresa. Whatever his orders and justification, the King shared the ferocious sentiments of his army.[27] The matter may best be left there.

8

The Military Philosopher

Hohenfriedeberg reinforced another development favourable to Frederick during the summer of 1745. In London there was growing impatience with Austria and with what was regarded as Maria Theresa's intransigence. There had never been much concern in England about the rights and wrongs of the Silesian issue: the continuing preoccupation of Austria with Prussia simply served, in British eyes, to distract her from efforts against what should be her chief enemy, France. As to Prussia, it was known in London that Frederick had hoped for a French offensive in West Germany against Hanover as a means of putting pressure on a Britain which was subsidizing his enemies, as well as a means of distracting Austria from Bohemia at the time. This policy of Frederick's had, naturally, been resented: Hanover, contiguous to Prussia, was a sensitive point for the British court and government, where the latter mistrusted their sovereign's concern for his Electoral possessions but could not maintain total indifference to Hanover's security. And George II disliked and distrusted his nephew. Nevertheless continuing war between Austria and Prussia was not in the British interest and this mood suited Frederick who had long been seeking British mediation for a favourable peace.

On 19 August Charles Edward Stuart, having landed in the western Highlands of Scotland in the previous month, raised his standard at Glenfinnan. The Jacobite rising had begun and the more Britain could reduce her continental commitments the better for her. On 26 August a convention, the Convention of Hanover, was signed between Britain and Prussia, under which Britain not only guaranteed to respect Prussian possessions in return for a reciprocal guarantee of British possessions but specifically mentioned Silesia. In return Prussia undertook to evacuate Saxony and Bohemia when agreements with Britain were concluded. Frederick invoked God's name in swearing that he had never wished to annex Saxon territory.

The convention would not be ratified by Britain, however, until early October and meanwhile there was still a campaign for Frederick to conduct. The Convention of Hanover suited Frederick. It was an advance on the defensive alliance agreed in November 1742 and the reference to Silesia was consistent with his hopes and policies. It was, naturally, unwelcome to France. Frederick hoped that the convention might presage a general peace (not excluding some financial subsidies from Britain to Prussia) but the hope was not strong. He took secret steps to inform Charles of Lorraine of his intended dealings but received the cool reply that that prince had no information which would lead him to suspend operations of war.[1] Frederick had hoped that his gestures to Britain would induce Austria, as Britain's ally and beneficiary, also to think more warmly of peace but it did not look likely, although he naturally hoped that British influence would be exerted in that direction. He reflected, in his gloomier moods, that he might have simply upset France to little purpose.[2] Furthermore Louis XV had to swallow the (surely inevitable) election of Maria Theresa's husband, Francis of Lorraine, to the Imperial throne on 13 September, an elevation which Frederick had agreed at the Hanover convention not to block – his representative abstained, leaving Frankfurt the day before the election.

In fact Britain was pressing Maria Theresa hard towards acceptance of peace with Frederick but with absolutely no success. That resolute woman regarded her possessions as intolerably vulnerable while the King of Prussia was as much in the ascendant as he was, and the suggestions of the British Ambassador fell on deaf ears. She was, after long and disappointing delay, about to secure the Imperial crown for her husband. She had managed to conclude a new alliance with Saxony on 29 August. She believed that the way to deal with the Prussians was by beating them in the field. Nor was she alone. At the end of September the Tsarina Elizabeth decided that Russia would support Saxony 'if Saxony were again to be attacked by Prussia'. Frederick guessed – correctly – that the Russian Empress had conceived a strong hostility towards him.

Frederick had, by diplomacy, neutralized one potential enemy – Britain/Hanover. He had, by battle, reduced the capacity and the confidence of two more, Saxony and Austria – including the principal enemy. But he had, not for the first time, increased the distrust of himself by an ally, France, in signing the Convention of Hanover. He was, nevertheless, complaining bitterly at the French subsidies he was receiving, which were well below his expectations. He also, of course, grumbled about French strategy which had neglected to help his own campaign. He always had the spectre of a possibly hostile Russia. Matters could probably only be improved by another victorious battle. While conducting these complex and tortuous negotiations in several directions Frederick was marching his army through Bohemia, through enemy territory, followed at a respectful distance by the Austrians.

Frederick's encampments on this progression through northern Bohemia were harassed by the energetic enemy cavalry patrols which sometimes penetrated even to his own quarters. His movements were carefully observed by the enemy commanders – and he, as carefully, watched them during their regular reconnaissances of his own moves. His objects were forage and provisions; and he hoped, too, to exhaust an enemy frustrated by witnessing his march through Austrian territory. He was hoping to receive news, at any day, that the Convention of Hanover was having the desired effect in Vienna and that hostilities for the time being were over. His communications with Silesia were under constant threat from the enemy's patrols. He had won a victory in open field at Hohenfriedeberg but he was not dealing with a demoralized opponent. In Berlin Podewils was again worried about a Saxon raid into Brandenburg and Frederick told him not to be so timid – 'I don't know a bigger chicken-heart (*poule-mouillée*) than you'! Podewils was always nervous of Saxon reactions and Frederick was robust with him.[3] With sadness Frederick learned in their next exchange of letters of the death of Dietrich von Keyserlingk, 'Cesarion', beloved companion of early days.[4] 'We should have taken more care of him last winter,' he wrote wretchedly, signing (as occasionally) '*Votre fidèle ami*'.

In the last days of September Frederick, having crossed and recrossed the Upper Elbe, was marching north with the river on his right flank. Ahead were the Silesian hills and on the 29th he was encamped, watching the south, near the village of Soor and east of a place called Bürkersdorf. He aimed to withdraw for a while across the Silesian border and to reach the frontier between Bohemia and Silesia next day. And here Charles of Lorraine, with an army of 40,000, decided to attack him.

The ground was undulating, with a mass of thick woods west of the village, the Königsreichwald, offering possibility of a concealed advance. A low hill, the Granerkoppe, rose dominantly about a half-mile north of Bürkersdorf. Charles of Lorraine reckoned that he could march unobserved through the Königsreichwald, emerge opposite Frederick's camp east of Bürkersdorf (less than a mile from the edge of the woods) and deploy for battle before the Prussians had much time to reach the ground and to form. This move would, incidentally, also threaten the Prussian northward communications. Charles decided, as a first essential step, to send a strong detachment to occupy the Granerkoppe – which was about equally near the edge of the woods.

There was a thick early morning mist. Covered by this and the preceding darkness, Charles managed to push sixteen heavy guns, thirty squadrons of cavalry, some mounted infantry, some grenadier companies and ten musketeer battalions to the crest of the Graner-koppe, all during darkness. From the Granerkoppe the Austrians could dominate the Prussian deployment when it happened: it was key ground. The main body of Charles's army then moved out of the Königsreichwald and formed up facing Bürkersdorf on a frontage of about four miles. The Prussian army was suffering from the necessity to make detachments for protective or logistic purposes and they were outnumbered by almost two to one.

At five o'clock on the morning of 30 September Frederick received the first reports of enemy to the west. He gave orders for the alarm to be beaten and galloped with Leopold Max of Anhalt to see what he could. This, though not much, was enough to show that he was facing a major attack. It was also clear that the Granerkoppe, whose tactical significance was evident, was occupied by the enemy.

The Prussian regiments, according to established system, fell in without necessity for further orders. Frederick intended to form a line roughly parallel to the Königsreichwald and to the enemy, and to do this by marching his leading troops – who would become his right – towards the ground east and north-east of the Granerkoppe, moving on the east side of Bürkersdorf and occupying the hill itself; the remainder would then front left and advance direct on the enemy centre (as it later proved to be).

The leading cavalry squadrons moved round the east of the Granerkoppe and then started to climb. They were able partially to escape the line of fire of the Austrian artillery on the crest and – going up a steep convex slope – met and worsted approximately double their number of Austrian cavalry, deployed in front of the infantry. The Prussian cavalry task was to clear the enemy cavalry so that the infantry assault could go in – a task made particularly difficult by the lie of the ground with the slope protected by a small, steep valley. The task, however, was discharged and the Austrian cavalry withdrew to the shelter of the Königsreichwald.

The way was now clear for the advance of the Prussian infantry. Six battalions came forward, ordered to advance up the slope and straight towards the Austrian guns and infantry in position. The distance was 500 yards. It was eight o'clock in the morning, the early mist had cleared and there was nothing to protect the advancing Prussian lines.

It was a gallant but costly attack, one of those operations where the price in blood is horribly high but where the operational benefit justifies that price because of lives ultimately saved by victory. There are echoes of Marlborough's assault on the Schellenberg before Blenheim, and, like Marlborough, Frederick saw that he must commit more and more to the attack as the leading battalions suffered and fell. Within minutes he ordered forward another five battalions – grenadiers and musketeers – from the second line of the right wing. Casualties were frightful. The Queen's young brother, Prince Albrecht of Brunswick, lay dead. The first line wavered, fell back and merged into the second. Eventually the whole mass, or those of it still alive, reached the crest of the Granerkoppe and the battery position there. The dominating feature of the battlefield was in Prussian hands.

Meanwhile Frederick's centre and left wing battalions, which he had intended to hold back until he had mastered the Granerkoppe,

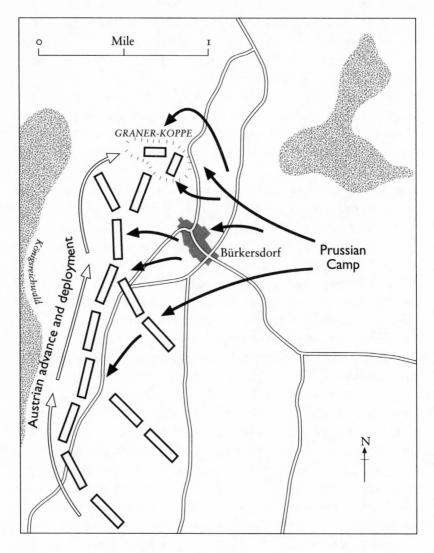

Soor, 30 September 1745

moved forward – by whose orders or none is unclear – through Bürkersdorf and south of it. At first they were checked by an Austrian battery to their immediate front but were then led forward by another brother-in-law, Prince Ferdinand of Brunswick, later to be the victor of Minden and much else. These battalions then advanced and charged with the bayonet, a charge which drove the Austrians from the field with heavy casualties. The action was over by midday. It was an expensive battle for both sides in proportion to the numbers engaged. Frederick lost just under 4,000 men, with 850 dead: and Charles of Lorraine lost 7,500. Once again, however, the Prussians had the best of it. They had won.

Frederick acknowledged, with the candour and modesty which were among his most attractive qualities, that Charles of Lorraine had taken him by surprise at Soor, as the battle was named. In a long letter to Podewils he paid generous tribute to the Austrian troops. He had underestimated his opponent's enterprise and had allowed a large enemy force to approach his west flank unobserved until dangerously late. He might also have commented on his failure to hold the Granerkoppe from the start, although it could have necessitated a dangerously large detachment. Thereafter the Prussian army had done all that could be wished – drill, discipline, cohesion all admirable. The initiative shown by subordinate commanders (subordinates trained by Frederick) had been excellent. The victorious outcome, Frederick said, owed little to generalship and everything to the quality of the army itself. He wrote that he had been in trouble at Soor, but the army had got him out of it – although he added, justifiably, in a letter to Podewils next day that his own *'promptitude et courte résolution'* had had something to do with it![5] Full of praise for his troops though Frederick was, his own assurance and confidence was now immense. In the same letter he said that the battle could explain George II's remark to the Austrian minister in London, to the effect that the King of Prussia could do more in a day than Charles of Lorraine in six weeks. To Anhalt-Dessau he wrote that 'our men, both cavalry and infantry, are all-conquering!'*[6] 'If our negotiations don't go well today they never will,' he told Podewils.[7]

* *Überwindlich.*

Frederick's personal baggage had been caught by enemy patrols, due, he said, to the incompetence of the responsible officer. His ciphers had been captured and compromised: he wrote hasty instructions about consequential security. More personally saddening was the capture – or, as he expected, killing – of his beloved whippet bitch, 'Biche'. He loved Biche and Biche loved him.

About the loss of his clothes, tents, tent furniture, silver and musical instruments Frederick was philosophic. He wrote to Fredersdorff[8] on 2 October that he had lost everything and needed 10,000 thalers from his treasurer, Koppen. Fredersdorff managed all personal matters and was the conduit of instructions and wishes between the King and every sort of court official. The King's household officers with their high-sounding titles, Masters of Household, of Horse, of the Wardrobe – all (wrote a French visitor, marvelling) were overseen in every particular by one man, Michael Gabriel Fredersdorff, four years older than the King, still simply entitled 'First' Valet and personal secretary; man of power and indispensable friend. To Fredersdorff Frederick would write about his health, often casting ridicule on doctors ('*Grosse Idioten!*')[9] and giving his own robust theories on medical matters. To any hint that Fredersdorff himself might be unwell Frederick was solicitous: '*Gott bewahre Dich und mache Dier wieder gesundt* [sic]'.[10] Letters to and from Fredersdorff tend to be dominated by bodily ailments and money; and personal administration.

Telling Fredersdorff of his losses, he mentioned first the loss of his horses, Anne-Marie and Champion; then referred to members of the staff, Cabinet Secretary, cryptographer, personal doctor, who were still missing; then gave a few names of the dead, including two generals, von Blanckenburg and von Bredow. He also referred to his dead brother-in-law, in a sadly unfeeling way – 'Not much loss' – which reflects his lack of love for his wife and is certainly unendearing. Frederick could and did dissemble – elegantly – in diplomacy and courtly compliment. Privately, and about his true feelings, never. On this occasion – unusually – the sad Queen complained bitterly to her youngest brother-in-law, Ferdinand, who was only fifteen – 'I'm accustomed to his [Frederick's] manners but on such an occasion, when one of my brothers has died in his service, such manners are *too* cruel!' A week later Frederick wrote a brief, slightly kinder letter – 'He was a brave man. I'm amazed he wasn't killed long ago.'[11]

On 6 October Frederick resumed his march north towards Silesia, taking his own time; and on the 19th the army crossed the frontier. From the battlefield he also wrote to Fredersdorff for more snuff – he took a great deal of his favourite Spanish snuff, spilling it copiously so that his clothes, especially as he became older, were often snuff-stained. And Biche was not dead. A few days later, after some anxious requests, she was returned by her captors to Frederick's camp a few miles south-west of the battlefield and quietly introduced to his quarters by Rothenburg while the King sat alone at his table writing letters, unaware. Biche leapt on to the table and put her paws round his neck: and he was seen to weep.

Frederick was carefully watching the reactions or inaction of the British Government in the aftermath of the Convention of Hanover, now ratified. He had been promised subsidies from London and at the end of October he pressed for these to be paid a full year in advance.[12] So far there was no indication that British efforts to promote peace were having much effect in Vienna but these were early days and Frederick was concerned to maintain his new accord with London. He offered six Prussian battalions for service against the Jacobite rising (troops, he made clear, who could only be used in Britain and must be sent back to Germany when the emergency was over). If these were insufficient to deal with the business for George II he could send considerably more. He could, however, send none at all until peace had been negotiated between himself and Maria Theresa – a perfectly understandable point of pressure.

Meanwhile – and equally understandably – Frederick was aware of a reproachful note struck in his communications from Paris,[13] where the Convention of Hanover rankled. He tried to test the idea of a possible peace between France and Britain, leaving Austria isolated, but he knew the chances were thin. There was the Jacobite factor: and, as would increasingly dominate the century, the rivalry between French and British in distant continents. On his own borders there seemed little hope of relaxation. With the realization that the Austrians would not accept his victories at Hohenfriedeberg and Soor as decisively ending the campaign, and with the Tsarina's undertaking to support Saxony against him 'if attacked', Frederick seemed to be opposed by two implacable women.

The Swedish minister to Saxony was, effectively, Frederick's agent in Dresden. He kept the Swedish minister to Prussia well-informed, and the latter had good relations with the Prussian court. Frederick returned to Berlin at the end of October and learned from these and other reliable sources that Maria Theresa, far from yielding to pressures from London and the imperatives of the battlefield to seek peace, was preparing a winter campaign, launched from Saxony and planned to threaten Prussian communications to the troops in Silesia and Bohemia. If this were pursued vigorously Brandenburg itself might again be threatened; and at the beginning of November 1745 Frederick learned that an Austro-Saxon enemy army was advancing northward out of Lusatia,[14] the area of Saxony round Gorlitz and Bautzen, while an Austrian force was also on the march to join the Saxon troops quartered near Leipzig. There should, he reckoned, be a counterstroke devised, perhaps of a different nature from his battles hitherto. 'More than ever,' he wrote to Maurice de Saxe on 6 November, addressing him in acknowledgement of compliments to a 'connoisseur of war' in the recent fighting, 'more than ever am I sure that in every country one needs to make a different sort of war.' He left Berlin on 16 November and hurried to join the army.

The army, expensively victorious at Soor, had withdrawn northward across the hills into Silesia, and Frederick decided to lead it westward, against the eastern flank of the enemy in Lusatia. On 23 November he crossed the river Queiss at Naumburg, the eastern border of Lusatia, and on the same day his cavalry fell upon the Saxon army in camp at Hennersdorf, taking nearly 1,000 prisoners and seizing the magazine at Gorlitz. The Austrians then withdrew through Zittau to the frontier of Bohemia. The counterstroke, because of the speed and energy with which it had been organized, had succeeded.

But the enemy were resilient. Further west an Austrian force – 6,000 under General de Grunne – had joined the Saxons near Dresden and at the beginning of December Frederick learned that Charles of Lorraine had led the main body of the Austrian army out of Bohemia to join them. Frederick was at Bautzen, nearly seventy miles distant.

Nearer the enemy, however, was another Prussian army, 25,000 strong, which the Prince of Anhalt-Dessau, the Old Dessauer himself, had been assembling for some time. Frederick had planned that this army should be ready to invade northern Saxony from the direction of Halle and it was already on the march southward by the Elbe at Torgau towards Dresden. Frederick was in touch with it by his fast-riding couriers, and was able to send regular information and operational instructions. He also sent, on 2 December, a detachment from his own army, fifty cavalry squadrons and ten infantry battalions under General von Lehwaldt, to join the veteran Anhalt-Dessau at Meissen; and proposed to march with the residue of his army towards Dresden. The enemy would be threatened from two directions.

On 13 December Anhalt-Dessau reached Meissen and united with Lehwaldt on the west bank of the Elbe – a combined force of some 33,000 men. With these, on 15 December, he beat a combined Austro-Saxon army at the battle of Kesselsdorf, south of Meissen, in a ferocious frontal assault against superior numbers. The Prussians lost 3,500, including 1,000 dead, at Kesselsdorf: the Saxons left 3,000 dead on the field and lost 5,000 prisoners to the enemy. It was a triumph, and after it the two wings of the Prussian army, Frederick's and Anhalt-Dessau's, were united. When the two commanders met outside Dresden on the morning of the 17th, Frederick dismounted, uncovered and embraced his distinguished old kinsman.

It was a happy conclusion to a frustrating few days for Frederick. He had chafed at what seemed the slow progress of the western wing of the Prussian army under his most illustrious – and oldest – commander. 'I cannot pretend,' he had written to the Old Dessauer on 9 December, with a good deal of moral courage, 'that I am wholly content with your Highness's operations – you are moving so slowly!'[15] There were some additional and hurtful expressions, although on the following day he had sent something like amends.[16] Frederick could be brutal in dealing with subordinate commanders, however distinguished. The Old Dessauer was sixty-nine now. He had been at war for many of those years since the siege of Namur in 1695, serving with Eugen and Marlborough in most of the campaigns of the War of Spanish Succession, a marshal since the year of Frederick's birth, a disciplinarian and trainer of troops whose reputation was second to none in Europe. He, more than any man, had formed the incomparable Prussian infantry which Frederick had used to such effect; and he, more than any man, had interceded with Frederick William when the Crown Prince was used so cruelly. Now that Crown Prince was himself king, commander-in-chief; and was prepared to rebuke him, Prussia's greatest hero, for slowness!

The Old Dessauer had, of course, been something of a military oracle to Frederick when young; but the truth was that the great old man had become slow – slow and cautious. He had not welcomed the Silesian adventure. He had seen a great deal of war and had not wanted to end his days as witness to a Prussian reverse. A devout Lutheran, he always spent time before battle praying and he prayed hard on 15 December 1745 – and won for Frederick the great fight of Kesselsdorf, his last battle, in which he charged at the head of his own regiment and had three bullets through the tunic. The King's embrace, all slights forgotten, marked the end of a great warrior career (the Old Dessauer died two years later) and of the second Silesian war. Kesselsdorf had tipped the balance decisively. Dresden surrendered to Frederick on 18 December and peace with both Austria and Saxony was signed there on Christmas Day 1745. By this peace Frederick's possession of Silesia and Glatz was recognized, while he recognized the Pragmatic Sanction and the Imperial dignity of Francis of Lorraine.

Frederick was delighted that peace was agreed, as he had long hoped. He also wrote on Christmas Day 1745 to the French Ambassador, Valory.[17] It was a sharp letter. As far as the recent campaign went, Frederick observed, he had been wholly abandoned by his allies – which was largely true. He had, he said, received inadequate subsidies and been helped neither by troops nor by some strategic diversion. In these circumstances, which France could long have foreseen, he had had no alternative but to make peace. France was complaining, but Frederick's reaction to complaints was justified. Prussia had waged the war in central Europe single-handed; and France had profited thereby. The point was made with waspish courtesy and equal firmness in a letter to Louis XV sent through Valory on the same day.[18] '*Je n'entre point dans les raisons qu'elle peut avoir d'abandonner ses alliés à leur propre fortune; cela fait que je sens doublement le bonheur que j'ai de m'être tiré d'un pas très scabreux par la valeur de mes troupes.'*

In his *History of My Time*, Frederick was harsh about his own performance in the second Silesian war. He spent some time on this work immediately after the Peace of Dresden and wrote that no general had committed more faults than he. He had underestimated the logistic difficulties of campaigning in Bohemia, the problems created by the awkward country and passes between Saxony and Silesia. He had underestimated the skill of the Austrian commanders. He had, as before, made over-optimistic assumptions about the effect of French initiatives on Austrian operations. Strategically he had found himself isolated and outnumbered, and had extricated himself only through the superior quality of the Prussian army and through the good fortune, as he put it, of being able to fight three battles. Without these he would have been faced with the wholly unacceptable terms which Saxony (backed by Russian resources) and Austria, still bent on recovery of Silesia, would have sought to impose.

There was some over-reaction here. Frederick's assessments and appreciations had been faulty on occasion but he had recovered from the consequences of error with commendable speed and resilience, he had regained his balance. In these self-castigations, however, he never blamed himself for that which many historians have criticized – the decision to go to war at all. On that his conscience was completely clear. The odds had been piling up against him and his duty to Prussia had been to strike first and to hope to emerge with an improved situation. He never wavered on this.

His situation, in fact, was only to a limited extent improved. The Peace of Dresden had given Prussia respite. The outcome of the war had reflected the ever-increasing military reputation of the Prussian army. Frederick's possession of Silesia was again recognized – as frequently happened and was as frequently overturned by another Austrian attempt at recovery. Frederick wrote that the war had been necessary if Silesia was to be held and Prussia respected, and this was a tenable viewpoint but he knew that the roots of the issue were not affected. These lay in the reluctance of Austria to acknowledge the reality of Prussia's increased stature and importance, as well as

Frederick's acquisitions of territory. He emerged from the second Silesian war less with euphoria than with a continuing sense of insecurity. He also emerged from it with a near-exhausted treasury, although he knew that it had also placed severe strains on the resources of the enemy.

Frederick's immediate preoccupations were strategic and military but there was a good deal of diplomatic business to transact and influences to exert or forfend. He frequently declared, in his letters to his embassies, astonishment at the credence given to malicious stories about his intentions. He ascribed this, in the main, to the ill-will of Austria and to some extent (varying with the season) of Hanover. In the years immediately following the Peace of Dresden he was as watchful as ever. He realized, with reluctance, that his fellow-sovereigns were suspicious of him; and he was suspicious of them. Moltke later remarked that perpetual peace is a dream (and, he added, not even a beautiful dream). Frederick was of the same mind. He was always restlessly uneasy about the security of Prussia; about the intentions of Austria; and about the policy of Russia.

Frederick concluded a defensive treaty with Sweden, a treaty unpopular in both Russia and England, and later joined by France. There was a large Russian army in Courland, near Prussia's borders, and Russia was equipping a fleet of galleys in the Baltic. Why? He mistrusted the behaviour of Russian troops, particularly Cossacks and Irregulars when passing near his own domains.[19] He heard that it was being said that his power was now dangerously great and that he had designs on Polish Prussia. Why?[20] At the same time he conveyed good wishes to the Tsarina and, since he had heard that coaches had been ordered for the Russian court from coachmakers in Berlin, he trusted that 'Madame ma Sœur' would accept a particular coach as a personal gift.[21] He was always intensely suspicious of the close relations between Russia and Saxony, sure that these would lead to an attack against him one day (a justified suspicion). Count Brühl, the Saxon chief minister, was, in Frederick's view, 'Le dernier des misérables', and he told Valory that the French were taken in by the Saxons so often he had lost count.[22] Not until 1748 would there be anything resembling a general peace in Europe, albeit one of short duration. Meanwhile, in 1746 and 1747 Frederick's letters and anxieties were those of a sovereign surrounded by the alarums of war, even if not actually waging it.

And much of Europe was, indeed, still at war. It was an uneasy time and Frederick's uncertainties and irritability show in the curtness with which he sometimes handled his envoys. His style was generally most courteous, full of acknowledgement and gratitude for a discerning report, a perceptive opinion. But, 'I should tell you I am displeased (*mal content*) with you,' he wrote to Andrie, in London, on 10 May 1746. Andrie seemed, he continued, to be ill-informed as well as inept at handling the various damaging stories which were current about the King of Prussia. He was particularly sensitive about failures at news management of this kind.

He was also sharp over style and detail. His man in Vienna had sent a long 'apologia' in code. Frederick: 'I like seeing code used only for *interesting* matters!'[23] and to his envoy at The Hague, von Ammon, who was representing him at Aix-la-Chapelle during the treaty* negotiations, he was explicit in his snubs: 'You should take care to avoid small and superfluous details in your reports, such as the fact that you had to spend a night at Roermond – all these personal matters which are not of the slightest interest to me!'[24] And to von Mardefeld, in St Petersburg, he wrote in July 1746 that the Ambassador found it rather too entertaining to report the goings-on in the Empress's apartments which in ordinary times might amuse the King but in critical periods like the present '*ne me paraissent guère intéressants*'! Frederick kept his envoys on their toes and it is unlikely they always looked forward to his correspondence with enjoyment.

Sometimes they showed their hurt. In a letter to Mardefeld later in July, referring to an earlier exchange, Frederick soothed his ambassador's feelings: 'You indict me wrongly, dear Mardefeld, if you suppose that for a *single moment* I have doubted your loyalty.'[25] Loyalty was not at issue but accurate information was. An Austro-Russian treaty was hatching and since there was now peace Frederick had sent his chief minister's nephew, Otto von Podewils, as Envoy Extraordinary to Vienna to keep in touch with events in that and other directions.

* The Treaty of Aix-la-Chapelle marked the definitive end of the War of Austrian Succession. The negotiation took a long time.

Podewils reported at the end of July that the proposed agreements seemed purely defensive; he had talked to a number of other ambassadors including the British Ambassador, Robinson, and been reassured. Frederick would remain less easy about it – anyway he had a poor opinion of Robinson,* who was, he believed, besotted with Maria Theresa. Dealings between Austria and Russia would always need very close watching indeed. Bestuzhev, as Podewils in Vienna agreed, was anxious to give any Austro-Russian agreement a more offensive character but was at present unable to get his way.[26] Frederick was right to be anxious: there were secret clauses to the agreement, learned much later, which were unmistakably aimed at Prussia. Frederick also learned, with considerable suspicion, that George II, in his capacity as Elector of Hanover, was proposing to accede to the same agreement.[27]

As members of what could loosely be called the earlier anti-French alliance, the Austrians and British had been promised an expedition of 30,000 Russian troops, allegedly to march to the Low Countries, to join against the French. Frederick regarded this without enthusiasm. He doubted whether these Russians would move as soon or as fast as their allies hoped, but their real purpose, he knew, had been to deter Prussia from any moves to support France against Hanover. This Frederick found understandable – at an earlier stage of the war (which was now over as far as he was concerned) he had certainly pressed for a French demonstration against Hanover and a counter-demonstration, involving in this case Russian troops, had been comprehensible if unwelcome; but now matters were different.

French policy he found equivocal. They seemed unable to decide whether they wanted a general peace, as Frederick favoured, or continuance of the war, in some form, in some places, for some objects. In fact France was moving towards desire for a general peace, but their backslidings (as Frederick saw it) in the recent campaign gave him little warmth of feeling towards them. The French were still, however, conducting a campaign in Flanders and Frederick was following its course closely. He admired Saxe's conduct of operations and had written to him in flattering terms in October 1746 to tell him so, signing, '*votre affectionné ami, Fédéric*'.[28] Saxe, now Marshal, inflicted

---

* Thomas Robinson, later 1st Lord Grantham.

defeat on the Dutch states-general in the following May, 1747, a defeat followed by an internal revolution in Holland which brought to power again the house of Orange as Stadtholders. The French now held the initiative in the Netherlands, despite British support for the Austrians and Dutch.

Militarily this support did not amount to much and in July 1747 an allied army – Austrians, Dutch, British, under the command of the Duke of Cumberland – was defeated at Laufeldt. 'This will teach Cumberland,' Frederick wrote, 'to distinguish boldness (*audace*) from rashness (*témérité*).' There was an idea current, of which Frederick disapproved, that a marriage might be arranged between Cumberland and Frederick's sister, Amelia (who never married and was later abbess of Quedlinburg). The British were disillusioned by the progress of the war and to a large extent by the cause of Maria Theresa, a disillusionment which gratified Frederick. The negotiations which led to the Treaty of Aix-la-Chapelle began in January 1748, and in the same month Frederick sent an affectionate letter and portrait of himself as a present to his cousin, the Prince of Wales. He always hoped that the death of George II, when it came, would give an opportunity for improved relations between Britain and Prussia.

In the event George II was succeeded not by his eldest son but by his grandson, later George III; and not until 1760. One personal contact, perhaps useful for the future, was, however, made at this time. The British Government sent to Berlin as envoy Henry Legge, who had been private secretary to Sir Robert Walpole. He was four years older than Frederick, had already been a Lord of the Treasury and the Admiralty, would be Chancellor of the Exchequer for several years, including during the Seven Years War, and was rated by some the most acute financial mind of the age. He was charged with some negotiations about moneys allegedly owed to Britain from Silesia, 'The Silesian loan',[29] and this negotiation was unsuccessful; but he was also empowered to sound out Frederick about an alliance between Britain and Prussia once the war was over. It would be over when the Treaty of Aix-la-Chapelle was finally ratified, and meanwhile the two men talked, according to Frederick, '*particulier à particulier*'.[30] The authorities in Hanover were always concerned at the possible threat to the Electorate from Prussia – was that reasonable, London wondered?[31]

Legge was a devoted friend of William Pitt, later Earl of Chatham: and Pitt, who at the time held a junior position in the British administration, would one day be the ruling spirit of British policy and a loyal friend to Frederick. Legge (although according to one story* he had been treated by Frederick badly, and 'duped') may have left on Pitt's mind a favourable impression of that King who had once talked to him about the affairs of Europe, *'particulier à particulier'*. He reported that Frederick was particularly in awe of the power of Russia.

Frederick's acquisitions of land were confirmed to him under the Treaty of Aix-la-Chapelle, a treaty concluded between France and Britain as principals and accepted, with some scepticism, by their respective allies. The limited objects for which he had first gone to war had been achieved and he had never over-reached himself by trying for ends beyond his means. Britain made renewed attempts to get Frederick fully to endorse the Pragmatic Sanction (still Maria Theresa's dominant desire) but his reaction was that, in so far as there was anything of that left to do, Austria had never fulfilled her engagement to him under the Peace of Dresden, by which the Empire would have guaranteed his possession of Silesia. He had agreed at that time to endorse the Sanction and he was still waiting for Austrian recognition, as promised. For Frederick the underlying situation, the situation based on power, was unchanged. Austria was unreconciled. Hanover was nervously hostile. Russia constituted a brooding menace. France had failed to exploit diplomatically her strong military position in the Low Countries at the war's end; she would not be sorry to see Frederick once again embroiled in war with his own neighbours.[32]

Although Frederick's attention to detail and mastery of the nuances of European diplomacy inspired respect, there were dangers in it. He had a knowledge few of his officials could equal, but faced with this expertise – an expertise combined with an autocratic and often intolerant temperament – men were tempted to report in a way they knew would be congenial to the King's own views, to tell him what he wanted to hear. A letter starting, as often, *'vous méritez mon approbation'* no doubt warmed the ambassadorial heart but might be followed[33] by congratulations on coming to share a mistrust or an

* By Horace Walpole.

opinion already known to be Frederick's. Frederick could intimidate – the perennial risk of the powerful character – and could thereby risk diminishing the frankness of the advice he received.

But he could always endear. He knew how to sweeten rebuke if he felt he had wounded unduly. 'Don't be so *angry* with me!' he wrote to le Chambrier in Paris. 'The Devil isn't as black as he's painted in Geneva! Remember that if false zeal is the attribute of fanaticism, moderation is that of the true Christian!'[34] Le Chambrier had been reporting what was said in France about Frederick's religious views and Frederick had responded sharply, but added this emollient postscript. Nevertheless he kept le Chambrier (and all of them) in a certain state of tension. 'I should tell you,' he wrote to him, 'that it is tedious for me to read in your dispatches, almost word for word, what *I* have written to *you*!' He had told le Chambrier what he should say to the French ministers; le Chambrier had done so, and in reporting had repeated the instruction. Frederick was easily irritated.

More seriously, he wrote to le Chambrier at the end of 1748 about the situation in France. Could the French, despite their great resources, possibly maintain their considerable army and also aspire to rival Britain at sea? Would not France, in her efforts to preserve her position in India and elsewhere, fatally weaken herself in Europe and at home? Did the French, therefore, not inevitably regard the present situation in Europe as an armistice rather than a genuine peace? Frederick might have argued from his own premises that France, involved in a great maritime and colonial competition overseas, had all the more reason to hope for peace in Europe, but he did not do so. He felt certain – the greatest miscalculation of his life so far – that France would never desist from continental rivalry with Austria, while neither peace nor trust were possible between France and Britain. He saw no reason not to keep his lines open to both the latter nor to discourage their mutual suspicions. There was, he felt, fundamental instability in the rival and incompatible ambitions of the great powers.[35]

In July 1749 Frederick was told by a reliable source that the Russian Empress Elizabeth, 'disturbed by the perilous situation in Sweden', had decided to send a corps of Russian troops into Swedish Finland 'as a precautionary measure'. His sense of general unease was increased and was hardly diminished by a further report that Saxony had assured

Russia of its support against Swedish aggression.[36] Nothing came of all this which, as a 'crisis', had petered out by February 1750, but it indicated the fragility of the general situation. The various powers were watching each other with unceasing suspicion; and they were all around Prussia. Frederick shared in a universal nervousness, and his own reputation for bold and perhaps pre-emptive action increased rather than diminished the tensions in Europe. Despite the end of the war which his own actions had originally launched, the continent was an armed camp.

It was unsurprising, therefore, that in the aftermath of the Peace of Dresden, and after the conclusion of the Treaty of Aix-la-Chapelle, Frederick's immediate preoccupations were strategic and military. He is thought to have suffered at this time (at the age of only thirty-five) a very slight stroke, which never recurred, but his energy was unflagging. He began further works in Upper Silesia – a new fortress was constructed at Schweidnitz and Neisse was fortified. He set in hand correction of the army's manpower deficiencies – not least by the simple if brutal expedient of conscripting into its ranks Austrian and Saxon prisoners of war. And he set down in writing what he reckoned were the lessons of the war.

Frederick was an indefatigable military author and many of his writings were alluded to, revised, corrected as his life went on. His *Military Instructions from the King of Prussia to his Generals* and *Particular Instructions to the Officers of the Army* were not published until many years later but were first drafted by Frederick in the period immediately following the second Silesian war and it is seldom hard to connect particular maxims or instructions with incidents in that war. The first chapters of the *Military Instructions* were written and described as *General Principles of War* and were very comprehensive.[37] He also began composing his *First Political Testament*[38] (completed in 1752), which has an extended military section. Some of this is duplicatory, but taken together expresses Frederick's mind and experience at that time. Since Frederick wrote in French his works had to be translated into German.

In these *Instructions* Frederick described in some detail the characteristics of Prussian troops, their virtues and defects; and he set out certain very human principles of handling them. 'Take trouble to see the cavalry and infantry get on with each other,' he wrote. 'The infantry are more inured to hardship and if they get good quarters they'll fight to keep them!' He knew them well after regimental command in peacetime and after two campaigns. He enjoyed moving among them, talking to them at their campfires, exchanging jokes and banter. To them he was 'Fritz' – increasingly '*Alter Fritz*'. With them he was relaxed, although all knew his strictness. 'We didn't see you earlier today!' a soldier called from a bivouac after one battle. Frederick smiled sardonically and opened his coat; two Austrian bullets fell to the ground. He tolerated – enjoyed – familiarities called out on the line of march. It was ever clearer to his soldiers that the King shared their dangers and hardships to a degree rare in that or any other age. This was not the least of the traits which would mark him as great. The soldiers were at all times aware of him, felt his presence, sensed his powerful concern with every detail.

Frederick referred in the *Instructions* to half the Prussian army being 'of our own people' and half of foreigners 'enlisted for money' (he might have added 'and not always voluntarily'). The army of 'our own people' was based on the cantonal system, a strong, robust territorial system which associated the army with the people, but the losses on campaigns would always necessitate incorporation of many who were not Prussians. Prussia was small, and one of the motives for expansion by any state was to get an increase in recruiting grounds. Many princes besides Frederick were often impelled to recruit to their armies prisoners of war, *en bloc*. In an age where nationalism in the modern sense was virtually unknown while most combatants were Germans, under whatever sovereign, this was a less difficult proceeding than might appear, although local and regional patriotism was strong. It underlined, however, one ever present hazard: the incidence of desertion.

Desertion accounted for a considerable proportion of the casualties in all armies. It was one of the prime duties of Frederick's officers to keep desertion numbers down; the possibilities of men slipping away from the ranks unperceived often limited operational choices, frequent rollcalls were intended to reduce opportunities, and punishments were harsh. When the troops were in barracks a deserter generally earned a flogging for the sentries of the barrack guard. Villages were given a cash reward for betraying a deserter. In the field a deserter might hope to hide in the countryside, perhaps try to join another army. If recaptured and identified he could hope for little mercy. But desertion could be reduced, too, by inducement – by a reputation for decent treatment and good administration. Frederick, for reasons both of practical advantage and of humanity, was sharply aware of the need to look after soldiers well. They must be paid regularly. His soldiers, he wrote, should be better fed than almost any troops in Europe – he knew how much a man's food contributes to his contentment and his conduct, and a soldier assured of a good meal at the end of the day had solid reason for staying at his duty. Frederick went into meticulous detail, writing orders about field bakeries, field ovens, the scale of provisions, their transportation and protection (by a convoy system). He was always alert to the necessity for sufficient grain storage in the right conditions. Drink was almost as important as food and Frederick's instructions dealt with the need to cover all distilleries and breweries with a system of requisition (at fair prices) so that the soldier should never lack his dram if it could possibly be managed.

Care of horses was as vital for the army's efficiency as care of men. By Frederick's calculation an army of 100,000 men needed nearly 50,000 horses. He did not believe in ox-drawn carts and his draught horses – and artillery horses – were particularly important to him. Prevision and provision of forage was crucial. Forage meant territory, and foraging parties – drills for which he laid down in great detail – provided a frequent motive for phases of a campaign. He was by now very experienced about the terrain of Silesia, Saxony, Bohemia. He knew which territories could feed his horses and which could not, and it formed a large part of his calculation. Remount systems, too, were essential to plan and supervise – and were, he wrote, often as difficult as they were important.

Terrain affected more than logistics. Besides the fertile areas and grasslands of intrinsic value, Frederick had by now marked all the principal topographical features which would influence operations in central Europe. He had noted a number of possible 'camps' – ground where he or an enemy could assemble a force, defend it, communicate with it, debouch from it – as well as the chief lines of strategic communication, mainly rivers. He was familiar now with the hill passes between Bohemia and Saxony, between Silesia and Moravia. He knew that the Silesian villages, full of widely separated low-built houses, were indefensible. He had covered, during his campaigns, a great deal of ground by personal reconnaissance – which he exhorted his officers never to neglect. He said that he 'carried his maps in his head', which was probably true; but he had done a good deal of survey and had built up a considerable corpus of terrain intelligence, including town maps, which would do much for him in the future. He wrote a good deal in the *Instructions* on the subject of reconnaissance, about the officer's need to appreciate the salient points of a piece of country. How many troops could it contain? Which is the vital ground? How would troops be best deployed so that all would have freedom to act without confusion and without being prevented by some natural feature – Villeroy, he wrote, had neglected this at Ramillies and placed his left wing behind a bog, where they were impotent.*

In assembly areas or primarily defensive deployments the troops must be kept busy – active and fit. There must be sufficient entrenchment and fortification for protection, although Frederick's temperament and, increasingly, experience led him away from defensive and entrenched positions unless absolutely necessary. Decision, he wrote, must be sought from battle, and battle meant manoeuvre and attack – 'It is battle that decides the fate of nations.' Nevertheless Frederick was specific about the details of entrenchment where necessary, about siting, about reconnaissance of approach and withdrawal routes: and he was very specific indeed about patrols, giving detailed composition of early warning patrols and the system for cavalry reconnaissance patrols. These last, he said, were so important that the commander himself (and he meant Frederick) should where possible brief and debrief them personally. As for night patrols he laid down in considerable detail their composition, specimen objectives, equipment and clothing. The object of some patrols would be to obtain prisoners and thus information.

Frederick wrote in equal detail about orders for troops on outpost duty, their numbers, their drills, if and when they should unsaddle horses; and he wrote, again in detail, about the alertness, at all times,

* Presumably the river Greet – a harsh judgement of questionable fairness.

of troops in camp or billets; their need for familiarity and practice of what to do in case of alarm, their drills at darkness and dawn. Much of what he wrote was, of course, the sort of detail which would find a place in field service regulations, in standing orders by whatever name. It demonstrates, however, his sense that the King was responsible for everything – then, once settled by regulation, it became a matter of discipline. He was equally exact in orders for troops on the march. During an advance to actual contact there must be precise orders for advance guards about dismounting, watering and so forth. There must be absolute silence, and no smoking. Advance guards – mainly composed of hussars and grenadiers – must 'fix' an enemy, carry out preliminary reconnaissance; then the commander would have orders ready for the main body when it came up.

Frederick argued strongly and surely incontrovertibly against winter campaigns. He had, he wrote disarmingly, begun one himself – the first Silesian war. The political situation had left him no option. Had he delayed it would have needed several more campaigns to achieve his object. In the main, however, winter campaigns made appalling demands on men, horses and logistics. To go into winter quarters gave opportunity for recuperation, rest, training, equipment and saddlery repair.

Besides these excellent precepts and a sequence of standing orders which would be found sound in essentials, with minor changes of idiom, at least until the Second World War, Frederick laid down a number of more general operational maxims and these, too, are of enduring interest – and, sometimes, validity. The *objective* of operations, he wrote, is the defeat of the enemy's *army*. Whatever manoeuvres are undertaken, the aim should be a battle on favourable terms with a main body of the enemy. Outflanking marches, ingenious manoeuvres, may be justified but are inherently risky since they complicate coordination, divide one's forces and consume time (he might have added that they may exhaust one's own men before battle is actually joined, a charge sometimes made against Frederick himself). And to divide one's own force is always dangerous: 'He who divides his force will be beaten in detail.' He cited his own failings, notably at Soor: 'I should have been defeated, and deservedly so. I was saved by the presence of mind of my generals, and the valour of my troops.' It was natural that his operational maxims involved examples from his experience hitherto; and although Frederick could be vainglorious on occasion and sometimes give himself the benefit of the doubt he was also capable of great, and endearing – and, in a commander, unusual – modesty. He knew and wrote that Mollwitz represented little but a missed opportunity – he should have crippled the Austrians thereafter.

The necessity for striking with a concentrated blow had impressed itself early on Frederick's mind and he could on some occasions claim that he had done so, but he was frank in admitting that his battles had not all been intended – or devised – by him. Two out of the four he had fought had been forced by the enemy. 'I am not writing my own panegyric. I have often erred through inadvertence. My officers are expected to profit by my mistakes and they may be assured I shall apply myself with all diligence to correct them.' Such disarming admissions (albeit at first intended only for his own eyes) might be found in Turenne, perhaps; in Slim, undoubtedly; and in Frederick. And although his apparent scepticism about manoeuvres and his emphasis on firepower, mass and assault may seem unimaginative, Frederick was a great believer in the use of feints, raids, demonstrations; in everything which could confuse or mystify an enemy, everything which might lead him, rather than oneself, to disperse his forces. He was certainly not unsubtle. He was surprisingly dismissive of night attacks. With the weaponry of his day, of course, they held fewer advantages than would come in an era of devastating observed artillery or machine-gun fire but, although he acknowledged the element of surprise which might be achieved (and often himself used darkness for approach marches), he disliked the inevitable confusion night attacks produced and he probably reckoned they increased the possibilities of desertion. The battle-winning element was the excellently drilled and disciplined Prussian infantry with their well-rehearsed fire control. And their effect was maximized in daylight when they could be seen and strike terror. Each infantryman must be trained to fire four rounds a minute (a standard increased in some circumstances to five or even six). Then there could be a 'rolling fire', platoon by platoon, each platoon firing a volley.*

* But see also Chapter 5 above.

Above all Frederick believed in the offensive: in speed, energy, movement. He discussed various tactical manoeuvres. There could be the device of attacking in two successive lines, where the first may pretend weakness, fall back, induce pursuit and expose the advancing enemy to one's fresh second line, attacking strongly. Something like this, he wrote, had happened at Hohenfriedeberg (although in writing this Frederick was surely imposing a retrospective order on events, in particular on the actions of Prince Leopold Max. Every commander tidies up a battle when he comes to write its history – as Erwin Rommel observed two centuries later, 'the best plan is the one made when the fight's over!'). But in these instructions, these examples, Frederick first wrote of that 'attack in oblique order', that *Schrägangriff*, which has become associated with his name. In essence the manoeuvre was a 'refusal' of one wing and reinforcement of the other, thus achieving, in theory, overwhelming superior strength at a chosen point, breaking into one of the enemy's wings or flanks, reinforcing this *Schwerpunkt* and rolling up the enemy line from that direction.

There has been argument about when and how often he actually employed it – some regarded it as already exemplified at Chotusitz, even Mollwitz (although hardly by Frederick), while others put its first use in 1757. Nevertheless the theory was set out by Frederick in his writings in the 1750s, immediately after the Silesian wars. The 'oblique order' attack was further refined to a drill, whereby the attacking, reinforced wing of the army would advance in echelon, with the leading battalion twenty paces ahead of its neighbour and so on. Frederick first practised it on the parade ground at Potsdam in August 1751.[39] And during this period Frederick was ceaselessly experimenting with and practising alternative movements of what would now be called close order drill – deployment from column of route into line and vice versa; forming mass, forming extended line on leading companies. The Prussian infantry, he was determined, must be absolutely 'handy' on the battlefield and their effectiveness never be impaired by sloppy or ill-thought out movements.

He interspersed his operational maxims with a good many purely tactical injunctions. Avoid attacking in built-up areas; they swallow up men. If cavalry have to attack the enemy in a village they must avoid the enemy outposts, must go in at the gallop, fire at all windows, create maximum confusion; and – a very Frederician remark – take strong steps to prevent looting and pillage or your force will disappear. If a town is to be taken the essential prerequisite is detailed knowledge of its layout as well as its fortifications; Leopold Max's success at Glogau had been exemplary in this regard. As for Frederick's own taking of Prague, it had been easy – the garrison had been too small for the defensive perimeter.

Frederick wrote a good deal on many occasions about the handling of cavalry. He was always alive to their expense as an arm. He was firm that they should be handled with care, husbanded, kept out of enemy artillery fire, kept in reserve when an enemy defensive position was being attacked, preserved fresh for the true opportunity when the infantry and artillery had prepared the way. They must be really well-trained, their officers must have been attached to other arms and understand the whole business of battle. As for cavalry actions, light cavalry, hussars, were by definition unsuitable to meet a mass of heavily armed, heavily mounted opponents in shock action and should in principle be kept for patrol duty, advance guards, outposts, forays. He accepted, however, that the light cavalry – who now practised the charge at the gallop – on the basis of their horsemanship and dash might, on occasion, literally, make weight.

On the various standard operations of war Frederick produced some more maxims – 'Nothing is more difficult, not to say impossible, than defending a river line.' He reckoned that an enterprising enemy would always get across a river somehow, somewhere; that the defender would have deployed too many men in an ineffective attempt at linear defence; and that the attacker, after penetration, would have too good a chance of rolling the defence up. If the task had to be undertaken there must be methodical patrolling, the minimum of troops used in attempts at static defence, and counter-attack routes reconnoitred, with roles practised. It all has a very modern ring. And on the conduct of an operational defensive he wrote wisely, albeit without great originality, of the use of deception; of disguising the size of 'camps', pretending to hold a longer line than in reality, simulating great boldness when actually wishing to avoid battle and – conversely – lulling the enemy into a false sense of security when oneself intending to attack. And where there are enemy fortresses, deploy so that a number of them may be simultaneously threatened by one centrally placed force.

These were admirable precepts in which Frederick set down for others and for posterity what he felt he had so far learned about the military art. Being the man he was, he accompanied them with a long poem, 'L'Art de la Guerre', published in 1751 as a separate work and alleged by him to be inspired by Marshal Saxe's *Pensées*. But besides theory and instruction there were actual organizational changes to be made in the army; there was training; and there was – which went well beyond the military sphere – the whole matter of intelligence.

Frederick had, earlier, greatly increased his artillery. He had allocated field guns to infantry battalions for their immediate support. Reorganization would continue almost throughout his reign, an evolution of the artillery arm. At this stage – between the end of the second Silesian war and the start of the Seven Years War in 1756 – many changes were still aspirations rather than achievements but he was working towards them, a gradual process. He was moving towards an organization which would give two six-pounder guns to each infantry battalion in the 'First Line' instead of the three-pounders, and a heavy battery of ten twelve-pounders for every five battalions. For the 'Second Line' battalions the organization would substitute long three-pounders for the six-pounders.* Like all expensive equipment programmes this took time to achieve but it started. In 1759–60 – by which time another war had begun – Frederick formed a 'light artillery', comparable to a British horse artillery arm, troops who were expected to get into action in under a minute. For all his artillery Frederick placed great emphasis on speed into and out of action, and on the training of his artillery with other arms.

As to tactical handling, Frederick laid down that for the reduction of fortresses and defended places his heavy artillery would be massed in siege batteries. In an attack operation the aim would be to produce concentrated fire, both direct and in enfilade, on the enemy wing selected for the *Schwerpunkt*. In a defensive operation Frederick wrote that the artillery plan was vital and that the 'second-line' artillery

* And see Chapters 5 and 16.

(definition imprecise and dependent on the army's organization and deployment at the time) must deal with possible enemy break-ins, and cover the flanks.

Frederick, throughout life, devoted much thought to training, to the selection and training of officers, and to the whole subject of command. There were comprehensive instructions for the officers of the Prussian army, but who were these to be? There was no doubt about the importance he placed on his officers. The mainstay of the Prussian state was and must remain the Prussian officer; and the responsibility for selection, training, promoting and nurturing the Prussian officer corps lay with the throne. 'The King of Prussia,' he wrote in his *First Political Testament*, 'must, of necessity, be a soldier and the head of the army. It is shameful when soft and idle princes give others the command-in-chief,' and the quality of the officers was vital. He observed, making clear that he was writing from experience, that in battle 'the conduct of colonels decides the destiny of empires'. Frederick maintained a firm policy that his officers should be members of the Prussian nobility. When battle thinned their ranks in wartime he modified this, but when peace returned he enforced it and justified it.

Frederick was too intelligent to suppose that only those of noble blood could possess the necessary qualities. On the contrary he was, on occasion, particularly cutting about the *Adel*, the nobility, of Prussia. He was equally cutting about his royal relatives and connections, what he called in his *Political Testament* 'an amphibious sort of creatures called princes of the blood, neither sovereign nor subject, difficult to govern, who should be excluded from public affairs and only given commands if talented'. He was sometimes ambivalent on the subject – in 1769 he wrote that while service in the law, in finance, in diplomacy and in the army was certainly a laudable ambition for a nobleman 'all would be lost in a state if birth were valued above merit'. But his design was less to do with the army than with society. The landowning class, whether rich or comparatively poor, was large. Each family, with its many branches, represented a local power centre. Frederick was determined to bind these power centres to the Prussian crown, and it was a natural corollary that their sons should aim to receive commissions in his regiments. The tradition of their order was not and must not be self-enrichment, but self-denial and service. And if an estate (with permission) was sold to a non-noble family the purchaser acquired not only land but commensurate responsibilities. One son, for instance, would – must – serve in the army. Just below the surface Prussia was still a society not of the Enlightenment but of feudalism.[40] Just as the cantonal system integrated the ranks of the army with society as a whole, so the officer corps was virtually an extension of the order of nobility. Frederick expected young men of noble family to wear his uniform unless there were good reason against.

Thus, over time, Frederick knew them all and in many cases knew them well, personally. He had an excellent memory for names and faces. He marked those who were gifted and he was ready to promote young. He took great trouble over the training of officers at all levels of seniority, and he was adamant that officers, however junior, should be treated with dignity. He was strict in laying down their regimental duties, in every detail; they must always, for instance, attend 'stables' when the horses were being groomed. The system and its ethos was inspired, directed and supervised by the King. Duelling had been prohibited by Frederick William and Frederick thought it barbaric and generally absurd, but he also thought that there were occasions when it could be a justified reaction to insult or injury and he rescinded the prohibition.

The pay of officers was low until they reached Captain's rank (normally at about the age of forty, but the outstanding were generally accelerated). Frederick's attitude to the manning of the officer corps was mirrored in the higher civil service, where posts were almost entirely taken by members of the nobility. These men – forbidden to take part in trade or commerce – were, in the King's view, members of families on which the state depended and which the state should nurture, provided that their behaviour was loyal to the crown, and that they did not exploit their fellow-men or seek to enrich themselves. And when writing of the care and morale of his soldiers Frederick wrote much good sense: 'Many people wish to command without having learned to be commanded themselves!' The commander, at every level, he wrote, should learn from 'cunning old troopers'. Soldiers will always grumble, but where the commander has reason to suspect real discontent he must instantly seek its causes. Above all, 'Have the soldiers had their dues?' Rewards and punishments should both be equitable and prompt.

Frederick thought a good deal about intelligence. He wrote in what often seems remarkably modern terms about the handling of sources and agents, taking much personal interest in detail. As to sources he was generally suspicious – Wellington wrote that 'there is a good deal of charlatanism in what is called procuring Intelligence', and Frederick would have heartily agreed. Ordinary agents, he said, recruited for money, could probably give some simple, practical information about the enemy: 'Where?' but little more. There were agents 'under compulsion' whose reliability would differ, case by case. 'Important' agents (and Frederick at times had several) might be invaluable, but if detected by the enemy they might always be 'turned' and the commander needed to be sensitive to that possibility. 'Double' agents, playing with both sides, could be used with care, for disinformation; to mislead.

Frederick also took much trouble to plant agents in foreign capitals; 'sleepers' who could be activated if tensions increased and relations worsened; 'seducers' – he maintained a number of handsome young men in Vienna who could beguile and get information from highly placed ladies at the Austrian court. He was very alert to compromise of ciphers, as sometimes happened, and would personally direct the 'damage limitation' thereafter. He was his own intelligence chief, although a Colonel von der Goltz handled coordination. And during this decade, when relations with France were still on the whole good, he often deliberately shared covert intelligence – intercepted dispatches sent *en clair* and so forth – with the French Ambassador.

On military intelligence, he wrote, the essence lies in interpretation. An enemy's physical configuration may be one thing, his future intentions another. To assess the latter correctly needs shrewd projection – not only 'Where is he deploying, where are his light troops, his reconnaissance forces?' but also 'Where is he establishing his depots? What potential is he giving himself?' In the matter of deduction Frederick laid down a maxim, a sound one. 'Assume that an intelligent enemy will attempt that enterprise which is likely to give you the greatest annoyance.' Be ready, in other words, to seize opportunity but reject wishful thinking and convenient assumptions.

In the oversight of the army's training and preparations – and, to a certain extent, in the coordination of intelligence about foreign armies – Frederick relied a good deal upon a key figure in his circle, General Hans Karl von Winterfeldt. Winterfeldt, a bluff Pomeranian field commander, was somewhat older than Frederick and had much charm. He acted as confidential associate and something not unlike a chief of staff. He understood Frederick's mind, was methodical, experienced in military matters and able to translate concepts into practical systems with minimal fuss. He had first met Frederick in the distant days when the Crown Prince had visited the front and met Prince Eugen in 1734. To some in the new Prussian army (and in the royal family) he was an object of some suspicion, as would be likely to attach to any intelligent confidant, but he was from these days very close to Frederick (who showed him his own military writings for comment) and of his devotion and ability there is no doubt; and equally no doubt that he hated the French.

Frederick now felt himself an experienced *Feldherr*. His self-confidence was strong and he had had plenty of practice in the actual technique of command. His system was modified as his experience lengthened but certain features were constant. If possible, on the eve of battle he held a conference – a conference at which he was completely dominant but which enabled him to put subordinate commanders in his mind and allocate particular tasks. He did not believe, he said, in 'councils of war' as such: a commander generally only resorted to a council of war when he didn't want to fight.

He generally slept very well before a battle. On the day itself Frederick would place himself – sometimes unwisely – where he reckoned personal influence would be most necessary. His presence – his voice above the crash of battle at crucial moments – was undoubtedly effective. Orders, naturally, could only be conveyed beyond his immediate surroundings by message, and he would dismount and scribble a note, often using the back of the nearest staff officer as a writing desk. He spent long hours in the saddle, and rode boldly and fast. He preferred English horses, browns or chestnuts if possible, and maintained about twenty saddle horses. On campaign he travelled light – a few uniforms, six shirts, a couple of velvet coats for grander occasions, always half·a dozen snuff boxes (he owned about a hundred and thirty). The picture is of a man restlessly energetic, watchful, impatient and quicker in mind than other men; a man brave, ingenious, a master of his craft; a stickler for discipline and propriety but combining at times wit with the severity. And, despite the severity, often unexpectedly solicitous and sensitive.

Perhaps Frederick's greatest gift to his army was his insistence on initiative. A higher commander cannot be everywhere. Other generals 'may be shot dead at any time'. A commander, once able to assess a situation, must take responsibility for action within his area of influence whatever his seniority. This development of initiative regardless of formal instructions was laid down by Frederick as a principle and was described as late as in 1905 as his enduring legacy to the Prussian army.[41]

Frederick could accept bluntness when it meant sincerity. On one occasion he sent a page with a decoration to a particular captain whose courage and conduct he admired. The captain sent the page – and the decoration – back to the King with a message. It was, he said, the acknowledged custom that a page bringing such a decoration should be given by the grateful recipient a present: eleven ducats was the usual tariff. This captain, a poor man, couldn't afford them: 'Tell the King I've done my duty without this sort of ornament. I need my money, and I don't need this!' Many sovereigns would have found such brusque manners insufferable and it is unlikely they would have been exposed to them. Frederick simply sent the page back again, carrying the decoration and a note from the King: 'My dear — I completely forgot that I owe you 100 ducats! Forgive me – here they are.' The page was given a double tip of twenty-two ducats. Nobody was deceived; but Frederick's heart was generous, and the army knew it.[42]

PART III
1750–56

9

Sworded Aesthete

Throughout his campaigns Frederick was conducting the business of state from his field headquarters. He was doing his duty as commander-in-chief, as sovereign and as lawgiver – simultaneously, and with total commitment to each function although it was inevitable that the concerns of war had priority while war lasted. He did his best to reduce administrative paperwork during wartime – 'Collect revenues, leave everything else and don't pester me with trivia,' he said – but it was always considerable. His determination that normal economic and public activity should continue as far as possible imposed strains, not least on himself; and the policy of 'business as usual' was inevitably affected by the shortages of manpower and resources which campaigning had produced. Furthermore the absence of the King – 'chairman' of the General Directory albeit seldom attending – inevitably and adversely affected the conduct of affairs on occasion. Nevertheless it is remarkable how well matters ran, and by the beginning of 1746 he was back at Potsdam and for the next few years could devote himself in congenial surroundings to the concerns of peace, although security preparations would never be far from his mind. And one of the chief concerns, in his view, was the state of the administration of justice.

Frederick, autocrat that he was, was nevertheless passionate in his pursuit of equality before the law. He established mixed military and civilian courts to try disorders involving troops in garrison towns. He called himself, proudly, *l'avocat du pauvre* and *le roi des gueux* – king of the beggars and the poor man's advocate. Denial of a man's just rights enraged him; and so did impunity of the guilty. His instincts were humane – he had abolished the judicial use of torture at the beginning of his reign. He worked with the 'Grand Chancellor', Samuel Cocceji, on Prussian jurisprudence. Cocceji, Frederick wrote, was a man whose 'virtue and integrity were worthy of the highest point of the Roman Republic',[1] and although the sovereign was the sole legislator in the Prussian state he consulted carefully before anything was enacted. He was, however, less interested in reform or augmentation of laws than in their equitable administration. He considered that lawyers, everywhere, had too much power and made too much money. Late in life he gave his view that the French nobility were being ruined and would be replaced by avaricious lawyers.[2]

Frederick wrote that when he came to the throne of Prussia a rich man could buy justice – or, at least, could buy the services of an eloquent advocate who could win a verdict for him.[3] He not only introduced a new penal code (called by his name) but modified procedures. Henceforth advocates could not employ oratory. Eloquence, in his view, had no place in justice. Advocates must simply state the causes and arguments and prove or disprove pleas by evidence alone, heard before a panel of judges. The King – the executive – must have no hand in the administration of justice (beyond his responsibility for the wise framing of laws) although he must ensure that the selection of judges was made with impeccable integrity. A death sentence, however, must be confirmed by the King himself; and compared with other European countries Frederick endorsed the execution of remarkably few of his subjects – no more than about ten a year. For two decades of his reign the only death penalties ratified were in cases of homicide by soldiers.

The Frederician reforms made all courts the King's courts. Court fees were paid into one fund and court officials were paid fixed amounts. Delays in justice – trial backlogs – were eliminated. Promotion in the judicial service was to be based on merit – with academic qualifications demanded – rather than influence. The powers of the Justice Department were also widened – the superior courts in each province had ultimate authority over the appointment of pastors as well as teachers; and a Consistory for Higher Education was established which gave the state considerable authority over universities.

Courts of law, churches, educational establishments were thus brought together under the aegis of the Prussian state; and there was inevitable tension between the governmental system Frederick had inherited – the General Directory – and the new style; in particular between the minister who had administered Prussia in Frederick William's day and Cocceji whose outstanding abilities made him the chief standard-bearer of reform. Frederick's own personality, ardent though he was for reform, was sometimes an impediment.

The *Code de Frédéric* was admired. Nevertheless his praiseworthy determination to remain uninvolved in particular cases was sometimes overtaken by his zeal for the right. In one famous instance late in Frederick's reign a Pomeranian miller named Arnold, who had earlier been a soldier, brought an action against a landowner, Count von Schmettau. Arnold (although Frederick only discovered this later) was a notorious litigant. He alleged that von Schmettau had leased land to another count, von Gersdorf, who had diverted water from a stream (von Schmettau was a riparian owner). The diversion, allegedly, had ruined the Arnold mill's operation. The court found for Schmettau, ruling that Arnold, if really injured, could bring an action against Gersdorf but must meanwhile pay his proper rent, which he had refused. The miller appealed and at a retrial the verdict again went in Schmettau's favour.[4]

Frederick heard about this and demanded to see the papers in the case. He then sent a personal commission of inquiry to investigate the facts and report. Their report confirmed that the facts were as the miller alleged and that his business was indeed injured.

Frederick wrote in his *First Political Testament* that 'The Sovereign becomes an accomplice of crime if he fails to punish', and he now intervened, alarmingly. He supposed he had discovered an instance of abuse of power by the mighty and proud, an instance of the machinery of law operating against the small man, an instance for the exercise of kingly authority, as ultimately responsible that right be done. He sent for the magistrates who had given the verdict for Schmettau, dismissed them from their posts and ordered them into arrest. He reversed their verdict and ruled in the miller's favour. He ordered the landowner to pay costs and restore the flow of water to the litigious Arnold. The matter became widely known.

Then rumours began and a further investigation on the spot was ordered. Embarrassingly for Frederick, it was found that the Arnold mill was upstream from the Count's land so that the diversion of water could have had negligible effect on the mill's operations. The magistrates were freed. The Count's payments of costs and damages were annulled. The verdict was restored. The King was blamed.

The case, notorious in its day, is very indicative of some of Frederick's qualities, both bad and good. He was or could be hasty; could act before a true judgement might be formed. He had accepted the inadequate evidence of his commissioners and it must be suspected that he had done so because it coincided with his prejudice – he supposed he had found the sort of case of abuse of position which he most loathed. Then he had, peremptorily and inexcusably, acted against magistrates whose own conduct and findings had been impeccable. All this was despotic and the reverse of what he always claimed as a chief ambition – that Prussia should be a *Rechts Staat*, built on law.

Yet Frederick's motive was noble. He believed that his power existed to do good, to right injustice, to defend the oppressed. In this instance he got matters very wrong, but his heart was sound. He genuinely believed in the rule of law, rather than arbitrary diktat, and had mistakenly supposed that he was strengthening legality by exposing and punishing corrupt practice. It demonstrated however – and probably also to him – the hazards of personal interference in the judicial process. Another miller owned a property near Sans Souci, which was coveted by Frederick when he was expanding and beautifying the place. The King's agents saw the miller but he refused to sell. 'Doesn't he know,' Frederick said to them, 'that I can *take* it, if necessary?' But when they again confronted the miller he said, 'No, I'm not afraid of that. We've got *courts* in Berlin!' And this gave Frederick great and understandable happiness.[5]

Frederick enjoyed opportunities to use his wit in reconciling the claims of justice with the prejudices of men. In Silesia the Catholic population had looked with suspicion on his assumption of power, although he had largely conquered this suspicion by the scrupulous equality of toleration he extended to both religions. On one occasion a Catholic soldier, apparently devout, was convicted of stealing jewels from a statue of the Virgin in a church. The soldier denied it, and claimed that Our Lady had miraculously given them to him; and the case came to Frederick's attention.

Frederick assembled certain doctors of theology and put to them a question. Could Our Lady be believed capable of giving away treasures which had been presented to Her? The theologians, unsurprisingly, replied that it was highly improbable but that there was no actual doctrinal tenet which would define it as impossible! Frederick thanked them. The soldier had already been sentenced but his story had not been disproved and Frederick was ready to allow a miraculous explanation if not theologically condemned. Tongue well in cheek, he had had to consult the beliefs of his Catholic subjects and he now annulled the sentence. He said that he, naturally, had no power to forbid Our Lady from giving. But, he added, he would in future punish with death a soldier or anyone else who *accepted* such a gift!

Frederick not only loathed inequity, real or fancied, in the administration of justice; he was also infuriated by any arbitrary misuse of power by proud individuals. He had an excellent system of internal posts and communications, whereby post horses were hired to travellers by the agency of local postmasters in all towns. The postmasters, generally retired military officers, were answerable to the King for the collection of dues, for proper payment to the owners of horses and for the recruitment and conduct of postilions. The system worked well and economically but on one occasion personal dispatches were being carried to Frederick, who was at Breslau, from the Empress of Russia. The Tsarina's courier was the later-to-be-famous General Suvorov; and Suvorov experienced delay which he reckoned was due to an idle postboy. He remonstrated and was met with impertinence. He beat the postboy with his cane.

At the next stop Suvorov was arrested and brought before the magistrates but was allowed to proceed when he identified himself. When he ultimately reported to Frederick in Breslau he was received with great charm and hospitality. The King asked whether he had had a pleasant journey and Suvorov told him the story.

Suvorov said afterwards that the change in Frederick's demeanour was dramatic. The King said icily, 'General, you may think yourself fortunate!'

And Suvorov realized that he was in the presence of a monarch to whom laws and regulations were sacred, as were the established rights of the state's employees, however humble. It was the King's duty to protect postboys in the course of their duties, against no matter whom.[6] Frederick heard later of a distinguished French traveller who struck a postilion, who hit back and threw him out of the carriage with his valise. The Frenchman wrote indignantly to Frederick who told him to be less free with his stick in future – 'What an infernal country this Prussia is,' said the Frenchman to others, 'where you cannot thrash a postilion without bringing blows on yourself!' Frederick liked that.

In theory Frederick governed Prussia through departmental ministers. There was no 'cabinet' in the modern sense of shared responsibility, but by occasional conference, and above all by incessant correspondence, he ensured that all knew what was going on. His senior ministers, corporately, composed the General Directory of Prussia. And, remarkably, Frederick produced in May 1748 a new *Instruction for the General Directory* which acted as a guidance document for the entire machinery of state and which remained in force for many years. He was also greatly concerned with local, regional administration, laying down in much detail the principles of 'Land' and 'Kreis' government and the powers the Landrat (for instance) should or should not possess. There would always be tension (but also the need for cooperation) between such personages as the Landrat, elected by his peers to watch the interests of the landowning community as well as those dependent on them; and the servants of the state.

In central government there were ministers for war, for finance, for religious matters, for posts and communications. Each departmental chief was served by about four 'privy finance councillors'. These were departments of state and each department had a corresponding sub-department in each province of the kingdom. Furthermore each province was supervised by one of the ministers of the General Directory, so that ministerial responsibility was both functional and territorial, a minister being responsible for several provinces. The Prussian domains were so widely separated and so dissimilar – ranging from East Prussia and Pomerania to the Rhineland territories of Cleve and Mark – that there was necessarily some decentralization and variation of practice. Frederick, furthermore, created a new 'Fifth Department'[7] of the General Directory without territorial responsibilities but concerned with aspects of economic policy; a centralizing measure which was to coordinate 'industrial and resettlement programmes'. This Fifth Department was characteristic of one aspect of Frederick's character and rule. He was often impatient with the established systems he had inherited and he found the entrenched bureaucracy conservative and, in his view, obstructive. His way in such cases was to create a new organism, responsible to him, to deal with the particular matter or matters he thought were being addressed with insufficient imagination and energy. The result, frequently, was resentment. Men muttered that they wished old Frederick William was back. Battles for influence in particular spheres were surreptitiously waged, and there was inevitable mistrust between factions. Such mistrust, naturally, became mirrored in the Provincial Boards, which were themselves images of the General Directory. At one point Frederick began sending for the Provincial Board presidents personally and discussing with them – which was predictably resented.

In all this Frederick often misjudged the extent to which a tried and established system – even with imperfections – can be superseded by improvisations or *ad hoc* devices without ultimate inefficiency. The Prussian tradition had been one of collegiality – of discussion and tacitly shared responsibility. That had been Frederick William's way, despite his bluster; and he had personally presided over the General Directory. Frederick did so seldom. He had ideas – sometimes very good ones – and looked for a gifted individual to put them into effect. Sometimes it worked. Often it did not, and Frederick found himself withdrawing to the embrace of the traditional. He made attempts, for instance, to strengthen the Fifth Department, and make it an effective economic planning and development department. Ultimately he had to settle for making it a statistical and information centre.

Frederick modified the system therefore, by improvisation rather than fundamental structural change; and it was in practice more centralized than the organization might theoretically permit. Submissions came to Frederick, and a few brief marginal comments of his conveyed decisions. His well-trained and immensely hard-working secretaries could translate the King's will on every issue, great or small, into appropriate directives. In practice Prussia was governed from the King's study. Or from his tent.

Finance and the economy, naturally, occupied much of Frederick's mind and time. From the first he had realized the need for both a strong army and a healthy exchequer, and unless the latter was well-managed it would be depleted by the former. Soon after the Silesian wars Frederick revised his *General Instructions* to deal with what he considered certain imperfections of administration. There were, he thought, too many examples of bad accounting, and superficial records of taxation. Officials were not cooperating with each other; he was temperamentally inclined to be suspicious of them.

There was no direct taxation in Prussia. Frederick regarded excise as the most equitable way of raising revenue, but it must, in his view, be tempered by policy. Raw materials, for instance, if needed for home manufactures, must be duty free. Imports of goods Prussia herself was capable of producing must be charged. His revenues, like those of most contemporary sovereigns, came from these dues and duties, from dues on tolls and canal transport, from postage, and from a tax on the sale of certain commodities, a sort of value added tax. Canals were crucial; Brandenburg is a flat country and the great waterways of Elbe and Oder, with their tributaries, needed systematic development and connection. Projects were initiated, and, despite the predictable 'turf wars' within the bureaucracy, were driven through to completion, not least through the energy of the King.

There were farmed concessions of various kinds, and profitable state monopolies in certain manufactures, notably silk, wool, porcelain and, of course, arms; later he set up a tobacco regulatory board which was profitable. There were also the revenues from the royal manors. Frederick's personal expenditure was met entirely from his privy purse, from his personal wealth such as it was, and since he was by far the largest landowner in Prussia he enjoyed a financial independence greater than most of his fellows.

Frederick avoided interference by regulation unless it appeared absolutely necessary. He encouraged initiative and aimed to govern in cooperation with his senior ministers and officials. Nevertheless some support was given to essential industries – mining, forestry, linen – where it was reckoned (rightly) that the potential was good but that temporary conditions were working against success; and 'support' could take the form of import control, as well as a centrally directed felling policy in the case of timber. He made mistakes; and an expert Frenchman, de la Haye de Launay, told him late in life that Prussia would do better if protection and state subsidy were abolished. 'That would be premature,' Frederick said. He feared a 'sucking-in' of unnecessary imports if all controls were dismantled, and he may have been wrong. Nevertheless Prussia, an agrarian economy, had become self-sufficient in industrial goods within a few years of the acquisition of Silesia; and Silesia was crucial.

Frederick somewhat exaggerated the significance of monetary matters, which he probably did not entirely understand. He tried to control currency movements by edict – for instance ruling, in 1747, that nobody could take more than 300 thalers out of the country. Two years later he enlisted a new director of the mint from Brunswick, Josef Graumann, who was to be a member of the General Directory. Graumann, who taught Frederick a good deal, met a certain amount of predictable hostility. In 1753 a central bank was established; the pressures of war and consequent inflation lay ahead.

Frederick later* introduced a state-run lottery, organized by an Italian, recruited for the purpose, who was reported to have run a similar enterprise successfully in Genoa. He appreciated the hazards (a huge profit for the Exchequer was promised) and set up a team of bankers and accountants to supervise. Like a number of Frederick's schemes this route to pain-free revenue-raising proved disappointing, and its Italian founder of questionable integrity.

Frederick, however, was obsessed, throughout life, with the necessity of living within his means and of securing Prussia's economic position; and he was very aware that wars can seldom be financed out of current revenue and that they lead to a necessity to finance deficits. He always took trouble to amass a 'war chest' in time of peace, to set aside from various state receipts particular sums as a contingency reserve for war. He regarded this aspect of his duty like the head of a great corporation, mindful of his overheads, his cash flow, his balances. Because he watched Prussia's finances as he did he became proverbial, gaining a name as something of a miser. He believed that trade must be encouraged, that manufacture must be

* See Chapter 18.

encouraged – and did all in the royal power in both directions – but he never neglected the significance of agriculture, or of education in agricultural development: stock breeding; planting; forestry; price stability supported by state purchase; drainage and the maintenance of dykes.

Frederick also pursued active colonization policies in newly acquired territories, which were often underpopulated. During his reign 900 new villages were founded in Prussia, and 300,000 individuals from other lands swelled its population. Settler peasants were to become owners of land. Nor did Frederick mind their origins provided they were hard-working – people came from all over Germany and beyond, Catholics, Protestants, Mohammedans from Tartary. He planned for this to be the concern of the General Directory's Fifth Department. All were welcome if they worked and conformed. He wanted Prussia to be a land of opportunity, and to many it was.

The whole Prussian enterprise and all its departments needed accurate administration conducted with scrupulous honesty. Prussian officials had to pass demanding examinations but their integrity was prized above all else. If an official was found guilty of financial irregularity, or even of tolerating some temporary procedural irregularity in order, for instance, to tide over imbalances between accounts, Frederick was merciless – 'To think the world is populated only with rascals is misanthropic, but to suppose every two-legged creature without feathers to be an honest man is imbecile!'[8] He knew that the state's servants, supervised with severity though they were, cheated on occasion. He knew that there were excisemen who took bribes to allow in some imports duty free when the rules demanded duty. No system is utterly immune.

Frederick invited to Berlin a well-known Frenchman, Claude Helvetius, who had a great reputation for skill in revenue management. With his advice on method, Frederick established a large inspectorate to supervise the excise. This was reportedly unpopular but it is questionable whether the unpopularity derived from the fact that many inspectors were French, and unfamiliar with Prussian ways, or from the abuses which they checked. Some observers, while loyal to Frederick, thought some of the Helvetius ideas unsound and ultimately counterproductive.[9]

Frederick's care for the finances of the state was wholly honourable and his provision for the future, including the possibility of war, was a model of prudence although ultimately inadequate to the demands. If he was asked to furnish troops to help another sovereign he costed them exactly. When the contingency was to help Sweden in 1750 he told the Foreign Affairs department that ten squadrons of dragoons, 1,600 men, would cost him 140,000 *écus*. An infantry regiment (1,750 men) would mean 75,000 per annum.[10] Nevertheless Frederick's careful management would prove unequal to the cost of a *protracted* war: and a protracted war was to begin in 1756. For this Frederick would have to seek subsidy from an ally; or to depreciate the currency, with its longer-term problems. He would also need to rely on exactions from occupied territory, notably Saxony, which would be bitterly resented. This lay in the future.

Some concerns were already evident. Finance was not the only sinew of war which was to exercise Prussia. He realized, from the Silesian wars, that the whole matter of support for the army in war – responsibility of the General Directory – needed a separate department of state; forage, procurement, storage. He thus established another (sixth) department in 1746. He had always taken trouble to store grain and taken equal trouble with the means of transport, the commissariat, the strategic communications of Prussia and the Prussian army if it took the field in neighbouring lands. But there was also the matter of *matériel* and war supplies. The country's manufacturing capacity, particularly of gunpowder, would after a while prove inadequate and Frederick would need to import from both Holland and Britain. Prussia's factories had been expanded during the recent war but it would, in the event, prove necessary also to buy arms in from Sweden and Holland.

The greatest sinew of war was population. Enlargement of territory meant that Frederick's subjects had increased by as much as 50 per cent since the Silesian wars;* but there were still four times as many human beings in France as in Prussia, three times as many in Austria, uncountable numbers more in Russia.

---

* The population of Prussia was reckoned to have doubled by the end of his reign, despite the ravages of war.

Meanwhile there was peace, and Frederick could again devote himself to its duties and its pleasures – to administration, to the arts, to education, to friendship, to the dictates of humanity. He now built the '*Invalidenhaus*' in Berlin for 600 pensioners from the army and concerned himself much with the care of disabled servicemen, appointing a general with special responsibility as 'Inspector'. The *Schloss* at Potsdam had been his main residence when not in Berlin itself, but in May 1747 he moved into the newly completed Sans Souci and this fascinating rococo palace, constructed in a descending sequence of terraces and source of many disagreements with the architect, Wenzeslaus von Knobelsdorf,* became the place most associated with his reign and his personality. His reputation as ruler, warlord, liberal philosopher and patron of the arts rode high in Europe; and at this time he began to be referred to as 'The Great'.

Frederick's routine at Sans Souci closely resembled that he followed wherever he made his headquarters and held his court, for when he was on campaign many of the officials he required for the business of state accompanied him, although the chief minister – still Podewils at this time – remained in Berlin, exchanging letters on most days with his master. Foreign ambassadors sometimes rode in the King's suite. Only operations disturbed the pattern of the day.

By the standards of the time Frederick's was a small domestic household. There were five footmen, six 'running footmen' who could take messages and precede the King's carriage on journeys, and two pages. There were no valets as such and the King's wardrobe was so comparatively meagre that valets were hardly needed. Frederick was paternal to servants, addressing them often as '*Mein Kind*', my child; and his relationships with those who served him were sometimes eccentric but remarkably human. On one occasion a soldier-orderly was given money by Frederick for the specific purpose of buying a watch. He was required to know the time and never did. Instead of buying, he sent the money to his home – a misappropriation of royal

---

* Who had embellished the old *Schloss* at Potsdam, had planned the new residence Frederick had built at Rheinsberg, later given to Prince Henry, and also designed a new wing at the palace of Charlottenburg in Berlin.

bounty. Frederick instantly discovered – he discovered every deceit. The man was in severe trouble but was pardoned and kept on as an orderly. Some time later Frederick was ill with a fever, medicine was prescribed and the patient refused to take it.

'Take it away!'

The same orderly was on duty and was convinced from what he had heard that the King's life depended on taking the medicine. He forced it down Frederick's throat and when Frederick recovered from the indignity, from his rage, and from the fever, he rewarded the man.

Throughout life, and wherever he was, Frederick rose early, although he gave himself a little longer in bed – a small, narrow bed at Sans Souci – after the age of sixty. He was up at five o'clock in summer, sometimes earlier; and before six in winter. He took only a few minutes to dress – he got straight into his clothes rather than first spending time in a dressing-gown; and he generally wore the same blue uniform coat of the 1st Life Guards, with its red collar and cuffs, and with the star of the Black Eagle. He habitually wore his breeches and top boots (seldom polished) rather than stockings; whatever the day held Frederick was always ready for the saddle, or for parade. But his first concern was with his correspondence.

After he had dressed a page brought in the great mass of letters and papers addressed to the King. Frederick sorted these into three piles as he looked through them: requests to be granted, requests to be refused and papers requiring further consideration.[11] He was rapid in deciding on what pile a paper should be put but he was surprisingly patient with the importunity of some requests. 'He presses me so often and so boldly,' he said of one petitioner, 'that he can't be *completely* in the wrong!'[12] This was perhaps generous to excess: but it was kind.

At exactly eight o'clock the Cabinet Secretary, August Friedrich Eichel, was admitted. Eichel was a kindly, tolerant and immensely hard-working man. He had risen from humble origins, was the son of a sergeant in the army, and was regarded as the man in all Prussia who knew most of what was going on, and of what was in the King's mind – he gave long service and died in harness in 1768.

Eichel was given the three piles of papers, with indications of the King's preliminary consideration; and then passed them to a team of four secretaries who worked in the next room to Frederick's apartment or lodging. The secretaries looked through the letters, calling out a summary of each, audible to Frederick who was now taking breakfast – a cup of chocolate and some fruit. When appropriate Frederick would, from where he sat or stood, dictate a reply, calling to the secretary who would scribble. Copies were then made. These were 'writers' rather than confidential secretaries but their responsibilities and knowledge were inevitably wide.

A new personal secretary to Frederick, a *Vorleser*, Claude Etienne Darget,* had taken over duties from the beloved Jordan in January 1746. Darget grew very close to the King, was often more literary adviser than secretary; and Frederick naturally wanted a man in this position whose mother tongue was French. Frederick's grasp of the German language (as shown by letters, for example to Fredersdorff) was so inelegant and ungrammatical that the secretaries must have had a prime role in producing his more official German language communications – which are articulate and correct. These secretaries had little time for anything but a quick breakfast of some soup, and supper in the evening. At four o'clock in the afternoon all letters were presented to Frederick for signature, a process which usually took about half an hour – he signed 'Friedrich' if the text was in German, 'Fédéric' if French. At five o'clock, signed and sealed, they were given to couriers. Frederick was adamant that any letter or submission to him must be confined to one page only and the rule, whether or not exactly obeyed on some occasions, helped the dispatch of business.

The secretaries had been dismissed at nine each morning and the principal aide-de-camp, a general, admitted. At ten o'clock in the morning there was the 'parade', a military occasion with the Potsdam garrison or the Household Troops, an occasion on which Frederick often personally exercised one of the Guards regiments, an occasion symbolic of the King's character as commander. And at midday Frederick dined.

Dinner at the King's table was an extended, formal affair which lasted until two or even three o'clock in the afternoon. Sometimes a

---

* Darget had been secretary to the French Ambassador, Valory, but there does not seem to have been any doubt about divided loyalties, or, indeed, security, although on one occasion Frederick, briefly, suspected him of betraying a document to Voltaire.

light collation was taken in the Chinese teahouse which he built in the gardens before the great war of 1756 began; but dinner was the central point of the day, attended by considerable numbers, and with conversation animated and lively. Frederick employed twelve cooks – well-paid and of several nationalities, German, French, Italian, English, Russian. They worked under the kitchen superintendents, grand functionaries who presided at the sideboards in gold-laced coats. Frederick lived what was, by the standards of royal households of the day, a comparatively simple life, often derided for parsimony; nevertheless he took an interest in food. His written exchanges with Fredersdorff were often concerned with procuring some particular fish or ingredient. He liked well-spiced dishes, and was very fond of fruit (he planted a large number of fruit trees at Sans Souci). During dessert a pencil and paper were put beside his plate and he personally wrote orders for dinner on the following day. He preferred French wine to any other, especially champagne to which, regrettably, he sometimes added a little water. He liked Tokay and often sent presents of it to various members of the family. He drank a good deal of coffee.

Some have found the reported conversation at Sans Souci somewhat forced and pretentious with its parade of what may have sometimes appeared ostentatious over-cultivation. It suited Frederick, however, and when his boon companions disappeared he missed them sadly.

After dinner, and before his letter-signing session, Frederick walked or rode. He had a strong streak of hypochondria, feared illness (although he mocked hypochondria in others) and cared a good deal for his health. His letters to Fredersdorff are full of reports and injunctions on the subject; he suffered painfully from stomach cramp. He believed in regular exercise.

If Frederick walked one of the court would accompany him. It was not a coveted privilege since he walked extremely fast and was impatient with slowness in a companion. If he rode it was generally with only one groom accompanying. It was said that he rode without great skill or elegance and he certainly rode very short, but he rode boldly and fast, kicking his horse to a gallop as soon as possible. He was fond of horses, preferring English browns or chestnuts, although the old Mollwitz grey was not neglected. Frederick named his horses personally. His two other favourites for many years were 'Caesar', who died only shortly before Frederick himself, and 'Cerberus', a particular love of Frederick, with white stockings, which he was to ride at intervals for most of the Seven Years War to come. Because he loved his horses he was anxious for them on campaign; and although he was prepared to ride Caesar or Cerberus on the line of march he preferred to change his mount for battle. It was against his usual practice, therefore, that he gave orders for Cerberus to be saddled on that day in August 1759 which saw the fight at Kunersdorf, one of Frederick's most terrible reverses. At the last minute something made the King change his mind, and he rode another from his string, Scipio, in the battle. Scipio was wounded. Cerberus was unscathed.

Frederick continued to ride throughout life but as he grew older he had his chosen horse ridden for half an hour before he mounted. He often had horses – besides Scipio – wounded under him; and killed under him at Chotusitz, Hohenfriedeberg, Hochkirch, Liegnitz and Torgau. His only serious accident not in battle, however, was at Potsdam in 1755 when he was returning to Sans Souci to meet his mother, the Queen Dowager. He was riding a new horse and came down heavily, cracking his head. He recovered quickly and – characteristically – blamed nobody but himself for the mishap. Once, after a gallop from Potsdam to Charlottenburg, he came down in front of the *Schloss* itself but fell in deep sand. 'It wasn't the horse's fault,' he immediately said to the anxious *Stallmeister*. 'Look out now, don't get under the horse!' he would cry out to the crowds of young children who would gather round when he rode out from Potsdam. 'This way, Your Majesty,' they would squeal. 'This way! we'll lead you!'[13]

And in the evenings, as at '*La petite colonie de Remusberg*' in former days, there was supper – informal, agreeable; and music. He sometimes supped in a small room in Sans Souci where a table was engineered to sink beneath the floor for replenishment between courses, and there were no servants.

It is the particular glory of monarchy, when combined with a sufficient degree of autocracy and when presided over by a prince of learning and cultivation, that a constellation can be gathered and a brilliant court formed by the prince's initiative. His personal patronage, free of committee and officialdom, enables bold choices and finances them;

his encouragement liberates and advances the scholar and the artist beyond the likely achievement of either bureaucracy or the market. So it was with the Stuart kings, especially James I – and his son until sadly overwhelmed by politics. So it was with Louis XIV. And so it was with Frederick, more constrained financially but with as good tastes as any.

There were comparatively few entertainments produced at Frederick's court, but music continued to play an absorbing part in his life. His flute-playing had contributed to that stooping, bowed appearance of the head familiar from many portraits. He liked to improvise, walking around his rooms in the morning before the Cabinet Secretary's eight o'clock visit – he said that a little flute-playing helped his mind and his imagination. His adagios, his slow movements, were much admired. He always loved composing – sonatas, fugues, church music.

As a performer Frederick, like most people, could slip. On one occasion the distinguished court musician Johann Joachim Quantz, flautist and composer, who had first come to Berlin in Frederick William's day (persuaded from Dresden by Frederick's mother to instruct the Crown Prince), was present when Frederick was playing orchestrally with others. Frederick was responsible for a flute solo in a new unrehearsed piece at one of the regular six o'clock concerts, features of the day at Sans Souci. He made a mistake and the place was lost. Quantz, never particularly tolerant and a professional musician before a courtier, snorted nasally and very audibly. Carl Philipp Emanuel Bach, son of the great Johann Sebastian, was also at Frederick's court and covered the awkwardness by improvising a few piano phrases to tide over. The other players were imperturbable and Frederick finished his solo. The leading violin was Franz Benda, one of two distinguished musical brothers, linchpins of Frederick's musician court; and Frederick asked him a few days later to tell him frankly whether he'd got the piece wrong, made a mistake.

'Yes, sire.'

'Then you'd better write out the score again,' said Frederick, 'and this time write in Quantz's catarrh!'[14]

Frederick loved both opera and ballet and enjoyed talking to experts about both; he built the new opera house at Berlin. The Berlin opera was paid for from his own purse – admission was by ticket but tickets were free. The pit of the theatre was largely occupied by soldiers and their wives, the latter generally perched on their husbands' shoulders, and there were, of course, reserved boxes – the opera house was designed by Knobelsdorf.

And the King was solicitous in a way few realized except those who knew him personally. The Berlin carnival started in December each year and lasted for six weeks. Frederick worked, as librettist, with the director of the Berlin opera, Karl Heinrich Graun, on some adaptations and pieces performed there. During the carnival of 1751 the part of Fedima in *Mithridates* was being taken by a singer who had an accident, a fall, the night before the final grand performance. On the evening itself she felt very weak and was really unfit to perform. She was determined not to fail the company on the great occasion and put forward all her strength. In the third scene of the first act, however, there was a particularly testing aria and she deliberately changed the texture and weakened it a little to bring it within her compass.[15]

Frederick noticed. He noticed everything. The singer was not a particular favourite of his but he was disturbed and asked what the trouble was. Nobody could tell him and after the act was over he sent behind stage and discovered she was in her room and obviously unwell. He said that an understudy ought to take the part but the singer sent word that although a little weak she had strength to carry on.

'She should *not* try her strength,' said Frederick. 'She should go home!' He was worried, and although he knew the girl had little more to do he was heard to say, 'I wish it was over!' Before the third act he sent for the *Kapellmeister* – 'That aria of Fedima in the third act should be *cut out*!' It was. Next day Frederick sent anxiously to see whether all was well. Such artists were his children.

Late in life he was delighted to be introduced to the Vienna ballet producer Noverra. 'We know him! We've seen him in Berlin! He imitated everyone, including our ballerina and made everyone die of laughter!' Noverra was unsure how to take this and Frederick at once became serious and professionally interested – 'Your ballets are good, your dancers are graceful, but it's a *hunched* grace – you make them use shoulders and arms too much . . .'[16]

The King's criticisms may have been matters of opinion, but they were expert and involved. Frederick was delighted to get the famous – and very beautiful – dancer Barbarina Campanini, 'La Barbarina', to Berlin. Barbarina had had many lovers, including Prince de Conti, and Frederick secured her services by having her, in effect, kidnapped. She was paid handsomely, given leave to travel when she wanted and granted five months' holiday a year; and Frederick encouraged the improbable story that she was his own mistress. She had left her Scottish lover, James Mackenzie,* taken Frederick's friend Algarotti as a lover, and ultimately married the son of Frederick's reforming chancellor, Cocceji.

Frederick had always loved dancing and all to do with it – it had been forbidden at Frederick William's court and he had learned secretly. Dancing once came up in conversation with Frederick's rather serious Secretary, de Catt, at a critical moment during a campaign: 'I'll show you the right steps!' said the King, and did. Then, 'What would people say? Am I not mad?' And de Catt, like all of them, hugely enjoyed the contrasts in Frederick's personality.

Frederick was fond of pictures. He had studied the history of art extensively, and he began his magnificent picture gallery at Sans Souci in 1754; the ceilings in it were by Van Loo. The King's preferred dealer was Gotzkowski, who had dealings all over Europe – and who also sometimes acted as a special confidential diplomatic courier of sensitive correspondence.[17] Gotzkowski, reputedly the richest man in Berlin, obtained two Raphaels for Frederick from a collection in Rome; Frederick wanted to see them before agreeing purchase. The Roman owner protested that he could not risk sending such masterpieces on approval without a price being both agreed and paid. Furthermore the King of Poland, Augustus III, had already offered 30,000 ducats.[18] Gotzkowski pointed out that in Poland a purchaser paid a tax on value – if the pictures could be obtained for the King of Prussia the net figure, unreduced by tax, could go to the vendor. Whatever the calculations, a deal was done and Frederick got his pictures; and in 1742 he had bought the famous collection of antique statuary and artefacts made by Cardinal de Polignac.

---

* Younger brother of the Earl of Bute and great-grandson of Sir George Mackenzie of Rosehaugh, whose name he took.

But above pictures and marble in his affections were his books. He maintained identical libraries at Sans Souci, at Potsdam (where a grand new palace would later be built), at Berlin, at Charlottenburg and at Breslau. In each library the books were arranged in exactly the same order, shelf by shelf, so that he could at once recognize what he wanted. His general system was to divide his books between 'study' and 'amusement' – the latter he read once, the former he would return to and consult or reject as inadequate. He therefore bought five copies of any book he wanted.

Frederick's lifelong depreciation of the German language made many enemies in the critical sense. Germans thought that so learned a prince should and could do more for native German culture rather than model his tastes and his works almost exclusively on the French. Certainly Frederick was a poor German scholar, his letters in German are barely literate and his constant denigration of the language must have offended. When Dieudonné Thiebault, a Frenchman, appeared at court to be interviewed for a position Frederick told him it would be a condition of employment that he should never learn German. French dominated his literary taste – he was contemptuous of Shakespeare's plays – 'these ridiculous farces, worth of Canadian savages, sinning against the rules of theatre'.[19] His greatest admiration was for Racine, whose work he loved reading aloud, often weeping freely. He relished Molière – later French writers of comedy such as Beaumarchais he thought wretched in comparison. He liked putting poetry into prose in his mind, to test its sense before abandoning himself to its music. Frederick was a poor linguist despite his marvellous feeling for the French language. He spoke (rarely) a little Italian. He had learned Latin, to his father's fury, but was no expert – he sometimes wrote formal letters to a brother sovereign in Latin but there must have been some help at hand; and he knew no Greek.

Frederick planned the first Royal Library in Berlin and it was ultimately built in 1774. A librarian of learning and distinction would be needed and two French sages, Voltaire and d'Alembert, pressed the claims of a French author of the Enlightenment, the Abbé Delille de Sales. The Abbé had written a book (regarded with suspicion in France) entitled *Philosophie de la Nature*. Frederick asked what German the Abbé knew? The Abbé, probably aware of the King's tastes, answered 'None!' The appointment was for an official to deal with scholars in Berlin. The job went to another. Frederick was practical as well as prejudiced.

Frederick was a lover of learning. He was devoted to the *idea* of academic education. He felt that it was a prerequisite of both civilization and prosperity. He associated the philistinism which had separated him in sympathy from his father with the backward condition of much of Prussia. From his first day he had been determined to make his kingdom a shrine of enlightenment and scholarship. Soon after his accession, in 1741, he had persuaded Leonhard Euler, Swiss and the greatest mathematician of his day, to come to Berlin from St Petersburg and accept the post of Professor of Mathematics which he held for twenty-five years. Frederick collected sages as other men collect stamps. To the consternation of many in 1773 he offered asylum to the Jesuits when their order, under papal interdict, was proscribed in some other, including Catholic, countries – in Portugal in 1759, France in 1764, Spain in 1767; he admired Jesuit achievements in the sphere of education, their dedication, established by Ignatius Loyola himself, to learning and enlightenment rather than superstition and narrowness of mind. Voltaire was now in regular communication with him. Diderot, on the other hand – another great rationalist philosopher and rebel against Christian orthodoxy – had referred disobligingly to Frederick in his *Encyclopédie* and was not welcome in Berlin. And not all Frederick's enthusiasm was for sceptics – he read Fénelon with great admiration.

Frederick's restless intellect found satisfaction in details of the academy of sciences (at whose head he placed Maupertuis) and in dealing with professional appointments there. His ceaseless efforts to bring the foremost minds in Europe to Berlin were evidence of his unfailing energy in the field of academia; and he took great personal trouble – at a different level – over the establishment of a 'civil-military academy for young gentlemen' in Berlin. He ruled on details of the curriculum (grammatical purity; rhetoric; history of the liberal arts; logic; ancient and modern history; geography; the writing of letters). Metaphysics and morality were to be taught, with the aim of inoculating young minds against superstition of any kind. There was to be physical exercise, riding, dancing, football. The young gentlemen were never to be struck if they merited punishment, but might be put on a bread and water diet, made to wear the dunce's cap, be deprived of privileges, including the privilege of wearing a sword. He was insistent that learning must be made a pleasure and he signed the rules personally. They undoubtedly reflected one of his many gestures of condemnation of his own upbringing.

In the field of general education, however, Frederick's achievements were unspectacular. There was considerable illiteracy in Prussia, despite a law imposing universal education: law was one thing, the means of giving effect to it was another. Frederick founded a large number of new village schools, he improved teachers' salaries and conditions, but when he died there would still be much to do and it may be that the King's essential intellectualism – and temperamental autocracy – detached him somewhat from enthusiasm for popular educational advancement. Prussia was still a largely feudal society, with the ordinary agricultural labourer a serf, bound to an estate, well clad and shod by comparison with many lands, but owing the lord of the manor three days' labour as his due.

Frederick's greatest happiness, always, lay in the companionship of chosen friends, although many of the 'beloved members of the Bayard Order' were now dead or soon would be. Frederick was only thirty-four when the recent campaign ended but some of his favourite people were older and their numbers were reducing. Dietrich von Keyserlingk, 'Cesarion', had died during the war, and on 3 January 1746 Frederick's beloved tutor, Jacques Egide Duhan de Jandun, died – Duhan was one of only four or five people Frederick longed to see when returning from campaign, and would write to Fredersdorff to arrange.[20] He had made Duhan director of the Liegnitz Academy and had asked him to keep the King posted on what people were saying when he rode off to the first Silesian war. Friedrich Rudolph von Rothenburg died in the winter of 1751 – a Catholic convert, he had been a friend since the siege of Phillipsburg, in the distant days when Crown Prince Frederick had accompanied his father to Flanders and met Eugen: '*Gestern ist Rothenburg in meinen Armen gestorben,*' Frederick wrote to Wilhelmina on 29 December. His sister understood better than anyone what the loss of old friends meant to her somewhat isolated, always difficult, but undoubtedly beloved eldest brother. In the preceding month, November 1751, Jules Offray de la Mettrie died at the age of forty-three. He was an author who had been expelled from Holland, a former French army surgeon, who had written a book aiming to explain all phenomena in purely materialist terms; he was probably the only avowed atheist in Frederick's circle. Frederick, certainly no mystic, found his work superficial: 'A good doctor of philosophy, a bad writer. One could enjoy his company if one left his books unread.' De la Mettrie, a practical joker with wit and imagination, had amused Frederick, although he had been caught out in the unpardonable offence of gossiping outside about the conversation at the King's dinner table.

Some were not dying but deserting. Algarotti, the attractive and rather boastful Venetian who had dazzled Frederick with his charm when first coming to Rheinsberg in the happy 'Remusberg' days, fell passionately in love with the beautiful Barbarina, left Potsdam to go to Italy in 1753 and, despite Frederick's orders, stayed there. He remained in communication; he organized consignments of fish from Venice (Frederick particularly liked tunny); but he did not return.

It was, perhaps, d'Argens – Jean Baptiste de Boyer, Marquis d'Argens – who gave Frederick the most consistently satisfying companionship during this middle period of his life, including the whole of the Seven Years War. D'Argens was a Provençal, a free-thinking philosopher who wrote *La philosophie du bon Sens* and had made his name with another work – *The Jewish Spy*. He had been harassed by the authorities in France on account of his views, had settled first in Holland and then in Württemberg, and had moved to Berlin in 1740. Frederick had made him Director of Philosophy at the Academy and was extremely fond of him, chuckling at his notorious hypochondria and his superstition, for like many 'free-thinkers' he was superstitious about customs and practices, appalled, for instance, if thirteen people sat at table. But d'Argens was a good-humoured and good-natured man with whom Frederick felt at ease and who, in turn, saw his task as keeping the King happy and on occasion cheering him up. His vivacity and good manners did much for the atmosphere at Sans Souci where, as at every court, there could be feuds and jealousies. He was thought weak by some,[21] but it was said that at no time in the thirty years of his service with Frederick did d'Argens cause embarrassment or hurt anybody; and his affection for his sovereign was undoubtedly complete.

Frederick enjoyed absurd practical jokes. D'Argens was, for a while, appointed director of the theatre in Berlin and, in 1749, married a talented but plain dancer, Mademoiselle Cochois, of whom Frederick initially disapproved, although later he spoke of her with warmth – 'full of wit, knowledge, talents'.[22] On one occasion d'Argens took a fine dress worn on stage by his wife in the character of a queen, and had it converted into a sumptuous dressing-gown for himself. He was relaxing happily in this garment in his own rooms one day, and sent word that he was not well enough to attend the King's evening supper circle. Frederick at once put on black clothes, made some of his entourage do the same, and processed to the d'Argens quarters where they found the Marquis in bed, in his splendid dressing-gown. The visitors surrounded the bed as if bringing the sacraments to one *in extremis* and poured some oil over the dressing-gown 'as a sign of grace' in this crisis of his health.[23] Such horseplay no doubt pleased the sycophants but it was unendearing. To d'Argens, however, it was part of the complex individual whom he admired and loved but in whom, as he knew, a touch of malice was never far submerged. D'Argens had rooms at Sans Souci, where his family were, predictably, lonely. Frederick had them refurnished and showed his friend round them after completion, indicating a library with an array of titles on several shelves representing the Fathers of the Church. Between the splendid covers of each the pages were blank; a very Frederician joke.

Another very Frederician joke was played on a Pomeranian pastor who had, Frederick heard, referred to the King as a 'Herod'. The pastor was summoned to appear before a consistory court and Frederick, disguised, presided. There the unfortunate pastor was cross-examined by the 'President'. Herod? This was an interesting analogy. Which Herod? Herod Antipas? Antipater? Of what date was the Herod referred to by the pastor, and what characteristics impelled him to this comparison? The wretched man, after displaying total ignorance, escaped to his parish.

D'Argens did a great deal for Frederick's morale in bad times, particularly in war. Some years later, when they were on campaign together at Leipzig, the Marquis was worried that Frederick ate nothing at supper. It was a moment of crisis for the campaign, for Prussia, for Europe. He went to the royal quarters and found the King sitting on the floor with a dish of fricassées from which he was feeding his dogs, making them take their turns checked by a small stick he was holding. D'Argens clapped his hands with delight – 'The five greatest powers in Europe are combined against the Elector of Brandenburg and are no doubt asking, "What's he doing at the moment? Making an alarming plan for the next campaign? Collecting funds for it? Strengthening his magazines, his reserves of men and horses? Designing negotiations to split his adversaries?" No! He's sitting quietly on the floor, feeding his dogs!'

In some there might have been sycophancy in this remark but with d'Argens it was spontaneous. He greatly admired Frederick and the longer he knew him the more he found to admire. Commenting on Frederick's letters, he said, 'From them I truly encountered his sublime spirit.' Frederick addressed verses to him at a low moment in Prussian fortunes, after the Austrians had taken Schweidnitz in 1761 –

> Aujourd'hui des revers le poids nous importune;
> Demain l'inconstante fortune
> Nous favorisera, Marquis, et nous rirons!
> Ne murmurons donc plus, et cessons de nous plaindre
> D'un mal qui ne saurait durer –

'Things are terrible today, but tomorrow we'll be laughing and luck will change.' Whatever d'Argens's view of the verses, the sentiment compelled respect. He could provide the companion, the foil, Frederick needed at such moments. He could understand Frederick's near-despair at a political and strategic situation seeming to offer little hope, but he could also understand the artistic need for self-dramatization, the need which made the King write at the same time –

> Esclave scrupuleux de devoir qui me lie,
> Un joug superbe et dur m'attache à ma patrie –[24]

This sort of mood might arouse cynicism or simply irritation, but d'Argens knew the man well enough to detect the mix of sincerity and contrivance. He revered but did not flatter. And he always appreciated

Frederick's *bons mots*. 'People say that kings are the images of God on earth,' Frederick observed. 'I look in the mirror and say "So much the worse for God."'

As close in spirit to Frederick as any were the two Scottish brothers, George and James Keith. George Keith, 9th Earl Marischal, was nineteen years older than Frederick and as a very young man had served under Marlborough. Although a Protestant (with a Catholic mother), he had found himself unable in conscience to accept the Hanoverian succession in Britain and had taken part in the Jacobite rising of 1715, and – with his brother, James – in the brief expedition with Spanish help to the Scottish Highlands in 1719, the expedition defeated at Glenshiel. Although George Keith succeeded his father in that year, his honours, titles and lands had been taken from him by attainder after the 1715 rising. He had been condemned to death *in absentia*, and had lived in Spain until entering the service of the King of Prussia at the age of fifty-four in 1747.

Frederick came to trust him utterly. He was 'Milord Maréchal', 'Lord Maréchal d'Écosse', was given the Order of the Black Eagle and was sent to Paris as Prussian Ambassador in 1751. Frederick was told that his uncle George II had taken strong exception to this appointment – indeed there was discussion in London about a rupture in formal relations – and he sent a letter to his envoy in London which came as close as communications between eighteenth-century sovereigns could to telling his uncle to mind his own business.[25] He also – generously – insisted on paying Marischal the sum in life rent on his attainted Scottish properties which had been agreed by Prince Charles Edward as compensation for Jacobite staunchness – a considerable sum, since the Keiths were a rich family. Frederick was determined that there should be no attribution of misfortune to his service for Prussia.[26] The recompense was sadly needed – Marischal was dependent on it and managed (an unusual achievement) to persuade Frederick to increase the expenses proposed for him as Ambassador in Paris by 4,050 *écus*. After his time in Paris Frederick appointed him governor of the Hohenzollern-owned principality of Neuchâtel in Switzerland, until relieved by the previous Prussian envoy in London, Michel.

It was a curious coincidence that, at the same time, Frederick's channels of diplomatic communication with France were by two Jacobite noblemen, the Scots Earl Marischal in Paris and the Irish Earl of Tyrconnel, who was for two years French Ambassador in Berlin. Frederick was fond of both of them, particularly of Marischal. Marischal had been anxious whether his earlier politics might prejudice his ability to mind Frederick's interests and Frederick reassured him – he had never been involved in negotiations with France or anyone else about the Stuart cause.[27] There were at this time various tentative Jacobite plans to upset the British Government in London with French help, and Marischal was often approached to sound out Frederick's reactions – one agent in the matter was a prominent Oxfordshire landowner by name Dawkins, an archaeologist, explorer of Palmyra and Mesopotamia – but Frederick thought such schemes hare-brained; and when Charles Edward paid a covert visit to Berlin he saw James Keith, Marischal's brother, but not the King. Marischal, gratifyingly, was not only pardoned by George II in 1759 but enabled to succeed to his principal ancestral lands in 1760 and to buy back others (at a low price and with none bidding against him) in 1764. 'I believe the Pretender himself could get his attainder reversed if he would apply to the King of Prussia!' wrote Horace Walpole. Despite this, Marischal ultimately returned to live in Potsdam where Frederick built a house for him and where he was, until his death in 1778, near the man he certainly esteemed most in the world. The King would often walk beside his chair when he was old and infirm.

Marischal's brother, James Keith, was three years younger. He, too, had been 'out' in the 1715 rising, had obtained a colonelcy in the Spanish army, and had then left it for the service of Peter the Great who gave him command of a Russian Guards regiment and under whom he became a highly esteemed general serving against Sweden. He had served as second-in-command to General Münnich, sometimes called the 'Prince Eugen of Russia'. In 1747 he joined his brother in Frederick's service and Frederick immediately made him a field marshal – his reputation was high. There were few barriers of nationality or blood for an able and ambitious soldier of education, particularly one of noble family; and James Keith, besides his military ability, was a brilliant linguist, an accomplished man of letters with many contacts among the literary establishments of Europe. Scotsmen, in particular, were to be found in most courts, often in high positions. When James Keith had been in the Russian service he had been sent as head of an embassy to negotiate with the Ottoman sultanate and had – resplendent in the uniform of the Tsars – been received by the Sultan's representative, the Grand Vizier, equally resplendent with huge ceremonial turban and robes. Keith had expressed the lofty and friendly sentiments of the Emperor of all the Russias. The Sultan's ambassador had replied with equally high-flown sentiments. During the short interval which followed Keith heard a murmur from the Sultan's ambassador. He listened more carefully – 'Eh, Jamie,' the other was muttering, 'I'm unco happy, far frae home, to meet one I remember as a laddie in Kirkcaldy!'[28] The Grand Vizier's father had been a bellman in that town, James Miller by name.

James Keith was just such a man as Frederick liked to have in his circle and he was soon made governor of Berlin. He used to translate for the King's benefit various speeches reported from proceedings in the British Parliament. He would be one of Frederick's closest companions until his death in battle at the King's side.

Richard Talbot, Earl of Tyrconnel, was appointed to Berlin in April 1750. A Jacobite, he had been taken prisoner by the English when trying to join Prince Charles Edward in 1746, and had later been exchanged. He had then fought at Laufeldt, was forty years old when he became French Ambassador, and was apparently inexperienced in politics. Frederick wondered whether Tyrconnel had the knowledge for so important an embassy but he liked him and told his brother, August Wilhelm, that Tyrconnel seemed *aimable* but with an underlying sadness which Frederick contrasted with Valory's cheerfulness and which he ascribed (rather surprisingly) to a residue of English blood, probably needing two generations to expunge.[29] Tyrconnel's melancholy may have had physical causes; he died in Berlin of a haemorrhage in 1752. In retrospect Frederick once described him (reasoning obscure) as somewhat *méchant*, presumably ill-natured, and it was clear that he and Frederick did not always get on well although he also spoke of him with affection. He was relieved by one, La Touche, who, Frederick remarked on his first arrival, 'will suit us better than Milord'.[30]

Tyrconnel had succeeded Valory, a long-serving ambassador at

Frederick's court who had got to know the King very well. Taking over from a favourite of Frederick's, Valory had at first bored him with his unquenchable flow of military reminiscence but affection had succeeded irritation, and now that he was retiring in 1750 to live at Étampes Frederick was sad. He called Valory 'the King of England's poodle' ('*toutou*') for his readiness to see the British point of view, and wrote to him that in his future, gentle, philosophic life Valory would continue reminiscing about the War of Spanish Succession, while remembering that others, too, had fought in it; that Frederick William himself had served. Valory's orchard at Étampes must become the garden of the Hesperides, and his home the palace of Antinous, but he must not altogether forget the Philosopher of Sans Souci.[31] The French Ambassadors to Prussia were having a demanding time in this decade between the end of one war and the beginning of another, since alliances and relationships were shifting and uncertain.

The British Ambassadors to Prussia were, from Frederick's viewpoint, of uneven quality. When he was Crown Prince there had been Sir Charles Hotham, at the time of the abortive 'English marriage' negotiation, who left after a furious row with Frederick William and was succeeded by Colonel Guy Dickens. Both Hotham and Dickens had been indiscreetly approached by Frederick in his despair in those days and had been sympathetic but cautious; he had initially liked Guy Dickens but later described him (when Dickens was serving at the Russian court) as violent, hot-tempered, very vehement and very vain as well as personally very prejudiced against Sweden.[32] There had been John Carmichael, Earl of Hyndford, who had done a great deal of negotiating during the Silesian wars and whose efforts had had much effect in leading to the Treaty of Breslau. Frederick, nevertheless, found him personally unsympathetic. There had been Thomas Villiers, later Earl of Clarendon, who had served briefly at Vienna, then at Dresden, before coming to Berlin in 1746. Frederick liked him at once – 'His ways of thinking and behaving are exactly such as to gain my confidence'[33] – and to his satisfaction managed to keep him for two years, until 1748. Then there had been Sir Charles Hanbury-Williams, at Berlin for only a few months, who, although noted in London as a wit and versifier, was antipathetic to Frederick. He later served in Dresden and in St Petersburg; and whatever his personal views Frederick would find his presence there very useful to Prussia. Frederick told his man in London not to ignore Hanbury-Williams, insignificant though he might appear: 'Small men can often make more trouble than big ones.' Fortunately for both Britain and Prussia one of the most outstanding ambassadors of the time, perceptive, courageous, high-minded and congenial to Frederick, would soon be appointed to Berlin.

D'Argens, Algarotti (until he deserted), de la Motte Fouqué, the Keiths – these, with others, were Frederick's intimates, the regulars; there were the ambassadors, whose personal relations with the King were of considerable importance; and there were frequent visitors. If Frederick heard of somebody of interest being within reach of Potsdam he wanted to see him. Marshal Saxe visited in 1748; Frederick was later given Saxe's *Rêveries* on war by his brother, August Wilhelm, and kept it by his bedside saying that it had stimulated his own poem 'L'Art de la Guerre'. There were chosen ministers. And there were members of the family.

Frederick was revered as head of the house of Brandenburg by his brothers and sisters. He was, *in loco parentis*, a strict brother. He was certainly loved by his elder sister, Wilhelmina; feared somewhat by his next elder brother, August Wilhelm, 'the Prince of Prussia' ten years his junior, and his father's favourite; and an object of some jealousy to the next brother, Henry, who was fourteen years younger than the King. Henry had already made his name as a soldier at Chotusitz and Hohenfriedeberg, and he thought Frederick lacking in warmth and fraternal affection. He was given the Rheinsberg estate by the King as well as a magnificent palace in Berlin and later in life a fine set of rooms in the Potsdam Neues Palais; was to hold high command (and deserve it) at a very young age, received handsome tributes from Frederick later in life, but suffered from a congenital suppressed resentment not infrequently found in younger sons, especially if gifted – and Henry was very gifted. Like Frederick he was a man of many and varied talents, cultivated, musical and intelligent. Like Frederick he established at Rheinsberg a brilliant court, rivalling the King's own. Like Frederick he was enchanted by France and things French – and, being without final responsibility, could indulge a prejudice in that direction without risk of it becoming mistaken for a policy. Like Frederick he would become one of Prussia's most distinguished field commanders. Small in stature, he was both charming and vain; and had a most attractive wife of whom Frederick was fond, but whom he later deserted, caring little for her as a woman. He would differ with his eldest brother on many aspects of policy and strategy as time went on.

Within Frederick's court and family, whether inspired by politics or by personal factors, there were jealousies, antipathies and intrigues. These were observed with amusement, and no doubt sometimes encouraged, by the King. Frederick liked playing men off against each other. He liked mocking, and seeing how much the mocked would tolerate without rejoinder. He liked provoking. He loved argument and he was rough in debate, pressing a point without mercy, testing the strength and justification of an opinion, enjoying the cut and thrust. His companions had to be careful, and the skilled knew how far they could go. Frederick disliked excessive familiarity; contradiction had to be courteous rather than too direct or abrasive. Above all he would not tolerate betrayal of his conversation to others outside the circle. But Frederick was extremely considerate, especially to strangers who might be unsure of themselves and nervous. A poor schoolmaster-curate made his way to Potsdam from his home in Jena, 250 miles away. He had something of a grievance and no money; and in the gardens at Potsdam was presented to the King by some off-duty officers who, mocking somewhat, told him how to behave. Frederick listened to everything, asked a great deal, satisfied his complaint and personally arranged that the hungry curate had a sumptuous meal in Sans Souci.[34]

The experienced knew that it was best to let the King talk, to keep quiet when he was giving vent to his sometimes cruel mockery, to keep powder dry. They knew that Frederick respected – and did not mock – sincerely held opinions if they could be rationally defended. They knew that his frankness was a sort of compliment – he took the view that equivocation was an injury. All men appreciated the range of his mind and his conversation, his courteous turn of speech, his wit and the beauty of his speaking voice – despite a few eccentricities; he pronounced 't' as 'd'. 'He ennobled any theme,' said the Prince de

Ligne, himself a man of great charm and high talents. 'He could take the first words of your conversation, twist them and derive from them a point of great interest.' All found it fascinating to talk and perhaps spar with Frederick, even when it was intimidating.

But as in every court there were tensions. And these were never greater than when, in July 1750, Voltaire again arrived in Berlin.

10

Penalties of Prominence

Frederick, with wars to run and a kingdom to rule, had been very busy since his and Voltaire's last encounter in 1743 and he had been only an intermittent correspondent, but his letters to Voltaire had been increasingly positive in tone, more confident, less the intellectual supplicant addressing the master, more the equal searcher after truth; and it may be that, whether knowingly or not, this altered tone struck the recipient and jarred a little. Voltaire was very conscious of his position – the emperor of European thought and letters. Emperors do not relish equals. Frederick, now, was unafraid to express his views about a book in the uncompromising terms of one not particularly expecting disagreement. This had been so for several years: 'The Anecdotes on Louis XIV's private life have given me pleasure,' he wrote in December 1746,[1] 'but I can't say I found anything new . . . contemporary authors in every age are accused of succumbing either to the bitterness of satire or the idiocy of flattery.' '*J'ai été ravi*,' he told Voltaire on one occasion (not the first), '*de voir les changements et les additions que vous avez fait à votre ode.*' This was not the language of a humble apprentice.

Frederick had made clear, however, that he expected another visit by the great man to Berlin: '*J'ai la folie de vous voir!*' he wrote in June 1749.[2] As in former days they exchanged literary criticisms and Frederick, as before, asked approval or advice on his own compositions, particularly his verses. Voltaire's responses were fulsome – '*J'ai toujours pris la liberté de vous aimer*' – but he needled here and there. He had heard that d'Argens (nicknamed 'Isaac') was making disobliging remarks about Voltaire's previous time in Berlin. It was certainly true that d'Argens saw through him, but 'I pardon him with all my heart, the best fellow in the world', the great man told Frederick, somewhat unctuously.[3] He was staking out territory.

Voltaire was fifty-six years old. His recent life and reputation had been uneven. After being several times passed over for election to the French Academy he had succeeded in 1746, and had also regained for a little the smile of Louis XV, writing, for instance, the libretto for the '*comédie-ballet*' composed by Jean-Philippe Rameau for the Dauphin's marriage in 1745. He was, however, the object of powerful and mixed feelings as he always had been, and his limited favour at court had not everywhere increased his popularity. He had been living in the house of his mistress, the Marquise du Châtelet, in Lorraine.

On 10 September 1749 the Marquise died after giving birth to a baby who also soon died. She was forty-three.* There was now less reason to resist going to Berlin if Frederick really wished it, but Voltaire was unsure how their relationship had survived six years without personal contact. He would have grimaced had he known that Frederick, that very month, had told Algarotti how, in Voltaire, a noble genius was linked to a mean soul – 'the malice of a monkey – but I need him for my French studies'. Voltaire had asked Frederick to honour him with the '*Pour le Mérite*', the most illustrious of Prussian awards, and received no reply.

But at the end of December 1749 Voltaire received a long and gracious letter from Frederick, expressing the hope that he would come to Berlin during the forthcoming year;[4] and this was followed by another, with eighty-four lines of the King's verses.[5] Voltaire was in raptures. It took some time to settle affairs and resign certain commitments in France but in June 1750 he set out for Prussia. His decision was not popular at the French court, where Louis XV turned his back on him. There were few hopes in Paris, as once, that this privileged friend of the King of Prussia could influence policy in a way helpful to France.

From the start there were shadows over the relationship. Voltaire was more financially dependent than he had been, and no Cardinal Fleury was seeking his services. Frederick seemed gracious, but remarkably assured in those literary matters where he had formerly acknowl-

---

* The father of the child was the Marquis de Saint Lambert.

edged himself a pupil. And Frederick was understandably touchy about his own writings, and especially his verses, confident though he might appear. He particularly deplored the idea of his work getting into unauthorized hands. When Valory had asked for a poem of the King's of which he'd heard and wished to send to Louis XV, Frederick courteously declined, saying that he had nothing but affection for Louis, but that the book might fall into other hands – theologians, politicians, purists! Then what ridicule might ensue! That a *king* should write a poem in six stanzas, should invent a heaven, criticize earth! That a German should attempt rhyme in French! Frederick's sensitivities, considering his position and his reputation (and that of Voltaire), are wholly understandable.[6]

Voltaire reached Berlin on 10 July 1750 and travelled to Potsdam on the same day, to find four welcoming lines of verse from Frederick. His niece, the young widow Mme Denis (with whom he was in love), had been charged by him to dispose of his personal effects in France and to join him when she could; and at first all seemed harmonious. Wilhelmina of Bayreuth visited Berlin in August and was enchanted by Voltaire. Frederick, also in August, made him a Court Chamberlain, approved for him a 20,000 franc stipend and guaranteed 4,000 to Mme Denis provided she stayed with Voltaire and kept house for him.[7] Enclosed with twelve elegant lines –

> *L'Éclat n'est rien pour vous: votre belle âme n'aime*
> *Que la sublime gloire et l'immortalité*

– were the Chamberlain's key and the Cross of the *Pour le Mérite*.

At first they happily teased each other with schoolboyish riddles. '*P/viens a Ci/sans*' – ('*Viens souper à Sans Souci!*') Frederick wrote, and received the reply – '*J a P*' ('*J'ai grand appétit!*') It is uncertain to what extent Voltaire was blind to Frederick's scepticism about him. Neither he nor Frederick would have been deceived by gracefulness of compliment – this was a game which it was well-mannered to play. But, words apart, it seems probable that Voltaire supposed his reputation and his intellectual dominance would keep him in something like security, and it also seems probable that in Frederick's mind the obvious self-interest Voltaire had in behaving himself would keep matters on a steady course. And Frederick, of course, while perfectly alive to the mischief-making which was Voltaire's forte, enjoyed the tensions, the feuds, which beset these men of talent who circled around him. The question was whether the mark would be overstepped.

It soon was. In February 1751 Frederick wrote a severe letter of reply from Potsdam to Voltaire, whose house was in Berlin.[8] Voltaire had complained that he was being slandered. The King had been told, he protested, that he, Voltaire, had committed financial irregularities. Some of the royal circle, unworthy of their positions, had misled their master. He named names.

This was a culmination. What had happened was this. Voltaire had been trying to make some money – illegally. He had asked a Jewish jeweller, by name Hirschel, to buy for him at a discount some Saxon exchequer bills which were repayable at par to Prussian subjects, thus guaranteeing a profit. Voltaire was not a Prussian subject and the deal was illicit. To finance it he had given Hirschel a money draft on a Paris bank, and in return for this had accepted some diamonds as surety until the Saxon stock was received. The stock was delayed and didn't arrive. Then Voltaire, in effect, stopped the cheque. Hirschel asked for his diamonds back and accused Voltaire of switching some of them for inferior stones while in his keeping. He threatened to take the case to the courts (although in the event it was settled). The matter came to Frederick's ears and the indignity of the whole thing infuriated him – the barefaced subterfuge of Voltaire pretending to Prussian nationality in order to cheat, the squalor of a stopped cheque and allegations of diamond substitution, the fact of the transactions and accusations being widely known in Saxony as well as Berlin, all this touching a known favourite and confidant of the King. Frederick was enraged. He continued to regard Voltaire as a genius but now also thought of him as an avaricious rogue. And then he received this actual letter of complaint from Voltaire as if he were the injured party rather than the culprit.

His response was icy. Voltaire, he wrote, had had the effrontery to advise on who should and should not be the King's trusted servants. In doing so he had vindictively pursued innocent men against whom he had a grudge. On the contrary, it was he who had indulged in financial malpractice and proved unworthy. Furthermore – a separate charge – he had most improperly discussed with the Russian Ambassador matters which were no conceivable concern of his and had implied that he did so on the King's instructions. He had also interfered in some personal affairs of members of the Prussian court. Frederick's letter ended with cold anger: 'If you can decide to live as a philosopher I will be happy to see you. If, however, you give yourself up to the flames of your passions . . . you will give me no pleasure by coming here and had better stay in Berlin.'

Voltaire's letters – and poems – were henceforth abject. Frederick's were few, brief and confined to literary criticism, although in October that year, 1751, he sent twelve verses of a complimentary ode almost in the old manner – '*Quel avenir t'attend, divin Voltaire!*'

Voltaire knew, nevertheless, that his hold on Frederick was weakening to the point of extinction. He tried to curry such favour as might be. When Rothenburg, a man he knew to be near the King's heart, died, he told of his admiration, and said that the dead man had agreed to be Voltaire's executor.[9] He failed with d'Argens, who had never liked Voltaire, but Frederick recognized that the two were unequal: 'D'Argens has just returned from France,' he wrote to Wilhelmina, 'and has had a *prise* with Voltaire – a jenny wren taking on an eagle! You can guess who won!' Frederick once said that Voltaire should be put in a cage like a parrot – 'and take care what you say in front of it!'

By autumn 1752 a storm was brewing again. In September Voltaire wrote to Mme Denis (who was away on a visit to Paris) that he proposed to negotiate through the Duke of Württemberg a life interest policy on both their lives, uncle and niece, financed by funds he intended to transfer from Berlin, presumably to Stuttgart. She could, he wrote, count on his imminent departure.[10] He was restive.

He was also extremely nervous. A letter he received from Frederick in December 1752 shows why. It began with the words, '*Votre effronterie m'étonne.*'[11] This was, or soon would be, the crux. It had come from an instance of hatred among academics, a ferocious condition. It affected Voltaire. It also affected the President of the Prussian Academy of Science, Frederick's protégé, Maupertuis.

Pierre Louis Moreau de Maupertuis, a Breton from St Malo, was a mathematician and scientist of international reputation. A man of somewhat quarrelsome temperament, he had been one of Frederick's earliest acquisitions for Prussia among the intellectual élite of Europe. 'From the moment I ascended the throne,' Frederick had written to him in June 1740, 'my heart and my inclination incited in me the desire to have you here,'[12] and Maupertuis at once prepared plans for the Academy, with Frederick writing impatiently throughout the first Silesian war, in which the mathematician accompanied the King. Their exchanges of letters and verses were of outstanding charm and wit. He was, said Frederick, brutally honest although with the sourest face in the world. He was now fifty-four and Voltaire had described him as a bore. He had agreed to the appointment in Berlin for sound practical reasons, not least because he had fallen in love with a Prussian noblewoman, a von Borcke, and married her. Frederick said that only Newton could be compared to him.

Maupertuis had developed a mathematical principle known as that of 'least action'. Now a Professor Samuel König, writing in The Hague, claimed that the correct elements of this principle had been formulated not by Maupertuis but in a letter from Leibnitz to another mathematician, Heimann, in 1707. This was to deny originality to Maupertuis and the König paper was denounced as promoting a forgery (the Leibnitz letter). König appealed to the public and Voltaire, who knew König well and disliked Maupertius, took up König's cause. He published a letter (anonymous) 'to an academician in Paris'. Maupertuis was deeply and understandably wounded by this assault from, so to speak, within the citadel and Frederick, appalled by this attack on the scholarship and integrity of his President of the Academy, most unwisely published a reply (again, anonymous, but known by all to be the work of the King). The row was now public, scandalous, undignified and enjoyable.

Voltaire returned to battle with a pamphlet, a more extended attack on Maupertuis (not confined to the mathematical point at issue) which he called '*Diatribe du Docteur Akakia, Médecin du Pape*'. This was a sardonic piece of buffoonery which pretended to make Maupertuis's own work the subject of a critique for the Inquisition. Frederick, when he heard of this, ordered it to be withheld from publication, although he could not resist having it read to him and laughing at it with relish.[13] It was, however, a brutal onslaught on Maupertius and the King was furious. On 27 November Voltaire wrote a penitent letter to Frederick,[14] promising good behaviour, but by then the matter was out of control. The *Diatribe*, despite Voltaire's promise to the contrary and Frederick's instructions in Berlin, had been published in Paris and in Leipzig. In Prussia Frederick ordered all copies to be bought up for destruction, and the book to be publicly burned. Hence '*Votre effronterie m'étonne!*'

Voltaire was told he could leave Berlin whenever he chose. He wrote that he 'needed to take the waters at Plombières' and Frederick responded coldly that pretexts were unnecessary. Voltaire was free to go.[15] He was, however, to return to the King the Cross of the Order of *Pour le Mérite*, his Chamberlain key and a volume of Frederick's writings which he had been given in confidence for comment. Frederick observed in the same letter that having neither the vanity nor the idiocy of certain authors he could only regard the feuds of men of letters as a disgrace to literature. The letter was carried by a page, ordered to wait while it was read; and Maupertius wrote at the same time to Mme Denis that she should prevent her uncle making a fool of himself.

Frederick, very naturally, was particularly concerned about getting the draft of his compositions back. Not only had he heard (and would hear again) of the ridicule poured by Voltaire on some of his writings but there were disobliging references to other sovereigns and European personalities which could have caused trouble in the wrong hands. Three lines of a letter from Voltaire to Fredersdorff acknowledged 3,000 *écus* of his pension; and he left Berlin, never to return, on 26 March 1753.

The last chapter of 'Voltaire in Prussia' was reminiscent of *opéra bouffe*. Voltaire and Mme Denis (referred to by Frederick as his 'Medea') travelled via Gotha, Leipzig and Frankfurt. While they were on their way Frederick discovered that he had been deceived and disobeyed. Voltaire had removed the Chamberlain's key entrusted to him; and he had also removed his confidential copy of Frederick's poems which the King feared – with reason and with anger – could be exposed to the public, without his approval and probably accompanied by ridicule. The couple reached Frankfurt, a free city of the Empire not under the jurisdiction of Frederick or any other prince. Prussia maintained a Resident there, by name Freytag.

Freytag was sent urgent instructions from Berlin to recover from the travelling philosopher and his companion the important items which he had removed. He went to Voltaire's hotel with his demands. Voltaire explained that his luggage had not yet arrived from Leipzig. He undertook to remain in Frankfurt until this happened, which it did two weeks later when the articles were duly handed over.

Freytag, although Voltaire now appeared to have leave to travel on and had discharged his obligations, decided that he had better detain the travellers and seek further instructions. He forcibly prevented an attempt by them to leave Frankfurt. Voltaire extracted the maximum from this situation, which had arisen from error, and told Frederick (and the world) that his wrongful detention had exposed Mme Denis to violence and ignominy, described in highly coloured terms. Frederick, wisely, took trouble to tell his ambassador in Paris (now '*Milord Maréchal d'Écosse*') what had happened. He regretted Freytag's mistake – Freytag had exceeded his instructions – but he was unmoved by Voltaire's indignation. He attributed Voltaire's behaviour to a desire to replace Maupertuis as President of the Academy, but whatever the substance in this Frederick's letter was otherwise a fair, factual record of the 'Dr Akakia' affair; and he asked Marischal to do his best to correct Voltaire's calumnies, which would undoubtedly be spread in France. If the book of Frederick's writings were to appear in France it should, if possible, be recovered. He referred to Voltaire as '*Le plus ingrat et le plus méchant des mortels*'[16] and apologized for giving his ambassador such absurd tasks, '*ridicules commissions*'. The *ridicules commissions* were completed in so far as possible and in June 1753 Frederick wrote that he 'abandoned Voltaire to his destiny'. He had not been mollified by learning that the great man had applied to Maria Theresa to enter her service, but had been amused by her response; '*Ingénieusement*', as Frederick told Marischal with relish, the Queen had said that Voltaire belonged not in Vienna but only on Parnassus.[17]

Henceforth, although time brought some conciliatory exchanges, Frederick kept Voltaire at arm's length. Nevertheless, in spite of the fury which had marked their parting and in spite of periodic reports of malicious libels circulating in the capitals of Europe which he easily traced to Voltaire,[18] Frederick could never forget the effect Voltaire's mind and writing had had upon him and he was grateful. He described Voltaire as 'the most malevolent madman'; as 'an abominable character, false, a cheat'; as 'the greatest rascal alive'; but he knew that he had been in touch with genius, however morally flawed. He knew that in a formative period of his life the master of European literature had commented in detail on his own draft writings, page by page and sometimes word by word: he had enjoyed a rare privilege,[19] and he continued to read Voltaire's works with huge admiration. Nor could he resist writing to the author about them.

Both men, in their later letters, periodically returned, with allusions, to their quarrel. Frederick followed Voltaire's fortunes in his struggle against intolerance and superstition, the battle which had brought them together, although – with the experience of an actual ruler – he now believed that it was a mistake to let men insult established beliefs; liberty could too easily provoke disorder and worse evils. Toleration was admirable but one should not authorize outrages against that which people revere, whether intelligently or not. In 1766 Voltaire wrote, 'I forgive him everything!'

When a superb bust of Voltaire by Pigalle was commissioned Frederick made a particularly handsome contribution, and Voltaire was touched. And on Voltaire's death in 1778 Frederick wrote a noble 'Éloge', which was read to a session of the Berlin Academy by the public orator. Characteristically he had composed it during a campaign.

The period of peace after the Silesian wars had given Frederick more time to devote to his own historical writings. He wrote his *History of the House of Brandenburg* over a considerable period and often revised it. A complete edition was published with royal approval in Berlin in 1751;[20] the book took the Hohenzollern story up to the time of Frederick's accession and the death of his father. It included, in very direct and lucid language, an account of the various transactions whereby the Electors had enlarged their possessions or failed to; and it thus acted as something of a statement of historic claim when dealing with such matters as the accessions of Jülich, Berg, Cleve, Ravensburg. But the 'Brandenburg History' became impassioned and dramatic when dealing with the horrors of the Thirty Years War, and such incidents as the sack of Magdeburg by Tilly in 1631: 'Everything that the licence of the soldiery can invent when nothing bridles their passions; all that the most savage cruelty inspires in men when only blind rage possesses their senses – all this marked the conduct of the Imperial troops, with armed men running through the streets slaughtering the old, the infants, men, women, children . . .'

Magdeburg had indeed been a horror and Frederick wrote with feeling. It was only a century ago, and the enemy of Prussia was still the same, or so it seemed. Indeed in many directions – in his handling of the history of the Polish question, in his treatment of the Swedish incursions into Pomerania – Frederick set out very clearly in the form of recent history the parameters, as he saw them, of the European situation he had inherited. And his portraits of the great personages of the previous century – Richelieu, Condé, the Great Elector – were eloquent and perceptive. Admiration for French achievements everywhere broke through – 'Francis I had tried in vain to draw the Arts to France; Louis XIV fixed them there. His protection was striking, as Greek taste and Roman elegance were reborn in Paris' – and he had only harsh words for his own grandfather, Frederick I of Prussia, who was possessed by blind hatred of all things French. When he dealt with the reign of his own father, Frederick William, Frederick's filial piety was now evident. He wrote (accurately) of the old king's charitable foundations for old soldiers and their families, of his care for the Cadet Corps, of his zeal in the organization of the army, although he was frank in recording – as he had often complained – that Frederick William's supervision of his cavalry was inferior to that of other arms. But basically the 'Brandenburg History' was a factual record, clear, even-handed and elegant, a tribute to Frederick's forebears which was by no means simply adulatory. It shows, however, a proper pride in lineage, from the opening sentence: 'The House of Brandenburg, or rather of Hohenzollern, is so ancient that its origins are lost in the mists of time.' There was a careful and by no means fiercely prejudiced piece on the effect of the Reformation on Prussia.

But the 1750s were marked by a good deal besides the exasperating behaviour of Voltaire and Frederick's literary compositions.

In 1748 and 1749 Frederick had been concerned about events in Scandinavia. It had seemed possible that war might break out between Sweden and Russia and Frederick had made clear that in that unfortunate contingency he could take no part, anyway at first. He had felt it necessary to give certain contingency orders to his troops in Königsberg and East Prussia and to their commander, General von Lehwaldt. A Baltic war would be a dangerous and unwelcome distraction and his concern continued through the years to 1752. He saw the hand of Austria behind the quarrel (he saw it in many places!). He suspected that the Austrians were using the cover of their 1746 treaty with Russia to make trouble in the north, and trouble in the north could too easily involve Prussia. He kept a highly mistrustful eye on the relationship – too warm for his liking – between the Empress of all the Russias and the Empress-Queen, Maria Theresa. In 1749 he learned that the Tsarina Elizabeth, troubled by 'the dangerous situation in Finland', intended to send a corps of Russian troops into Swedish Finland.[21] Elizabeth had just decided to leave St Petersburg for a year and spend it in Moscow, at some inconvenience to her court, a decision Frederick supposed linked to internal politics. He feared that the move into Finland presaged war – '*Violà les Russes qui vont entrer en Suède et par conséquent la guerre qui va commencer!*' – but on that occasion Russian plans were in some confusion and the immediate crisis passed.

Nevertheless the Russian situation continued to worry, and Frederick learned with pleasure that Sweden had made an alliance with the Turks, which should act as a counterweight to Russian pressure on Scandinavia. He also learned – with less pleasure – that it was being said in Russia that Frederick had been promised 20,000 French troops if he were to be involved in a northern war. There was nothing in this and he suspected mischief-making – he was determined that Prussia should *not* be involved in a northern war, and, indeed, determined that there should be no northern war at all if it could be prevented.[22] He worked out in May 1750 the cost of sending military help to Sweden, if such were done, unit by unit.* He told his ambassador in Russia not to discuss Russian intentions in Finland with any of the Russian officials; he was to appear to know nothing, to be uninvolved – 'I have very special reasons for giving you these orders'.[23] Frederick had declared his friendship with Sweden and he suspected

---

* See Chapter 9.

that these Russian demonstrations were a ploy to show the inutility of Prussian good will. The fish should not rise to that bait, these gestures were best ignored, and in August 1750 his ambassador (von Warendorf) assessed actual Russian aggression as unlikely.

Anything which happened in Russia, however, was of interest, generally suspicious interest, to Frederick. He heard in December 1750 of a new secret treaty being proposed between Russia, Austria and Britain, whereby each would guarantee all the possessions of the others against all comers and dangerous contingencies – a treaty to which, he understood, Holland and Poland – 'The King of Poland', that is Saxony – might be invited to accede.[24] He probably heard of this in communications to and from Vienna – the Austrian diplomatic codes had been broken. It made him nervous – although far-fetched, any internal constitutional change in Sweden (there was a struggle between Royalists and Republicans) might be regarded as invoking such a treaty.

At another extreme of political significance he heard that in St Petersburg there was an unprecedented campaign against prostitutes and loose women. Why? Why this *grande persécution contre ce sexe féminin?* Why this behaviour *aussi rigoureuse*? Inspired by the Empress? By the Russian minister, Bestuzhev? What was the rationale?[25] In April 1751 the old King Fredrik of Sweden died and Frederick's sister, Ulrica, became Queen. Frederick sent her his ideas about the defence of Finland,[26] and she wrote asking for the ideas of 'his friend, Keith', since Keith was expert in Russian methods. Finland was a huge area and troops were scarce. Ulrica possessed her own ciphers and kept Frederick well informed.

Frederick mistrusted Russian attempts to draw Denmark into a combination to put pressure on Sweden; but he also had reservations about the evident desire of France to enlist Swedish support – it was unclear how that might turn out. His chief desire was to keep politics quiet in the Baltic area and on the northern frontiers of Prussia. It was, in his view, of paramount importance that Sweden should not give Russia the slightest pretext to regard Swedish policy as hostile, and he warned Ulrica strongly to that effect in November 1751. There was no doubt, he wrote, that Russia, armed by the Austrians, was her real enemy, but there must be no *'prétexte de pouvoir vous attaquer*.[27] He accepted that overt aggression might be improbable at present, but Russia – and Austria – no doubt hoped to seduce Sweden with soft *'emmiellés'* words into dependence on the Tsars.[28]

Frederick wrote to Ulrica that all ceremony should be kept out of their private letters. He was glad to hear that her husband, Adolphus, had undertaken to maintain the constitution. In their exchanges his part was prudent, pacific, sometimes perhaps a little alarmist, never aggressive, and on occasion Ulrica told him his suspicions were unjustified. Frederick was, however, as free from illusions as ever. When he was told (not in this instance by his sister but by his embassy in Stockholm) of a suggestion that the child Prince Gustav, his four-year-old nephew, should be formally betrothed to the little Princess Magdalen of Denmark (also aged four), Frederick wrote tartly that Sweden had never been defended by the marriages of princesses hardly out of their cradles. Instead the most pressing need was to reinforce the troops in Swedish Finland.

Family matters were inseparable from diplomatic dealings. Frederick's most loved relative would always be Wilhelmina. He was her *'très fidèle frère et serviteur'*. She alone, he wrote in October 1747, could inspire in him a love of life which otherwise seemed to have vanished.[29] It was, naturally, to Frederick that Wilhelmina appealed for advice when her husband, the Margrave of Bayreuth, received an appeal from France at the beginning of 1751. He was asked to promise that, in the Imperial Diet, he would never oppose the wishes of France. In return the Margrave would receive a subsidy sufficient to finance 15,000 soldiers – computed as 30,000 *écus* in peacetime, double that in war. The King of France had a natural and unceasing desire to exercise influence in German affairs, although his only formal status was as a guarantor of the Treaty of Westphalia which had ended the Thirty Years War. What did Frederick think?

Frederick was familiar with offers of this kind. In October that year he was consulted by the Duke of Württemberg about a similar proposition,[30] whereby France would underwrite 4,000 men in time of war; the Duke was feeling aggrieved by French reluctance to contribute any of the money in advance. It was, of course, true in those days, as now, that princes were without influence and impotent unless they could deploy or offer the assistance of armed forces. In the first case Frederick knew that Bayreuth was pressed for money. He advised Wilhelmina that some bargaining might be in order. Men *could* be brought on to paper strength but only enrolled (and therefore expensive) if the need actually arose – that was one device. Another would be to hold out for an increase in the proposed subsidy – Frederick thought that improbable; he knew that France was in touch with many German princes and was unlikely to raise the bidding but it might be worth trying.[31] His own purse, he added hastily, was empty!* And this exchange with Wilhelmina culminated in hoping that she could pay him an *informal* visit, '*une visite de bonne amitié faite en robe de chambre*', so much more agreeable than cold official visits with their ceremony and etiquette, boring to both parties, and leading only to grateful relief when all was over.[32]

He could always write to Wilhelmina without inhibition. 'You were quite right in guessing that the Margrave of Schwedt [their brother-in-law: he had married their sister Sophie] wouldn't die!' he told her in February 1752. 'He made his brother come to him and received him with that bawdy vulgarity you know well. And tell me why the Margrave of Ansbach so much wants me to renew our family agreements? He has sent here a sort of lunatic whom he describes as a Cabinet Minister, one von Hütter . . .' and so forth. It was an undoubted relief to be able to pour out his concerns and sometimes his contempt for his fellow-princes to someone whom he loved and who understood.[33] Most of the overtures he received from such as Ansbach were because they were short of money.

The year which ended with the breach with Voltaire, 1752, began with more matrimonial suggestions for Frederick's youngest sister, Amelia, a beautiful girl who had been suggested, a few years previously, as a bride for the Duke of Cumberland; and now a match was being considered with the (widower) King of Denmark, a prospect Frederick regarded without enthusiasm. It did not happen. In the world of European diplomacy the various players moved to one side or back again like dancers, without dramatic change of position. Frederick could be a severe head of the family and they were all somewhat in

* Bayreuth ultimately settled for 35,000 rather than 30,000 *écus*, about £10,700.

awe of him. He could be harsh. He could, however, also be and generally was considerate. August Wilhelm once applied to Frederick for permission to go to Sweden and was refused – politically the visit would have raised difficulties at that moment. Frederick's ample letter of explanation – 'Your application is innocent, reasonable and fair: I hate having to tell you it's impossible'[34] – was frank and fraternal, and at this time his letters to August Wilhelm, 'the Prince of Prussia' (there was a sad breach later) were lively and affectionate.

The diplomatic dealings, the jockeyings, the position-taking, all occupied a great deal of his time. Dealings with Austria always contained the seed or threat of trouble. Frederick received periodic complaints from Vienna about Prussian administration in Silesia, often relating to the treatment of religion – complaints he firmly rebutted, secure in his knowledge of the toleration he had enforced there from the beginning. There were many exchanges in 1750[35] about obtaining the Electoral dignity of 'King of the Romans' for Maria Theresa's son, Joseph. It was a matter for the Imperial Diet, a sort of playing field where the German Electors and their patrons, whether within or without Germany, played politics, for the most part for comparatively small stakes. Maria Theresa was strong for the idea and was supported by, among others, George II of Britain. It became something of a litmus test for identification of sympathies towards the Habsburgs, and a bargaining counter within Germany. Frederick, demonstrating a certain neutrality, suggested it might be best to wait until the young man came of age – he had been born in 1741.

Then Frederick heard secretly from his man in Dresden, von Malt-zahn, that the Austrians were hoping to put Charles of Lorraine, Maria Theresa's brother-in-law and Frederick's old adversary, on the throne of Poland, a ploy, supported by Russia, which would require a vote in the Polish Diet.[36] Brühl, Frederick's arch-enemy at the Saxon court, was a vigorous supporter of the Czartoryski family in Poland, to whom the governance of the country, such as it was, had been virtually sub-contracted and who were in a close relationship with St Petersburg. The Czartoryskis were bitterly opposed by other great Polish families, Radziewills, Potockis, Lubomirskis, all living as petty sovereigns in that divided land. Frederick suspected that Brühl was involved in the plan to push the candidature of Charles of Lorraine whatever the effect on Saxon interests.[37] He was concerned, and he wrote a long letter on 18 December 1751 to Louis XV which specifically addressed the Polish question. If it were true, he wrote, that Austria and Russia planned to place Charles of Lorraine on the throne of Poland by armed force (as would be necessary, he said), was this tolerable? Frederick thought not. What would be the reaction of France? He set out the military options.[38]

A coalition consisting of Prussia, France and Sweden might be formed to protect Poland from the imposition of an unwanted sovereign. Such a coalition would be confronting the power of Austria and Russia. The latter could have numerical superiority in the crucial theatre, Poland. France might hope to create a diversion elsewhere, but this would be likely to make matters worse by arousing the hostility of Britain and whatever German princes Britain might enlist or subvent, as well as the Dutch. Sweden could do little against Russia in the north – geography protected Russia. The outcome would be that the whole weight of such a war would fall on Prussia, which could not simultaneously defy Russia and Austria. Coalition war for Poland thus looked impracticable, but another option might be to involve the Ottoman Turks, a project difficult to arrange but offering a better chance to preserve the peace of central Europe. There was continuing Ottoman ferment* on the southern flank of the Russian – and Habsburg – empires which might help both Prussia and France.

This was a curious letter of Frederick's. He had written a more general letter[39] to Louis shortly before, a letter in which he had described peace in Europe as hanging by a thread, and he was undoubtedly anxious at the reports he was receiving of combinations – Russia, Austria, Britain – aimed at himself.[40] But Frederick's letter, specifically mooting and then summarily dismissing the idea of a coalition to protect Poland, is puzzling. He later supposed its contents had become known in Vienna,[41] which cannot have been assumed as unlikely but which complicated matters, and if arranged by Frederick himself stimulates the query, 'Why?' His letter began by positing an Austro-Russian ploy to dominate Poland by the intrusion of Charles of Lorraine. It assumed that this was imminent and would be intoler-

---

* *'Fermentation à Constantinople'* was Frederick's expression.

able to both France and Prussia. It continued, however, by deducing that no military attempt to foil this would succeed. And it ended with the suggestion – surely far-fetched, however theoretically rational – that the matter might be solved by enlisting the Ottoman Turks, who had in living memory ravaged much of southern Russia and reached the gates of Vienna. It was unlike Frederick, generally so pragmatic, to begin with a firm declaration and end with a pipe-dream. A surely very credible impression may be gathered from this letter that his real object was to discover whether Bourbon hostility to Habsburg pretensions – and, perhaps, Romanoff pretensions – was as strong as it had been and as he hoped it still was. One way of discovery might be to raise an alarum over Poland.

Frederick ended his letter to Louis of 18 December with a near-passionate statement of the shame such an increase of Austrian power would bring to Europe, followed by a cooler observation that there might, nevertheless, be less risk in suffering it than opposing it. His letter can only be interpreted as an attempt to take the temperature and perhaps find a little reassurance; an attempt by a deeply uneasy man. His unease would before long prove justified.

Frederick's relations with Britain and Hanover were correct rather than cordial at this time. He always hoped they would improve when George II died – he was sufficiently aware of the British constitution but he nevertheless supposed, not unreasonably, that the personality and prejudices of the sovereign could be significant. He was, therefore, sad when he heard that the Prince of Wales, 'Poor Fred', had died in March 1751. He had hoped that the succession might help Prussia. Now the heir presumptive was a boy of thirteen about whose character he made anxious inquiries. It was depressing, too, to learn at the end of that year that a new alliance, similar to the one hatched in December a year earlier, was being mooted: Russia, Austria, Britain, with Holland and Saxony to be invited to accede later. It was, in fact, a proposal to revive the earlier alliance, and then manoeuvre Sweden into it, thus detaching her from friendship with France and – of course – 'checking' Prussia. This did not happen but there were aspects which were troubling and Frederick wrote a good deal about them.[42] In his view *Les deux cours impériales*, Vienna and St Petersburg, were showing a distressing propensity to get on together, while London had not lost what he called its inexplicable *penchant* for Vienna. He comforted himself, however, by ascribing this largely to British hostility to France, and consequential tenderness for so implacable an enemy of France as Austria.

Frederick spent a good deal of time and correspondence on the subject of money. Sometimes this was domestic: he watched Prussian expenditure with a sharpness of eye which was often mocked. He would write a strong letter to an ambassador about his personal expenses (while very generous if he thought it deserved). Sometimes he wrote about foreign trade – he asked his Paris embassy to explore a complaint he had received from the merchants of Stettin about French wine duty. Sometimes there were problems about the Silesian debts – referred to by Frederick as '*dettes anglaises hypothèques*', monies claimed by Britain on the so-called Silesian loans,* about which Lord Hyndford – previous British Ambassador in Berlin and now in St Petersburg – visited Prussia in January 1750 to conduct a negotiation. Frederick immersed himself in a great deal of financial detail where such international disputes were concerned and he must have enjoyed mastering them. Where a case was sound he always tried to be cooperative. In the Silesian case, however, he reminded Hyndford (never a favourite of his) of the piratical behaviour of some British ships on the high seas. Was there not a countervailing point in the debate? Should not some debt perhaps be written off to indemnify his Silesian subjects? He thought so.[43]

Frederick also spent a surprising amount of time on matters of security, on the safeguarding of secrecy. Because he dealt with so much personally – and expeditiously, with rare efficiency and decision – he felt deeply involved in the detail of such matters. He addressed rebukes to his ambassadors or ministers if he thought a code misused or if a communication were, in modern terms, to be overclassified. If a code were compromised he would send a personal instruction on how to limit the damage. And because he sometimes shared highly sensitive information with a privileged third party – notably the French Ambassador during that period when relations were happily close –

* See Chapter 8 and note.

he was very alive to the dangers of this practice being betrayed.

An example arose in February 1750. The reliable and experienced Valory was still in post in Berlin. Frederick had shown him a piece of information under customary oaths of confidence and non-attribution. The Austrian Government, Frederick learned, then became aware that Frederick had shared this particular knowledge with the French. He learned this because his own men had broken the Austrian diplomatic code. It was then a matter of discovering how the Austrians had come by their knowledge while, obviously, concealing the fact that he knew they had; and, above all, concealing the fact that their ciphers were compromised. Such problems recur in every age. Frederick traced the breach to Hanover where, he reckoned, the Hanoverian authorities had themselves broken the French diplomatic code and were thus aware of what Frederick had told Valory – a piece of information then either shared with or obtained by Austria. He wrote to Valory more in sorrow than in anger, and suggested that all codes be changed for his successor, Tyrconnel.

But Frederick's absorbing interest was in the production of position papers, documents to help clear his mind, to take stock of the general situation of Europe and the particular problems confronting Prussia. The first of these, called by him a Testament, was produced in 1752; the *First Political Testament*.

The *First Political Testament** was a long document. Frederick began it by recording the principles which guided him in the government of Prussia. There were sections on law, on finance, on government machinery, on the character of the various peoples of his dominions. He listed the rules which should govern the conduct of the nobility, the principles of equity which should regulate the conduct of both noble and peasant, and the duties of each. He wrote at length about industry and the local economy in each district of Prussia. Partiality, probably defensible, can certainly be discerned; Silesia is '*Cette belle province*' – there were fewer crown leases there than elsewhere, the nobility paid more towards the state revenues, the peasantry less. The Testament contained sections on military matters, in many cases duplicating his other military writings and instructions. But there was

* Not published in full until 1920.

also a long part on the state of Europe and the foreign policy options which faced or would face Prussia. Even as he wrote the European situation was changing, and the formidable decisions to be made some four years later – leading to his greatest period of trial – were not exactly anticipated in 1752. His 'Testament', nevertheless, gives much of his thinking at that moment.

Frederick began this foreign policy part of his paper with Austria. All powers are potential enemies but Maria Theresa, '*La plus sage et la plus politique entre elles*', is predominant. Of her, his chief enemy, Frederick was wary and admiring. Her father had left his realm in such a mess that the daughter became dependent on English subsidies for existence but now she was working without remission to reduce this dependency. Her husband, now elected Emperor, was less prejudiced against Prussia than his wife but it was Maria Theresa who counted.

Personal admiration for the sovereign did not dilute Frederick's prejudiced view of Austria and the Austrians. Vienna, he knew, was irreconcilable. Austria was 'of all powers the one to whom we have given greatest offence'. 'I've seen young Lobkowitz,' he wrote of a promising young nobleman. 'He has wit and conscience and is so agreeable I have trouble believing he's an Austrian!'[44] But he thought he knew (and was so far pretty accurate) how '*La Cour de Vienne raisonne*.'

Of all the powers, it was France on whose attitudes Frederick thought he could count with a certain assurance. France's antipathy to Austria was a constant factor in European affairs and it indicated that Berlin, whatever the difficulties, should maintain close relations with Paris. The difficulties were real. Frederick had not changed his mind about what he saw as French backsliding in the recent war, where he thought he had shouldered an unreasonable proportion of the burden. To say that he distrusted France is to say nothing – in foreign affairs Frederick trusted nobody and regarded trust as wholly out of place; but he had cold words about French policy which other generations have echoed, and he stated as a principle that in dealing with the French one must always be on one's guard: 'The way of their policy is to push us, their allies, to the front as much as they can, and then to play "*derrière le rideau*" a part which doesn't suit us but which exposes us to the resentment of other powers and places our fate in French hands.'[45]

Nevertheless it must be right for Prussia to stay close to France. Not only were the two nations bound by common hostility to Austria but they were like men who have married two sisters – in this case Silesia and Lorraine, both former provinces of the Empire – and have an interest in making common cause. Although France was the premier monarchy and the most powerful single state in Europe, the French crown and government were too dependent on luck and personality, Frederick wrote. Princes were given a bad education. That said, the worst thing for France would be the eclipse of the ruling family.

The impetus in European affairs during the last half-century, Frederick continued, had been provided by France and Britain. The King of England was personally prejudiced against the King of Prussia: his behaviour was imperious and disagreeable, and as Elector of Hanover he hoped to make a claim to Mecklenburg when the present line of dukes expired, and to divide it from Prussia – and if that happened it might be necessary for Frederick to chase Hanoverian troops out and occupy the duchy '*L'épée à la main*'. He would not hesitate – there was no difficulty in proving Prussian rights to the succession – but this should not be an imminent problem. Anyway, the Kings of England were likely to take less and less interest in Hanover. It was impossible to say whether England would preserve much influence in Europe. She was respected under Cromwell, less so afterwards. The dynastic question seemed settled, and was largely religious – and used by France simply to destabilize England. Frederick had reacted with vigorous disapproval to an idea that the unfortunate Stuart claimant to the British throne should come to live in Prussia, an idea mooted by a Jacobite emissary, by name Graham, in May 1748 but not pursued.[46] Above all England and France were bitter competitors in distant oceans and on distant continents. There was no reason why this hostility should lead directly to war in Europe, but it might.

As to Russia, there was no fundamental reason why there should be hostility between that Empire and Prussia, but Prussia must always watch the situation on the eastern flank. Potentially, Russia would always be the greatest danger. War with Russia should always be avoided – they disposed of cruel, savage hordes, Tartars, Kalmuks, tribes which burn and devastate. To girdle Russia, Prussia needed a defensible eastern border, sufficient influence in Poland to make reality of a border on the Vistula. And Poland presented an enigma, a confusion, a problem. There was a Polish constitution which was simultaneously aristocratic – primitively so, giving power to factions of powerful families, reactionaries remote from the development of European civilization; and anarchic. Poland – this was a recurrent theme of Frederick's and it inevitably surfaced in the *First Political Testament* – might well give birth to the next serious European war. The nobles were divided between adherents of Russia, like the Czartoryskis, and adherents of Austria. The monarchy was elective. The King was at present a German prince, the Elector of Saxony (although Frederick resolutely addressed Stanislas, Duke of Lorraine, exiled from his Polish kingdom, as '*Majesté*', and 'King of Poland' in letters). The Saxon royal family of Wettin had converted to Catholicism thus qualifying for election to the Polish throne. The situation in Poland was of inevitable importance to Prussia, not least because Polish territory separated one part of Prussia from the rest.

Russia would always have designs on Poland. But great internal changes were bound to come in Russia – Frederick included in this section of the *Testament* some disobliging comments on the Tsarina Elizabeth. Prussia would be best served by civil war in Russia, and its disintegration: meanwhile, be watchful. A stronger Sweden, a Scandinavian counterweight to Russia in the Baltic region, would be of advantage to Prussia.

Within Germany, within the Empire itself, Frederick turned to Saxony. Saxony was Brandenburg's near neighbour – only a day's ride from Berlin. There were frequent difficulties on the border – Prussian officers in pursuit of deserters beyond the frontier were occasionally subjects of complaints, complaints as to which, in Frederick's view, his ministers were sometimes excessively legalistic and over-scrupulous in seeing the Saxon point of view.[47] Saxon behaviour was often absurd. Frederick learned that the Saxon court had complained to Rome because the Papal Nuncio in Dresden had not been given a Cardinal's hat, as had those in Vienna, Madrid, Lisbon and Paris – and threatened that if this were not righted the Nuncio's mission would have to close! Such ludicrous outbursts ('*incartades*') would get them nowhere, Frederick wrote. To him this was typically Saxon.

Nevertheless, Saxony mattered. If Prussia were distracted elsewhere she could be defenceless against a Saxon enemy whereas if Saxony were under Prussian control there would be significant additional strategic depth to defence. That said, Frederick wrote that it would be unnecessary and undesirable ever to absorb much territory west of the Elbe. If Saxony were to join forces with Maria Theresa in hostility to him it would be easy to invade that country, and it should be done. The only other territorial acquisition which he would welcome if events moved that way would be in the east – Polish Prussia. These two acquisitions would help make Prussia defensible – against Russia, and against Austria. Prussia, a land power, could not afford a navy; but there was always a potential threat in the Baltic, and Prussia should have Danzig, and a small coastal fleet despite the expense. Above all Prussia must never acquire colonies overseas.

Frederick described his thoughts about possible territorial acquisitions – Saxony, Swedish Pomerania – as '*Rêveries politiques*' and it is unsurprising that historians have cited them as evidence that – contrary to his assertions – the war which was to begin in 1756 was not primarily a defensive or preventive war against a formidable coalition of enemies but planned from the start as an aggressive war of conquest.[48]

It may have been unwise to spend so much ink on '*rêveries*', but Frederick was not writing for publication. He was committing innermost thoughts to paper, even when those thoughts were dangerous or transient. This part of his *Testament* of 1752 became a battleground for a '*Historikerstreit*' about his real intentions and thus his guilt or innocence for what happened later. It may be best not to deduce too much from Frederick's speculative fancies but to concentrate on the facts of power, the 'correlation of forces' as they presented themselves to the King of Prussia at the time of writing. For in his mind Frederick returned always to Austria – to the house of Austria, to the Habsburgs, to the Imperial crown.

At present, he wrote, nobody could challenge the Habsburg dynasty for that crown – nor should they. It was certainly not something to which a King of Prussia should aspire, although there was no legal reason to exclude a Hohenzollern – or, for that matter, a Protestant. But it would be a mistake. Prussia had no natural frontier and must be strong within its own borders, compact. Its sovereign must be devoted to defending those borders rather than pursuing the will-o'-the-wisp of a vain title devoid of actual power. Conceivably one day a Bavarian prince, particularly if the Palatinate were united to Bavaria, might think differently about Habsburg pretensions, but not yet. And at present Austria, with or without the Empire, was irreconcilable.

The *First Political Testament* is more impressive when Frederick is writing about the practical principles of Prussian kingship than when it becomes a contemporary survey. His assumptions were too subject to changing circumstances and much of his forecasting was simply wrong. To a modern reader, however, many of his concerns have a curiously familiar ring. There is the concern with the internal fragility of Poland, the sense that Poland is vulnerable and yet may at any time provide a *casus belli*. There is the admiration for France, tempered by the feeling that France may always use others as stalking horses in a policy while keeping her own options open and her decisions concealed. There is the question mark posed over British policy towards involvement on the continent. There is the even larger question mark over the future development of Russia – menace? or chaos? There is, above all, a sense that Prussia is surrounded by unpredictable forces. And there are shrewd aphorisms: 'Don't threaten: dogs which bark don't bite'; 'Politics consists more in profiting from favourable circumstances than preparing them in advance.'

Frederick's words about Austria might have been penned even more vigorously had he been able to look forward one year, and the sense of being surrounded by potential enemies and ill-wishers might have been more pronounced. The first months of 1753 were marked by rumours, reported to Frederick as current in Paris, Dresden, Vienna, London and St Petersburg, that Frederick was preparing to invade Saxony; that he was getting ready for war. Furthermore it was being put about (and credited, he thought, by his uncle, George II) that he was simultaneously contemplating an invasion of Hanover.[49]

Frederick did his best to dismiss these rumours as ludicrous but they were, nevertheless, sinister. They strengthened his sense of isolation, and the mistrust which he so often evinced – to excess, but frequently with reason – aroused the same feeling in others. He watched with a sharp eye the movements of troops reported near his borders from time to time – in Livonia, in Bohemia. Europe throbbed with suspicions. There had been a time when the feelings and intentions of Prussia had been of only domestic German interest. No longer – the Silesian wars and Frederick's personality had changed all that. He had propelled his kingdom into a prominence which would now be a constant factor in European affairs and it carried penalties as well as opportunities.

There were good reasons for Frederick's anxieties besides the rumours of his own imminent aggressions, rumours he denounced as absurd. In 1753 Wenzel Anton, Count – later Prince – von Kaunitz-Rietberg, became State Chancellor to Maria Theresa, and her principal policy adviser.

Kaunitz, a contemporary of Frederick in age, had been Governor of the Austrian Netherlands, and then had represented Austria at the peace negotiations at Aix-la-Chapelle in 1748. He had been sent to Paris as ambassador in 1750, a congenial posting and one where he formed two opinions which largely guided his life and his career. The first was that the greatest menace to the house of Austria was the King of Prussia. The second was that, to outface and if possible destroy Prussia, Austria must form an alliance with France.

In cultivating a French alliance Kaunitz, while ambassador, had only limited success. Paris was not yet ready for the sort of overturning of alliances which would be involved in an understanding with the traditional enemy in Vienna, as well as in a breach with the counterweight – however difficult and unpredictable – in Berlin. But Kaunitz was clear in his own mind that there could be no security for the Habsburgs while Prussia remained as strong as it was and in possession of Silesia. To him this dictated the forming, somehow, of a major anti-Prussian alliance. He embodied all that Frederick feared and often supposed, and gave reason to the latter's policies. Frederick admired Kaunitz as a man of outstanding talents.

Frederick's envoy in Vienna, Klinggraeffen, reported at first on Kaunitz's 'honeyed words' and the agreeable sentiments about Frederick which he expressed to all.[50] But Frederick soon realized that with such a man advising Maria Theresa (and wholly in accordance with her own views) peace would never mean more than an interval between hostilities.

Kaunitz's policy took time to ripen; Frederick did not for a while appreciate the flexibility his enemies were now prepared to show. He was, however, unsurprised to receive reports in April 1754 that the Austrian Commissary General had told Maria Theresa he would only need six weeks' notice to guarantee the equipping and assembly of an army of 50,000 men in Bohemia: and could support them with eight regiments of Hungarian hussars. There were also reports of artillery horses being bought (Frederick was told of 1,600). This was apparently being done with Russian connivance. Frederick was unclear whether this was designed for effect, for threatening pressure; or for war. His reaction was to buy horses himself and to share his information with France – surely still his dependable ally in any confrontation with Austria.[51] The French ministers were somewhat dismissive, and Frederick, anxious not to appear to scaremonger, said that he, too, did not take these reports very seriously. He would, however, have been gratified by a little more French concern. He detected straws blowing in a wind.

The French were in something of a dilemma. They did not want to be involved in a general war with the British but events on both sides of the world, in America and India, were pulling in that direction. France, like England, was a maritime power, both Atlantic and Mediterranean: and a colonial power. Both were great mercantile powers. There were now frequent challenges to France on the high seas – under various pretexts. French merchant ships were sometimes being seized by the British. The great French settlements and trading posts in North America and southern India were threatened. Against this background France did not want involvement in another European war whether against or at the side of Prussia, Austria or anyone else – the Peace of Aix-la-Chapelle had ended one long struggle (somewhat indecisively) and there was surely little reason for another. As to the situation in central Europe, France was no more interested than before in the integrity of Habsburg possessions. Habsburgs were rivals, competitors, potential enemies. Hohenzollerns had until recently been, if sporadically, allies. Kaunitz had a difficult task.

As the game went on, however, there were cards he could play and he played them with skill. Personal factors were in some cases inimical to peace, or to good feeling between France and Prussia. The *maîtresse-*

en-titre of Louis XV, Mme de Pompadour, was extremely powerful: in December 1750 Frederick had sent a concerned letter to his man in Paris, Chambrier, asking for an urgent analysis of her influence on foreign affairs.[52] By 1751 she was exchanging letters as something like an equal with Maria Theresa. She was reported to be attached to the British interest and particularly hostile to Prussia. Frederick told Marischal, now in Paris, not to get involved in current intrigues to replace Mme de Pompadour with the exquisite Miss Murphy in Louis's affections[53] but the former was perfectly aware that the King of Prussia habitually mocked her among his intimates in particularly offensive terms. She was sympathetic to the ideas Kaunitz had promoted while in Paris. One woman, however powerful, could not switch the policy of a great nation overnight, but – although Frederick was slow to appreciate it – one of the major assumptions on which he based his policy, the continuing hostility between France and Austria, was becoming fragile.

A trick in the game was next to be played in northern Europe. Frederick was right in his *Political Testament* when he reckoned that Hanover would be of diminishing interest to the British – it was not a cause for which a British sovereign could arouse much enthusiasm in a British parliament. And a clause in the British Act of Settlement of the Crown specifically ruled out British war to defend territories not belonging to that crown – in other words Hanover. Nevertheless Hanover was still a factor, and during 1753 Frederick's letters, particularly to Stockholm and St Petersburg, were full of references to George II's suspicions about Prussian intentions, suspicions sharpened by certain movements of troops. These suspicions were unjustified, but they were used to promote a subsidy agreement between Britain and Russia, an agreement which would evolve two years later into a full Anglo-Russian treaty. This treaty was ostensibly defensive against Prussia or France but it was clearly aimed as a counterweight against Prussia; the British Ambassador* to St Petersburg had been charged with seeking a guarantee that a corps of Russian troops would be

---

* Guy Dickens, previously in Berlin and in Frederick's view now an unbalanced, hasty, ill-tempered man, certainly no friend to Prussia and engaged in making all the trouble he could. Frederick often encountered the malice (as he saw it) of diplomats who had crossed his path and failed to be enchanted.

made available in Livonia to operate in the Baltic area in support of Hanover against Prussia if required, a matter under discussion in August 1753.[54] From Kaunitz's standpoint the ultimate destruction of the King of Prussia – his aim – would need the cooperation of Russia. Austro-Russian relations had certainly improved and provided Poland did not become a bone of contention could improve further. Russia had territorial ambitions in the Baltic area as well as in Poland. Russia was short of money. Britain had plenty of money.

Frederick hoped that these Anglo-Russian transactions (he had copies of them all) if sent to Marischal for disclosure in Paris would help demonstrate the troubles he was having. Both in December 1753 and June 1754 he showed supporting documents to the French. It was, however, increasingly clear that these disclosures were not having the desired effect of increasing the sympathies of France. Marischal's dispatches sometimes hinted at coolness and scepticism in the French chief minister, the Marquis de Saint-Contest. 'I am not surprised,' Frederick wrote in October 1753, 'that he has no indications of these negotiations – but I can vouch for the authenticity of what you've shown him.'[55] The existing Franco-Prussian treaty – the defensive Treaty of Breslau – was only valid until March 1756.

Frederick's most important *point d'appui* at this moment must be supposed to be in Paris. The quality of his representation there and the reliability of communications mattered greatly. Frederick, unfortunately, made mistakes in that respect which would be mistakes in any age. His ambassador was the highly esteemed 'Milord Maréchal', the Earl Marischal. No more loyal servant existed, but some of their dealings – trifling in themselves – suggest that Frederick did not get the best from him. He wrote to Marischal on such matters as finding a really talented cook, an expert with sauces![56] He made this domestic request with apologies – Marischal had already applied to resign and Frederick's letter to him of gratitude and farewell is a model of elegance and affection.[57] But at the same time Frederick had instructed a subordinate at the Paris Embassy, Baron von Knyphausen, to send him periodic personal reports (with the Ambassador's knowledge) on points of detail about what was going on in France. No disloyalty was involved – Knyphausen was to do all under the supervision of Marischal – but it does not suggest a relationship of total confidence at such an important time. In some exchanges[58] Frederick gave the impression that he thought Marischal's 'feel' for French sensitivities might be inadequate or exaggerated – Marischal had suggested that Saint-Contest might take umbrage at one suggestion, instructed by Frederick. Knyphausen's reports gave satisfaction for a while although he was soon rebuked for not making them more interesting! The disaster in international relations which was already, unperceived, approaching Frederick surely had some roots in the inadequacy of his lines to and from Paris.

Marischal, at his own request, resigned. Knyphausen's reports did not give satisfaction for long. They were, Frederick told him, contradictory and superficial – they gave the impression of gossip culled from one or two women he knew and there was no serious analysis; and the King said strongly that he was dissatisfied.[59] This was a particularly stinging letter but Frederick was justified in feeling mystified. There was a new ministry in France – Saint-Contest had died and the Comte de Rouille was now effectively Foreign Minister. Frederick hoped that Knyphausen would form new and useful relationships with the men around Rouille but it did not seem to be happening. On 26 October 1754 the King wrote icily that unless Knyphausen gave better service there would have to be a change.[60]

The wretched Knyphausen tried, at the end of that month, to make his reports more interesting and sophisticated by some discussion of the Polish situation, only to be told, crushingly, that Frederick did not need instruction on Poland from that quarter. He expected to be told what was happening in France. On 26 November – and it is impossible not to sigh with relief – Frederick told Knyphausen, graciously, that his last dispatch was interesting. He ended his letter with a more general point – Knyphausen was to emphasize to Rouille that Frederick had always worked for peace and friendship with France.

For Frederick was worried. During 1754 he had sent his *Stallmeister*, Sainson, to England to buy saddle horses; and two consignments, of twenty-two and twenty-eight, had been purchased.[61] In the autumn manoeuvres of 1753 at Doberitz he had exercised sixty-one squadrons of cavalry, forty-nine infantry battalions and fifty-one pieces of artillery – the largest assembly ever.[62]

*

In seeking to promote friendship between Austria and France, Kaunitz had, inevitably, a problem with Britain. Britain was traditionally the ally of Austria and the enemy of France. There must be a question of how the new alignment, if it happened, would appear in London; and of how that would affect the British attitude to Prussia. At all times Prussia was the target of Kaunitz's policy.

Background circumstances were initially favourable, from Kaunitz's point of view. Frederick was disliked by his uncle, George II, and knew it. There were periodic disobliging references to Frederick in the British Parliament, which he would always (he said) treat with the contempt they deserved.[63] And Frederick's attitude in the matter of the Silesian debts had been regarded by British ministers as, on occasion, insulting.[64] But, more importantly, the Anglo-Russian treaty, based on money, had undertones of hostility to Prussia. In some contexts, therefore, Britain was locked into an anti-Prussian stance which could be to Austria's advantage, particularly if more life could be breathed into the long-standing Austro-British friendship, as some in Britain hoped. The British had made friendly gestures. They had supported Maria Theresa's move to get her son made 'King of the Romans'. They had concluded subsidy agreements with both Bavaria and Saxony – presumably hoping that in certain circumstances those states might be induced to make common cause against France. For Kaunitz it must be a question of whether these tendencies and gestures could ever be strong enough to offset Britain's deep hostility to France. Would this hostility now extend to France's future ally (if matters went well), Austria?

Frederick's system had needed the neutrality of Britain, which he tried to obtain by avoiding threats to Hanover, and by a correct rather than effusive relationship with Britain's enemy, France. Cool correctness with a neutral Britain, cool cordiality with France, correct wariness with Russia – if these were maintained Prussia should be able to face the hostility of Austria and a European balance looked possible to maintain. These were the calculations of 1754 and 1755, and it is remarkable that for a long time Frederick failed to perceive what was happening. He saw some things clearly. He was certainly right to see that British policy would be concerned less with Europe than with the mercantilist struggle with France. It was understandable that he disliked the implications of the Anglo-Russian treaty, with its hostility to Prussia, although he was reluctant to take Russian enmity too seriously. He often asserted that no real conflict of interest existed between Russia and Prussia and he tended to dismiss reports from St Petersburg of Russian military preparations as *'une illusion toute pure'.*[65] Russian military measures, he said, were taken in order to justify British subsidies, no more. In spite of this somewhat complacent reasoning Frederick realized that the indefensible frontiers of the Russian Empire produced an endemic sense of vulnerability which might lead to a search for increased security in a Russian 'forward policy' – and British subsidy might help support such a policy. And there were, it was true, signs of a strengthening of the Russian army near Prussia's eastern borders, just as there had been during the Russo-Swedish tension of 1749.

Poland was an added source of insecurity under almost any combination of circumstances; the internal situation of the country was frequently such as to give one or other neighbour an excuse to interfere. The constitution tended to make succession a matter of inevitable intrigue – even war. Bestuzhov was an enemy and an Austrophile. The Russian Tsarina was lazy and pleasure-loving. And Frederick was (in 1753) informed by his agents of the secret clauses of the Austro-Russian treaty of 1746 which envisaged the dismemberment of Prussia with Russian agreement or connivance.

Nevertheless, Frederick felt able to cope with such Russian threat as existed. He did not believe that all things were as they appeared. He thought it uncertain that the Russians would get as much English money as they supposed – it might turn on such unpredictables as the British Parliament and the reluctance of the Pelham brothers – the Duke of Newcastle and his brother Henry – the latter, Frederick reckoned, sympathetic to Prussia as well as hostile to expenditure.[66] And although Frederick was particularly sensitive about British subsidies to Russia he was encouraged by a dispatch from Paris, early in 1754. The British Ambassador to France, the Earl of Albemarle, had told Saint-Contest (then in office) that there would not, in fact, be an Anglo-Russian subsidy agreement. Furthermore the Frenchman had responded to Albemarle that if Prussia were, in consequence of such an agreement, actually to be attacked by Russia, ostensibly to help

Hanover, she could count on the support of France. Frederick wanted – needed – dispatches like this with their implication that Franco-Prussian understanding was a constant factor. '*Recht! Sehr gut!*' he wrote in the margin.[67]

His tragedy was to believe it.

I I

Quadrille to Distant Gunfire

Frederick could, if provoked, show a most undiplomatic anger. He was infuriated by anything he thought offensive to the honour of his family and equally enraged by presumption – by an official exceeding his duties and his place. Sometimes it did not matter that the official in question was not Frederick's, but the servant of another prince. An example occurred in October 1754 – unimportant in itself but showing his style of business.

Baron von Seckendorff, chief minister to the Margrave of Ansbach (brother-in-law of Frederick, he who had sent 'a sort of lunatic' as envoy to Frederick somewhat earlier!), wrote to Frederick's minister, Podewils, complaining of the financial mismanagement and debts of Frederick's other brother-in-law, the Margrave of Bayreuth. There was animosity between the two Margravates and the letter implied that Frederick, as head of the house of Brandenburg (to which both belonged), might help to improve matters. There had been a convention between the two, approved by Frederick, two years previously.

Podewils reported to Frederick. It was clear that Ansbach, or at least Seckendorff, was making trouble and Podewils wrote to the King with diffidence.[1] If it were true that Bayreuth was bankrupting himself and his state it might not be a matter of complete indifference to Frederick. On the other hand the King might wish to remain unconnected. What was the royal will?

Frederick wrote sharply, and few could write more sharply. He wrote for the record. He was astonished, he said, at the absurdity of Seckendorff's letter. It was gross impertinence to talk of Bayreuth's mismanagement, considering that Ansbach itself was almost bankrupt. This scoundrel (*'faquin'*) Seckendorff – who was a nephew of Frederick's old enemy of the 'English marriage' project – was trying to make trouble between two Margraves and to ensnare Frederick in his deplorable plots. Frederick wished that Ansbach could know Seckendorff's real character! There was more, and Frederick's instruction to Podewils was simple: 'send him a copy of this letter!' Podewils did so, earnestly imploring the recipient never to refer to the matter again! Frederick could certainly not be accused of hiding behind his officials. He was, of course, particularly indignant because the matter touched Wilhelmina, whom he had recently visited for a few days. Her health was not good, she had needed for health reasons to travel to Avignon, and there were insinuations of domestic extravagance in the Seckendorff letter which angered her loving brother.

Such matters were irritants only. And there were other minor irritants: the young hereditary prince of Hesse-Cassel (George II's son-in-law) became a Catholic, which could only gratify Vienna. The main thrust of Frederick's correspondence at the end of 1754, however, showed optimism, particularly about Franco-Prussian relations and Franco-Austrian enmity. He heard from Knyphausen – still nervously keeping his place in Paris – that the envoy had had a good interview with the new French minister, Rouille. Frederick sent back a genial letter of something like advice. He hoped that the French were not complacent about their possessions in America – when a British fleet, with reinforcements embarked, reached that continent it might be hard for the French to avoid being turned out![2] It was a letter, neutral but friendly as to France, which could only have been written if the relationship was unclouded by particular suspicions. And when he wrote, for Rouille's information, a long letter of complaint on 28 December 1754 about Austrian behaviour he could hope – almost assume – that it would find a sympathetic reader.[3]

The new year, 1755, coincided with the death of the Sultan and the possibility of upheavals in the Balkans. Frederick observed that he hoped differences between France and Britain would be peacefully settled, but that if one were to suppose war inevitable between the two it would be best that it should come now, when Austria would be uneasy about the aftermath of changes in Constantinople, rather than at some time when her hands were free to 'create diversions'.[4] He meant 'best for France'. 'Diversions' created by Austria would, all too probably, involve Frederick: at France's side. He sent new ciphers and orders to his commander in the county of Glatz, de la Motte Fouqué, and further secret instructions 'for use in time of war' to the Prussian commanders at Schweidnitz, Neisse, Cosel, Brieg, Breslau and Glogau. He might be ostensibly writing about Franco-British rivalry in distant territories, or about Austria's relations with Turkey (an emissary had left for Constantinople to sound out the Porte on a possible defensive and commercial treaty between the Ottoman government and Prussia) but his mind was never far from Silesia, the Oder, the Elbe.[5]

In February 1755 Frederick wrote to his ambassadors in both London and Paris that he would bet ten to one on war between France and Britain, perhaps without deliberate intent, probably confined to maritime operations. He sometimes described this as inevitable and he calculated how it might go. The objects of war would be maritime and commercial supremacy as well as colonial domination in America and India. He was well-informed on the number of warships each power could put to sea. This – and money – would be the decisive factor. His sympathies were with France.

Britain, Frederick thought, was determined on war. British proposals being put to France, from what he heard of them, seemed clearly unacceptable, and intended to be so. He hoped France could reach agreement with Spain – the Spanish would not look on increased British power in the Americas with enthusiasm. Frederick was anxious to avoid any suspicion that he was stoking the fires, '*que je voudrais souffler le feu*'.[6] Nevertheless he was now writing of war as a certainty. He wrote on 5 April to Klinggraeffen, his man in Vienna, that he was assuming the King of England and his ministers would try to make hostilities general after the first shots were fired. British policy, he said – and British diplomacy in both Austria and Russia – was directed to this end; the broadest possible coalition against France.[7] He had seen it all before. Subsidies were being offered to German princes (like Brunswick, who was also now receiving subsidies from France). The German princes were usually short of money and open to offers. Frederick kept himself informed. War was unavoidable.

To what extent did he wish it? Reason suggests 'not at all'. The time of renewal of the Franco-Prussian treaty was approaching and he supposed that if war between Britain and France spread to Europe there would be French pressure on him to take part and to launch operations against Hanover, which would almost certainly involve Russia without much prospect of advantage for Prussia. When Rouille discussed an offensive against Hanover 'in case of war', Frederick sent a discouraging reply. Such operations, he said, were easier to talk about than execute. There were 60,000 Russian soldiers in Courland, on Prussia's borders, while Saxony – her near neighbour to the south – had understandings with Britain, to say nothing of Austria.[8] Rouille responded (flatteringly) that the threats to Prussia of Russia and Austria were well appreciated but that operations by either were likely to be too slow to frustrate the King of Prussia![9] Such genial exchanges with Paris were still possible and Frederick could regard them, whatever their outcome, as part of the natural order of things.

If, as Frederick now assumed, Austria were ultimately to be involved on the side of Britain in a war against France, Prussia would probably, albeit reluctantly, be engaged. He had experienced plenty of war against Austria with the remote and inadequate military support of France and he had learned its hazards – among others it was always uncertain what part Russia would play. He would be ready for war on his borders if it happened, but he preferred the idea of Franco-British hostilities confined to the high seas and remote continents, or even not happening at all, although he believed that the situation of the two great maritime powers made conflict inevitable.

As to the ultimate outcome, whatever his sympathies, Frederick was sure that the British situation was inherently stronger. On 7 April Knyphausen wrote from Paris an optimistic dispatch on the strength of France's financial resources, a dispatch which Frederick found superficial and unconvincing. Knyphausen had recently been doing a little better; this was a relapse, and Frederick's response makes the reader, two and a half centuries later, flinch for Knyphausen.[10]

I have received your report of 7th April which has greatly shocked me with its pitiful reasoning. You have attempted to compare the advantages France possesses in Europe with those available to England and I don't wish to disguise from you that I have never received any account from one of my representatives at a foreign court as feeble and insubstantial as yours; nor one so packed with self-evident errors and absurd exaggerations ('*gasconnades*') the product of a youth without experience or background . . .

There was much more. Frederick told him that he was listening to *petits-maîtres* who never left Paris; the King could have learned as much from a boy still at college. He had studied foreign state finances with the expert eye of one who was his own Treasurer and he knew Knyphausen's analysis was facile wishful-thinking, characteristic of a young man perhaps overawed by the splendour of the court to which he was accredited. Frederick was, on the contrary, well aware of the fragility of the finances of the Kings of France, their dependence on the sale of offices and monopolies, their cash-producing but enfeebling grants of nobility for office with consequential tax privileges; their corruption; their extravagance. Brilliant management had sometimes massaged the ills of the system but it was opposed at all points to Frederick's principles and, greatly though he admired much in France, he thought Knyphausen's impressions ridiculous. The King of France, he wrote, had his eyes closed to the deplorable situation of his affairs.[11]

Frederick's opinion was well-based but it is possible that the ferocity of his rebuke derived, perhaps subconsciously, from another source. Frederick may already, without admitting it to himself, have needed to believe in the ultimate inner strength of Britain more than that of France. He may have already felt the shadow of isolation, disquiet about the French connection. His language throughout this pregnant year and the next shows on most occasions a sense of vulnerability rather than ambition, let alone aggressive intent. He was, as ever, particularly sensitive to any news of relationships between Austria and Russia; and he reacted with suspicion to a report that the aged Russian general commanding in Livonia, George von Browne, had visited Königsberg incognito and was *en route* to Vienna or Prague to see his relation, Field Marshal Maximilian von Browne, an old opponent in the first Silesian war where he had fought at Mollwitz and later served under Traun. Browne, aged fifty-one, was the son of an Irish *émigré* who had been made a field marshal after service for Maria Theresa in Italy and was now effectively commander-in-chief in Bohemia. Were these two concerting contingency plans? It was natural to worry, although Frederick supposed the former, George, was probably visiting a daughter who was being educated at a convent in Prague. Meanwhile he followed with great interest all that he could learn of the strength and movements of French and British naval forces in the Atlantic. In June he toured the Prussian Rhineland provinces, Cleve and Wesel, hoping to see Knyphausen who could travel there from Paris. He learned from Podewils that the French Ambassador in Berlin, La Touche, had been taking soundings about renewal of the Franco-Prussian defensive Treaty of Breslau, due to expire in June 1756.[12]

Also while at Wesel Frederick decided to travel *incognito* into Holland with two companions and to visit Amsterdam. On the boat to Utrecht by canal he saw a fellow-traveller, one Henri de Catt, who was a student and was planning to visit a distinguished professor at the university. Frederick accosted him: 'What is your name, sir? Come in here [Frederick had a cabin], you will be more comfortable.'

De Catt had no idea who the man was, and they talked of politics, philosophy, religion, the state of Europe. Frederick declared that he had studied philosophy a good deal and they discussed its principles. He knew least, he said, of politics: and invited de Catt to call on him at his inn, perhaps to sup. De Catt had made other arrangements and could not accept; and Frederick left for Arnhem in the small hours of the following morning. Six weeks later de Catt had a letter from Potsdam and first learned the identity of this argumentative and deeply impressive stranger. Frederick offered him a post at court of which illness prevented acceptance, but in 1757 the offer was to be repeated.[13]

There were other changes pending in his intimate circle in Berlin, for at about the same time Maupertius, with some embarrassment, appealed again for Frederick's help. A girl in Berlin was parading an infant and threatening 'a certain gentleman' with exposure as the father unless he paid. Blackmail. Now the same girl was trying the same trick in respect of the ex-President of the Academy, Maupertuis. Maupertuis was confident he was *not* the father – 'I took scrupulous precautions, the same care as a veritable *père* would have taken!' – but he had paid up when she acknowledged in writing that the child was not his. The girl took the money and returned to get another golden egg from the goose who had already paid eighty *écus*. She was arrested and committed to Spandau but then released and Maupertuis, in some panic, appealed to the King for protection.

Frederick was highly amused, confirmed the girl's release but placed her under very severe injunctions were she ever to approach Maupertuis again. He gave Maupertuis leave to travel to Italy 'for his health'.[14]

Frederick's jaunt into Holland was a brief holiday from the pressing business of renewal of treaties and the dangers of European war. Formal renewal of alliance, albeit defensive, with a power – France – about to engage in a major war (as Frederick saw it) was not to be undertaken lightly. On 8 June 1755 British warships actually exchanged fire with French off the coast of America. The crisis which would before long involve most of Europe was first developing at sea, as Frederick had supposed it would. The French Government initially showed restraint, wishing to fix the onus and odium of hostilities on Britain and hoping that peace might yet break out. There was, as yet, no seizure of British ships in French ports as proposed by the more warlike French ministers.[15] Frederick regarded this as timidity; it would alienate rather than encourage others such as Austria, Sweden, Denmark. Frederick was commenting on all this as a *soi-disant* ally of France, albeit not one committed to support specific actions. 'The conduct of the court of France in present circumstances could hardly be more feeble,' he wrote to Michel, his man in London.

He expected that the next few months would see renewed attempts by Rouille to get him to move against Hanover as a diversion and he briefed his ambassador carefully. The present time was inauspicious for such an operation. Might not France, instead, seek to enlist the support of Denmark? There was personal animosity of the Danish sovereign towards George II, whose Electorate of Hanover was contiguous to the Danish king's province of Holstein.[16] And – a remarkable suggestion which, predictably, came to nothing – might not this *'funeste guerre qui selon toutes les apparences entraînera la plus grande partie de l'Europe'*[17] be prevented by the joint mediation of Frederick and Maria Theresa? He floated this idea in a letter to Klinggraeffen in Vienna on 2 August and followed it with a letter to his brother-in-law the reigning Duke of Brunswick, ten days later. Brunswick, he thought, might further the proposal by his contacts with the Hanoverian court* – the Duke had been trying to get some sort of commitment from Prussia in case Brunswick were menaced by France and Frederick used him as something of an intermediary with London. Could war still not be pre-empted by mediation?

Frederick in the role of mediator was a difficult proposition to credit for many of the courts of Europe, and for none more than that of Vienna whose sovereign was cast as co-mediator with her own most inveterate enemy. But Frederick was encouraged – or encouraged himself – in what must with hindsight be regarded as fantasy by his sense that the British Government (as he supposed) was worried by Austrian lack of enthusiasm for the British anti-French cause, a cause which had formerly bound Britain and Austria together. If the British were, as Frederick (reasonably) reckoned, anxious for their connections and possessions in Germany, and if they suspected their Austrian former ally of being lukewarm about war with France, might there not be a chance for peace? At least on the continent of Europe? And for the King of Prussia to play a useful part in brokering that peace? He was, after all, not without influence in Germany. His army, probably the best in Europe, stood on the borders of Hanover, the King of England's fief, and of Bohemia, treasured possession of Maria Theresa. He was the nephew of George II. His friendship and alliance with France, even if not yet formally renewed, was an accepted fact of European affairs.

In all these exchanges Frederick was pursuing peace – a peace which would be for Prussia's benefit. He felt his position was strong and might be pivotal. He wrote again to Brunswick in September 1755 to say that he was uncommitted as to what should happen when his formal treaty with France expired in the following year. He was a free agent – open to offers by Britain or others. He certainly did not want to reduce his value as an intermediary or friend by giving the impression that he was absolutely committed to France or to anyone else.[18] He was anxious to discover the personal attitude of Mme de Pompadour to all this and Knyphausen told him that she was now very hostile to Britain (she had earlier been thought friendly to that

---

* There were several branches of the Brunswick family. George II was Elector of Hanover and Duke of Brunswick-Lüneburg; Frederick's sister, Charlotte, had married his wife's brother, the Duke of Brunswick-Wolfenbüttel, who was also cousin to Frederick's general, the Duke of Brunswick-Bevern.

country) but that her hostility (or so it was reported) was constrained by her financial difficulties. English credit was important to her; Frederick's private information was that the lady had managed to move between £30,000 and £40,000 equivalent from France into British funds.[19] Knyphausen reported that Mme de Pompadour was certainly involved in all important matters of state. Less convincingly, he wrote that she displayed *le plus grand attachement* for Frederick! Frederick was not inclined to believe this. He knew that she was aware of and resented the brutal sarcasm he often indulged about her person and character. He knew that she and her circle described his court in scandalous terms as unnatural. He called his greyhound bitches his *'Marquises de Pompadour'* – adding 'but less expensive'.[20]

Frederick thought it possible – and hoped – that France might prefer a war confined to maritime operations. He nevertheless reckoned that if war came the British might well again deploy troops, probably Hanoverians and German auxiliaries, in the Low Countries. Then France would once again find an enemy on her own borders. Surely France had an interest in preventing war, in negotiation if it could honourably be done?[21] Meanwhile he thought French reactions to British moves feeble. Feebleness would make peace more elusive by encouraging obduracy in the British.

In all this Frederick had miscalculated and continued to miscalculate. He learned with equanimity of harsh messages between London and Vienna; apparently Austria was indignant that the British were contemplating a major war without prior discussion with allies, of which, surely, Austria was one. Frederick supposed this fitted the general picture he had formed – of an Austria reluctant to underwrite a British war effort beyond some absolute minimum, resentful at lack of consultation and determined to exact a large price in British subsidies for any effort against France demanded from Austria herself. Austria, he imagined, was mediating a lukewarm attitude, a position from which to bargain. But Frederick was wholly mistaken. Kaunitz had done his work well. Austria was not mediating lukewarmness. She was preparing to change sides.

Kaunitz needed a decisive breach between France and Prussia. For him, Prussia was the enemy. France, Austria's accepted enemy hitherto, was inching towards war with Britain, Austria's ally hitherto. This was a familiar pattern but now Kaunitz needed French rapprochement with Austria and disenchantment with Prussia. He also hoped for Russian support if Russia could be seduced from her dependence on British subsidies. In this way Prussia could be isolated, hemmed by Russia, by Austria, by such of the German states as Kaunitz could enrol in an anti-Prussian coalition, and, ultimately, by France. Only Britain would be outside such an anti-Prussian camp, and Britain, primarily concerned with her struggle against France at sea and in America, would be unlikely to bring much relief to Prussia – except, perhaps, with money. It was a grand design, long nurtured.

It was also a design which Frederick showed few signs of recognizing. In September 1755 – with war still not formally declared between France and Britain – he was complacently writing to ask whether the British Government would do anything to gain his neutrality or whether they were indifferent,[22] and writing by the same post of his satisfaction that Belle-Isle, whom he regarded highly, was again in favour in France.[23] These were the letters of a sovereign who reckoned he had advantages to offer, that he was himself comparatively unthreatened, that he could maintain neutrality, and that he – as ever – wished France well.

But straws were again beginning to blow in the wind. At the end of September Klinggraeffen reported from Vienna that a friend 'who moved in very well-informed circles' had heard it said that Frederick had warned France against designs on Hanover 'which he would oppose, and that this had created coldness between the King of Prussia and France'. Rumour, gossip, disinformation, trouble-making – insubstantial and baseless – all this might be; but why? Frederick asked sharply, describing the story as pure nonsense. Kaunitz was reported to be in a bad mood with the British minister in Vienna, Sir Robert Keith: and Frederick suggested that the British might be jibbing at the Austrian price demanded for fielding troops against the French. Such an explanation for a *froideur* fitted his unchanged preconceptions. He continued to think and write that the French were showing weakness and lethargy in their reactions to such British outrages as seizing vessels at sea.[24] They were not encouraging others who wished them well but respected strength. Frederick also learned that the French were discussing certain 'arrangements' with Saxony, a state often to be found among Prussia's opponents. That meant money.

Had France lost direction, confidence and self-respect? A new French Ambassador Extraordinary to Prussia, the Duc de Nivernois, had been nominated and Frederick told Knyphausen to discover his instructions so that he, Frederick, could be prepared, an order which took some time to obey. He presumed that Nivernois would seek to conclude a new Franco-Prussian treaty when the present arrangements ended, in the following May, 1756; and he looked forward to finding himself in a strong position to strike a bargain. His envoy in London, Abraham Michel, had told him that the British were wondering with some unease how far Frederick might go to help France. They were awaiting anxiously the outcome of Nivernois's embassy. They realized, Michel wrote on 30 September 1755, that if the Russians (following a British subsidy agreement) were to move troops into any part of Germany Frederick would react,[25] and the situation become fraught. The British thus put a price on his friendship, and the French were sending a distinguished Duke with, presumably, another price in his pocket.

Frederick was gratified by the sense that the great contesting parties might compete for his friendship. He told Michel that the British were right – Russian troops moving into Germany would bring him into the war against Russia's British friends and paymasters; by this he hoped to keep his price high. As to France, Frederick began to take a hard line which would have rejoiced Kaunitz's heart. France was apparently negotiating with Saxony about subsidies and on 18 October Frederick wrote to Knyphausen[26] that if these negotiations succeeded he would not renew his treaty with France. He confirmed the point ten days later.[27]

Frederick may have been too precipitate. It may be that a more accommodating attitude would have postponed, even averted, the breach with France which was what his enemies most desired. In the event his diplomacy culminated in a quarrel with France and an agreement with Britain, and the latter has been defined by his critics as the cause of the former. It is hard to be certain what was cause and what effect but it is surely arguable that Frederick's ultimate agreement with Britain was effect rather than cause; that he had, in fact, lost the initiative in foreign affairs; lost it to Kaunitz but failed to realize the loss for some time.

Frederick was certainly uneasy. He wrote to Klinggraeffen in Vienna in November that the Austrian Government seemed to be disagreeing with British ideas for the war against France, while the French Government seemed to be distancing themselves from ideas of a land campaign against Britain and Hanover. Might there, he wondered, be some 'trickery afoot?' Some secret Franco-Austrian agreement that Austria would give no support to Britain provided France agreed not to attack in the Low Countries?[28] Frederick was still thinking in terms of the two irreconcilable enemies, Austria and France, nevertheless doing some short-term trading against the overarching phenomenon of world-wide war between France and Britain. Frederick was right in supposing that discussions were under way between France and Austria. He was wrong in supposing that what was hatching was confined to France's impending war with Britain. What was hatching – and this would not be clear to him for some time – was the destruction of Prussia.

Nevertheless Frederick, during that autumn of 1755, had an increasing sense of being isolated and hemmed. To the south Austria was as intransigent as ever and Saxony was in the pocket of Russia, while negotiating, it seemed, subsidies with France. In the east Russia had secured her subsidy treaty with Britain but during November Frederick heard of talks between Vienna and St Petersburg about ultimately dismembering Prussia. He hoped to maintain his own neutrality between France and Britain and had indicated that he was in no hurry to renew a formal treaty with France, while always writing of French difficulties with the sympathy of an ally. The British hoped for his neutrality. The German states of the Empire (except Hanover) had largely succumbed to Kaunitz's pressure or cajolery and were prepared to oppose Prussia. It was in this atmosphere that Frederick decided he needed more friends.

On 13 January 1756 the Duc de Nivernois arrived at Potsdam. Frederick found him delightful – a polished, witty man, exactly what Frederick liked a Frenchman to be. Nivernois was the only foreign ambassador ever to be invited to stay at Sans Souci. For his part Nivernois found Frederick entrancing, and was at once drawn by the beauty of the King's voice and diction as well as by the vivacity of his wit. He thought Frederick touched by vanity, and perhaps impetuosity;

but respected his obvious indifference to what others thought of him. The Duke had been briefed in Paris that Frederick might be contemplating some formal understanding with Britain – a prospect disturbing to France. He was charged with clarifying the situation, and perhaps promoting a tentative resumption of the Franco-Prussian treaty, despite Frederick's recent rejection. Nothing secretly agreed between France and Austria would have yet precluded this.

The Duke was received with due pomp. At their first meeting Frederick soon became relaxed and friendly, leading the conversation to philosophy, to the state of the French Academy, to matters interesting, cultivated and neutral. Nivernois soon made clear that he was hoping for some more substantial political discussion. Frederick suggested another, private, audience later and Nivernois gladly assented.

It took place. But in the interval between the two audiences Frederick had agreed to sign the final form of what became the Convention of Westminster, a convention whose draft he had approved ten days earlier, a convention whereby Prussia undertook to help defend Hanover against attack. Formally it was a promise to join the British in resisting any incursion of foreign troops into Germany.* For Britain it effectively disarmed any idea of a Russian threat to the Electorate. To most of Europe, however, it was at that juncture, and unmistakably, a declaration against France. What other foreign troops than French could intrude into Germany? Only the Russians; and there was already a Russo-British agreement to cooperate in defence of Hanover against outsiders, specifically France or Prussia which could now be seen as unnecessary in respect of Prussia if Prussia was signing up as Britain's ally. The cap only fitted France. The Convention of Westminster secured Hanover, and the British hoped that by antagonizing France it would have the effect of drawing Frederick firmly into the British camp. George II had with some reluctance suppressed his sentiments about the King of Prussia – 'a bad friend, a bad ally, a bad relation, a bad neighbour, the most ill-disposed and dangerous prince in Europe'.[30]

At their second and private audience Frederick told Nivernois all

---

* Frederick insisted on the term 'Germany' rather than 'Holy Roman Empire'.[29] He stated that the purpose of the convention was to keep Germany neutral.

about the convention, to the Frenchman's astonishment. At the same meeting he took the opportunity to send particularly affectionate messages to Louis XV, saying that France should look elsewhere (than to Prussia) for allies and suggesting that an understanding between France and Austria would be most natural. Until recently he had assumed the antipathy between Habsburg and Bourbon to be so ineradicable that this sort of *ballon d'essai* could be no more than a jest. Times had changed.

It has been easily assumed by critics that Frederick's action in signing the Convention of Westminster was gratuitous, in causing an avoidable breach with France, and was a cynical step towards a European war on which he had already decided, for his own purposes. In fact Nivernois was convinced that Frederick genuinely wanted peace not war and there seems no overriding reason to dismiss Frederick's own *exposé* at the time. He told Nivernois that the convention was an expedient, surely tolerable to France if properly understood. It committed Frederick to no sort of hostilities unless they were forced upon him. It was a purely defensive treaty which would help keep Russia out of Germany; and a neutral Germany, which the convention was designed to ensure, would be of no harm to France. As to Prussian ambitions, her military strength (he demonstrated to Nivernois) was only half that of her enemies – among whom he certainly did not include France.[31] And it was a well-established fact that Frederick had unresolved reasons for dispute with Britain and his uncle. Hanover occupied some territories in Mecklenburg claimed by Prussia: Prussia had occupied Ostfriesland to which Hanover had a counter-claim. Frederick had supposed his mother to have been willed a legacy by her father, George I, which she had never received. Frederick was said, furthermore, to be habitually sarcastic about George II and his conduct in action at Dettingen. These things were personal, private, perhaps insignificant, but they argued against any pro-British prejudice in the King of Prussia.

Nevertheless Nivernois indicated courteously that France would regard Frederick's rapprochement with Britain as an unfriendly act.

French hostility took a little time to evolve, but when it did the Convention of Westminster was seen in France as an outrage. To

France, by that time, Britain was the enemy, although the two countries were formally at peace and in that same January Frederick was again mooting the improbable idea of mediating between them. At first, however, there was a certain calm. Knyphausen saw Rouille on 20 January and received the impression that he was not as opposed to Frederick's proposals for 'German neutrality' as had at first appeared. It was not, however, an agreeable interview and Rouille showed resentment at negotiations clearly undertaken by Frederick with Britain in secrecy from his ally, France.[32] For the Franco-Prussian treaty was still in force until midsummer.

Frederick's reaction to this indignation was clear and surely defensible. He saw no reason to have consulted France. His treaty with France was about to expire and nothing in the Convention of Westminster threatened her. Frederick pointed out, furthermore, that he had specifically excluded (by an additional and secret article) the Austrian Netherlands from the 'German' area to be kept neutral, so that France's hands were free in a traditional campaigning ground. He was not disposed to be too alarmed by French protests. He was told that Mme de Pompadour was strongly inclined to peace – she was worried about her debts and averse to any policies which might take Louis XV away from the pleasure and idleness he enjoyed in her company. France had, Frederick supposed, long given up ideas of trying to persuade him to move against Hanover as a French ally and he thought there need be no great reason for French opposition to his policy. He wrote to Knyphausen on 10 February 1756 asking whether his *démarche très innocente* had really inflamed the French ministers against him?[33]

It had. French hostile reaction became more formal with a seven-point protest from Rouille, which concluded that the Convention of Westminster was extraordinary, was contrary to the spirit of treaties signed between France and Prussia and was inconsistent with Prussia's true interests. If Austria and Russia were to attack Prussia France could help her. Britain not at all.[34]

Frederick returned a cool but sharp reply. M. Rouille, he wrote, seemed surprised that a King of Prussia should take into account the security of his own kingdom. Alliances are based on mutual interest and, as to Rouille's accusations of breach of agreement, nothing had been done against any article of any treaty,[35] a theme he developed point by point. He told Knyphausen that the French were only angry and surprised because a King of Prussia had failed to ask their permission – a concept without precedent. Frederick was in high spirits as he often was when he felt he had tweaked the nose of at least one major power. He thought Rouille's expostulations unreasonable and out of order. Although his dealings with Paris were with Knyphausen, 'Milord Maréchal' was still in France and Frederick wrote to Marischal playful letters about the situation. Because he had made an agreement with King George, 'People will tell you, *Mon cher Milord*, that I am a little less of a Jacobite than I was! Don't hate me for it!'[36]

Frederick persisted for some time in the belief, real or assumed, that the French had no reason to be disturbed. They could pursue their world-wide struggle against Britain and concentrate upon it – Frederick was unconcerned with that. He bore no enmity towards France and actually discussed with Nivernois renewal of the Franco-Prussian treaty in some form. And although the French were naturally upset by the suddenness and secrecy of Frederick's proceedings it is hard to accept French anger as well-based. The Convention of Westminster somewhat eased Britain's strategic situation, particularly in respect of the defence of Hanover, but it did little to affect the main Franco-British struggle. France, of course, had previously hoped to divert Britain by a threat to Hanover and had matters been different it might have been possible to persuade Prussia to mount that threat. That was now out of the reckoning – it had been mooted as recently as December 1755.[37]

Nevertheless Frederick was soon writing to Knyphausen that France had turned her hatred and anger against him rather than her principal enemy, England. The French were haggling ('*chipotages*') with Austria. Knyphausen suggested a letter from Frederick direct to Mme de Pompadour, an idea the King regarded with distaste. Knyphausen also reported the increasingly frequent interviews between the Austrian minister in Paris, Count Stahremberg, and the French ministers.

But most powerful rulers at some time in their careers suffer a particular delusion, often a strong impression formed earlier which circumstances have conspired to invalidate. Frederick wrote to Knyphausen in February 1756 that 'It remains a constant and unchanging truth that it will never be in the interest of France to work for or contribute to the aggrandisement of the house of Austria.' And Frederick still had only inklings rather than positive perceptions of what threatened him. He had felt isolated, and reckoned he now had the limited support of Britain. He had upset France but he felt this might pass as logically it should. Nevertheless in mid-March Frederick was disturbed to hear that the French minister in Vienna, the Marquis d'Aubeterre, was ostentatiously avoiding contact and courtesies with Frederick's man, Klinggraeffen.[38] By the end of the month he was *for the first time* writing to his envoys in London, Vienna and Paris about this astonishing development: an axis might be forming between Paris and Vienna! D'Aubeterre, in Vienna, was frequently closeted with Kaunitz, although in early April Frederick was still incredulous.[39] There were also indications that Austria was seeking to unite the German Catholic princes and to divide the Empire on religious lines against Prussia, a distressing prospect.

The strength of French anger at the Convention of Westminster is easier to explain by their own contemplated behaviour. There had been confidential talks between the French and Austrians over several years and the French, of course, recognized that an improved relationship with Austria would be hard to reconcile with Prussian friendship beyond a limited point. But when an Austro-French alliance was actually signed, as it was, in May 1756 at Versailles, the French protested that Frederick had driven them into this alliance by his own perfidy; the French regarded as an insult and an outrage the action of one they had at least pretended to consider an ally. The contention of perfidy is hard to reconcile with the brief (three short articles) and very moderate terms of the Convention of Westminster; a convention primarily concerned with Prussian neutrality and peace within Germany. Frederick, in his instructions to his envoys, insisted that the latter were the sole objects of the convention, and its terms support him. The real cause of French reactions and of the *Renversement des Alliances*, as it was called, was the readiness of France to abandon Prussia and make common cause with Austria. It was a French *renversement*.

The fateful treaty signed at Versailles pledged France and Austria to support each other if attacked by a third power, specifically excluding

Britain; an exclusion which preserved Austria from involvement in the impending Franco-British struggle. In the existing situation it could only refer to mutual support against Prussia. Under the treaty, furthermore, Austria was to have a free hand to reconquer Silesia with French blessing, although this was not formally written down. France seemed to get little from the treaty; the conduct of Austria was wholly consistent. Frederick was told by Klinggraeffen that his convention with Britain was regarded most unfavourably by Kaunitz although in its effects, of course, it was exactly what the latter wished. Masks were now coming off. In March 1756 Kaunitz had already suggested to Russia a combined Austro-Russian attack on Prussia and was told that the Tsarina was in full agreement with the idea. In June Russia and Austria formally renewed their alliance, although it was not actually signed until January 1757.

Meanwhile Russia started to mobilize her army, a slow and laborious proceeding; and Austria, less laborious and with advantages of recent military reform and new regulations on the Prussian model, issued orders for mobilization in July. These powers, unprovoked, were preparing for war. A great offensive coalition, the grand object of Kaunitz's policy, was being organized against Prussia. Frederick was now threatened by an alliance numbering, in sum, 90 million people against a Prussia with 5 million. His only potential ally was Britain, little interested in the affairs of the continent unless they could be made to embarrass France.

Frederick was facing a new situation. He might, perhaps, have anticipated it when he agreed to a convention with Britain but his letters give the impression of a man trailing rather than ahead of events. He at all times preserved the courtesies and compliments which mollified eighteenth-century disputes. Nivernois continued at Potsdam, grateful for the charming way his stay there had been marked. Frederick sent graceful messages of his continued regard for the glory and interests of the King of France; and continued, too, to protest – with increasing vigour and a good deal of credibility – that he wished only for peace and neutrality, the peace of Germany and the neutrality of Prussia. The warlike measures reported from Austria and Russia could not be ignored but he could truthfully say they were not responses to any moves of his own – or not yet.

Frederick had remarked Austrian preparations in Bohemia and Moravia as early as December 1755; and he was now writing to his ambassador in London with references to France as to a common enemy of Britain and Prussia. He was, however, still confident – still nourishing illusions. On the Austro-French treaty he wrote that an agreement between Paris and Vienna was so unnatural it could not last.

There was one happier development for Frederick in the anxious spring of 1756. On 11 May a new British Ambassador, Sir Andrew Mitchell, arrived at Potsdam, the first for six years. Frederick had heard that Lord Tyrawley, a well-known Irish soldier, had been nominated. Tyrawley was a veteran of many wars and a man of great distinction. He was, however, seventy-four years old. Instead, Frederick had tried to get Villiers, previously in post. He got Mitchell.

Andrew Mitchell, a Scot, had legal training, was widely read, cultivated, of catholic interests and very stable temperament. Four years older than Frederick, he had been a member of the British House of Commons since 1747 and in Scotland was a close friend of the distinguished and moderate Lord President Forbes of Culloden. A widower, he had been under-Secretary of State for Scotland and was experienced in public affairs.

Mitchell was to accompany Frederick through most of the war which was now tragically imminent, and became one of his intimates, a favoured companion who understood the King without excessive deference but soon with genuine affection. Mitchell watched Frederick at some of the most testing moments of his life, and saw his own task as the development of real understanding between Britain and Prussia. He kept offensive and trouble-making tales (of which there were plenty on offer) out of his dispatches and wrote with fairness and perception. He also wrote with honest admiration. He wrote, among other things, that amidst many attractive qualities Frederick accepted literary criticism better than any author he'd ever met! In the business of diplomacy he told his masters in London that it was necessary to be frank with the King of Prussia and say what one thought even if unpalatable; and that he took it well.[40] For his part, Frederick loved him and respected him. He described him as the Englishman (*sic*) who interested him more than any he had met, with his wide historical and literary knowledge and his great integrity; and at the end of his life, Mitchell returned to Berlin, and lived there until his death.

At their first meeting, on his day of arrival, Mitchell had a very frank general exchange with Frederick on the European situation.[41] They discussed the sympathies of the various German princes and the military potential, as Frederick saw it, of the great powers. Mitchell told him that, contrary to Frederick's expectations, Britain hoped for the support of Russia in any continental war. If this meant that British influence (and subsidies) could pre-empt Russian moves against Prussia it would, naturally, be most welcome to Frederick, but he doubted it and thought this would be the key factor on which peace in Germany depended. He was sceptical about whether Russia could be kept for long at bay and at peace, but he told Mitchell that in his view nothing would happen in that year to 'disturb the peace of Germany'.[42] He impressed the ambassador with his obvious desire for peace. He assured him that if, following Anglo-Russian agreements, Russian troops were brought into north Germany as British allies in defence of Hanover Prussia would give them facilities; but he hoped it would not arise. One long-standing trouble was settled by the Convention of Westminster. The protracted haggling mixed with irritation which had been caused by the matter of the Silesian loan was at last resolved – and by a compromise agreed by both sides. In a secret declaration Britain agreed to pay Frederick 'a reasonable sum' (£20,000) in extinction of all Prussian claims against wrongful actions by British privateers. In return Frederick agreed to lift the sequestration of assets he was holding against repayment to Britain of the balance – capital and interest – of the loan.

Diplomatic relations between France and Britain had been broken off nearly a year previously, and hostilities had been taking place abroad and at sea. Formally, however, the two great maritime powers were at peace; and Mitchell now told Frederick that war was about to be declared, as happened on 9 June. They talked of Austria. Mitchell was as clear as Frederick that the principal motive of Austria was and always would be the recovery of Silesia. He reckoned that the Austro-French alliance was designed to produce a French invasion of Germany, directed at Hanover. They discussed very frankly the possible actions of Russia. If Russia, because of what was now believed of her understandings with Austria, actually invaded Germany (as opposed to arriving as British allies in defence of Hanover), Britain could send a fleet to the Baltic. The British Government still believed, however, that Russia would remain on peaceful terms with her neighbours. The more Frederick, either personally or through his ministers, listened to Mitchell's advice on the lines to follow, especially with Russia, the more his respect for the ambassador's judgement grew, although in the latter case it was to prove optimistic and mistaken.

It was a curious time. Because we know what was so shortly to come, and what was already being planned by some, there is a sense of unreality in the letters and dispatches of that summer, a comparable sensation to reading those of 1914. Every court and capital had its internal dissensions, its 'peace party', its partisans of one or other great power. Knyphausen's reports from Paris were full of the doubts of some men of influence about the new orientation of French policy – Belle-Isle, now back in France, restored to office and always admired by Frederick, was said to be so hostile to the house of Austria that he found events intolerable. But Frederick, previously inclined to clutch at straws, was now sceptical. Austria, he said, was now determined to embroil France in Germany as an anti-Prussian ally and would probably succeed. He wrote in June that the Habsburgs had three unchanging objectives – to establish despotism in the Empire, to ruin the Protestant religion and to recover Silesia. In all this they regarded the King of Prussia as the main obstacle. This was a somewhat desperate analysis: but Frederick was feeling somewhat desperate.[43] He sensed, and it was true, that his most recent campaigns might be the last wherein events were directed by antagonism between Bourbon and Habsburg. The implications were bleak.

Now was a time for hard intelligence on what the various powers were actually preparing to do. Frederick had for some time had a good source in the Austrian Embassy in Berlin, a secretary, Maximilian Weingarten, who was in love with a Prussian girl; and another, a clerk by name Frederick Menzel, in the Saxon Foreign Ministry in Dresden, who had the essential safe keys and was in Frederick's pay. From these he learned the details of the plans to attack him. The Austrians intended to persuade the Russians to launch operations against East Prussia when war came, while themselves marching from Bohemia through Saxony (enrolling the Saxons *en route*) to invade Brandenburg. Another Austrian army would move into Silesia and join hands with the Russians at present concentrated round Smolensk, who would cross the Polish border. Frederick believed that it was hoped at a later date to bring Sweden into the alliance against him.

Frederick was also getting intelligence from Russia and this, too, was disturbing. The British Ambassador in St Petersburg was his old enemy Hanbury-Williams, whose relations with another old enemy, Bestuzhov, were at present good;* and Frederick was getting the benefit (through Mitchell, whose contact with Hanbury-Williams was regular and rapid) of the Bestuzhov–Hanbury-Williams exchanges. In June it was reported that the Austrians were making considerable headway in turning the Tsarina against Britain, and thus against Prussia (which took little doing). False rumours were being spread about Frederick's war preparations in the north – that he had, for instance, a concentration of 100,000 men at Königsberg; and he learned of this disinformation, too, from Menzel and Weingarten. It was reported that the Russians had huge troop concentrations near Riga, which supported Frederick's own intelligence from his Austrian and Saxon sources. Couriers from St Petersburg to Berlin via Riga took ten or eleven days and used their eyes on the way. They were reporting roads crammed with military traffic.[44] This was all the more convincing in that it ran against the optimistic prediction of Mitchell in the previous month – Mitchell was having to accept that his earlier views had been at fault, and did so honestly. The present assessment was consistent with Frederick's own view that Austria would 'move earth and Heaven to inflame (*débaucher*) Russia against Britain',[45] although it was Prussia rather than Britain which stood in the first defensive line.

Frederick, therefore, reckoned that whatever pretext was found or invented, the Russians and Austrians had decided to attack him. Their mobilizations, their movements, all he learned of their plans, offered no other interpretation. They would launch coordinated operations

---

* Although Mitchell wrote later in the year that Hanbury-Williams was now in bad odour in St Petersburg.

against him from south and east, through Saxony and Bohemia into Upper Silesia and from Livonia and Courland* into East Prussia. His relations with France were still correct, if cool. He knew it was openly said in Paris that he was describing the French Government as too feeble to justify anyone's confidence,[46] but whatever ill will was being spread he reckoned the French would try to avoid commitment to land operations in Germany as long as possible. He was anxious to discover at what point France would play an actual part in the grand design against him. That there would be a part he was sure – he did not believe the huge Russian troop concentrations in Courland and Livonia, as well as the Austrian concentrations in Bohemia and Moravia, had been organized without the knowledge of France. France must be at the least a fellow-conspirator. The greatest power in Europe might before long actually be numbered among his enemies. As to Saxony, von Maltzahn wrote from Dresden that Count Brühl's references to Russian military preparations were made with such obvious insincerity and affectation they could deceive nobody. Perhaps, Frederick wrote to Knyphausen in June, a secret part of the Austro-French Treaty of Versailles had provided for France to take care of the British and of Hanover while Austria dealt with the Prussians.[47]

There were also stories of a large French subsidy – 800,000 florins – specifically to enable Austria to recover Silesia.[48] Battle lines were being drawn and, as always in the approaches to war, dangers and differences were being magnified by rumour and mistrust. Frederick sent orders to Field Marshal von Lehwaldt, commanding in East Prussia, and gave instructions for the recall of men on leave as well as for certain precautionary troop movements and transport concentrations in East Prussia and Pomerania. Lehwaldt had reported, on 25 June, that he reckoned some 70,000 Russian troops were moving towards the frontier. Frederick also sent orders in considerable detail to his commanders in Upper Silesia, at Schweidnitz and Cosel, including orders for fortress defence. These orders naturally made people thoughtful in Berlin. Was the King once again about to march? Only Valory, now back again at the Prussian court, raised the question with Frederick's minister, Count von Finckenstein. Was not the whole

---

* The Baltic provinces bordering East Prussia on the Gulf of Riga.

Prussian army on the move? What did it all mean? Finckenstein replied smoothly that his only certain knowledge was that Frederick's dearest wish was to preserve the peace of Europe.[49]

This might well be, but he had given up hope of doing so. In a long justificatory exchange with the French Government in July 1756 Frederick again went through the reasons which led him to mistrust Austria, and which had led him to the Convention of Westminster. His justification absolutely contradicted French accusations, whether of bad faith or inordinate ambition. He knew that the Austro-French Treaty of Versailles envisaged benefits to France in the Netherlands, which Austria could afford; but also envisaged the dismemberment of Prussia and the removal of her Rhineland possessions, to the benefit of Austria, Saxony and the Palatinate. He knew that he was the designated victim of a huge concerted attack, which would be justified as a defensive measure against the aggressive moves of the King of Prussia. His enemies would decide when.

'I am between war and peace here!' Frederick wrote to Abraham Michel in London on 6 July.[50] He learned with satisfaction that the British, in spite of considerable strain on their maritime resources, hoped to make good their promise to send a naval squadron to the Baltic,[51] which remained a promise unfulfilled. London was still optimistic that the Russians could be kept friendly. Frederick did not share this optimism – he read the signs differently. He continued, however, to send courteous messages to St Petersburg. His moves and preparations were causing the chancelleries of Europe to buzz and he was unconcerned by the fact. 'Negotiations without arms,' he wrote, 'are like music without instruments,' and his own instruments would always be tuned. The Prussian army was assembling. Soon it would be ready. In that and in that alone lay the kingdom's security.

Faced with this sort of situation Frederick acted according to his own philosophy. He chose the path of courage and pre-emption. He had defined it in his earliest writings. Certain that war may be forced upon him at a time and in circumstances of his enemies' choosing, the wise and responsible prince must move first. A miracle might yet save the peace of Europe – but he did not think so. He wrote a tender letter to Wilhelmina on 12 July. 'We're preparing for all eventualities here, nevertheless trying not to give offence to those determined to take it!' He took the waters. Strains might soon be imposed on his frame. He was forty-four.

Frederick decided to give something of an ultimatum to Maria Theresa. He listed all the warlike preparations of which he had been informed, in Bohemia and Moravia, with full details; and he told Klinggraeffen, in Vienna, to seek an audience with the Queen-Empress and ask what her measures were intended to convey? Would she explicitly state that there was no intention to attack Prussia this year (1756)? Or the next? He kept Andrew Mitchell, in Berlin, informed of every exchange and at an audience on 21 July gave him the draft of an agreement between Prussia and Britain which went well beyond the indefinite and conditional terms of the Convention of Westminster. Mitchell told Lord Holdernesse* in London that if Prussia received from Austria 'a fair and favourable answer' Frederick reckoned he could secure the peace of Germany for 'this year and the next'; and seriously wanted to avoid a breach with France.[52]

In Potsdam Valory had an audience with Frederick on 26 July. Podewils was present.

Valory: 'I'll pawn my head that the Queen-Empress has no intention of attacking Prussia.'

Podewils: 'Will the King of France *guarantee* that?'

Frederick: 'Wrong! France will promise not to *assist* the Queen-Empress against me, *if* I promise not to assist the King of England? I shall do no such thing. I will fulfil my engagements to the King of England!'

Frederick told Mitchell afterwards that he had no intention of being talked to 'as one talks to Dutchmen', and told what treaties he could or could not keep. He was in excellent humour. He was sure that the French would make no move in support of Austria for some time, if ever; and he never neglected to show even Valory, of whom he was fond, that Kings of Prussia were not to be lectured by French ambassadors, however distinguished. He told Mitchell how his *démarche* in Vienna was going. He knew that Maria Theresa would tell Klinggraeffen that Austrian measures were purely defensive and were

---

* Robert D'Arcy, 4th Earl of Holdernesse, Secretary of State.

purely Austria's concern. Frederick then proposed to have Kling-graeffen tell her all Frederick knew about the Austro-Russian plan to attack him, a plan whose execution had, he was sure, only been delayed because of Russian unreadiness.

Having faced the Queen-Empress with this, Frederick next intended to tell the French of his full awareness of Austro-Russian intrigues. They were no doubt privy to them but perhaps unaware of the extent of Frederick's knowledge of them. 'This will naturally occasion some messages between these courts,' Mitchell told his own government, probably with some satisfaction, 'and he [Frederick] thinks that towards the end of August the French will find the season too advanced for them to attempt a march into Germany by way of diversion.'[53]

It was unlikely now that anything could deflect events. Judgement of Frederick's conduct turns on the sincerity and justice of his belief that Austria, Russia, and ultimately France, were intending to attack him at a time of their own choosing; and of that there seems little doubt. He was getting detailed reports from von Maltzahn in Dresden of the military deployments being agreed between Saxony and Austria, as well as accounts of interviews with Kaunitz himself in Vienna; and Kaunitz was speaking with confidence of the coming conjunction of Russia, Austria and France against Prussia.[54]

Frederick waited with some impatience for Klinggraeffen's report from Vienna. 'I have,' Frederick wrote to Wilhelmina, 'entered into a negotiation with my enemies. I want them to declare their intentions and thus justify my conduct to the world.'[55] And he wrote to her again on the next day, 29 July, a letter overflowing with love and concern for her health. 'I have many reasons for anxiety of which you furnish not the least violent. Deign at least to give a little calm to my heart and realize that nobody loves you and cherishes you more than your old brother.'

Klinggraeffen's audience with Maria Theresa had taken place at the palace of Schönbrunn on 26 July – the Queen-Empress had written her sentences on a sheet of paper and read them out to the ambassador. They were so uninformative as to constitute an uncompromising rebuff. 'Affairs, generally, are at a point of crisis. The Queen-Empress has judged it appropriate to take these measures for her own safety and that of her allies. They threaten nobody.'[56]

Writing from Potsdam on 2 August, Frederick told Klinggraeffen at once to seek another audience and to leave Maria Theresa in no doubt about what Frederick knew and its implications. It was not Austria or the Habsburg domains which were threatened. It was Prussia – threatened by 120,000 Russians and 80,000 Austrians. Frederick reiterated his demand for a solemn assurance that no attack on Prussia was intended in this or next year. Were he and the Queen-Empress at peace or at war? It was for her to decide.

Frederick had few illusions about how all this would go. His intelligence had conveyed Austrian plans and intentions beyond possibility of doubt. On the same 2 August he gave Schwerin command of the army of Silesia with 24,000 men and a defensive mission against the Austrians who would debouch from Bohemia and Moravia. 'War is inevitable,' he wrote to Wilhelmina on 9 August. It was the Prince of Prussia's – August Wilhelm's – birthday and Frederick gave him a picture by Wouwermann which was much appreciated. His family, including his soldier-brothers, August Wilhelm and Henry, were anxious. They revered, and to an extent feared, the King; but they were well informed and they could see something of the odds Prussia would encounter. Henry – always sceptical and somewhat jealous of Frederick's motives – was particularly unconvinced; he also thought the King was influenced by Winterfeldt, of whom he disapproved. Podewils, too, was anxious. Would it not be wiser to wait? Events might fall out unexpectedly well. Enemies might fall out with each other. Podewils maintained good relations with Valory, and the old Marquis, formerly so good a friend, was naturally unhappy. The British, too, were anxious. They still hoped Russia might be kept from joining Frederick's enemies and they were concerned as to how much he might or might not be able to do for the defence of Hanover if his hands were as full as he seemed to expect.[57]

Frederick replied that the hostile powers had, he knew, agreed to postpone, but only postpone, action. They were determined to attack Prussia. He realized that Kaunitz understood his tactics perfectly – understood that Frederick sought to put Vienna in the wrong. He had good information from those close to the Austrian chancellor. The stately dance of diplomacy concealed little and Kaunitz was confident that Frederick could be shown to the world as an aggressor if he moved; and Frederick knew it.[58] Yet Frederick's best resource, his only ultimate defence, was to strike first – to strike first and to place reliance on his own speed and resolution in action; and on the skill and discipline of the Prussian army.

Klinggraeffen was meeting delay in Vienna. Kaunitz had reported his second *démarche* to Maria Theresa, who had asked for something in writing; on which Klinggraeffen had reported again to Frederick. Frederick was furious. Why had the ambassador not been ready with a paper? It had been clear from the preliminary exchanges with Kaunitz that this would be necessary, and time had been lost. 'You've spoiled my affairs!' Frederick wrote on 13 August, with a stinging rebuke on the ambassador's incompetence. Klinggraeffen must present a paper instantly to the Queen-Empress and inform Frederick of the answer not later than 21 August.[59]

On the 25th Frederick received Maria Theresa's reply to his second approach. He told Klinggraeffen, acidly, that it was not in any proper sense a reply at all. It did not address the fundamental question of whether Austria wanted peace or war.[60] Instead, it denied the existence of any offensive treaty with Russia, but wholly abstained from disavowal of Austrian intention to attack Prussia.[61]

Frederick told Mitchell exactly what had happened and what he intended. He ordered Klinggraeffen to seek one more audience and to reiterate a request for an assurance of peace, as already besought. If such an assurance were given he would order the withdrawal of any troops who had marched. Mitchell, a shrewd observer, was convinced of the sincerity of this – Prussia was ready, he wrote to Holdernesse, but Frederick was clear nothing would ultimately be gained by war, while sadly sure that now it must come. 'Both interest and inclination lead him to wish for peace.'[62]

A few weeks earlier Mitchell had seen the King in his study. Frederick had pointed to a portrait of Maria Theresa which he always kept there. 'That Lady wants war,' he had said, 'and she shall soon have it.' Frederick regarded his operations as essentially defensive and he maintained to the very end that the war was a defensive war. In such a situation only an indecisive and inadequate fool of a prince stood still and allowed his foes to set the pace and timing of events. Others thought, and have argued since, that although Frederick's desire for peace was genuine he would seize any chance to acquire Saxony, as a territory too close for comfort to the vitals of Prussia; more important, even, than East Prussia.[63] But whatever Frederick's priorities and contingency planning in 1756 his main object was to improve his defensive position in a war he did not want but thought inevitable. He was unsurprised and unconcerned to learn from Paris a week later that in Rouille's view the terms of his ultimatum to Maria Theresa had left her with no power of dignified response.[64] On 24 August he gave a general order about administration of the kingdom to his ministers on the General Directory – 'Comply with my instructions of 1748. Don't plan any economic development projects.'

On 28 August, the Prussian army invaded Saxony. They were on the march towards Bohemia. Frederick explained, with some speciousness but little sign of bad conscience, that this was a regrettable necessity, that the troops would behave perfectly and that his regard for the Elector-King and his family was as high as ever. What was to be the Seven Years War had begun.

PART IV
1756–63

12

Into Hostile Territory

'This morning, between four and five o'clock,' wrote Sir Andrew Mitchell to Lord Holdernesse on 28 August 1756, 'I took leave of the King of Prussia. He went immediately to the parade, mounted on horseback, and after a very short exercise of his troops put himself at their head . . .'[1] Next day Frederick led the Prussian army across the border into Saxony. With one brief exception in the following January he would not again dismount in Berlin until the end of March 1763.

Frederick was in a merry mood. '*Je vais rendre une petite visite à mon gros voisin*' – off to pay a visit to my fat neighbour, the Elector of Saxony – he wrote to Wilhelmina.[2] If his health was adequate he was always stimulated by the physical challenges of a campaign – his stomach often betrayed him and he was plagued by painful haemorrhoids but if digestion was in order he suffered the discomforts with remarkable stoicism. He was often treated with enemas and medicines but would say, firmly, 'we must not coddle ourselves' and be in the saddle for longer than healthier men. He had divided the army for the campaign against Austria and Saxony into three wings, a total of 58,000 men. On the right Prince Ferdinand of Brunswick was to march to Leipzig. On the left the Duke of Bevern was to move through Lusatia to the east bank of the Elbe. In the centre, under the immediate command of Frederick himself, the troops were to advance through Torgau on Dresden; the point of convergence was given by Frederick as Pirna, south-east of Dresden, on the Elbe. Far to the east Schwerin, with a further 25,000 men, was to hold Silesia.

In spite of his certainty that the Russians had planned to attack him, Frederick had a poor opinion of their initiative and believed that

Field Marshal Lehwaldt, with 20,000 men in East Prussia, could deter or outface them. Lehwaldt had behind him a reserve corps of a further 8,000 men under the Prince of Hesse-Darmstadt, in Pomerania. Frederick, therefore, was committing some 83,000 men (out of an overall army strength of 126,000) to the campaign against Austria and Saxony; and in December – after one battle – he tipped the balance further by ordering Hesse-Darmstadt's reserve corps into winter quarters in southern Saxony.

Meanwhile Dresden was defensible. It was a large city and could accommodate a sufficient garrison to man the defences. Through the city ran the Elbe, a principal artery of any campaign, while to the east the approaches were dominated by heights incorporated into the defensive system. Dresden was defensible; but in September 1756 it was not defended: the Saxons had withdrawn from their capital.

There was, for a while, no clash of arms. Frederick was anxious to preserve for as long as possible the appearance of a friendly prince simply seeking facilities for his troops on their march to conduct operations against an intransigent enemy, Austria. Augustus of Saxony, King of Poland, wrote on the day after Frederick crossed the frontier that he hoped the Prussians would show strict discipline – he was, he said, surprised by the actions of the King of Prussia which he thought inconsistent with treaties existing between them, and he hoped for reassuring explanations.[3] Frederick replied that his own desire for peace was well-known but that the hostile intentions of Maria Theresa had forced him to act. He accompanied this with a thrust at the Saxon chief minister, Brühl, 'a man whose ill intentions are only too well-known to me'. Frederick's exchanges with Augustus continued for several weeks with Augustus protesting that he was being treated as an enemy and that the Prussians should leave his realm and Frederick responding that this was impossible (although his regards for '*son bon frère*' were irreproachable), since he had been forced to embark on war and the safety of his troops demanded their movement through and supply in Saxony. There were plenty of detailed conditions proposed and opposed touching such matters as freedom of navigation on the Elbe. Augustus, although initially he had troops in the field confronting Frederick's, tried to be conciliatory on details but stuck to his main demand: that the Prussians should quit Saxony.[4]

On 9 September Frederick entered Dresden. His immediate objective was Bohemia and the main Austrian army under Maximilian von Browne. The Prussian line of communication to Bohemia ran through Saxony. When Augustus asked Frederick for safe personal passage to Poland it was granted without argument. His remonstrances at Prussian invasion of the Saxon royal residences in Dresden were dismissed cursorily,[5] and Frederick did not neglect to use this first brief stay in Dresden to seize Saxon state papers of which he had earlier learned from his agent, Menzel, and to share their contents with the British Ambassador, Mitchell, who sent copies to London.[6] He also hoped (in vain) that the direct evidence these provided of hostile Saxon intentions might strengthen the hand of his representatives in Paris in their task of justifying Prussian policy.[7] His language showed him on the defensive on this subject, sure though he was of Saxon malign intentions. He realized that a good deal of effort must be devoted to advocacy. Silesia had been comparatively straightforward – his cause, he had been convinced, was good in law. To invade Saxony, another sovereign's possession, was in a somewhat different category. He learned with satisfaction that Mitchell had received George II's permission to join Frederick's suite on campaign.[8] All the messages from England were now encouraging.

Frederick found the Saxon army was in position at Pirna, a very defensible 'camp' in that dramatic and mountainous territory through which runs the Upper Elbe. He decided to leave them unmolested and to continue his march towards the Bohemian frontier, moving by the west bank of the river. He supposed – wrongly – that there would be plentiful forage in Bohemia. He did not know where Browne would have concentrated the main Austrian forces but he felt confident – he told Prince Ferdinand that his initial task in Bohemia would probably be over by about 16 September.[9] His leading troops crossed the border on the 13th.

In Silesia Schwerin was in the area of Glatz, where he reckoned he was both covering Lower Silesia and preventing – or deterring – Austrian moves to reinforce from the east Browne's forces in central Bohemia. He was, clearly, outnumbered if the Austrians were to make a concentrated effort against him but Frederick was confident that his own operations would take the pressure off Schwerin, and he was right.

Browne had in the field an army of 34,000. He knew that the Prussians would act offensively and probably with rapidity – that was Frederick's reputation. He needed to deploy where he could meet the enemy on ground of his own choosing and, with good luck, win a victory on points, inflict casualties, prevent or inhibit a further Prussian advance, gain time. He selected the ground west of the Elbe near the town of Lobositz. Frederick, to invade Bohemia by the Elbe valley, must come that way. The ground itself was in many places suitable for defence, broken, affording plenty of cover. Browne hoped to entice the Prussians into an attack which they would not, he thought, win decisively; and meanwhile to send a mobile force to reinforce the Saxons at Pirna. He covered his deployment with an advance guard, charged with breaking up the Prussian advance when it came and getting it bogged among the patches of swampy ground which lay across the front of an enemy approaching from the north.

The Austrian army had experienced considerable reforms since the last war. It was now better trained and disciplined, better logistically supported and better financed. The Austrian artillery, which had been evolving over much of Frederick's fighting life, had greatly improved under its director, Prince Joseph Wenzel of Liechtenstein, Frederick's old friend and mentor. Browne had a formidable force at his disposal; and Frederick did not know where he was.

On 24 September Frederick supposed his enemy was at Kolin, many miles east of Prague. By the 28th, however, his patrols had located their approximate whereabouts near Lobositz; and he joined the army at Aussig, only ten miles downstream from Lobositz. He had in hand sixty squadrons of cavalry and twenty-eight battalions of infantry. Aussig, he wrote, was a poor place to concentrate an army and he determined to leave it, find the enemy and beat them.

Frederick felt confident – perhaps over-confident. He had assured Prince Ferdinand on 19 September that there was nothing to fear.[10] His main anxieties were logistic. He was deep in enemy territory and the Elbe navigation (which anyway had a limited capacity) was not certainly clear. His progress was slower than he had forecast. To adventure too far into Bohemia before his supply lines were assured would be dangerous and he would not do it. On the other hand a successful manoeuvre to occupy Lobositz might ease the forage situation.[11] He advanced by the Mittelgebirge, the hills bordering the west bank of the Elbe, having formed an advance guard of eight infantry battalions with ten cavalry squadrons and eight squadrons of hussars. The advance guard was to follow the main road which ran from Aussig towards Lobositz, parallel to the river; and he divided the main body into two – one column to move by a place called Pashcopolo and a second to follow the advance guard.

Frederick accompanied the advance guard – moving by Turmitz to another place called Wellemin, which he affectionately told Wilhelmina had put him in mind of her. He arrived there an hour before sunset on 30 September. That night he slept in the open. He reached Wellemin in time to reconnoitre forward personally and to observe the Austrian army, which he described as probably numbering 60,000 men. In fact Browne had considerably fewer than this. Few commanders in history have underestimated the size of the forces opposed to them.

While Frederick pointed out the ground to his senior generals the Prussian army moved up into position opposite the Austrians. Frederick's orders for deployment were straightforward. The enemy's right rested on Lobositz, his left on the river Eger; and Frederick resolved to rest his own wings on high ground, notably the hill of Lobosch which rose to a height of 1,300 feet to the north of Browne's position, dominating both the Austrian right flank and Prussian approaches to it. From Lobosch hill, the Prussians exploring it could see Lobositz, two miles to the south, and the enemy cavalry deployed chequerwise between Lobositz and the village of Sullowitz to the south of that place; but Lobosch hill itself was occupied by the Austrians – in fact by 2,000 Croat light infantry. A lower hill, the Homolkaberg, rose from the plain about a mile to the south of Lobosch, and was ungarrisoned.

The morning of 1 October was foggy. It was unclear to Frederick whether the Austrians were simply deploying a rearguard to cover their crossing of the Elbe which lay behind them or were anticipating a major defensive battle; he suspected the former but acknowledged that his own poor eyesight might be misleading him and asked the opinion of others who might see more clearly. At six o'clock in the morning Frederick ordered the infantry forward in two columns, with his cavalry forming a third line behind them. The Prussians debouched

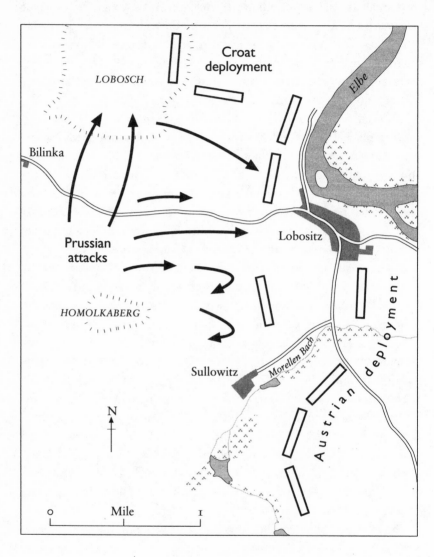

Lobositz, 1 October 1756

from the high ground to the open ground between hills and river. Frederick at once placed a battery, probably of about ten guns, on the Homolkaberg, a good observation point; and rode there himself. One thing was clear – any attack towards Browne's left would be complicated by the Morellen Bach, a stream which crossed the southern half of the front, just as any attack towards the Austrian right would be overshadowed by the Lobosch hill.

Browne's position was well chosen. He was ready to disorganize a Prussian advance from the west and to inflict casualties before there was a clash of main bodies, if there was; and Frederick, unsure of what his enemy was trying to achieve, perhaps acted with excessive confidence. His first move was to launch eight squadrons of his cavalry, with more following them up, as a reconnaissance in force against the Austrian centre and left. This manoeuvre led to setback: Austrian cavalry, handled expertly, beat them back and as they withdrew they found themselves caught by direct artillery fire from concealed gun positions. Then a second wave of Prussian cavalry – over forty squadrons – launched a second attack, without orders, between Lobositz and Sullowitz. This attack also failed. The ground over which Frederick's squadrons were attacking was too broken and difficult. Men and horses became enmired in the Morellen Bach and an Austrian counter-attack sent the Prussians smartly into retreat. Meanwhile accurate Austrian artillery and infantry fire was taking a heavy toll and Frederick reckoned, perhaps belatedly, that to clear the enemy from the Lobosch feature was a prerequisite for any success.

He did so, but it was a stiff fight. In his own account of the battle, written immediately afterwards,[12] Frederick described his cavalry as succeeding in beating the enemy's cavalry at the start of the action despite the artillery and infantry fire on their flanks. He had, in fact, committed them – or allowed them to commit themselves – in unfavourable conditions, with a concealed enemy skilfully manning positions for enfilade. The taking of the Lobosch feature itself was, to an extent, a repetition of the assault on the Granerkoppe at Soor – a savage, expensive task directed by the Duke of Bevern,* with

---

* First cousin of Frederick's Queen – their fathers, sons of Ferdinand Albert of Brunswick-Bevern, were brothers.

Prussian battalion after battalion fed into the fight. The Austrians attempted to frustrate it by a move to turn Frederick's left and this caused him to deploy his last two battalions to his left and to change direction with his main body, turning them, too, to their left while strengthening his depleted centre with what he had left of his heavy cavalry. Eventually the infantry of the Prussian left wing carried the day and fought their way into Lobositz itself, having driven the enemy from the Lobosch feature. The troops were by now short of ammunition and tackling the Austrians at the point of the bayonet.

The action had lasted seven hours. Browne ordered a withdrawal behind the Elbe and the Eger, covered by a cavalry rearguard and destroying all bridges. His main body, behind the Morellen Bach, had not been engaged. Lobositz was a curious episode in Frederick's career – an expensive battle which, because there was no attempt to follow it up, appears wholly indecisive in terms of the invasion of Bohemia. The Austrian main army was still in the field, its movements largely unaffected, although there had been a reminder – salutary from Frederick's point of view – of what Prussian discipline and Prussian determination could do when it came to a fight. Frederick wrote to Keith on 14 October that he had complete confidence he could now maintain himself in Bohemia, with superiority of numbers. The confidence might seem rooted in optimism rather than fact or logistic calculation,[13] but Frederick planned a major expansion of the army during the winter when he would be keeping it in quarters and he was probably anticipating this. He was to write buoyantly to Wilhelmina in January – enjoining absolute secrecy – that by mid February he would have increased his numbers to 210,000, and this was why he had been keeping so quiet.

Over the Saxons Frederick could claim victory. The force which Browne had sent to support them at Pirna had been headed by Frederick's deployment of an intercepting cavalry detachment and the Prussians could now concentrate all necessary strength against the Saxon army. That army surrendered on terms on the same day, 14 October, that Frederick wrote so confidently to Keith, although they had held several weeks' provisions at Pirna. For the whole first phase of campaign and its comparative success Frederick, characteristically, gave all credit to the men of his army. He had once again been gladdened by what he had seen of their conduct. 'You know them,' he wrote to Moritz of Anhalt-Dessau. 'After this trial nothing on earth is impossible for them!'[14] In his account of the fight at Lobositz he wrote that he had never witnessed such courage, infantry and cavalry alike, in those 'he had the honour to command'.[15] He could only mention their losses, he said, with tears in his eyes. All this is assuredly sincere – casualties affected Frederick deeply. There is, nevertheless, an impression in his account of a Frederick somewhat shaken by the ferocity of the experience, almost as if there was an element of the unexpected. It may be that he was unprepared for what was undoubtedly a better Austrian army than he had encountered before.

Frederick himself left the battlefield before the issue on the Lobosch feature was finally settled. He rode towards Pirna, stopping, however, at the village of Bilinka only a few miles west of Lobositz, beneath Lobosch. To leave the field before final tactical success was curious but he had confidence in Brunswick-Bevern, who was overseeing the final stages of the victorious Lobosch assault, and he may have been more anxious about the possibility of Browne reinforcing the Saxons and concentrating on the Prussian deep flank than was in the event justified. Frederick has also been criticized for not exploiting victory. It has been suggested that he might have marched forthwith on Prague and Vienna – Prague lies only forty-five miles to the south – leaving Saxony alone; instead he had blunted his sword in an indecisive action without follow-up. This ignores the overall strategic situation and Frederick's vulnerability until he could be better balanced in logistic terms. He was anxious about supplies and forage. He had always, furthermore, made clear that he thought winter campaigns, unless absolutely unavoidable, were a bad thing, wasting and exhausting an army.

Instead Frederick settled down to consolidate victory over the Saxons. First, there were the terms of capitulation, with details to be decided on exactly how Saxon officers were to be treated; their sovereign, the Elector, King of Poland, had surrendered as a prisoner of war, and was allowed to go to Poland with all his family, accorded royal honours – he took the road to Warsaw on 18 October. Conditions were imposed on the future service of officers and the troops under their command, conditions which led to certain acrimonious exchanges between Frederick and Major-General von Sporcken, responsible (in Warsaw) for Saxon compliance – exchanges savagely ended by Frederick in December, 'I wash my hands of the matter! That is the last reply you will get from me!'[16] He was also indignant to hear that Brühl was spreading stories that Augustus, despite Frederick's safe conduct, had not been safe – an absurd allegation, since he had been wholly at Frederick's mercy.

The Saxon soldiers, after capitulation, were to be enrolled in the Prussian army. Frederick, probably unwisely, formed ten new regiments from these, agreed a financial allocation to cover their costs, and assigned to them Prussian officers, not of the highest quality. He underestimated the simple patriotic feeling of the Saxon soldiery. This was to sow the seeds of a probable increase in desertion rates and it indeed happened that, early in 1757, two regiments in a mutinous condition had to be disbanded – leading Frederick to investigate making up numbers by an appeal for recruits to the Landgrave of Hesse-Cassel. On Saxony itself Frederick imposed a harsh system of exactions, ultimately to cover more than one third of the cost of his campaign.

Frederick forbade irregularities, looting, plunder. He wrote in forceful terms to his commander in Lusatia, General von Normann, that he had heard of instances which Normann would be responsible to the King for stopping instantly.[17] When the wife of Brühl, whom he loathed, wrote personally (but humbly) to him about the seizure of some of her furniture by hussars in the Prussian service, Frederick answered at once that he would inform himself of the facts and would never allow her property to be misappropriated or misused.[18] His exchanges with the Brühls, however, continued for some time; on the whole disagreeably. And benefits could be obtained without flagrant illegality, from the occupation of Saxony. Frederick's favourite picture dealer, Gotzkowski, got possession of the patents at the porcelain factory of Meissen and went into production in Berlin – an enterprise which ultimately failed, and was taken over by the King.[19]

Frederick hoped that diplomatic advantages would flow from judicious disclosure of extracts from the Saxon documents seized in Dresden, documents which might show Saxon perfidy and aggressive intent.

Such propaganda initiatives need skilful handling and Frederick, who had sent a chestful of papers to Berlin, ordered Podewils and Finckenstein* to prepare and edit the material. He was then irritated by what he reckoned was lack of imagination on their part. Instead of a carefully constructed propaganda coup, an effective *exposé* of Saxon improprieties wholly justifying Frederick's incursion, they simply made proposed extracts for Frederick's approval. These, taken straight, were inadequate to make the necessary point and the ministers had struck the predictable difficulty that to prove the blackheartedness behind the Saxon papers it would be desirable to include additional information, which they possessed but which came from intercepted diplomatic dispatches. Was this acceptable? They put the dilemma to the King.

Frederick wrote back sharply. He said he did not want a simple sequence of extracts such as they had submitted, he wanted a convincing polemic. His ministers were causing delay and wasting his time. Their initiative should have been sufficient to suggest to them what might be done without further recourse to authority – 'work more and consult less! Act and don't await orders! Adieu. Fédéric.'[20] His mood and impatience were understandable. It looked decreasingly likely that the bold move he had planned, the pre-emptive war to discourage the coalition of his enemies, was having that effect.

His eyes were particularly on Paris and on French reaction to his moves. In September he had been writing to Knyphausen there with a certain complacency, saying that, as predicted, French ministers had at first reacted with violence to his crossing the Saxon border but that calmer counsels would probably soon prevail. They didn't. On 21 October Knyphausen was summoned by Rouille. He was to leave Paris. Relations between France and Prussia were to be broken off.[21] Valory was being withdrawn from Berlin – he left at the beginning of November after exchanges of great affection with Frederick who was, he said, simply writing to an old friend rather than to the envoy of France. Whether this rupture would have the military consequences which had always threatened but which Frederick had hoped his boldness might discourage was uncertain.

---

* Count von Finckenstein was Podewils's 'alter ego' and successor.

At least the open hostility of France would further warm the friendship for Prussia felt in England, and Frederick wrote that he trusted his operations would be perceived in London as essentially helpful. When he learned something from his sources in France about French intentions in India he naturally passed it to Mitchell – information probably known already, but strengthening Frederick's credit in the passing; just as did reports of French intentions against Hanover.

But Frederick's enemies were slowly gathering and a great question mark hung over the policies of Russia. His information in that quarter came largely from the good communications between the British Ambassador in St Petersburg, the uncongenial (to Frederick) Hanbury-Williams, and the highly congenial Andrew Mitchell in Berlin. From this channel Frederick learned – and believed – that the only reason why the Russians had not yet moved against him was the grievous shortage of recruits. Hanbury-Williams reckoned they would not undertake operations before June 1757. The Russians had, however, undertaken to the Austrians *as long ago as January 1756* that they would march against Prussia when they could.

On the outcome of this Frederick was inclined to scepticism – 'Winter will calm them down!' he wrote; and Hanbury-Williams made clear to his authorities that the Chancellor, Bestuzhev, seemed amenable to a bribe. But the dispatches from St Petersburg also made very clear that the King of Prussia had more enemies than friends there. Frederick hoped that British diplomacy – and money – would help him in that quarter. Hanbury-Williams himself, despite his personal disapproval of Frederick, was now playing the part of a friend – and was ultimately rewarded by a handsome portrait of the King, delivered, sadly, after the ambassador had died, to his home in England. Frederick also heard that the Tsarina's health was poor and told the Dowager Princess of Anhalt-Zerbst (somewhat prematurely) that he hoped her daughter might in future bring a helpful influence to bear.

Militarily Frederick could certainly not be complacent. He had seen enough at Lobositz to appreciate that the Austrians were formidable. They had used ground with skill, been steady when steadiness was required, and their artillery had been devastating. The Austrians were still in the field, wary but little damaged, although he was sure Browne would attempt nothing before the spring. As for the sustenance of the

Prussian army, northern Bohemia could furnish disappointingly little
– the land was *totalement mangée*, he told Wilhelmina[22] on 24 October,
and he resolved to winter in Saxony. 'No more battles this year!' he
wrote to her a few days later. Frederick already had some misgivings
about the strength of his army for the tasks he envisaged. Their quality
was admirable but were there enough of them? He started to plan –
'Everything we've done this year is only a prelude to next,' he wrote
to Algarotti.[23] He was sure 1757 would be a year of decision. And, to
his sister Ulrica, the Queen of Sweden, he wrote on 4 January of that
year that his situation could be compared to that of Charles XII when
Charles came to the throne of Sweden and found three great powers
planning his destruction. 'It is that which made me undertake this
war but we've still achieved nothing. Next year will decide the fate
of Germany and myself.'[24]

Frederick's move into Saxony has been criticized as failing to win
a decisive victory, as giving his enemies time and as confirming France
in her enmity. Nevertheless he had knocked Saxony out of the war;
and French hostility was by now, sadly, assured by the Convention
of Westminster although Frederick for some time – unrealistically –
supposed that when the French saw him in the military ascendant
they might reconsider friendship.

Although he paid a visit to Berlin for a few days in January 1757,
Frederick governed Prussia and conducted his negotiations from Dresden or at Lockwitz, nearby, until 20 April. Between 20 November and
10 December 1756 he wrote several assessments of the situation,[25]
papers which served to clear his mind and keep his ministers in it,
papers also intended to keep the British informed and stimulated –
Mitchell was given copies even when they were not specifically written
for him, as some were. Frederick was free with suggestions about
what Britain might do for what he assumed was now the common
cause; and he often responded to communications from London with
appreciation of the generous sentiments but also with expressions of
hope that words would, before long, be followed by action.[26] At an
audience he gave Mitchell on 9 December he asked bluntly when
London was going to bestir itself.[27]

Frederick's anxieties about the strength of Britain's commitment were understandable. There was sympathy in England for his pre-emptive strike but Britain was an old friend of Austria, despite Austria's recent attachment to France; and Frederick learned without great surprise in February 1757 that the Austrians were trying to persuade the authorities in Hanover – and thus their sovereign – that the French could be brought by Austrian pressure not to attack British possessions in Germany. He knew that some of the Hanoverian ministers had hoped to check the tide of events and to seek an understanding with Austria, so greatly did they dislike the idea of cooperation with Prussia. This would leave Hanover, through the good offices of Austria, in what Frederick indignantly described as 'a false neutrality'; unmolested.[28] It would be a false neutrality indeed – Maria Theresa was proposing to ask Britain/Hanover for unchallenged passage of an Austro-French army of 25,000 men through Hanover to attack Prussia. But British reactions to this were robust although, Frederick heard, Hanoverian were less so. He did not underestimate the historic mistrust between Hanover and his own realm. Nor was he blind to the dichotomy of George II's role as Elector and King, with what many reckoned was dubious identity of interests between Kingdom and Electorate.

Frederick considered French intentions in a *mémoire raisonnée* of 20 November 1756. In Germany, he wrote, all was still to play for – 'the dice are on the table'. Having acquired Minorca the French would certainly reinforce their troops in Madras and in Canada but they would aim to keep Britain on the defensive in the Channel area; and they would send an army of 50,000, perhaps 60,000, to attack Frederick's Rhineland possessions and march by Wesel into West-phalia and towards Hanover. They would start operations in March or April. Wesel could only hold out for ten days. It should, however, be possible to assemble in Westphalia an anti-Austrian German army to confront the French – 5,000 from Brunswick, 3–4,000 from Gotha, 35,000 Hanoverians and Hessians (he presumed). To this, despite his major preoccupations in southern Germany and Silesia, he should be able to contribute 8–10,000 Prussians. That should be sufficient to do the job, although it would be best if both Denmark and Holland could be enrolled as allies and if the latter could continue what he called a 'barrier of ports' to complicate French operations; Ostend, Bruges, Antwerp, Malines. An allied army should be concentrated first in the area of Hameln on the Weser. Bases for westward operations should be prepared there and at Dortmund. A major action should not be sought but a generally defensive campaign envisaged in Westphalia, on the line of the Lippe. Britain, perhaps, might threaten some diversions, descents on the Norman or Breton coasts for instance; and might not Britain, to compensate for the loss of Minorca in the Mediterranean, seize some other position there? Corsica?[29] At all times Russia must somehow be kept inactive, a precondition of Prussian contribution.

In floating these ideas – which were in most cases perfectly defensible in their own right – Frederick was, of course, demonstrating to London that he was not narrowly concerned with the interests of Prussia; on the contrary, he had a wide geostrategic understanding. He was also insinuating British involvement, partly because of Hanover but largely because of interest in opposing France, into the complex of German affairs. It was certain, he wrote, that while France was preparing or undertaking action Austria would be seeking to organize the maximum number of German princes *against* Prussia. Maria Theresa would concentrate an army of 130,000 in Bohemia and demand help from France – probably a corps of not more than 24,000 men, he thought – to help drive the Prussians from Saxony and intimidate any German states friendly to Britain. By these formulations Frederick sought always to line up British interests with his own concerns – and plausibly so. The Austrian plan of operations would be to invade Lusatia from Bohemia with one army and Lower Silesia with another, having sent Croat and Saxon cavalry to range Upper Silesia.

The forum of discussion about action by the German states was the Imperial Diet, due to meet in Ratisbon at the beginning of 1757, and Frederick would have to exercise his influence as well as he could. 'I will support their liberty despite themselves!' he wrote to Wilhelmina. 'Let it never be said that while a Prussian lives Germany lacks defenders! Please God, the pride and despotic spirit of Vienna shall be humbled!'[30] Frederick was fighting for what he regarded as the good old cause. Hanover, it must be hoped, was now firmly if reluctantly on his side: Brunswick also. Some, like Bavaria, must be assumed as in the opposite camp. Saxony was now occupied territory. Some with votes in the Diet were waverers – Frederick wrote a furious letter to his brother-in-law, Ansbach, on 17 January, when he heard that that prince had succumbed to Austrian blandishments or bullying and changed the instructions to his representative in the Diet,[31] a letter unlike most of Frederick's, with their courteous phrases even to declared enemies. It ended uncompromisingly – 'Let none say you have injured me with impunity and if God lets me live you'll repent this – and soon!' And Frederick had heard with anger in November that the Duke of Württemberg, Wilhelmina's son-in-law, was in touch with the Austrians, who were hoping for a Württemberger contribution to the anti-Prussian coalition.[32] The Duke, indeed, was soon to serve in the Austrian army confronting Prussia.

The diplomatic battle swung to and fro, largely to Frederick's disadvantage. In January the Diet approved plans for a 'German' army of 100,000, a 'Reichsarmee', the 'Imperials', to oppose the pretensions of the King of Prussia. For what it was worth this was a victory for Vienna, a declaration of war on Prussia, but it left Frederick unmoved. 'I mock the Diet and its resolution,' he wrote to Wilhelmina in February. 'I fear not all these grand projects of my enemies. People will see, in the spring, that it is Prussia, its strength and above all its discipline, which will be a match for Austrian numbers, French impetuosity, Russian ferocity, great bodies of Hungarians – everyone who opposes us.'[33] To Schwerin, in Silesia, he wrote, however, that the coming campaign would be 'très rude'. He despaired of nothing. What was needed was 'vivacité, prudence, intrépidité à toute épreuve'. Frederick's courage was high. It was certainly true that his enemies found many difficulties in assembling and equipping a united force from the smaller German states – primarily Bavaria, now Württemberg, Hesse-Darmstadt, the Ecclesiastical Electorates of Cologne, Trier, Würzburg and Mainz, and the Palatinate. Some small principalities – Brunswick, Hesse-Cassel, Schaumburg-Lippe, and Hanover of course – were on Frederick's side; and there was undoubtedly a difficulty in animating the Reichsarmee. 'Against whom?' men asked. And to many besides Prussians now the King of Prussia was a German hero.

The number and potential of his enemies was, however, daunting, although Frederick doubted whether threats would materialize as rapidly as some feared. There might be delays in French activity. On 5 January 1757 there was an attempt (inflicting only a minor wound)

on the life of Louis XV by a deranged miscreant, Robert Damiens.*
Frederick wrote courteously sympathetic expressions of concern to
his enemy and fellow-sovereign,[34] but he supposed this might have
some effect on French operations in the Netherlands and Rhineland.
He knew, however, that France had hopes of persuading Sweden into
a pro-Austrian stance, threatening what had been Swedish Pomerania,
and Frederick trusted that, to deter this, the British might deploy a
squadron of the Royal Navy to the Baltic, an idea often mooted and
as often disappointed despite Mitchell's urgings. In Germany, when
the French ultimately marched to the direct support of Maria Theresa
(as he must presume they would) he envisaged them joining Austrian
troops withdrawn from the Netherlands, in the area of Nuremberg.[35]

All this was speculation. As ever the attitude and intentions of
Russia were menacing – 'Russian ferocity' – but obscure. Frederick's
information from St Petersburg was that his withdrawal into Saxony
after the battle of Lobositz had been regarded by the Russians as an
indication that Prussian power was crumbling and that it would soon
(but, he also learned, not until June) be time to send the long-proposed
help to Maria Theresa. 'Help' would probably take the form of 80,000
Russian troops and a large number – over 30,000 – of 'irregulars',
Cossacks. A convention was signed at St Petersburg binding Russia
to provide these troops as a compact with Austria and to fight until
Frederick was defeated. In every agreement made between his enemies
Silesia was mentioned, as the thorn in the international flesh. Frederick
took this calmly. 'I'll play my part and you must play yours,' he told
Mitchell, who was the bearer of this information, on Christmas Day
1756,[36] and he exchanged cheerful letters with his uncle, George II.
He knew that the Tsarina had ordered Field Marshal Count Apraxin
to prepare operations against Prussia and that Apraxin was singularly
unenthusiastic. The Russian army was in no fit condition to take

---

* Damiens was soon executed, after torture and with abominable cruelty, in the Place
de Grève in Paris, before a large and enthusiastic audience. The punishment included
the flesh being torn from the body by giant, red-hot pincers, molten lead being poured
into the wounds and the limbs then pulled from the body by outward driven horses.
Penalties for attempted regicide were understandably ferocious and the statutory sentence for high treason in England was also gruesome. The Frederician code, albeit strict,
had no provision for equivalent savagery.

the field, there were few competent officers, serious deficiencies, an inadequate cavalry. An expedition, whether into Lithuania against Memel or into Silesia, would be dangerous for them. Not only Apraxin but also the younger members of the Imperial family – the Grand Duke Peter and his remarkable wife, Catherine – were disposed to be friendly to Prussia.

But Frederick was not complacent about Russia. He learned at the end of January 1757 that the Tsarina had told Apraxin to make ready for operations whatever the condition of the army, the roads or the weather! This information reached him through the good offices of the reigning princess of Holland and he was grateful for it and for her friendship.[37] It contrasted, he said, with most of his situation – surrounded by *'femmes furieuses'* – Elizabeth, Maria Theresa, Pompadour.[38] He anticipated a Russian march into Lithuania, and thence to Warsaw; and all this would be in return for French and Austrian subsidies, on which he was well informed.[39] The number of his enemies was indeed great and their intentions certainly malign; and so far his offensive operations did not seem to have persuaded them to desist. He sent instructions – the same instructions he had used before – about what should happen if he were to be killed (everything must proceed according to plan) or be taken prisoner, in which case no attention must be paid to orders purporting to come from him; and absolutely no regard must be paid to his personal safety.[40]

February 1757, however, brought good news to Frederick. On the 18th William Pitt, later to be Earl of Chatham, spoke in the British House of Commons – a powerful speech urging wholehearted British support for the threatened King of Prussia; and on 20 February Frederick was told of the firm and final British decision to make common cause with him in his war against Austria and France. He understood that what had seemed coolness towards cooperation on the part of some Hanoverian ministers derived among other things from their ownership of lands in Saxony and consequent sensitivity about Prussian policy there. It was to be hoped that a better spirit would now prevail, although he knew that the French, in particular, would always try to drive a wedge between the interests of the King of England and that king's interests as Elector of Hanover. Frederick himself mistrusted the Hanoverians and it has to be said that they mistrusted him. He had, however, a good man, von Schmettau, as his representative in Hanover.

Pitt had been out of office in England for some time but from December 1756 was Secretary of State and leader of the House of Commons under the premiership of the Duke of Devonshire. Although he again had two months out of office, from April to June 1757, his passionate resolution to carry on war against France with energy until the end was strongly supported by much of the country. When he returned to power in June it was at the head of a War Administration which lasted until 1761. And although he had a reputation for scepticism about the interests of Hanover (and somewhat offended George II thereby), no better development could have been imagined from Frederick's point of view. Pitt's implacable hostility to France was not particularly sympathetic to Frederick, but he reckoned he saw in Pitt a spirit of resolution and imagination; and that he liked. After Pitt's February speech Frederick sent a personal message of gratitude to 'The Great Commoner'. The advent to power of Pitt brought Prussia a subsidy of £700,000. It meant that there was a friend and ally of Prussia prepared to act in northern and western Germany, a reliable support with, however, one deplorable lapse which Frederick, mercifully, could not yet foresee. 'It has taken a long time and much pain for England to produce a *man* but she's finally done so!' Frederick remarked some time later to Mitchell.[41]

In his letter of appreciation to George II Frederick – never backward in making suggestions about command in other armies – urged that consideration be given to placing the Duke of Cumberland at the head of a British continental army, a recommendation which was acted upon but which he would have reason to regret. In the immediate future, however, all seemed encouraging. As to the quartering of Hanoverians (and Hessians, contracted to Britain) in Westphalia, Frederick expressed himself happy to give them free lodging – he suggested Minden, Bielefeld, Herford and small places like Petershagen. In a letter to Mitchell confirming this in March, Frederick nevertheless told him that the Hanoverian ministers in touch with his own gave an impression of indifference to British interests – of, perhaps, still hankering after that 'false neutrality' which had earlier been mooted. It bothered him and it should, he suggested, bother

London too.[42] He complained, courteously, to Mitchell that the British seemed somewhat unconcerned with continental affairs. In February, however, the British Parliament had approved support for an 'army of observation' for the defence of Hanover if required; and the Duke of Cumberland, as suggested by Frederick, was appointed to command it, and sailed for Germany on 10 April.[43] His instructions from his father came by the medium of the Hanoverian rather than British ministers.

In mid March Frederick sent a general appreciation of the military situation to Schwerin. The French, he now reckoned, would cross the Rhine with 80,000 men – more than his earlier estimate because they would be joined by Austrian troops from the Netherlands. Fifty thousand of the enemy would besiege Wesel and 30,000 march east towards Magdeburg. In Bohemia Browne, with the main Austrian army, would not move until he calculated that Frederick himself was moving against the French. At that moment he would reckon he could concentrate superior strength against the Prussians. Browne probably considered Frederick something of an amateur; a prince enthusiastically playing soldiers. His plan would be to keep the Austrian army ready at the right moment to invade Saxony, while with smaller forces to range through Silesia from Moravia. If this were coordinated with a French offensive from the Rhine all the odds would be against Prussia.

To deal with Browne Frederick produced alternative 'projects', contingency plans with detailed possibilities of enemy deployment and proposed counter-moves, and sent his papers for comment to Winterfeldt, whose opinion he valued, and to Schwerin at Neisse. Browne might stand on the defensive and await a French move to join him; he might advance towards the French; he might try, himself, to advance into Saxony. In these various cases Frederick suggested the appropriate counter-deployments, allocating troops to tasks, to march routes and so forth.[44] It was detailed work, based so far on supposition. He knew that Browne's headquarters were at Prague and those of his subordinate, Prince Ottavio Piccolomini, at Kolin, thirty miles east of Prague along the great highway, the Kaiserstrasse. He supposed the Austrians were quartered on a wide front between Pilsen, west of the Moldau, and Königgrätz on the Upper Elbe. In some cases, for instance if Browne operated northward towards Zittau, in Lusatia, Frederick was prepared to draw back towards Bautzen.

From Neisse, on 24 March, Schwerin sent thoughtful comments on Frederick's contingency plans.[45] He saw the various hazards to which each of Frederick's contingency counter-moves might be exposed and Frederick, agreeing in principle with his ideas, wrote to thank him – '*vous êtes un vieux routier!*' – and their exchanges were crucial in making up Frederick's mind in a sense very different from his plans hitherto.

He decided that he would not develop any of his 'projects' in response to Browne. Instead he would take the offensive and Browne should dance to his tune. Despite the huge superiority in numbers of their enemies to north, west, east, south, the Prussians would attack. They would defeat the Austrians before French intervention or Russian intervention could be effective.

Frederick therefore now proposed to invade Bohemia; to do so on a broad front and extremely soon.

On the right Prince Moritz of Anhalt-Dessau would advance from west Saxony towards the valley of the Eger, with 20,000 men, creating maximum disturbance. In the centre the Duke of Bevern, whom Frederick planned to reinforce to about 16,000, would operate south to Reichenberg and towards the valley of the Iser: these operations, initially limited because of the considerable Austrian forces – probably 30,000 – opposite, would be facilitated by the actions of Schwerin. For on the extreme left Schwerin, with 34,000 Prussian troops from Silesia, would operate inwards, westward, towards Bevern. The Austrians, aware of this threat, would seek to avoid the pincers of Bevern and Schwerin, due to close somewhere in the Elbe valley. They would run, and subsequent operations would depend on the Austrian line of withdrawal. Frederick, in the centre but on Bevern's right, would march with 40,000 men up the left, west, bank of the Elbe by the familiar route through Lobositz. He would unite, thereabouts, with Moritz, cross the Eger and march on Prague. He was concerned about forage; the combined forces would number a great many men and a great many horses and Bohemia, he reminded Schwerin, was *radicalement mangée*.

This was a great concept, a true 'operation', and Frederick took considerable trouble to keep it secret – *'notre affaire secrète'* he called it to Schwerin.[46] Only a tiny number were told details. If his moves went as planned he could surprise the enemy and considerable numbers might be trapped in the area of the Eger and its confluence with the Elbe; and his strategic concept, which might lead to considerable victory over the Austrians in the first phase, should lead, in a second phase, to their flight to the Prague area. In the first phase his operational plan, involving the movements of widely separated forces in some sort of coordination, was much affected by where the various enemy magazines and supply depots were situated. These were essential to his own campaign, especially those at Jung Bunzlau on the Iser, at Budin, at Leitmeritz, and at Königgrätz.

Frederick's correspondence conveys much excitement. His ambitious concept involved a decision to pass to the offensive, to ignore for a while the huge threats building up against Prussia from various directions, to coordinate an invasion of Bohemia by widely separated forces – all this had been hatched in comparatively few days. In the last week in March he had digested and agreed Schwerin's comments. On 7 April he received Mitchell in audience and told him, without details, that he planned a *coup* which should encourage his allies, upset Austrian plans, discourage the French and make the Russians think twice before involving themselves.[47] The organization of such an operation with the communications of the day – and winter was hardly over – on a front of 140 miles including much of the Riesengebirge, and its completion in less than a fortnight, bore remarkable witness to Frederick's energy and power of decision as well as to the training and professionalism of his troops.

Frederick put the minimum in writing until it was absolutely necessary in order to get the troops on the move in time, and even then he kept much of the concept locked in his heart. On 10 April he told George II[48] as much as he felt he could, well aware that detail could change with the enemy's reactions. In his letter to his uncle he wrote that Browne, according to his latest information, seemed to have divided his army into four parts. Thirty thousand were based in the city of Eger, presumably intended ultimately to join a French army marching from the Rhine via Bamberg and then to move north through

Erfurt and threaten Prussia's western frontier at Magdeburg; 50,000 were at Budin, the confluence of Eger and Elbe, centrally placed; 30,000, he reckoned, were on the borders of Lusatia, presumably intended to pre-empt or defeat a Prussian irruption into Bohemia from the north: 30,000 were at Königgrätz, to watch and ward the Prussians in Silesia and Glatz. In total Frederick was hugely outnumbered and knew it.

Frederick told his uncle – the letter of 10 April could not be read until operations were well developed – that, based on this enemy deployment and the existence of depots, he intended that his right wing, Moritz of Anhalt-Dessau, should draw the enemy's eyes westward by operating towards the Eger; this, he told Mitchell at an audience a week later, was essentially a deception, a distraction,[49] which had already begun. In the centre Frederick himself proposed to move to Aussig and to march south by the Elbe valley. On the extreme left Schwerin would march to seize the depot at Jung Bunzlau and then effect a junction with Frederick at Leitmeritz, while in the centre Bevern would advance south from his position at Zittau against the Austrians facing Schwerin, and, Frederick wrote, *leur donnera la chasse* before uniting with the latter. Browne would be confused by these operations from all directions and would withdraw southward. Frederick anticipated being on the Beraun, south of Prague, by midMay and then being 'balanced' to confront French or Russians and 'to help his allies'.

To an extent this was probably written for effect, although it gave the outline of the Prussian operation accurately enough. It also showed the range of Frederick's concept and certainly exalted his potential as an ally. But Frederick only disclosed when they were about to happen the essential moves which he hoped would really confound Browne. This depended not only on Schwerin taking Jung Bunzlau (it was in fact taken by Bevern before he got there) but on Schwerin marching with such energy that, in conjunction with Bevern's troops, he would trap the Austrians watching the Lusatian border between pincers from north and east – trap them east of the Elbe or north of the Eger. The success of the plan depended on the detailed moves made by each commander, their direction, timing and speed. These matters were not easy to coordinate from a distance and Frederick could only try to impart urgency with his pen. 'We're all ready!' he wrote to Schwerin on 11 April. 'Hurry now! Ignore everything except essentials!'[50] Whether or not a battle had been fought Schwerin's troops, augmented if all went well by Bevern's, must march to the Elbe and join him at Leitmeritz. If that were not done, if Schwerin allowed himself to be pushed or drawn instead to the east, to the middle Elbe at Kolin or Königgrätz, Browne would be able to withdraw into central Bohemia, Frederick would probably need again to retreat into Saxony and the whole project would fail. He told Schwerin, striking an unusually harsh note with so distinguished a commander, much his senior, that his orders must be obeyed *au pied de la lettre*.[51] And when some of Schwerin's Saxon regiments were reporting deserters, Frederick, exasperated, told Schwerin that at such a moment it was unimportant if 2,000 deserted – '*Ne pensez point à ces f— Saxons! Pressez-vous donc!*' His eyes were on the hoped-for junction of Schwerin with Bevern, preferably behind the Iser at somewhere like Münchengrätz.

But all went well although not exactly as Frederick planned. Bevern, on his march south from Zittau, met a force of 28,000 Austrians north of Reichenberg on the Neisse; met them and, on 21 April, beat them in a battle which lasted eleven hours and which he followed by the capture of the magazine at Jung Bunzlau towards which Schwerin had been moving. On the same day Frederick wrote to Schwerin, exultant: 'Here's a miracle, dear Marshal, our secret has been kept and our enemy surprised!'[52] Next day his own advance guard started to march south to join forces with Moritz. He crossed the Eger at Koschtitz and outflanked the Austrians at Budin. The effect of his march was to lever Browne's forces out of position south of the Eger at Welwarn and to force them into a retreat towards Prague.

The concept had now to change, and rapidly. Whereas, earlier, Frederick had envisaged Schwerin and Bevern marching towards the Elbe at Leitmeritz and closing a comparatively shallow trap, Bevern's victory of 21 April and his junction with Schwerin meant that this arm of the Prussian army could form an eastern pincer, could march south from Jung Bunzlau and then swing west. Frederick's troops would form the western pincer and the pincers would meet at the Bohemian capital. The effect of these manoeuvres, intelligently modified as they had been, was to clear the Austrians from northern

Bohemia. Frederick, as he had forecast, was now following up an enemy running for Prague. At the end of April he heard that the Austrians were encamped on the Weisserberg, the White Mountain, scene of the battle which had launched the Thirty Years War.

Browne, suffering severely from tuberculosis, handed over command of his army on 30 April to the Archduke Charles while still remaining himself in the field. On 2 May Frederick was again standing before Prague.

At Prague Frederick faced a dilemma. For a systematic siege the place would need considerable forces, deployed as a besieging army. The garrison was large, the perimeter enormous. While the main body of the Austrian army was in being and within reach, concentrated or able to concentrate for battle and dominating much of the surrounding country, a siege was virtually impossible. It must, anyway, mean men, equipment and time. Frederick was short of all. He would have about 64,000 men, and the Archduke Charles had about the same number as well as the garrison of the city. Frederick's best hope was to beat the Austrians in open field: unless he did so he would be compelled to withdraw. It was a dilemma which often faced a commander whose manoeuvres had successfully brought him to the surrounding of a fortified place but whose strength would not enable him to subdue it, and whose army needed supply.

In seeking a battle with the main Austrian army, Frederick had to accept that the enemy's position was strong and that an unsubdued garrison of Prague on the Prussian flank or rear made it stronger. Charles had crossed the river Moldau and had deployed his Austrians east of the city, facing north on the general line of the Kaiserstrasse with their centre several miles from the centre of Prague. Their line was along a plateau rising to the Taborberg, a low hill just south of the great highway.

Frederick felt optimistic. He ordered Schwerin and Bevern to march towards him as rapidly as possible. He told Mitchell on 4 May that the determining fight between Habsburgs and Hohenzollerns might be about to take place. He had hoped to fight west of the Moldau but Charles's movements meant that a major engagement could only take place east of Prague and a major engagement was what Frederick reckoned he needed. He nevertheless kept Keith with 30,000 men west of the Moldau. This gave him a reserve if a new situation arose, it gave him a potential interception force if the Austrians, after defeat, tried to escape west of Prague, and it gave him a firm 'foot on the ground' if matters went awry. This decision inevitably meant that Frederick was shorter of men for the main action than he might have been, although he would still slightly outnumber Charles when Schwerin joined him; and it has been criticized as weakening him at the point of decision and leaving troops out of battle for contingencies which did not arise. Wellington at Waterloo has been similarly criticized for the deployment of Hill's corps to the west of what became the actual battlefield: but such criticisms are easier to mount – and harder to refute – when the whole business is satisfactorily over.

Frederick determined to manoeuvre, to march round the Austrian right flank with a wide and deep movement. He needed Schwerin's and Bevern's men, to level the odds, and when they arrived in the early morning of 6 May, having marched through the darkness under the ferocious exhortations of the King, they formed the Prussian left wing. Frederick, with the main body, had crossed the Moldau by a bridge of boats and by six o'clock in the morning of 6 May the army was united again.

Frederick at once ordered Schwerin, with Winterfeldt, to reconnoitre ground to the east, towards what seemed to be the Austrian right in the direction of the villages of Hostawitz and Unter Poczernitz just north of the Kaiserstrasse. He wanted to start his manoeuvres as quickly as possible and soon the main body of the Prussian army east of the Moldau was on the move east along the Prosek ridge at about the same altitude as the Kaiserstrasse and separated from it by a shallow valley through which ran a stream, the Roketnitzer Bach. At a certain point they would turn south on their great outflanking march.

The movement developed and it was soon clear to the Austrians what was happening. A threat might soon appear – how soon depended on the energy of the Prussian advance – to the Austrian deep flank. To counter this, an infantry force with twelve regiments of cavalry was redeployed to the village of Sterbohol and the ground south of it. The Prussian outflanking movement was led by the seventy-three-year-old Schwerin himself, determined to reach an advantageous

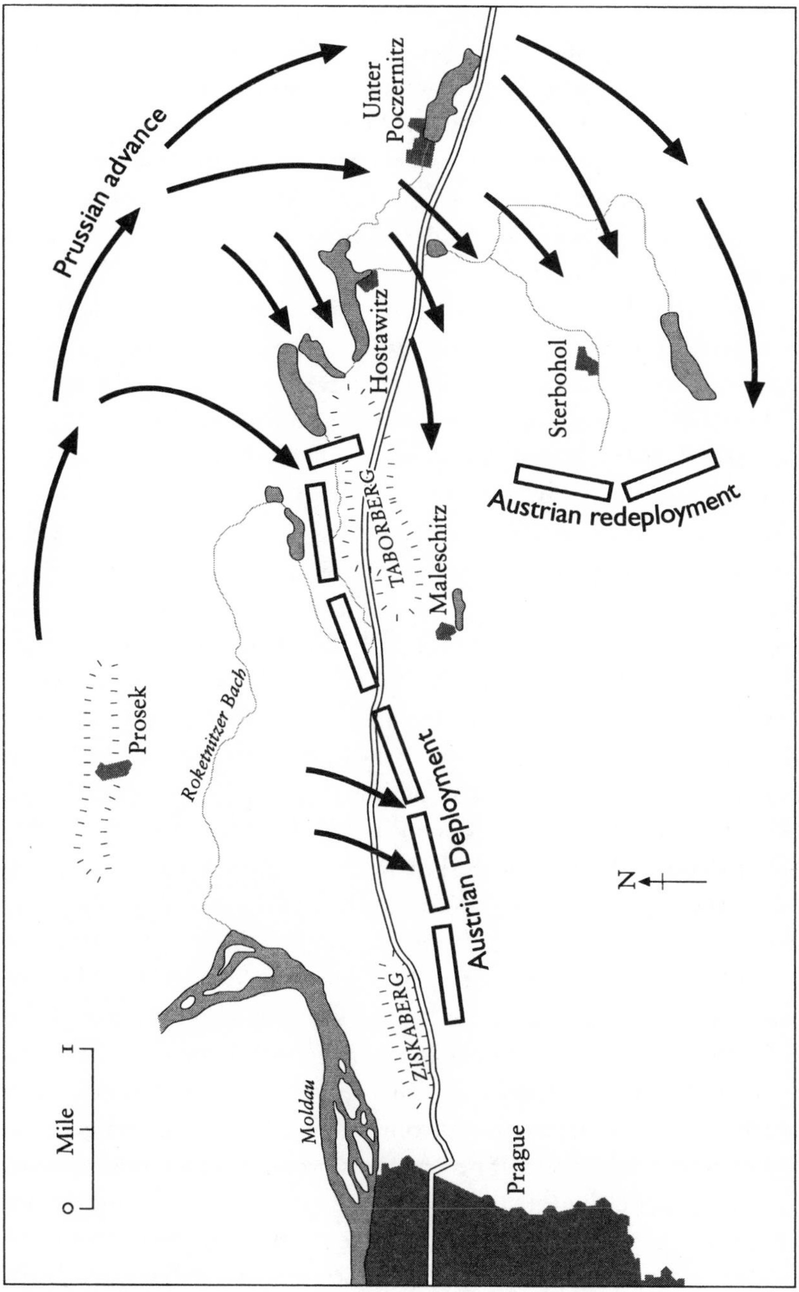

Prussian advance

Unter
Poczernitz

Hostawitz

Sterbohol

TABORBERG

Maleschitz

Austrian redeployment

Prosek

Roketnitzer Bach

Austrian Deployment

N

Mile

1

0

ZISKABERG

Moldau

Prague

Prague, 6 May 1757

position on the plateau facing west, south of the Kaiserstrasse. He pushed his cavalry on as fast as possible. They were largely unsupported by artillery since the guns were getting stuck in the infuriatingly soft going (drained fishponds, acting as a sort of polder), in which wheels, men and horses all became bogged, as well as in the narrow streets of Unter Poczernitz. Schwerin drove his leading infantry battalions, fourteen in number, to get round somehow and to form a firm west-facing front. He was determined to pre-empt the arrival of the Austrians in strength.

Frederick galloped to Sterbohol. He was worried at the possibility of committing the army 'piecemeal' and he was anxious at what seemed the difficulties and delays of the advance but he found Schwerin as determined as himself. If they could win a forming-up place facing west south of the Kaiserstrasse, the terrible 'moving walls' should once again settle the matter.

But the ground was defeating them. And now Austrian artillery fire from the higher ground behind Sterbohol began to inflict casualties in the struggling regiments. Some of them showed signs of breaking and at about eleven o'clock Winterfeldt, riding with the advance guard, was hit by a musket ball and fell, badly wounded. Schwerin himself, riding forward to rally the men of his own regiment, fell dead in front of them with most of his head removed by canister shot; and at the same time Austrian infantry began to counter-attack the Prussians extending north from Sterbohol.

At this stage of the battle the Prussians seized an opportunity. There was a gap between the right of the main Austrian north-facing line and the left of the forces redeployed to face Schwerin's outflanking movement. Into this gap, east of the Taborberg, twenty-two Prussian battalions began a westward advance, south and west of the village of Hostawitz. The initiative was taken by regimental commanders, catching the impulse from each other in the confusion of battle, and under the general direction or encouragement – impossible to exercise in any detail – of Bevern. The Prussians broke through and began to do what Frederick had always hoped – roll up the Austrian north-facing line from right to left. At the same time fresh squadrons of Prussian cavalry under Lieutenant-General von Ziethen moved round a small lake at the extreme south of the battlefield and attacked the southernmost Austrian cavalry who had moved to that flank. Ziethen, one of the great names of the war, had been marked early by Frederick. Small, ugly, weak-voiced, quarrelsome and too much given to drink when young, he had once killed a man without justification; and had crossed swords with Frederick in peacetime when, at a great concourse of commanders at Spandau in 1753, he had chosen to remain silent although asked to give his views on some proposed new cavalry manoeuvres. When ordered by the King to speak he had been barely subordinate – 'I'd know how to react if the situation actually arose!' Thereafter he had been given the cold shoulder by Frederick, and had applied to resign although war seemed imminent. Frederick had then seen him personally – 'so faithful an officer cannot leave his king and fatherland at such a time!' – and Ziethen had succumbed and thrown himself at the King's feet. Reputation wholly restored, he was now an immensely effective cavalry commander, nearly sixty years old, a man of vigour and audacity.[53]

Meanwhile on the ridge, where Austrian east-facing positions had been hastily taken up among earthworks north of the Kaiserstrasse and west of Hostawitz, four Prussian battalions under Major-General von Manstein drove them into retreat. By early afternoon the Austrians had been routed on their right, southern and eastern wings, by the Prussian turning movement through and round Sterbohol. In the centre they rallied behind a gully which ran north from Maleschitz and inflicted heavy casualties on the Prussians: but on their original north-facing centre and right a fresh Prussian infantry attack led by Prince Henry broke in and threatened them from a new quarter. By three o'clock in the afternoon the Austrian army, defeated, was retreating towards Prague.

Frederick had defeated a numerically superior or equal army in position – and a strong position. He had been suffering personally from a serious stomach disorder and had been frequently sick throughout the day. By the evening he felt shattered. He had won a battle, and it had to a great degree gone as he had intended, but he had lost over 14,000 men – more than the enemy as it transpired. The effectiveness of the Austrian defensive fire had reduced Frederick's belief in the all-conquering moral effect of his advancing infantry. The loss of Schwerin – Schwerin who had once fought at Blenheim, 'one of the greatest generals of our century', he wrote to George II[54] – and the incapacitating of Winterfeldt, to whom he was devoted, hit him hard. There had been terrible casualties among those infantry. He described the battle of Prague as one of the most murderous on record.

Having launched the original manoeuvre which set the stage for battle, Frederick had not much intervened, nor needed to even if it had been possible, although he had strengthened Schwerin's resolve (which hardly needed it) when he first arrived at Sterbohol and saw the possibilities of further attack by the left wing. For the most part the opportunism and initiative which had decided the day, which had led the Prussians to exploit the gap on the Austrian right, which had led to cavalry success in the south and to Prince Henry's break-in in the centre – these had been the work of subordinate and regimental commanders – Ziethen, Manstein, Prince Henry. Frederick's, certainly, was the concept which had led to victory – and it was indeed a victory. The tactical conduct of the battle had not been his and he did not claim it. His army was now east of the garrisoned city of Prague, into which had poured most of the Austrian survivors of battle and which, he must hope, would shortly be so short of supplies that capitulation would follow. The loss of Prague might be sufficient to discourage Austria from continuing the war. Browne, serving voluntarily under the Archduke, had been mortally wounded, dying on 26 June.

Capitulation might be encouraged by a bombardment, and at the end of May the Prussians, who had laboriously set up siege batteries with heavy ordnance shipped up the Elbe and transported overland from Leitmeritz with all the delay which that involved, opened fire with heavy cannon and siege mortars. Frederick had heard that another Austrian army under Field Marshal von Daun, said to number 14,000, had appeared on his eastern flank but had withdrawn towards Kolin, thirty-five miles to the eastward.[55]

13

Kolin and After

The summer of 1757 was approaching. Frederick had marched into Saxony nine months earlier. He had invaded Bohemia, withdrawn and invaded it again. He had wintered in an enemy capital among an enemy sovereign's papers and palaces. He had fought and won two battles beside Bevern's victory on the road to Reichenberg.

The capital city of Bohemia was holding out and the Austrians were still in the field, but while the King of Prussia could maintain the momentum of his campaign it might be that his bold attempt to disrupt the plans of his enemies would succeed. 'I am obliged,' he told Wilhelmina, 'alone to defend Germany's liberties, privileges and religion. Germany is at present in terrible crisis.' He was engaging greatly superior numbers but he was engaging them near-singly so far, and far from the borders of Prussia itself. He was periodically plagued by stories of Hanoverian intrigues – the latest was a rumour that Frederick himself was in negotiations with Vienna, a story Mitchell scotched.[1] 'The King of Prussia,' the latter wrote to Holdernesse, 'frankly said that he wanted to do all the harm he possibly could to his present enemy.' Mitchell reckoned that the Hanoverian ministers were frequently playing false by both Prussia and Britain.[2] If the Austrians were again to show themselves for another beating, Frederick had dreams of marching west thereafter, with Austria eliminated, to beat the French before they could develop an effective offensive themselves. All this was consistent with Frederick's philosophy: when threatened, attack. When outnumbered, choose a target and, again, attack.

Despite setbacks and disappointments his record, so far, was one of an unbroken sequence of victories, although some of them had been narrow; and some of them had been expensive. As to allies, he was disappointed in Britain. There had been no response to his request for a British naval squadron in the Baltic and he thought the British disunited and half-hearted; 'The English are no longer the same people,' he told Mitchell early in June. 'Your want of union and steadiness has dissipated the natural strength of your nation and if the same conduct is continued England will no longer be considered of great importance in Europe.'[3]

In the next months there would be radical changes in the nature of the war and in the fortunes of Prussia. In north Germany his enemies were to range freely for a while but at the end of six months Frederick, by a brilliant series of victories, would defeat the greatest powers in Europe and make 1757 the most glorious year in Prussian military history between Fehrbellin in 1675 and Leipzig in 1813. First, however, Frederick and his army would face something like annihilation.

The bombardment of Prague which began on 29 May was undertaken with twenty twelve-pounder guns and ten twenty-five pounders, together shooting some 30,000 shells. There were, additionally, twelve heavy mortars, each throwing a huge fifty-pound bomb, of which the army had 6,000. The bombardment followed a storm which had destroyed bridges and threatened to divide in two the besieging Prussian army. It caused many fires and killed many people. It had not, however, brought capitulation and thus had not seemed to have had great effect when Frederick learned disturbing news from eastern Bohemia. By the end of the first week in June he knew that the Austrians had assembled a fresh army in the east. This was not Daun's '14,000' thought by Frederick to be hastily withdrawing towards Kolin; this was said to be of formidable size – a figure of 55,000 was alleged, which Frederick was disposed to doubt. There was, however, no doubt about a threat from the east to the Prussians around Prague, and Frederick, having previously deployed Bevern with 24,000 men in the area of Kolin to keep the Austrians at a distance on that flank, now had cause to wonder whether his measure would be sufficient. Bevern had meanwhile captured supply depots, including one at Kolin.

The Austrian army in question was under the command of Leopold, Count von Daun. Daun had proved himself, in the war of Austrian succession, as a careful, prudent commander who had been trusted by Traun – and Traun was an object of veneration to Frederick; Daun had fought at Chotusitz, Hohenfriedeberg and Soor, and been made a field marshal in 1754. Now a number of men who had escaped from the Archduke Charles's army after the defeat outside Prague had joined him and he was, it appeared, moving towards the Prussian army. Frederick did not know much about Daun as a commander, since the latter's position so far had been subordinate. It is, however, likely that Daun, an acute man, knew rather more about Frederick. Frederick's first thought was that Daun had orders to avoid battle. He was wrong.[4] Daun intended to raise the Prussian siege of Prague and that would probably mean fighting.

Frederick decided to take a small force to reinforce Bevern and to get a 'feel' for the situation on this flank. 'Leopold Daun is being reinforced,' he wrote on 6 June to Keith, who was with the besieging force at Prague. 'We must prevent him [interfering with us], must put together all we can, attack him, and chase him as far away as possible.'[5] He left the siege of Prague and rode eastward on 13 June with sixteen squadrons of cavalry, fifteen guns and four battalions of infantry. Next day he joined Bevern, who had marched from Kolin, and absorbed the latest information. It was clear that this might be a threat to take seriously.

It might, also, be an opportunity. He sent word to Prince Moritz of Anhalt at Prague to join him – to join him and to bring all the troops who could without difficulty be withdrawn from the army investing the city. Moritz acted swiftly and within forty-eight hours Frederick had 35,000 men in hand. By nightfall on 17 June he knew that Daun had deployed his army – and he accepted that it was over 50,000 and that the Prussians were seriously outnumbered – facing north along the line of the Kaiserstrasse, the great highway running east from Prague to Kolin, about fifteen miles east of his earlier battlefield. The Austrians appeared to have taken position on a number of low ridges, south of and parallel to the Kaiserstrasse, ridges of diminishing height until crossed in the east by the highway itself. Of these, two were prominent – the Przerovsky Hill about one and a half miles south of the Kaiserstrasse, a long east-west running feature, and the Krzeczhorz Hill, immediately west of the village of that name and about one mile from the highway.

Frederick had absolute confidence in his army. He knew it was outnumbered although he was probably ignorant – or refused to take in – the extent of the disparity. He reckoned that if he marched the Prussian army eastward, straight down the line of the Kaiserstrasse, it would be possible at a certain point to wheel the marching columns right – south – and climb what looked to be an easy gradient; and thus to bring them on to the higher ground on the Austrian right. If he had marched sufficiently far he would have outflanked the enemy and could form a west-facing front of assault. Then the irresistible Prussian infantry would, once again, roll up the enemy from the flank. The left flank of the Prussian approach march, including the great wheel, would be protected by the cavalry who would thereafter be kept in reserve. Frederick gave his orders to his generals and pointed out the ground from the upper floor of an inn on the Kaiserstrasse, east of Planian and ten miles west of Kolin. At about one o'clock in the afternoon of 18 June the troops moved off, straight down the Kaiserstrasse. It was an exceptionally hot day.

The initial right wheel off the Kaiserstrasse was scheduled to take place opposite the village of Krzeczhorz. The Prussian advance guard of seven battalions was commanded by Major-General Hulsen, followed by the division of Lieutenant-General von Treskow. Before the movement had got far two things were evident. First, Daun had certainly extended his own position to his right – to the east; second, there were Austrians in Krzeczhorz. It was clear from this that the first phase of the Prussian manoeuvre, the outflanking march, would be more difficult and would (if practicable) take longer than planned. And Frederick took a fateful decision. The bulk of his army were still in line of march along the Kaiserstrasse.

It appeared to Frederick that he might save time and still achieve his object by changing the line of his approach. A wood, 'Oak Wood', lay immediately south of the village of Krzeczhorz and Frederick gave the order for a short cut to be taken by Hulsen's battalions, marching in column of route. They and those following them were to make straight for Oak Wood, whence they could deploy to carry out the original concept, appearing on the Austrian right flank and progressively reinforced by the rest of the Prussian army.

For this to work, however, the Austrians who had occupied the

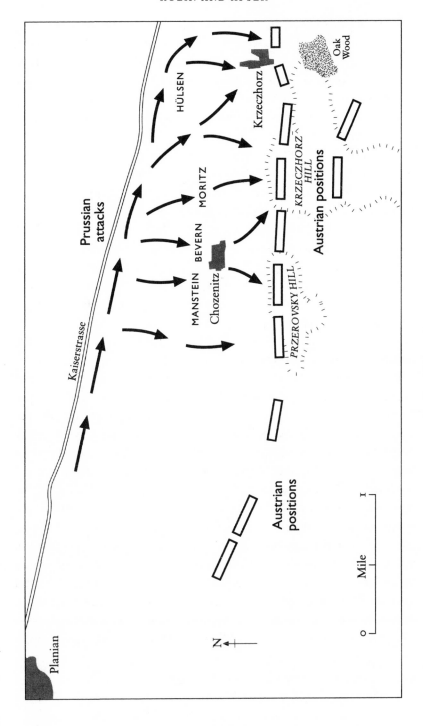

Kolin, 18 June 1757

Oak Wood

Krzeczhorz

HÜLSEN

KRZECZHORZ HILL

Austrian positions

MORITZ

BEVERN

MANSTEIN

Chozenitz

PRZEROVSKY HILL

Prussian attacks

Kaiserstrasse

Austrian positions

Planian

N

0   Mile   1

village and those who had been redeployed from Daun's reserve to his right needed to be fewer than they were and either cowed or remarkably inactive. In fact, Daun had extended his right with an entire division and Frederick soon realized – and it must have been with despair, whatever the several records – that he was marching up a hill towards an unbroken enemy force in position and with an enemy-garrisoned village on his flank.

Frederick responded to this situation in the only way he could. He ordered the advancing troops to wheel their platoons into line ready to engage. Prince Moritz, seeing that the battle would soon be one of Prussian lines advancing uphill towards a deployed enemy in strength, hesitated and Frederick barked his order again. Into line! The Prussians, therefore, were moving forward in a frontal attack, uphill, outnumbered, and with no favourable circumstance whatsoever. There was nothing to do but press on in this desperate manoeuvre. Moritz's men were falling in swathes before the Austrian heavy artillery and infantrymen in position on the higher ground. They, like their commander, saw that this was disaster and said it aloud. Moritz, himself, called out that the battle was lost.

Further mishaps made the day ever more fearful. Croat sharpshooters had been harassing the flanks of the Prussian line of march along the Kaiserstrasse and General von Manstein, commanding the detachment immediately following Moritz, organized a quick attack to clear them, an attack which ultimately involved his whole force of five battalions. This operation – which reached further than Manstein intended – involved what became a subsidiary attack against the Austrian centre, and an expensive one although Manstein took the village of Chozenitz and began to climb the Przerovsky Hill.* But by late afternoon the general situation was a Prussian army, extended in line and struggling upwards over dead and wounded comrades, in a battle which looked to have no possible outcome except disaster and a battle their king had certainly not designed or intended. At seven o'clock in the evening, nevertheless, the Prussian infantry had reached the crest of the Krzeczhorz Hill in an attack to which Frederick

---

* Manstein's action was selected for special condemnation by the German General Staff in their history of the battle (*GGS*, Vol. 3).

committed every man he could find alive. This attack seemed, at long last, to have opened something like a gap in the Austrian line.

The attack was led by Bevern, whose regiments had been on Frederick's centre right as they marched along the Kaiserstrasse. The Austrians were now running out of ammunition and it seemed for a little possible that, once again and at the last moment, Prussian energy and sheer dogged courage could snatch an improbable victory. Austrian cavalry, counter-attacking towards the village of Krzeczhorz, were themselves attacked on their right flank with ferocity and effect by the Prussian cavalry of General von Krosigk, who was killed in the battle. But although Bevern's battalions had made a gap it could not be exploited. It was too late. The Prussian army had been worn down by its repeated attacks, its appalling casualties. The Prussian breach, furthermore, was sealed on the ridge by Austrian initiatives, and by a great cavalry counter-attack, with both Austrian and Saxon squadrons, from Oak Wood. By eight o'clock that evening the last trick had been played. Small groups of Prussians were straggling back towards the Kaiserstrasse. Frederick had lost 14,000* men, the Austrians only 8,000. He had also lost forty-five guns, twenty-two colours and a major battle. The Austrians bivouacked on the field they had won.

Frederick was completely shattered. When he had seen what, from whatever cause, was unfolding – a frontal attack, uphill, against a strongly posted enemy in position (and one in greatly superior numbers although he is unlikely to have realized it at the time) – he had ridden to every quarter of the field attempting to inspire, to rally, to turn the tide. When the Prussian attack faltered in the ascent of the Przerovsky Hill he had drawn his sword and himself advanced at the head of the Anhalt regiment. To Manstein's battalions, wavering in their assault of the same objective, he had roared (as became legend), 'Rogues, would you live for ever?'†[6] He was everywhere; and everywhere it became more apparent as the hours passed that he had involved his magnificent army in a stupendous disaster.

---

* Losses were of the dead, wounded and missing. Of the Prussian army 9,600 were killed at Kolin, and 1,600 horses.

† *'Kerls, wollt ihr denn ewig leben?'* The story goes that an old grenadier called out, 'Listen, Fritz, I thought for thirteen pfennigs pay we'd done enough!'

Criticism of Frederick came fast and has slackened little with the years. Why did he take on superior forces, while still leaving Prague under siege and a large number of Prussian soldiers there? It is unlikely he appreciated the odds: perhaps his over-confidence, his trust in a winning streak, led him to reject unpalatable information – it would not be a unique example. Why did he change his plan and the line of the approach march? He was probably most influenced by the factor of time. He would not have been the only commander in history to find that a planned manoeuvre was taking longer than it should and then to try to save precious minutes by adopting a variant; it was, however, a disastrous variant with the enemy deployed as they were. Why did he deploy the advancing troops into line and lead them into an uphill battle against odds? It is likely that he found this the least awful of the choices available, once the troops were committed to advance from a direction he had not planned. A battle against the Austrians on higher ground was now inevitable, so the Prussians needed to form line to fight it.

It may also be that Frederick thought he saw an opportunity which was not there. He may have first supposed that he might catch the Austrians in the actual process of reinforcing their right to counter Hulsen – supposed that he could, in effect, catch Daun doing something which he had probably already done. For this, speed was needed above all things; the most direct and simple route, the fastest pace. This could have led Frederick to march the leading echelons across the chord of an arc, towards Oak Wood, hoping or assuming that the Austrians so far deployed could be brushed aside. Then he might, having gained a lodgement on the Austrian right flank, have simply 'fed' the battle so vigorously that a Prussian force with preponderant strength could be built up where he wanted it. But the way the fighting developed, the strength of the Austrians in position, the actions of Manstein – all made nonsense of such hopes if Frederick entertained them.

There may have been elements of some of the foregoing in Frederick's mind and motives. It is unlikely we shall ever know. All that can be known is that the formidable King of Prussia had suffered a major defeat. The taste of defeat is bitter but he wrote to George II without equivocation on 20 June: 'after eight consecutive battles won, here is the first one lost. But I despair of nothing. I only need a little time to restore the troops and I'll find a way of making good the situation.'[7] To 'Milord Maréchal' he wrote that Fortune had turned her back on him – she was a woman, Frederick was unchivalrous, Fortune had smiled instead on the ladies who were at war with him.

Frederick rode from the terrible field of Kolin to his previous head-quarters at Lissa, north-east of Prague. Every year the anniversary of the battle, 18 June, would fill his mind with dark memories. He collapsed on a bale of straw and was for some time incapable of initiative. The army, clearly, had to be withdrawn and he gave orders to his brother, Henry, to see to the details, which he did with competence. On 20 June the siege of Prague was abandoned and the army rallied northward, based on Leitmeritz.

Then Frederick began to recover. He wrote to Keith on 25 June that he hoped to win enough time to repair matters – fast.[8] He needed to regain freedom of movement for the army, to provide for the defence of Silesia, to protect his communications with Prussia and to ensure supplies. He heard that Daun, predictably, was marching towards Prague but exactly where he was Frederick did not know – he had lost touch. He told August Wilhelm, the Prince of Prussia, to take command of 35,000 men, about half the army, and cover the approaches to the Elbe. He, himself, would join him later. Meanwhile he rode to Leitmeritz, establishing his residence at the episcopal palace there on 27 June.

At Leitmeritz Frederick found Mitchell and told him about the battle. His account was restrained and dignified. He did not blame others, although he said that the 'too great ardour' of some of his troops (he meant Manstein's command) had embroiled the Prussians in an unintended way. His written account, dated 22 June, was bare and unadorned by comment. Later he told de Catt that the battle might have been won. 'He has now,' Mitchell told Holdernesse, 'recovered his spirits.'[9] He was showing resilience. 'I have seen the King of Prussia great in prosperity, but greater still in adversity,' the ambassador wrote. Frederick recognized, however, that there must not, or not yet, be another battle unless he could be confident of winning it.[10]

The size of the campaigning area over which he had to meet threats to Prussia was uppermost in Frederick's mind, as well as the costs of another campaign if he had to fight one – and it was pretty clear that he would. He carefully sounded Mitchell about the possibility of a British subsidy to help keep him in the field – Frederick had always disliked the idea of subsidy and the dependence it implied but he had to face the fact that simultaneous Austrian, French and Russian incursions could reduce his revenues disastrously. Mitchell undertook to do what he could, and was impressed by Frederick's obviously genuine embarrassment. Frederick sent an affectionate and philosophic line to d'Argens in Berlin – 'Had I been killed at Kolin I would have reached a port and feared storms no more.'[11] The energy and stylish phrasing of Frederick's letters immediately after Kolin show a king who was far from demoralized. But then a different and considerable blow of a different kind fell. His mother had been ill for some time and on 28 June Frederick heard that she was dead. His grief was great.

During the next few weeks Frederick took stock of the strategic situation. Some of the dangers to Prussia were immediate in space and time, others slightly more remote. Most immediate was, obviously, the danger from Daun and his Austrians in Bohemia who might invade across the Riesengebirge into Lusatia, occupy southern Saxony and threaten Brandenburg itself. Frederick reckoned that he had placed a strong enough force under August Wilhelm to deal with this threat, at least until he could himself march to reinforce. He told his brother to try to maintain himself in Bohemia until mid-August if he possibly could. The essential, he said, was to cover the routes north and ensure his depots and magazines were well protected by his deployments – the whole army depended on them. If the Austrians were to move north August Wilhelm was to occupy strong positions so that if he were attacked it would be on ground of his own choosing, and if possible he should thereafter get behind the Austrians and threaten to cut them off.[12] Frederick could not give him detailed deployment orders since it would depend on what the enemy did in that area – if he did anything; and when August Wilhelm wrote in July asking how he should manoeuvre[13] Frederick replied, no doubt with some exasperation, that he could not prescribe details. His brother had sensible generals with him and all Frederick could do was to tell him what must be achieved.

Far to the north and west the French had started their march to the Rhine in March with nearly 70,000 men under Count d'Estrées. They had then begun a movement through Westphalia directed on Hanover, and in their path was a smaller force of Hanoverians under the Duke of Cumberland. Cumberland had commanded against the French at Fontenoy. On several occasions Frederick lamented that he could do little to help him, which was undoubtedly true, although a small number of Prussian troops – not of the highest quality – were detached to the Duke's command to help. They were withdrawn from the 'Army of Observation' soon thereafter. On 16 July the French crossed the river Weser.

Also in the north Sweden had now indicated readiness to support Kaunitz's grand coalition with a military contribution – a corps of 17,000 men, to form part of an expedition against Pomerania, where the Swedes had ambitions to recover territory. And in the north-east it appeared that the lumbering Russian forces under Apraxin were now actually on the move towards East Prussia. The enemy were, therefore, threatening to irrupt into north Germany from two if not three directions. Meanwhile another French army, under Charles de Rohan, Prince de Soubise, was now advancing east from Strasbourg, aiming to cooperate with the 'Imperial Army' – the *Reichsarmee* established under the resolutions of the Diet at Ratisbon – to deal, perhaps finally, with the King of Prussia.

'It was not the army,' wrote Napoleon, 'that defended Prussia for seven years. It was Frederick the Great.' This would appear vividly true on a number of occasions, and the first of them was during the months after Kolin.

The most immediate threat was the nearest – the Austrians in Bohemia and the vulnerability of the Prussian depots and magazines in Lusatia. In mid-July, while the French in Hanover were advancing on Cumberland, August Wilhelm was manoeuvred into losing the important road junction of Gabel, north of Niemes, and uncovering the vital magazine of Zittau, north of the border, in the face of superior forces. The situation in Lusatia was thus a disaster. 'You make me

357

pay a high price for the confidence I reposed in you,' wrote a furious Frederick;[14] and he followed it up with further letters of great bitterness – 'You will never be anything but a pitiful general!'[15] In a letter to Wilhelmina he referred to their brother's *sottises*.[16] Frederick rode from Leitmeritz to Lusatia, to see August Wilhelm as rapidly as he could, and told him at Bautzen he would never command an army again. He was, said Frederick, like a spoiled child. And when August Wilhelm declared that he had better leave the army he received further terrible letters: 'You want to run away? To flee, while we fight? While we fight to preserve Prussia for you and your family? Blush to the roots of your being at what you propose!'[17] Frederick later assured August Wilhelm that he had never accused him of cowardice,[18] but his words had been brutal and many thought them intemperate beyond what was justified. The King's savaging of August Wilhelm was the talk of Berlin, where the story ran that Frederick told him he was only fit to manage a harem![19] Nevertheless Frederick reckoned that the whole army had been endangered and its supply situation put at risk by incompetent operational handling. He wrote on 30 July that his brother, by his *mauvaise conduite*, had put everything into a desperate situation.[20]

August Wilhelm deeply resented this treatment and thought it unjust. His friends reckoned that he had received inadequate guidance: and Frederick's ferocity probably owed something to the soreness of his heart after Kolin. Having left the army August Wilhelm died of a stroke a year later, and Frederick undoubtedly felt and expressed remorse.[21] He wept copiously when told, and went for a long, solitary ride. He believed that he had sent clear instructions to his brother, particularly about the primacy of Zittau: but his brother had not thought so, and now, after their awful exchanges, his brother was dead. August Wilhelm, said Frederick, 'had the best heart in the world', but was indecisive and worried excessively. Frederick knew that Henry – who had been particularly close to their dead brother – resented this treatment[22] and he wrote to him in piteous terms;[23] but that breach was never fully sealed.

Immediately, however, there were 100,000 Austrians drawn up north of Zittau, at Lobau, and Frederick decided he would face another general action: would attack. It was Prince Henry who persuaded him against this. Henry pointed to the strategic situation, to the threats from every quarter, to the uncertain situation in Hanover and East Prussia, to the news of a fresh French enemy to the west, to the questionable outcome of a battle with the Austrians at the moment. Frederick admired and respected Henry. Henry, unlike the others, had never been bullied by Frederick William. Frederick had a high regard for his character although he thought him prone to pessimism, but 'amiable, full of parts and bravery, as generous as a king',[24] and he took his advice. He decided – or at least he wrote – that the Austrian position was 'inattaquable'.[25] Instead of attacking Daun, Frederick moved to Dresden and gave new orders. He took immediate steps to cover Silesia – Bevern, with 40,000 men, would be responsible for that and would give early warning of any move from the south against Brandenburg. Frederick would lead the rest of the Prussian army – reduced by now to about 25,000 – and would march west to find and defeat this new French army and the 'Imperial army' they had come to support; defeat them and prevent any junction between them and the French forces confronting Cumberland. After a successful battle he might march north, to within supporting distance of the Hanoverians.

Frederick declared himself very disappointed with the performance of the British Government so far. Could there not be British diversionary attacks on the French coast? In Germany surely Cumberland, King George's son, could not be abandoned – Frederick told Mitchell in July that 'he could not persuade himself England would sit tamely still'. He often reminded him of the efforts of Marlborough – a British army to reinforce Cumberland would be the most effective way of restoring the situation.[26] He spoke even more strongly – it was a misfortune, he said, to have allied himself with England in her decadence. Frederick thought British hesitations largely derived from fear of antagonizing Russia. Mitchell, while properly loyal to his own authorities, was sympathetic; and there was still no British naval squadron sailing towards the Baltic, while the Russians had blockaded and raided Memel. Then, on 26 July, the French defeated the troops led by Cumberland at Hastenbeck on the Weser.

Frederick could only hope that his troops under Lehwaldt, deployed at Tilsit to defend East Prussia, would be steadfast in the face of what might be numerically overwhelming Russian forces. With reason, he felt himself beleaguered on every side and it did not help that he still despised some of his nearest enemies. 'Prince Charles,' he wrote to Keith on 11 August, 'drinks, eats, laughs and lies! . . . oh, how sweet it will be to rub out that proud, arrogant race!'[27] Frederick had received from Mitchell news of an intended British subsidy* with suitable gratitude but Mitchell – and this continued for some weeks – felt deeply depressed about Prussian military prospects, and said so. He felt that Frederick, in his despair, might be forced again to seek an accommodation with France – disastrous for England.

Frederick, having assembled his troops less those assigned to Bevern, now set off on his march westward to meet and confound the French and the 'Imperials'. He left Zittau on 25 August and advanced west through Saxony. The success of this venture inevitably depended to a large extent on the enemy; if they withdrew, kept out of his way, he would be beating the air and probably abandoning a more critical area of campaign. He must count on Cumberland keeping the French busy in the north and on the comparative inactivity – for which he was, in Frederick's view, well-known – of Daun. The Prussian army was led west under Frederick by a strong, mainly cavalry, advance guard under Friedrich Wilhelm von Seydlitz, an officer who had received very rapid promotion and had distinguished himself at Kolin. Seydlitz, nine years younger than Frederick, was a cavalry *beau sabreur* above all things – tall, slender, immaculate, a superb horseman with a famous, instant, 'feel' for tactical situations, entirely practical with no intellectual pretensions, a notorious pursuer of women and a legend throughout the army for his daring and leadership. Frederick admired Seydlitz, an attraction of opposites, and stood slightly in awe of this aloof, glamorous and gifted young subordinate who, he recognized, was unimpressed by the royal moods, tirades or anger. Seydlitz was certainly the man to lead a bold operation and Frederick's expedition westward might turn into such.

The Prussians marched through north Saxony, Erfurt, Gotha, and the enemy apparently made no response. The march was something of a triumphant progress, with Frederick's arrival everywhere greeted with curiosity and a good deal of enthusiasm. But there was no battle,

* 4 million thalers – about £170,000 per annum from 1758 until 1761 inclusive.

and when he reached Gotha he heard disturbing news: the Austrians had moved some forces north from Lusatia and were advancing – in what force was unsure at first – into Prussia itself.

Frederick, beset by enemies, always hoped that at some time there would be renewed opportunity for a favourable peace, although his military situation made it improbable. It was, nevertheless, desirable, in his view, to keep open lines of communication across the chaos and tension of war and on 6 September he wrote to the Duc de Richelieu (who had taken over command of the French army in the north from d'Estrées). It was a courteous letter to the effect that, while Frederick appreciated Richelieu was not at present in a position to negotiate, the nephew of the great cardinal was surely designed by nature for the signing of treaties as well as for the winning of battles! An association between France and Prussia which had lasted sixteen years must, he suggested, have left *some* residue of comradely feeling – '*quelques traces dans les esprits*' – and the letter, full of compliments, was an appeal to consider the possibilities of peace.[28] It was not an approach which would have gladdened London.

It is unlikely that Frederick hoped for much from this. Richelieu replied with equal courtesy that to contribute to a general peace 'with a hero such as Your Majesty' would no doubt be even more acceptable to the King of France than a victory, but that the Duke had no ideas on how such a 'desirable consummation' might be brought about![29] Correspondence continued, distant but courteous as befitted distinguished adversaries. Richelieu was, in fact, on the point of producing an even more desirable consummation. His own troops had entered Hanover itself. Cumberland's troops, outnumbered, were pinned against the north German coast after the battle of Hastenbeck and Cumberland received from his father, the King-Elector, permission to sign a capitulation agreement with the French at Klosterzeven, by which there would be a cessation of hostilities,* Cumberland's troops would be disbanded and the French would be, in effect, free to march in whatever direction they chose.

---

* The capitulation was disowned as 'shameful' by George II, but this was to abandon Cumberland who acted with authority.

The Convention of Klosterzeven was to some extent negotiated by two very pious Lutheran counts, Lynar and Reuss, and the Prussians intercepted a letter from Lynar which said that the idea of the convention had come to him as an inspiration from the Holy Spirit, to check French progress as once Joshua had made the sun stand still in its course; in order to save Hanoverian blood. 'We may leave Lynar somewhere between Joshua and the sun,' Frederick observed harshly.[30] He took the news, Mitchell remarked, more calmly than expected but reports of this capitulation, which reached him on 17 September, were a grim development for him. He had just entered Gotha, and received news of Austrians actually approaching Berlin, although this turned out to be little more than a raid and they would stay there only one day (on 16 October). In the east, however, Lehwaldt had been heavily engaged with the Russians under Apraxin on 30 August, at Gross Jagersdorf near Königsberg, a battle which had seen heavy casualties on both sides and left the destiny of East Prussia uncertain.

Frederick forbade excessive talk about the situation vis-à-vis the Russians, in a vain and unusual effort at mitigating bad news by suppressing it. He realized that he must call off his westward march, retrace his steps, balance his forces for this new situation. He directed that the Prussian ministers and the royal family should move from Berlin to Magdeburg. He had written his letter to Richelieu on the day he heard about Gross Jägersdorf and it was now very clear that the situation in Saxony and with the French must mean battle rather than peace. He decided to march east again, still ready to tackle the French and the Imperials if the chance offered, but to make for the area of Bautzen and as a start to lever or drive the Austrians out of Lusatia. He ordered Moritz, from Torgau, and Seydlitz, from his own army, to move towards Berlin and put a stop to Austrian intrusions there. Meanwhile he marched to the Elbe, via Leipzig, crossed the river at Torgau, and set up his headquarters at Grochwitz, east of the Elbe and centrally placed. In Berlin they were saying at court that 'All Europe has sworn to destroy us,' and many fled the city.[31]

By October the news in some quarters had become slightly better. Frederick learned on 23 September that the unexpected outcome of Lehwaldt's battle at Gross Jagersdorf was a decision by the Russians to retreat eastward – Russian casualties had been huge and Frederick sent warm congratulations. He wrote with considerable bitterness to George II about the Klosterzeven capitulation and Hanover's redis-covered 'neutrality', pointing out – understandably if not with absolute accuracy – that he had only renounced his long-standing agreements with France because of *toutes les belles promesses* he had received from England.[32] That notwithstanding, Frederick was soon reassured that Berlin was not under serious threat; and for a while about East Prussia. If he could again concentrate the army while still leaving Silesia covered he might find the chance for the major battle which had eluded him on his round march to Erfurt, Gotha and back.

The times, however, still seemed grim. Much of Prussia was being ravaged, he had lost revenue-producing provinces, he would be short of money for the next campaign, he was using up his resources. He wrote to Wilhelmina at the beginning of October worrying about finance and giving her some advice – diamonds were poor security for a loan now, nobody was accepting them although he hoped she was looking after hers.[33] To Finckenstein, Minister of State, he wrote on the same day that '*Nous avons toute l'Europe sur les bras.*'[34] And there were personal sadnesses: Winterfeldt, whom he greatly liked although his brothers did not, 'a man of soul, my friend', had been killed in a skirmish in Lusatia. '*Hélas! Croyez-vous que les Graces favorisent les malheureux?*' he wrote in a melancholy letter to his sister Amelia. He persisted in thinking – for his love of France never disappeared – that the hostile conduct of France entirely derived from the evil influence of Austria.[35]

Mitchell, however, reported on 30 October that Frederick, who had moved back now to Leipzig, was full of ideas about campaigns in 1758.[36] The French under Soubise seemed to be moving forward at last, something Frederick's westward march had failed in tempting them to do – moving forward, together with the Imperials under Prince Joseph of Sachsen-Hildburghausen, a field marshal of the Empire. Here, at last, was a target; and – or although – Soubise had been reinforced from Richelieu's army after Klosterzeven, according to Frederick's information, by twenty battalions and fourteen squad-rons of cavalry.

This concentrated the King's mind wonderfully. Dark thoughts about the intractable evil of Austria and pessimism about the immediate situation seemed to have dissolved. Frederick was now talking about getting Lehwaldt, after his expulsion of the Russians, to march west, to attack the Swedes and drive them from Pomerania. He – Lehwaldt – could then march to the Elbe, join whatever troops the British might put in the field, and act against the French in north Germany either under Ferdinand of Brunswick, or Frederick himself. Fantasy at such a time? Perhaps – but, nevertheless, the germ of an idea which would one day find fulfilment at Minden and Warburg.

Frederick had, a week earlier, sent orders to Moritz in the Berlin area and to Ferdinand at Magdeburg to join him, moving by Halle. He now heard that the enemy, the French and the Imperials – referred to by Frederick as 'the Circles'* – had recrossed the river Saale to the west bank. An uplift in Frederick's spirits often meant that he scented battle. He now gave orders to his own army – once again concentrated – to cross the Saale to the west bank on 3 November. Meanwhile he moved to Weissenfels, where he had spent some time during the abortive September march west and east again. From Weissenfels, on 31 October, he wrote to Keith – 'The enemy is assembling opposite me. From my window I can see all his cavalry!'[37] 'All his cavalry' represented about 7,000, in an army of some 41,000 of which 30,000 were French.

Keith had been separated from him with a strong detachment watching the Saale near Merseburg. Now he had returned and Frederick had the whole army in hand. Frederick had been told, with some exaggeration, that the combined forces of Sachsen-Hildburghausen and Soubise numbered 60,000 compared to his own host of 21,000; but he was, nevertheless, outnumbered by more than two to one.

Frederick knew that the enemy were assembled south of Mucheln, he believed facing north, and he drew up his Prussians about four miles distant from them, facing west, with his right resting on the village of Bedra and his left at Rossbach where he established his headquarters. The country is open and rolling, the slopes are easy and the hills are undramatic while giving good observation. There are few obstacles

---

* Troops assembled for an 'Imperial' force had earlier been reckoned by the districts – *Kreise* (circles) – which furnished them.

to the movement of men and horses. In front of the Prussian right was higher ground, beyond the village of Schortau, from whose summit the enemy camp and movements could be clearly seen. Frederick rode there and observed that they now appeared to be facing east. Facing the Prussians. He had supposed that there might be a chance of attacking their right flank, but this was now clearly impossible. The French were strongly posted and Frederick abandoned any idea of attacking them. He would watch and wait.

Soon after dawn the Prussians observed the enemy forming columns and moving south, apparently towards Zeuchfeld which lay opposite but about three miles distant from Rossbach. Their intentions were unclear. They might be refusing battle as they had so far done. Frederick occupied the Janus Hill plateau behind his left flank, and placed a battery of guns there. He then redeployed most of his cavalry to that flank, moving concealed by the slope, and thus extending his left.

From the observers on Janus Hill, at a certain point in the early afternoon, the report came in that the enemy were now marching not only east from Zeuchfeld, but north-east. The direction of their march had been changed so that it was clearly now planned as a great outflanking movement round Frederick's own left flank; and this movement was comparatively close, and comparatively vulnerable. The enemy were led by a mass of cavalry.

This was the opportunity he had been hoping for ever since learning that Soubise and the Imperials were moving into Saxony.

Frederick did two things. He ordered Seydlitz to move east from the end of the Janus Hill, the Polzen Hill, with most of the Prussian cavalry and to prepare to head the approaching enemy – to check them and ready them for a counter-blow. At the same time he gave orders to Ferdinand of Brunswick, commanding on the right wing, to begin marching the Prussian infantry southward so that the enemy's outflanking movement could be met by infantry in position. The Prussians would be moving by a shorter route than the enemy and able to take post forming an angle into which the enemy would have to march.

It worked perfectly. The prescience of Frederick, the competence of Ferdinand, the skill, initiative and tactical brilliance of Seydlitz and

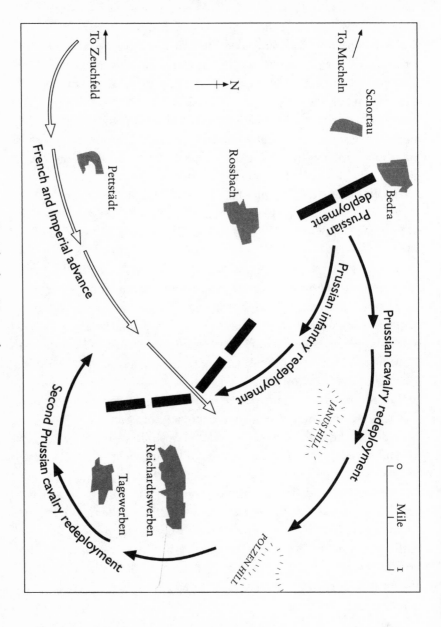

Rossbach, 5 November 1757

the superb training and stamina of the Prussian infantry ensured it. Seydlitz's first wave of cavalry, followed by a second – thirty-two squadrons in all – headed the enemy cavalry as they breasted the Janus plateau, charged them at great speed, and drove them back in disorder past Reichhardtswerben. Then Seydlitz, without waiting for orders, redeployed the Prussian cavalry to a position south of Tagewerben whence they could attack the French south flank as they marched on towards the presumed Prussian left flank. Lastly the Prussian infantry, marching through an exhausting afternoon, reached their appointed positions west of Reichardtswerben where they formed, as Frederick had designed, an acute angle into which the French and Imperials now advanced – unsupported by their cavalry which had been driven from the field, devastated by Frederick's artillery, and taken by his infantry from front and both flanks.

The French columns were massacred. The day was decided in minutes. The flight and the killing lasted until Soubise's men reached Pettstadt. By nightfall Frederick had lost just over 500 men while enemy losses, including a considerable number of prisoners, amounted to 10,000 together with twenty-two standards and colours. These losses were divided between French and Imperials with the majority (although not a vast majority) French. It suited Frederick at this time to represent the battle as primarily a victory over the French; and one whose prime effect was to free his hands to face dangers elsewhere.[38]

The entire situation in Saxony had been transformed. 'We have beaten them *totalement*,' Frederick wrote to Podewils. 'Heaven has blessed the just cause. Let there be Te Deums and artillery salutes and *feux de joie* at Berlin, Stettin, Magdeburg!'[39] He found that quarters were planned for him in the castle at Burgwerben near the battlefield, but when he got there he discovered it was already full of wounded French officers and told them not to disturb themselves, having his bed put up in the pantry of a house nearby. He saw among the French soldier-prisoners a man he recognized as a deserter from the Prussian army and things might have gone badly for him as Frederick asked why he'd earlier deserted.

'Sire, the situation was so bad.'

'Come and fight for *me*,' said Frederick, 'and if I lose we'll both desert tomorrow!'

Hugely outnumbered, Frederick had seen his opportunity and taken it. Not until Salamanca in 1812 would a French army attempting an outflanking manoeuvre be so cut to pieces. Frederick, using the superb tactical talents of Seydlitz (who was slightly wounded, but remained at the head of the cavalry) had controlled the course of battle. It was the beginning of the revenge for Kolin.

Seydlitz always spoke his mind. 'What a pity,' he said to the King, 'that Your Majesty is not omniscient.'

Frederick looked a question.

'Simply,' said Seydlitz, 'that Your Majesty yesterday sent a decoration to General von —. Nobody deserved it less. That his regiment did well was owed to its colonel and the two majors commanding battalions. General von — lost his head.' Ziethen rode up at that moment and Seydlitz appealed to him for agreement and got it.

A few weeks later the same regiment again distinguished itself. Frederick gave Seydlitz three decorations and told him to give them to the colonel and the two majors: 'Tell them they've earned these earlier.'[40]

The enemy's flight after Rossbach was marked by more than customary atrocity, at least according to the reports reaching Frederick. Destruction was indiscriminate, churches and altars were defiled, the country people treated deplorably – and all this, as Eichel remarked piously, done by so-called saviours of Saxony![41] Fugitives were being cut down or taken prisoner as far as Erfurt.

Frederick could certainly not afford to rest. In the north he sent instructions to Lehwaldt for deployments and operations in defence of Pomerania.[42] He met Mitchell's transmission of a British suggestion that he should now march north to help liberate Hanover with courteously veiled irritation. He pointed out what he was doing to fight the enemy in his own domains, to purge them of Austrians – would the British, he inquired, help with that if it came to it? Surely so, Mitchell replied, with what conviction is open to question.[43] Frederick, however, made one suggestion – King George had asked him to propose a commander to fight the French in the north for the allied cause and Frederick offered the name of his brother-in-law, Ferdinand of Brunswick, if he were acceptable and willing. It was a sound and fruitful offer. Although Frederick did not yet have a full and formal treaty with England, matters were moving in that direction and would reach fulfilment in April 1758; it was clear that Prussian victories would assist the process. There was a strong tide of opinion in Britain in favour of limiting any future continental commitment: but there was a countervailing tide in favour of supporting any really effective opponent of France.

But Frederick's immediate problem was Silesia. While he had been marching to drive the enemy from Saxony and south from Lusatia, the Austrian army of the Archduke Charles had moved east into Silesia, had been ravaging the country and had defeated Prussian contingents at Landshut, Liegnitz, Schweidnitz and Breslau. They were apparently having things all their own way against Bevern, who was in command there, and Frederick decided, immediately after Rossbach, that he must march at once to the beleaguered province. '*J'y marche incontinent*,' he wrote on 7 November to George II, who was greatly cheered by the news of Rossbach.[44] Frederick, therefore, set off, moving by Leipzig where he assembled the army, by Torgau, Königsbruch, Bautzen, Gorlitz to Naumburg on the Queiss which he reached on 24 November after very hard marching. He sent Keith with a force almost as large as his own into Bohemia to demonstrate, to make what he called '*Diversion und Luft*',[45] even to appear to threaten Prague. Seydlitz was recovering from his wound in Leipzig, comforted by a hospitable and beautiful Saxon lady.

At Naumburg Frederick heard that Bevern had won a battle against the Austrians round Breslau and wrote the good news in all directions, saying that he could now operate to cut them off. Unfortunately the news was false. Bevern had indeed fought but had been beaten and driven east across the Oder, whence the residue of his forces later joined Frederick; and he himself, on a solitary patrol, had been taken prisoner. Frederick was compelled to write several letters regretting his own precipitation.

The situation was most serious. Breslau appeared to have surrendered without a battle. Schweidnitz, after a short siege, was in Austrian hands, Bevern having failed to attack from what Frederick described as '*appréhensions frivoles*'.[46] Frederick gave orders to concentrate all possible troops at Parchwitz on the Katzebeck river, a tributary of the Oder. He himself reached Parchwitz on 28 November. He had with him now about 35,000 Prussians: and they had for the most part covered 200 miles from the field of Rossbach three weeks earlier.

At Parchwitz Frederick addressed all generals and commanders down to battalion level on 4 December, an address which became famous. He spoke in German. There was no ambiguity about the task. The Prussian army was to find and destroy the main Austrian army commanded by Charles of Lorraine. That army had now left their temporary base and baggage and moved westward towards the Prussians – 'The fox has left his earth,' he told Prince Ferdinand, 'and how I'll punish his pride!'[47] Frederick knew, and his hearers knew, that the Austrians outnumbered them, although he underestimated by how much – he was, in fact, outnumbered by slightly less than two to one. 'I must conquer or die,' he told his officers. 'We shall be fighting for our glory, for the preservation of our homes, our wives, our children.' With an echo of Shakespeare's St Crispin's Day, he said, 'If anybody prefers to take his leave, let him have it. He will cease to have any claim on my beneficence.' And he ended with a simple call which aroused the enthusiasm of all – 'Good luck, gentlemen. In a short while we shall have beaten the enemy or we'll never see each other again.'[48] Few doubted the critical nature of the moment. Frederick, not for the first time, gave orders as to what should happen if he fell. He asked to be buried at night, without pomp or ceremony, at Sans Souci. On his death all commanders must swear fealty to the Prince of Prussia.[49] He had about 12,000 cavalry in 128 squadrons and slightly under 24,000 infantry; and his artillery numbered about 160 guns. The Austrians were numerically superior in all arms, and especially in infantry. Their total was over 60,000.

The weather was freezing cold. There had been a light fall of snow during the night of 4 December and Frederick was moving about in the darkness before dawn. He greeted the Garde du Corps, standing dismounted before the first troops moved. 'Good morning, Garde du Corps.' 'Same to you, Your Majesty.' 'How goes it?' 'Bloody cold!' was the answer: and Frederick came back at them – 'Patience, lads! It's going to be hot, later!' At five in the morning the approach march began.

Frederick knew that the Austrians were drawn up in line west of

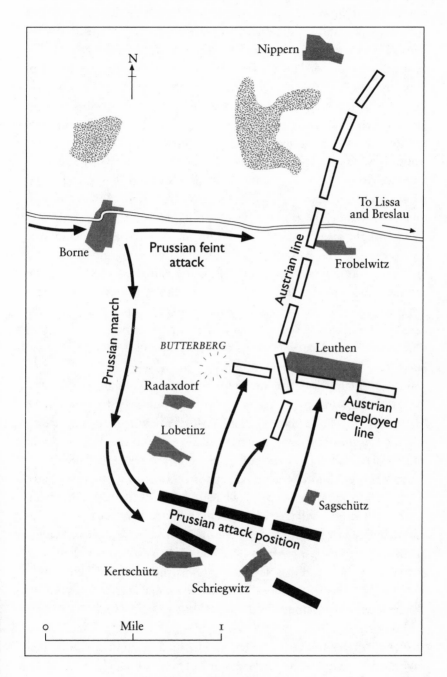

Leuthen, 5 December 1757

the Oder, facing west. He knew the terrain well. Besides the Silesian wars he had conducted peacetime manoeuvres and tactical studies there. He moved the army in four columns preceded by an advance guard and he himself rode with the advance guard, or just ahead of it, with a scouting detachment of hussars and *Jäger* light infantry. He moved east towards Breslau, to find and fix the Austrian line, and discover where its extremities were. He then intended to demonstrate against the Austrian right, as he expected it to be, to feint towards it frontally with cavalry. He then proposed to lead the army south, to find the Austrian left, to wheel and march round it until he could form a front at right angles to the enemy flank and roll it up. It was, to a large extent, the classic attack in oblique order.

When light allowed Frederick found that he was approaching the centre-right of the Austrian line – an appropriate point for a feint, but involving thereafter a long southward march by the main body behind him in order to reach the enemy flank. The Austrian line – longer than he had expected – covered about four miles. The Prussians needed to march south for two miles before wheeling. Their march was observed and actually presumed by some to imply a withdrawal in the face of clearly superior force.

The landscape was flat but Frederick was able largely to conceal his southward march by using the configuration of the ground he knew so well. His 'demonstration', east of the village of Borne, was intended to simulate a movement against or round the Austrian right and in this it had been successful – the Austrians reinforced their right wing as Frederick intended. Having passed Lobetinz on their southern march the Prussian main body wheeled left and formed up in front of and astride the villages of Kertschutz and Schriegwitz, with Sagschutz in front of the right of the line. They were now deployed facing north on a frontage of just over a mile. The Austrian left flank was 600 yards ahead; and just beyond that was the village of Leuthen.

The great wheel took time. The movement had started in darkness. While it was happening Frederick rode to an isolated wood near Radaxdorf, inside the angle of the march, where he came under artillery fire from both sides. He was concerned about time – December daylight was limited. Nevertheless at about one o'clock in the afternoon the army had reached its assault stations and the first Prussian attack against the Austrian left flank took place; an assault by Prussian infantry, by the 'moving walls'. The infantry were supported – very impressively – by artillery batteries moving from fire position to fire position on the low ridges parallel to the line of infantry advance. On the right, eastern, flank Frederick massed a large part of the Prussian cavalry under Ziethen, who moved level with the main advance and defeated an Austrian cavalry counter-attack launched from the north, from behind the original Austrian position.

Charles (and Daun was with him) was taken in flank by concentrated Prussian strength. He tried to redeploy the Austrians to face south-ward, astride Leuthen. This new deployment was attacked by the Prussians in mid-afternoon, with the heaviest fighting taking place around the houses, farmsteadings, and walls of Leuthen itself. The Austrians had established a battery of guns on a ridge behind Leuthen which checked the centre left of Frederick's advance, and there was a massed cavalry counter-attack – seventy squadrons under General Lucchese – which threatened Frederick's left flank from the area north of Radaxdorf; but this, in turn, was routed by forty squadrons of Prussian cavalry under General von Driesen, who had been held uncommitted near that village. Meanwhile Frederick had managed to deploy some of his own guns on a ridge called the Butterberg, which had the effect of neutralizing the Austrian artillery from west of Leuthen.

With the defeat of their cavalry and the inexorable Prussian advance, the Austrian infantry began throwing away their arms and fleeing eastward. They had suffered severely. The battle was over by four o'clock. Frederick was master of the field.

Snow was falling lightly. Frederick was determined to press on, even if with only a few troops, to reach Lissa five miles away where there was a bridge across the Schweidnitzwasser. He hoped to get across it and prevent the enemy forming a new front behind it, and in this he was successful. Hurrying forward with Ziethen, he reached Lissa at eight o'clock and spent the night in its *Schloss* where, remi-niscent of Rossbach, he found all available space crowded with wounded Austrian officers whom he greeted with affability. 'Good evening, gentlemen, is there room for me?'

Frederick had lost under 6,000 men, including many lightly

wounded; his first estimate was optimistic, putting his losses at 2,000 dead and wounded.* The Austrians lost 10,000 and a further 12,000 prisoners of war. Frederick's victory was complete.

The troops had shown high spirit, excellent discipline and admirable cooperation between all arms. The perfection of drill and order on the march of the enormous host meant that exact distances and timings were enforced according to Frederick's design – an exactitude which no other army could have matched and which bore witness to superb organization and training. Commanders had shown praiseworthy initiative, acting, as Frederick had always taught them, to deal with immediate situations which they could assess more instantly and accurately than any higher authority, however gifted; Driesen's coun-ter-attack was made on his own responsibility. Such responses in an army imply a high standard of training and an equally high level of moral courage. There are always attractive reasons for hesitation or inactivity.

The enemy had been recently successful and had notably worsted the Prussians at Schweidnitz and Breslau. Their tails had been up. Now they themselves had been decisively beaten, and beaten by numerically inferior forces, in one of the greatest battles of the century. They had, however, also been beaten by one of the greatest com-manders. Frederick had devised the battle and been in full, personal, control. He had been captain as well as king and general. A bemused young officer in the advance guard, apparently surrounded by Austrian and Saxon cavalry, with barely the strength to hold the colour, remembered Frederick suddenly riding up, his unmistakable voice sending something like an electric current through the ranks: 'Now children, *frisch heran*, look lively and in God's name onwards!'[50] He had timed the army's movements and judged each situation perfectly, from his initial feinting against the Austrian centre and right to his gallop to the bridge at Lissa. The French had been driven headlong from the field at Rossbach; now the Austrians were seeking escape – and escape out of Silesia. It was a triumph, a deliverance from the

---

* Even in his *Histoire de mon Temps* he only put his loss at 2,600: almost certainly an understatement, although casualties always depend on definition and are notoriously difficult to record accurately. The General Staff history records total Prussian losses at 6,380, including 1,175 killed. Of the Austrians 3,000 were dead.

two most renowned powers among the coalition of Frederick's enemies, and the battle which Napoleon said would, by itself, place Frederick among the greatest commanders of all time.

Frederick's, like most German armies, was a singing army. As the Prussian troops, near-incredulous at the scale of their victory, began to assemble and march from the snow-covered field it was always remembered how one single, penetrating soldier's voice was suddenly heard, and was almost immediately joined by the whole host in a great, spontaneous gesture of thanksgiving and relief, with the bands of the regiments taking up Rinkart's great hymn,[51] known thereafter as the Anthem of Leuthen – 'Now thank we all our God . . .'

> *Nun danket Alle Gott*
> *Mit Herzen, Mund und Händen!*
> *Der grosse Dinge thut*
> *an uns und allen Enden.*

14

A Loathsome Trade

The Austrians were hunted back past the walls of Breslau, which capitulated with its garrison of 17,000 on 20 December.* Liegnitz, with 3,400, followed suit a week later. The completeness of the victory was deeply gratifying; Frederick's instruction to Ziethen, who led the pursuit, referred to the enemy's *'grosster Confusion und Consternation'*.[1] His letters were triumphant, especially to Wilhelmina, whose health was more and more fragile (she died within the year), and Frederick's greatest happiness was in sharing success with her and hoping to cheer her. *'Adieu ma chère, ma charmante sœur,'* he wrote, saying that the only hope and consolation left to him was to kiss her before dying.[2]

Frederick knew perfectly well that his hour of triumph was ephemeral, that much lay ahead. His mood, however, was understandably confident and authoritative. He was without boastfulness. 'He talks,' wrote Mitchell, 'with the modesty of a hero whose magnanimity is not to be affected with the smiles, nor with the frowns, of fortune.'[3] He dispensed criticism, regardless of to whom, as freely as ever. To Keith, illustrious veteran, he wrote on 17 December of an 'unfortunate and fatal decision' (by Keith) to withdraw from Chemnitz to Leipzig – 'Please God that you have not already carried out this plan, which would make me think you off your head!'[4] August Wilhelm's congratulations were acknowledged with a severity which showed no softening: 'Although you could not have held a command, it would have been better for your reputation if you had at least been present.'[5] He rallied Prince Henry, but gently: 'All men, whoever they are, do foolish things

* Including twelve generals and 300 officers.

(*sottises*)! the best simply do the least deplorable!'[6] And he told Henry that the latter was seeing the overall situation too darkly – '*trop noir*'.[7] He sent word to Podewils at Magdeburg that the royal family could return to Berlin. Mitchell at this time suspected Henry of contemplating some sort of personal initiative towards a negotiation with the French without Frederick's knowledge – he was always very conscious of Henry's jealousy of the King.[8]

The months after Leuthen exemplified the grand strategic character of Frederick's problems and the diversity of his enemies. They also showed how easy it was to miscalculate priorities.

Frederick hoped that the French had received a sufficient knock at Rossbach to make another French incursion into southern Germany unlikely. The Imperials they had come to reinforce in that campaign now amounted to little. In the north, however, to which he had moved after Rossbach and Leuthen, Ferdinand of Brunswick, with a mixed army of Hanoverians, Brunswickers and some Prussians, was still conducting a campaign in defence of Hanover, a matter of marches and manoeuvres, to threaten the French first from one then another direction, aiming to prevent them consolidating their position, and ultimately to lever them into withdrawing westward. Frederick, who had warmly recommended Ferdinand for allied command, watched all this with attention and, often, anxiety. He sent frequent letters of operational advice or remonstrance, letters which never actually sundered relations between the two men. Ferdinand was Frederick's brother-in-law, brother of the solitary, unhappy Queen of Prussia, but that would have helped him little had his abilities not been high.

There was, however, a good deal of Frederician interference in operational detail. Ferdinand, wrote Frederick, had been *séduit* by Hanoverian influence as to the direction of his marches. He had moved on Celle: it would have been better, and might have split his enemies, to march by Nienburg and Minden.[9] There was much of this sort of thing. Frederick's chidings were impeccably courteous and he was generous with praise when he thought it deserved. Ferdinand was '*mon cher Ferdinand*'. But Ferdinand knew that Frederick was looking over his shoulder.

Ferdinand, as he intended, eventually procured by his manoeuvres a French movement westward, out of Westphalia – and without the cost of a major battle. 'Once you turn towards Paderborn, they'll run for Düsseldorf and the Rhine,' Frederick told him happily – and accurately – in March 1758.[10] He learned with anger of French outrages on the civilian population and he warmly praised Ferdinand for threatening reprisals: if the French did any more burning, he wrote, the Prussians would respond in kind, and he drafted a letter for Prince Henry to send to Richelieu to that effect. But Frederick also heard that Cardinal de Bernis, now French chief minister, believed in the possibilities of peace.

Nevertheless a good deal of Frederick's diplomatic energy was directed to trying to get a British army deployed in north Germany. It might be that Ferdinand's efforts were keeping the French at a distance for the time being but the future might be very different. If there were campaigning in that area in the autumn of 1758 or in 1759 a British effort could be decisive, he told Mitchell.[11] From the time of Rossbach he had been particularly scathing about British efforts, or lack of them. He had, however, been scrupulous in his own dealings; when Hanoverian envoys had suggested to his ministers in Berlin that after the war certain bishoprics – Paderborn, Osnabrück, Hildesheim, part of Münster – might be joined to Hanover in return for renunciation of Hanoverian pretensions to Ostfriesland, Frederick had said that such talk must be kept entirely secret and that proposals like that could only be considered with British concurrence. Meanwhile, he asked, where were British troops?[12]

He was met by protests at his criticism, following the current line in London, that a military contribution would be expensive; the financial effort would prejudice trade. 'Security comes before trade!' Frederick observed, saying that even 8,000 men would make a significant difference to the likely balance of forces.[13] Hanover was a legitimate pressure point. Frederick's possessions were threatened by Sweden as well as by Russia, just as were the King-Elector's by France. Britain was at peace with all but France, but British soldiers on the ground would be an earnest of the fact that the King of Prussia was not friendless, as well as possibly, in the future, affording the opportunity to deal a blow at a French army, an operation surely dear to British imaginings.

Instead Frederick received British protests and requests that he himself do more to help Hanover. He showed his irritation frequently.[14] 'Having received until now absolutely no help from Britain whether by land or sea,' he wrote to the embarrassed Mitchell on 23 January, 'to balance my own part and my powerful diversions against our common enemy —' and continued that the proposed subsidies might be regarded in the light of indemnities for his losses. He reckoned he knew the reason for British hesitations. Favourable though opinion in Britain was now reported to be towards him, Pitt, Chief Minister, was hostile not to Frederick but to the idea of any further continental commitment on land. Britain's resources were, Pitt argued, primarily required for the world-wide maritime and colonial struggle with France. Pitt was prepared to buy allied soldiers with subsidy rather than see a single Englishman in Hanover. Even in the matter of a British naval squadron in the Baltic Pitt raised practical difficulties. And when Cumberland had assumed command of the 'Army of Observation' he had, he believed, been led to expect that Prussian support would be greater than in fact happened.

Frederick understood all this and handled it with skill. He instructed his man in London (Knyphausen had now been sent there as Envoy Extraordinary) that the question of a British continental contribution to the allied cause should be managed *pas à pas*; Pitt, he said, had 'vertigo' at the idea![15] But in time the British would come round. Meanwhile, when George II, in April, made some reference to British troops perhaps coming to Frederick's help, Frederick deliberately responded with coolness that he hoped it would not be necessary. Knyphausen's instructions were threefold: to get a British squadron to the Baltic, to get an increase in Hanoverian troops (since the British, for the time being, would not commit any of their own), and to negotiate an increase in annual subsidy. Given these points being made, Frederick announced he was ready to sign a formal agreement. He would not, beyond a certain point, play the part of *demandeur*, however. He knew that the British needed him in the field and he did not place too low a price on himself. Mitchell had been temporarily replaced and when the new British Ambassador in Berlin, General Yorke, reported that the King of Prussia had decided to delay signing the agreement which had just been negotiated there was consternation in London.[16]

The Baltic area continued to need a good deal of Frederick's attention. His sister, Ulrica of Sweden, wrote in January (saying, credibly, that she was risking much by such a communication) that she hoped her brother would soon be clear of annoyances from the Swedes – a few changes of personality in Stockholm would achieve it.[17] The annoyances continued, however, and demanded a certain precautionary deployment of Prussian troops. Ulrica wrote gleefully (she was devoted to Frederick) of the long faces of Swedish ministers at the news of Leuthen. But, more significantly, there was word in January 1758 of a new Russian offensive in preparation. It would be directed at either Pomerania or Silesia, possibly both. The Austrians, predictably, were trying to target Silesia. Frederick knew that there was a new Russian commander-in-chief, Count Fermor. Russian troops were already over-running East Prussia.

Frederick, at first and for some time, took the news from the east with surprising equanimity. Lehwaldt, at Stralsund in northern Pomerania, still commanded the army which had survived Gross Jägersdorf, and Frederick prepared reinforcements for it. 'There's hardly anything to fear from the Russians,' he wrote to Wilhelmina at the beginning of January. 'When I've dealt with the Swedes I'll have my hands free and can bring whatever help is necessary.'[18] The Tsarina Elizabeth, he heard, was ill. Russia was, in effect, competing with Sweden for territorial gains in the Baltic region and Frederick, encouraged by the memory of how the Russians had withdrawn after a hard fight with Lehwaldt, was confident: over-confident. 'The King of Prussia,' Mitchell observed, 'amidst all his great and superior qualities and with the most penetrating understanding is by no means exempted from the common weakness of humanity of believing with wonderful facility whatever is agreeable and with the greatest difficulty whatever is contrary to his wishes and interest.' It was true.

But the last quarter of Frederick's concerns, as so often, was in the south. He had given the Austrians the most severe beating in recent history and he had won time, but Austrian power was still great and broad-based. The Austrian army under Daun, who had replaced the Archduke Charles, was still in the field. There would, inevitably, be further attempts to recover Silesia and probably to drive the Prussians from Saxony unless Vienna could be brought to think seriously of peace. This, Frederick thought, would probably require another resounding military success. Meanwhile there were limits to the extent that southern Germany could be denuded of Prussian troops. Silesia and Saxony were within reach of an Austrian army once it recovered and he knew that Leuthen had not inflicted such damage as to make recovery impossible.

Frederick's war chest was low. He occupied all Saxony, and his exactions there were necessary to that war chest but they were often hard to obtain. Keith told him of difficulties in getting the agreed sums from Dresden and Frederick replied, harshly, that it was no use trying to be tactful, to *ménager*, be easy on, the Saxons. The monies due must be produced; or taken. He was not pleased to receive further periodic acrimonious communications from Countess Brühl, who complained about her properties, and alleged that a Prussian colonel had looted one castle. She was reminded by Frederick of Saxon outrages and of how 'the allies of the King of Poland' had ravaged Prussia. The colonel in question, he said, had been warned of arms concealed at the Brühl castle.[19] He had acted with propriety.

But despite his internal problems in the occupied territories, despite his shortage of funds and despite his multiplicity of enemies, Frederick decided that he must again take the offensive against Austria. One more effective blow could produce conditions in which Vienna might talk peace. Frederick was unimpressed by civilities from Kaunitz, who wrote in January – to the King, personally – warning of how a French wine merchant in Boulogne (name and present whereabouts unknown) had called out in public, 'Will nobody find a knife to rid the world of the King of Prussia?' This, said Kaunitz, had come to the ears of the Emperor and Empress who, much shocked, had instructed that Frederick be warned. Frederick, aware of the vitriol he inspired in reports from Vienna, was not impressed by this uninformative and unctuous communication and dictated the reply to be sent. All owed 'to the civilized century in which we live a horror of assassination', but it would be desirable if the century could also mollify the bitterness of '*plumes indécentes*' used against great princes.[20]

Frederick therefore decided to invade Moravia. He had business to finish in Silesia and Schweidnitz must be taken, but as soon as that and the weather permitted he proposed to march across the mountains and besiege the city of Olmütz. The Austrian reaction, he presumed and hoped, would be to march to the relief of that important place. Then Frederick would again face Daun in open field and perhaps inflict a final defeat upon him, such a defeat as would lead Vienna to yearn for peace. He showed optimism, or at least demonstrated it – perhaps for her good – when he wrote to Wilhelmina at the end of March that he hoped soon to mount a '*grand coup*' against Maria Theresa.

He had been having difficulty in getting replacement English horses – his normal price was £75 from a dealer named Castle and he had sought Mitchell's help. That excellent Aberdonian had reckoned to knock at least 25 per cent off the price, and suggested to the British authorities that a personal present from George II of twenty or thirty such horses might be a sensible move.[21]

Frederick's invasion of Moravia could be criticized on several counts, in addition to the retrospective point that it failed in its strategic object; it did not effectively reduce the ability of Austria to recuperate and challenge him again, nor lead her to parley for peace. In spite of his buoyancy he seems to have underestimated the difficulties of reaching so far into enemy territory after a busy and expensive campaign which had lasted since the previous summer. He was short of money and he was short of men. Of his total of 170,000 about 50,000 could be regarded as necessary to man garrisons.

Olmütz would necessitate a siege. Frederick – who, when he made the decision, was still besieging the important centre of Schweidnitz – was short of the means for besieging, the resources both material and human for siege warfare. He wrote to his man in The Hague, von der Hellen, on 24 December – might there be some skilled engineer officers in the Dutch service who would contemplate serving under Frederick? He was looking for captains or majors with high professional reputations, Protestants if possible (in Silesia with its religious ambivalence this could be desirable). He could offer a major 512 *écus*, a captain 360* per annum.

Then there were the operational problems. In marching on Olmütz

---

* About £7,000 per annum in modern (1998) equivalent.

Frederick would be, in effect, marching across Daun's front – Daun had the Austrian army deployed and presumably licking its wounds round Königgrätz – and this might, he hoped, tempt the cautious Austrian to move against his western flank. But it might not. Daun might choose simply to harass the Prussians with his light cavalry, always formidable, and in particular harass the supplies and reinforcement columns of the besieging force. He might, and Vienna might, be content to live with a Prussian siege of Olmütz for an inconveniently long time.

For the next operational problem was with time. The approach march and the preparation of investment would use a considerable period out of the campaigning season. Even the time being taken to reduce Schweidnitz was disconcerting and Olmütz would be a much harder nut to crack. Time might not have been a pressing factor if no other dangers pressed but Frederick, although sometimes affecting insouciance, knew well that the Russian danger would have to be faced again during 1758 and it was unlikely his deployments so far would prove sufficient. If affairs in the north required a major effort it could not be managed while his hands were full with a difficult campaign in Moravia.

Then there were the actual operational risks which a Prussian army besieging Olmütz would encounter. To besiege Olmütz was one thing, to keep the besieging forces supplied and secure from raiding forces from outside was another – and likely to be expensive in manpower and resources. If Frederick failed to give enough weight to these difficulties they could soon be brought sharply home to him; but he was not a man to desist from an attempt because of dangers or difficulties. De Catt noted that whether in great or small things if Frederick was told that something was difficult he at once tried to do it. He was too wise a soldier to suppose that campaigns are always won by flouting the odds, but his temperament was sanguine and he had a healthy belief in the virtue of boldness in war.

On 16 April General von Treskow took the capitulation of Schweidnitz. Prussian losses had been seventy killed and 137 wounded. Austrian losses were 3,450 prisoners of war, including 250 officers. The Austrians had lost a further 3,500 men during the siege, largely through sickness. It had taken too long: Frederick had opened the siege on 18

March and reckoned it should be over by 1 April. The spring days mattered. He had, probably wisely, asked Keith to come from Saxony and supervise the last week of the operations.[22] His own headquarters had been nearby and he now began the march to Olmütz, by Neisse, where he concentrated the army; and by Troppau.

On 27 April Frederick set up his headquarters at Neustaedtl, near Neisse. At Neisse he harangued a reception committee of ecclesiastics. He distrusted them and showed it. He told them he knew they had a propensity to spy – 'an infamous profession!' – 'Take care!' he said. 'If I perceive disloyalty I will have you hanged from one of the towers of this town!'[23] Frederick had not earned a name for atrocity but when he spoke like this there does not seem to have been much inclination to disbelieve him. But although on such occasions his demeanour could be rough, many remarked his obvious unhappiness at the sufferings of the people in war. 'A man must be very barbarous,' he observed at this time, 'to trouble without reason poor devils who have nothing to do with our illustrious quarrels!' And when he found a peasant robbed of his horse – doubtless his most valued asset – by a *vivandière* he summoned a corporal and ordered him to give the woman twenty strokes with his cane.

Frederick reached Olmütz on 29 April. Based at Schmirschitz, eight miles south-west of the city, he deployed his troops covering the south and east of the place while Keith covered the north and north-west. The siege train, including the heavy siege artillery, was to move to join them under de la Motte Fouqué and arrived on 20 May. Olmütz was then blockaded and all the laborious preliminaries for an eighteenth-century siege were in position by the end of the month.

From the start the siege went badly – slowly and badly. The army's engineer, General de Balbi, took the brunt of Frederick's criticism and impatience with the engineering works and with the engineers. On one occasion the wretched de Balbi was lashed by Frederick's tongue for the best part of an hour and many, including Keith, thought the King unfair. There was a lack of equipment and insufficient men for the works. Siege work was highly labour-intensive, with the opening of trenches up to the point at which parallels could be dug and then further trenches towards the ultimate storming points, as well as protected battery and mortar positions. Not all the shortcomings and delays were Balbi's fault – he had, ultimately, done well at Schweidnitz. The first parallels were dug on 27 May.

June passed. Frederick wrote to Keith indignant complaints about the ineptitude of his siege artillery officers.[24] Both reinforcements and supplies for the besieging force were becoming urgent. A huge convoy – 3,000 wagons – was organized and moved from the north towards the Prussian lines. It was bound to exercise a magnetic attraction on the enemy if they retained any sense of initiative: and they did. The Austrians assembled a strong force to attack the convoy and did so on 30 June, trapping it on the road between Domstadtl and Altliebe, between Olmütz and Troppau. The convoy was broken up by Austrian cavalry, with great effect. Ziethen, summoned earlier from the area of Landshut, counter-attacked unsuccessfully; and then Austrian cavalry from the west, under General Loudon, counter-attacked the counter-attackers with considerable success. The Prussians were worsted with 2,300 casualties. Only 100 wagons got through.

Loudon, who played a critical part in this action, was to prove a thorn in Frederick's side for a long time. Gideon Loudon was another of those European soldiers of fortune whose family origins were Scottish – an Ayrshire family settled in Livonia in the fourteenth century – and who served more than one crown. Four years younger than Frederick, his father had been a lieutenant-colonel in the Swedish service and he himself had been a Russian cadet. Anxious for active employment and a commission, he had travelled to Germany in 1743 to find the first Silesian war had just ended with the Peace of Breslau. He had at once gone to Berlin and, aged twenty-six, had managed to obtain an interview with the King of Prussia. Frederick told him there were too many applicants: 'I can't give a squadron to every foreign officer visiting Berlin!'[25] Loudon therefore moved to Vienna in the spring of 1744, was received by Maria Theresa and was given a captaincy in the Austrian service.

Loudon had fought against the French in Alsace and by 1753 was a lieutenant-colonel and soon to be a general with a considerable reputation for boldness. He had also studied Frederick's recent campaigns with care as well as the military reforms associated with his name. He was in most things the opposite of his superior, Daun: hasty where Daun was deliberate, vigorous where Daun (although Frederick often under-estimated him) could be accused of lethargy. Somewhat later, and in time of peace, Loudon met Frederick, not on the battlefield but at a banquet, where he had taken a modest place. 'Come here, Marshal Loudon,' the King of Prussia called to him, 'I would rather have you beside me than opposite me!'[26]

Frederick received the news of the destruction of the great relief convoy on 1 July with impressive calm. Introspection and loss of confidence can plague any man as age overtakes him and so it was with Frederick. 'I know my destiny no more,' he told Marischal in 1758. 'Whence do I come? Where am I? Whither going?' But despite such moments he showed his greatness, as so often, in the handling of disappointment. 'The school of misfortune is a good school,' he observed; but in the immediate situation he knew the game was lost. He must abandon his plan. The siege of Olmütz would be a long affair, perhaps impossible; and it looked increasingly difficult to maintain the blockade. Indeed, the Austrians, moving by Kleinowitz and Dobrawillitz, sidestepped the main besieging force and actually established contact with the garrison from the south. Frederick had to accept that supplies to the besiegers had been interdicted, that the blockade had been penetrated and that the siege must be lifted. He had hoped to provoke Daun to a major battle which the Prussians could win, and Daun had not obliged. 'I have lost the ascendancy I won last autumn and winter,' he said, and it was painfully true. He must quit Moravia.[27]

To get the besieging army away without finding himself facing a battle on Daun's terms and Daun's ground needed adroitness. Frederick wanted to avoid too predictable a main withdrawal route and therefore marched the army not north-east to Troppau, their previous line of approach, but north-west by Zwittau and Leitomischl (in each of which was an Austrian supply depot) across the hills between Moravia and Bohemia. He decided to make for Königgrätz on the Elbe, where Daun had earlier based himself on the fortified camp there. From Königgrätz, which he reached on 14 July, he determined to turn through a right angle, north-east to the county of Glatz and the area of Landshut. He reached his destination in good order with all artillery and baggage. The invasion of Moravia was over. Frederick soon learned that this was as well. Crisis had sharpened elsewhere.

The Russians under General Fermor were devastating all Prussia east of the Oder.

The Russian invasion had been agreed with their Austrian allies at a conference in April. Earlier hopes that the Russians would march to support the Austrians in Bohemia and Moravia had been set aside in favour of a direct onslaught on Prussia which should draw the Prussian army away from the south, and – having taken Frankfurt – culminate in an offensive towards Berlin itself.

Frederick, at the beginning of April, before marching to Moravia had written to Lieutenant-General von Dohna, who was about to take over command of troops in the Baltic area from Field Marshal von Lehwaldt. Dohna had been 'shadowing' Lehwaldt before assuming responsibility, with all the frustration such a situation often begets. The two men did not get on well, as Frederick knew, and he told Dohna that the marshal was an old man and that it behoved Dohna to control himself (*se gouverner!*).[28]

In another letter a few weeks later Frederick had told Dohna[29] that his own chief preoccupation was with the Austrians – he had written from his headquarters at Schweidnitz which was still under siege – and that the only enemy distractions he could imagine would be from the Russians or the Swedes. Dohna should so operate as to frustrate them. Fermor, the new Russian commander-in-chief, was thought to have an army of 45,000 men and he must be kept out of Pomerania. Dohna should cover the port of Stettin, on the estuary of the Oder. The Swedes must be made or induced to conclude a peace (Queen Ulrica's optimistic messages had led to nothing), and if Dohna was forced to confront the Russians he should beat them and then turn to face the Swedes. It had all sounded comparatively simple and Frederick had made clear that these matters were secondary to his preoccupation with Austria. Now everything was different.

Frederick left Prince Henry, based at Leipzig, in command in Saxony and the Margrave Carl of Brandenburg-Schwedt, his brother-in-law's brother, in charge in Silesia. He himself marched north with only a small part of the army – 11,000 men, composed of thirty-eight cavalry squadrons and fourteen infantry battalions – to join Dohna. Dohna had inherited from Lehwaldt (reinforced by Frederick in March) about 26,000 men; twenty-nine infantry battalions, thirty-six cavalry squadrons, two regiments of heavy cavalry and 128 pieces of artillery. Frederick's reinforcing troops would now produce an army of 37,000 and would still, according to available information, be outnumbered by Fermor's Russians; but he did not wish to march with more, and give the impression to Daun that he was altogether abandoning south Germany. The weather was exceptionally hot. The march was demanding, but even more demanding, Frederick knew, could be the coming battle with the Russians. He issued harsh orders at this time. Infantry officers and NCOs must be ordered to shoot on the spot any soldier who, unwounded, left the line and his comrades.[30]

Frederick's Prussians reached Liegnitz on 10 August, Dalke on the 15th and Crossen on the Oder on the 18th. Frederick read Cicero during much of the march; when he used his carriage he always read a good deal and also, almost invariably, used the time to memorize poetry – his memory was prodigious and he could quote at length with a range and accuracy which astounded all. Everyone who saw him was impressed by his demeanour at this time. He had had to abandon one campaign, strongly and perhaps misguidedly cherished. He was faced with the invasion of his homeland by superior numbers. He had had to reorder all his plans, was facing new challenges. He was deeply troubled by news of the ill health of Wilhelmina – loving letters went to her from almost every staging post. His firmness and equanimity were evident and admirable. As usual he tried to carry out acts of justice or mercy where he found occasion – he stayed one night at a monastery in Silesia and heard moaning sounds which he traced to a cell where a monk, after some misdemeanour, had been kept in close confinement, with frequent floggings, for over a year. Frederick intervened.[31]

At Crossen he began to hear more of the disasters being visited on Prussia. Villages everywhere were being looted and burned, women and children were being butchered.[32] He marched on to Frankfurt on the Oder where he could hear the Russian guns bombarding Custrin, island-fortress between Oder and Warthe, place of early imprisonment and grim memory. Frederick needed in these crucial days to order his and Dohna's marches so that the Swedes who were deployed near the north coast should if possible be kept from joining the Russians. He needed to watch the situation in Prince Henry's area. He needed to manoeuvre in such a way that neither his nor Dohna's troops were exposed to battle on unfavourable ground. He was in daily touch with Dohna. If both Swedes and Russians were to act with skill, rapidity and in unison he would be in trouble.

The Prussian army, Dohna's and Frederick's contingent, was united at Manschnow, west of Custrin, on 22 August. Frederick's men had covered 160 miles in eight marching days. Some twenty miles north of Custrin a bridge of boats had been built across the Oder by 23 August but Custrin itself had been burned to ashes. Frederick visited it and inspected what was left of his former quarters.

Frederick brought the army across the Oder at Alt-Gustebiese into a concentration area south of that place and east of the village of Darmietzel. South of Darmietzel a stream, the Mietzel, runs into the Oder a few miles north of Custrin. Because of the very wooded country observation was difficult and Frederick had no clear idea of how Fermor was deployed, except that he was south of the Mietzel. The Russians were all east of the Oder. Frederick examined local foresters – these were state forests – and had a good picture of the terrain and its difficulties. He also acquired them as guides for the army through the forests which lay south and east of his concentration area. Frederick probably also knew the country from early visits, not least from when he had been diligently studying Prussian local government and administration as a prisoner-prince in the fortress of Custrin.

South of the Mietzel were thick forests which continued as far as the three villages (from west to east) of Quartschen, Zicher and Batzlow, each about two and a half miles from the next. Two miles south of Batzlow was the village of Gross-Cammin, and a further mile south were some marshes, the Warthe marshes. South-west of Batzlow and two miles west of Gross-Cammin was Wilkersdorf. Two and a half miles west of Wilkersdorf was the village of Zorndorf, itself about three miles south of a line drawn through Quartschen, Zicher and Batzlow.

Some low marshy land, difficult to traverse, ran south from Quartschen to a point near the west edge of Zorndorf: this was the Zabern Grund. A similar strip of wetland – the Langer Grund – ran roughly parallel, two miles to the east. The battlefield, as it ultimately became, was roughly within the rectangle Quartschen–Zicher–Wilkersdorf–Zorndorf, and was for the most part confined to the ground between the Zabern and the Langer Grund.

Frederick assumed, correctly, that Fermor would deploy for battle clear of the forests. Frederick had no intention of attacking directly from the north. Wherever Fermor's line and flanks were – and Frederick did not know – the King could not contemplate a march through forest paths with a deployment thereafter in the face of the enemy, probably in near darkness. He needed room for an effective deployment of the army. The line Fermor decided to adopt and the direction to face would clearly depend on what Fermor learned of Prussian moves, but it seemed likely that he would face east: for Frederick planned to march round the east of the general area in which the Russians must be.

Frederick, in fact, decided to assault from the south, from a forming-up place between and astride the villages of Zorndorf and Wilkersdorf. This would necessitate a long approach march, screened on its flanks by cavalry. Having brought the whole mass from the north to the south of the enemy he planned an attack 'in oblique order'. The 'refused' wing would be on the right, under Dohna, and would be deliberately inactive at first, deployed between Zorndorf and Wilkersdorf. The *Schwerpunkt* of the attack would be delivered by the Prussian left wing, taking off from the area west and in front of Zorndorf.

The *Schwerpunkt* would consist of two waves. Leading it would be an advance guard of eight battalions under General von Manteuffel, and following up would be a further fifteen battalions in two echelons, commanded by General von Kanitz. The cavalry were divided. Some – five regiments – were part of the right, or 'refused' wing under Dohna. The majority, however – thirty-six squadrons under Seydlitz – were to cross the Zabern Grund after moving round with the whole army on its great circular march, and to advance northward, parallel with Manteuffel's infantry but beyond the wetlands; and would protect the advance of Frederick's left from Russian cavalry on that flank. The artillery were intended to play a vital part in the *Schwerpunkt*. Frederick ordered that two grand batteries, a total of sixty guns, be formed and deployed north and north-west of Zorndorf. They were to soften up that part of the Russian line – which might be an east-facing right flank but was in fact a south-facing right flank – where the Prussian blow was intended to fall.

On the evening of 24 August, with the Prussian army in or reaching its concentration area, Frederick managed to push some troops across the Mietzel stream by the Neudammer Mill where he made his head-quarters, and thus to get a small bridgehead in the woods across the river. This would be the launchpad for the great approach march.

Having designed his battle in outline Frederick set the troops on the march in appropriate order for the positions he intended them to take up before the attack itself. The march – about eight miles – was to be from the concentration area south-east towards Batzlow. Passing both east and west of Batzlow, the army would then turn through a right angle to the south-west and aim for Wilkersdorf. Between Wilkersdorf and Zorndorf they would form up, facing north, while Seydlitz would take the left-wing cavalry beyond the Zabern Grund. The troops moved off, led by Manteuffel's advance guard, at three o'clock in the morning of 25 August. Frederick rode with the advance guard. Even before dawn, as well as after, it was evident that visibility would be poor whatever the weather – and the weather was particu-larly hot. The Russians had burned every village and murdered all the inhabitants, and black smoke was drifting everywhere mixing with the dust a mighty army, horse, foot and guns, inevitably raised.

During this approach march Frederick saw a huge assembly of wagons near the Warthe marshes, beyond Gross-Cammin. These were, obviously, the Russian baggage train and no doubt vital to the enemy's logistic support. This could wait, he reckoned. His eyes were on the coming battle and he knew well that there can be no victory if subsidiary objects are allowed to distract a commander's aim. The sight must, however, have helped somewhat to confuse his perceptions of how Fermor would be deployed. In fact Fermor had originally, and understandably, faced his army north, towards the Prussian concentration area, with the logistic train to their right rear. He had now – when he realized the nature of Frederick's movement – in effect turned them about, to face south, and in this configuration their train lay well to their left front. Frederick presumed for some time – a

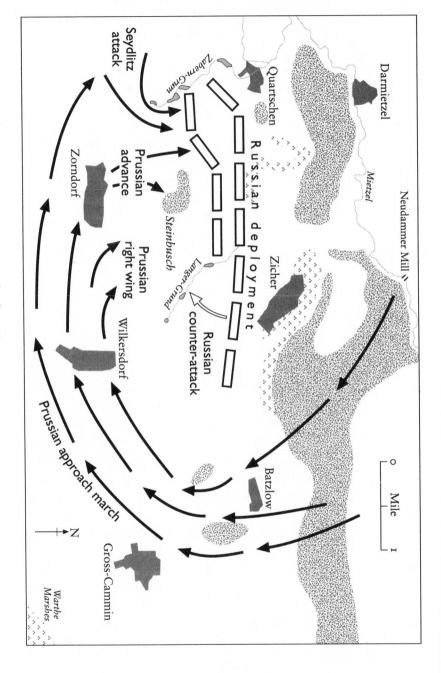

Zorndorf, 25 August 1758

reasonable presumption – that he would find Fermor initially deployed facing east, and that when he reached Zorndorf he would be somewhere near the enemy's right flank. In the event the two armies would be facing each other. At one moment a hussar approached Frederick and stammered out a report – he'd seen a Russian battery move into the next wood and reckoned he must at once tell the King. Frederick was sceptical: 'I've heard stories of plenty of batteries!' and the hussar rode away saying, 'That's a lesson to me never to make a report.' Seydlitz observed this and told the King he knew the hussar personally – 'A first-rate man!'

'Get him back!' said Frederick, and when the man rode back: 'I didn't fully understand your report, my son.' And then – 'A bright hussar. He'll go far.'[33]

The head of Frederick's great column passed Zorndorf at eight, and at nine o'clock in the morning of 25 August the Prussian army was in position. The guns of their great battery opened fire towards the north-west, with the morning sun behind them. Shot was falling short and after a while the guns were moved forward and firing recommenced. It did not, however, appear that the Russians were breaking under this cannonade. They were standing firm, and at about eleven o'clock Manteuffel's men, followed by Kanitz's, began to march forwards.

Very soon things began to go wrong. The left wing of Manteuffel's leading battalions, for what reason is uncertain, began to move further away from the Zabern Grund than was intended. This gave an opportunity for Russian cavalry to attack their left flank, and the Russians took it – fourteen squadrons, who did great execution. At the same time visibility was so poor that Manteuffel's battalions marched almost to the Russian lines before smoke and dust cleared and Russian fire was opened – point blank, infantry and artillery fire alternating with savage cavalry assaults against the Prussian left, which suffered appalling losses.

To make things worse, Kanitz's battalions – tasked with immediately following up Manteuffel to give depth to the main attack, as this was – began to wheel somewhat to their right, away from the designated thrust line and through a wood, the Stein Busch, with its inevitable effect on order and cohesion. They were attempting, or their commander was attempting, to maintain contact with the right wing of the army, the 'refused' wing under Dohna. This was a less important object than the immediate support of Manteuffel. The consequence was that Kanitz's men emerged from the Stein Busch opposite the Russian left-centre (so far untouched by the artillery bombardment); the Russians were well capable of dealing with them and did so.

Frederick thus found matters in disarray on his left. His infantry were trying to attack, on too wide a front and on slightly divergent axes, in the face of terrible fire and superior forces. His battalions, exposed to ferocious cavalry attacks, had suffered severely and were in some cases and places breaking. The country, broken by woodland, made movement and control doubly difficult. Frederick had sent messages to Seydlitz beyond the Zabern Grund telling him to intervene, but that independent-minded commander had sent word back that he hoped the King would trust his, Seydlitz's, judgement as to where, when and how.

And that judgement was good, although to Frederick it must have seemed for a while doubtful. When it was clear to Seydlitz how dire was the situation of the advance guard and of the whole left wing of the army, he managed to get his entire force, thirty-six squadrons, across the Zabern Grund. Ahead of him was a mass of Russian horse, mingled with infantry, cutting into Manteuffel's battalions. Seydlitz formed three columns, each of twelve squadrons and each formed on a three squadron front. He charged. The Russians of Fermor's right wing broke and began to run for the woods south of Quartschen and to straggle back towards the Mietzel.

Frederick had been trying to rally Prussian battalions he found behaving less well than the way Prussians should. Now he rode to the right, to the refused wing where Dohna's fifteen battalions and five cavalry regiments were drawn up. And at that moment thirty-six Russian cavalry squadrons under General Demiku, moving from the Russian left east of Zicher, fell on Dohna's centre and right-hand battalions south of the Langer Grund. Frederick brought two regiments from his left, from Seydlitz, which joined Dohna's regiments and together with them charged the Russian cavalry from a point near Zorndorf village, with great effect.

It was time for a more general advance. Any advance by Dohna's battalions had been checked and threatened by Demiku's action but now Frederick himself and Moritz of Anhalt-Dessau began to urge them forward. The sons of the Old Dessauer were of uneven quality. Moritz was the third and youngest. 'Prince Moritz, as brave as his sword, is a very *singular* man,' Frederick once observed.[34] 'There is no better holiday for him than a fight!' So it was now. Dohna's battalions moved forward among scenes of indescribable carnage and a good deal of drunkenness. No quarter was given on the field of Zorndorf. Prussian soldiers, hardened to warfare, were shaken by the ferocity and hatred shown that day. The armies were near disintegrating in a merciless orgy of alcohol and bloodlust. At 8.30 in the evening the Prussians, or some of them, had reached the ground between Quartschen and Zicher where the Russian main line had deployed that morning, while a good many Russians found themselves, after extraordinary and generally unintended manoeuvres, nearer Zorndorf and, as at dawn, south of their enemies. Casualties on both sides were horrendous. When they could calculate, the Prussians found they had lost nearly 13,000 men. The Russians had lost 18,000,* with 2,000 prisoners, twenty-four colours and six generals in captivity. Neither army was in a position to exploit or follow up the situation. The armies drew apart with nightfall and on 1 September Frederick learned that Fermor had withdrawn eastward to Landsberg, thirty miles from Custrin. It was perfectly possible that a Russian offensive might be resumed, but their losses had been frightful and Fermor withdrew to carry out some indecisive sieges on the Baltic coast and did not return. Frederick wrote of a victory, in confident terms. Mitchell told the British authorities of the remarkable courage shown throughout by the King of Prussia, taking the colours of a battalion in his own hands and leading them forward: 'His firmness of mind saved all. The Russians fought like devils incarnate.'[35]

Frederick had been appalled by the savagery of the day. 'We have beaten the Russians and haven't had great losses,' he told Wilhelmina, but he had, in truth, been shaken.[36] War with Russia should always

---

* Frederick wrote that they had counted at least 26,000 Russian dead on the battlefield. The General Staff history, more restrainedly, gave the figure as 6,600 dead – but also 12,500 wounded and a further 2,500 missing or taken prisoner.

if possible be avoided, he wrote – 'They dispose of Kalmuks, Tartars, cruel savage people who devastate and burn. Russia is, ultimately, the most dangerous power in Europe'[37] – the field of Zorndorf was in his mind when he wrote thus several years later. He had often been somewhat dismissive of Russian military performance: now with the fear and mistrust there was a good deal of respect. 'Of all our enemies,' he wrote to Henry, 'the Austrians understand war best, the French are the weakest, the Russians the most savage.'[38] And he told Finckenstein to try to get details of Russian atrocities well-publicized in the press of France as well as Germany.[39] He wrote of 'the barbarities the devils commit . . . the slaughter of women and children, the mutilation of prisoners . . .' Little of this was exaggeration. He moved to Tamsel on 27 August, where the von Wreech family had once shown kindness to a sad young prince and where he had experienced calf-love for the young Frau von Wreech. The house had been sacked by Cossacks, and a murdered woman's body, raped and pierced by a pike thrust, was lying by the main door.[40]

Frederick had been concerned at what he saw as lack of the old impeccable discipline and fighting spirit among some of his infantry – some, indeed, had run, despite the draconian orders he had issued during the march from Saxony. The cavalry and the artillery, he conceded, had done well. He had been shaken by the casualties. His favourite *Flügeladjutant* or ADC, von Oppen, had been brought in dead with twenty-seven wounds in his body. Next day, however, he calmly explained the battle to de Catt. He had promised to instruct him in warfare and he seldom failed to do so. 'Do you know of any prince,' he teased him, 'who is as much a *pedagogue* as I am?' He, himself, had been everywhere, as usual. The actual conduct of battle, the tactical plan, gave him no regrets. The approach march had been long and arduous but it had enabled the Prussians to deploy on fair ground and they had done more damage than they had suffered. Seydlitz should, perhaps, have been awarded the palm; but 'The King,' said Seydlitz. 'It was the King alone who won it.'[41] And Seydlitz was no courtier.

But Zorndorf marked Frederick. Depictions on canvas or in the theatre of eighteenth-century battles can convey an elegant, an almost ceremonious scene, uniforms colourful and graceful, troop formations symmetrical; scenes made for accompanying music whether of triumph or disaster by Handel, by Telemann. In reality the eighteenth-century battlefield was, as in other centuries, a horrible place. The ground was littered with the bodies of dead men, or men bleeding to death, or men with severed and shattered limbs, men in agony. The air was filled with the shrieks of pain of the wounded – sometimes made more hideous by the howling of unfortunates found and being tortured for the amusement of their victors before death released them. The stench of an abattoir was heavy in the air. At Zorndorf the frightful screams of the fallen, victims of parties of vengeful Cossacks patrolling the field, could be heard on the far bank of the Oder.

Frederick now learned that his brother Henry, in Saxony, was facing a concentration of 100,000 Austrians and Imperials (commanded by Prince Frederick of Zweibrücken) under Daun. Henry had about 45,000, including 24,000 under Carl of Brandenburg-Schwedt in Lusatia. The Austrians were apparently concentrating near Dresden among the rocky hills round Stolpen, east of the city, a dominant position and castle overlooking the whole plain between Dresden and Bishopswerden. Frederick also learned that Daun had ordered a gun salute to celebrate 'the victory of Zorndorf' ('Supremely ridiculous!' he observed). He knew the campaigning grounds of Saxony extremely well by now. Daun's communications with Bohemia ran through Zittau, with Silesia through Bautzen. On 2 September, with sufficient volumes of Cicero to entertain him when he took to his carriage, Frederick set out for Saxony. He was accompanied by 15,000 men, leaving twenty-one battalions and thirty-five squadrons of cavalry under Dohna to watch the eastern front. In Prussia itself there were skirmishes, some of them large-scale against the Swedish troops who had made the incursion into Pomerania. Some 15,000 Swedish troops under Count Hamilton had been marching and counter-marching among the wetlands and lakes south of Stettin, but their logistic support had betrayed them and they had failed to effect that union with Fermor's men which might have threatened Frederick in the days before Zorndorf. He learned with approval at the beginning of October that the Swedes had just had a beating, with heavy losses, at the field of Fehrbellin by a Prussian force led by General von Wedell. Hamilton had marched by way of Frederick's old battalion home of Neuruppin.

*

The Russian army withdrew eastward. Apart from a detachment to besiege Kolberg on the coast, Fermor's whole force would be behind the Vistula by the end of November.

On 11 September Frederick joined Prince Henry in Saxony. Daun's army outnumbered him and Frederick did not intend to seek a major battle unless he was given a favourable opportunity. Instead he proposed to manoeuvre, to keep Loudon's cavalry patrols at a distance by counter-patrolling; to threaten Austrian communications whether with Silesia or Bohemia. He heard that Neisse was being besieged and said that he would, no doubt, soon have to 'run over there again! Always on the run!'[42] He intended, therefore, to shadow Daun and watch. He relied on his instinct for battle to keep him out of trouble. Meanwhile he stayed in his camp at Schönfeld near Dresden, collecting such information as he could and writing, usually every day, to Prince Henry. When he moved, as he would, on the tail of Daun, it would, clearly, be necessary that his own positions in the face of superior numbers should be defensible and that his own supplies (which would soon be urgently necessary) were assured. He eventually moved east from Dresden in the early hours of 6 October. Daun was on the move and Frederick set off towards Bautzen with a small force of 'free' battalions and light cavalry, to be followed by the rest. At the first disputed river crossing this advance guard suffered some 320 casualties but learned that Daun, having moved from his position among the 'rocks of Stolpen', had redeployed first to Neustadt, a short way east of Stolpen, and then to a position at Kittlitz, west of Gorlitz. 'You may count on it,' Frederick wrote to Henry on 8 October. 'Daun, with his whole army, is between Hochkirch and Lobau.'[43] He had supposed that Daun might move south, into Bohemia.

Frederick now reckoned that he could threaten Daun frontally, from the west, and at the same time make a strong detachment to embarrass and perhaps deter any further Austrian march eastward to Silesia. He had already detached General von Retzow with 9,000 men on 28 September and ordered him to move to Weissenberg, north of where Daun was now reported to have deployed, and thus beyond Daun's presumed right flank. Thence Retzow was to operate towards Reichenbach, between Lobau and Gorlitz. This might threaten not only Austrian communications with Silesia but also those running south through Zittau to Bohemia. Daun's moves seemed to fit his concept and on 11 October Frederick moved the main Prussian army, short of Retzow's detachment as it was, to a position in and around the village of Hochkirch, five miles west of Kittlitz, where the road from Plotzen met another small road running south from Rodewitz, two miles to the north of Hochkirch. Frederick's left-hand troops of the main army were around Rodewitz, his right were round and in Hochkirch and the tracks running west and south from it. He made his headquarters at Rodewitz.

Daun, Frederick knew, was deployed to his east and south-east, from a point south of Weissenberg (which Retzow was due to occupy) to somewhere south and south-east of Plotzen. Frederick understood that the Austrians had decided to deploy round the village of Kittlitz, and Kittlitz did, in fact, lie behind Daun's centre. Frederick reckoned that Daun would abandon this position – and Kittlitz – as he felt the Prussian threat to his communications.[44] In front of Daun's right, south of Weissenberg, was a commanding hill, the Strohmberg. Frederick ordered Retzow, as part of the operation against Weissenberg, to occupy this hill. Retzow, however, found that the Austrians had already done so.

Frederick felt secure against any offensive movement, not only because of his estimate of Daun's character but because he had secret intelligence from Daun's private secretary who had been suborned and who gave Frederick a full report on Austrian intentions or lack of them.[45] Unfortunately the private secretary had been discovered in his treachery (by the enterprising Loudon) and had been promised his life by Daun if he fed Frederick false information. He was, therefore, 'turned' and the effect was to lull Frederick. Daun, therefore, had some cause for confidence. He had at his disposal sixty-three battalions of infantry and eighteen squadrons of cavalry. He knew that he was not regarded as a 'thruster' by his distinguished opponent but he also knew that the numerical odds were greatly in his favour – Frederick had about 35,000 men to Daun's 80,000. Daun had been on the ground for several days and had done a good deal of personal reconnaissance. He had observed the Prussians take up position as they had arrived. His right was dominated by the Strohmberg which he had occupied and placed heavy artillery thereon. His left rested on wooded hills, the

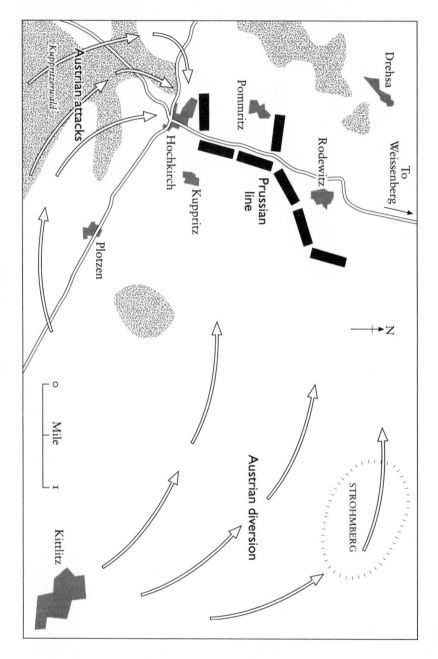

Hochkirch, 14 October 1758

Kuppritzer Berg, which overlooked Hochkirch itself from a distance of under a mile, and he filled these woods with light cavalry. He decided on a general attack. He believed he could deal the King of Prussia a resounding and with luck unexpected blow. His attack, furthermore, would be a variant of Frederick's own 'oblique order'. He would demonstrate with twenty battalions towards what he presumed was the Prussian centre and left along the Hochkirch–Rodewitz road, and would move his main army westward into the cover of the Kuppritzer Berg woods and attack northward to take the Prussian right at Hochkirch in flank.

Frederick, for what seemed to him good reasons, had been dismissive of the likelihood of serious attack. Keith and others had pointed to the proximity of the Kuppritzer Berg woods to the troops around Hochkirch; they provided a perfect covered approach. Frederick had replied that he, not Daun, would make the next moves and would lever Daun out of his present position. Keith had remarked that the enemy deserved hanging if they failed to attack, so great was the opportunity. Frederick disagreed. It is a matter of remark how much his infrequent disasters derived from over-confidence and underestimating his enemy.

Daun agreed with Keith's assessment although he didn't know it. He believed his hour had come. He was right. The Austrians, having moved through the wooded hills to the south of the Prussian right wing, began to go forward in the early morning fog of 14 October as the village church clock of Hochkirch struck five.

They achieved complete surprise. The Austrian approach march had been quiet and well-ordered. The Austrian artillery began playing on the Prussian camp where tents were still standing and men had not yet stood to arms or deployed into line of battle. In the three right-hand Prussian battalions men were stumbling about in the obscurity of darkness and fog as the Austrian cannon roared and as, soon after, the leading Austrian battalions of their main army emerged from the Kuppritzer Berg. Daun had made a demonstration from his own right against the Prussians south of Rodewitz but the main attack was coming against Hochkirch by his main force which had marched west, south of the Prussian positions, and was now falling on their right flank from the south with massive preponderance of strength.

Frederick, at Rodewitz, believed that he was hearing the sounds of a skirmish – '*Pandours*,' he said, Croat and Hungarian light cavalry probing his right. As he heard the thunder of Austrian artillery he realized, belatedly, that this was a serious attack – Daun had taken the offensive, as Frederick had refused to believe he ever would. He galloped south to Hochkirch where he found desperate fighting going on round the church and churchyard whose walls made it a defensible point, held by a Prussian battalion under a leader of legendary courage, Major von Lange, who fell with eleven wounds. Keith was there – worried about what he thought insouciance on the King's part, he and Prince Moritz had ridden there as soon as sounds of battle started. With Moritz he was organizing small-scale local actions with any troops to hand. To try to give coherence to an action where the men have been taken utterly by surprise and are disorganized is a desperate business; and at Hochkirch it was made more desperate by Austrian gunners who had taken charge of Prussian guns – overrun by the Austrian attack – swung them, and were firing at point-blank range into Hochkirch and its defenders.

Soon after six o'clock on the morning of 14 October the Prussians, somehow, retook Hochkirch at bayonet point. Most of the houses were on fire and there was indescribable confusion. Shortly afterwards the Prussians themselves were again driven out, northward and eastward. Keith, that great and sagacious old warrior, was hit by a musket ball and fell from his horse, dead.* Moritz was severely wounded and was carried from the field. One of Frederick's brothers-in-law, Frederick Francis of Brunswick, had his head taken off by a cannon ball; his grey horse with the prince's richly embroidered saddlecloth galloped riderless around for more than half an hour. Frederick could be dismissive of his wife's relations (and hurt her thereby) but in the case of Frederick Francis he had said in the previous year that he would one day make a great commander.[46]

The Prussian right wing was being smashed to pieces. The lane

---

* He had already been wounded once when death found him. A monument was erected to him at Hochkirch by a kinsman, Sir Robert Keith of Craig, who was British minister to Saxony from 1769 after a distinguished military career, and whose father, also Sir Robert Keith, had succeeded Robinson in Vienna before appointment to St Petersburg in 1758.

running past the high churchyard wall was a river of blood and was named the Blutgasse thereafter. A cavalry counter-attack from the west against the Austrian left was defeated by Loudon's cavalry, operating on the left of the Austrian infantry columns. At about seven o'clock the Austrian right wing from positions north of Kittlitz began to move against the Prussian left wing round Rodewitz, and by ten o'clock on that terrible morning this wing, too, began to fall back.

The King had been in the thick of the fight at Hochkirch. His horse had been killed by a musket ball in the chest and Frederick was covered with its blood. He had prevented more men being committed to what he realized was a futile and expensive struggle in Hochkirch itself. He had tried to organize the cavalry counter-attack which was frustrated by Loudon and the Austrian cavalry. 'Where are my horses?' he shouted and was told, 'Behind that defile.' Only then, after six hours of battle, did he ride back a little despite earlier urgings. When he realized that the battle must be broken off and as many troops as possible extricated, he tried to organize a defensible position round Pommritz. As soon as he could he assembled and withdrew the survivors of the army. It was necessary to march them – a defeated force – through a defile at a place called Drehsa and to do this in the face of the enemy. Frederick conducted this operation very personally and coolly, sending his cavalry first and covering the whole withdrawal by his remaining artillery. Beyond the defile he at once took up a new defensive position at Doberschütz. This was Frederick the tactical commander, wholly in control of himself and the immediate situation, and he aroused the admiration of Prussians and Austrians alike.

Frederick had lost 9,000 of his best men. He had lost many of his best officers. He had lost twenty-eight pairs of colours, two standards and over 100 guns. He had lost James Keith, a man close to his heart. Moritz of Dessau, wounded, had been taken prisoner and was to die of cancer in 1760. The King showed de Catt, that evening, the small gold box which contained pills, sufficiently poison-bearing to kill him. He carried the box on a ribbon round his neck and was more than once close to using it – 'How I *loathe* this trade to which I am condemned!' he said. He thought of the things he might have done differently, the chances which might have fallen otherwise, his refusal to give credence to inconvenient intelligence, his exaggerated confidence in one agent. He knew the disaster was his own fault – 'Don't think I'm trying to justify myself,' he said to his *Vorleser*, describing the events of that fearful day, 'I have committed mistakes, follies. May it please God to make them the last! O, God! give me the wit to mend them – splendidly!' He prayed, he said, for a 'cessation of these stupidities on both sides! Then all could go quietly home.' But he nevertheless said, whether with bravado or commendable resilience, that Daun would derive no benefit whatever from Hochkirch – and it was true that the Austrians had lost almost as many men. The battle did not mark a significant turning point in the war. Frederick, Frederick said, would somehow still come out of it all right.[47] And he was now hopeful of Turkish initiatives in the Balkans towards the Danube which would embarrass Vienna.[48]

Frederick's miscalculations had, nevertheless, been serious. He had reduced his main army by detaching Retzow and thus increasing the odds against him. He told Henry that he would have won if he had had only eight more battalions, but lack of forethought as well as lack of soldiers had betrayed him.[49] He had made a false appreciation about Daun's capacity and intentions. He had neglected battlefield intelligence about enemy deployment on the Kuppritzer Berg and indulged in wishful thinking. Strategically, he had not succeeded in physically interrupting or preventing Austrian reinforcement of Silesia.

Tactically Hochkirch was a calamity. Operationally and strategically it had not done the Austrians great good. Psychologically, however, Frederick had been worsted and the Prussians sent, bloodied, from the field. That was a great deal, and he told Henry frankly that he now had too many regiments on whom he could not rely.[50] He sent word, through Mitchell, to London – with reluctance – that he needed financial support if he was to carry on with a war in which he had, so far, borne the main burden.[51]

But in spite of this Austrian moral success there was still considerable reluctance to face Frederick again in open field. Frederick, having sent his baggage train into Lusatia, marched the army to Gorlitz whence he crossed the Neisse and the Queiss into Silesia, harried by Loudon's cavalry. He had been reinforced by eight battalions and five cavalry squadrons from Prince Henry's command and now hastened to raise the siege of Neisse, beset by the Austrians. He did so on 7 November.

It was then time to return to Saxony. Daun, Frederick heard on 13 November, was before Dresden and had summoned the Prussian garrison to surrender without success; the defending commander, General von Schmettau, had carried out his threat to burn much of the suburbs in order to blind and disrupt an Austrian attack. Frederick's Prussians marched back to the area of Dresden on 20 November 1758 and found that Daun and the main Austrian army had moved south into the Bohemian hills. The Imperials had withdrawn to Leipzig.

On 17 October, immediately after Hochkirch, Frederick was told of Wilhelmina's death.* Next day his letter to Henry, concerned with the move of various battalions, simply ended with a line: '*Grand Dieu, ma sœur de Baireuth!*' 'I lose all who are dear to me,' he told de Catt, sobbing. 'One after the other!' and so it seemed; and he often referred gloomily to his little gold box.[52]

---

* Wilhelmina's beautiful daughter, Elizabeth, became Duchess of Württemberg, admired by all, and probably Frederick's favourite niece. Her marriage failed.

15

'I Am Lost, Prittwitz!'

Frederick decided to spend the winter months in Breslau. The army was in winter quarters either in Saxony or in Silesia around Landshut and Frederick was suffering from a severe influenza-type fever in the exceptionally cold weather of the end of 1758. He was advised to travel by coach rather than on horseback, and rejected the suggestion roughly unless this was absolutely necessary – 'Do you take me for an old woman? What would the army say?' Nevertheless the King, just forty-seven, was remarked as having aged a good deal in recent months. He was also, at this time, particularly unkempt in his appearance. Not only was his coat habitually snuff-stained but he took pride in his old patched clothes. 'When my mother was alive I was cleaner!' he said frankly. 'Now it all looks well-worn and old but I like it a hundred times better than when new!'[1] He was pleased to get a letter of condolence from Voltaire about the loss of Wilhelmina – 'The unfortunate love to be spoken to of their afflictions,' he observed perceptively. Voltaire's letter told him that although the writer was old his heart would always belong to Frederick and to '*l'adorable sœur que vous pleurez*' and would never age. Frederick had asked Voltaire to compose a tribute to Wilhelmina – dissatisfied with the first draft, he requested a further effort and when it arrived in March 1759 Frederick said it was the first piece of genuine comfort he had received. Voltaire's was still the pen of a magician. He wrote for Voltaire a reply enclosing an offensive poem about Louis XV which he had written to amuse the philosopher – '*Votre faible monarque, jouet de la Pompadour.*' He was, however, persuaded that this would make unnecessary trouble and that it would be best not to enclose it.*

---

* But he sent it a few months later!

Frederick, as usual, was restoring his spirits and allaying his anxieties with reading and with literary composition. He was composing a study of Charles XII at this time. He also amused himself with some satirical pieces on his enemies, including an imagined letter from Mme de Pompadour to Maria Theresa demanding abolition of a supposed College of Chastity. He talked with accustomed mockery about Augustus of Poland – 'my great brother whose idea of fun is to kick the bottoms of his jesters!'[2]

Although with his own share of hypochondria and often referring to his ailments, Frederick was genuinely solicitous about others, with plenty of theories to try on them. A drummer of the Guard had a high fever which the medical men seemed unable to bring down. Frederick prescribed some drops of vitriol and a large glass of water every half-hour, and the drummer recovered. As in more peaceful times Frederick loved arguments, verbal fencing, philosophic duels. In these he changed his mind – or at least his position – frequently and with obvious enjoyment. He boasted – at first sight an improbable boast but it may have been so – that he had actually persuaded his father to look again at the works of Christian Wolff, the philosopher who had defended Confucian principles and been dismissed from his teaching post at the University of Halle for irreligion; and that Frederick William had done so.

Frederick's mind, indeed, went back often these days to his formidable parent and he usually defended him. He spoke once of a recurring dream he had: he was seized by soldiers, bound, taken from his room to be sent, he knew, to Magdeburg. His offence was to have loved his father too little. The connection with the nightmare of Custrin is evident but the loss of Wilhelmina, too, brought early years often and painfully to his mind.

He spent time, as he always had, reading and reciting his beloved French poets and dramatists; Racine was his favourite. He claimed to like putting poetry into prose in his mind to test it for sense and sensibility before surrendering himself simply to its music. When he read aloud or recited it was with great skill and feeling, although he could not stop himself mocking any phrase he disliked by giving it an exaggerated emphasis. His memory for poetry was immense – was, indeed, immense in every direction. Like most people he became furious with himself if he could not remember a name – 'This is absurd! I know it perfectly!' On one occasion he found it impossible to recall the name of a particular opera, saying he wouldn't sleep until it came to him. At one o'clock there was a knock on de Catt's door – an orderly from the King, with a note. 'It was *Montezuma*! I shall now be able to sleep and I wanted to spare *you* insomnia!' De Catt, of course, had slept perfectly well until awoken by Frederick's message.

Frederick always enjoyed making efforts on behalf of old friends, especially when misfortune hit them. James Keith had been killed at Hochkirch and Frederick now again tried to persuade George II to restore the elder Jacobite brother, 'Milord Maréchal', to his forfeited honours and estates. He wrote a well-phrased letter,[3] tactful and persuasive, to his uncle George, pleading Marischal's cause – Marischal cared nothing for possessions, he said, but always hoped for restoration of the right to succeed one of his Keith cousins (the Earl of Kintore) who had just died. Marischal was about to be sent by Frederick to represent Prussia as ambassador to Spain; and from Spain he was able to send reports (about Spanish intrigues) which were helpful to Britain when communicated to London. No doubt influenced by this, he obtained his pardon from King George in May.

There were plenty of concerts at Breslau that winter. And Frederick's mind went often to Sans Souci, his beloved creation. He sketched aspects of it for his entourage. He was, he said, determined to build a mausoleum there; and in all his testaments he maintained that he, ultimately, must lie at Sans Souci. He quoted Chaulieu – '*La Mort est simplement le terme de la vie, un asile sûr, la fin de nos maux.*' But he knew that such escapism was temporary. The new year of 1759 would bring plenty of fresh evils. 'This polished century is still very ferocious,' he told d'Argens, and on the last day of 1758 a new alliance was concluded between Austria and France.

The century was indeed still ferocious. In north Germany Ferdinand of Brunswick had fought a most successful campaign in the latter part of 1758, crossing and recrossing the Rhine itself and keeping the initiative. Frederick was delighted – 'The King of England,' he told Ferdinand, 'must be convinced by events that there are other ways of defending Hanover than sitting behind the Weser . . . Be an imitator, dear Ferdinand, of Arminius who, in the same region, fought for the liberty of his fatherland; and see that Soubise and Contades suffer the fate of Varus!' – the reference was to the great defeat of the Roman legions at the battle of the Teutoburgerwald in AD 9.

Ferdinand, now a Prussian field marshal, had his forces strengthened. The artillery were increased and the total brought to sixty battalions of infantry and seventy-seven squadrons of cavalry. Ferdinand hoped for an opportunity to attack the French who had again adventured into Franconia from the west, an idea which came to nothing – indeed Ferdinand himself would be worsted by the French at Bingen in April 1759. Nevertheless Frederick had confidence that Ferdinand, in his manoeuvres to defend Hanover, would hold his own and wrote often to animate and encourage him. This confidence would be tested in June when a French army again advanced through Hesse and in Westphalia, taking Münster and then Minden. Frederick could send little but advice.

In Saxony Prince Henry had 30,000 men and proposed to raid Austrian posts and magazines across the frontier in Bohemia when the spring came – manoeuvres at Aussig, Lobositz, Leitmeritz and elsewhere, blessed by Frederick and carried out with particular skill. Henry marched and feinted against the Imperials in May and June – no major battle but much damage done to the enemy's logistics, all watched with high approval and generous congratulations by Frederick, who was for most of the spring at Landshut. Henry kept the initiative and Prussian-occupied Saxony seemed secure. In Silesia Frederick's old friend de la Motte Fouqué, with 13,000 men (later reinforced to about 20,000), matched Prince Henry with a slightly less successful raiding policy, stimulated by Frederick.[4] Frederick held the main army, about 50,000, under his own hand to move to whichever quarter might need reinforcement or emergency action. Action against Daun. Or against Fermor. 'No sooner does one project fail than he is ready with another; no disappointment discourages him, no success elates him beyond measure,' Mitchell told Newcastle in May. But at the same time he wrote to Holdernesse of Frederick's 'ardent desire for peace' – 'It is impossible to describe the fatigue of body and mind which this hero king daily undergoes.'[5]

Frederick was, as usual, running his intelligence service very personally – not always with very happy results as Hochkirch had shown. He spent a good deal of his time weighing information, testing it against other evidence, trying to deduce intentions. His letters were full of conjectures. He now planned to insinuate an agent, a Brunswicker, into Russian headquarters in the guise of a Dutch officer visiting the Russian army, charged with gaining the confidence of the Russian commander-in-chief. Before the agent was activated Frederick drafted careful instructions for him and advised how he might gain access to Fermor. Having done so he was empowered to offer Fermor 100,000 *écus** as a down payment and an annuity of 10,000. If money did not suffice he could also convey the promise of a field marshal's rank in the Prussian service.[6] If Fermor agreed terms the price would be timely information on all Russian movements. Frederick's instruction – to be handled according to strict covering orders – was to be kept *sine die* by a Prussian official in Hamburg. Unfortunately, before it could be used, Fermor was replaced by General Saltykov, a particular favourite of the Tsarina. Whether there was a connection between this and Frederick's intended ploy may only be surmised; Russian counter-intelligence has usually been of high quality. And some – including the devoted but observant Mitchell – reckoned that Frederick was too parsimonious in paying for information – 'In this army spies are paid too sparingly, consequently the intelligence is none of the best.'[7]

Saltykov, aged sixty-one, commanded 70,000 men. He was faced by Dohna, still regarded by Frederick – with some justification – as being deficient in initiative and offensive spirit. It was clear, however, that Dohna would be heavily outnumbered by any serious Russian offensive unless he were reinforced: his army numbered 23,000. Small measures could help and Frederick had, in March, sent General Wobersnow with a detachment on a deep raid into Poland to destroy the supply depot at Posen.[8] Both the Russians and the Austrians had, he knew, been buying and storing grain on a large scale.

But Frederick faced a familiar situation. 'My enemies are increasing on all sides,' he said to Mitchell in January 1759, 'and they are nearer to me than they were last year!'[9] The enemy were indeed likely to

---

* About £30,000.

outnumber the Prussians in any isolated encounter but might always have the tables turned on them by the fast-moving troops of the fast-thinking King of Prussia, able to reinforce any threatened quarter, operating on interior lines. There was now, however, a determined if belated attempt by Russians and Austrians to combine, to synchronize the timing of their movements. They outnumbered the Prussians in total, many times. All that was necessary was to prevent Frederick reinforcing either front by posing a sufficient threat to the other. A plan was made; it was laborious and difficult as is the way of all allied planning but it gave a fair promise of success. 'Europe is united to crush me,' Frederick observed, sometimes, no doubt with a gesture of self-dramatization, 'but I have two resources – my little gold box and a little of my old luck!'[10]

He often referred to his 'little gold box' of poison pills. As to his old luck, that was soon shown to be in short supply. Frederick talked often and gloomily of the necessity of peace, in terms which Mitchell and others found both moving and convincing. He reiterated, often, how much he trusted to the integrity of Pitt.[11]

In confronting his enemies Frederick, reasonably, hoped much from the divergence of political objects among them. Of the French he observed sourly that Choiseul, the French minister, was now 'the slave of Vienna'.[12] The French naturally wished to threaten Hanover and distract the British, their principal enemy. Frederick wrote to George II in June, lamenting the implacability of their common enemies and suggesting some sort of joint peace initiative, at some time, by Britain and Prussia.[13] The Russians wanted to extend their power in the Baltic as well as in Poland: their eyes were on East Prussia and Silesia. The Austrians wanted to recover Silesia, they always had, they always would. Frederick undertook a small expedition at the end of April to relieve General von Treskow who was holding Neisse against Austrian siege.

These divergent objects gave Frederick a chance, he reckoned, that coordination of Austrian and Russian manoeuvres might be found too difficult – 'It is a fortunate circumstance,' he wrote to Ferdinand at the beginning of the year, 'that our enemies can't decide their operational plan for the next campaign!'[14] Nevertheless both Russians and Austrians could too easily menace Silesia; and he knew that there was also a hope in the enemy camp that the Swedes might create another complication for him by attacking Stettin.

Frederick did not for some time wholly give up hope that his enemies' difficulties would lead to inactivity and allow him to remain on the defensive. He was encouraged by Prince Henry's ravaging of Austrian depots and the effect that must have had on Austrian war-making potential: 'They won't be able to cause you much trouble!' he wrote to Henry at the end of April, 'and Daun will wait until the Russians move.'[15] Nevertheless there was no doubt that Daun – 'the great Marshal' or simply 'Leopold', as Frederick ironically called him, no doubt with several grains of resentment for Hochkirch – was in position to take the offensive at some time during 1759. Daun had 100,000 men. He was capable of – and carried out in May – major raids across the border into Lusatia. His western flank was covered by 35,000 Imperials of the *Reichsarmee*, able to threaten Leipzig. If his operations could be coordinated with Saltykov's Russians from Poland, Frederick could be faced with a huge preponderance of force against him in Silesia. And through Ferdinand Frederick learned (by a secret source) that this was indeed the ultimate plan. The French were to occupy Prussian attention in north Germany and the Austrians were to make another major effort in conjunction with the Russians in Silesia.[16] Frederick was short of men against such a combination. Even small measures could help and in March he had sounded out the Danes about the possibility of getting 10,000 men from them for an annual subsidy of 300,000 *écus*.*[17]

Saltykov, a somewhat opaque character, a court favourite with a reputation for being sluggish, had his main army in central Poland, based on Posen. The north-facing Austrians were quartered with their right wing at Neustadt on the frontiers of Glatz and their left around Trautenau. They had, Frederick knew, left winter quarters in May and their scouts were often inspecting Prussian camps from the heights of the Riesengebirge. If Frederick moved prematurely against one opponent he could give the other a clear run. He supposed they expected him to take the offensive and was determined on this occasion to wait. He learned in June that both Russians and Austrians were

---

* About £100,000. The request was refused, Frederick told Mitchell, with laughter.

preparing an advance, the Russians towards the Oder at Glogau, the Austrians into Lusatia. The summer had been filled with such reports and some had been baseless. Meanwhile, in July, Frederick took up a strong and defensible position at Schmottseiffen, near the upper course of the Queiss river. He knew he might have to march at some time to prevent a junction of Russians and Austrians but if he moved too soon he could be beating the air.

Then in mid-June Frederick learned that in the east the Russians were, indeed, advancing – had been advancing for some weeks. Dohna, in this contingency, was intended to move against them – Frederick wrote, angrily, that he was moving like a tortoise;[18] he had hoped that Dohna would 'fix' Saltykov and threaten his communications. It soon appeared that Dohna had done nothing of this – was, in fact, withdrawing without a battle.

Frederick was having difficulties with generals. He had sent General von Wobersnow to 'assist' Dohna in early June and Wobersnow had initiated an operation against the Russian supply lines, as he supposed the King desired. The operation had come to nothing and Frederick's subsequent letter to him must have left ineradicable marks, describing him as incompetent, alcoholic, dilatory, irresolute and an example to the whole army of how not to behave: '*Alle sottisen die man im Krieg Thun kann haben Sie gethan!*' There were two pages and each line was harsher than the one before.[19] Now Frederick, disgusted with Wobersnow and disappointed with Dohna, replaced the latter with General von Wedell. Wedell understood – somewhat simplistically – that the King expected him to take offensive action. He was given command of all Prussian troops – about 28,000 – beyond the Oder. Meanwhile Daun, by Frederick's information at the end of June, was also moving – crablike past Frederick's southern flank, towards Lusatia.

Then came news that Wedell, who had just assumed command and on whom hopes had been pinned, had been outmanoeuvred by Saltykov who was showing a good deal more skill than his reputation suggested. The Russians, apparently, had marched round Wedell and taken up a strong position between the Prussians and the Oder at Crossen. Then, observing what seemed to be (and was) a simple and unsubtle operation by Wedell's men to attack straight towards them, they had deployed their artillery to maximum effect and sent the Prussians from the field after a bloody encounter at Paltzig on 23 July, costing Wedell 8,000 men. The wretched Wobersnow had redeemed his previous performance by getting killed. The Russians were advancing on Frankfurt.

There was now no doubt about Frederick's duty and no options open. He must march again, with what reinforcements he could, to the lower Oder. Prince Henry, in whom Frederick's confidence in operational matters was total, must manage any direct threat from Daun to Lusatia while de la Motte Fouqué, with his force of about 20,000 in all, must contain the Austrians in southern Silesia. Frederick assigned about 40,000 to Prince Henry and set off northward on 31 July. He took with him twenty-nine battalions, thirty-five cavalry squadrons and seventy pieces of artillery, aiming to combine with Wedell's survivors and confront Saltykov – Saltykov who would by then have no doubt been reinforced by Daun with whatever Daun thought he could contribute to a campaign on the Oder.

So far Daun had been sluggish, taking his time, it seemed to Frederick, from the comparative slowness of the Russians. Now he could simultaneously become bolder against Prince Henry or de la Motte Fouqué and send reinforcements to the Russians. He sent, in the event, two corps – a total of 40,000 men – and one of them was commanded by Loudon. Loudon had started from Lauban, near Frederick's own camp, and marched north by the valley of the Queiss, through Sagan. According to Prussian information he had three cavalry regiments and ten infantry battalions with him; had moved northward and then been withdrawn again.

Frederick respected him – 'I hope there will be an opportunity to bury all this *Landonnerie*,' he wrote on 18 July.[20] He was to be disappointed. Loudon was soon on the march again, and Frederick, on the move himself now, was disappointed in his hope of overtaking and intercepting although he captured the baggage train of the other Austrian corps (General Hadik) moving to support Saltykov. When the Austrians joined the Russians, having crossed the Oder to the east bank on 2 August, the Austro-Russian army numbered 64,000. Saltykov's losses against Wedell and on campaign in Poland had been more than made good by this augmentation. Daun, meanwhile, had been personally ordered by Maria Theresa to march in maximum strength to meet and beat the King of Prussia but was conscious of the still considerable Prussian forces in Saxony and southern Silesia. He had sent two strong corps to the Oder already and he hastened slowly.

Frederick joined Wedell's men on the west bank of the Oder on 6 August. The situation, he said, represented *une crise terrible*.[21] He had been angry when he had learned of Wedell's defeat at Paltzig – a young staff officer had brought the news and Frederick had at first exclaimed at what sounded like ineptitude. He was disappointed since he had supposed Wedell – young, eager – had the qualities he was looking for after the sluggish and unenterprising Dohna. Frederick, however – although Wedell had now lost the King's confidence – was generous. He forgave him. His own judgement of the man's abilities had been at fault and he knew it. He was now joined by a corps of troops from the Berlin area under General Finck and this brought the total of Prussian troops on the Oder to 48,000 – fifty-three battalions of infantry, ninety-five squadrons of cavalry and 140 pieces of heavy artillery. Saltykov outnumbered him by about three to two overall, and more than that in guns, of which the Russians disposed of 250.

Outnumbered though he might be, Frederick decided he had no option but to cross the great river and attack. The enemy, in considerable strength, was within a short march of Berlin and he knew from the campaign of Zorndorf what a Russian occupation meant to the wretched inhabitants of Prussia. On the night of 10 August the Prussians moved north and crossed the river by a pontoon bridge at Göritz, south of Custrin, thereafter turning south and marching parallel to it on the east bank. Frederick's information was that Saltykov was deployed along a ridge running south-west from the village of Kunersdorf and he confirmed this by a personal reconnaissance during 11 August. The enemy appeared to be entrenched along the line of hillocks which formed the Kunersdorf ridge. Between this ridge and the Prussians were wetlands, bordering a narrow waterway, the Huhner Fliess. Frederick intended to avoid these by marching eastward, turning south and then fronting up facing west, to dominate the enemy's eastern flank. This, as at Zorndorf, would necessitate a march over thickly wooded ground. The approach march was scheduled to begin at two o'clock in the morning of 12 August.

The weather was extremely hot. Night brought little cool and mosquitoes were everywhere. When day broke on 12 August Frederick, who was with the leading troops, was able to see for the first time the ground in the planned sector of attack, the Russian eastern flank. He could now see that when the enemy reacted to his movement and faced east their position would be extremely strong. The ground to the east and south-east of the Russian line was marked by a series of ponds south of Kunersdorf village which would have the effect of greatly constricting an attacker's operations. The enemy's north-eastern flank rested on a low hill, the Muhl Berge, about 500 yards north of Kunersdorf itself, and between this, the village, the ponds and the surrounding woods, the defenders had plenty to their advantage: the attackers little. This was certainly not a case of a vulnerable flank to be taken in oblique order by a reinforced Prussian *Schwerpunkt*.

Frederick mounted his replacement horse, Scipio. By half past eleven in the morning he had managed to get his heavy artillery, more than sixty pieces, into position to support the attack. The guns were deployed in three positions on small hills ringing the Muhl Berge, and their fire was intended to destroy the Russian artillery on the Muhl Berge by concentric bombardment and to soften up the Russian north-east flank in the same area. The Prussian line of attack was to be formed east of Kunersdorf village facing west. At the same time a strong corps – Finck – was deployed at right angles, in the north, facing south behind the Huhner Fliess, on the route of the Prussian approach march. Finck was intended to make a diversion, to keep the enemy's eyes on the north, while Frederick smashed him from the east.

The Prussian artillery fire succeeded in its aim. The Russian guns on the Muhl Berge were silenced. The Russian troops there – five large regiments – suffered frightfully and were then destroyed by the advancing Prussian infantry of Frederick's right wing; and Frederick now managed to deploy some of his own guns on the Muhl Berge. There was the usual confusion caused by smoke and dust, exacerbated by the extreme heat, but all seemed set for a further march forward

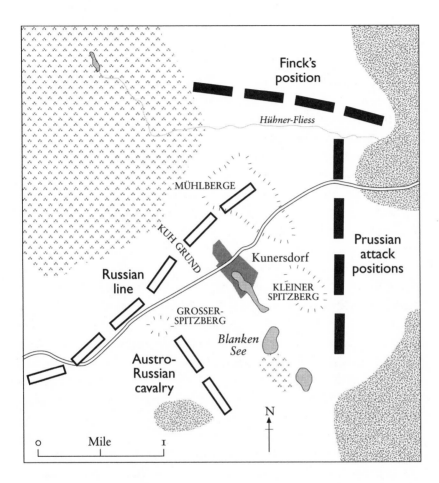

Kunersdorf, 12 August 1759

by Frederick's right wing against the north-eastern flank of the enemy, north of Kunersdorf village. Frederick proposed to lead them personally, and at the same time he ordered Finck's troops from the north to advance across the Huhner Fliess and engage. It was early afternoon.

West and north of Kunersdorf, however, and lying across the line of attack of the Prussian infantry, was a shallow valley, the Kuh Grund. Based on this Saltykov formed a new local front – narrow, and confined by the village on the right and the wetlands on the left. To this new front Saltykov hurried considerable reinforcements, marching from west and south-west. The battle had now become a savage contest at close quarters on an impossibly narrow front.

Frederick tried to win some elbow room by driving his centre and left-hand battalions through Kunersdorf village. The ground was too confined for effective cavalry action except in the comparatively open space south of the village between the various ponds. Here there were confused cavalry engagements, small-scale because of constricted terrain, and inconclusive. Seydlitz was wounded, and after his successor, the Prince of Württemberg, was also wounded, General von Platen assumed command of the cavalry. In the late afternoon Platen tried to attack another small hill – the Grosser Spitzberg – deep in the Russian position, west of Kunersdorf, but was driven off by artillery fire and by an Austrian and Cossack counter-attack, led by Loudon. All cohesion had now gone from the Prussian attack. Finck's battalions, attacking with great courage, had all been held and driven back. The exhausted troops had suffered terribly from the Russian guns pouring shot into the confused mass, friend and foe alike, as well as from the close-quarter fire of greatly superior numbers of Russian and Austrian infantry. Then they saw their cavalry apparently chased from the field by triumphant Austrian cavalry and Cossacks. Frederick tried to rally some battalions and to make a stand on and around the Muhl Berge but that flank was now being swept by Russian guns, firing at low angle. The Prussians had lost the battle, and defeat was emphasized by an appalling thunderstorm.

Frederick had had two horses shot under him, just avoiding serious injury himself. He had several musket balls through his coat, one deflected by a snuffbox. He had more than once nearly been overrun by Cossack cavalry. His life and liberty had been saved on one occasion by a troop of Ziethen's hussars, led by Captain von Prittwitz: 'I am lost, Prittwitz!' 'Not while there's breath in our bodies, Your Majesty!' The Prussians, in considerable disorder, struggled north in small, shattered parties, across the Huhner Fliess. That evening, 12 August, Frederick himself crossed the river to the west bank at Reitwein, certain that all was lost for Prussia and himself. The night air round Kunersdorf was made hideous, as after Zorndorf, by the shrieks of the wretched Prussian wounded being tormented and butchered by the Cossacks.

Frederick wrote a line to Finckenstein. He could, he said, no longer exercise command. He had only 3,000 men surviving and the army was in flight. In the short term command would be exercised by Finck and the troops must henceforth obey Prince Henry. To control east–west movement across the Oder and limit the effects of panic he gave such orders as he could. But – 'a cruel reverse! I shall not survive it. I think everything is lost. *Adieu pour jamais.*'[22]

It was, perhaps, his only complete failure of nerve in the war. Everything was not lost, but losses were grim. Next day Frederick returned to the east bank. There seemed to be about 18,000 survivors able to be reorganized into coherent units. He had lost 19,000 men – 6,000 killed – together with 172 guns and twenty-eight pairs of colours. Three generals and many officers were among the dead, including the distinguished poet Ewald Christian von Kleist, a battalion commander, whose lyrical verses on the beauties of nature had been published three years earlier. Kunersdorf was a disaster, and largely a disaster of faulty tactical appreciation. Frederick was short of reliable reconnaissance cavalry and had been mistaken about the significance of the ground. This failure, together with his usual tendency to believe the enemy would collapse under his initial hammer blows, had led to defeat. The Russians had got a second wind after losing Muhl Berge.

Frederick resumed active command, despite his depths of depression, on 16 August, four days after the battle. He wrote that day to Finckenstein that if the Russians crossed the Oder and actually marched on Berlin, 'We'll fight them – more in order to die beneath the walls of our own city than through any hope of beating them.'[23] But on the same day Saltykov and the main Russian army did cross the Oder to the west bank – Loudon and his Austrians had crossed on the previous day. The enemy in great strength were now concentrated within fifty miles of Berlin.

Frederick managed to assemble about 33,000 men, including many lightly wounded but able to bear arms, and to march, at Fürstenwalde on the Spree, twenty miles east of the capital. Some of the Prussians had behaved badly in battle, throwing away their arms, and Frederick ordered every such case to be given twenty strokes of the cane – in the circumstances a remarkably light punishment.[24] Daun, Frederick learned, was now marching north from Saxony with the rest of the Austrian army. He calculated that he faced a combined enemy force of not less than 90,000 and his army was shattered. The only chink of light in the strategic situation – too small and remote to do much for Brandenburg – was that Ferdinand of Brunswick, with an Anglo-Hanoverian army, had on 1 August smashed the French at Minden, news which Frederick had received on 4 August. Meanwhile Saltykov, Loudon and Daun were advancing on Berlin from east and south. In view of Ferdinand's success, they might not be supported by a French offensive from the west. But they were unlikely to need it.

Nevertheless Frederick's enemies had lost nearly 20,000 men and they, too, were shaken. Ludwig Ernst Coeper, who was acting for Eichel as Cabinet Secretary, wrote on 21 August from Furstenwalde that matters did not seem absolutely desperate.[25] And there now occurred what Frederick himself called the Miracle of the House of Brandenburg.[26]

The miracle lay in what seemed the inexplicable failure of Frederick's enemies to follow up their victory. Instead of exploiting success and occupying Berlin, Brandenburg and wherever else they chose, the Austrians and Russians at first remained inactive and then, despite their initial advances, began to withdraw. September was marked by a recoiling of the enemy on all fronts.

There were reasons apart from any divine intervention. Kunersdorf had been expensive for the enemy as well as for the Prussians. The usual discord between allies with different priorities, a discord on which Frederick had counted, began to tell. Daun was concerned about his lines of communication from the south and the presence of Prince Henry in Saxony and southern Silesia; and that excellent commander, when he heard of the disaster of Kunersdorf, immediately began to move north to Sagan from his base at Schmottseiffen to threaten those communications. Saltykov, by an agreement between Russians and Austrians, was also to an extent dependent on communications with the south and shared Daun's anxieties. He did not wish to be drawn too far west of the Oder, and was soon to withdraw to the Vistula whence he had started. The immediate crisis seemed to have passed as Daun moved south again to manoeuvre against Henry in Saxony.

Henry – and Frederick – was content to have drawn Daun's attention southward, and he spent the next weeks in the sort of balletic movements opposite the Austrians which were such features of eighteenth-century warfare. Henry's own troops had been uninvolved in the horrors of Kunersdorf and his own judgement and initiative were unimpaired. Frederick wrote to him on most days, coordinating movements, exchanging views on the immediate probabilities, discussing how best to inconvenience Daun, and how best to cut communications between Daun and the Russians (a measure which became unnecessary as Saltykov withdrew). Frederick's own confidence was recovering. He was always resilient but resilience was sorely tested in the days after Kunersdorf. He had never before felt such a sense of irremediable disaster, felt literally so suicidal. But within days in late August and as September passed there was a fresh note of restored spirit in his letters. 'You won't be surprised,' he wrote to Prince Henry on 1 October, 'to hear that the Russians have crossed the Oder, but that Loudon has gone with them! They'll go to Poland and Loudon will go to Upper Silesia, aiming at Troppau and Jagerndorf. I can't yet tell what I'll do . . .'[27] This was Frederick once again in charge of events and when he wrote to Finckenstein about the difficulties of finding troops to oppose the Swedes he simply added, 'But I'll do what I can.'[28] Frederick had recovered his calm. To de Catt he remarked that in war one can neither hope too much nor despair too much: 'A little firmness and a good heart will restore everything.'[29]

There were, however, fresh setbacks. In Dresden General von Schmettau surrendered to the Imperials on 4 September with what he thought was permission received earlier from a demoralized king. He was mistaken and Frederick made the fact very clear with a somewhat unreasonable display of anger. By mid-October Henry had withdrawn to Torgau on the Elbe and Frederick was starting to goad him: 'The ground between Torgau and Leipzig is flat and it's there you can attack the enemy. If you never want to take risks you can achieve nothing!'[30] This may have seemed unjust to so successful a commander, whose judgement Frederick respected, but Henry was himself depressed at this time and seeing matters darkly; and Frederick deliberately struck an optimistic note in letters, particularly after British successes against the French in Canada. 'The enemy are withdrawing in Saxony into Bohemia. You'll see – the French will make peace, they're as much in need of it as us. Don't worry about your own situation – I can be with you in four hours with cavalry reinforcements. In eight days things will turn from black to white – we'll have peace before the spring.'[31] This may have all contained an element of morale-boosting encouragement, but Frederick knew that some (and Henry was one of them) felt deeply pessimistic about the odds facing Prussia, and about the continuance of the war. The truth was that there were murmurings in the army that Prince Henry might now lead them more successfully than their king – a lost battle is a mighty destroyer of confidence in the leadership.[32] And all knew that there was jealousy and always had been between the brothers. Mitchell wrote later that he trusted they would always be in different armies – 'There cannot be two suns in the same firmament.'[33]

In one respect they were more at one than Henry perhaps recognized. Frederick's letters at this time were full of his yearning for peace and of his optimism about it. He wrote to Finckenstein at the end of October that after British successes against France in America, at sea and in Germany, France had been so badly damaged by British power that she would accept whatever terms the British imposed:[34] 'And what of the advantages for *us*, in Europe? Britain will have the dominant role in Germany, held for so long by France. This is good, since it will at the same time fend off the potential influence of Russia. Britain and Prussia can sufficiently counter-balance Austria.' And to help matters along Frederick, using third parties, tried to suggest to the Russian ministers that the French were now very divided from the Austrians and were so keen to make peace that the Russians could find themselves 'left in the lurch' (Mitchell's expression). Some communications he received from Russia hinted that the Russians, too, might not be averse to peace.[35] And, Frederick asked with delicacy, might a judiciously offered present of money in some quarters help in St Petersburg? All of this arose from French discomfiture in Canada. Quebec had fallen to the British on 12 September.

The Prussian army, too, was beginning to recover. Henry had about 60,000 men and in November Frederick, after some long and hard marches from the Oder, joined him at Elsterwerda, north-west of Dresden. He had been encouraged by Ferdinand's successes against the French and had urged him to greater efforts, to push the French altogether out of Germany while Frederick and Henry harassed Daun, threatened communications between Bohemia and Saxony, and tried to lever Daun into evacuating Dresden.

But there were reverses in this somewhat twilit period beside Schmettau's surrender of Dresden. In November 1759 Frederick sent Finck to Maxen, west of Pirna on the Elbe, with 15,000 men. Maxen is on a plateau and a force maintaining itself there could command the roads from Bohemia to Dresden. 'You will have there a very good, secure position,' Frederick wrote to Finck.[36] Unfortunately Daun was a much improved general and one, furthermore, who had learned at Hochkirch that if a Prussian army could be isolated from the main force (as Finck was) and were outnumbered it could be beaten. He occupied high ground which dominated all withdrawal routes from the Prussian position and attacked it on 20 November from the south-west while General Lacy attacked from south-east and north. Each – Daun and Lacy – had as many men as Finck and after suffering an undetected enemy approach march and a massed attack in overwhelming numbers Finck lost half his guns and part of his force. Next day he surrendered with all the survivors – 13,000 men. He spent the rest of the war in Austrian captivity, was ultimately court-martialled, and was sentenced to a year's fortress confinement. There were further resentful letters from Henry: 'Whoever commands under the King loses by it in honour and reputation,' the latter wrote to their brother Ferdinand. 'He has thrown us into this cruel war and only the valour of generals and soldiers can extricate us . . .' Henry reckoned that Finck had been deployed in an impossible position.[37] And soon Mitchell was again writing home of irreparable breaches between the King of Prussia and his brother.[38] This was to exaggerate the underlying sentiment, but undoubtedly transient feeling ran high.

Maxen was a bitter blow to Frederick, who had now established his headquarters at Freyberg, south-west of Dresden, and who wrote grimly to Finckenstein of the possibility of losing Saxony.[39] And Maxen was followed by a smaller but deplorable affair at Meissen, where General Diericke had been guarding the Elbe. Diericke was attacked with stronger numbers, surrendering with 1,500 men. Frederick was predictably enraged by these two humiliating reverses. Winter was now coming on – heavy snow fell in early December – and the troops were existing in most disagreeable conditions.

The year of 1759 had been a year of bloody defeats. The Russians had withdrawn but would probably return unless induced to look more favourably on peace. The Austrians had scored too frequently for comfort. Even the French were showing signs of resilience against Ferdinand and had pushed him back towards Hanover – they had a new army commander, the Duc de Broglie, with a good reputation. In December Kaunitz was reported as saying that the King of Prussia was near-destroyed.

Apart from Ferdinand's triumph at Minden the brightest point in a dark year had undoubtedly been British successes against the French in Canada. Frederick, however, knew that the British were as reluctant as ever to increase or even renew their continental commitment. They did not wish to antagonize Russia and Sweden and endanger their timber trade by maritime activity in the Baltic, so often requested by Frederick. Yet by something of a mirror image of British strategy the French, too, planned (Frederick understood) to limit their commitment in Germany so that they could concentrate effort against Britain; and intended to threaten England again with some sort of invasion in order to draw British eyes away from their now commanding position in Canada.

None of this looked likely to be of much immediate help to Frederick, and were there any serious French threat to England it would be the reverse, although this seemed to him most unlikely. French plans of this kind were dependent on improvement of their maritime position and so far from that happening the French fleet was almost destroyed on 29 November at the battle of Quiberon Bay. But the French were finding the war a great strain on their economy, and so were the British – and so was Frederick. He told Henry on 1 January 1760 that he had come nearly to the end of his resources. Prussia's finances – always a strong point and the pride of her king – were suffering and Frederick, unhappily, presided over a debasement of the currency and an inflation which helped his immediate budgetary problem at the expense of the long-term reputation of the Prussian mark.

There was no doubting Frederick's desire for peace and in the first months of 1760 he undertook initiatives directed towards it in many different directions. He believed, with some justification, that both France and Britain, despite their rivalry, might be ready for some sort of accommodation and he made many suggestions, directly to London and through third parties to Paris – and even tried personal letters to a trusted intermediary* in France. He received, through this intermediary, communications from Choiseul, declaring how much Louis XV desired peace, but also contending, understandably, that the surest way to peace appeared direct negotiation between France and Britain. This had to be regarded with reservation by Frederick. Choiseul, Frederick said, was too much the creature of Vienna, although strongly denying it, protesting that it was not he who had concluded the Treaty of Vienna.[40]

He talked a great deal with Mitchell. He wrote to his great friend the Duchess of Saxe-Gotha. He sounded out 'Milord Maréchal', at his listening post in Madrid, on how matters in Europe seemed from there. The burden of all his communications was the same: could not a general peace be initiated at a conference jointly called by France and Britain, with Prussia supporting? There were, surely, no territorial questions which could not be settled, given good will; and this fearful war must, somehow, be stopped. He wrote – and believed at the time of writing – that Austria and Russia would decline to attend such a conference, but a start could surely be made. And although Frederick was naturally very concerned that any negotiations leading to peace should take account of Prussia, there is no reason to suppose him anything but sincere in believing that the war, by now, was to the disadvantage of everyone.[41] His correspondence in all directions was

---

* Bailli de Froullay, who had earlier been befriended by Frederick in Potsdam.

full of tentative peace plans, hypothetical horse-tradings of territory, ideas tried on envoys in London, The Hague, or on Finckenstein. Frederick, like any power engaged in coalition warfare, was concerned that Britain, his only ally, should not make a *separate* peace, to the exclusion of Prussia, and he was gratified to learn through confidential exchanges in neutral capitals between French and British representatives that the former had explicitly disclaimed any desire to get Frederick to give up Silesia at a peace conference.[42] It was good that this was so, for what it was worth; and even better that Britain had apparently taken so supportive a line. But Frederick – although probably seldom truly optimistic about peace – genuinely dreaded the continuance of the war. He told Ferdinand of Brunswick that he regarded the prospect with 'trembling'.[43]

This was understandable. He called the Kunersdorf campaign the most frightful he had ever undertaken. Prussia was still facing a huge combination of enemies. The Russians were still rumbling beyond the Polish horizon, ready to irrupt again and sack and burn if war resumed; and with, perhaps, even more dangerous long-term consequences they were making themselves almost acceptable in East Prussia, as if in a province which could one day be Russian – to such an extent that late in life Frederick, scenting disloyalty, never visited the region. Maria Theresa was still intransigent. Silesia was still threatened. The Austrians were preparing to besiege Neisse. If nothing came of peace initiatives with France – and Frederick sometimes suspected the French were only playing for time, were not really serious – they would probably again march to menace Hanover during the year. Frederick periodically considered an understanding of some kind with the Ottoman Government which might again be induced to distract Austria, although how effectively had to be doubtful.

Frederick's anxieties were, therefore, powerful and his health was fragile. He looked old and emaciated at forty-eight. He spent the winter of 1759–60 in Saxony at Freyberg, occasionally meeting Henry, by appointment, at somewhere like Torgau where they could compare notes and ideas. The stress of incessant campaigning, marching and battle was telling. He had gout in both feet, arthritic pain in knee and hands.[44] His youngest brother, Ferdinand, wrote with worries about the King to receive a robust reply: 'I am only a man, dear brother. Affection leads you to solicitude for me but the state existed before me and, if God pleases, will outlast me!'[45] Ghosts of earlier quarrels sometimes returned to annoy. De Catt was sent, anonymously, a pirated copy of Frederick's verses, one of those volumes he had been especially anxious to recover from Voltaire – particularly sensitive because containing scurrilous tirades against other European personalities. Frederick supposed Voltaire was making free with it – 'The scoundrel! Voltaire!' But he then wondered if another might be responsible. Darget? He fulminated and spent two months amending to produce a sanitized version.[46] He hoped to believe something better than the worst about Voltaire – Voltaire sent him *Candide* in April 1760 and Frederick read it four times and described it as 'the only novel you can read and re-read'. And Voltaire periodically sent him letters with thoughts about political negotiations which Frederick read with a certain irritated resignation.

The army was recovering. Its numbers, both of officers and soldiers, were being made good, largely through the wholesale enlistment of Saxon and Austrian prisoners in the ranks and through the commissioning of very young cadets. Frederick saw some young officers of his guard apparently ragging together like small boys and 'Are your ears dry?' he teased one of them. 'Sire, I am young but my courage is old,' was the reply, which both pleased and saddened the King. He longed for a time when he would no longer need to lead children to war. He learned something of bookbinding and started to try his hand at it. 'We should try everything,' he told de Catt. 'Undertake everything.'

There was reorganization. Frederick reduced some infantry regiments to a single battalion, amalgamated several and did something of the same, albeit less drastically, to the cavalry. He reorganized the artillery, grouping heavy guns into artillery brigades and ordering the casting of new guns. He formed a horse artillery arm, a '*Reitende Artillerie*' he had been meditating for some time – light six-pounders, each drawn by six horses with three of them ridden. He had few illusions about the odds against him in the next campaign if there were no peace. He told Mitchell in February that he reckoned his enemies could number about 230,000 in sum if they acted in unison (which they could probably do after midsummer), while he might produce 90,000 to oppose.[47] The overall standard of the army was not – could not be – what it had been; and he planned to stand on the defensive as long as possible.[48] Nevertheless he appeared to Mitchell, as ever, robust and candid. He knew that Daun hoped for renewed Russian cooperation come spring or early summer although he supposed that, as previously, he would not initiate much until sure of Russian support; and he knew that the Russian generals had been granted leave of absence from their troops until 1 June. There must, therefore, be some time before a main enemy offensive, probably in Silesia.[49] Peace might come later this year, but probably not before other storms had burst. He knew that there was discouragement in the Prussian army itself about prospects – he acknowledged it frankly. But he did not want London to regard his cause as lost, although it was important that the dangers of his strategic situation be seen clearly. So far Pitt had been staunch.

By the end of April 1760 Frederick's main army was in position at Meissen, numbering some 55,000. Henry, with 35,000, was at Sagan between Neisse and Oder, and could watch and ward the Russians. Lieutenant-General Henri-Auguste de la Motte Fouqué was within reach of the Silesian fortresses with a further 12,000 round Landshut in the Riesengebirge. On the enemy side Loudon had 40,000 men in Upper Silesia. Daun, with the main Austrian army, some 25,000 stronger than Frederick's, was concentrated round Dresden although Frederick heard that he was having logistic difficulties and might even need to withdraw into Bohemia. Daun had, in June, detached a corps – General Lacy – east of the Elbe. Frederick heard this, and also heard that a strong force of Imperials were marching from central Germany to reinforce Daun. He decided to cross the Elbe, and, leaving two bodies of troops on the west bank, to attack Lacy before reinforcements could reach Daun. He crossed to the east bank north of Dresden on 15 June. Lacy was thought to be at Moritzburg, immediately north of the city.

Frederick gave several reasons for this venture. There was, of course, the hope of pre-empting Daun's reinforcement. There was also news that Glatz was threatened by Loudon, that Fouqué needed reinforcement and that 16,000 Russians had crossed the Vistula and were advancing towards Posen. Frederick's magazine at Wittenberg as well as Leipzig and the country round Halberstadt and Magdeburg were all threatened, and this indicated to him, he said to Finckenstein, that action was necessary, '*quelque coup hardi*'.[50] It was aimed at Lacy.

Franz Moritz Lacy was yet another Austrian commander of Irish Jacobite stock – his father had followed James II and been in the Russian service, while he himself had been a colonel with the Austrians at twenty-five and had fought at Lobositz, Leuthen and Hochkirch. Now he withdrew his corps, with some adroitness, so that Frederick's operation misfired although he captured Lacy's baggage train. Frederick wrote with considerable disappointment that his own situation was deplorable. Loudon was obviously aiming at Breslau, while Daun was undamaged Frederick couldn't leave Saxony, and the Russians were on the move.[51] He set up his headquarters at Gross Dobritz, just east of Dresden.

Seven days later, 26 June, another fearful blow fell. The Austrians under Loudon had attacked the Prussians in Upper Silesia on the 22nd with devastating success.

16

Confidence Restored

Gideon Loudon regarded his superior, Leopold Daun, as dilatory and unenterprising. He himself had decided views on the strategy to adopt. Frederick should be kept moving from one area to another by ceaseless blows – from the Austrians in Saxony and Silesia, from the Russians towards Berlin. The blows should be not only ceaseless but so violent that Frederick would have no option but to react, and expose himself elsewhere. The theory was simple, and had inspired the allies in the recent campaign, but the practice required energy and tactical imagination. Loudon did not believe Daun possessed these, despite his victory at Hochkirch.

Throughout May and June 1760 Frederick had been following as well as he could the movements of this vigorous and resourceful commander. On 8 May he supposed Loudon in Lusatia – he had apparently joined another Austrian force at Zittau.[1] Alternatively he was preparing to move towards Lower Silesia, in which case de la Motte Fouqué would need to redeploy to cover Breslau and Schweidnitz. Frederick was somewhat dismissive of what he heard of Loudon's manoeuvres, claiming that he found them 'almost incomprehensible'.[2] He said that Loudon seemed to be marching to every place in Glatz and Silesia and inspecting each for the possibilities of a siege, although Frederick knew he hadn't the resources for a siege. Why, Frederick asked rhetorically, undertake these marches, to Frankenstein, to Silberberg? It was all most questionable, *'douteuse'*.[3] Presumably the ultimate aim was an attempt on Neisse, probably in June.[4]

One thing, however, was certain. If Loudon undertook action by concentrating all available forces, de la Motte Fouqué would be unable to cope.[5] It was as it had long been – too many enemies, too many points to cover. And, as it also had frequently been, Frederick's mind turned to the possibility of disorganizing his enemies and redressing the balance of forces by a successful battle, by one *'heureuse action'* which would intimidate the other side and recover the initiative. 'Our situation is abominable,' he wrote to Henry from Meissen on 30 May. 'One doesn't know where to turn.'[6] He had not given up hope of some Ottoman intervention to distract Vienna, and conducted a long correspondence with his man in Constantinople, Karl Adolf von Rexin.

Outside the garrisons of fortresses and magazines the Prussians in Silesia numbered about 13,000. Based on Breslau, Schweidnitz and Neisse, they maintained positions in the Bohemian and Moravian hills, dominating the county of Glatz from Landshut and Upper Silesia south of Breslau. It was a large area and necessitated widely separated detachments; and on 23 June the Prussians round Landshut were suddenly attacked by Loudon from several directions in the small hours of the morning, and the various detachments beaten in detail. At the end of the day de la Motte Fouqué and 8,000 men were prisoners in Austrian hands; and 2,000 were dead. Fouqué, with three sabre cuts, had fought like a hero. 'He furnished an example,' Frederick wrote, 'of what courage and strength of will can do against superior numbers, however great. His action that day can be compared to that of Leonidas at Thermopylae.'[7] But less than a thousand survivors straggled north into Breslau. Loudon had sacked and pillaged Landshut. Once again 'the fair province' seemed the enemy's for the taking. A week later Frederick, who was at Gross Dobritz, near Meissen, started eastward towards Silesia. For Frederick Silesia was Silesia, and whatever the dangers to Saxony or elsewhere he knew that he, himself, must march.

He left Gross Dobritz on 3 July and crossed the Spree at Nieder Guntz near Bautzen on the 6th. There he learned that Daun, with the main Austrian army, was also marching towards Silesia, and was ahead of him. This meant that if Frederick continued his march he would find greatly superior forces already deployed against him. The defeat of de la Motte Fouqué had deprived him, temporarily, of Silesia and he would win it back – nobody could doubt his resolution on that point – but meanwhile it would achieve nothing to march the

main Prussian army into a losing situation. His immediate task must
be to keep the army in being and use it effectively wherever opportunity
offered. For the moment, although it was hard to accept, this would
not be in Silesia: but Daun's eastward march had left the Austrians
weaker in Saxony and Frederick decided to retrace his steps and
march towards Dresden. The loss of the Saxon capital in the previous
summer still rankled and now he might – just – have enough men and
guns to achieve local superiority and seize the city. The garrison of
Dresden numbered about 14,000: but within reach were Lacy with
20,000 men and about the same number of Imperials. Frederick
reckoned that a serious threat to Dresden would at least bring Daun
back from Silesia and give hope of some restoration of the situation
there. A 'serious' threat meant that it must be visible and violent. He
deployed his guns and began a bombardment of the Saxon capital on
19 July. His only hope must be rapid capitulation. He certainly did
not have the means for a serious siege.

Prague had not fallen to bombardment. Dresden did not fall to
bombardment. Unlike Prague, however, Dresden began to burn –
many of the buildings were wooden and whole areas of that beautiful
city were destroyed by fire. The garrison did not capitulate. Frederick
was also in some danger if he tried to maintain any sort of blockade.
Daun, as Frederick had hoped, reacted to the western march of the
Prussians by turning his army, too, around and retracing his steps.
He was soon deployed near Dresden on heights east of the Elbe. There
the Austrians were in position to attack the Prussian bombarding
artillery positions and on 21 July Frederick was obliged to evacuate
his guns – and lost three battalions of their covering escorts in so
doing.

Frederick's attempt on Dresden had failed. He had incurred a certain
amount of international criticism by the bombardment. He had drawn
Daun back from Silesia but it seemed certain that the Austrians would
now return to exploit their success there. On 29 July Loudon took
the fortress of Glatz after only a few hours of combat and followed
that (after an unsuccessful attempt to summon the garrison of Breslau)
by taking Liegnitz and Parchwitz. Now Daun was joined by Lacy and
they set off with their combined forces to join Loudon's victorious
men. The Austrians numbered 90,000.

Frederick could only react. With the uneasy sense that he was, unavoidably, doing exactly what the enemy planned for him, he once again set out eastward. His residual force numbered only 30,000 now, but he hoped for junction with Prince Henry's army of 35,000. Henry was deployed to ward any Russian westward move towards the Oder, but on hearing of the disaster to de la Motte Fouqué he had at once appreciated that the next act would be played out in Silesia and he would relieve Breslau on 5 August. His instinct, as usual, was admirable although his action carried risks. Saltykov was thought to be moving west from his positions round Posen, whither he had withdrawn after Kunersdorf, and to have detached a corps of 25,000 men under General Chernyshev to operate with Daun, Lacy and Loudon in Silesia.

Frederick had only one ray of light in his darkness – in Hesse Ferdinand of Brunswick had beaten a numerically superior French force, taking nine colours and many prisoners, at Emsdorff on 16 July. At the end of the month the King again set out for Silesia, leaving his headquarters at Dallwitz, near Dresden, and crossing the Elbe at Hirchstein on 1 August. He was in a good deal of pain – he had fallen from his horse, which trod on his foot, and was badly bruised. He drove his army hard – many men collapsed from heat – and reached Bunzlau in Silesia in five days. His object was to place the army somewhere whence he could prevent a junction of Russians and Austrians, and where he could find terrain on which to meet Daun on favourable terms. Nothing could alter the numerical imbalance. He told Henry that he thought there might be a decisive battle somewhere between the Queiss and the Bober – somewhat out of reckoning as things turned out, but not a great deal.[8]

The Austrians and Prussians had both again been hurrying on parallel routes towards Silesia, assessed by both as the critical theatre of the campaigning season. Daun had first occupied the former Prussian camp at Schmottseiffen. The Austrians were now concentrated between Wahlstatt and Kossenden, south-west of Liegnitz, and Frederick was at a small place called Hohendorf on the Katzbach river, a tributary of the Oder which runs past Liegnitz. From there he wrote to Henry on 9 August 1760, saying that he thought matters would come to the point of decision in very few days. Four days later he wrote again:[9] 'Here's my idea!' He had moved his headquarters into

Liegnitz itself and proposed to march thence towards Merchwitz, which is north-east of Parchwitz, and get some supplies from Glogau. He then intended, he said, to cross the Oder. The Russians were thought to be already at Wohlau, ten miles east of the river opposite Parchwitz, and if this were so Frederick planned to outflank them and move to join Henry so that their forces would again be concentrated. If the Russians were not at Wohlau Frederick proposed to go there himself – it was a useful road and valley junction point. After that, manoeuvres would depend on Austrian, and perhaps Russian, moves. The essential must be that his and Henry's movements should be coordinated; and it is striking how open and consultative he was in exploring plans with his brother. There was little of the didact, still less the rival, in these communications.

But all this was theoretical, contingency planning only, and the operations east of the Oder never happened. The Russian corps under Chernyshev appeared to have crossed the Oder to the west bank but then recrossed it again, eastward, and to be no longer a factor in the immediate situation. Daun, Frederick learned, had sent Loudon with 24,000 men across the Katzbach river with orders to front westward and act as a stop force while Daun, with the main mass of the army, would advance against Frederick – presumably, correctly, to be at Liegnitz – from the south. The Prussian army numbered 30,000; Daun had 80,000 and knew of his superiority. The Austrians reckoned that Frederick was trapped. He would be caught between Daun and Loudon.

Frederick, however, had formed an accurate idea of the enemy plan and he set out northward in the early morning darkness of 15 August. He occupied high ground at a place called Pfaffendorf and sent out strong patrols. Two of these, at two o'clock in the morning, reported enemy columns of both cavalry and infantry approaching from the east, by Bienowitz. This was Loudon.

Frederick was then able to occupy some more rising ground, which dominated the roads an approaching enemy must use. Still in darkness, the Prussians reported enemy about 600 yards away. Frederick by now had some guns in position and they opened fire. To the south, where Frederick put Ziethen in command of a right wing facing across the Katzbach, there was no contact. Frederick had, necessarily,

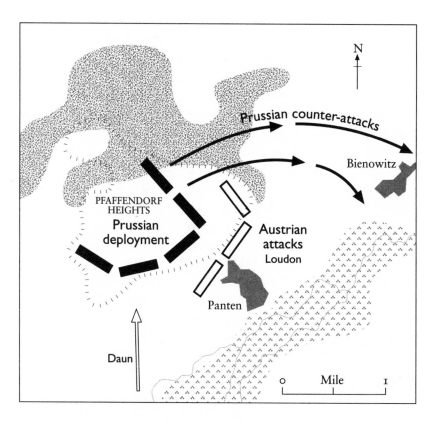

Liegnitz, 15 August 1760

deployed facing both east and south but only to the east was he engaged.

Loudon's attack against the Prussian centre, west of the village of Panten, was beaten with heavy casualties – about 2,000 Austrian dead were counted on the field next day and the Prussians took more than 5,000 prisoners. The Prussian counter-attack which followed was by Frederick's left wing and was directed towards the Katzbach, smashing *en route* Loudon's right wing in positions astride Bienowitz to which they had recoiled after an initial attack on the Prussian left, an attack which had made some headway before being defeated. Thereafter the confused battle revolved on an axis with the Prussian left driving through the Austrian right while the Austrian left was held by the Prussian right. And the Prussians won.

Frederick halted the Prussian advance before reaching the river – the whole affair had lasted only two hours and was over by six o'clock in the morning. It had been a straightforward battle of Frederick against Loudon – the main Austrian army under Daun were hardly engaged. Daun had intended to move forward just after dawn but had hesitated and lost valuable minutes. By the time that he had recovered them he could see that the Prussians were already victorious. Liegnitz was to an extent won by artillery, warned, in position and ready for the attack. It was won by timely battlefield intelligence which had enabled Frederick to deploy promptly and face both Loudon and Daun. It was won by what Frederick described, perhaps a little smugly, as the perfect exactitude with which he and his opponents could divine each other's minds – 'two enemies who make war against each other several years running acquire a clear understanding of how each other thinks, of what plans each is making.'[10] He did not say, but observers did, that it was also won or helped by the physical courage shown by Frederick himself throughout the actions, one horse wounded, shots through his coat, a page's horse killed by cannon fire, his personal grooms mortally wounded.[11] And it was won by the moral ascendancy which Frederick, despite some terrible defeats, had established. Daun had known that Frederick was deployed ahead of him, albeit outnumbered. But it was Frederick, and Daun had hesitated: and he who hesitates is lost.

Loudon withdrew and the Austrians prepared to withdraw from Sile-

sia. Daun had hoped to cut Frederick off from his fortresses and magazines, notably Schweidnitz; and the hope was frustrated. Frederick
could now move freely – but circumspectly – in southern Silesia. He
marched to Breslau where his troops temporarily united with Prince
Henry's; then established his headquarters at Bunzelwitz, a few miles
north of Schweidnitz, and moved shortly afterwards to Dittmansdorf,
nearby. He approved an order to the army on 16 August containing
particular congratulations and commendations. And next day he wrote
a letter to Lacy[12] which typifies a pleasing aspect of his character – Lacy
had lost his baggage and his maps in an affair on 11 August –

... although an opponent of the cause for which you are fighting I am not
so blind as to refuse justice to your high qualities. It is not hope of advantage
which impels men of honour like you, and I realize that the loss of your
baggage is insignificant; but because I believe it possible to conduct war
honourably ('*faire bonne guerre*') although espousing different causes I
try, when opportunity offers, to bring courtesy and good manners into a
profession which itself is sufficiently hard and cruel. When the operations
of this campaign begin to reduce in their intensity the surveyors of my army
will work to copy your maps and I will take pleasure in sending them to you
as soon as they are completed ...

The victory of Liegnitz, like so many other victories in this endless
war, was indecisive. It produced no final shift in the balance of forces
in Frederick's favour. It restored the immediate situation in Silesia
and it to an extent avenged de la Motte Fouqué, but it was clear that
the war would go on. Nevertheless Liegnitz was highly creditable to
Frederick and confidence in him spread back throughout the army.
The stains of Hochkirch and Kunersdorf began to be washed clean.
Liegnitz had reflected the speed and energy with which he had reacted
to the loss of his forces in Silesia when de la Motte Fouqué was taken,
it reflected his resilience when disappointed in not taking Dresden, it
showed his undiminished resourcefulness and courage in the face of
greatly superior forces. His marches and manoeuvres as well as his
tactical handling had been admirable. And Frederick, once again, had
been in the thick of it. He had been up all night before battle, riding
to the various regiments in the darkness, dismounting when they were
in position, talking to the men round a campfire, chaffing, encouraging.

To the army he was *Alter Fritz*, their own man, model, master and mascot. The charisma was restored.

The Russians had again withdrawn eastward beyond the Oder and September 1760 was largely occupied with skirmishing in Silesia as Frederick, from a secure base in the hills bordering Glatz, aimed to make the Silesian plain too hot a place for the Austrians to venture. He gave orders to Prince Henry to leave 14,000 men east of the Oder to watch the Russians and again to join him with the rest of his troops. At the end of August the King had about 50,000 men under personal command. There were isolated engagements, some significant. An attack on a Prussian column by eight Austrian battalions was defeated by two Prussian regiments, including 'Prince Henry's', and sixteen Austrian guns were taken. Frederick was re-establishing dominance.

But the shift of the war's centre of gravity to Silesia carried inevitable penalties. At the beginning of October the Russian generals Todleben and Chernyshev raided Berlin with over 17,000 men. They were soon joined by Lacy, marching from the south with 18,000 Austrians and reaching the Prussian capital on 7 October. Frederick had outmanoeuvred and beaten Daun and Loudon. Now Berlin, Potsdam, Sans Souci were being occupied by an enemy who was still ranging at will over large parts of Germany. In Silesia the news was that Loudon was marching south in Upper Silesia to invest Cosel on the Upper Oder, but the main threat was now in Brandenburg itself and Frederick left his headquarters in the hills south of Schweidnitz and set out for the north on the day before Lacy's troops reinforced the Russians in Berlin. On 11 October he reached Sagan.

It appeared that Lacy was moving west and then south from Berlin and that Daun, who had taken the main Austrian army to Saxony after defeat at Liegnitz, was marching from Bautzen to combine forces with him. The Imperials had moved to the west, via Leipzig. The Russians had withdrawn their forces from Berlin but were probably meditating another more general offensive from Poland towards the Oder. Daun, when joined by Lacy, would have a solely Austrian force – the combination confronted by Frederick at Dresden. It appeared that the two – Daun and Lacy – were planning to unite on the middle Elbe, probably at Torgau.

Frederick found this credible – he knew the Torgau position well, and knew its strengths. The unknown factor at the moment was the Russians – where were they, after their raid on Berlin? How soon would they make another forward movement and in which direction? At one point he had information that they were contemplating a deep advance towards southern Saxony, which seemed improbable,[13] but this was soon followed, more credibly, by news that they were still in the region of Frankfurt on the Oder. Frederick sent orders to his local commander in Silesia, Lieutenant-General von der Goltz, to march to cut off Loudon from his supplies if he was really advancing to Cosel.[14]

The enemy's occupation of Berlin had been brief and remarkably merciful. The garrison, under Lieutenant-General von Rochow, had largely consisted of the very young, the very old and the recently very unwell; and after resisting the first Russian probes had quite evidently had no chance for sustained defence. A large number of alleged combatants – about 16,000 – had moved westward out of the city and slipped past the Russians on the evening of 8 October 1760 and von Rochow had then negotiated a surrender of the city.

An indemnity of 4 million thalers* was demanded of the inhabitants, but Frederick's favourite picture dealer, the brilliant merchant Johann Gotzkowski, managed to negotiate a reduction by about 60 per cent with the Russian commander. There was a certain amount of looting and wanton vandalism, including at Charlottenburg palace and the Queen's palace at Schönhausen, but there were few atrocities.† A guard from the Austrian Kaiser Regiment was mounted by Prince Esterhazy on Potsdam. Frederick's collection of classical statuary was smashed at Charlottenburg, but public buildings were not destroyed and private property was on the whole respected. A good many horses found new, Russian, owners and the surrounding countryside was plundered. Compared to the sort of horrors produced by later wars, however, the 1760 raid on Berlin was a mild business. The most

---

* About £700,000.

† Although 100 cadets – eleven- or twelve-year-olds – were marched to Königsberg by the Russians in distressing conditions; and Frederick recorded to Finckenstein (and told him to publicize) the barbarities committed by Cossacks or Croatians, including the spoliation of graves.[15]

merciful aspect of the affair was its brevity. This was largely due to the enemy's nervous reaction to the news that Frederick was on the move.

Frederick's army, having marched northward from Silesia, was reinforced by troops from the Berlin district. He now had about 50,000 men and 250 guns and it was clear to him that he must move towards the Elbe. It was uncertain where his enemies would join, but Daun, with Lacy's contingent, would have about 55,000 men: so that, for a little, odds would be not far from even. The Russians were in Poland, watched by Prince Henry. The Imperials had withdrawn westward. Daun would be anticipating an attack by Frederick and would aim for a defensible position of strategic importance. This would very probably be Torgau. Frederick began to march westward, leaving Sagan on 11 October, moving by Lübben (eighty miles), where he spent five days from 17 October, and reaching Wittenberg (sixty-five miles) three days later. He needed a bridge across the river, marched to Coswig on the east bank, crossed on 26 October and set up his headquarters at Kemberg, on the west bank, on the 28th. From there he marched south, to Duben and then to Eilenburg, eighteen miles south-west of Torgau. There, he gave out detailed orders for the advance to what would certainly be another major battle.[16]

Torgau was a fortified place on the west bank of the Elbe. The permanent bridge across the river had been destroyed but a boat bridge had been put in place. Frederick knew Torgau and soon discovered the main features of the Austrian deployment – the enemy were (or would be when Frederick advanced) on a gentle plateau west of the town, facing south. Their left would rest on Torgau's fortifications and their right on some wooded hills, among which were the villages of Suptitz, Grosswig, Weidenhain and Roitzsch, places up to eight miles from Torgau itself. On the forward slopes of the ridge were vineyards and at their feet were ponds, marshes and wet ground.

Daun knew that the Prussians' initial advance would be from the west and south-west. Tactically, the river and Torgau's fortifications made any attempt to outflank his left impracticable while the wetlands and woods on his right would make such an attempt against his right laborious. His main position – the ridge – had excellent observation

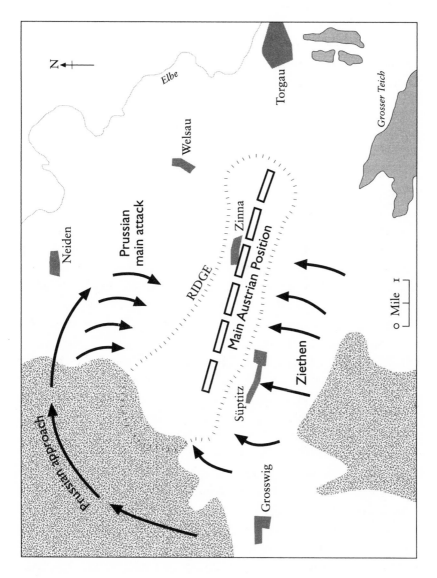

Torgau, 3 November 1760

and few obstacles to movement, whether by defender or attacker; but the villages of Zinna and Welsau on the part of the ridge nearest Torgau would also complicate an attacker's task. Daun was very extended but he was strongly posted.

For Frederick it was clear that any attempt to outflank the enemy needed a movement round the Austrian right, or western extremity. The wooded hills there offered the only chance of a concealed approach march although it would be a long one – a Zorndorf. How to achieve any sort of surprise was, obviously, a problem to which there might be no solution; Daun's eyes would certainly be on his western flank, his right. Frederick decided that the best device would be a *strong* diversionary attack against Daun's centre, around Suptitz, from the south and south-west. There might then be a hope of marching around Daun's right and attacking him from the rear – again, a Zorndorf, but perhaps more successful.

A strong enough diversionary attack necessitated division of the army, perhaps to a dangerous degree. Frederick placed Ziethen in command of the diversion and allocated to him 18,000 men, of whom 7,000 were cavalry. He was to attack the Austrians on the plateau from the south-west, where he could avoid the ponds and swamps, and was to attack in that quarter with such energy and persistence that there could be no chance of Daun redeploying or drawing on troops to face the main Prussian attack from the north when it came. The timing of such a diversion was obviously critical and it is not known precisely how Frederick instructed Ziethen on this point. All that can be said is that the timing was not effective.

The strength of Ziethen's diversionary force – and if it were weaker it could accomplish nothing – left Frederick with a main body of only 30,000, of which 6,500 were cavalry. The main body had about twelve miles to cover before reaching a forming-up place for their attack – a formidable distance before battle began. Frederick moved them in three distinct columns. With the first column – fifteen battalions – rode Frederick himself. The second, twelve battalions, was commanded by General von Hulsen; and the third, a mixed column with four battalions and thirty-eight squadrons of cavalry, was led by Prince Georg Ludwig of Holstein-Gottorp. The main attack, from the north, was planned by Frederick as a refused right and a *Schwerpunkt* from his left. As the approach march continued, however, and fresh information came in, Frederick had second thoughts about the battle plan. It appeared that Daun was more concentrated than supposed and was facing in three directions, including west. It also appeared that a *Schwerpunkt* by the Prussian left (as it would become) against the Austrian right might find itself beating the air – Daun was more closed in on the other flank than supposed. These second thoughts, which led to revision of orders and deployment for battle, only came after time had been spent on the approach march. They caused, inevitably, some delay.

Frederick set the main army on the move from camp at Langen-Reichenbach, nine miles south-west of Torgau, at 6.30 in the morning of 3 November 1760. Ziethen moved to take position for his own part at the same time. The weather was wet and cold. Both Ziethen's and Frederick's advanced elements were soon detected by Daun's outposts and his Croatian light cavalry – Daun was well covered by standing patrols and it had never been likely that the Prussians would achieve much surprise, if any. It was not long before Daun appreciated the nature of the threat. A large part of the Prussian army was moving round his western flank and in due course would be behind it, north of it. Meanwhile another part, perhaps equally large, was confronting the southern and south-western faces of his position. He made minor changes to his defensive deployments, marching eighteen battalions to cover the north and west flanks. Frederick, reaching his intended forming-up place at about one o'clock in the afternoon, found the enemy in position and covering every axis of advance he planned.

Frederick, nevertheless, decided that the attack from the north must be launched as devised. At two o'clock he ordered the first wave forward – ten infantry battalions, advancing in the face of Austrian artillery in position but themselves virtually unsupported by guns because of the lie of the land. When the first line was stopped they were exchanging musket fire at point-blank range with the Austrians and over half the leading echelon were casualties – had fallen within minutes of the start of battle. Frederick ordered forward another wave of battalions in line – his troops were still arriving after their difficult march through the woods and they had to fight off an Austrian cavalry counter-attack, led by Daun himself.

The Prussian cavalry had been left somewhat behind by the difficulties of the approach march and the changes which Frederick had found necessary to make when the situation became clearer to him. At 3.30 in the afternoon they came up with their own infantry and went into action, to be themselves counter-attacked in turn by Austrian cuirassiers. At about this time Frederick – in the thick of it as usual – was stunned by a spent musket ball and slipped from his horse. He pushed aside help – *'Ce n'est rien, ce n'est rien'* – but had been badly bruised, had a very painful breastbone and was temporarily carried from the field. He had had three horses shot under him. At four o'clock the light was already beginning to fail. Frederick, already aware of huge losses, assumed at one point that he had lost the battle. He rode to the little church at Elsnig between the battlefield and the Elbe and by candlelight began to prepare withdrawal orders.

They were not necessary. Ziethen – with exactly what orders as to timing is uncertain – had delayed his own attack until about four, and when he first moved his men made little headway. The Austrians on the plateau seemed to be standing firm and Ziethen became concerned for his own left flank. He was confused – like everyone – as to what was happening to the main attack, Frederick's attack, and he moved some of his troops northward by a causeway between ponds, towards the western flank of the Austrians holding the ridge. By now in both armies there was a good deal of chaos. Stragglers were leaving the ranks, there were dead and wounded everywhere, and there was an almost total loss of coherent command. Daun, lightly wounded, had also had to leave the field. The Austrians were exchanging point-blank fire with Ziethen's men in the smoke and dusk.

But at that moment General von Hulsen, who had been wounded earlier in the day, climbed on a gun, ordered the nearest men to drag it forward, and yelled to the nearest drummers to beat the charge. Sufficient Prussian troops heard and responded and at last the Austrian defenders began to retreat in a confusion which was by now matched by that of their enemies. They straggled back off the higher ground, towards and ultimately across the Elbe. Many were said to have reached Dresden, fifty miles away. They had had enough.

Frederick had lost at least 17,000 men, although a large number of 'stragglers' rejoined their regiments, as often happened, and improving medical treatment of the wounded was already bringing men first counted as casualties back into the ranks in a comparatively short time. The Austrians had lost 18,000 – a total assessed by Frederick a week later at 20,000, together with fifty guns. He reckoned he had won – 'We have beaten Daun and the Austrians,'[17] he told Finckenstein that evening, writing in considerable pain. It was, however, certainly not a decisive victory. He at first underrated the Prussian casualty bill, putting it at only 9,000 including 1,500 prisoners: it was considerably more and the infantry, as usual, had suffered most.* He has been condemned for seeking battle at all; but, as so often, he believed that he must maintain a moral superiority. To go into winter quarters with Daun secure in Dresden and dominating much of Saxony would be to surrender that superiority.

As to the tactical conduct of the battle, Frederick has been criticized for dividing the army, although a strong diversion, which involved division, was surely the only device by which he could hope to distract the defenders, at least somewhat. There seems to have been poor coordination in the timing of Frederick's main attack and Ziethen's manoeuvre, but such things are not easy to arrange, while ground made movement and coordination particularly hard. The shift, by Frederick, of the centre of gravity of his own attack was also unfortunate, in that it lost time, but to attack towards a point where Daun was hardly deployed would have been futile. The pressing of the attack in the face of horrendous casualties has also been criticized, as it has in every age and in many battles of Frederick's, or Marlborough's or Napoleon's, or Haig's. Circumstances alter cases. Once the troops were committed to battle for what seemed a tactically vital feature (as was the Torgau plateau) the attack had either to be broken off with all that that involved for the morale of the army and the psychological balance of the campaign, or sustained until victory. Frederick sustained it after an interval of doubt and he won. Victories are sadly often expensive businesses and wars involve death and suffering on a distressing scale. Some of Frederick's subordinates certainly thought battle unwise – it was avoidable, and winter was

---

* He also exaggerated the enemy casualties, and admitted as much to Prince Henry, who had queried his figures, while disclaiming any intention to deceive.[18]

approaching. Nevertheless from Frederick's point of view Daun at Torgau had cut him off from many of the resources of Saxony; and he needed them.

Frederick, in a good deal of pain, rode to Leipzig on 8 December and the Prussian army went into winter quarters in Saxony and southern Silesia. He had told d'Argens in October that although he could recover or hold Leipzig, Wittenberg, Torgau, Meissen, the enemy would keep Dresden and the border hills which would enable them to attack again next year: 'The Queen of Hungary's determined on war.'[19] There seemed little doubt that for the campaigning season of 1761, if there was one, Frederick would be on both the strategic and operational defensive. Manoeuvre would need to be principally directed to the protection of his supplies and to threatening those of his enemies. Dresden was still in Austrian hands, and Frederick's periodic hopes that Daun would find it convenient to abandon it did not materialize. His information was that Daun was likely to have 60,000 Austrians in Saxony in the spring and that Loudon would have a larger number, perhaps 70,000, in Silesia. The Prussian fortresses and magazines – Breslau, Schweidnitz, Neisse – would all be threatened at some time or other; manpower would never permit sufficient garrisons in all of them to make them safe against the maximum attack which could be mounted.

As for combined Austro-Russian operations, it was likely that, as in the past, the Austrians would wait for a Russian initiative: and this was always unlikely before high summer. At some time it would come.

Two days after the battle of Torgau Frederick learned that his uncle, George II of England, had died on 25 October 1760. For Frederick the death of his uncle was not a particularly grievous blow. They had never liked each other and Frederick had often supposed in earlier days that Anglo-Prussian relations might improve with the accession of the Prince of Wales; and thereafter (when 'Poor Fred' died) when the young prince who now became George III succeeded. Since those days, however, Britain had become Prussia's ally – an ally whose most useful function was the provision to Frederick of a considerable subsidy: slightly under £700,000 per annum at the time of George II's death.

This subsidy enabled Frederick to play his part in coalition war; and without Britain as an ally helping in this way, albeit not supplying a large military effort on the continent, Prussia would indeed be alone. The size of the subsidy was, naturally, a matter of frequent negotiation and Frederick was from time to time asked to justify his requests. To put them in perspective, a corps of 40,000 men required, for a campaigning season, just under 6 million *écus** – forage, rations and pay all included but not allowing anything for payment to contributing princes. Frederick reckoned that this calculation, which he showed to Mitchell, sufficiently justified his arguments for the scale of the subsidy.[20] But approval for the principle, of course, needed continuing political perception in London that to back Frederick was in the British interest; and the next months were largely dominated by diplomatic and political exchanges bearing on this perception.

On his uncle's death Frederick wrote in appropriate terms to George III. He also wrote personally to Pitt.[21] He knew that the support he had in Britain owed much to the energy and policies of Pitt and in his letter – with justification beyond courtesy – he said that he, Pitt, was perhaps the only man in Europe with the wisdom and temperament to bring this ruinous war to an honourable conclusion. Frederick expressed his total confidence, but he knew that the survival of ministers under a constitutional monarchy as much as under an autocracy could be subject to mood. The great struggle between Britain and France for maritime and colonial mastery had gone Britain's way and Frederick knew that one upshot of this success could be renewed questioning by British ministers of their country's continental commitment and thus their support of Prussia. The war was expensive for everyone and even the British purse was not bottomless. Many in Britain regarded the war on the continent as by now a German civil war and one in which Britain's friend, Frederick of Prussia, had difficulty in surviving, while elsewhere Britain had conquered and was triumphant.

Pitt had been resolute in his opposition to French pretensions. He had enlarged Britain's possessions, interests and ambitions. He had been to Frederick a steadfast friend so long as France was Frederick's

---

* Something under £2 million.

enemy. The French were reported to have been discouraged by Prussian success at Liegnitz and Torgau. They were supporting the manoeuvring of Broglie's army and the Imperials in central Germany, notably in an occupation of Hesse; and they represented in that quarter a threat to Hanover to which London could not be indifferent. But did the French really want to continue war indefinitely? Frederick hoped and believed not. He never relished being at war with France and when he was told by his envoys in Sweden, Holland, as well as by his sources in Russia and Vienna, that the French wanted peace[22] one part of him wanted to believe it. The first soundings for peace might well come between France and Britain – he thought that appropriate, and said so. In such a negotiation Britain's position was strong and he told Mitchell in January 1761 that he could have no sort of objection of principle to such a negotiation.

But if this happened the terms must be right,[23] a point to which Frederick returned often and sharply in the following months. There should be a *general* peace, not one simply limited to Franco-British hostilities. France should evacuate Westphalia, withdraw French troops from Germany; and give no help to Maria Theresa. Frederick was always aware of the old alliance between Britain and Austria, recollection of which had not disappeared in Britain, while he never under-estimated Kaunitz – 'a clever head and a very great politician'.[24] He knew that Kaunitz believed Prussia almost at the end of her resources. His task was to prove Kaunitz wrong; and Austria, too, was in economic difficulties, if not crisis. As an occasional accompanying theme to his commentary on possible Franco-British peace soundings he sometimes again mooted a British diplomatic effort to detach France from the Austrian alliance.[25]

Frederick, therefore, was friendly to the idea of a peace initiative: he had consistently welcomed it and he knew that, as things were, a genuinely productive initiative would probably have to spring from Britain and France. What he feared – with reason – was a negotiation which excluded him, which took no account of the situation on the continent and which could leave him, yet again, isolated, threatened and alone. In the spring months of 1761 there were many exchanges about a possible peace conference of all the belligerents and Frederick welcomed the proposal if it were to lead to a true and general peace.

It should, he said, follow a general armistice (*suspension d'armes*) by *all* parties.[26] He disliked suggestions for a long, dragging, haggling conference, accompanied by military operations in which all parties would manoeuvre with military forces to improve their negotiating positions at the conference table.

Meanwhile prospects for peace and the general European 'correlation of forces' were inevitably affected by the current military situation. The Prussian army was in winter quarters. So were most of the Austrians. In central Germany, however, Prince Ferdinand with his Hanoverians was responsible for confronting a French and Imperial force which had occupied Hesse-Cassel, and Frederick complained bitterly to him at what seemed culpable inactivity in chasing them out.[27] A Prussian detachment was part of Ferdinand's force and Frederick saw little point in leaving it with him unless more was done.[28] This was a British as well as German interest and he made sure that Pitt was aware of his feelings. Of course friction between France and Hanover in northern Germany was helpful in maintaining British interest in continental warfare, but there was a reverse side to this: French military success would lead to French intransigence and away from inclinations towards peace, encouraged as they would be from Vienna and St Petersburg.

The military situation in central Germany, therefore, played its part in the diplomatic game beyond any strategic significance it might have; and this situation fluctuated. In February 1761 Ferdinand's forces had a modest success in Gotha and Cassel; General von Sporcken's Hanoverians and General von Syburg's Prussians defeated a Franco-Imperial force, taking 3,000 prisoners and four colours – '*Cette belle expédition*', Frederick called it, delighted,[29] and he told his sister Ulrica that the French certainly desired peace and the desire would be greatly increased 'now that we've chased them out of Hesse'.[30] Ferdinand's achievement, he told his friend the Duchess of Gotha (who had complained bitterly at the situation), would probably contribute an essential element to the search for peace, peace which was desirable for 'the good of Germany, of humanity, and of all the belligerents'.[31] He used to address her as '*mon adorable Duchesse*', a favourite correspondent.

But this limited military success and Frederick's optimism in

February were succeeded by bad news within weeks. By the beginning of April Ferdinand's troops were confronting not one but two French armies in Westphalia. Frederick reckoned that their situation was difficult and that this could help Austria to needle France into continuing the war (*aiguillonner*)[32] as well as weaken Britain's (and Prussia's) negotiating position. He thought the need for a negotiation was consequently more urgent – Britain still held the strongest hand – but he observed to Knyphausen that 'the majority of British ministers, as I've often remarked, have only a vague idea of what happens in foreign countries, outside England!' Lord Holdernesse had been replaced as secretary of state in London by the Earl of Bute, and Frederick was unsure how things would go from his point of view. He told his sister, Princess Amelia, that in spite of the proposals for a peace conference Austria was not serious. It would, he told her, be his sixth year of war and all he could hope was to defend himself.[33]

He was extremely angry when told in June that Pitt, whom he admired, had actually asked Knyphausen to inquire what sacrifices Prussia would make for peace. 'None!' was the answer,[34] to be delivered without equivocation. The reaction achieved its object, although Frederick thought it tactful to write direct to Pitt in July referring to 'misunderstandings' by his envoy in London and making his position (and its historical justification) very clear indeed.[35] There were rumblings from Saxony, where Henry – and many others, including Mitchell – thought Frederick's demands on the population unreasonably harsh; with fifty Leipzig merchants arrested as sureties of payment by the city of a demand for 2 million crowns. Frederick pushed such remonstrances aside. The war was going on and the war had to be paid for.[36]

So much for diplomacy. One gleam of light for Frederick, although of uncertain real consequence, was that his man in Constantinople, von Rexin, signed a treaty of friendship between the Ottoman Porte and the King of Prussia on 2 April – to the indignation of all his enemies. The effect was more presentational than practical, but Frederick reckoned it had some value. In the military sphere Frederick learned that the Austrians and Russians were intending, in collusion, a repeat performance of their campaign of 1760.

*

Frederick had a new intelligence source on Russian plans. General Todleben, who had commanded the Russian force in the joint Austro-Russian raid on Berlin in 1760, had been in charge of an expedition against Kolberg on the Baltic. At some point he had been successfully approached by a distinguished Jewish merchant, 'le juif Sabatky', in Frederick's employ. Persuaded by Sabatky and Frederick's money, Todleben agreed to give advance warning of Russian intentions. The payment was not only for information but for Todleben's undertaking to treat humanely all Frederick's subjects affected by his operations in future.[37] As for Russian plans, it seemed they proposed (again) to send a corps of 25,000 to try to join Loudon in Silesia while another corps would advance through Pomerania towards Kolberg. The main body would probably march towards Silesia; but all of this would happen only 'when the grass was green'.

Frederick had this information in early May 1761. He knew that there were changes in the Russian army and system. Saltykov had been relieved by Field Marshal Count Buturlin and it seemed likely that Buturlin would have in total over 25,000 men to deploy. The Russian logistic and supply system was also said to be greatly improved. On the southern front, by the beginning of May Loudon seemed already to have left winter quarters and begun operations in Silesia. It was depressingly clear that, once again, Frederick would be driving his army now east, now west, now north, to deal with the numerically superior enemy forces in Silesia, in Saxony.

And, if all went badly, in Brandenburg.

Frederick had sent his orders to Prince Henry on 21 April.[38] Henry was to look after Saxony. He was to have 30,000 men and Frederick understood that Daun, when he took the field, intended to concentrate his own forces in Saxony, while Loudon – with 70,000 men – had been told to remain in Silesia and prepare to cooperate with the Russians. It was painfully familiar and Frederick's situation was as hard as ever. He decided to march to Silesia with the residue of the army – 30,000 – and to reinforce his local commander, General von Goltz. He had been for some time in camp at Meissen and he crossed the Elbe on 4 May, reached Gorlitz on the 8th and then set up his Silesian headquarters at Kunzendorf, near Schweidnitz, with the army bivouacked along the nearby ridges. He had some re-formed cavalry regiments, and had tried to make good some of his infantry shortfall by the formation of eight new 'free' battalions, operational from 1 May. These were units of volunteers and adventurers from many different countries and backgrounds, with differing experience and motivation. Their quality was uneven, and Frederick's army of 1761 was certainly not the superbly drilled and disciplined instrument it had been earlier.

Frederick's intention was to intercept an attempt of the Russians and Austrians to join forces, an attempt which, as previously, would bring them together in south-eastern Silesia. He exchanged almost daily letters with Henry about the movements which might be made to frustrate this and he eagerly awaited news from Todleben. Eichel had written to the latter on 30 May in discreet terms – Frederick was 'Der Principal', Todleben 'Der Freund'. Would the Russian march be directed on Breslau? Or Glogau? Or Frankfurt? Information on Austrian plans would also be appreciated![39]

Todleben was also sending information by the medium of Gotzkowski (Frederick's ubiquitous dealer and entrepreneur, who had played a part in reducing the Russian demands on Berlin), but it was through his more direct link that Frederick had his report from Todleben on 20 June,[40] a report whose substance he had already gleaned from a different source on the previous day.[41] It appeared that Daun intended to march into Lusatia while the Russians advanced towards the Oder at Crossen, having detached a corps to operate with Loudon and another to move on Kolberg. 'It is the same sequence as in '59,' Frederick wrote. There would be further news of enemy plans and changes to enemy plans before he left Kunzendorf on 7 July and moved to Pilzen, south-east of Schweidnitz. But Loudon was on the move. The news from the north was good – on 16 July Ferdinand had again beaten the French in Westphalia, near Lippstadt.

Loudon had been given the command-in-chief in Silesia. He was now responsible directly to Vienna and not to Daun. His orders were to wait until joint operations could be mounted with Buturlin and it might be a long wait – Buturlin appeared even slower to move than Saltykov had been. By the second week in July the Russians were still only a few miles south of Posen, although undertaking to advance south, towards Brieg. Loudon hoped to manoeuvre Frederick into

abandoning his strong position near Schweidnitz by threatening Prussian communications with Neisse. He knew that Frederick would seek
to frustrate his own junction with the Russians, and it might *also* be
possible to anticipate that – to frustrate Frederick's frustration – by
intelligent anticipation. He first took position at Frankenstein between
Breslau and the frontier hills. The Russians had undertaken to cross
the Oder to the west bank at Leubus, thirty miles north of Breslau,
and did so on 12 August when Loudon and Buturlin met.

Frederick perfectly understood what Loudon was intending – a
junction with the Russians without the necessity to fight a major
action before it took place. He realized that it might be impossible to
prevent this junction – and it happened on 19 August. He would
certainly attack Loudon on the march, he said, if opportunity offered,
but it might not.[42] He confessed that Loudon's individual moves
somewhat puzzled him but this was a characteristic war of manoeuvre,
war of threat and counter-threat, march and counter-march.
Manoeuvre was always constrained by supply. Frederick could draw
on Neisse, Schweidnitz, Breslau, whilst at this stage Loudon was
supplied from Bohemia and the passes over the Riesengebirge were
vital to him.

The Austrian and Russian junction of armies might be somewhat
tentative but it would produce a combined force of 130,000, and
Frederick decided to take up a strong defensive position and defy
attempts to attack him. These manoeuvres were taking up the enemies'
time and consuming their resources, and he was occupying the efforts
of greatly superior numbers at no loss. He now created a defensive
camp at Bunzelwitz, where he had temporarily paused after the battle
of Liegnitz, only two miles from Schweidnitz; and work began on 20
August. It was an open position, based on a network of villages, with
connecting and very well-dug trenches and ditches within an eight-mile
outer perimeter. The ground outside the defensive perimeter was
extensively mined, with pits and *chevaux de frise* interspersed between
the minefields. Frederick had always studied field engineering although
seldom having occasion to practise it.

All fronts of the camp were covered by artillery – 450 guns, with
interlocking arcs of fire; and the Prussian army, sixty-six battalions
of infantry and forty-three squadrons of cavalry, stood ready behind

the defences. Within the perimeter life was hard and rations short. Frederick spent every night with his men in one or other battery position. Bunzelwitz was a formidable place to attack. Loudon, nevertheless, tried to persuade Buturlin to agree a joint Austro-Russian assault, and dates and plans were agreed; and ultimately cancelled.

Frederick, when sure of this, felt free to move – towards Neisse, for much-needed replenishment. The investment had been difficult for the defenders – too many men had been confined in too small an area for too long and disease was taking its toll. Frederick had, however, engaged the attentions of two enemy armies at negligible cost for three weeks.

Having left Bunzelwitz, Frederick intended not only to replenish his own army but to threaten Loudon's communications with Moravia. Unfortunately he was facing a commander as quick to seize opportunities as he was himself and after he had taken the Prussians towards Neisse Loudon assaulted Schweidnitz and took it by a brilliantly executed attack on the night of 1 October. The Austrians took 4,000 prisoners and over 200 guns. Schweidnitz was an important depot, fortified by Frederick in the Silesian wars, and Frederick was appalled – just as Maria Theresa was highly gratified. He described its loss as '*presque incroyable*' and was sceptical of reports that the garrison had done their best.*[43] Thereafter neither contestant in Silesia felt strong enough to seek a major battle at that season of the year and in December both went into winter quarters. Unfortunately, with Schweidnitz in their hands, the Austrians could in many cases take up winter quarters on the Silesian side of the border.

In spite of the fact that in the north Ferdinand of Brunswick had successfully confronted the French in Germany, manoeuvring with great skill in the area of the Lippe and the Weser, Frederick's strategic situation was as bad as it had ever been at the conclusion of a campaigning season. He longed for peace and in some of his letters was optimistic about it, but peace on terms he could accept seemed a concept which was forever slipping beyond the grasp. The Prussian

---

* In his *Histoire* Frederick ascribed the loss of Schweidnitz to the information given to the Austrians by an Italian Major Roca, one of his prisoners, who had bribed his way to much intelligence.

economy, through good management of essentials and by its system, had survived these years astonishingly well but it was now in a fragile condition and there had been another forced devaluation of the currency. Frederick had not inflicted a defeat on the enemy since Torgau – and Torgau had been expensive and in some minds something of a Pyrrhic victory.[44] He had lost a valuable Silesian fortress. Prince Henry, in Saxony, had been levered by Daun out of the camp of Meissen. The Russians, it was true, had withdrawn into Poland, but on the Baltic Count Rumanzov, with a Russian force, had attacked and obtained the surrender of Kolberg; and with Kolberg in Russian hands the Baltic was something of a Russian lake with all that that implied for the vulnerability of Pomerania and northern Brandenburg. The Swedes, nominally at war, might trouble him little in Pomerania and were being contained by the skirmishing of a small Prussian force; but the northern coast lay open to his enemies. Frederick had long tried to persuade the British to send a naval squadron to the Baltic but he had failed; and – in some ways the worst blow of all – Pitt had resigned office in August and been succeeded by the Earl of Bute. Pitt – described by Frederick as the only British minister who combined real firmness with ability – had wanted an immediate British declaration of war against Spain and had failed to carry the cabinet with him.

Bute, generally reckoned to be the lover of the widowed Princess of Wales, Augusta of Saxe-Gotha, had inevitable influence over the mind of the youthful king. Bute was known to be an enthusiast for peace with France and for an end of the war for Britain. Frederick could accept this in principle, but unless Britain were loyal to her Prussian ally there could be disregard of the pretensions for which Prussia had been fighting for so long, an end to subsidy (and, sure enough, Bute was soon expressing hopes that a smaller sum would be acceptable), and Frederick facing Austria and Russia alone once again. In the 'weighting' between allies which can have a decisive effect on grand strategy, Britain, because of her maritime successes, was in the ascendant: Prussia, because of the strain of five years of war and appalling losses, was in decline and her negotiating position with her ally correspondingly weaker. Bute might be as bad a friend as Frederick chose to believe but the situation really reflected the correlation of forces rather than personalities. Such exchanges as there were with St Petersburg offered little hope. The sky was dark and Frederick's survey of the strategic situation sent to Finckenstein on 10 December held little cheer:

The Austrians are masters of Schweidnitz and the mountains, the Russians are behind the length of the Warthe from Kolberg to Posen ... my every bale of hay, sack of money or batch of recruits only arriving by courtesy of the enemy or from his negligence. Austrians controlling the hills in Saxony, the Imperials the same in Thuringia, all our fortresses vulnerable in Silesia, in Pomerania, Stettin, Kustrin, even Berlin, at the mercy of the Russians ...[45]

Yet everybody, in every country, longed for peace.

Frederick still had optimistic dreams of some great Ottoman initiative against Russia, against Maria Theresa's Balkan lands. His letters to Constantinople and to his representative, Boscamp, with the Khan of Tartary grew ever longer. He made pictures of a campaign next year with a mixed Turkish and Tartar force of 200,000 – including 30,000 Tartars – operating against Belgrade, or into Tartary.[46] These might be fantasies and few shared them. The war seemed endless and the future for Prussia black indeed. A British historian has written of that period:

A little, desperate, haggard man, his face unwashed, his clothes old and much soiled with grease and Spanish snuff, was still hanging on among the Silesian hills, with a following of war-battered veterans as ragged and desperate as himself ...[47]

And the 'little, desperate, haggard man' was painfully conscious of how many soldiers had been consumed by war. Of 5,500 Prussian officers in 1756, 1,500 had been killed; and that included the best, as it always does. Over 100,000 of his men had fallen in battle. He had lost 120 generals. His famous clarity of mind was not always what it had been; there were occasions when subordinates, including (perhaps predictably) Prince Henry, complained that the King's orders were sometimes confused and confusing.

Then, in January 1762, there came the second miracle of the House of Brandenburg.

17

The Second Miracle

'The Messalina of the North is dead,' remarked Frederick with notable lack of chivalry. '*Morta la Bestia*,' he wrote to Knyphausen[1] on 22 January 1762. Elizabeth Petrovna, Empress of All the Russias, had been ill for some time. Her accession to the throne in 1741 had been to a large extent due to her own courage and initiative when she, daughter of Peter the Great, had persuaded the Preobrazhensky Guards Regiment to support her in a palace revolution. Beautiful, sensual, extravagant and indolent, she had nevertheless played a considerable personal part in Russian policy during the war and had been led, not least by her mistrust of Frederick, to join Austria and France in the anti-Prussian coalition. Her policy had been one of friendship with Austria and uncompromising hostility to Prussia; and she had recently signed a secret convention which would procure East Prussia for Russia. On 5 January 1762, at the age of fifty-two, she died.

Elizabeth had no legitimate children. She had named as heir her nephew, Peter, son of a beloved sister, the Duchess of Holstein-Gottorp; and it was this feeble-minded and unstable young man for whom Elizabeth had sought Frederick's advice in finding a bride. The young Princess of Anhalt-Zerbst had been recommended and duly married to him, and although it is uncertain whether the marriage was ever consummated Sophia – later Catherine – had produced a son, Paul, and was herself in high favour with the Tsarina Elizabeth. Now her husband was on the throne.

Unlike his aunt Elizabeth the new sovereign, who assumed the Imperial dignity as Peter III, was famous or notorious as a dedicated admirer of the King of Prussia – 'one of the greatest heroes the world has ever seen,' he wrote. He openly referred to Frederick as 'my master'. His fascination with military minutiae seemed like a caricature of Frederick William of Prussia. He wore Prussian uniform and tried to introduce Prussian drill and exercises into the army. Frederick was well aware of this admiration but was at first uncertain of the effect the succession would have on European politics and the course of the war. He was, however, optimistic and with reason. Since a state of war existed between Prussia and Russia direct communication was difficult, but he managed to get messages through the laborious and rather slow channel of his own lines to London – Britain was not at war with Russia. He lost no time in sending warm congratulations through the medium of the British Ambassador in St Petersburg, Sir Robert Keith. He sent Baron von Goltz as a special envoy, instructed to keep in close touch with the British Ambassador and to start negotiations for the conclusion of the war between Prussia and Russia; and to sow maximum mistrust of Austria and Saxony.[2] He soon learned that Tsar Peter would be particularly gratified by the decoration of the Black Eagle (which Frederick himself always wore) and conferred it instantly. His personal letters became ever warmer – with George III, however, kept fully informed. 'I put all my confidence in Your Imperial Majesty,' Frederick wrote to Peter on 20 March. 'Where else could I put it? I pledge a faithful and undying friendship'[3] – and he referred to the Tsar's 'Truly German heart'. Peter's truly German heart led him to summarize for Frederick's benefit reports from the Russian Ambassador to London, Prince Galitzin, which indicated that Bute's government would only support Frederick to a limited degree; and that Bute hoped for Russian military pressure on Frederick which would sharpen his appetite for peace.[4] In forwarding to Frederick these somewhat disobliging references the Tsar added that he, himself, naturally, was ready for peace.

All this was, on balance, agreeable to Frederick, although it did not improve Anglo-Prussian relations. That the British were now lukewarm in their support for him, he knew; he also heard that the British were making secret overtures to Austria and suggesting for themselves some sort of honest broker role over Silesia, stories which Mitchell (who had been ill and absent from Frederick's court) was at pains to deny as trouble-making and to correct – not to Frederick's satisfaction.[5] The British had attempted to conceal the fact that they were, in effect, conducting tentative peace negotiations whose effect, if successful, would leave Frederick isolated, and his awareness of this confirmed his bad opinion of Bute. In these exchanges, too, the British had recognized that there should be some Prussian reduction of claim in Silesia – the most outrageous idea of all to Frederick.[6]

But there were difficulties in the sudden and enthusiastic rapport with St Petersburg. Much of Frederick's recent correspondence had been with his man in Constantinople, von Rexin, and with his representative to the Khan of Tartary; and these communications (to which there had been no replies since November) had all been directed towards getting an initiative by Ottoman and Tartar forces – what some thought his fantasies. Fantasies or not, the encouragement of a great Oriental incursion into the Tsar's domains was inconsistent with the newfound affection between Hohenzollern and Romanoff, and Frederick told von Rexin to concentrate the minds of the Sultan's ministers on action against Austria, at least at present.[7] He also told von Goltz in St Petersburg to explain everything very fully to the new Tsar – the desperate straits in which Prussia had been, the redirection of Ottoman antagonism from St Petersburg to Vienna and so forth. It must have been, at times, a demanding diplomatic task.[8] Frederick, as recently as February, had been writing to Prince Henry about the imminence of this (Ottoman) *'bonne diversion'*;[9] against Russia.

But these complications were minor when set against the huge, near-miraculous benefit of removal of the direct Russian threat. An armistice was agreed in March, and on 15 May a formal treaty of peace and friendship was concluded between Russia and Prussia. Frederick was, naturally, delighted with this diplomatic coup, telling few and keeping the prior negotiation confidential, even from the British, until all was final – he authorized Mitchell to be given a copy of the treaty on 24 May. These proceedings brought some coolness in London.[10] And Mitchell was puzzled by instructions from his authorities to remonstrate over the conduct of Prussian ministers in England. 'What have they done?' he inquired, without satisfactory answer. The answer, however expressed, was that they had discovered what the British were doing in respect of Austria. It was a bad time in Anglo-Prussian relations and one consequence was a decision of the British cabinet at the end of April not to renew Frederick's subsidy

– as Bute had threatened unless Frederick dropped his proposed treaty with Russia, which he had no intention of doing,[11] and as was decided largely at the insistence of Bute with Newcastle demurring. The British wanted by now to be clear of continental war, the earlier the better.

Apart from loss of subsidy, the benefits were practical and immediate. Russian troops were to withdraw from Prussian territory. And matters went further: on 1 June a treaty of alliance was signed between the two powers, under which a Russian force of 20,000 under Chernyshev would cooperate with the Prussians against the Austrians in Silesia. Frederick undertook to help with logistic support. From hovering menace the Russians had become allies. The eastern flank appeared secure.

Frederick could oblige his new friend in other directions. The Tsar was making hostile noises towards Denmark, where there were unresolved disputes concerning the Duchy of Holstein, and was proposing Berlin as a *venue* for a negotiation under Frederick's auspices. Frederick found this entirely acceptable,[12] and his letters began to prepare Finckenstein's mind for an international conference. The Tsar, Frederick wrote, preferred to drink burgundy at dinner, and liked a glass of English beer after it. Prince Ferdinand of Prussia* would receive His Imperial Majesty on his entry into Prussia from Pomerania.[13] Frederick, himself, unfortunately, had a war to fight but the Prussian welcome would be warm.

The spring and early summer brought other good news. On 24 June Ferdinand of Brunswick, outnumbered, fought a successful if inconclusive action against the French at Wilhelmsthal. At the end of May the Swedes had made peace with Prussia. Frederick was sardonic – 'Have I really been at war with Sweden?' he asked: they had bothered him little of late. In Constantinople matters were going very slowly – on 12 May Frederick told Prince Henry that agreements were being held up by something new to him, called Ramadan, which was apparently preventing the transaction of all business at the Sultan's court.[14] Nevertheless his mood was comparatively buoyant. The realignment of alliances had thrown him a lifeline and he told Ferdinand of Brunswick that the enemy alliance's 'string of beads' (*chapelet*:

---

* The youngest brother.

rosary) was beginning to unravel.[15] He was pleased, too, with the arrival at his headquarters (he was still at or near Breslau) of his nephew, Frederick William, son of August Wilhelm, whose mother had been a princess of Brunswick and sister of Frederick's queen. Frederick was encouraged by the tall* young man's promise – he loved music and the King said that one campaign would greatly improve him in both body and mind.[16] Sadly this favour was not long-lasting.

The situation in Germany, however, was still challenging. After the Tsarina Elizabeth's death Frederick told Henry, optimistically but accurately, that there could now be little to fear in Saxony, Henry's area of responsibility.[17] Henry was having difficulties there. The Prussian exactions were bearing very hard on the people and Henry remonstrated a good deal. Frederick referred to his brother's *indulgence deplacée* – inappropriate kindness – and told him without equivocation that he needed the money (he was also irritated by Henry's suggestion to give up the command in Saxony). He told his brother that he would do well to remember how the French had treated Hesse, had treated occupied Prussian territories, how the Russians had behaved wherever they had marched.[18] But in Silesia the war was continuing and a new campaigning season had opened.

Frederick's army there numbered 76,000. Daun had over 80,000 men. He held Schweidnitz, the key to the campaign, and with 40,000 had taken up a strong position north and east of it, in Frederick's old camp at Kunzendorf. Loudon had something over 20,000 men near Silberberg, north of Glatz; and the Austrian General von Brentano had about 7,000 on the Zobtenberg, north of Schweidnitz and south of the field of Leuthen. Frederick had no intention of attacking superior forces. His plan was to wait until he was reinforced by his new allies, the Russians, under Chernyshev and then, with superior strength, to manoeuvre Daun out of his positions. If he could be levered out of them, or defeated, Schweidnitz would be isolated from the main Austrian army and the situation in Silesia transformed.

The next move, therefore, depended on the arrival of the Russians. On 29 May Frederick wrote to the Tsar about the forthcoming junction of his army with the Tsar's '*braves troupes*', a junction which would

---

* 'He makes us all look like pygmies!' Frederick wrote in September.

assuredly force Daun to withdraw; and[19] on 30 June the '*braves troupes*' crossed the Oder, marching towards their Prussian allies. The junction was effected and the combined forces started their advance against the Austrians in position at Burkersdorf. Frederick believed it might be possible to jockey Daun out of his position by moving against his magazines in Bohemia, using Prussian cavalry and Cossacks from Chernyshev's corps. Although the conduct of the latter appalled the local population, the Austrians – unappalled – stood firm. Daun was well-posted at Burkersdorf in the hills north-east of Landshut, and it appeared that a battle would be necessary to dislodge him.

The Burkersdorf position was strong. Daun, facing north and north-west, had been forced by Frederick's manoeuvres to make detachments and he was out-numbered by the Prussians on the actual battlefield, but he had wooded hills and several villages strengthening his right. A curving ridge behind a deep valley running past Dittmannsdorf and Reussendorf gave him a natural north-west-facing defensive line, and another narrow valley through which ran the small Weistritz stream gave shelter and concealment to the troops in the northern part of the position. Frederick, in full consultation with Chernyshev, advanced from the north, made his plan and gave orders for the attack. It was intended to take place on 18 July.

On 18 July, however, Frederick's letter to Henry was brief and bleak. '*Je vous donne la triste nouvelle du détrônement de l'Empéreur de Russie.*'[20]

Tsar Peter's behaviour had not endeared him to powerful circles in St Petersburg, and after so short a reign his wife, Catherine, was as popular as he was despised. One July morning Peter drove to the Peterhof and found it deserted. Catherine, assisted by her lover, Gregory Orlov, had appealed to two of the Guards regiments and had driven to the Kazan cathedral, where the Archbishop, primed and prepared, proclaimed her as sovereign. In a few hours she had obtained from her abject husband a letter of abdication; and within days he was 'dead of a gastric disorder'. Murdered. Henceforth Catherine of Anhalt-Zerbst, aged thirty-three and soon to be known by her subjects and by history as 'The Great', was Empress of all the

Russias. One of her first decisions was to make peace, instantly, with Austria; and word of these dramatic events at home now reached Chernyshev, readying himself and his troops for battle at Bürkersdorf.

On 18 July Chernyshev had already received word from St Petersburg to redeploy his troops, moving away from the Prussians. Frederick wrote a brief line of friendship to the new Empress, hoping the newly established relations between their countries would continue,[21] and revised his plans. The Russians were under orders to start marching homeward, by Smolensk, back into Russia; out of Silesia, avoiding Prussian territory. Chernyshev understood, however, that the new Tsarina intended to maintain peace with Prussia. She simply proposed to stop making war on Austria – not '*se mêler dans la guerre présente*' as Frederick told von Goltz philosophically in the following week.[22] His immediate concern was to disguise from Daun that he was now confronting the Austrians at Bürkersdorf unsupported by his Russian ally.

He sent for Chernyshev on 18 July and persuaded him not to withdraw the Russian troops for three days. Frederick could and did make no attempt to involve the Russian general in actions against the Austrians – this would have been to invite him to treasonable disobedience. If, however, he would simply remain inactive for three days the Russian *presence* (this was how Frederick reasoned to himself) could have as significant an effect on Daun's mind as if they were still allies. This was a difficult effort of persuasion – to suggest to a loyal Russian officer that he could observe the *letter* of his orders (for the timing of the movement of troops was inevitably for their commander to decide) while allowing himself to take a covert liberty with their *spirit*. And Frederick's effort was successful. The power of his personality, his charm, his voice – all succeeded. Chernyshev left his presence weeping and exclaiming how magnificent a man was the King of Prussia, and how he longed to be in his service. The Russians would not strike camp for three days. And during that time Frederick would make no move with Prussian troops. The effect was to be produced within Daun's mind.

Not until 21 July, therefore, did Frederick launch the Prussian attack. His manoeuvre had worked well. Chernyshev's Russians remained in position on the western flank astride the villages of

Seitendorf and Seifersdorf. This would constitute a (passive) demonstration and sufficiently engage Austrian attention towards the north-west while scrupulously abstaining from engagement. They had *'Spectateurs geblieben'* as Eichel wrote to Finckenstein, describing the battle afterwards.[23] For the main operation Frederick took great trouble over timing and harmonization, always difficult and notably imperfect on some occasions in the past. He attacked with three separate columns, Generals von Wied, von Mollendorf and von Manteuffel from north-east, north and north-west respectively. The attack from the north-east – von Wied – was to set the pace and act as signal to the others; and Frederick, having galloped to each of the attacking columns, joined Wied himself. Wied's attack was to be astride the village of Leutmannsdorf, while Mollendorf, conforming to the sound of Wied's battle, would attack towards the small valley of the Weistritz beyond the village of Bürkersdorf; at the same time or very shortly afterwards Manteuffel's columns would advance from the north-west past Hochgiersdorf.

It worked admirably. By early afternoon the Austrians had retreated and the Bürkersdorf position was in Prussian hands. The battle had been distinguished by the well-planned movements of widely separated columns, given separate and distinct objectives and left to reach them by the tactics which seemed best to individual commanders. It was not, and could not be, a great unified action, but in terms of technique and command it marked a significant stage in Frederick's career. Daun withdrew into the county of Glatz and abandoned Schweidnitz. And Schweidnitz capitulated on 9 October after a long and demanding siege, largely supervised by Frederick himself and involving much sapping and mining.

Frederick's last Silesian campaign had been won. Daun had made one attempt to raid the Silesian plain from his position in the hills and been driven back by Frederick on 16 August. It was, he told Prince Ferdinand, an affair in which five of his battalions, led by the Prince of Bevern, had beaten five Austrian battalions – everyone else of the considerable host had been spectators.[24]

The next few months were largely occupied by Frederick in diplomacy, and in particular in relations with Britain. Frederick conceived a great

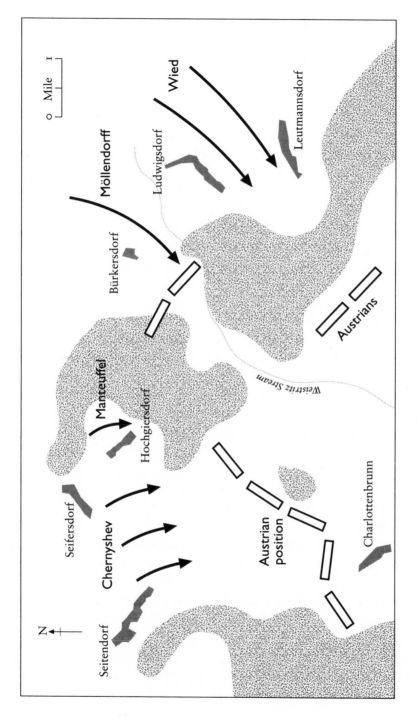

Bürkersdorf, 21 July 1762

distaste for George III's new minister, Bute, and reckoned that he would be false to their alliance when he could. The distaste was entirely understandable. Frederick reckoned Bute had been the moving spirit in stopping his subsidy, and he knew that he had been urging the Russians not to withdraw their troops even after the peace negotiation with Austria so that Frederick would feel under more pressure. Bute had also (Frederick understood) implied to the Russians that Britain would be perfectly happy to see them in possession of East Prussia. It was no secret that Bute was particularly anxious for peace, 'and was sacrificing Britain's allies', Frederick wrote indignantly to Ulrica of Sweden on 20 August 1762[25] – 'England is on the point of making peace with France.' The 'sacrifice', he suspected, took the form of agreeing to withdraw troops from places in Westphalia and the Lower Rhine which belonged to Prussia – notably Wesel – and making it all too simple for France to occupy them herself in the aftermath, unless a specific agreement were made which Bute showed no signs of contemplating. Bute suggested, when challenged, that it would be simple for Frederick to prevent any French move by using Ferdinand of Brunswick; but Ferdinand had been told nothing by London and Frederick angrily commented on the impossibility of him, the King of Prussia, using troops for such a specifically Prussian duty who were in the service of the King of England for an allied purpose. Why could not the British make their views clear to Ferdinand?[26] Nevertheless Frederick asked Ferdinand to do exactly as suggested, whatever the proprieties.

There were further recriminations. Frederick was accused of making peace with both Russia and Sweden without consultation. He was to an extent vulnerable, although he had arranged for Keith, the British envoy in St Petersburg, to be kept informed. Frederick, however, pointed out that it was Prussia, not Britain, which had been at war with these two powers. Quite different was the case of France, with which power Prussia as well as Britain had long been at war, but with which Britain was conducting unilateral negotiations without apology and with possible detriment to Prussian interests. Furthermore, Britain (Frederick believed) was secretly in communication with Austria and would always, if she saw advantage, concede Austria's claim over Silesia.[27] These exchanges in September and October marked a low point in Anglo-Prussian relations in the closing stages of the war. Frederick referred to Bute as a man with a head made of metal and entrails made of brass; with a rude play on his name he called him a bullying lout ('*Butor*') with no common sense who made Frederick despair of the human race. He hoped that when the British Parliament were reassembled in November they would force the minister's removal. Bute, said Frederick, was sacrificing his country's interests to France, while making a virtue of wishing to distance British policy from European concerns and of proving his credentials in that sense to British public opinion. He was the lover of the Princess of Wales and exerted improper influence thereby. He was treacherous to an ally, the King of Prussia. He was squandering the benefits won by the great Pitt. And he was surely too unpopular to survive in British politics – he was a Scotsman, furthermore![28] Frederick was most indignant – he asked Knyphausen for a pen-portrait of the new Secretary of State, Lord Halifax, and trusted that Bute's demise would not be long delayed.[*]

The war was still going on, and in Saxony Henry suffered a minor reverse in October but won *une petite victoire* against the Austrians at the end of the month.[30] He manoeuvred the Imperials out of the position they had taken up on the Saxon-Bohemian border hills south of Freyberg – taking much booty and over 4,000 prisoners. Frederick acknowledged his report with jubilation – 'Your letter has made me twenty years younger!' Their nephew, the tall, gangling Frederick William, was now with Henry. 'Make him *dance* if possible!' Frederick wrote. 'Although I don't expect there's much dancing at Freyberg.'[31] Frederick sent Wied from Silesia in October with strong reinforcements – twenty infantry battalions and fifty squadrons of cavalry. He still hoped to take Dresden.

But in November there was a new development – the best which could be imagined. Baron von Fritsch, a senior Saxon diplomat, arrived at Frederick's headquarters. Frederick had left Silesia and was now at Torgau, then at Meissen, then at Leipzig. Fritsch was empowered to discuss Maria Theresa's 'sincere desire for peace'.[32]

---

[*] Bute was, indeed, unpopular but survived in office until April 1763. Cumberland, too, thought Frederick badly treated in the peace negotiations.[29]

This was not entirely surprising to Frederick. He had told Finck-enstein in the previous week that he foresaw the need for a shrewd negotiator in Vienna before long – *'un homme habile'*. The truth was that the whole of Europe was exhausted. Losses had been fearful. Treasuries were depleted. Countries were devastated. People were wretched. Frederick met Fritsch on 21 and 22 December and opened a negotiation which ultimately led to a peace conference in the Saxon royal castle of Hubertusburg.

Frederick had no difficulty in agreeing to discussions although he knew that there would be hard bargaining. He wrote to the Tsarina in St Petersburg, reiterating for her the main historic points of the Prussian case – he had heard that certain intrigues in Russia were under way to set her against him. The war, he said, had been like a fire and the great thing was to remove inflammable materials; the causes of war.

The bargaining continued for a few weeks – very few, considering the length and intensity of the war. Frederick supposed at one point that he might have to concede in the matter of the Rhineland duchies, and accept Münster instead, but it didn't come to it. He fought hard for Glatz, and the Bohemian mountain passes; and won. There was much argument over the duties and taxing of Silesian produce. The negotiation, however, was based on the agreements of Breslau and of Dresden after the Silesian wars – and Frederick's possession of Silesia was not challenged. He himself made something of a virtue of propos-ing to withdraw all his troops from Saxony! And it was true that at one point he had had ideas of taking it.

He wrote to 'Milord Maréchal' that the negotiation was being conducted with warmth but he was hopeful.[33] 'We are in agreement about everything and will sign next week,' he told Henry on 2 February, 'and this war which has cost so much blood, pain and loss will be over.'[34] Signatures took place on 15 February. Frederick knew that Maria Theresa – and Kaunitz – were heartily sick of war, although he reminded Prince Henry of the fable of the cat and mice – 'the cat remains a cat!'[35] He set out from Breslau at the end of March for a tour of Silesia. Only when that was over would he return to the capital of Prussia.

*

The war had greatly benefited Britain in terms of maritime superiority and imperial expansion in India, America and the Caribbean. France had suffered to an almost exactly commensurate degree; and Spain also, for the Spanish had intervened on France's behalf in 1761 and had paid penalties in the West Indies. Russia emerged from the war unweakened but wary, as did Sweden; and in the following year an eight-year treaty was signed between Russia and Prussia. Austria was seriously diminished by the war. She had finally lost Silesia, suffered enormous losses of men and treasure and, above all, had forfeited – perhaps for ever – hope of recovering her pre-eminent place among the German states and the powers of Europe. That forfeiture was mainly due to the performance of the Prussian army and the resolution of its commander and sovereign.

Prussia, despite terrible material and human losses, emerged in one way a winner. Prussian soldiers were now respected and feared throughout Europe and their King's military skill was held in some-times exaggerated esteem. The war on the continent, as Frederick from first to last insisted, had been waged for the extinction of Prussia. A coalition of the greatest continental powers had come together to crush this upstart northern kingdom. Instead its King had struck first, continued striking and refused to be crushed. Prussia, small as she was, with no naturally defensible frontiers, would henceforth be one of the principal powers in Europe; but Frederick wrote in his *Histoire* that the war had cost Prussia 180,000 men and that her sufferings exceeded those of others; and it was probably true.

Frederick had made many mistakes during the war and in his better moments recognized them. He had, however, shown a near-unflagging offensive spirit. He had been determined to force a decision on the battlefield where one had been possible and often the decision to fight had itself been brave and difficult. He had recognized after Kolin that it was going to be a long war. Tactically he had learned fast and applied what he learned with rare skill. His failures had not been for lack of resolution. He reckoned that he had always been fighting for Prussia's life; and she unquestionably lived.

Now the sense that the King they had not seen for so long would be returning, the King who had been defending them on frontiers, near or remote, who was known to have been devoting his every hour to their service – this sense was very alive in the population of Brandenburg. They were tired of his war and their sufferings in it but Frederick's sense of duty, his appetite for work on their behalf, was as legendary as his military prowess. It was known among the Berliners that at long last their King would be coming back to his own people, his own capital, on 30 March 1763. Celebratory decorations were improvised. A newly gilded coach into which the King could transfer from his travelling carriage was prepared. Crowds gathered. The militia, who had been issued with new uniforms, were paraded. Excitement mounted. Frederick would first be riding to his principal (and unloved) palace of Berlin. He was expected soon after ten o'clock that morning. The morning passed. The afternoon began to turn into a cold evening. Light faded.

There was no sign of Frederick. He had quietly decided that he wanted no tumult, no celebrations, no expressions of rejoicing. D'Argens, one of the few who could always talk frankly to him, expostulated. He told Frederick that this was a great occasion. Prussia had been at war for nearly seven years. Her life had been threatened by a huge coalition of enemies. Her capital had been occupied, looted. Her ultimate salvation owed everything to her sovereign, and he had a duty to give his people a sight of the man who had worked and fought and conquered for them for so long. To ignore that feeling would be arrogant and churlish.

Frederick was unmoved. He said that d'Argens knew perfectly well he had wanted no fuss.[36] He was determined to return home by a circuitous route, and late, avoiding the crowds and the celebration. He wanted no triumph, no acclaim. Perhaps there was a touch of that austerity, that disdain for popular emotion, which would later lead Wellington to deplore cheering of himself – 'I hate that cheering. If they cheer on one occasion, they'll hiss on another.' Perhaps Frederick was even more tired than he appeared. The hours and days spent in the saddle in all weathers, the ceaseless stress and anxiety, had undoubtedly taken their toll; and he often appeared an old man. Portraits show a very different Frederick from the full-faced, handsome and robust figure of the Silesian wars; now he acquired that lined, cynical, trouble-plagued expression with which posterity is more familiar; and he was more bowed and hunched than earlier. He was just fifty-one, but he had been in the thick of ten of the most terrible battles of the century, with their sounds and smells of the abattoir, their crash of cannon, their screams of tortured and dying men and horses, their confusion, their extraordinary demands on body and mind. He had made a detour and visited the field of Kunersdorf across the Oder on his journey back to Berlin – Kunersdorf, where he had appeared to companions as if deliberately seeking death, Kunersdorf, after which he had resigned command pleading illness but in reality suffering acute clinical depression.[37] Frederick's memories were vivid and varied: and many were appalling, although he had always managed to find solace in a little music and in writing, versifying at the most unpromising times – he had composed a charming brief poem for de Catt at a late crisis in the war and his letters, whatever the strains of business, were frequently enriched by witty and graceful flourishes, illustrations, *jeux d'esprit*.

Perhaps now – indeed, it is probable – the faces of men he had known, men who had served him, some of whom he had loved, came almost intolerably before his eyes. It can happen, particularly in the hour of triumph. Victory can beget a particular, mingled sense of sadness and anti-climax, stronger than relief or satisfaction. Rejoicings can appear peculiarly out of place, however rational they may be. Whatever his feelings, Frederick made his way in his campaign coach late and quietly to the *Schloss* where the diplomatic corps and some of the family were gathered. He greeted them briefly, supped and rose from the table at midnight.

In the darkness of the early hours of the following morning, for the first time in nearly seven years, a light could be seen behind the shutters of Frederick's study window. Business as usual. The King of Prussia was at his desk.

PART V
1763–86

18

Family Circles

Prussia had suffered horribly, losing from various causes about one tenth of its population. Over 160,000 Prussians had died in battle or from wounds, sickness or privation. Some noble families had been almost wiped out in all their branches, so savage had been the losses of officers. The army had lost more than 60,000 horses.

Frederick's first task was the restoration of the Prussian economy, and the repair of the enormous amount of damage done. It was a task he attacked personally and immediately. It is, however, remarkable that in spite of a devaluation of the currency and an inevitable inflation; in spite of great material losses and state expenditure which no subsidies had fully balanced; in spite of maintaining and reconstituting armies (to a large extent, it is true, by the conscription of prisoners of war) which would have taxed the resources of far larger states than tiny Prussia as she was at the outset; in spite of all this Frederick emerged from the war solvent.

Much rebuilding was urgent. Prussia, like most of Germany, had been ravaged by the war. Parts of it had been overrun by enemy armies, with Saxons behaving worse than the Russians. Towns and villages had been destroyed, forest and farmland devastated; and Cleve had suffered as badly as Brandenburg. But after a tour of Silesia in August 1764 Frederick wrote that already 2,000 houses burned in the war had been rebuilt, that 4,000 had been restored in the New Mark and a further 2,000 were planned.[1] There had also been serious neglect of agriculture – when on campaign Frederick had always had an eye for that, and even during the battle of Kunersdorf he had noticed poor cultivation in the country beyond the Oder. He now set in hand remedial measures, drainage, dykes, afforestation. Impressed by what

475

he heard of progressive farming in England, he explored such possibilities for Prussia, but disappointingly. The soil of Brandenburg and the traditions of the agricultural community were not conducive to the emergence of a Coke of Norfolk.

Not everyone had behaved well. There were instances in some provinces of Landrats fleeing their posts and even cooperating with the enemy before *force majeure* made it inevitable – and inevitable it had in some places been. In East Prussia officials had been compelled to take oaths of allegiance to the occupying power.

Natural disasters sometimes put back the work of rehabilitation. A huge fire in Königsberg in November 1764 made many homeless and Frederick, anxious, did what he could for the unfortunates, while flooding from the Oder caused great damage in Silesia shortly before his death and caused him – most unusually – to divert funds from another part of the state budget to help alleviate the suffering. He built up financial reserves specifically to deal with such calamities.[2]

And Frederick – it was probably something of a gesture – also started to build a new and very splendid palace at Potsdam, the Neues Palais, a formal and magnificent baroque building designed for ceremonial events and grand entertaining. It cost 3 million thalers, was completed in 1769 but was used before on occasion – Frederick was present at a performance of Hasse's[*] oratorio *The Conversion of St Augustine* there in July 1768. 'The music was beautiful,' he said, 'but as for Augustine he preaches tolerance in some works, persecution in others; predestination in some, free will in others! The chief effect of divine grace should be to correct imperfect reasoning!'[3] Potsdam was his true capital and he would one day lie in the garrison church there, a church whose ornamentation was primarily military and which Frederick seldom if ever visited for purposes of worship.

Every aspect of the state's economy needed Frederick's attention. The population was falling and measures to encourage its growth were urgent. He always wanted to improve the lot of the farming

---

[*] Johann Adolf Hasse, born near Hamburg, made a great name in Dresden, in Italy and in London. In Dresden his wife, a beautiful singer, became one of the many mistresses of Elector Augustus the Strong. Thence Hasse (and his wife) went to Vienna. Most of his manuscripts had been destroyed during the Prussian bombardment of Dresden.

population, but it was not always easy to do so without unreasonable penalty to the landowners who had, incidentally, suffered dispro- portionate human losses as officers in his army. Frederick often found the problem intractable and the result of particular measures was not always what he intended.[4] He had written in his *First Political Testament* that the Sovereign must 'hold the balance between peasant and gentleman' and it remained difficult to do. Frederick had always a taste for reform but socially he was a convinced conservative, forbidding the alienation of noble estates without his leave.

The currency had been depreciated; Frederick had regretted the step but it had happened. By 1760, in mid-war, the silver mark was producing 30 thalers instead of the pre-war 18, a devaluation of some 65 per cent. There had to be recourse to loans – a consortium of financiers had managed this successfully and become rich thereby: Ephraim and Son, Moses Isaac, Itzig, Gumpertz and the ubiquitous Gotzkowski. Now there was price inflation, primarily in the cities; and speculation in bills of exchange. The financing of the war had, almost inevitably, been out of the hands of the General Directory and undertaken by shrewd individuals. There had been some corruption and much profiteering.

Frederick now had to restore fiscal rectitude. He was helped by the fact that the Prussian bureaucracy was the most efficient in Europe, largely the achievement of Frederick William, but he drew on foreign expertise in reordering finances and taxation. 'You are in a country,' he wrote to Knyphausen in London, 'which is the resort of many human beings in whose breasts nature and the love of liberty inspire notions unknown to the rest of the species!' and he told him to find and recruit a financier for his service, 'a man fertile in the invention of systems', to offer advice. It was at this time that he experimented with a lottery; Knyphausen suggested not an Englishman but an Italian, by name Calsabigi, who had reformed the workings of the lottery at Genoa.[5] Frederick engaged him, and the lottery proved disappointing. He also engaged Helvetius, a famous French *philosophe* who had held the appointment of 'farmer general' of France. Helvetius, who had fallen into disfavour in France because of his liberal ideas, arrived in Berlin with a high if uneven reputation and Frederick drew for a short while on his acknowledged probity and wisdom. The state, as Frederick knew, was being cheated by corrupt excisemen who took bribes to turn a blind eye to illicit imports, and Helvetius recommended the establishment of an inspectorate and advised how to recruit it. It was formed – an unpopular measure – with nearly 5,000 inspectors: and was a necessary reform since there was a need to reduce imports as well as eliminate corruption.[6]

The Helvetius reforms, however, led not only to the Inspectorate but to a new system, a 'General Excise Administration', which should be separate from the General Directory – in effect a separate ministry. It was a 'tax farm' on the French model and managed at the highest level by some clever Frenchmen. It took over from the traditional bureaucracy much of the task of revenue raising; and, predictably, it attracted a good deal of odium. The separation of 'Revenue, Customs and Excise' from 'Treasury' – Government – proved effective in revenue raising terms. It was, however, unpopular and seemed to many another indication of Frederick's prejudice in favour of French over Germans, not only in literature but in the skills of the civil service. Nevertheless the friction generated accelerated a desirable trend already under way – the increased professionalization of the Prussian civil service; although it had always been regarded as having the most efficient tax-collecting system in Europe.

Frederick also instituted tolls on the Rhine for river traffic, another unpopular measure with other riverine powers and their merchants. Whatever the King's financial initiatives – and many thought them often ill-judged – prices were rising and the cost of living in Berlin caused much hardship.[7] The Prussian State Bank (guaranteed by the Treasury) was inaugurated in 1765.

There were many bankruptcies in Prussia in the aftermath of war. Even the great Gotzkowski was in trouble – he had made a huge fortune by speculation but he had most recently bought an enormous amount of Russian army grain and the price then moved against him. Frederick was worried but felt he could not act directly and other finance houses were reluctant to help. Eventually he bought Gotzkowski's porcelain factories (the *Königliche Porzellan Manufaktur* (*KPM*) was set up in 1764) and arranged for a special Court of Inquiry to review the bankruptcy. In the end the renowned merchant paid 50 per cent of his debts.[8]

Work, therefore, dominated as it always had; and there were tours to be made of most parts of Frederick's dominions. His own resilience took a little time to reassert itself. He was bent, grey and suffered from chronic digestive problems. 'I am very old, dear brother,' he told Henry, 'useless to the world and a burden to myself.'[9] Such melancholy was understandable, not least because so many of his most loved friends and companions were no more. Buildings might be familiar but atmosphere had dissolved. 'I am a stranger here,' he told his sister Ulrica of Sweden after returning to Berlin. 'Seven years of war have changed all.'[10]

Sans Souci gave him undiluted pleasure, however. His mind had often turned to it during campaigns, he had delighted in describing its details to de Catt and others. He was proud of the grapes he was growing in its glasshouses, and often sent presents of them to Henry at Rheinsberg. But in a letter to Ulrica he said he felt that his family was disintegrating.[11] 'Our poor family won't last long. Sister Ansbach [Frederika] is heading for total ruin: Sister Brunswick [Charlotte] and I are almost toothless: Sister Schwedt [Sophia] is dropsical: Poor Amelia [Abbess of Quedlinburg] gets no better despite the waters of Aix-la-Chapelle: Brother Henry is a hypochondriac: Brother Ferdinand only enjoys brief intervals of health. In ten years there'll be none of us left!' Not all Frederick's family letters were so mockingly gloomy but his spirits were often low. And Wilhelmina – and, of course, August Wilhelm – were dead. His springs of mood from despair and self-pity to ribald exuberance had always been extreme. Whether there was manic depression in the clinical sense can probably never be known.

But Frederick took interest in his younger relatives, in nephews and nieces, and his tone with them was most affectionate. 'My dear Child,' he wrote to a favourite niece, the Princess of Orange-Nassau,* after she married, 'your relations are all well and delighted to hear of the enthusiasm which accompanied your entry into The Hague – people write to me that "The Princess has won all hearts . . ." what joy for me to know my dear so loved and valued. What pleasure you give your old

---

* Daughter of Frederick's brother August Wilhelm. She was the dominant partner in her marriage with the Stadtholder, and conducted a good deal of Dutch policy.

uncle . . .'[12] And he sent her some Tokay from his own cellars. Later she sent him herring from Holland – he had always liked fish – and he told her she was 'the daughter of a brother I always loved'[13] and praised her wisdom which transcended age. Marriage-broking within the extended family took a good deal of his time; marriages were alliances, however remote, and could affect policy; but there was affection as well as calculation in his exchanges. The King was lonely.

He was especially devoted to August Wilhelm's second son, his nephew Henry. Henry died of smallpox, aged eighteen, in 1767 and Frederick composed a eulogy which he read aloud to Dieudonné Thiebault, breaking down with obviously heartfelt grief. To his brother, Henry, he wrote, 'It is a *coup de foudre*. I loved him like my own son'; and his letter reporting the death was stained by his tears. He had hoped for a marriage, one day, between this nephew and another niece, the daughter of sister Ulrica of Sweden.[14] He ordered the eulogy to be read before a huge throng, at a public session of the Berlin Academy.[15] His '*Eloges*' or funeral orations were excellent: he would have been greatly in demand to speak at memorial services. Nor were these always on the world's distinguished – he wrote movingly of a shoemaker he esteemed, Mathew Rheinhardt, 'by his abilities, piety and virtue more deserving than princes'.[16]

And Frederick was very ready to back members of the family in difficulties. When Dorothea of Württemberg (another relation) complained that her allowance from the reigning Duke was greatly in arrears, Frederick wrote sharply.*[17] He took family responsibilities seriously and his reputation was such that few willingly crossed him. He was, however, frank as well as obliging and in the case of this particular princess he told her that he thought her unwise to travel to France to take the waters. However pure her motives, he suggested that expenditure of this kind would give the Duke a very ready excuse to stop her funds.[18] He later had further reasons for dissatisfaction with Dorothea.

The family gave periodic trouble as well as comfort. Frederick was

* Three Württemberg brothers succeeded each other. Dorothea had married the youngest, Frederick Eugen, and was mother of another Frederick – and of three beautiful daughters whose marriages caused Frederick frequent anxiety. Dorothea was born Brandenburg-Schwedt – daughter of Frederick's sister Sophia.

by no means pleased with all of Sweden's policies, and he tended to blame his sister, Ulrica, the Queen. He thought it dangerous and absurd that the Swedes took insufficient pains to keep on good terms with the Russians – 'I try to prevent you embroiling yourself with a formidable power on your doorstep!' He knew such warnings annoyed Ulrica but he said that, as an honest brother, he must convey them.[19] He spelled the Swedish situation out to her very plainly, 'not as a prince but as a brother', in February 1768: 'Sweden has a pro-Russian and a pro-French faction. If the former feel weak they will appeal to the Empress Catherine, who will send 20,000 troops to help them. Has Sweden means to resist? And if Sweden is to be rescued from the yoke of Russia is it to be under that of France? You make me tremble for you!' Ulrica was being somewhat bellicose vis-à-vis Russia and Frederick suspected she was getting French financial subventions, perhaps 200,000 *écus*.[20]

Frederick was fond of his sister Amelia, although her own attitude to him was variable; his concern for her health was genuine. A strikingly beautiful woman, who never married, she was somewhat similar to Frederick himself – dogmatic in conversation and one who enjoyed mockery (of others). She had a taste for such absurdities as fortune-telling with cards, and shared the results with Frederick.[21] Perhaps because sometimes so close to him, she was a little mistrusted by other members of the family, notably brother Henry.

Charlotte, Duchess of Brunswick, tiny and energetic but 'almost toothless', shared Frederick's taste for literature and had learned from him. Unfortunately her lovely daughter, Elizabeth, had married, unhappily, her cousin 'the Prince of Prussia', August Wilhelm's elder son and Frederick's ultimate heir, generally held to be congenitally unfaithful. She was divorced by him for reasons which led Frederick to condemn and confine her to the fortress of Custrin, of evil memory. An elder (Brunswick) brother, Wilhelm – another nephew of Frederick – reckoned that he had condoned his sister's offence (probably adulterous) and asked in honour to be dismissed from the Prussian army – he commanded a Guards regiment.* There were other Brunswick

---

* Request refused. He later served as a volunteer in the Russian service and died very young on campaign.

troubles from time to time. Prince Ferdinand, Frederick's illustrious brother-in-law and military colleague, was on one occasion furious with a certain cavalry colonel whose regiment he had found to be below standard. He ordered the regiment to be drilled for an extra two hours by its colonel; the order was disobeyed; Ferdinand placed the colonel on arrest; the colonel appealed to Frederick, who (for reasons which are unclear) supported him. Ferdinand at once complained that his authority had been undermined, and resigned.[22] His indignation was understandable, but peace was ultimately restored between these two brothers-in-law. It was good that it should be so – Ferdinand had been an outstanding commander and was himself a distinguished patron of learning and the arts. He visited Frederick at intervals in his later years, outlived him and died in 1792, at the age of seventy-one, a comparatively poor man.

These were essentially family squabbles, even when the position of the relative in question implied some official significance. They gave Frederick trouble and the court something to talk about but they preserved him from boredom and the humdrum. And this was desirable, for although there was an active social life with masked balls and so forth in post-war Berlin, his own circle was almost no more – the men who had once stimulated his mind, responded to his wit, lightened his frequent shadows. Maupertuis, the sour but brilliant Breton, had died in 1759, with Voltaire still writing spitefully to Frederick about him as late as in 1760 – 'What fury still animates you against him!' Frederick had replied in that April.[23] Occasional exchanges with Voltaire had taken place throughout the war and continued sporadically – exchanges often full of recriminations, now in prose, now in verse; recriminations part mock, part genuine. Voltaire's last letter would not be written until 1778, when the philosopher was eighty-four. It ended affectionately: 'Live longer than me! May Frederick the Great be Frederick the Immortal!'[24]

'Milord Maréchal', to Frederick's joy, returned to Potsdam in 1764 from Aberdeenshire, where he had been living without much enjoyment since recovering his estates. Frederick gave him a plot of land on which he built a small house, adjoining the grounds of Sans Souci, where the old Scot tried to act as peacemaker in the incessant quarrels which erupted in 1765 and after between Jean Jacques Rousseau and David Hume. There was a gentle respect widely accorded to Marischal – addressed as 'Father' by Rousseau. Frederick needed little reminding of the bellicosity of philosophers.

Algarotti, of the original 'Remusberg' circle, where he had been known as 'the Swan of Padua', had left Frederick never to return. He had been a companion of an earlier, adventurous, less sobersided Frederick – long ago they had visited Strasbourg together incognito, with Frederick travelling as '*Commandant* Dufour'. A man of reputedly encyclopaedic knowledge, and reputedly attractive to both sexes, he had died in 1764. D'Argens, ever faithful, was still at court. And Frederick conducted an affectionate correspondence with d'Alembert, perhaps the greatest scholar of his time, who visited Potsdam in 1763 but who nevertheless resisted all Frederick's invitations to join his court and would (satisfactorily) resist similar invitations from Catherine of Russia. Frederick had first met d'Alembert at Wesel in 1755 and greatly liked him; 'a very *nice* man!' he had described him to Wilhelmina on that occasion. Their letters continued until his death in 1783. 'Your works will live, mine will not,' Frederick told him, and d'Alembert, from the first, had been greatly struck by Frederick's modesty as well as the huge spread of his attainments. But correspondents were not companions, and anyway d'Alembert was emotionally attached to the distinguished Mlle de l'Épinasse in Paris.

Winterfeldt, the clever, sophisticated, militarily gifted Winterfeldt, had fallen in battle as had so many others including Keith, Schwerin and a fair number of Frederick's family. Henry, however, was installed at Rheinsberg, which Frederick had presented to him on his marriage to Wilhelmina of Hesse-Cassel and where he had established a brilliant small court, now almost rivalling the King's.

Frederick was reading as avidly as ever and urging its merits on his brother:

In reading a miser fills his memory rather than his money bags. An ambitious man conquers error and can praise himself for dominating by reason; a voluptuary finds in poetry delight for the senses, and gentle melancholy; A man full of vindictiveness can cherish, inwardly, the insults which men of learning trade in their polemics; the lazy man reads novels and comedies which entertain but do not exhaust; the politician travels through history and can find, in every age, men mad, vain, and as mistaken in their wretched conjectures as in our own time![25]

Frederick's appetite for justice was undiminished. His *Code*, his *Project des corporis Juris Fredericiani*, on which the great Samuel Cocceji had laboured so hard, aspired to combine Roman with German law, and had been completed in 1751 although it would not come fully into effect until 1794, after his death. But he was as alert as ever in seeking to remedy what seemed misuse of power, authority or status. When a niece pleaded for a Dutchman of good family who had, it appeared, behaved violently on the highways of Cleve and was in trouble, Frederick told her he had done all that conscience permitted. He had examined the case and had halved the man's sentence to eighteen months in prison: 'It is not punishment which is a disgrace but the commission of crime. What would come of public safety if we punished commoners and excused noblemen?' He retained his humour where appropriate in dispensing justice. The magistrates of a small Brandenburg town had arrested and charged a citizen with slander of God, the King and the Magistracy. The case came to Frederick. 'To slander God,' he wrote, 'is proof of ignorance and only the accused can suffer. I forgive slanders of myself happily. But to slander the *Magistracy*[26] deserves *exemplary* punishment. Half an hour on bread and water in Spandau!' Frederick was unchanged. He was also, as ever, cutting about many of his fellow-princes in Germany. 'The Prince of Zerbst is a lunatic and if his sister weren't an Empress would have been locked up long ago.'[27] 'The Duke of Württemberg will continue his stupidities as long as he lives!' And so forth.[28]

D'Argens, one of the few from an earlier circle, remained with Frederick until 1769.* A lively, jovial, hospitable man, he regarded it as his function to keep the King in a good humour and he largely succeeded. He could talk freely and if necessary critically to him; he understood him; and he could approach him about particular matters which, if brought up by others, might earn a devastating rebuke. Not that d'Argens could always escape Frederick's irritation. On one occasion Frederick took him by the nose, when he suspected him of

---

* He returned to France, to Frederick's anger, and died two years later.

being taken in by some supplicant to the King, and led him several times round the room – 'That's how you're led, by the nose, by whoever wants to make a fool of you!'[29] On one occasion, however, soon after Frederick's return to Berlin, d'Argens handed him a petition. It was from one Moses Mendelssohn; and d'Argens – a particular friend – had advised him to submit it to the King, and volunteered to present it.

Mendelssohn,* a mathematician and brilliant philosopher, was known as 'the German Socrates'. A member of Berlin's *Mittwochge-sellschaft*, an association of distinguished men of letters, he was an uncompromising champion of free speech as a moral necessity in any society. He was a great admirer of the English school of philosophy, notably of Locke. A Jew, small, deformed and born in poor circumstances, he had worked his way from being a humble sweeper to the direction of a major commercial concern, as well as acquiring great learning. And he was now one of the foremost figures of the Jewish community in Germany.

Mendelssohn, unsurprisingly, was also a notable champion of Jewish rights. The eighteenth century was a period of increasing Jewish emancipation, particularly in Germany, but there were legal disabilities, largely connected with rights of residence. The European leaders of the Enlightenment were not particularly generous-hearted to Jews, tending to regard Judaism as superstitious and obscurantist. Enlightenment had certainly not driven out traditional antisemitism. Nevertheless Jews enjoyed more tolerance in Frederick's Prussia than, probably, in any other European state.

But Jews in some areas needed royal permission to marry and then, as an obligation, if Berliners, had to buy a specified amount of porcelain from the Berlin factory. It had long been held as axiomatic – and Frederick regarded it as a fact of life – that the Jewish community in any city created so powerful a financial caucus, to the possible detriment of Gentiles and Gentile traders, that Jews needed residence permits and were thus subject to a certain degree of control. This bore particularly hard on the relatively impecunious Jew – the wealthy merchant, once established, was welcome. When Frederick occupied certain districts

---

* Grandfather of the composer Felix Mendelssohn.

of Poland an edict was issued that Jews with less than 1,000 crowns of capital were to leave the territory.

Mendelssohn wished for the status of *Schützjude*, 'protected Jew', which would give him unrestricted right of residence in Berlin. He was a man of great and acknowledged distinction, his connections were illustrious: Lessing – *doyen* of German philosophers – was a close friend. Through his translations of some of the Bible, Mendelssohn was known not only as the German Socrates but as 'the Luther of the German Jews'. His application for the *privilegium*, as the unrestricted residential status was called, seemed certain to succeed, although he said that it saddened him to apply for something which should belong by right to any man prepared to live as a law-abiding citizen. A new edict had been promulgated in 1750, laying down among other things that the *Schützjude* status was heritable but could only be bequeathed to *one* child.

But there was a complication. Mendelssohn was a great friend of the distinguished Jewish linguistic scholar Raphael, and Raphael had antagonized the Jewish Elders. The Jewish community was regulated very strictly by their own authorities and some leading Jews (including Mendelssohn) were struggling to emancipate their co-religionists from the more rigid and intolerant practices and rules of their own people and to bring them more into the general European cultural mainstream. While Frederick was away at the war the Elders had tried to have Raphael expelled from Berlin and d'Argens, as a friend, had taken up his cause. It was, however, an expulsion which the King's courts declared they had no power to prevent – it was an internal Jewish matter. D'Argens felt this inherently unjust. He was also concerned that such a precedent might extend to the internationally distinguished Mendelssohn, who also had his disagreements with the Elders. He therefore persuaded Mendelssohn to petition the King for the *privilegium*.

Mendelssohn was at first reluctant. He thought this something of an intrusion. The King was still leading his army – the war had not yet ended – and 'What right have I,' he asked, 'to exceptional treatment, if the state has overriding reasons to limit the number of people of my race?'[30] Nevertheless d'Argens persuaded him to write out an application and in April 1763, the war over, he gave it to Frederick.

Then there was silence. D'Argens knew that Frederick admired Mendelssohn's work and could not believe the King reluctant to perform an act of manifest justice even though it might offend the leaders of the Jewish community. He tackled him one day when Frederick was on the way to his own apartments. Frederick nodded. 'Mendelssohn shall have his *privilegium*. The application must have been lost.'

D'Argens wrote out a new application in his own name: 'A bad Catholic and philosopher requests a bad Protestant and philosopher to grant the *privilegium* to a bad Jew and philosopher.'

He handed it to Frederick with the words 'Don't lose it again!' Mendelssohn received *Schützjude* status and the *privilegium* in October 1763. He admired the King, just as the King admired him. When others discussed Frederick's apparent agnosticism about eternal life he would say, 'The King *deserves* to believe in immortality of the soul!' Faith as reward. He sometimes offered criticisms of Frederick's writings, taken on the whole in good part. The first synagogue to be founded in Potsdam was built in 1766, and Frederick observed, sensibly, 'To oppress the Jews never brought any prosperity to any government!' Both the prosperity and the cultural integration of the Jewish community increased in the years following the Seven Years War.[31] Nevertheless he recognized that the prejudices of others existed, and when Mendelssohn's name was proposed as first choice for the chair of speculative philosophy at the Academy Frederick demurred. It would be the first Academy election after that which had formally elected the Empress of Russia and he thought the juxtaposition might give offence.[32] But Mendelssohn was unequivocal. 'I live,' he wrote, 'in a state in which one of the wisest sovereigns who has ever ruled mankind has made the arts and sciences to blossom, and a sensible freedom of thought so widespread that the effect has reached down to the humblest inhabitant of his dominions.'[33] Kant wrote in similar terms of Frederick's care for freedom of conscience.

Gradually, as peace and civility succeeded war and crisis, something like Frederick's earlier community of like minds began to assemble again. In March 1765 Dieudonné Thiebault arrived in Berlin. He had been recommended by d'Alembert and was hoping for a post as Professor of Literature at the Academy. He had had a long journey but was immediately received by the King, to suffer two hours' remorseless questioning. Frederick surprised him.

'Give me your word of honour not to learn German!' Thiebault spoke no German, and Frederick told him it was a half-barbarous language with a poor, imitative literature. They talked of other men of European letters. Frederick said that Jean Jacques Rousseau was mad.

'He was in trouble! We offered him a house and a pension.' 'Milord Maréchal' had seen to it, and Rousseau's response had been to ask, impertinently, what was being done for those who had lost limbs in Frederick's service. This had been in 1762, and Frederick had been enraged.

Thiebault got his professorship and Frederick enjoyed verbal sparring with him. This sometimes involved Colonel Karl Guischardt, a former officer of the 'Free Battalions', son of an official in Magdeburg, who was fascinated by Frederick and was used by him as something of a butt. Guischardt was a well-read man, a historian and naturalist, but had, unfortunately for him, earned his position as butt by an early show of pretentiousness. He had praised the physical endurance of Roman soldiers for the weight they could carry on the march, compared with the modern Prussian. Frederick looked at him – 'Really?'

He ordered in a soldier from the Guard, told him to remove his equipment and hang it on Guischardt. 'Our captain may not in future pass judgement so lightly!'

Frederick kept him standing, equipped and laden, for an hour. Guischardt was known to be making notes on life at court and when he died in 1775 Frederick bought up all the dead man's papers.

Frederick gave Guischardt the name of 'Quintus Icilius', famous centurion of the 10th Legion at Pharsala, and would sometimes say he felt too exhausted for conversation; would Quintus Icilius and Thiebault please talk – their intelligence and exchanges would soon stimulate him. They might begin, but after a short while Frederick, exhausted or not, would interrupt. And then never stop talking. He might start the conversational ball rolling.

'Why did God not enable men to foresee the hour of their death?'

Quintus Icilius might try to keep things going with a flight of excessive cynicism which he supposed congenial. This would be put down – devastatingly – by Frederick. After inflicting such a humiliation, however, Frederick would be quiet, conciliatory. He would change key. His moods were as fluctuating as ever. And he liked trying his own compositions and often sardonic verses on Thiebault. Thiebault might laugh.

Frederick – 'What, sir? What are you laughing at?' And so it continued. Part genuine intellectual and literary exchange, part play-acting, part bullying. Seldom dull. Thiebault, a Catholic, refused to be drawn by Frederick's periodic raillery. He was, himself, prepared to challenge – respectfully but firmly – the validity of Frederick's written discourses, challenges which met a mixed reception. But the great trouble Frederick took with his own reading and literary criticism always impressed.

Frederick still enjoyed teasing. He was mischievous. 'What news in Berlin?' he called out at his dinner table once in 1767.

'The talk is that there'll soon be war again, sire.'

'What nonsense! They talk about war because they've nothing left to talk about!'

Frederick said the public needed different stories on which to feed. He told a reliable friend to send a report to the two most prominent Berlin newspapers – 'I'll dictate it!'

The story ran that, as reported from Potsdam, there had been on 27 February thunder, lightning, rain, hail – a storm greater than anybody remembered. The sky had darkened and one of a pair of oxen being driven into town by a farmer was struck. There had been many human casualties. A brewer had broken his arm. Windows in one street were all shattered.

The reports, wholly invented by Frederick, were published and people talked of nothing else for a while. There was much correspondence in the papers and other European press took up the story. In the following year the phenomenon was mentioned in a book by a professor at Wittenberg. Frederick chuckled. It had taken minds away from absurd and undesirable speculations about war.[34]

Peace had come, but the King was still always and primarily the warrior-leader of the people, the commander-in-chief. He held a great banquet after the war, entertained his generals at it and, like every successful commander in every age, fought past battles again. He talked with his old subordinates of the fights they had seen, the mistakes made, the triumphs, the accidents. In Berlin (a remarkable gesture to subordinate commanders) he erected statues to honour Seydlitz, Keith, Schwerin, Winterfeldt. He was working on his next *Politische Testament* (to be completed in 1768) and it would have a military section.

Prince Henry was at the banquet, and Frederick turned to him. 'Now let us drink to the only general who did not commit a single error!'[35] It was a striking tribute. Frederick and Henry had often differed sharply. Henry had thought the war might have been ended earlier had Frederick shown more readiness to compromise. Compared with Frederick, Henry had tended to caution, to shrink from risk, but his judgement in action had been good, and his ability to predict and prepare also good. A humane man, he had thought the treatment of Saxony and the exactions therein harsh, and had said so; and had gained the actual affection of the Saxons. Like his brothers he tended to regard Frederick as aloof and lacking in affection. Like them he had mistrusted some of those close to the King, particularly the influence of Winterfeldt while Winterfeldt was alive. He had resented Frederick's treatment of August Wilhelm. He had a fair portion of ambition of his own and could be touchy, suffering some of the jealousy which can plague younger sons; and when Henry sulked, as he sometimes did, Frederick generally humoured him, although Henry took it amiss when the King sharply reminded him, after the war, that he was again a regimental officer (as colonel of a regiment) and should be dressed as such. Small, handsome and charming, Henry had won the last pitched battle of the war, at Freyberg. Frederick valued him highly and had on most occasions taken him into his confidence and treated him well; and now the unique encomium – 'The only general who did not commit a single error!' His huge correspondence with Henry, mostly about campaigning business while war lasted, is full of affection as well as gossip and family news.[36] His legacy to Henry in his will was to 'the Victor of Freyberg'. It was sad that there had been so many times in life when jealousy and resentment had soured their personal relationship.

Frederick's inspections of his regiments at Potsdam resumed, in all their strictness. Men remembered long afterwards the terrifying nature of the King's unwavering stare, the look in his very blue, very cold and very beautiful eyes as he cross-examined some uneasy officer about his command, his duties and his men. Despite the frequent shabbiness of his own appearance, Frederick was a stickler for correctitude in military matters and dress. There were conventions, as at all courts, and when two French officers, visiting Berlin, disregarded the applicable convention Frederick looked them up and down. One was wearing stockings rather than boots and Frederick's stare transfixed him.

'Your regiment?'

'Régiment de Champagne, sire.'

'Ah,' said Frederick, 'we've not forgotten the old saying, I see, "Champagne laughs at order!" '[37]

There was no doubt that as a result of wartime conditions the quality of the army had gone down. War improves some of the standards of an army; battle experience and ordering of logistics in combat conditions correct the unrealities and sometimes the false priorities of peacetime. Some very basic things can, however, deteriorate with neglect and these now needed correction and got it. Frederick wrote in 1767 – with the war now four years behind him – that things were getting better, discipline and training were improving, but that it would take another three years for standards to be what they had been.[38] There had been dilution of quality and the first remedy lay with rigorous insistence on the quality of officers.

Frederick had reformed the Prussian Cadet Corps early in the war. He cared deeply about it and nearly 3,000 young men passed through it during his reign. The Cadet Corps was fed by junior cadet schools at Stolp in Pomerania and at Külm in West Prussia. After completing his course the cadet served first in the ranks of the army with non-commissioned officer's rank and status before becoming Ensign (*Fähnrich**). The first full commissioned rank was that of lieutenant (drawing very little pay); and the most important step was to a captaincy, which carried company command. The system had served Prussia well in the long war just ended and it needed watching, nurturing and protect-

---

* Perhaps comparable to a midshipman in the Royal Navy.

ing. It placed emphasis on the homogeneousness of the officer corps as a band of brothers, reared in the same *ethos*, sharply observant of military hierarchy on duty but taught to be social equals when off. The uniform of Prussian officers was the same, whatever their rank.

Frederick reckoned that he knew his army well. He had always demanded very scrupulous administration: soldiers must, for instance, be paid regularly and correctly at all times. He thought he knew well the different characteristics, as soldiers, of men from the various regions of his kingdom. He esteemed Berliners the least and Pomeranians the most – the best infantry in the world. In his private order of merit he next placed men from Halberstadt and Magdeburg, the areas beyond the lower Elbe. Then there were the Silesians, people of outstanding appearance, whether the Lutherans of Lower Silesia or (just behind them) the Catholics of Upper Silesia and Glatz. Rather surprisingly he put below the Silesians the men from East Prussia; and below them again those from West Prussia and Prussian Westphalia, although in respect of the latter he had a special word of commendation in his writings for the natives of Minden and of Herford. In all these generalizations and stereotypings – no doubt as unfair in particulars as most such – Frederick appreciated that the native – Prussian – element in his army had in war generally been less than half, so dependent had he become on foreigners, deserters from other armies, and impressed prisoners of war.

Education and literacy naturally absorbed him. He reverted in his next *Political Testament* of 1768 to the education of princes. The prince, he wrote, must from the age of twenty be given actual experience of government: and, because he will be a military leader, of military command. He will then get to know the junior officers of the army and assess them; some will one day be his generals. They, in turn, must encourage intelligence and literacy in all under their command – regimental commanders were to inaugurate regimental libraries. And care of the soldier's family must receive humane attention at all times. A given number of wives could accompany the regiment on campaign,* but otherwise they must remain in the Regimental District, in quarters, and be given a small allowance both in

---

* As in e.g. the British army. In Prussia the number was generally five per company.

money and rations at state expense. The wives of officers must also live in the Regimental District. Letters to soldier husbands, of whatever rank, must be postage free. There were, of course, a tragically large number of widows and orphans and already by 1758 Frederick had founded at Potsdam a military orphanage, the Waisenhaus, for the children of dead or destitute soldiers; in that year there were 2,000 children therein. The wars had been a terrible experience and at that time there were still four years of war ahead. The problem of abandoned babies also exercised him greatly – in 1768 he founded homes to care for them in Berlin, Breslau and Königsberg and placed great importance on their (expensive) administration.

In this 1768 *Testament* Frederick again considered the situation of Prussia, strategically.[39] Some things had changed, improved even. Some dangers had receded. And 'If we have no colonies in Africa or America,' he wrote, 'I congratulate my successors. Prussia needs a good army, but not a fleet.' His words reflected long experience – he had been ruling for twenty-eight years – and considerable thought. The Prussian Levant Company, based on Emden, and designed for the China trade in 1765, did not last long. Nevertheless the Prussian coastal trade and shipping increased during Frederick's reign. He never wavered, however, in his view that Prussia was a land power and must not be seduced by temporary circumstances into any other direction. The quality of the army, and in particular of its leaders, was what mattered.

Always scrutinizing the performance of his own officers, particularly the seniors, Frederick recorded in this *Testament* incidental notes on the character and potential of some of those already well-tried. Ramin, Wunsch, Stutterheim, for instance, were 'not bad'. Mollendorf 'will be good' (he was one of the heroes of Bürkersdorf!). Lastwitz and Wolfersdorf were first class, although the latter 'should never be entrusted with a defensive position'. Bülow, admirable. Manstein, '*très bon*'. Others were described variously as 'brave', 'of limited vision', 'too soft'. Thadden was firmly assessed as 'of high quality when not drinking'. Zastrow and Alvensleben were 'good'. Most of the rest were 'mediocre'. In the cavalry Seydlitz surpassed all.

There can always be dangers when, after a major war, the affairs of the army are in the dominant hands of a high commander with great prestige and a record of victory; and the greater the dominance the greater the dangers. His confidence and his achievements can induce certainty that the recipe for success lies simply in repetition of formulae he has tested and proven. His impressions, the lessons his own mind has received in historic circumstances, may be so indelible as to exclude all others. His authority has acquired an aura of infallibility; and all this may arise in a war-weary state and army, eager for relaxation from the austerities of war and ready to suppose new thinking to be unnecessary and probably unsound. Britain, for instance, underwent such a phase after the Napoleonic wars when the long and distinguished shadow of Wellington tended to stunt military progress. Men simply asked what the Duke would have thought, and ceased to think themselves.

Such eras are liable to lead an army towards pedantry, stagnation, concentration on minutiae and precedent rather than objectivity and innovation. The danger is clearly greater when the recent hero is not only sovereign but, like Frederick, has both taste and aptitude for recording his impressions, the lessons of his experience, the key to his victories in writings which acquire (at least in the author's eye) near-Scriptural authority. It is fascinating for posterity but may have been unfortunate for Prussia that Frederick, to all Europe now a towering military figure, chose to write so much, so soon, on the military affairs of the Prussian kingdom. Great though his achievements were in organization and in the field, wise though most of his measures and his writings were, the terrible clouds of Iena and of Auerstadt might have been prophetically discerned in the sky at this time.

It would, however, be a mistake to suppose the later Frederick simply a theorist or chronicler, still less a reactionary. On the contrary, he wrote frequently to Henry about experiments with battle drills, cavalry formations, undertaken at Potsdam. He tried out 'attacks with squares, in the Russian manner', he told him in 1771. 'It may be good against Turks but not against a European enemy with a considerable artillery.' He conducted the army's manoeuvres in Silesia until 1785, the year before he died. In that year, entertaining foreign notables as usual, he charged at the head of the Prussian cavalry in pouring rain, cursing them for not going hard enough. He was seventy-four.

Alexandre Berthier, a young French cavalry captain and one day to be Napoleon's superb chief of staff, attended the manoeuvres of 1783 and remarked, particularly, the incredible liveliness of the King's eyes. Three years later, on Frederick's last manoeuvres, another French visitor* was the young Marquis de Lafayette, who would always remember 'the most beautiful eyes I ever saw'. Frederick drove his body as ruthlessly as his mind until the end.

In the *Political Testament* completed in 1768 Frederick showed little change in his scepticism about human nature, about the affairs of the world, or about religion. His Enlightenment prejudices were still with him. Christianity was 'an old metaphysical romance, filled with marvels, contradictions and absurdities, born in the ardent imagination of Orientals'. Frederick, the *philosophe*, was still eager for a fight with any intellectual ready to take him on, although, as one of his readers shrewdly observed to him, the King's scepticism was so frequently and ostentatiously paraded that it might be thought he was a little uncertain of it; even a little uneasy.[40]

He reiterated in this *Testament* his main convictions on the duties of the prince. His private personality must be kept distinct from his role as embodiment of the state. He must, however, be 'not only first servant of the state but the last refuge of the unhappy, the father of the orphans, the succour of the widows, obliged to care for the meanest and least fortunate'. There is no reason to doubt Frederick's sincerity in this regard and Prussians knew it, just as they knew and respected his industry – knew and respected it even when they grumbled at his military demands or mocked his financial stringency. He was 'Fritz', master, father; harsh, fair, unselfseeking; a 'character', a winner of battles; their lord, but in a curious way one of them.

He never minded the grumbling or the mockery. He was told that a citizen of Berlin had been heard to refer to him as a tyrant, a despot; to speak treason. Frederick – 'What resources has this man? Can he raise an army of 200,000?'

---

* A British visitor was the Duke of York, George III's son, who married Frederick's great-niece, and was for long commander-in-chief of the British army – and, until 1803, Bishop of Osnabrück.

'No, sire. He is poor, a private individual.'

Frederick chuckled. 'Well, *that's* all right!'

The Prussian press was subjected to strict political censorship but the King was indifferent to purely personal attacks and Prussia was the most tolerant state in Europe in this respect. Once, when he was riding out with a groom at Potsdam, he saw a crowd of people peering up at something posted high on a wall. Ordered by Frederick, the groom investigated and reported that the people were looking at an offensive caricature of His Majesty, deriding his meanness. 'Hang it lower!' called Frederick loudly, 'so that they don't have to crane their necks!' There was a roar of cheers from the crowd and the caricature was instantly destroyed. He was sensible and pragmatic about military articles by serving officers. Colonel von Manstein had asked leave (before the war) to publish some memoirs about his service in Russia. 'Yes', was Frederick's ruling, 'provided they contain no personalities'. Preliminary censorship was necessary to ensure no damage was done to international relations, but after that an officer and his pen were free.

His tolerance extended – remarkably – to criticisms of himself by officers. A colonel during the last phase of the war wrote a frank and hostile critique of Prussian strategy, and his paper was captured with his baggage by an Austrian cavalry raid – and then recaptured by the Prussians. The paper was then discovered and sent to Frederick. Frederick made annotations on the colonel's comments: sent the paper to him – 'this seems to be yours!' – and rewarded the stupefied man some time later with the command of a regiment.[41]

But in this post-war period, the 'sixties', Frederick's main concern, as ever, was with foreign affairs. In the west he remained suspicious of the French, although he agreed in 1768 the draft of a commercial treaty;[42] a treaty which was never concluded due, in his view, to the indecision and incompetence of the French minister, Choiseul. He presumed that French actions in the Mediterranean, where they took possession of Corsica, would arouse British sentiment and perhaps lead to war; but it did not happen. Formal relations with France, and an exchange of ambassadors, took time to re-establish, in 1768. And Frederick ultimately concluded that the real loser in the war would turn out to be France. The French had gained nothing in Europe and lost much in distant continents. And they were gravely weakened internally.[43]

As to the British, Frederick was for a long time still smarting with indignation at the conduct of the Bute ministry, although war was now behind him; and when he was told that there was disquiet in London at resumption of relations between himself and the King of France he declared himself wholly indifferent.[44] When the British (Lord Rochford*) referred to their previous subsidies and to future relations, Frederick took a high line: 'The King of Prussia only takes subsidies if all Europe is in arms against him.'[45] This was fair; and he remarked that with the British one never knew with whom one would be dealing – ministers, personalities, opinions, veered and switched. Knyphausen had been withdrawn at British request, following their request for the removal of Mitchell, and Frederick was disgruntled. 'I don't understand,' he told his ambassador, Count von Maltzahn, in January 1767, 'how the British Government can hope to find new allies when it has so grossly deceived those who have rendered essential service to England.'[46] In this he showed a certain lack of realism, most unusually. He often seemed blind to the very different aims of Britain and Prussia. Britain had been concerned with a world-wide struggle against France, a struggle in which the European balance of power was only one factor, and the King of Prussia only one small piece on the chessboard. Prussia, on the other hand, had been fighting for her life and Britain was her only ally. Coolness or worse in that ally could mean death. Pitt, himself, had come to modify his opposition to continental commitment, but it is actions which speak and Frederick thought British actions too often unimpressive. Bute – unfairly – personified this in Frederick's mind.

This was a prejudice which would fade little. Frederick relished any circumstance which might discomfort Bute (who was, in fact, out of office from April 1763). Bute's second daughter married Sir George, later to be Lord, Macartney and Macartney, who had been an envoy in St Petersburg for three years from 1764, was then appointed ambassador but never took up the post. Frederick said that the

---

* William Nassau van Zuylestein, 4th Earl of Rochford, Secretary of State from 1766. An honest man, generally thought to have no great ability.

Russians had found him insufferable, with 'the arrogance and haughtiness of the young Englishman. He has outraged the Empress with his behaviour.'[47] Macartney may not have outraged her as much as Frederick liked to imagine, since she gave him a very fine snuff box; but he had other ambitions, was trying to get a seat in the House of Commons and had already offered £2,000. His posting to St Petersburg was cancelled and Lord Cathcart, a veteran of Fontenoy and previous ADC to Cumberland, was sent instead.

Frederick hoped that Bute would be mortified by Macartney's unacceptability; petty, perhaps, but indicative of his intense dislike and distrust of that Earl.[48] He was told, and believed with alacrity, that Bute had taken bribes from the French during the negotiations leading to the Peace of Hubertusburg.[49] When he learned that Cathcart would travel to Russia by sea he supposed the influence of Bute had led to avoidance of a route through Prussia. There was, therefore, chilliness between Frederick and his former British ally and he seldom neglected the chance to pass a disobliging remark about the British. Harris[50] spoke in 1772 of Frederick's 'hatred to England' as being great, citing his imposition of duties on British imports to the port of Danzig, where British merchants had long enjoyed privileges.

'Hatred' is too strong. Frederick took a considerable if sometimes disapproving interest in what went on in England. He was quick to detect ill will. He generally thought British policy feeble. He was appalled by what he heard of the public insults and jeering sometimes endured by the sovereign, saying that he would prefer a simple gentleman's life than to rule in such a country. And he was surprised the British were not taking more seriously what he reckoned would be a great deal of trouble with their American colonies.[51] He kept in touch with the internal situation in Britain, the condition of Parliament and the agitation over John Wilkes – with a certain *Schadenfreude* but also with disquiet. Frederick did not like upheaval in the established monarchies of Europe, whatever his relations with them. He hoped, he wrote, that the British Government would not show indecision, and he thought they were giving an impression of weakness in America which would encourage others, notably France, to take chances; but he equivocated somewhat and noted that in the sort of situation the British were confronting, 'violent measures of repression tend to have worse consequences than at first imagined'.[52] He always watched carefully changes of personality in foreign governments. From the summer of 1765 there were new ministers in London, although for a long time Frederick could not accept that Bute was no longer powerfully influential. He had an obsession and it was by no means entirely fair. Bute had followed a policy vis-à-vis Prussia and continental involvement which did not differ *in essential motivation* from that of Pitt.

In fact the new British secretaries of state, the Duke of Grafton and General Conway, were not ill-disposed to Prussia. That might be so, Frederick told von Maltzahn, but while Bute was a member of the Privy Council (in this, misunderstanding British systems, not for the first or last time) there could be no real good will.[53] Conway had briefly given up the Secretaryship in the summer of 1767 and Frederick hoped for a return of Holdernesse, but it didn't happen. Conway came back. Nevertheless, when Grafton and Conway were first appointed Frederick wrote that 'these men will try to counter-balance France, Austria and Spain. They will try to unite with Holland, Russia and *me*!' It seemed a reasonable expectation. Conway later visited Potsdam in 1774 and was immensely struck by the elegance and symmetry Frederick had insisted on everywhere, including in the new houses of humble artisans.

Sir Andrew Mitchell, however, was now back in Berlin, and doing good work, as ever, in warming these chilly relations. Mitchell had returned to Scotland to stand for the constituency of Kintore in his native Aberdeenshire and had been helped by such good offices as 'Milord Maréchal' could provide, now that the Keith lands – which included Kintore – had been restored to him; the two men were particularly friendly. The British wished, in the 'sixties, to form a new alliance in northern Europe – Britain, Prussia, Russia – to counterbalance the influence of what was called the Bourbon 'Family Compact' between France and Spain. Some of the other German princes and Scandinavian monarchs might usefully be brought into such an alliance. Frederick's immediate response, a natural one, was to inquire whether Austria was likely to be associated with the Family Compact in some way? He had heard without anxiety (in 1766) of the impending marriage (although it did not happen until 1770) between the French heir, son of the Dauphin, and the Austrian Archduchess, Marie-Antoinette.[54] Nevertheless relationships between Vienna and Versailles needed watching and his considered reaction to the British idea – conveyed to Mitchell at an interview on 4 December 1766[55] – was that the proposed alliance might arouse suspicions. To the British this was equivocation. The alliance would be purely defensive; they were simply suggesting a pact to help maintain the precarious European stability now being enjoyed. To Frederick, however, such a pact could foreshadow again a continent dividing itself into armed camps.

Frederick reckoned, not unreasonably, that British policy was always concerned with maximizing the forces potentially hostile to France; and he was keen that, as far as Prussia was concerned, every step should also be consistent with his present policy of maximum harmony with Russia. The proposed alliance might meet that principle but there could be disadvantages. He was unconvinced of its merits. He had a long interview with the Russian Ambassador, Baron von Saldern, in May 1766[56] and there were references to a possible '*système du Nord*' as the British had proposed. The only object of such a system would, Saldern said, be a durable peace and a balance of power; and in such a system there would be both active and passive powers. Frederick cut in: 'Fine and fair. What are you going to say to these active and passive powers?'

Saldern remarked that the King's powerful eyes could not fail to recognize that only Russia, Prussia and Britain were active powers in the north.

But Frederick was still disgruntled with Britain. 'At present she is nothing! The King is the most feeble man alive, he changes his ministers as often as his shirts. There's just been another change – the Duke of Grafton is out!* Perhaps Egmont† will take his place, the biggest supporter of Austria that exists. Don't place any reliance on Britain, I beg you!' And when Saxony was mentioned Saldern reported that the King's eyes had changed their expression as he said that he, Frederick, knew how to deal with the Saxons. He tried to convince

---

* He had, it was true, just resigned at the time of this interview but would soon be back as First Lord of the Treasury, and virtually Prime Minister after the Earl of Chatham's health broke down.

† John Perceval, Earl of Egmont.

the Ambassador that there was nothing to fear from the Family Compact. Austria and the Bourbons were now feeble. Anyway the Emperor could now be numbered among his friends. There was little danger of war. Why invent coalitions?

That might be true at present, Saldern observed, but it might not always be so. War might not originate in Europe – 'Wars in America generally end in Europe.' Frederick replied that this would not always be true. He was optimistic about peace and he told Prince Henry in April 1767 that the Austrians were in no mood to get mixed up in any trouble. '*Messieurs les Russes*' could be as offensive as they liked without opposition from that quarter.[57]

Yet deaths of sovereigns and consequential upheavals could always send the European concert spinning into disarray. Three and a half years earlier, on 7 October 1763, Frederick had had the news of the death of the King of Poland, Elector Augustus III of Saxony. 'I jumped from my chair when I heard the news,' Catherine wrote to Panin, 'and the King of Prussia, I hear, leapt up from table!' The consequences, immediate and remote, had dominated the intervening period; and would continue to absorb Frederick's mind and care for much of the next decade, with echoes which can still be heard in our time.

Augustus III, Elector of Saxony and son of Augustus the Strong, left an eldest son who had succeeded him in the Electorate. Of his five daughters one had married the Dauphin of France and was mother of the future King, Louis XVI. His wife, a Habsburg, was a daughter of Emperor Joseph I, and thus first cousin of Maria Theresa. For his entire reign Augustus had been under the influence of Brühl, an inveterate opponent of Frederick; and Brühl died within weeks of his sovereign. Augustus's son and successor, Elector Frederick Christian, was in Frederick's words a 'mild and well-meaning man', who died two months after his father, leaving an only son, aged thirteen. The Polish throne – which was, in any case, elective – was vacant and it seemed likely that the so-called 'Saxon' period of Polish history had ended.

It had not been a happy period for either main party. Augustus the Strong of Saxony had offered his candidature for the Polish throne in 1697, at a time when Saxony itself was in appalling economic straits arising from the costs of war with Sweden. Districts of Saxony had been pawned or alienated and almost the only commercial ray of light came from the beginning of porcelain manufacture at Meissen in 1710. The Polish crown offered little beyond a kingly title to the hard-pressed rulers of Saxony and there was no compelling reason why they rather than other rulers should have sought it. Nevertheless Augustus had done so.

Thereafter the fortunes of Saxony and Poland had been inevitably if artificially intertwined, a circumstance which had often plagued Frederick. The constitution of Poland, a proud and historic nation, was such as almost to guarantee impotent government. The land was, for the most part, divided between huge landowners of ancient lineage; and they or their representatives met in the Polish Diet, an assembly in which each man was his neighbour's equal. In the Diet each member had a veto, the '*Liberum Veto*', over any measure or action, a system which, of course, demanded unanimity and made likely that no progress would ever be made on anything which mattered. There tended to be little discussion or debate in the Diet, but if one member dissented – or could be bribed or persuaded to dissent – nothing could be done. The only way to get action would then be through the superior bargaining power or actual force exercised by one or more of the great competing families or their supporters. The demand for unanimity is generally a recipe for stagnation and weakness.

Frederick described Poland's as internally the worst government in Europe except that of the Turks, a cruel tyranny of nobles over serfs, without laws or liberty, a sort of aristocratic anarchy. The Polish character, he said, in a letter to Henry, was arrogant, obsessed with *grandeur*, as well as 'slovenly, cringing and servile in the face of superior strength'[58] – a harsh and questionable judgement, undoubtedly written at a moment of considerable irritation. Many, however, would have agreed with it in respect of Poland's domestic condition; while in external matters Poland's impotence was not unsatisfactory to those (Frederick often among them) who preferred to see the country weak and divided.

The main players in the Polish game naturally sought foreign backers; and these main players were the great noble families, small sovereigns in their own right and certainly sovereign in the absoluteness of their domestic rule – the Czartoryskis, the Radziewills, the Potockis, the Lubomirskis; Prince Czartoryski, a man of great charm, at that time maintained a household in Warsaw of 375 personal servants, and there were, of course, far more in the country.[59] They had, sporadically, intrigued for the deposition of Augustus. During the Saxon period now coming to an end the Czartoryskis had been largely dominant; and their foreign backers had often been the Russian court.

The Czartoryskis had, before the recent events and deaths, argued for constitutional reform, including abolition of the *Liberum Veto* (which would, of course, have strengthened the central authority, the crown). This would have correspondingly diminished the authority of their fellow-princes and competitors. They had failed to carry their point and had hoped for Russian support, possibly military. Whatever the various factions wished, it was clear that the occupancy of the Polish throne was a matter of importance to Poland's neighbours. The Czartoryskis appeared to be supported by St Petersburg (although the Russians had no desire to see the Polish crown and central authority stronger); but the courts of Vienna and Berlin could not be indifferent. The French were known to be intriguing with the Saxons, who had come to regard the throne of Poland as something of a family possession.[60]

On the death of Augustus, Frederick at once wrote to Catherine and gave her frank advice.[61] The Empress should make her position very clear. If there were opposition to the Czartoryskis, probably taking the form of opposition to their candidate for the throne, the Russians would have a sound excuse to send troops into Poland. It would be dangerous to have ferment, even civil war, in so crucial a strategic area. There might be logistic difficulties in maintaining such troops, and Frederick would be happy to help. He was answered by a letter from Catherine[62] in which she thanked him and asked for his cooperation in seeing that no Saxon troops entered Poland, a request he had no difficulty in agreeing – and of whose content he courteously made the Saxons aware. All this had taken place in the months immediately following Augustus's death, and in September 1764 Stanislaus Poniatowski, a former lover of Catherine on whom he had fathered a child, was elected King of Poland to the considerable anger of, among others, the authorities in Vienna. His mother was a

Czartoryski. At the same time Prince Nicholas Repnin was appointed Russian minister in Poland, with wide authority from St Petersburg.

Stanislaus was crowned in November 1764 and Frederick wrote to congratulate him. He also wrote to Catherine. Vienna and Versailles, he told her, would both be furious.[63] He understood that Catherine did not wish to promote radical change of constitutional system in Poland which suited him well – in other words she wanted to keep it weak.[64] He privately reckoned that the ambition of Prince Czartoryski was boundless and his influence over Stanislaus probably excessive, but a new Russo-Polish treaty was in preparation and Frederick declared he was ready to accede to it provided there was nothing in it prejudicial to his interests. He was already, since March, committed to a treaty of alliance with Russia, and in the following year, 1765, he acceded to the new treaty and joined Russia in a defensive alliance – a long-lasting arrangement as it happened – which declared both sovereigns 'joint protectors of Polish freedom'.

There were both detailed and broader matters at issue here. A detail was a tariff proposed by the Polish Diet on all exports and this would make some commodities more expensive for Prussia – in particular horses, remounts for the Prussian army which Frederick wanted to buy in Poland and the Polish Ukraine in 1765, and which would cost him more. He protested, saying that he would be obliged to take counter-measures: and persuaded the Russians of his point so that the Polish *douane générale* was only partially applied – the Russian influence was already dominant. Frederick's threatened counter-measure was a *douane* on Vistula shipping at Marienwerder, south of Danzig, and he proposed to excuse payment to Russian transports so that, with Russian support, a more general agreement could be negotiated. He was glad to hear later that his horse purchases were welcome to all parties in Poland.

But the broader matter had been the succession itself, and at stake would soon be the whole destiny and orientation of Poland. Frederick had two main concerns: that Poland should not constitute an area of danger to Prussia; and that he should preserve harmony with Russia.

He had been convinced for some time that Prussia's future lay in friendship with Russia. In communications with his ambassadors he had very clearly taken Russia's part. When told by von Rohd, his man in Vienna, that Russian troops were being sent into Poland in April 1764 (no surprise to him), he had explained[65] that this was not to constrain (*gêner*) the Poles in their free election but simply to protect their republic and its liberties. By liberties, he meant liberties to elect a Russian, a Czartoryski, candidate to the Polish throne.

Frederick had few illusions about Russia – he never had had. He remembered his campaigning beyond the Oder. He remembered Zorndorf. Commenting to Finckenstein in 1766 on a recent dispatch about Catherine he wrote that he noted her '*ton despotique*, with which she was coming to treat all her neighbours' – 'I intend to manage our friendship, not to forge fetters for myself.'[66] But he knew it was unlikely to be easy. In the case of the Poles, however, he regarded their constitution as so fragile and inherently absurd that any firm initiative – in this case by Russia – was preferable to instability and vacuum. He did not think there were serious dangers in the situation. Saxony had had pretensions to play a part but neither Vienna nor Versailles had backed them. The French, although the Dauphine was a Princess of Saxony, had other concerns. The Austrians would fear involvement with Russia.[67]

The pretensions of Saxony had been voiced by the Dowager Electress, a Princess of Bavaria, widow of Elector Frederick Christian, the son of Augustus III who had been Elector for a bare two months; and Frederick's letters to her with their characteristic note of irony are amongst his most pleasing, if not always his most convincing. '*Elevé dans les camps et dans la Tumulte des armes*,' he wrote to her, '*je n'y ai point appris l'art de déguiser mes pensées. La vérité naïve, la conscience intime de mes pensées passent dans mes paroles ainsi qu'au bout de ma plume ...*' and more to the same effect. She had remonstrated over Russian actions which she was not alone in regarding as putting intolerable pressure on the Poles – 'Would it not be simpler to leave to the Poles the choice of their king and not to interfere?' – and Frederick had replied with flowery protestations of admiration for her sagacity. He had disarmed (or so he pretended to hope) an earlier remonstrance by saying he could not possibly write to so illustrious a princess with sufficient frankness. He would therefore pretend he was answering similar points had they been addressed to him by a (long-deceased) Saxon field marshal, by name von Wackerbarth. Under this fiction he proceeded to demolish the von Wacker-barth (the Dowager Electress's) points in devastating style, ending, 'You can now, M. le Comte Wackerbarth, return to the Elysian fields.'[68]

On this second occasion he wrote:

The affairs of Poland are so tangled and so subject to different interpretations that I leave them to political minds more skilled than mine. The questions put to me by Your Royal Highness are a little embarrassing. If one had inquired of a patriarch why the God of Abraham, of Isaac and of Jacob, had rejected Esau in his mother's womb in favour of Jacob, the patriarch would doubtless have replied that these choices of Providence and marks of divine favour are not for men to penetrate. I may say much the same about Poland. God, who appears not to wish the Czartoryski party to be worsted, has inspired the Tsarina to send Russian troops to Warsaw to support them. As for me, Madame, submissive as I am to the decree of Providence, I simply worship and hold my peace . . .

He enjoyed teasing her with elaborate compliments on every possible occasion – 'Your Royal Highness is universal, and would find herself as little out of order at the head of a Commercial College as in the company of Richelieu, or judging the Muses on Parnassus . . .'[69] It is unlikely that the Dowager Electress took all this with enjoyment. A Saxon prince, a brother of the late Elector, might have been a claimant to Poland. She was reckoned by Frederick to have ambitions for her own son in the same direction, and although not herself Saxon born she knew how Saxony had suffered in what Saxons regarded as Frederick's war. But Frederick was determined to do all he could to cement good relations with Russia.

Frederick's earlier dealings with the Ottoman Porte were, of course, known in St Petersburg, where they had caused anxieties he was able to soothe. He had long exchanges with Catherine during the summer of 1765[70] and was pleased to hear that there was in St Petersburg disenchantment with Vienna.[71] On the whole he was finding that his views were close to those of the Russian Empress. The Polish business seemed quiescent; Stanislaus was on the Polish throne; the discontents of Austria, Saxony, France had not amounted to a great deal. He knew that his Russian alliance was intensely disliked by the Austrians, who would do all in their power to make bad blood, as he often impressed on Rohd in Vienna; nevertheless he reckoned he could keep matters calm.[72] In Vienna the Emperor Francis, husband of Maria Theresa, died in August – 'Soon forgotten,' said Frederick, 'by everyone but his widow.'

But the Polish business was not quiescent, as very soon became clear; and Frederick was now to find himself paying the inevitable price of making Prussia a major power on the European stage.

19

'A Very Quarrelsome People'

The period between 1766 and 1772 was one of the most difficult Frederick ever experienced, and although it was not punctuated by actual hostilities involving Prussia, fear of another general European war was ever-present. Sometimes such a war seemed imminent. Frederick often wrote with deep depression about how fragile and impermanent were the prospects for peace; and not all of this was personal melancholy.

The situation was confused and it was hard to define and attack the root of the matter, to decide what was cause and what effect. The story, as so often, began and ended in Poland, although the dangers and involvements spread far beyond that unhappy country. And the Polish business first sprang from internal affairs. There was now a new king, Stanislaus, on the Polish throne – Catholic like most of his subjects. Of the Polish population of nearly 12 million about one-tenth were classified in religious terms as 'Dissidents' – mostly Protestants in Polish Prussia or Orthodox in Polish Lithuania. The majority of these were of the artisan or labouring class, but whatever their social status their religion had excluded them from political rights; or from such political rights as existed in Poland. Catherine, through her mouthpiece Repnin, demanded that these Poles should be given equality of treatment. Non-discrimination must be applied. She, the Tsarina, was their protectress – at least of the Orthodox. Legislation was drafted for approval by the Diet. And the *Liberum Veto* – as proposed in the stillborn Czartoryski reforms – should be abolished.

The Catholic noblemen of the Polish Diet regarded these proposals as outrageous. The Dissidents should be kept in their place and the *Liberum Veto*, cornerstone of their privilege, their liberties (and their impotence), must be retained. The Diet rejected the legislation.

Frederick was uneasy. He had hoped that Poland's internal affairs – with which, he often emphasized, he was not concerned – would be left undisturbed by Russian support for the new monarch wherever absolute justice might lie. The Austrians had indicated sympathy with the attitude of the Polish Diet. Frederick understood this, just as he understood Catherine's sympathy with the 'Dissidents' – indeed, when he heard the King, Stanislaus, was suggesting that Russian support for the Dissidents should be muted he said that it would be against the Tsarina's dignity to appease opposition in that way.[1] Nevertheless he feared an Austro-Russian clash with sides taken largely on confessional lines.

But he also feared the ultimate results of Russian attempts to impose change. He said privately that the intransigence of Catherine's attitude was hard to justify although he understood it, and the anti-discrimination which allegedly inspired it.[2] It was troublesome, however. When Saldern, at an audience in May 1766, said that Russian policy was straightforward – strengthen the Dissidents and give the King of Poland sufficient military support to enable him to suppress opposition – Frederick expressed worry. 'Why stir things up? Leave Poland in its lethargy.'[3] Frederick would not take an opposite line: he valued the Russian connection too highly. But he was uneasy. His reaction, he said, was *'complaisance, non pas faiblesse'*.

The situation became increasingly violent. The Diet was not in the least *complaisant*. After the refusal to enact the pro-Dissident legislation one faction petitioned Catherine to guarantee Polish liberties by empowering Prince Repnin to overrule other authorities, including the Diet; Repnin was duly empowered and began to enact the legislation and to rule virtually dictatorially. His reputation soon became one of a man intolerably overbearing to Poles, including Poles of high degree – and intolerably flirtatious with Polish ladies. He assumed great airs; the theatre was delayed for an hour when he was late, despite the King of Poland being already present in his box.

The appeal to Catherine had, of course, been a blatant attempt by one faction to crush the other. There were wholesale arrests by the Russians of all opposing the legislation; measures to give rights to Dissidents were enacted; edicts against them were repealed. The

Liberum Veto was, however restored. The whole package was guaranteed by the Tsarina.

The result was as feared by Frederick. There was a patriotic revolt against the Russian-supported regime. Frederick had detected the seeds of this earlier, when there had been attempts to establish within the Diet a permanent council, a sort of caucus with executive power. He had not believed such a council desirable – it might exercise power in the King's name but an increase in the authority of the King of Poland was, anyway, to be deplored, a view in which Catherine wholly concurred.[4] Her attitude to Frederick, like his to her, was wary but respectful and each valued their frequent gestures of friendship. Frederick had recently, in May 1767, invited her to be godmother to the newborn daughter of his niece, wife of the Prince of Prussia. And Catherine, like Frederick, was an enthusiastic correspondent with the intellectual élite of Europe, with Voltaire, Diderot, d'Alembert. 'Russia,' she said in 1767, 'is a European state'; and she 'Frenchified' the Russian court in a way which mirrored Frederick's own efforts. They shared a good deal.

The Polish patriotic revolt, as so often in Polish history, was led and inspired by certain bishops; and it led to the forming of a 'Confederation' in February 1768, directed at the assertion of Polish rights in the face of naked Russian domination. The first Confederation was led by a Krasinski, the second by a Potocki, and given French encouragement and limited support; and it soon developed into armed rebellion in the countryside with (or so Frederick alleged) considerable cruelties against the 'Dissidents' by the 'Confederates' as the rebels were now called.[5] The rebellion might be small-scale in military terms, but it was troublesome. It reflected a divided and unstable country; and unless it were quickly ended infection might spread, and with it complications. Frederick supposed the best solution would be a rapid extinction of the Confederate military rising; but that might be beyond the power and skill of the authorities – Polish, but now in reality Russian. His attitude was realistic, as always. Various Polish dignitaries on one side or other of the dispute sought his support, but he was cautious.[6] Sides were being taken by external powers and although he valued his relations with Russia – had he not promised logistic support to Russian troops when entering Poland on the King's election?

– he wanted to keep his cards in his hand. And privately he felt bound to agree with Austria, however reluctantly, in their criticisms of Russian conduct. He told Solms, his ambassador in St Petersburg, that the Tsarina must appreciate the realities of the situation and her dilemma (and his own).[7] If the Poles – or the 'Political nation' among the Poles – were wholly antagonized they would support any enemy of Russia in a future war.

The armed rebellion of the Confederates, although not militarily menacing to Russia, had dangerous consequences. There were raids and skirmishes in the countryside. In June 1768 Russian troops chased a Confederate force across the border into Silesia. Frederick was prepared to accept that this had been a genuine error and contented himself with a formal representation to Repnin, but shortly afterwards, in August, another Russian force pursued a large party of Confederates across the frontiers of the Ottoman Empire, reached Dubazar in Moldavia,* and burned the town after an indiscriminate massacre of Turks, Tartars and Poles. The Ottoman Government, fiercely indignant, ordered a concentration of 20,000 troops on the common frontier with Poland.[8]

In Constantinople, as Frederick put it, there was inevitably '*grande fermentation*'.[9] He speculated as to whether open rupture was inevitable. The lands between the Adriatic and the Black Sea had long been disputed territory for the forces of the Ottoman and Habsburg Empires; while those on the north-western and northern shores of the Black Sea itself had been equally disputed between the Ottoman and Russian Empires. These great empires, whose frontiers had for several centuries ebbed and flowed like tides, met in the Balkans and in southern Russia. Near or on the tidemark were the borders of Poland.

There could be little profit for Europe in a protracted war in the Balkans and the Ukraine between Turkey and Russia, and Frederick watched Turkish military preparations as closely as he could. He understood that the highest quality Ottoman troops were assembling in Bosnia[10] and he thought (mistakenly) that rather than an attack on Russia or Russian troops in Poland there might be a Turkish descent on the Dalmatian coast. This appears wishful thinking and somewhat

* In modern Romania.

elliptical: it is not immediately clear how it would have helped the Confederates in Poland or stung the Russians. It did not happen. Frederick, however, was hoping very hard that Turkish efforts would be peripheral and that the course of events would not run out of control. He thought Russian money might be offered to persuade the Turks not to interfere with Russian actions against the Confederates. He told the Russian Ambassador, Tschernyshev, that if Russian troops did not go too near the Ottoman frontier the Turks would not worry about what went on inside Poland, and there would be peace.

This, too, was wishful thinking. A few weeks later, in October 1768, Frederick was told that the Turks had asked Vienna for agreement not to impede or challenge troop movements, 300,000 men, from Bosnia and Wallachia, through Transylvania, to concentrate on the borders of Poland.

In Vienna Kaunitz himself assured Rohd that such agreement had not been given.[11] But Kaunitz reckoned that the Russians had behaved in a bizarre manner. They had attempted to impose a system (tolerance of Dissidents) on a Poland to which such tolerance was alien, whatever its theoretic merit. They had then entered Poland and committed outrages; and had crossed frontiers and committed others, not only in Ottoman territory but in Hungary. Frederick, when he read this, felt constrained to agree. Policy bound him to Russia but he now thought war was inevitable.[12] The Russians had misjudged matters, and Turkish reactions. The Confederates would join any war against Russia. Now, as he told Catherine, they were drunk with enthusiasm at the expectation of Turkish support and the miracles this would produce.

Nevertheless, although they probably had much popular feeling as well as Polish tradition on their side, Frederick had no sympathy whatever with the Polish Confederates and their cause, however much he deplored the likely consequences of Russian actions to suppress it unless these were to prove more rapid and effective than he expected. When leading Poles wrote to ask for his understanding he answered sharply, and ensured that his anger became widely known. In their attitude to the Dissidents, he wrote, these Polish nobles were apostles of intolerance. He could find no evidence of injury done to them, the Confederates, in their own religious beliefs. On the contrary:

Neither the Empress of Russia nor the King of Poland have wished to restrict the liberties of the Catholic religion. Christianity consists not in violence but in toleration . . . the first Christians were the most peaceful men on earth. They tried to convert heretics but didn't persecute them. England is Protestant, Holland is Protestant – that doesn't prevent Catholics, Orthodox or a hundred others from freely practising their religion. You won't, therefore, find it strange that I, who am very tolerant, perceive little convincing in your arguments . . .[13]

There was plenty of bigotry in contemporary Protestant countries and in their legislation, and to some Frederick's attitude was probably disingenuous, although it was true that religious toleration had long been a Hohenzollern tradition, fortified by Frederick's 'Enlightenment' convictions. But he found the Poles as fractious as they were troublesome, and he always had. 'Very *quarrelsome* people, the Poles,' Josef Stalin remarked softly at an Allied conference in the middle of the Second World War. He had just secretly murdered several thousand of their élite and consigned countless others to death or deportation. 'Very *quarrelsome* people!'[14] Frederick would have nodded to the sentiment although appalled at the criminal savagery which accompanied it.

Frederick could see little promising in a Russo-Turkish war, whatever its military outcome, and that outcome must be uncertain. Turkey would probably annex Podolia, bordering Moldavia and the Black Sea. Russia would send troops across the Hungarian frontier and provoke Vienna.[15] Frederick had obligations to Russia under his alliance, which still had three years to run, and these committed him to a subsidy of 400,000 roubles a year while Russia was at war. In spite of this he said he would be ready to negotiate an extension of the agreement – it might be a good time to extract some reciprocal guarantees from St Petersburg, for instance support for the successions in Bayreuth and Ansbach.[16]

The prospect of serious and prolonged Russo-Turkish hostilities was agitating the courts of Europe; and war on Russia had now been declared by the Ottoman Porte. Everyone recognized that the crisis had been produced by the situation in Poland, a situation which had run out of control. The Russian Government seemed to have been taken by surprise by the force of Ottoman reactions to Russian policy and to the actions of Russian troops. Frederick sent his good wishes to Catherine, adding some shrewd observations on the most important practical things to watch if preparing a campaign against the Turks – notably logistics, and the operational assessments of field commanders who might try to cover too much ground with the available troops.[17] But in every letter he emphasized that he was in no way involved in the internal affairs of Poland, he was simply discharging his treaty obligations to Russia in war, a war he hoped could be swiftly ended. In February 1769 he sent Count Lynar as a special emissary to St Petersburg. Lynar, a distinguished author of philosophic works, had spent most of his life in the service of Denmark but had a name as an international negotiator, a reconciler, a finder of solutions. He had once been active in negotiating the Klosterzeven agreements and was a shrewd politician whose mind the King respected. He now had ideas, shadowy as yet, whereby certain territorial offers to Austria and Russia, at Poland's expense, might play a part in bringing war to a satisfactory conclusion.[18]

The British asked whether Frederick envisaged actually sending troops to support the Russians. 'No,' he replied, only the subsidies to which he was bound by treaty.[19] The French, he learned, planned to send 100 officers under the Marquis de Conflans to help the Confederates in Poland and, therefore, to help the Turks.[20] The internal affairs of Poland, however much Frederick disclaimed concern with them, had a near-inevitable tendency to create widespread discord or to arouse greed. Russia, with Frederick's support, had embarked on a forward policy there in the aftermath of Augustus's death, but now Russian actions had brought much of the Polish nation into arms against them, and the Turks had reacted, understandably, to Russian outrages across their frontiers, outrages all caused by Russian perception of the need to suppress rebellion in Poland; and by consequential Russian heavy-handedness.

For the next few years, until 1772, Frederick's main concerns were with three great interlocking issues. First there was the Russo-Turkish war itself; how it would go, where it would reach, how it might be limited in its spread and its consequences, how it could be stopped.

Second, and inseparably, there was the situation in Poland, that situation which had produced the match to light the fires of war and which absolutely demanded some ultimate resolution to prevent recurrence. And thirdly – and again inseparably – there was the whole question of Prussian relations with Austria, with the attitude of Austria to the Polish question, the attitude of Austria to the Russo-Turkish war, the attitude of Austria to any settlement in the theatre of war, the Balkans. Other factors – the attitude of France, the attitude of Britain, the situation in the Baltic area – these played a part but from Frederick's point of view it was in each case peripheral. Austria was central, and in Austria there had since 1765 been a new situation. The Austrian Emperor, Francis of Lorraine, having died, the head of the house of Habsburg was thereafter his and Maria Theresa's son, Joseph: nominally 'King of the Romans' since the previous year, and on accession aged twenty-four.

The death of sovereigns could always affect international affairs, but in very differing degrees. When, five months after the death of Francis, the King of Denmark died, Frederick wrote to his ambassador in Copenhagen that this was 'an event which, to tell the truth for your eyes only, is hardly a great loss to the *système publique* of Europe'.[21] But a vacant Imperial throne was a different matter. The Empress-Queen, Maria Theresa, was still only forty-eight and as vigorous as ever but she was, Frederick reckoned, short of money and her heir would have difficulties; he calculated that Francis would have left 15 million thalers in cash* but this would have to be divided between all his children, for such was the system. He had not presumed there would be any immediate change in Austrian policy but supposed that Joseph would feel himself very dependent on the experience of his formidable mother,[22] and would probably be more rather than less reliant on the great Kaunitz – 'so splendid in great affairs, so petty and ridiculous in others'[23] as Frederick observed. Kaunitz, a widower, was in the throes of a notorious infatuation with a younger singer. Joseph's character would probably be significant.

A few days before Francis's death Frederick had received a pen-picture of the young archduke from von Rohd, Prussian Ambassador

---

* About £2,500,000.

in Vienna.[24] Joseph, it appeared, needed perpetual amusement and activity. He got up in the morning, went for a ride, and spent much of his day in the stables. During his first wife's time he had shown a taste for reading and music (she, a princess of Parma, had died very young in 1763). Those tastes had disappeared and Rohd also reported that the young man seemed bored by his new wife, a princess of Bavaria, a younger sister of Frederick's correspondent, the Dowager Electress of Saxony. Rohd suspected infidelity would soon follow.

Frederick had not welcomed Joseph's Bavarian marriage. When asked for matrimonial recommendations on the first wife's death he had supposed that Joseph would follow his own inclinations; he could think of no suitable Protestant princess – it was generally accepted that if there were she would make no difficulties about conversion. The most likely choices had seemed to him from the houses of Savoy or Portugal. Instead it had been from Bavaria, which he thought might complicate matters.[25] What Rohd had not reported at that stage was anything interesting about Joseph's mind.

There was much to report. Joseph might be young and apparently superficial in his tastes but he had, like Frederick, studied a good deal. Like Frederick he had read deeply in the works of the *philosophes* and of Voltaire in particular. He had come to a strong belief in religious toleration, matching Frederick's own. He had also formed a strong belief in the power for good of the state, a power which should be able to override individual and sectional interests. Joseph's ideal, at that time, was a rational, benevolent and enlightened despotism; an ideal probably shared by the best of his sovereign contemporaries, very much including the King of Prussia. Joseph was good-hearted, idealistic, wilful and not very clever. He showed early signs of impatience for reform in the name of reason, an impatience almost comparable to that of the French revolutionaries of a quarter-century ahead. His mother watched him with some unease; and Frederick, many of whose ideas were inherently sympathetic, hung a portrait of Joseph in his study, saying, 'I am obliged to keep my eye on that young gentleman.'[26] He had quickly promised his Electoral vote to Joseph, nevertheless; and he had been anxious to meet him.

In the summer of 1766 there might have been an opportunity. Joseph had made a short visit to Saxony in June and in several diplomatic exchanges a meeting between the two sovereigns had been mooted, at Torgau. It did not happen. The Emperor's programme (he was already Emperor) was such that time could not be made. Frederick, as Mitchell observed and reported to London, had been hurt.[27] It was something of a snub. He had told Prince Henry that a meeting was about to take place and given him permission to attend it if he wished. It might have been historic. He had informed St Petersburg, lest they heard and formed a wrong impression. Then – at short notice – cancellation. Frederick supposed Kaunitz had dissuaded Joseph, probably at French urging – neither the chancellor nor the Empress-Queen would wish to arouse the suspicions of France as might have followed an Austro-Prussian meeting of sovereigns.[28] He had reported the incident to the Dowager Electress of Saxony, who would certainly hear: 'We are puppets of Providence, Madame! and it goes its way, mocking our feeble attempts at wisdom!'[29] He had reacted with indignant warmth when he heard that the British Secretary of State, General Conway, had told von Maltzahn, Prussian Ambassador in London, that he hoped the intended interview would not have bad consequences for the peace of Europe.[30] That peace was still fragile.

Frederick had certainly wished to do nothing then in 1766 or later which would disturb that peace. He was determined to maintain a policy of friendship with Russia, a policy which had involved trying to understand Russian attitudes not only in Poland but in the Baltic region and towards Turkey in the Balkans and the Ukraine (it had also obliged him in August 1766 to convey to the Russian Ambassador in Berlin, Prince Dolgoruki, displeasure at the behaviour of Dolgoruki's young nephew, and hopes that the uncle could exercise authority to improve it!).[31] But he also reckoned, after a lifetime combating the power of Austria, that fences might be mended in that direction without upsetting the entire system of Europe which had precariously emerged from the war. And if fences were ever to be mended Austria would need to be sufficiently satisfied about the relations between Prussia and Russia; and thus about the future of Poland.

In April 1767 Frederick had told Rohd, in Vienna, that he had heard of something covert (*dessous*) going on in the matter of Poland – this was before the outbreak of Russo-Turkish war. The open game, the

Confederacy-forming, the Russian intervention, was one thing, but he thought there were suspicions in Vienna of *'un arrangement de partage pris entre nous'*, a proposal actually to partition Poland! His brief letter to Rohd simply expressed his understanding that Austria would oppose such an idea.[32] Undoubtedly the Polish insurrection and the Russian measures taken to suppress it were itching sores on the body of Europe, before and apart from the Russo-Turkish hostilities they provoked. And mistrust abounded.

When Count Nugent, Austrian Ambassador in Berlin, had an audience with Frederick in November 1768, he asked why Prussia was apparently making preparations for war. How did the King explain the extraordinary number of horses recently procured? Frederick replied that he would prefer to declare war than have it declared on him,[33] and Nugent was convinced of the King's good faith and peaceful intentions. Frederick was particularly fond of Nugent and he launched into a general discussion.[34] 'What's it to us if in Canada or anywhere across the Atlantic the French and English fight each other? Whether Paoli* keeps French hands full in Corsica? Whether Russians and Turks pull each other's hair out? So long as I and the house of Austria understand each other, Germany can keep clear of war. The Empress-Queen and I have waged expensive and ruinous war for a long time. What have we got from it?'

Maria Theresa would have found this ironical, and probably disbelieved its sincerity. But Frederick was genuinely persuaded that peace of the heart as well as peace by signed document might be possible between his house and the house of Habsburg. A meeting would surely help when opportunity offered – the abortion of the previous encounter still rankled. Nugent suggested an exchange of letters between sovereigns. Frederick nodded. But – 'I can't write first.'

Might not a third party 'broker' a fresh understanding, Nugent suggested? The Electress of Saxony? (He was referring to the Dowager Electress, Frederick's frequent correspondent.) Might not a meeting be contrived, Nugent said, during the next year's Prussian army manoeuvres, near the Silesian border? Frederick liked the idea – it would indicate a meeting in September 1769. But when he reported

---

* Corsican patriotic leader, defeated by the French in 1769.

the conversation to Finckenstein he wrote, prudently, 'Let's take one step at a time.'[35]

The critical scene of action at the moment was in St Petersburg, where Lynar was busy.

Lynar had a plan, a proposition – at least an outline of one – which he suggested might be discussed with the Russians, and, as a next stage, put to the Austrians. Under this Russia should offer to Austria the area of Zips in Austria, nominally in Poland, as well as the town of Leopol. In return Austria would support Russia against the Turks in the area of the Dniester. It would be a tidying up of some of the outer districts of Poland and relieve Russia of some Turkish pressure, all at the expense of Poland. Lynar suggested that this would have the incidental effect of disarming jealousy between Russia and Austria. Furthermore, to reimburse her for the costs of the Turkish war, Russia should – with Prussian and Austrian approval – annex whatever other parts of Poland the Russians found convenient. That was the Lynar plan.

The plan was discussed at length in St Petersburg and in Berlin. The Russian Foreign Minister, Count Nikita Panin – regarded by some as being Frederick's 'creature',[36] although it did not seem so to Frederick – doubted the usefulness to Russia of the proposed territorial acquisitions. Panin was not opposed to the idea of some attempt at concordat between Austria, Russia and Prussia but he thought the strategic object of the war now under way should be to chase the Turks not simply beyond the Dniester river, as was envisaged, but out of Europe altogether. Russia, he said, did not need more land. It simply needed to be free of the potential menace of the Turks – although this, of course, was a menace which Russian actions had aroused.[37] Frederick was sceptical of Panin's suggestions. Apart from all else (and the military situation was at the moment wholly uncertain), to drive the Turks from Europe must bring into sharp focus the potential rivalry between Russia and Austria in the Balkans; and Frederick doubted Austria's acceptance of such a plan as at present conceived. As to the Russians, Frederick had agreed to the idea of renewing his treaty with them, but objected to some of the accompanying detail;[38] and Panin seemed to be taking a good deal of time over the matter.[39]

Slowness on all fronts, both military and diplomatic, was now the Russian hallmark. Frederick expected, however, that in the Balkans they would soon cross the Dniester and occupy the Ottoman provinces of Moldavia and Wallachia.* A Russian army there, threatening the lower Danube, would not be welcome to Vienna and he hoped that the progress of the Russo-Turkish war – and, ultimately, the inevitable Russo-Turkish negotiations – would not create an unmanageable danger point in that area. Meanwhile the Russians had won an inconclusive victory at Chozim. Frederick told Prince Henry that the slowness of Russian operations was due to the idleness of their ministers and differences of opinion at the top. They were, he said, only saved because the Turks were even slower and even more irresolute.[40]

In Poland itself, Frederick told Catherine, the Confederates' behaviour was becoming more outrageous every day: 'They kill, massacre dissidents, one can only regard them as a swarm of wasps ...'[41] He thought she was ill-informed on Poland and took matters there too lightly – '*Elle traite trop en bagatelle.*' His own frontiers were being increasingly crossed by Confederates 'in hot pursuit'. He also supposed the Confederates were being encouraged by France – and, to an extent, Austria. Panin, he told Henry, was ignorant of matters in Poland, which did ill service to the Tsarina; and he was ignorant on much else. The Russians compared him to Richelieu whereas the two were, in reality, poles apart. He and his mistress, the Tsarina, thought anything could be solved by force.[42] They were proud. Instead, ingenuity would be needed. Nevertheless Frederick's letters to Catherine remained effusive, and he offered to send five or six Prussian officers to Russia as 'volunteers' in January 1769; he meant 'advisers'. He knew that there were many who would wish to make trouble between him and Russia. A nonsensical press report found currency in Holland, to the effect that Frederick was designing a treaty with France and Spain as well as Austria!

Frederick suspected the hand of Choiseul.[43] Negotiation of a suggested commercial agreement between France and Prussia was dragging, and in April Frederick broke off the discussions. He was now so sceptical about French financial management that he doubted

* Now Romania.

whether France could take much effective part in European affairs for a while, let alone contemplate war.[44] The Prussian envoy in Paris, von Goltz, had been seeking to obtain the commercial treaty and had seen Choiseul several times; he now told Frederick that the French were planning to support the Ottoman cause against Russia and would try to induce Frederick to join the same cause by offer of the bishopric of Warmie and the Duchy of Courland – unrealistic propositions, as Frederick noted with contempt: 'This shows what little sense there is in France at present!'[45] The French were supporting the Confederate (and passionately anti-Russian) cause in Poland, and when Frederick found Prince Charles of Courland, an uncle of the Duke, travelling via Glogau to join the Confederate forces he had him and his companion arrested and advised the Duke to send somebody responsible to escort them home. Prince Charles, who had married a Krasinski, was a keen supporter of the Confederates.

Frederick saw the hand of France everywhere, and thought it an inept hand. Choiseul, he said, was unstable, changed his views daily and acted without system.[46] And he reacted coldly to French behaviour where it fell below his standards of protocol. The French envoy in Berlin, Count de Guines, wrote direct to the King asking leave to present two visiting French officers and Frederick referred him to Finckenstein: 'I am not inclined to accept letters from foreign ministers who happen to be here or engage in direct correspondence with them.'[47] Choiseul had become something of a Bute, a *bête noire* to Frederick. He was, Frederick said, meddlesome, childish, arrogant, a confuser of business. There was *malignité* in his character.[48] For good measure Frederick relayed to Henry stories he heard of French atrocities in Corsica. French troops, he wrote, were indulging in indiscriminate massacres of the Corsican 'patriots', were killing everyone 'up to infants at the breast'.[49] His attitude to France was cool and he greatly mistrusted their proclivity – to take the Ottoman part in the Russo-Turkish war. They were also active for the Polish Confederates, and among a batch of Confederate prisoners taken by the Russians there were nine French officers.

Frederick's attitude to Britain, however, was equally cool at this time. He said in April 1769 that he had a strong aversion to the idea of liaison with Britain, because their conduct towards him in the war had made him mistrustful.[50] He had no wish to draw Britain into any treaties he might form with Russia – it would extend the latter too much. He was, however, very curious about Britain's increasing difficulties with her American colonies. He asked Mitchell if the British Government really hoped to settle their affairs there. 'Yes,' said Mitchell, 'our hopes are good.' Frederick was sceptical.[51] During the recent war there had been extensive contraband trade between the British American colonies and the French enemy and there had been a strengthening of Imperial control and garrisons as a consequence; together with such fiscal measures as the extension of British stamp duties to the colonies. Frederick doubted whether the evident resentment of this would blow quickly away, and he said so. He thought the British Government (of Lord North) weak and inept, and was unsurprised, probably with a certain malicious satisfaction, on hearing of British troubles with disturbances in Boston in the new year. 'They'll need great skill to avoid repercussions,' he said, and doubted if they possessed it.[52]

But Frederick's mind was at the moment concentrated on his forthcoming visit from the Emperor Joseph; this was now agreed to be at Neisse in Silesia, starting on 25 August 1769, during Prussian army manoeuvres.

Frederick now had great personal prestige among the sovereigns of Europe. Nevertheless he fussed a good deal about the details of the arrangements for the visit of the head of the house of Habsburg. It was not a state visit. Joseph was coming by invitation to see the troops of another monarch exercising in the field, and was taking the opportunity to receive his hospitality. But such events, with their attempts at informality and relaxation of protocol, can be more testing than the strictest ceremonies, and Frederick bombarded Rohd with queries. Would the Bishop's Palace at Neisse be suitable accommodation? Frederick's own court chamberlains would be in attendance on the Emperor – was that appropriate? He proposed a gun salute by the fortress batteries and hoped this would be regarded as in order. Would the Emperor like to dine tête-à-tête with his host, or with members of the family? Did Joseph intend to bring his own riding horses or would he like some of Frederick's at his disposal? Everything must be done to make the visit successful and enjoyable.[53]

The whole thing went excellently. Frederick met his visitor on the steps of the Bishop's Palace with every welcoming grace. Joseph had greatly looked forward to seeing Prussian soldiers and was suitably impressed. He was in the saddle at seven in the morning, riding out with the King to inspect the troops on manoeuvres; and, above all, he relished Frederick's conversation, his modesty, his charm. He noted with approval the way Frederick, reminiscing of his campaigns, appeared to give credit to his own subordinate generals. He was introduced by Frederick to the famous heroes of the war, to Seydlitz and others whose names were now European bywords. He listened to his host's analysis of battles, to the way Frederick assessed Joseph's own commanders – criticizing Browne, full of praise for Daun, Loudon, Lacy, above all for Traun. He thought Frederick's humanity very evident from his conversation, although it was perfectly clear that much of Frederick's talk was calculated, was for effect: and that he wanted to make Joseph wary of Russia. Despite his own staunchly pro-Russian policy, the King often adverted to the Russian danger. Frederick's unhappy experience of Austro-Russian *rapport* was still alive in his mind.[54]

Frederick was delighted with his guest, and with how well he later heard the visit had gone in Joseph's eyes. He was proud of the appearance of the troops – 'Your regiment were in splendid order, *mon cher ami*,' he wrote to de la Motte Fouqué. 'He is most polished,' he wrote of Joseph, 'and his manner won all hearts.'[55] But he told Finckenstein that this was a young man of great ambition, somewhat impatient of the check in which he was held by his formidable mother; a young man who would certainly try some large venture when free to do so. Venice? Bavaria? Silesia? Lorraine? 'Europe will go up in flames when he's in charge.'[56] This was ominous, but Frederick recognized that Joseph's authority was at present limited; and he promised his good will and his neutrality if there were some future war between Britain and the Bourbon monarchies. When the visit ended it was agreed that a return would be desirable during the following year.

Little actual business was done; the meeting was, however, symbolic. Prussia and Austria had been bitter enemies for many decades and to see the young Habsburg Emperor fêted by the King of Prussia seemed to mark the end of an era, whatever the next era held. Business would be done elsewhere, and there was a good deal of it. Frederick supposed that there would be no very decisive turn of events in the Russo-Turkish war for the rest of 1769, but in October he reckoned that the Russians were 'swollen with success' from their (minor) victories, and had deployed a corps to Jassy to keep order in Moldavia.[57] Russian success, not for the first time, was (for Frederick) like water running from a tap which was sluggish to get going but could become a dangerous flood, hard to stem. He had encouraged Catherine to play her part in Poland, and to be firm in the face of the Polish Confederates. He was uncompromisingly on the Russian side in the confrontation with the Ottomans which had followed. But like many before – and since – he was appalled at the heavy-handedness with which Russian policy was applied. 'I wish these confounded Russians had never left their own lair and that the Empress would be content with giving orders to Russians and not try to impose laws on Poles over whom she has no legitimate authority,' he wrote to Prince Henry in September 1769.[58] He learned that the Russian strategic plan was to arouse revolt in Montenegro against the Ottoman Empire, and also to influence insurrection in Georgia. They also, he heard, planned to send the Russian fleet to make an attempt on Constantinople. Frederick asked Rohd whether the Austrians viewed all this with equanimity?[59] He was Russia's ally, as far as subsidy and sympathy went, but he was not at war and he was deeply concerned about the way matters were running. The greatest need was for peace. Peace might need mediation.

Mediation in the Russo-Turkish war had been mooted since the day it began. Austria, as a neighbouring and interested power not directly involved, had been thought by some a natural mediator and Frederick had not been hostile to the idea. He thought that Russian influence in Poland – which he had supported – bid fair to become excessive, and a large role for Austria as mediator might help to check this. Prussia, too, was mooted as mediator in some quarters and Frederick initially regarded this as a good idea although he later cooled to it. He was sure the war should be stopped, but he did not under-estimate the difficulties of stopping it on terms which would be accepted by both sides and acceptable to all others, notably Austria, concerned with the balance of power in eastern and south-eastern

Europe. 'Nothing would be better,' he told Rohd in October 1769, 'than that Russia should charge me as mediator to end their war with the Turks, and that the Ottomans should charge Austria.' He believed that business might be done on that basis but it might not be easy to arrange.[60]

The principalities of Moldavia and Wallachia were central to the Russo-Turkish war, and their destiny would be central to any peace negotiation. They had been won by the Russians from the Turks in the course of the campaign of 1769 and it was possible that Russia would aim to keep them. For this to be reversed would need either a successful counter-campaign – which looked unlikely and would certainly take time – or would require the concerted diplomatic (and perhaps military) pressure of external powers; notably, and most nearly affected, Austria. These were Danubian principalities, but Frederick realized that the Ottomans were absolutely set on recovering them; and to prevent them becoming another flashpoint for conflagration, another Silesia, another Lorraine, would require considerable adroitness. It would also require plain speaking at times, and Frederick told the Russians early in 1770 that if they planned to keep the principalities after the war, they would be facing the prospect of another war: with Austria.[61]

Frederick had not mellowed in his treatment of his own officials and ambassadors when he thought their conduct inadequate, unintelligent or presumptuous. 'I entrust ciphers to you for important news, not for your grumblings,' he told von Goltz in Paris. 'You are silent on matters worthy of attention . . . your choice of sources of information is poor – I am dissatisfied with your reports . . .'[62]

He proposed to withdraw von Goltz, but when Solms, his man in St Petersburg, had the temerity to comment on this intention Frederick was particularly sharp. 'I haven't sent you to St Petersburg to give me advice on matters you're not asked to comment on. I've sent you there to carry out my orders, and I have no obligation to prove to your satisfaction my own dissatisfaction!'[63] He was equally savage at any attempt by another power to comment on his own appointments. When Finckenstein told him that the Russians were anxious to see the position of Prussian Ambassador to Denmark filled Frederick told him not to be so abject. 'You must not be so cowardly towards the

Russians. Do you want to be a slave? Russians must be resisted, they climb down (*mettre de l'eau dans leur vin*) when they see they won't succeed ... take shame at this deplorable weakness! Blush!' If he showed so little spine, Frederick told him, he would be replaced 'as the most cowardly and unworthy of ministers'. No power, he wrote, should presume to interfere in his, Frederick's, appointments.[64]

Frederick undoubtedly suffered anxiety that he might be too compliant towards the Russian point of view: that his assiduous courting of Catherine could easily become – or be taken for – weakness and subservience. He was unsparing in his gestures to her – he was keen to send her some Berlin porcelain ('the Prussian Service') of which he was justly proud. He kept its designs close to the style of his beloved Watteau, 'Watto' as he generally wrote him. He was loyal, by conviction, to the Russian connection but he was always walking a tightrope. The anxiety led him, of course, in the direction of Austrian rapprochement but he felt this should not go too fast. 'One step at a time,' he had told Finckenstein; and when Prince Henry urged the benefits of Prussian union with Austria, a union which would form a barrier to France, Spain and England, and which would be sufficiently formidable for Russia not to challenge[65] Frederick told him that this might come, but perhaps after his time. Maria Theresa must 'lose the habit of thirty years, the habit of hating me!' The young Emperor seemed to have good will, but he might change.

Frederick was moving cautiously in that autumn of 1769. He had, nevertheless, approached Vienna, in a low key and without commitment, on the possibility of Austrian mediation between Russians and Turks – an idea he had considered for some time and which would become more prominent, more urgent, and then diminish. Frederick 'would do all in his power[66] to help', he told Finckenstein and Herzberg, but he was increasingly conscious of 'the approach of old age. Louis XIV did nothing but talk nonsense at the end of his reign. The great Condé thought he was a rabbit. Marlborough lost memory itself. When Eugen commanded on the Rhine there were a few sparks among the embers but the Eugen of Cassano, Turin, Zeute, Belgrade, was no more.'

The passing years (he was approaching sixty) made him particularly zealous for peace, and for a secure Prussia in a more stable Europe. He was often lonely, although not sorry for a certain solitude and enjoying correspondence with favoured members of the family, especially the beloved Princess of Orange. 'I am alone here . . . we have no ladies who play the violin, no English Duchesses!' He added that 'we have had a Duke of Devonshire,* the most stupid of men, hardly made in the image of God!'[67] He told her he longed for her letters, provided he read, 'I'm well, I'm happy, I still love my old uncle.'[68]

The year 1770 began with the brilliant and immensely expensive marriage of the Dauphin of France, the future Louis XVI, with the Austrian Archduchess Marie-Antoinette. Such festivities, wrote careful Frederick, would help drive France to financial ruin.[69] And the French, to Frederick's irritation, were now sending as much money as they could – and more than they could afford – to Constantinople to help the Turkish war effort.

In Poland the situation was as troublesome as ever. The Confederates were behaving with great savagery to the Dissidents – and even to Catholics thought friendly to Russia. They wanted to force the abdication of Stanislaus, the King, unless he openly supported their cause.[70] To do so, Frederick warned him in January 1770, might conform to a recent resolution of the Polish Diet but it would bring him into open opposition to the Tsarina. The Polish situation could probably not be resolved until peace was achieved between St Petersburg and Constantinople. He had sent his ideas about mediation to the Russians but their reactions so far were vague, although he was sure Catherine would not be disinclined to a peace if the conditions were right. The Turks, he wrote to Prince Henry in May 1770, 'were beginning to talk peace'.[71] The good will of Austria might do much.

On 6 May Frederick received in audience the Austrian Ambassador, Count Nugent, who was leaving.[72] The King spoke flatteringly of the young Emperor, Joseph, and with admiration of the genius of Kaunitz, 'the greatest statesman Europe has had for a long time'. He spoke of the Russo-Turkish war.

'Now a secret – tell their Majesties that the Turks are keen for peace and will accept Austrian mediation.' Prussia, he said, was an ally of Russia. So was Britain. France was too committed to the

---

* The 5th Duke, future husband of Georgina Spencer.

Turkish cause to be a credible mediator. Frederick would, if desired, act as an intermediary with the Tsarina. The Austrians, he suggested, did not want the Russians as neighbours: yet Russian progress in the Balkan seat of war was making this likely. Nugent replied that Austria was scrupulously neutral. He also, however, observed that 'if one drew a line through Graudenz, Thorn, Posen to Glogau, between that and the Baltic – might be a convenient territory for Prussia?' In most conversations about the end of the Russo-Turkish war and the linked question of the future of Poland there were now tentative suggestions, hints, propositions which would one day take firm shape. *Partage.* Partition. But this would take time and Frederick certainly did not wish to take a leading part. His definite proposals at this stage, as expressed to St Petersburg in September 1770, were for a settlement of Polish differences whereby Dissidents would be prevented from becoming senators but that in return for this the Confederate rebels would give in to the royal authority (of Stanislaus) or be forced (chiefly by Russian arms) to submit; such a settlement to be guaranteed by Austria, Russia and Prussia. There was as yet no mention of territorial adjustments, but the concept of the three powers colluding in a Polish settlement was an augury although there was still a long way to go.[73]

Before this communication two important events had occurred. Frederick agreed his return visit to Joseph at Neustadt. And Prince Henry, after a visit to his sister Ulrica of Sweden, had accepted an invitation from Catherine to continue to St Petersburg: 'a purely friendly visit'. 'I don't think you can refuse!' Frederick wrote to him, although he said that it might not be very agreeable.[74] It seems to have been very agreeable indeed.

Frederick wrote a briefing letter to his brother before his departure, and arranged special ciphers for his communications. Henry was to do his best to persuade Ulrica to use her influence for peace between Sweden and Russia, a cause which Frederick, in the name of realism, had always pressed on her.[75] He was to try to urge Catherine towards peace with the Ottoman Porte, and moderation of any territorial demands (likely in Moldavia and Wallachia). He was to mix this with expressions of unstinting admiration for Catherine and for Russia – Frederick gave him a fulsome letter – '. . . the Mediterranean covered with Russian ships and ensigns which, deployed among the ruins of

Athens and Sparta, will bear eternal witness to the greatness of your glory . . .' Constantinople, he wrote, would soon tremble at the sight of a Russian fleet. There was more effusion than sincerity in this. Frederick had earlier deplored the idea of Constantinople trembling at the sight of a Russian fleet, but at the moment he needed to appear staunch for the friendship of the Tsarina.[76]

Catherine might be short of money, he told Henry, and the Prince should talk 'as an innocent' with foreign ambassadors to find what he could of the state of Russian finances. Prussia might help if it made the Tsarina more amenable. He had written separately to Panin complaining about the unpaid debts in Berlin of the Russian Ambassador, Prince Dolgoruki. He was amused to hear, some weeks later, that Prince Henry was being said in Poland to be visiting the Tsarina hoping for a grant from her of suzerainty over Moldavia and Wallachia after the Russians had beaten the Turks. And there were also stories that some Polish officers wanted Henry as their own king. But before the Russian visit took place Frederick had himself paid his return visit to the Emperor Joseph.

Frederick's visit to Neustadt in the autumn of 1770 was memorable, not least for a long series of conversations with the King of Prussia's previous arch-enemy, Prince Kaunitz.

Frederick had taken as much trouble with the minutiae of this visit as with its predecessor when Joseph had come to him at Neisse. He was accompanied by his brother, Prince Ferdinand, and gave him strict instructions, including on dress. As a compliment to his host Frederick intended to wear Austrian uniform (he held honorary rank) and told Ferdinand to do the same: a white tunic, braided and embroidered with silver and without a star or any other distinction. Neustadt is near Olmütz in Moravia and Frederick had ridden all the way from Breslau. Everyone was anxious to see the legendary King of Prussia, a small old man in Austrian uniform who had come on horseback more than 100 miles over the ground of some of his campaigns to meet the youthful Emperor.

The Prince de Ligne, a distinguished soldier and particularly cultivated and well-read, was in Joseph's suite and he immediately got on excellent terms with Frederick. He was exactly the sort of man Frederick most appreciated, a soldier, well versed in European history and literature, witty, entertaining. Ligne could make Frederick laugh, with his well-told historical anecdotes. He could – and did – quote from Voltaire and meet counter-quote from Frederick, always the happiest way of bringing minds into conjunction. He noted how Frederick, when he exclaimed '*Mon Dieu*', would clasp his hands together with pleasure, and how his conversation was so intelligent, well-informed and witty that he ennobled any theme. The King's mind could easily wander, but if his attention was held he was, said Ligne, an entrancing talker. And Ligne also said that Frederick struck him as not only a good but a very gentle man.[77]

For his part Frederick much enjoyed meeting Ligne.

'Was it your name, your letter to Rousseau, which was printed in the newspapers?' Rousseau had written a somewhat presumptuous letter to Frederick, chiding him for not making peace.

'Sire, I am insufficiently distinguished for my name to be used!'

Frederick was sceptical of such modesty. He had been kind to Rousseau, admiring his obvious genius while quite out of sympathy with his philosophy. 'The poor unfortunate must be relieved,' he told 'Milord Maréchal' in 1762. 'His only sin is in having peculiar opinions!' They talked of what one might most like to be in life. That would depend on age, said Ligne. A pretty woman until thirty, perhaps. A lucky and skilful military commander until sixty, certainly. After that, until eighty, a cardinal! Frederick appreciated this. They discussed Austrian generals. Frederick, as he had with Joseph at Neisse, praised Loudon, Lacy. Daun, he said, had always seemed to fear him, as if he, Frederick, like Jove, might always have an unexpected thunderbolt to hand. And it was 'your old Marshal Traun' who taught Frederick what he called 'the little I know. What a man!'

Frederick asked whether the French had improved as soldiers and Ligne told him that their discipline was worse than ever – not what they had been in Turenne's day. Frederick nodded – this accorded with his own impressions of French military performance at that time – poor administrative system, indifferent command. 'Yet they still won battles under Vendôme.'

'Yes. But they are like people who want to sing without knowing the music.'

'I'm fond of untrained, natural voices (*voix champêtres*),' Frederick said, 'they have inborn talents, courage, lightness of touch . . . it is impossible not to love them.'

'They need German or Swiss support, sire,' said Ligne.

But Ligne never missed an opportunity to make a political point where he could. He found Frederick, he said long afterwards, the man with the most magical gift of conversation, with the boldest, gayest, most brilliant traits he had ever met; and he was brave enough to say, 'If you and the Emperor were united, sire, all Europe would need to watch its step!' For that, however, Frederick kept his counsel for the meeting with Kaunitz.

To discuss campaigns with previous enemies is always fascinating, and the Austrian commanders enjoyed it as much as Frederick. They marked his advertisement of his own caution – 'I'm not as brave as you think!' But they also appreciated his easy transitions to other themes, to art, literature, religion, philosophy: gardening – 'I used Virgil's *Georgics* as a gardener's guide!' Ligne said Virgil was a great poet but a poor gardener, and Frederick conceded that the gardener at Sans Souci had said to him, 'You're a fool, and so is that book of yours!' It was, surely, all a matter of climate and climate had always betrayed him – 'Yet who would believe that God or the sun would refuse *me* anything?' And the Austrians remembered how, whatever the remark, Frederick would produce some absurdity to cap it and make them all laugh; and remarked, too, how charming was his voice – low, gentle, clear – as well as the range of his conversation.

Frederick's first meeting with Kaunitz took place on 4 September 1770. As he expected, he found the great Austrian highly intelligent and with excellent judgement. He also (as he told Rohd in a subsequent dispatch)[78] found him very opinionated – 'a political oracle, with others pupils he needs to teach!' Frederick recognized that to Kaunitz he was a simple soldier, in need of instruction. That may have been a mix of Kaunitz's manner and Frederick's sensitivity, since it is unlikely he expected the King to conform to the type of a straightforward military man.

They had a very long talk.[79] Frederick needed to impress on the other his belief that peace was urgent, and should come, if possible, that winter. His subsidy to Russia was a tedious drain on his purse, and if the war continued the Russians would soon be on the Danube, surely unwelcome to Austria and leading to the prospect of another general war which would be Europe's worst nightmare. The present war, said Frederick, was damnable (*'maudite'*). A war involving operations in Poland would probably involve Prussia – if they were confined to Moldavia and Wallachia he said that he might be able to keep out. The principalities might demand independence from Turkey, and a formula might be found which would achieve that without handing them to Russia. Affairs in Poland would probably settle themselves.

Frederick said that he probably knew Catherine better than Kaunitz did – a difficult woman. He suggested – a concluding suggestion which Kaunitz declined to take seriously – that Austria might try to deter Russia by threatening a breach in relations if the Russians – General Rumanzov – crossed the Danube, and might seek an undertaking from France to send 100,000 men to help in that eventuality?

Kaunitz was surely right not to make much of this – it was a *ballon d'essai* to get a reaction and the Austrian thought it childish. He compared the Prussian relationship with Russia to Austria's with France: essentially defensive. This helped contain the possible spread of any war. It had other benefits – it suited Britain, for instance, because it helped protect her from a continental commitment. In the present Russo-Turkish war he agreed that mediation might become useful, and perhaps both Austria and Prussia might play a part. In time this might be requested by Constantinople. This line was palatable to Frederick, who was always anxious about a possible Austro-Ottoman alliance. Kaunitz agreed with Frederick that if Britain were invited to be a mediatrix an invitation would also need to be extended to France; and the Russians would oppose France just as the Turks would oppose Britain because of British help to Russia and the Russian fleet.

They talked long about Poland. Frederick believed that the key to a Polish settlement was a Russo-Turkish peace. Kaunitz believed that a Polish 'arrangement' might precede that peace. Catherine herself might propose something, take the initiative and communicate it to Vienna and Berlin, suggest Austrian and Prussian guarantees, with agreement to force acceptance on the Poles? Frederick listened carefully. Kaunitz was emphatic – and there was no disposition to disagree

– that any settlement in Poland must satisfy 'neighbouring powers'. His tone throughout, as might be expected, was moderate, clear and not ferociously partisan.

This was far from the sort of suggestions made to Frederick in the previous July by the Polish Prince Sulkowski[80] visiting Berlin with a 'solution'; the solution had been to deprive Dissidents of all privileges, as agreed by the Diet, and to exclude the crown from all participation in financial management and military administration. Such measures – remote from any possibility of acceptance by the Tsarina, to whom Frederick reported in full – would simply have returned all power to the fractious nobles of the Diet. Sulkowski,* Frederick said, was a '*grand bavard*' (chatterbox) – 'like all the Poles I've ever met'. His ideas were remote from the cool realism of Kaunitz.

Frederick reported on his conversation with Kaunitz when he wrote to St Petersburg with his current thinking on Poland in September 1770. There was now an infectious plague affecting livestock in that country and a military cordon was established by neighbour states, including both Austria and Prussia, to prevent it spreading.[81] Frederick wrote briefly to Prince Henry telling him of his impressions of the Austrian troops: 'Infantry much improved. Artillery good. Cavalry pitiable.'[82] As for Kaunitz: 'He knows he's clever and expects deference. He treats the Emperor as a son.' Frederick heard later that the Duke of Gloucester (brother of George III), who had visited Neustadt at the same time, thought Frederick had been cold to him. 'When he was in Berlin,' Frederick remarked, 'he never called on me! Why should I talk to him first?'[83]

* Sulkowski, who had put his views to Frederick at an urgently requested audience, also asked for a loan and was told that loans were a matter for bankers not kings.

20

Cutting the Cake

Prince Henry set out on his travels in September 1770, first to Sweden then to Russia. His visit to St Petersburg was a great success. He arrived in October 1770 and stayed for more than three months. He was, like everyone, filled with admiration for the beauties of Peter the Great's noble new city, and he made a most favourable impression on Catherine – 'a hero', she said, 'who has given me friendship' – and charmed her. Henry, often supposed to be homosexual, was generally able to impress those of either sex on whom he turned his attractive personality. Later, in 1776, he would pay another visit at her invitation. He was delighted, when talking politics with her and with Panin, to find how relatively moderate Russian demands on the Turks seemed to be.

When the time for actual negotiation came (if it did), Henry supposed mediation might help, if acceptable mediators could be found. That last was the problem. Frederick reckoned that the greatest difficulty might lie in acceptance by Russia of Austria as a mediator. He sometimes declared that he had now renounced ideas of Prussian mediation, having often pushed them previously, and despite his belief that he might be acceptable to the Turks although a loyal ally of Russia. He was sincere in saying that he would do anything to promote peace, but some connections could have a reverse effect, including connections of his own. Austria on the other hand – and he now assiduously promoted the idea of Austrian mediation – was thought to be tied to France and Spain, and had renewed a treaty with the Turks, to Frederick's concern. Britain sometimes seemed keen to play a mediatory part but that would lead to a demand by France for a counter-balancing role and to the automatic opposition of Russia.[1]

To find mediators whose own interests would not cause instant mistrust, or upset any conceivable negotiation, was not easy. From time to time Prince Henry acted as a channel of communication, from Catherine to Frederick and vice versa, as the Tsarina tried out various ideas on the King of Prussia before floating them more widely.

In this advisory role Frederick – and Henry – played helpful and realistic parts. At the end of 1770 the Russians (who had won a decisive victory over the Turks in July) put forward proposals for the 'debatable lands' of Moldavia and Wallachia which they supposed might be steps towards settlement; these principalities might be detached from Ottoman rule altogether. Frederick – through Henry – told Catherine that this suggestion, if made *tout court*, would be seen by Austria as a barely disguised Russian acquisition and must lead to war between Russia and Austria. He said that he could not pass on such proposals – he would lose credibility and be regarded simply as an agent of Russia; and he made clear that in such circumstances, despite his friendship with Russia, he could not regard the cause as justifying a Prussian war against Austria.[2] At that moment the Russians were 'drunk with success', he said. There must be a restoration of moderation. He told Catherine by personal letter[3] that he could not put to Vienna suggestions which went too far beyond limited adjustments on the littoral of the Black Sea. Russian demands of this kind would drive the Turks more closely into the arms of Austria, with whom they had a treaty. The Turks would then give up Serbia to Austria in return for united action against Russia, and the war, far from abating, would be dangerously spread with no hope of Austrian mediation. The prospect of Austro-Russian war worried Frederick deeply in the early months of 1771. The business had all started with Poland but now it was rumbling dangerously in the Balkans.

Henry's first meeting with Catherine after his arrival in October 1770 had, not unnaturally, been largely concerned with the progress of actual military operations. The Prince had a deserved reputation as a soldier not far behind that of his formidable brother and Catherine wanted his views. She paid lip-service to the desire for peace, well aware that this was what Frederick wished to hear; but if peace did not come what should she do? Cross the Danube? Continue pushing her armies south?

Poland, 1772

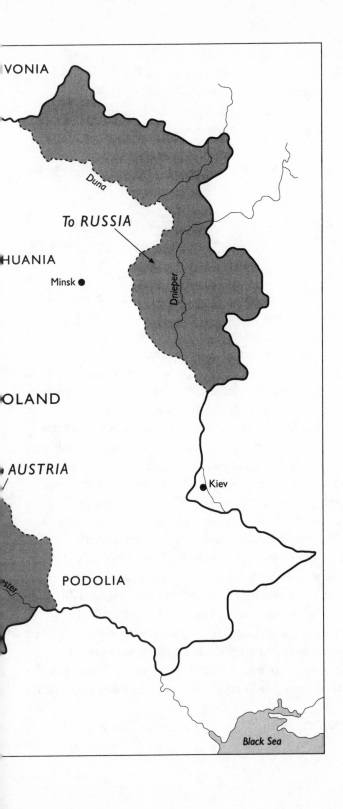

VONIA

Duna

To RUSSIA

HUANIA

Minsk ●

Dnieper

OLAND

AUSTRIA

Kiev ●

PODOLIA

ester

Black Sea

Henry made a point for consideration. Could Moldavia and Wallachia, 'the principalities',* actually *support* an army which crossed the Danube? And would not the terrain south of the great river produce difficult operating conditions? Furthermore, he wondered, would not a Russian advance south of the Danube cause particular anxiety to Austria? And, perhaps, France? Catherine laughed. She was well aware that he and his brother saw it as their task to press her towards minimum action, minimum extension.

'Well, we'd better have peace!'[4]

Then they had talked of Poland, for the first of many times; and Henry promised to tell Frederick what she hoped, and to suggest Frederick push it as far as possible with Vienna.

By the time Henry left St Petersburg Catherine had come to the view that the best hope of peace in the Russo-Turkish war would probably be from direct negotiations between the two principals. And Frederick had come to the view that the best thing he could do would be to continue trying to moderate Russian demands and using his influence. He could not, he now realized, be a go-between for Russia with Austria, any more than he could act as a formal mediator between Russia and the Ottoman Porte, although this was sometimes mooted. Nevertheless his friendly advice had prevented some misunderstandings. The Austrians had learned of the Russian ideas for Moldavia and Wallachia and, as he knew they would, rejected them as unacceptable. But, Frederick told the Austrian Ambassador, van Swieten, 'they'll lower their position, depend on it. They told Prince Henry it wasn't their last word.' And he, Frederick, Russia's loyal ally, had made clear to them that he would not support the indefensible. Van Swieten said that Austria appreciated Frederick was Russia's ally, but that Russian expansion should surely alarm him as much as it alarmed Vienna?[5] Frederick acknowledged it, but he was working for a different solution which finally won acceptance. Moldavia and Wallachia might become independent principalities, but to pre-empt that independence leading to Russian hegemony they could be under nominal Ottoman overlordship which need not involve a military presence. This would be a considerable concession; the Russians were in possession. Catherine

---

* i.e. modern Romania.

ultimately agreed but the issue came near to causing war in the following year, 1771, and all Frederick's powers of conciliation would be needed.

Henry's excellent service at St Petersburg included his insights into the Russian court and personalities. Catherine herself; Panin; Orlov, the huge and influential lover of Catherine who thought he could make the Russian monarchy, already absolute, more powerful by the elimination of any even slightly moderating influences. Henry's reputation, charm and personality had affected the Tsarina and although it would be some time before peace was achieved – Henry's first charge – the process of negotiating it, laborious and often frustrating, had been advanced by his visit. 'If one could arrange an alliance,' Panin told him, 'between Prussia, Russia and Austria, that would be the best thing of all.' And although Henry responded cautiously it was clear that a certain wind was blowing. It would have alternating periods of gust and calm but dangerously extreme positions taken by St Petersburg and Vienna had been averted. Russian demands and triumphalism had been moderated. Something like a settlement in the Balkans was in sight.

And – a separate matter although inevitably overlapping – conversations about Poland had been conducted amicably albeit without immediate prospect of conclusion. Panin had suggested that the conflicting Polish parties, the Dissidents and the Confederates, might be brought to negotiate directly an agreement between themselves.[6] Russia would be happy to guarantee such an agreement, jointly with Austria and Prussia. In Panin's eyes, 'Poland's neighbours have a common interest' – and Catherine was entirely content for conversations about Poland to be a feature of Austro-Prussian conversations.[7] She would press moderation on the Dissidents. Meanwhile the Austrians had taken possession of the area of Zips in Poland, historically a part of Hungary, which had featured in Lynar's plan, near the Slovakian-Polish border. It had long been a wealthy and semi-autonomous county, largely peopled by Saxon, Lutheran incomers. The Austrians were also claiming ancient rights over a district (Sandec) near Cracow; and the Russians were saying that if Austria set an example of that kind it would be wrong for Russia and Prussia not to follow suit.[8] Frederick was of the same mind – 'If the Austrians want to support their acquisitions in Poland the Russians should have part of the cake.'[9] His chief concern was to avert war between the two but he had not forgotten his agreement with Kaunitz that there should be a Polish settlement which satisfied neighbouring powers. And it was still important to end the war between Russians and Turks, a dangerous business.

Henry's visit to Russia drew a letter of particular gratitude and admiration from Frederick on the Prince's return to Berlin,[10] and he had earned it. And – explicit or implicit – the dismemberment of Poland was now clearly contemplated as a means to procure an amicable settlement between her neighbours. Henry had been left in no doubt of this by Panin. He had reacted very sensibly. As far as Prussia was concerned there would be no difficulties in absorbing Prussian Poland. Were more of Poland to be mooted there might well be trouble with other German states.[11] But, in Henry's words, 'the ice has been broken'. When, at a small evening party on 8 January 1771, Catherine spoke of the '*cordon sanitaire*' which she understood the Prussians had established in some Polish provinces to prevent the spread of cattle infection, she simply asked, 'Then why not occupy them?'

The seeds of an agreement over Poland had been sown. The rest of 1771, after Henry's return (he reached Potsdam on 18 February), was marked by cultivation of that difficult plant; several difficult plants.

In February the Russians announced that they proposed to deal directly with the Turks over peace. This was good as far as it went. One impediment was the detention by the Turks of the Russian Ambassador, Obreskov, who was being held in Constantinople in defiance of diplomatic protocol and whose release and safety were regarded in St Petersburg as prerequisites of progress in negotiation.

In Poland the Russians had now suggested a settlement on the lines put to Henry by Panin. There might be an internal settlement arranged between Dissidents and Confederates, guaranteed by neighbour powers; and – as yet a matter of hints and suggestions rather than hard proposals – there could be territorial 'adjustments', to satisfy the security concerns of those neighbour powers and perhaps to compensate Russia for the cost of the war. Russian troops would then withdraw from Poland.

Also in February the Russians made a further stipulation for any Russo-Turkish peace agreement; freedom of navigation in the Black Sea. Their proposed acquisitions vis-à-vis Turkey were, they claimed, for lands which were incontestably the Tsarina's. Certain Aegean islands should be ceded as entrepôts for Russian trade; and Russia would renounce claims to Wallachia and Moldavia.

And Obreskov must be freed.[12]

This seemed promising and represented a softening of earlier Russian positions, although not to the extent Frederick had hoped. Everything was likely to turn on Austrian reactions. The Austrians were by now extremely anxious about Russian expansion in the Balkans and had given notice that they were assembling an army on the Hungarian eastern frontier as a precautionary measure. This would 'ensure sufficient authority' for Vienna's negotiations.[13] Frederick thought this no bad thing – it was a time for sharing, at least to an extent, Austrian concern about Russian expansion rather than only for worry about Austrian intentions. The Austrians wanted to know whether, if they were forced to 'act' *outside Poland*, they could rely on Frederick to do nothing against Austrian interests? The implication was – 'would he remain neutral if the Austrians felt bound to move defensively in the Balkans?' The same point was put to him very frankly by van Swieten at an audience on 14 February, and Frederick had no difficulty in answering clearly and satisfactorily. His treaty with Russia bound him to support the King of Poland, Stanislaus, and to help Russia with subsidies in any war arising from the Polish situation. No more. No Prussian intervention in Moldavia and Wallachia, for instance, was conceivable.[14]

Meanwhile the Austrian occupation of the Duchy of Zips, a considerable territory including several towns and ninety-seven villages, was going ahead. Frederick took this with unconcern. Either Zips would revert to Poland after a Russo-Turkish peace or 'others will revive claims on Polish territory'.[15] By now he had little doubt which alternative would apply, and in separate exchanges with the Russians in February they said, and he agreed, that there could no longer be a question of 'conserving Poland in its entirety'.[16] He would, he said, 'imitate Vienna'. He would invoke 'certain ancient rights' and occupy some small province – to hand it back if the Austrians did the same;

or keep it. The accident that both Austria and Prussia had recently cordoned certain Polish districts because of the fear of cattle infection, the *'cordon sanitaire'*, might prove an administrative convenience. In this he was responding to Catherine's nod to Henry. 'The Poles,' Frederick wrote, 'would be the only ones with a right to complain, and, by their conduct, deserve consideration from neither Russia nor me!' Nor, he might have added, from Austria. He reckoned that with the great powers in agreement such adjustments would not be hard to manage, and would materially promote peace. He appreciated that the Russians had earlier and formally undertaken to keep Poland intact, but if the Austrians were set to acquire Polish land so should Russia. And Prussia. For his part he wanted little but the lands which bordered Prussia. Details could come later.

There was now little need for concealment by veiled language. Finckenstein gave open advice on the borders Prussia should look for in Poland. Take Marienburg. Take Pomerania up to the Netze. The initial occupation could be part of the *'cordon sanitaire'* measures[17] which had been initiated in 1770.

This was all still tentative, and the Turks were still at war. Reality was the deployment on the Hungarian eastern frontier of a newly formed Austrian army and the possibility, as Frederick expressed it in an April letter to Solms in St Petersburg, that the Austrians could soon, if they chose, march out of the Carpathians and hem the Russians between themselves and the Turks, forcing an evacuation of Moldavia and Wallachia and an end to negotiations except on dangerously changed terms. Delay in bringing peace was giving Austria time to assemble. There was war talk in Vienna. The French were generally supposed to be promoting the continuance of war and from Constantinople Zegelin reported that the French Ambassador could not leave his residence without an armed escort, so unpopular was he.[18]

On the other side Frederick understood that Orlov was pressing Catherine to raise her terms.[19] The Tsarina was possibly due to visit Berlin shortly, to which Frederick was not looking forward.[20] He knew that both Austrians and French were trying to sow mistrust between himself and Russia and in present circumstances it was only too easy to do,[21] although he was keeping Kaunitz well informed of his ideas. He believed – surely reasonably – that if Prussians and Russians could agree about Poland the Austrians would fall in with them,[22] provided the settlement there or elsewhere did not constitute a genuine threat to Austria. The Russians must have '*un morceau*' of Poland – and Frederick would only act with full Russian agreement. The Austrian army on the Hungarian border was a piece on the chessboard, a point of pressure, no more.

As to the principalities, any formula regulating the status of Moldavia and Wallachia would surely be acceptable to the other powers, if Russia could negotiate it with the Turks. When there was still difficulty about this in June, Frederick, near desperate, proposed another solution. Give the principalities to Poland! The Russians didn't want the Turks there, the Austrians didn't want the Russians there, such a cession would give the Poles three times what it was proposed to take from them! It is hard to believe Frederick was serious in this suggestion[23] and it was, predictably, dismissed by Austria.

By the summer of 1771 Frederick had reached agreement with Russia over Polish territory in the north of the country, whereby Livonia (the Baltic province between Estonia and Riga) should be Russian, Pomerellia (that is West Prussia) Prussian, to the Netze – extending Frederick's domains to the Vistula. Prussia and Russia agreed to guarantee the other's territories, and to continue negotiating a wider settlement with Austria, which was proving difficult. It was said that Kaunitz was being particularly suspicious.[24] Frederick saw his own role as, in his words, to *calmer les premières vivacités* in both St Petersburg and Vienna. He was still haunted by the fear that Austria and Russia would come to blows and the whole European settlement dissolve. Russo-Turkish peace talks were now under way, with every prospect of taking an extremely long time.[25]

Frederick sometimes felt near despair. The same problems recurred again and again, and he often complained that he was conducting a dialogue with the deaf. 'At the beginning of our alliance with Russia it was only a matter of the kingdom of Poland. Then the issue of the Dissidents. I warned them then that if they didn't manage things carefully they'd have war with the Turks. Nobody believed me. War came . . . one thing led to another' – thus to Solms.[26] To Panin, also in August 1771 – 'This is the only moment to avoid a general war –

next year, between Russia and Austria over Moldavia and Wallachia!'
If this happened, he told Henry, Prussia would be drawn in. Yet he
had, surely, suggested and promoted an acceptable formula for the
principalities, the debatable lands, and Russia had offered to renounce
claims to them. Now, however, he heard that Austria refused to
contemplate *any* dismemberment of the Ottoman Empire – which put
matters back to the beginning. At the same time Frederick heard that
the Turks had crossed the Danube northward with 120,000 men, so that
the tide of war might also be turning – and effectively counteracting
the tide of diplomacy.[27] When the Sultan proposed to Frederick a
'perpetual alliance' between the Ottoman Porte and Prussia, Frederick
had no difficulty in declining sharply, reminding him of his relationship
with Russia.[28]

Frederick assessed the extraordinary situation in September. If
the Austrians decided to break with Russia they would cooperate,
militarily, with the Turks in Moldavia and Wallachia and drive the
Russians north across the Dniester. At the same time they would try
to promote a general 'patriotic' anti-Russian union of Confederate
forces in Poland, where they would seek the election of another king.
Any 'diversion' mounted by Frederick would draw on him all other
forces of the German states. Russia, he said, wants everything, Austria
will concede nothing. War seemed inevitable unless conciliation was
given a chance.[29] He had pointed out to the Russians endlessly the
futility of acquiring or *seeming to wish to acquire* the two provinces,
Moldavia and Wallachia, which would be hard to defend, and whose
acquisition made peace impossible. He thought he had been successful.
He, himself, was wholly indifferent as to who possessed these places,
as he made clear in countless conversations with the Austrians. He
was now exasperated with both Catherine and Maria Theresa and he
thought other powers, when not meddling, irresponsibly blind to
the danger of the times. 'I admire the tranquillity of the British
Government, in the present situation in Europe,' he wrote waspishly
in September 1771. 'It smacks too much, however, of unpardonable
indolence, of complete lethargy.'[30] Britain, he said, 'after glorious
campaigns could be one of the first powers in Europe, an arbiter.
Instead, weakness and laziness had made her abject, ignorant of what
happened elsewhere in Europe, hardly ranking as one of its powers.'[31]

Portrait by Johann Heinrich Tischbein commissioned by Frederick as a gift to Sir
Charles Hanbury-Williams between the Second Silesian and the Seven Years Wars.
He was accustomed to present a portrait to previous ambassadors to his court

'Frederick was delighted to get the famous – and very beautiful – Barbara Campanini to Berlin. Frederick encouraged the improbable story that she was his own mistress.' *Die Barbarina*, *c.* 1745, by Pesne

'In 1753 Wenzel-Anton, Count – later Prince – von Kaunitz-Rietberg, became State Chancellor to Maria-Theresa, and her principal policy adviser.' Engraving by J. Schmutzer, 1765

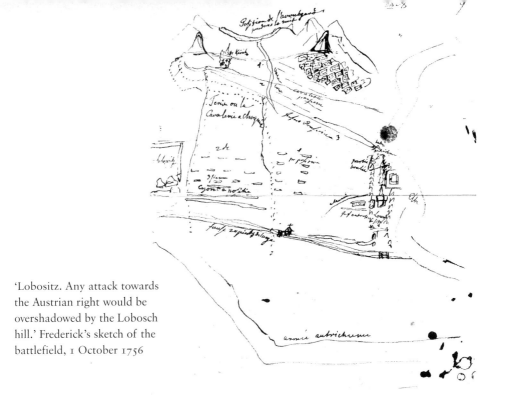

'Lobositz. Any attack towards the Austrian right would be overshadowed by the Lobosch hill.' Frederick's sketch of the battlefield, 1 October 1756

'Over the Saxons Frederick could claim victory. That army surrendered on 14 October 1756.' A contemporary engraving of the scene at Lilienstein by J. S. Ringk

'The bombardment of Prague which began on 29 May was undertaken with twenty twelve-pounder guns and ten twenty-five pounders. There were, additionally, twelve heavy mortars each throwing a huge fifty pound bomb.' Contemporary English engraving by P. P. Benazech

'The Prussians were moving forward, uphill, outnumbered, and with no favourable circumstance whatever.' An anonymous artist's depiction of Kolin

'There were murmurings in the army that Prince Henry might now lead them more successfully than their King, and all knew that there was jealousy and always had been between the brothers.' Prince Henry of Prussia, by Johann Heinrich Tischbein

'The only chink of light in the strategic situation was that Ferdinand of Brunswick, with an Anglo-Hanoverian army, had smashed the French at Minden.' Prince Ferdinand of Brunswick-Wolfenbüttel, undated, eighteenth-century German School

'In a few hours she had obtained from her abject husband a letter of abdication and within days he was 'dead of a gastric disorder'. Murdered. Henceforth Catherine of Anhalt-Zerbst, aged thirty-three and soon to be known by her subjects and by history as *The Great*, was Empress of all the Russias.' Portrait, *c.* 1770, by Vigilius Erichsen

'A negotiation which
ultimately led to a Peace
Conference in the Saxon
Royal Castle of Hubertusburg.'
Allegorical depiction of
Frederick, Maria Theresa
and (improbably) Augustus
III of Saxony, 1763, by
Johann David Schleuen

'Frederick also started to build a new and very splendid palace at Potsdam.'

'Sans Souci gave him undiluted pleasure.'

Unter den Linden, Berlin. Frederick's new opera house opposite Prince Henry's palace. Engraving, 1780, by Jean Rosenberg

'He was unsparing in his daily routine and in the parades and exercises through which he put the troops.' Frederick in his last decade. Engraving, *c.* 1777, by Daniel Berger

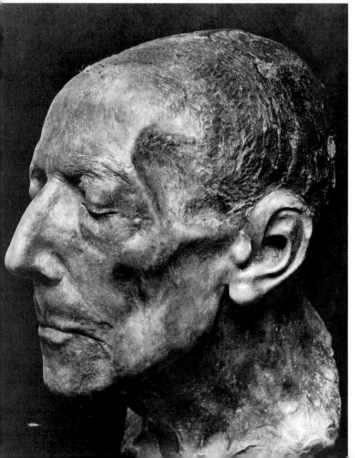

The death mask

He had watched with sceptical detachment, 'a tranquil spectator', he said, a dispute between Britain and Spain in the south Atlantic,[32] observing that Europe would be wholly uninterested whether Falkland* belonged to Spain, Britain or neither. Such far-flung acquisitions (as he wrote about New Zealand) were potentially expensive to the powers concerned and were distractions from the central issue, the peace of Europe. Where they brought commercial opportunities they might also be the occasion for discord between maritime powers.[33]

In January 1771 Sir Andrew Mitchell had died in Berlin. He had been with Frederick during both the darkest war years and the hour of glory and Frederick had been extremely fond of him. He was to be replaced by Sir Robert Gunning, whose appointment coincided with one of the cold periods in Frederick's relations with Britain and only lasted until the beginning of the following year, 1772. Gunning ('I have no desire to see *le Sieur Gunning*, and that goes for all the English who come here, their behaviour doesn't deserve the slightest welcome, it is perfectly clear what jealousy and hatred they have for me!')[34] had correspondingly little influence on the King or on events. He was succeeded in January 1772 by James Harris, later 1st Earl of Malmesbury, who had played a vigorous part at the British Embassy in Madrid over the Falkland dispute. Von Maltzahn told Frederick that Harris was an 'excellent young man, pleasant and smooth: a protégé of the Duke of Grafton'. He was certainly a brilliant diplomatist.

The Russians now decided to mark the start of 1772 by marching an army of 50,000 men into southern Poland, as a counterweight to Austrian pretensions.[35] They hoped that this move, combined with an offer ultimately to withdraw any claims to Moldavia and Wallachia, might persuade the Turks to take the Russian part in confronting Austria, although still at war with Russia. This was all complex, convoluted and – with hindsight – improbable, but such had been 1771. Frederick concerned himself with some relatively minor but significant issues while the great question of peace or war between Russia and Austria simmered. He wanted Danzig as part of whatever Prussia acquired from Poland – and the Russians were anxious that their trade might suffer and wished it to remain a free city.[36]

---

* He used the singular form.

Nevertheless the shadow of a wider war remained, and Frederick agreed contingency measures with Russia if Austria had resort to arms and took the offensive in Moldavia and Wallachia. A Russian army of 70,000 would invade Hungary from Poland. Meanwhile the separately agreed Russian army of southern Poland would deploy between Cracow and Sandomir. In case of war Frederick would create a diversion by marching into Bohemia and Moravia; areas he knew painfully well.[37] At the same time there were exchanges with St Petersburg about the terms on which Polish territory should one day be occupied. Panin had not previously supposed this would formally be annexation – simply an occupation of lands originally cordoned against disease, a *fait accompli*. The Russians hoped to get, sequentially, a Russo-Turkish peace agreement; Austrian reactions to this; and to conceal from the Turks any Polish partition agreement.

Frederick saw the matter pragmatically. When the Russian army was fully deployed in southern Poland would, he said, be the moment to act. There should then be a joint declaration by Russians and Prussians that certain territories would henceforth be administered as part of the domains of the Tsarina or the King of Prussia. In effect, annexation. There should be an oath of allegiance to the Tsarina, to show the arrangement was not tentative but final. The Poles would be presented with fact, citing the Austrian precedent of Zips. The Austrians would be inhibited from interfering by the presence of the Russian army of southern Poland. The Turks would be inhibited from interfering by the presence of General Rumanzov's Russian army in Wallachia. If, which he did not expect, the Austrians took an initiative, Frederick would, as agreed, create a diversion by invading Bohemia, and this would be decisive. Having reached this point in diplomacy the Polish partition would be essentially a military problem.

There were slips and back-tracking in the first months of 1772. The Russians changed the terms of entry of their 'new' army into southern Poland – and its composition, reducing it somewhat. Kaunitz began to take a very personal line in Vienna, adopting a somewhat dictatorial tone to the Russian Ambassador, Golitzin, and assuming a sort of governing authority (in his own eyes) over Russo-Turkish peace negotiations, demanding that more matters go through his hands;[38] Frederick reckoned the Austrian wanted hostilities prolonged, to weaken both parties.[39] There were more exchanges on the timing of Russian and Prussian occupation of Polish provinces – Frederick thought this should be when the Russians reached the Vistula.[40] The Poles would '*jeter les hauts cris*' but they always did, and an army on the Vistula would soon quieten them. Nevertheless drafts of a Convention on Poland were sent between Berlin and St Petersburg in January 1772, with comments exchanged soon thereafter; all taking place under an agreement as to what should happen if Austria intervened.

But Austria did not intervene and those particular fears of Frederick dissolved. Instead Austria looked for more practical advantages from the arrangements which Frederick and Catherine had negotiated with such difficulty between themselves. The Austrians represented, in January, that there must be 'equality of acquisition and a written promise to that effect'.[41] Frederick wholly agreed. There *might* be detailed discussion about portions but he could now feel that, after so much anxious manoeuvring, threat and counter-threat, troop deployment and counter-deployment, the Austrians – first in principle and within a few months in detail – were assenting parties to the arrangement; to the partition of Poland. Between Frederick and Catherine it was agreed that May or June would be the date of occupation of territory.

Before final agreement to the convention – the initial agreement in principle – the Austrians suggested that they might receive Glatz and part of Silesia, and cede claims to some of Prussian Poland.[42] The proposal received short shrift from Frederick. He told Solms that this particular exchange went well because he could point to 40,000 Russian troops in Poland.

The Russo-Prussian convention was signed in March in St Petersburg, with Austria expressing approval.[43] Final and formal Austrian accession took place in early August 1772; Frederick had insisted throughout that an Austrian 'portion' was essential if the Poles were not to regard Austria as their champion and thereafter blame losses, real or fancied, exclusively on Russia and Prussia.[44]

Thus a certain stability was produced in eastern and south-eastern Europe. Frederick was at last recognized as King not only 'in' but 'of' Prussia. It was agreed that Moldavia and Wallachia should nominally be part of the Ottoman Empire on the terms Frederick had proposed – the Turks had also pressed for the Crimea but Frederick, through his man in Constantinople, von Zegelin, believed he could dissuade them, and did. And in 1774, with the mediation of Austria and Russia as Frederick had originally planned, the Turks at last signed the treaty which ended the Russo-Turkish war, gaining Black Sea littoral territory and withdrawing their troops from Moldavia and Wallachia. For no party was the treaty disastrous. This grumbling war which had threatened the equilibrium of Europe and which had begun with the disturbances of Poland was at last over.

The 'portions' taken by the neighbouring powers at this 'first partition' of Poland amounted more to a cession of outlying provinces than a division of the main body. The effect, however, was to enlarge the territory and power of the partitioning powers and to leave a rump. There was a good deal of horse-trading over detail, and in some places possession had already been ceded in the previous years. Austria got Galicia, less Cracow, an accession of 1,700 square miles and in terms of area the second largest. Russia got the lion's share, about 2,000 square miles, much of Byelo Russia, the area of Vitebsk. Prussia had the smallest increase of territory, about 600 square miles. These included, however, the maritime provinces of Poland, less Danzig (which would be a free city, not under the Polish or any other crown); this latter concession Frederick had not welcomed but accepted. The territorial effect was to join East with West Prussia.

Considerable increases in population accompanied these cessions. The Prussian population rose by 385,000 and others were proportionate. The largest addition of humanity was Austria's – over 800,000. The partition meant that the kingdom of Poland lost one quarter of its territory and one fifth of its population. The outcome left Poland with a more internally balanced economy but with even less external influence than before. The convention also enabled the three partitioning powers to impose a new constitution and, at least superficially, more stability ensued. There still, however, remained an elective monarchy; and there still remained the traditional *Liberum Veto*, guarantor of Poland's impotence and correspondingly congenial to Poland's neighbours.

Russia, Prussia and Austria having taken so positive, and, as some would say, brutal a course in agreement, the ability of other powers to meddle in Poland's affairs was largely nullified. If the Tsarina had taken a strong line with the Czartoryskis earlier, Frederick thought and said, Poland might have been pacified sooner.[45] The internal struggle was now overshadowed by the darkness, as some Poles saw it, of partition. As recently as in November 1771 the King, Stanislaus, had been kidnapped by Confederates in the middle of Warsaw (with French approval as Frederick, scandalized, alleged![46]) but had escaped. It was symptomatic of what many besides Frederick regarded as a situation in need of radical reform. Poland was in chaos, he told the Dowager Electress of Saxony, in dismissing her earlier ideas (in 1770) of the Polish throne for her son;. ideas which he had described as incomprehensible.[47] Nobody could have wished to rule Poland. Now there was a new order.

The partition of Poland has been characterized as a ruthless expropriation of the weak by the strong. It did not cause unmanageable agitation in Europe at the time. The adjacent powers of Russia, Austria and Prussia had come to an understanding – with great difficulty – and agreed to plunder a largely defenceless neighbour. This was, arguably, an example of international relations conducted regardless of morality. Raison d'état, and that alone, dominated policy in St Petersburg, Vienna and Berlin. And a brutal example was given to others who, in the future, might consider that interest, security and material advantage could legitimately override contractual obligations and be held superior to any thought of respect owed by a state to the integrity or independence of another. Critics of Frederick, in particular, have seen his hand in the transaction as all a part of his cynicism and predatory inclinations: a predictable sequel to his invasion of Silesia.

Certainly the partition could only be feebly justified by appeals to law or to historical circumstances and dynastic rights; even Finckenstein, when advising on the boundaries of Prussia should aim to secure, had conceded that the historic claim was not strong.[48] Maria Theresa was said to weep tears of remorse although, as Frederick observed, the tears did not prevent her taking. Certainly the spectacle of three legitimate sovereigns conniving at the forced acquisition of a fourth nation's lands did something to weaken respect for legitimacy. Certainly the resentments produced among patriotic Poles who had been impotent to resist guaranteed a reaction one day. To suffer under a constitution imposed by external powers was hard, and could not last for very long; the revival of Poland would need another patriotic revolution with real rather than superficial reform – and a revolution indeed took place in 1791, by which time Frederick was dead and Europe had been shaken by even more profound convulsions.

The matter could be regarded differently, however. The outcome could be considered an example of reasonable cooperation by powers which all had an interest. It was not Frederick's design – and probably the design of none of them – that Poland should be annihilated, but that an 'aristocratic anarchy', dangerous to Europe, should be replaced. And despite the shock of the partition to Polish pride and feeling, despite the frowns of international lawyers and chroniclers, the actual condition of Poland improved. The imposed constitution, while still imperfect, gave a better chance of orderly government. The material condition of the people had a chance of betterment; so did their education. Foreign visitors soon commented on the great and beneficial transformation brought to the population of Polish Prussia by Prussian rule.[49] And critics of the partition should surely consider the deplorable and anarchic situation of Poland during the previous years – anarchy combined with domestic tyranny. Frederick looked at the matter pragmatically; certainly Prussia had profited, although it was a pity Danzig was not wholly hers. The partition had enabled peace to be brought to a large part of Europe, and had eased the negotiation of peace between Russia and the Ottoman Empire with Austria acquiescent. Against the real benefits could only be set traditional feelings in the 'lowest and most factional nation in Europe', a nation where 'the King sells posts, the women intrigue and decide everything, and their husbands get drunk'.[50]

This, like most of Frederick's comments on Poland, was harsh. In 1768 he had completed his second *Political Testament*. All the time he was continuing, amending and updating his *Histoire de mon Temps*, his commentary on his life and reign, works whose cynicism about human nature increased rather than diminished as the task proceeded: 'Only a man ignorant of humanity can be permitted to trust men!'[51] He could now complete his two volumes on the Seven Years War and begin the next, which would take his story to 1774. There is no hint in these of remorse for the treatment of Poland. In Frederick's eyes the people of this 'frivolous and superficial nation' had received benefits rather than the reverse; and the political nation had richly deserved to suffer such losses as there had been.

The apparent lack of scruple with which three hereditary sovereigns divided between them much of another realm caused a good deal of censure and cynicism: and has continued to do so. The reputations of Catherine and of Frederick were for a certain ruthlessness and rapacity; fairly or not, Maria Theresa had an allegedly more moral name; yet all cooperated in the dismemberment and Frederick wrote that never had there been such harmony of sentiment as that between himself and Panin over the Polish question.[52] 'Perhaps never has one seen,' he wrote, 'such perfect conformity of feelings as that which has existed between me and Count Panin.' The circumstance of Poland's being an elective monarchy surely had a good deal to do with the sentiment of the rulers of the partitioning powers. To annex for simple *raisons d'état* (and there were few others with any plausibility) the kingdom of a hereditary monarch, however practically beneficial the outcome, would have seemed an outrage against the principle not only of property but of legitimacy. Hereditary realms might be subject to dispute, but dispute was over title, comparable to lawsuit over an estate. An elected monarch, on the other hand, albeit crowned, owed legitimacy only to the elective process. In the case of Poland everybody recognized that this was a matter of backstairs dealing between powerful magnates, and of influence exercised by external powers. Popular suffrage, however limited, played no part and was anyway a wholly unfamiliar concept as conferring legitimacy to authority. The position of the elected King of Poland might appear to be strengthened by the assent which election implied but was in reality much weaker than the position of a hereditary sovereign, whose fellow-rulers would at least recognize the principle of their own legitimacy as bound up with his. That Poland, internationally, was weaker in consequence was something Frederick, Catherine and Maria Theresa accepted with complacency.

There was little disposition anywhere to regard the settlement as final, whether or not it was beneficial. 'We won't manage to tame these Poles easily,' Frederick wrote to Solms in St Petersburg in

November 1772. 'I foresee a second partition. And if that happens you will do your best to see that my portion is a good one. Thorn, Danzig, the Vistula to the junction with the Warthe, and the whole course of that river.'[53]

21

Relations with an Old Enemy

In August 1773 Frederick visited Seydlitz at his home at Minkovsky near Ohlau. He would never see the great cavalryman again. Seydlitz had been unhappy in his family life, with two divorced daughters (the younger, indeed, twice divorced), and Frederick had seen little of him in recent years until his last illness – he died shortly after this visit, in November. The heroes and the memories were slipping away.

Peace and general harmony sometimes seemed as remote as ever. It was not only the partition of Poland which suffered from grumbling after-effects. The Russo-Turkish war finally ended in July 1774 with the Peace of Kutschuk-Koinardsche but the settlement in Moldavia and Wallachia was fragile. There were arguments between Constantinople and Vienna, with St Petersburg deeply suspicious of both. The Austrians now had a foothold, earlier obtained by secret treaty from the Turks to Russian anger, in these principalities. Frederick was sure that Kaunitz's ambitions were for a major extension of Austrian possessions in Croatia, and perhaps for Venetian Dalmatia. As to Poland itself, Frederick had completed his part in the dismemberment of that country quickly and effectively. There would remain some dissatisfactions as the partitioning powers found their portions either indigestible or inadequate – Frederick was unreconciled to the situation he had ended with in Danzig – and there were a good many exchanges about the actual limits of territory which had allegedly been agreed.

It was likely that there would be further chapters to the Polish story but for the moment they could wait. Frederick's dominant policy throughout this period of his life – and one of the few constant factors – was his determination to maintain good relations with Russia. When he heard from Henry that Catherine was most unlikely to make concessions to him over Danzig he sighed and accepted, at least for the time being. When he heard that a party of Russian troops had been sent to protect the Jews in Warsaw against eviction from the 'Faubourg' following an order of the Polish Permanent Council,* his sympathy was with the Russians (who had had to withdraw) and he said so; the Jews were then forcibly expelled by Prince Lubomirski. He showered Catherine with letters of congratulation on the victorious end of the Turkish war. He followed with sympathy Russian difficulties with the ferocious rebel, Pugachev – *'cette hydre homicide!'*[1] – trusting that when he was captured Catherine would condemn him to death (she did). And he learned with considerable gratification that Catherine was anxious for another visit to her court by Prince Henry. The invitation, in September 1774, was to be present at the celebrations of peace, and Frederick was determined that his brother should go, although he suspected it would not be wholly congenial. He, himself, was relishing a visit from his sister Charlotte, Duchess of Brunswick, who enjoyed social life, entertainment, balls, concerts, and whose company had cheered Frederick a good deal – 'She loves her country and her family,' Frederick wrote to Henry; and he liked showing off the cultural achievements of Berlin – there had been a *diva* at the Opera since 1771 with extraordinary agility of voice and theatrical ability, Elizabeth Schmeling, and such distinction gave Frederick much pride. Charlotte continued her journey to Rheinsberg, to visit Henry.

Frederick had some difficulty in persuading Henry that his duty lay in acceptance of Catherine's invitation;[2] the Russian connection was at present crucial to Prussia's position and it was clear Henry had established a rapport with her. Frederick's relationship with Henry was, at this time, particularly gracious. Some commentators have emphasized periodic jealousy between the two; nothing of the sort can be detected from their correspondence, however suspiciously analysed. Frederick's expressions, consideration, gentle humour, all convey affection just as Henry's, despite rough words in private, exude admiration and respect. Frederick was anxious, and often wrote, that his brother should have some sort of supervisory role in the state after

---

* The Permanent Council, inaugurated after the partition settlement, had thirty-six members elected to two Houses, biennially. The King of Poland presided.

his own death. Henry was a devoted and talented servant of Prussia and Frederick's every line makes clear that the King appreciated it. Henry, furthermore, could argue, oppose. Sometimes he thought Frederick's suspicions – particularly of some line of Austrian conduct – a little paranoid and he would say so: sometimes rightly, sometimes not. At other times it was Henry who was obsessed with ideas of Austrian *revanchism*, and Frederick who would tell him not to fuss, that Austrian moves were routine. Neither had a monopoly of foresight or wisdom but their exchanges were frank and free. And in the spring of 1776 Henry eventually set out again for St Petersburg, more than a year after the initial invitation.

By this time Frederick had met the Tsarina's previous lover, the legendary Prince Orlov, who visited Berlin. He had naturally always followed Orlov's fortunes from afar. Orlov had been ill in 1773 and Frederick remarked that he had, it seemed, good natural sense and that 'in a year it's said he'll be up to all his duties, except f—ing! That's lost for ever!'[3] 'I tell you frankly,' he wrote to Henry,[4] 'I liked him better than the great majority of Russians I've seen. He gives an impression of candour and sincerity . . .' Orlov, however, had been replaced in Catherine's affections by Alexander Vasilchikov and in July 1774 Frederick noted that he had been completely disgraced. Vasilchikov was soon to be followed by the extraordinary Prince Potemkin. Frederick's long-serving ambassador in St Petersburg was Count Solms, and Solms periodically complained about the length of time it took to get anything done in St Petersburg, largely because of the Tsarina's '*dissipations amoureuses*' which led her to neglect business.[5] Through Solms Frederick kept Catherine well informed of the tides he thought running in central European affairs, with Henry – during what turned into another exceptionally successful visit – able to give a helpful complexion to all.

There were also, however, urgent and connected family affairs. Catherine's daughter-in-law, wife of the Grand Duke Paul, had recently died in childbirth. Frederick had worked hard to arrange the marriage and the loss was grievous for him as well as for the Russian court. Catherine was now looking for another wife for her son and was advised that the eldest of three daughters of Prince Frederick Eugen of Württemberg, Sophie, aged seventeen, would be very suitable.

Her mother was a Princess of Schwedt; Frederick's brother, Ferdinand, had married another Princess of Schwedt; and Frederick's sister, Sophia, had married the Margrave. Frederick had largely supervised the upbringing of the three Württemberg brothers, of whom Frederick Eugen was the youngest – ultimately each succeeded his next brother. They were the sons of Duke Karl Alexander, Imperial Field Marshal, who had become a Catholic, married a beautiful Princess of Thürn und Taxis, and died when they were very young boys, in 1737. They had all been educated in Berlin, so Frederick's influence as well as his relationship was strong; and the eldest brother, Karl Eugen, had married Wilhelmina's daughter, Frederica, in 1748, a marriage which had unhappily ended in divorce.

Sophie was a beautiful girl of sweet disposition. A difficulty was that she was already betrothed, to Ludwig, a prince of Hesse-Darmstadt (the Russian Grand Duke's deceased wife had also been a Hesse-Darmstadt). It was necessary to persuade Hesse-Darmstadt to give up Sophie and to win, thereby, the gratitude and protection of Russia. It was also proposed that, instead of Sophie, Ludwig should marry one of her younger sisters (still under age). Frederick was entrusted with the business and it was agreed that the Württembergs, with their eldest daughter, would come to stay in Berlin where the Grand Duke would pay a formal visit to Prussia and meet his intended bride. Hesse-Darmstadt, as Frederick pointed out, had few options but to acquiesce – he was completely impecunious.

Frederick took immense trouble over the Russian Grand Duke's visit on this occasion. Such occasions must be a credit to the house of Brandenburg. Visitors must see clearly that Berlin equalled Vienna in splendour, despite its reputation as a society where the men were totally absorbed in military matters and uninformed on all others. Henry had now reached Russia and was staying at Tsarskoe Selo; he would return with the Grand Duke, and Frederick's letters to him during the spring of 1776 are full of detail. How many dishes should be served at the midday meal? Forty? Or twenty? What sort of carriage would be suitable, and with how many horses?[6] Did the Grand Duke like tea, coffee or chocolate? Frederick went into the ceremonial at every point – the guards of honour, the placing of triumphal arches, the numbers of attendants.[7] He sadly recognized that he, personally, was less mobile than he had been and he would be accompanying a twenty-two-year-old. 'Parade the regiments at Spandau at eleven o'clock, and *stay mounted*,' he told his brother, Ferdinand, who would have the ceremonial command at one juncture. 'I can't walk! And if we can dine at ground level that will be good – going up and down stairs is very painful.' Frederick suffered from chronic back pains as well as piles. His gout was recurrent and agonizing. That October he had an abscess 'the size of an egg' in the groin, with continuous fever. But the Grand Duke's visit went ahead – he arrived in Berlin, escorted by Henry, on 21 July 1776; and Frederick said, with whatever sincerity he could muster, that Paul had gained the praise of all who met him.[8] The greatest satisfaction, however, lay in the annoyance Frederick claimed he discerned on the faces of the French and Austrian ambassadors. He wrote in warmly eulogistic terms to Catherine. He noted, however, with some anxiety, what he called the Grand Duke's 'natural vivacity',* which might cause offence and which he, Frederick, had tried tactfully to moderate.[9] Nevertheless all went sufficiently well. Sophie married, took the Russian name Maria Federovna and bore the Grand Duke four children.

Frederick now, more even than previously, was conducting all business with maximum secrecy. His natural proneness to suspicion had increased. He was, too, less socially agreeable than he had been, more liable to snub than joke, less happy sitting for hours at dinner with his intimates, more moody. He was also often ill-tempered with servants, a new trait. He broke his flute over the head of a hussar, a favourite orderly, and he gave up playing in 1772. He would aim kicks and cuffs when angry. Affability, which had once so marked him, was being succeeded by reclusive peevishness. The earlier charm had given place, sadly often, to harshness and sullenness. He was sometimes thoroughly inconsiderate. He would say that he proposed to attend guard mounting at Potsdam and cancel at the last minute. The servants called him '*Brumm Bär*', the grumbling bear. And, unlike his former self, he was angry if he detected this sort of resentful mockery, and punished it. When he found an orderly had called the King 'the Bear'

---

* He later went mad.

in a letter to his mistress he made him write a postscript – 'Several weeks will pass before I see you because I must now set out for Spandau'; and the man was then consigned to the Spandau guardroom, although only for a short time. This sort of thing was disagreeable. It was also out of true character.[10] More in character was the incident of a gardener new to Sans Souci who began work early in the morning and was approached by a man he didn't recognize, who remarked that he seemed to be starting work very early.

'Yes indeed! If the Old Bear arrived and nothing was happening there'd be the devil to pay!' Frederick chuckled. 'Quite right! Keep that in mind!'[11]

But despite fits of irritation he generally maintained an impressive control of ill-temper. He had suffered the loss of a large part of the handwritten manuscript of his *Histoire de mon Temps* – the chapters dealing with the Seven Years War – when the carelessness of a page allowed it to be burnt on the fire; and had, after a pause, simply said – 'Well, I'll have to write it again.'[12]

Frederick was getting visibly older and was conscious of it. He had always been somewhat contemptuous of the judgement of others and this was now more marked. He heard with sardonic amusement that Voltaire had composed some verses on war – 'I don't doubt he wants to give us some lessons on tactics!' Voltaire's verses (which Frederick did not see for some time) were disobliging about him:[13]

> Past master in this art, so full of horror,
> He is a more accomplished murderer than Gustavus or Eugene.

The poem ended – 'I *hate* these heroes – it is useless to tell me of their admirable behaviour. To the Devil with them.'

Frederick, despite Voltaire, increasingly felt that only he understood the world, and that on the whole mankind was a poor thing. This certainly applied to his fellow-sovereigns. 'Don't show surprise,' he told Henry, 'when the Emperor and the King of Denmark exchange witticisms – men, stupidly, attribute talent to anyone with power. Instead, such people should be treated like children who stutter, yet win approval for things which in an adult would be called mediocre!'[14] And he wrote with some amusement that he heard Maria Theresa treated the Emperor like a naughty little boy (*'polisson'*).[15] But despite his cynicism about royal personages, Frederick firmly defended the principle of monarchy and valued the respect shown to office and to form.

Henry's Russian excursion came at the end of an episode of particular family disturbance, troubling to Frederick. Some years earlier he had heard that the Queen Consort of Denmark, Caroline Mathilda, had been placed in arrest in the early hours of 18 January 1772, by order of her husband. Christian VII had been made to sign the order by his stepmother, the Queen Dowager, when the latter discovered that the young Queen was planning to have herself proclaimed regent, on the grounds of her husband's insanity. The Danish relationships were close. Caroline Mathilda was a daughter of the late Frederick, Prince of Wales, a sister of George III of England, and thus a near cousin of Frederick. Her mother-in-law, who had died some years previously, had also been her aunt, a daughter of George II and Frederick's first cousin. Her father-in-law, the late King of Denmark, had then married Juliana Maria, a princess of Brunswick-Wölfenbüttel and a sister of Frederick's queen; and it was this lady, now the Queen Dowager, who had taken strong action in respect of her stepson's wife.

The development was not entirely surprising. Christian VII was said to be often drugged and insensible. 'Is the King *rational*?' Frederick asked his man in Copenhagen, von Arnim.[16] Nevertheless the situation was packed with scandal. Johann Friedrich Struensee, a brilliant philosopher and physician, had gained a powerful position at the Danish court. He had spread the story, which some thought exaggerated, of the King's madness; had bullied him ostentatiously, had treated the Danes with undisguised contempt and had made himself virtually dictator of Denmark. He had also become the lover of the frightened young Queen Caroline, and was the supposed father of her child.

Struensee was not a Dane. He had been born at Halle in Saxony, and was generally hated. He was, however, formidably clever: Frederick wrote one of his imaginary *'dialogues des morts'* (a form he enjoyed) as a conversation between Struensee, Choiseul (object of dislike) and Socrates! The Queen Dowager's coup was popular and Struensee, lamented by few (although not all his rule had been bad), had been condemned to be beheaded, drawn and quartered; and the sentence was carried out at the end of April 1772. The Danish affair had horrified the courts of Europe, including the several-times-related Frederick, and was, of course, particularly difficult for the King of England. Frederick said that George III, despite his natural concern for his sister, could not possibly adopt a high tone on her behalf, given her behaviour. His best policy would be to take things as quietly as possible – and certainly not (as idle talk suggested) send a fleet to bombard Copenhagen! He wrote, with a certain *Schadenfreude*, to his niece of Orange saying what a consolation it was that theirs was not the only family to suffer public scandal![17] There was a royal divorce in Denmark and the unfortunate Caroline Matilda died, to Frederick's loudly expressed relief, in May 1775.

Juliana Maria, Queen Dowager of Denmark, his sister-in-law, maintained a lively correspondence with Frederick; she was one of the few to whom he wrote with frankness. He trusted her intelligence and her forceful actions in 1772 undoubtedly reinforced his esteem. Sometimes he even referred to her sister, his wife, in letters – 'She [Elizabeth Christina] is not entirely recovered from her inflammation of the skin – it's been necessary to make an incision. You would laugh at us, a couple of lame creatures from whom you couldn't make one healthy leg from the four!'[18] It would be pleasant to think that he was now more agreeable about that sad lady, by now and understandably a victim of hypochondria and depression, she whom her chamberlain, Lehndorff, called 'My good, fidgety, old queen',[19] while admitting that social intercourse was a terrible trial. Frederick sometimes assembled the family at dinner with her, but her pleasures were few and even when she hoped to show the gardens at Schönhausen to a visiting princess it poured with rain! But most of Frederick's letters to Juliana Maria were concerned with the affairs of Europe, and he complained at the frequency of letters in which she asked his advice and expressed her perplexity or distress. 'I have no ambition,' he once told Finckenstein, 'to be her political director!'[20] He sometimes found it necessary to humour her – she found fault with the Prussian envoy, von Arnim, for some alleged failure in protocol and Frederick, although believing him to be the victim of an intrigue, removed him. Relationships had become too bad for Arnim to act effectively in Copenhagen.

In family business, a particular – and increasing – source of Frederick's discontent was his lack of empathy with his heir, Frederick William, the Prince of Prussia; and he also disliked the Prince's mother, doubly his sister-in-law, a sister of his own queen and August Wilhelm's widow. 'I have here now,' he wrote to his sister Amelia, 'the good old Princess of Prussia. She's quite a burden and I wish she was already on her way back to Berlin. She and her son spread a cloud of boredom and distaste!'[21] Frederick William's marriage had foundered and ended in divorce; and he had married again, a Hesse-Darmstadt, although his mistress was the chief influence in his life. Frederick, nevertheless, took a great and responsible interest in his elder nephew's family. He wrote to him in March 1773 that he wholly agreed with the idea of finding a governor for his son, little Frederick William (born to the second wife in 1771), and taking him out of the hands of women – 'provided one could find the right person – not easy – and did not hurry over the choice'. And he concerned himself in the appointment.[22] Frederick longed for an heir he could trust and love; such a one had been Frederick William's younger brother, Henry, whom the King never ceased to mourn. He found Frederick William, by contrast, large, stupid, and a bore, although he was generally considered friendly and amiable. An inveterate pursuer of women, the Prince of Prussia was also extravagant, and was so congenitally short of money that he was said to be unable even to meet his laundry bills.[23]

But Frederick was naturally concerned with the fragility of the male Hohenzollern succession. After the Prince of Prussia and whatever descendants he could produce there came the family of Frederick's youngest brother, Ferdinand. Ferdinand had one son who died as a child and a daughter who also died young; and there were stories about Ferdinand's relations with his wife, Elizabeth Louise of Schwedt. Countess Hohenthal (later Lady Paget) wrote in her memoirs that 'Frederick the Great left nothing untried which could produce a male heir for the house of Hohenzollern and placed all his hopes on his sister-in-law, Elizabeth Louise. From his officers he chose one, Major von Schmettau, and entrusted him with this delicate mission; and soon the childless Elizabeth Louise was pregnant and brought a daughter into the world, who later married Prince Anton Radziewill . . .'[24]

Whether this exercise in outbreeding actually happened must be speculative. It was not true to say that Elizabeth Louise was childless – she had already produced two, who died young, before the infant who became Princess Radziewill. Elizabeth Louise had, however, many admirers. Lehndorff, the Queen's chamberlain, visited Ferdinand's court at Friedrichsfelde in 1771 (the year after the infant's birth) and noted: 'I would not like to be here long – a third person feels uncomfortable. The Prince is much alone, the Princess draws her ladies apart and spends a lot of time whispering with Schmettau, while the Prince prefers Marwitz . . .'

So that perhaps Frederick's anxieties had foundation. Nevertheless Elizabeth Louise produced another son, Frederick Ludwig, soon afterwards, a birth which delighted the King and was hailed with great joy and ceremonial gun-salutes.

All marriages and connections and disputes within his enormously distended family tended to be referred to Frederick. 'There are unfortunate quarrels between our sister of Sweden and her son,' he told Henry in 1775. 'I'm very annoyed. Our Swedish nephews are still very young, they've got spirit but little good will. I'm afraid it may come to a breach with their mother and I won't be able to prevent it . . .'[25] And he could never resist exchanging teases and quasi-irreligious views. When a Hesse-Darmstadt princess, because of a Russian marriage, was converting to the Greek Orthodox Church, Frederick noted that there was an ancient disagreement with Western Christendom over a central tenet of the Creed, the debate over the relationship between the Persons of the Trinity. He heard from the Landgravine of Hesse: 'The Empress [Catherine of Russia] has ordered me to tell your Majesty that as Head of the Greek Church she will prove to you, as sure as two and two make four, that the Holy Spirit proceeds from the *Father*, not from the *Father and the Son*.' Frederick quoted back the Council of Nicaea, as authorizing the change to *filioque*, but, 'I promise never to be *difficult* about this!'[26] He would intersperse this sort of thing with hard diplomatic business or family news; and it was the mix of the facetious, the affectionate, the formidable, and sometimes the learned, which gave his letters their especial flavour.

Family letters were also exercises in diplomacy. His relationship with his sister Ulrica of Sweden had always been warm, despite

Sweden's joining the coalition of his enemies in the war. When his brother-in-law, Adolphus Frederick of Holstein-Gottorp, King of Sweden, died in 1771 there was, however, something of a constitutional revolution. The new king, Frederick's nephew Gustavus, was pro-French and imposed a limited but stronger monarchical system in 1772. This was seen as something of a triumph for France and a setback for Russia. Frederick had always urged friendship with Russia, and he was concerned, although Gustavus later became one of the most talented sovereigns of the age.

He still savoured gossip. 'We have here an Englishwoman by name Mme *Coucou*,' he told Henry in July 1773. 'She may come to Rheinsberg and you'll be luckier than me, she hasn't shown herself yet . . .' This was Lady Coke, born a Campbell of Argyll and daughter-in-law of an Earl of Leicester whose honours had lapsed, a lady of famous eccentricity who had carried on a savage feud with her husband over many years. Frederick liked informing himself about every visitor. And he still enjoyed keeping his ambassadors up to the mark with frequent rebukes for the inadequacy, wordiness, or dullness of their dispatches, as well as for any complaints they had dared make. Von Arnim, when moved from Copenhagen, had relieved von Borcke at Dresden and had grumbled about the hardships of the journey. Frederick: 'I'll try to improve things and arrange roses and flowers strewn along the route. Messieurs, you have fragile nerves, health, chests! You need delicate preservation! You are collectors' pieces, precious, unsuitable for exposure to the fresh air. Fresh air is only good for *men*!'[27]

Frederick took pleasure in the fact that in 1773 he had welcomed the Jesuit order to Prussia; the order had been declared unacceptable in many, including Catholic, countries after dissolution by an order of the Holy See. His action outraged many of the politically correct Enlightenment. Frederick had always admired the Jesuits' work, particularly in the sphere of education, and he told the Catholic Dowager Electress of Saxony, frequent correspondent and friend, that: 'If your Royal Highness approves of the Pope [Pius VI was newly elected] it prejudices me in his favour. I only hope he won't persecute what's left of the Society of Ignatius. I've saved them from total shipwreck.'[28] Actions of this kind were thought contrary by much of the world, and Frederick enjoyed them the more.

He heard with less enjoyment, however, that this Saxon Dowager Electress was proposing to write her memoirs[29] and, *inter alia*, to say that the present Elector was really the son of a previous French Ambassador, the Marquis des Issarts. Frederick's reaction was commonsensical. It was known that the Electress had long wished to replace the Elector, Frederick Augustus, by her second and favourite son, Charles Maximilian – who was likely to be more under her influence. There had, indeed, been one appalling story, disbelieved by Frederick, that she had planned to poison the elder son.[30] Frederick simply regarded the present nonsensical tale as a further attempt by the Electress to push the fortunes of her younger son and discredit the paternity of the elder. That she, herself, would be incriminated by the allegation would trouble her little. And it was, Frederick said, inherently incredible. If there were anything in it, the time for disclosure would surely have been when the late Elector died; not now. Little of this disturbed Frederick's exchanges with the lady.

Throughout these years Frederick watched with an interested and on the whole unfriendly eye the troubles of Britain with her American colonies. His sense of having been betrayed, let down, by Britain in the Seven Years War went very deep. He could affect to discern the lingering influence of Bute in almost every unwelcome development. 'Their Bute has gone mad,' he wrote to Henry in November 1772. 'I maintain that he always has been, but by their inattention they've only just noticed!'[31] He was savage in his denunciation of what he saw as the follies of British ministers, bringing disaster upon their country by hamfisted policy towards the American colonists and then lacking the strength or strategic wisdom to deal with the ensuing situation. Nor was he always wrong. Throughout 1775 and 1776 he constantly told von Maltzahn, his man in London, that the American business would turn into something much bigger and with more lasting consequences than the British Government supposed.[32] At first he imagined that militarily the colonists could not last long – regular troops and artillery would surely be decisive[33] – but this did not continue and by August 1775 he was writing that, despite the bulletins, the British had been beaten by the colonists.[34] He was astonished at the improvidence and dilatoriness, as he described it, of the British authorities.[35] They seemed to be unprepared, short of transports, and not taking the matter seriously. He was surprised the government was not dismissed by popular indignation and ascribed it to parliamentary corruption.[36] He had initially been prepared to bet 'one hundred to one' on British victory. No longer.

Frederick also watched with some cynicism British attempts to raise more troops from elsewhere. He heard that they were negotiating for a Russian corps of 30,000 men in return for a large subsidy and did not think that Catherine would agree. There was a Scottish brigade in the Dutch service which Frederick did not think it possible for the Dutch to retain[37] if it were requested back, but it was very weak – six small battalions, 2,100 men. At the beginning of 1776 twelve battalions of Hessians were reported to be bound for America[38] and Frederick was asked by the Duke of Württemberg his opinion on a British request for a corps of 3,000 men. He advised the Duke to think carefully and to seek a British guarantee if the French – neighbours of Württemberg in Alsace – reacted with hostility, as they might.[39] He acknowledged the financial attraction of compliance, naturally; and Württemberg was poor. He was doubtful whether many of the German auxiliaries in the British service would remain loyal to their colours if chances of desertion offered. It was, however, clear that the American war was consuming numbers of men; and so would the garrisons which would be necessary afterwards, even if the fighting were brought to a successful conclusion.[40] He professed detachment from the whole business, and certainly was not minded to help – 'Only in the last extremity would I make another alliance with her [Britain]' – since the past had demonstrated British bad faith in fulfilling engagements.[41] He said that he wouldn't supply two files of Prussian soldiers to help the British, for all the millions imaginable. They had acted to him like an enemy, despite alliance; and were obstructive about his Polish acquisition and ambitions, particularly for Danzig. Even if the French invaded Hanover, he said, it would bother him little.[42]

The American colonists were maintaining agents in Europe and seeking some sort of representation, commercial and no doubt one day diplomatic. Frederick was properly cautious. These ideas were premature, he said. The only desirable import from America was

Virginian tobacco, and he could never do anything to protect trans-atlantic trade.[43] He also, and incidentally, spoke with the utmost horror of the trade in negroes which he called a blot on humanity. He could not possibly have a major breach with Britain by an improper association with rebels against the crown, a formally friendly crown. Nevertheless he was sure after some months that the colonists would win their independence and keep it – British policy, in fighting a war with no allies and with less than whole-hearted public support, was self-defeating.[44] Lord North's government would be turned out one day.

Frederick was unimpressed by the military operations of Howe, Cornwallis, Burgoyne, which he followed closely. He supposed that France must enter the war with maritime operations before long – he thought Britain might deliberately provoke this in order to produce more popular support and money for the war. There was now a new Chief Minister in France, the Duc d'Aiguillon, a man of no great ability. A struggle against France could touch patriotic British nerves, which a war against colonial kith and kin could not. On the other hand he could not believe France would neglect her opportunity, with Britain so committed in America. Since he had little disposition to help the British, when his permission was asked for the movement of troops through his territory from Hanover and Hesse he refused it, saying that earlier parties of that kind had committed disorders. Anyway, the independence of the American colonies was now inevitable; George III, he wrote, had got what he deserved.[45] Whatever happened it was all going to be very expensive[46] and take a long time, during which the British would think of little else. He heard that the extravagance and luxury in England was inordinate, he wrote somewhat unctuously.[47] Frederick was, nevertheless, unfailingly cour-teous to individual British visitors. General Conway, sometime Secre-tary of State, saw the King at Sans Souci in 1774 and recorded how graciously he was received – and how each of Frederick's dogs had a special chair to which it could climb, with a special step placed by it to ease the ascent! Conway was also deeply impressed by the planning and elegance of Potsdam itself.

There was now a new British Ambassador in Berlin. Harris – 'Honnête homme,' Frederick wrote approvingly, although they were never intimate – had been sent to St Petersburg, to Frederick's annoyance. His successor was Hugh Elliot – 'God knows what hare-brained Scotsman they'll find,' said Frederick. Initially the King made difficulties, telling von Maltzahn that he understood Elliot was very junior, 'only a captain', and not nobly born; Frederick would, he said, certainly one day show the British what he thought of this by replacing von Maltzahn by some 'old captain from a Free Battalion', a person of no diplomatic consequence.[48] Maltzahn did his best to clear things up. Elliot was young, certainly – he was twenty-five; but he was well-regarded, of an ancient Scottish family,* son of a baronet, a man of charming wit and character. He arrived in the autumn of 1776.

Elliot's start was inauspicious. One of the American agents in Europe, by name Lee, was in Berlin with companions. Their very obvious mission was arms purchase and Elliot, as almost his first diplomatic task, was watching them. Lee's portfolio case was removed on a June evening in 1777 from his room in the inn where he was staying and the contents were examined. Elliot was challenged on this and admitted that he had told his staff to watch the Americans but had not authorized the theft of documents. He was apologetic, and said that he would repeat his apology to the King. 'That's what I call a *public* theft,' said Frederick. He was angry at the breach of protocol, but somewhat impressed by Elliot's frankness. He said that no doubt this was the conduct taught '*dans l'école de Bute*',[49] and he remarked that his own tolerance was in sharp contrast to the ill will shown by Britain over such matters as Danzig! But 'Don't take it too severely,' he said to his ministers.[50] There was always something in Frederick which enjoyed a bit of rascality.

Elliot was a diplomatist of considerable intelligence and skill. He soon, however, fell in love with a very beautiful sixteen-year-old Berliner, by name von Krauth, and married her in 1778. And then the lovely young Mrs Elliot was unfaithful to her husband with a handsome aide of Prince Henry's, a Knyphausen. Elliot caught her *in flagrante*, removed her child, a daughter, and drove with the infant to Copenhagen.[51] Thence he set out in pursuit of Knyphausen, who was racing for Mecklenburg with Mrs Elliot, and caught them. Knyphausen at

---

* He was the younger brother of the 1st Earl of Minto, ennobled in 1797.

first refused a challenge, was attacked by Elliot with a stick and ultimately accepted. They met next morning (after Knyphausen had allegedly tried to make off during the night) and exchanged shots. After one shot Knyphausen signed a letter of abject contrition; and in 1783 there was a divorce, with the lady thereafter shunned by respectable society. By then, however, Elliot had been transferred to Copenhagen.

Prince Henry was infuriated by this flurry affecting his personal household. Such incidents enlivened diplomatic life and were not particularly unusual. 'Berlin,' Harris remarked, 'is a city with no honest man and no chaste woman. The women prostitute their persons to the best payer, the men are impecunious and extravagant.'[52] This was not the image of his capital that Frederick had hoped to cultivate. Harris thought it owed something to Frederick's own irreligion and neglect of moral duties, and it may be true that the general tone of Berlin was becoming somewhat decadent by the austere standards of a Frederick William. Visitors commented on the prevalence of unabashed prostitution, but also on the agreeable ease and informality which they found – in striking contrast to the caricature of Prussian stiffness they had expected.

Frederick's eyes were never far from Austria. He had accepted – connived at – the increase of Austrian territory at Polish expense in 1772. He had noted Austria's acquisition of territory in Wallachia by a secret treaty with Turkey in 1771. He frequently adverted to what he called Kaunitz's duplicity. 'They're relieving their man in St Petersburg, Lobkowitz, because he's honest!' he told Henry. 'He'll be relieved by the son of Kaunitz who'll intrigue against the Tsarina and us!' He reckoned that if any power were called upon to check Austrian pretensions once again it would inevitably be Prussia. It would never be possible to manoeuvre either France or Britain into opposing Austria, he told Henry in a long letter about the state of Europe at the beginning of 1775.[53] It was apparently hopeless to try to persuade the Turks to resist Vienna. The French appeared enmired in frivolity, accompanied by financial chaos.[54] Britain was absorbed in America and her troubles there; and Russia was exhausted, with the Tsarina determined (rightly) to concentrate on reforming the laws and (wrongly) to give enormous gifts to personal favourites. It could happen that, once again, Prussia might stand alone.

For Austrian pretensions were, once again, very real. In July 1775 Frederick wrote to St Petersburg of rumours – little more – that the Austrians had well-matured plans to partition Bavaria when the present Elector died; to divide territory with France, including the Austrian Netherlands – all largely nonsense. What was not nonsense, however, was an Austrian plan simply to take possession of the Bavarian Electorate – the richest in Germany. Henry – in this more alarmist than his brother – felt sure that this would happen and must be opposed. Frederick – a little incredulous – doubted if such a move could be prevented in the first instance. It could involve major war and the formation, somehow, of an anti-Austrian coalition which looked improbable. It would be better to persuade others such as the Elector Palatine and his heir, the Duke of Zweibrücken, to take the initiative. Prussia might act as support, as an auxiliary.[55] Frederick did not wish to anticipate events. He had a good intelligence source, the Palatine minister in Dresden, Baron von Hallberg.[56] He obtained a paper from the French Ambassador in Vienna which suggested that, when the Elector of Bavaria was dying, Austrian troops would occupy the Electorate and reclaim territories 'proper to Austria';[57] but it might not happen. He also periodically expressed the certainty that when he himself died the Austrians had plans to invade his domains (he meant Silesia),[58] but as to Bavaria it would be better to wait, to keep powder dry. Henry thought him complacent, but was soon absorbed in his own second visit to St Petersburg, which had been arranged at this time, and in the successful promotion of even closer Russo-Prussian relations as well as in the arrangements for the Grand Duke's visit to Berlin. He, like his brother, was sure that Kaunitz was doing his utmost to make bad blood between Frederick and the Tsarina.

Nevertheless Frederick welcomed any gestures of friendship from Vienna, and was delighted to hear that Joseph had ordered a ceremonial salvo of fire by five battalions of Austrian grenadiers, commanded by his friend Nugent;[59] a salvo fired by the tree near Prague where Schwerin had fallen, and done in Schwerin's honour, an act of courtesy and chivalry. Such civilities were appreciated but Frederick, despite reacting to Henry's warnings with a certain coolness, suspected that Joseph would, at some time, try his hand at 'an adventure'. Austria was the only quarter, he was persuaded, in which danger to Prussia lay. The head of the third division of Frederick's General Directory – in effect his foreign office – Wilhelm von der Schulenburg, an astute man, reported in early 1777 that it had been decided in Vienna to seize Bavaria by a *coup de main* on the Bavarian Elector's death.[60] Frederick, of course, always feared Russia, despite the friendship he had worked so hard to strengthen; but Henry told him his fears were now chimerical and Henry had the standing of something of an expert on Russia. Austria was a different matter.

Joseph was planning an unofficial visit* to France – Frederick thought it would largely be directed to soothing matrimonial relations between Joseph's sister, Marie-Antoinette, and her husband, Louis XVI, for whom Frederick had conceived a great contempt. If Louis, he said, could find a great minister, a Louvois, he might, save France, but at present mismanagement of finances was such that some sort of revolution was inevitable.[61] Joseph's visit might, of course, have more sinister motives, but by something of a reversal of roles Henry was now writing about Austria in a consolatory vein – 'Austria's policy is always measured. To begin a war against you would be a ridiculous course of action!' he wrote in September 1777.[62] He was replying to Frederick, who had told him of an observation of Kaunitz: 'The Imperial court should never tolerate the power of Prussia. To master it we must destroy it.'[63] Frederick's mistrust was strengthening again. When he received a gifted young Italian musician with an introduction from the Emperor he was charming to him. The Italian was looking for a position at the Prussian court, but Frederick was perfectly aware that his real task was to act as an informant for Vienna. He granted him an extended interview, marked by great friendliness. Next day, however, the Italian received the King's command: 'Leave Berlin today!'

Suspicions over the Bavarian issue went back a decade, to a time well before the more recent rumours which now had both Frederick and Henry in some agitation. They went back indeed to March 1767, when a certain Count Philip Sinzendorf had visited Berlin. Sinzendorf

* As 'Count von Falkenstein'.

was a nephew of the Grand Prior of the Knights of Malta, the Order of the Hospital of St John, a Catholic order of great age and prestige, sovereign in international law. Sinzendorf had been instructed to look into the possibility of a commandery of the Order in Silesia – an earlier bishop of Breslau had been a Sinzendorf. He had also been instructed to present letters of credence as an ambassador to Frederick.[64] His secret task, however, was to do his best to promote mistrust between Russia and Prussia and to insinuate some ideas about improved relations at that time between Vienna and Berlin. In this he had been Kaunitz's man.

Sinzendorf was of a familiar type, often found on the fringes of international dealings, without very clear position, plausible, agreeable. He was entertaining and popular, he knew everyone and he liked to quote everyone to everyone with a high show of intimacy. Acting almost as a freelance, he would appear on important occasions as if it were unthinkable they could take place without him. When Frederick had been about to meet Joseph at Neisse in 1769 his ambassador in Vienna, Rohd, had remarked sardonically that he would be surprised if Sinzendorf didn't turn up there somehow, 'to have a hand, to meddle!' And to report to Kaunitz.[65]

Frederick had been rightly sceptical of Sinzendorf. He doubted his credentials and his sharp nose scented the whiff of the charlatan. But such persons sometimes let drop something of more value than first suspected, and when, in September 1768, Frederick had heard that Sinzendorf was talking loosely about what would happen when the Elector of Bavaria died he had paid attention. And according to Sinzendorf the plan in Vienna had been, in that eventuality, to move Austrian troops instantly into the Electorate.[66] To take possession.

This might be the gossip of a professional intriguer enhancing his own reputation for inside information; it might be a trouble-maker with whatever motive; it might be a stalking-horse for Kaunitz's ideas. Rohd, when Frederick discussed it with him, had thought it should not be taken seriously. Nevertheless something scored in Frederick's mind. 'What interests me at present,' he had told von Goltz in Paris in August 1769, 'is to penetrate the intentions of Vienna on the Bavarian succession.' And in December that year he had written to Henry, almost as an afterthought, that 'the next possibility of advantage to our house will be when the Elector of Bavaria dies'; prudently adding – 'which may be forty years on'.[67] If there were to be 'possibility of advantage' (or the reverse) the other European powers would be concerned, and Frederick had sent to Panin in St Petersburg a précis of the genealogical background of the interested princely houses. These were the families of Bavaria and the Palatinate. Both, he wrote, were different branches of the Guelphs,* 'the most illustrious family in Germany'. The present head of one branch was the Duke of Zweibrücken, of the other the Elector of Bavaria. The Habsburgs, he had emphasized, *could have no pretensions to either Bavaria or the Palatinate.*[68]

This was somewhat to simplify a complex issue. It was true that Karl Theodor, the Elector Palatine, was head of the so-called Rodolphic branch of the family and that his heir was his nephew, the titular Duke of Zweibrücken. It was also true that the head of the other, the so-called Wilhelmine branch, was the Elector of Bavaria, Max Joseph; and that by an original arrangement, dating from the fifteenth century, the lands of the one would revert to the other in case of extinction. There were, however, more recent arrangements and more controversial factors. First, Bavaria itself had alternately grown and diminished with the years; the Emperor had claimed Lower Bavaria as an Imperial fief by a treaty of 1426 (allegedly renounced three years later). Second, the Dukes of Bavaria had acquired various lands which might, in case of dispute, also revert to the Emperor rather than pass with the Duchy of Bavaria. Next, the Treaty of Westphalia of 1648, still a 'sacred canon' in German affairs, transferred the Upper Palatinate to the south-eastern neighbour, Bavaria, although it was to revert to the Palatines if the Bavarian line were extinguished.

This was genealogical, legalistic, almost antiquarian. More recently and relevantly the Bavarian Elector, Max Joseph, had made a secret family compact in 1766 reiterating the right of the Elector Palatine to succeed to Bavaria; Max Joseph, last of his line, had no immediate family. This family compact was supported by a formal will in 1769, and was renewed in 1771 and 1774. The matter – which to an extent seemed almost straightforward – was complicated by the fact that

---

* Now in most cases known as Wittelsbach.

Karl Theodor's nephew and heir, Zweibrücken, was, by this compact, to have the right to be consulted by his uncle if there were any question of a change in these arrangements; and Zweibrücken learned – and told Max Joseph – that his uncle, the Palatine Karl Theodor, was secretly negotiating with Austria about what should be his, Zweibrücken's, inheritance. Kaunitz – and his young master – had their eyes on Bavaria.

Many factors, therefore, affected Frederick's definite and simple statement of the case, as given in 1769. Time had passed, and it was clear that there might be analogies with Poland, an analogy drawn by those who pointed to the relative backwardness of Bavarian system and government (although Max Joseph, a generous and humane man, had done much for education and economic reform); and the analogy was further emphasized by the existence of powerful neighbours. Austria was thought to have already tried to buy off the claims of the Elector Palatine, not without success.

There were practical advantages, Frederick reckoned, in possessing Bavaria. The strategic position, commanding the Upper Danube, was good. The annual revenue at present was 6 million *écus*.* The population could support an army of 20,000 men. Were Austria to have ambitions in that direction, she could probably expect the opposition of France, but France might always – as had often been rumoured – be offered the Austrian Netherlands as a *douceur*, although such an offer would undoubtedly meet the strong opposition of Britain.

And Austria, surely, must meet the opposition of other German states. Notably, once again, Prussia.

Frederick was still impressive for a man of his age. On the autumn manoeuvres of 1776: 'Mounted from 8.30 until 11,' a French visitor noted – 'gave an audience from 2.15 until 4.30 – standing all the time, no support for any part of the body, no resting of hand on table, eyes clear, colour good . . . half-way through the conversation lifted head and drew shoulders back – talked of poetry, the Jesuits, the theatre, education, literary anecdotes . . .' The King was in most ways unchanged. He spoke with animosity of the Poles as well as with undying hostility for the memory of Mme de Pompadour.[69]

---

* About £18 million, in contemporary terms, or around £1,100 million today (1999).

At the end of December 1777 Frederick wrote to his man in Vienna, Josef Hermann von Riedesel, that he understood the Elector of Bavaria had a sort of smallpox.[70] On the night of 29 December Max Joseph died.

'If the bugle sounds,' Frederick had told Henry, 'we must mount our horses once again!' It seemed that the bugle might now be sounding. Sinzendorf's story of many years before as well as von der Schulenburg's recent assessment and Henry's prognostications had been accurate. It was Austria's intention to occupy Bavaria.

Within days of Max Joseph's death, on 3 January 1778, Kaunitz signed a treaty with the Elector Palatine which recognized his rights as Elector of Bavaria but which conceded Lower Bavaria to Austria, as in that (allegedly renounced) treaty which had lasted only three years three and a half centuries before! This arrangement, if it was allowed to stand, removed from Bavaria one third of its acreage, including the richest land, and accepted Karl Theodor's effective vassalage to Vienna. This was the 'partition treaty'. It was an imposed partition, long planned. It was also in direct contravention of the Elector Palatine's formal announcement a few days before that he would only accept the inheritance of Bavaria undivided.

On 15 January 1779 Austrian troops moved into Bavaria. Frederick heard, two days earlier, that this was imminent and wrote at once to St Petersburg that it would be *diametrically opposed* to the constitution of the German Empire.[71] Kaunitz, it was clear, hoped for the support of France, so zealously courted over the years of war and before; and also had in mind (as often forecast by Frederick) a possible trading, in case of difficulty, of the Austrian Netherlands (to France) in return for the rump of Bavaria (to Austria, with French approval). France, however, disappointed Kaunitz. The French were on the point of going to war with Britain in support of the American colonists, and over Bavaria they decided on neutrality. The British, like the French, were concerned with America. They suspected Frederick of encouraging the French in their support of the Americans. The affair of Hugh Elliot and the American agent, Lee, had not generated much sympathy in Britain for the Prussian point of view; and there was certainly no disposition in Britain to help check the ambitions of Austria or anybody else.

In Berlin there was suspense. Few people supposed that Prussia, which had fought for so long for its independence, and to curtail the power of Austria, would easily tolerate this unilateral move. The 'partition treaty' was clearly an imposed treaty and Karl Theodor now a creature of Vienna. The map of Germany was in danger of being forcibly redrawn by Austrian power. 'One would have thought,' Frederick wrote in his *Histoire*, 'that the partition of Poland would be the last remarkable event in the King's reign. Destiny ordained otherwise.'[72] Germany now looked to Frederick.

22

The Last Campaign

Frederick moved carefully. The crisis was not unexpected but he believed that on this occasion the mobilization of opinion might be as important as the tribunal of arms. It must be possible and was certainly highly desirable to rally as much German sentiment as possible – and not only German sentiment – against Vienna.

Frederick sent for all relevant documents in order to check his facts – treaties going back to the fourteenth century, the will of the Emperor Ferdinand III who died in 1657, the texts of certain articles of the Peace of Westphalia in 1648, copies of the laws of the Empire applicable to alienation and dismemberment.[1] He sent urgently to learn what he could of the Elector Palatine's intentions. He made sure that his man in Paris, von Goltz, was fully briefed on the legalities of the situation so that the French should be clear about it. He was suspicious of Austro-French collaboration although hopeful of French support for the Elector Palatine if he stood by his rights. The French were, he reminded everyone, joint guarantors of the Peace of Westphalia and if they stood apart on an occasion like this they could expect no influence in German affairs in future. 'Demonstrate all your eloquence!' he exhorted Goltz. 'France might even be a gainer!'[2] But he thought it more likely that French policy would be feeble for four reasons – the age of the octogenarian chief minister, Maurepas; the bankruptcy of the French crown; the absorption in rivalry with Britain; and the Austrian connections of the Queen, Marie-Antoinette.

Frederick was getting different and often conflicting reports every day. Some said that Austrian troop movements had been cancelled – troops were simply being held poised at the frontier. Some said that the Elector Palatine had already conceded to Vienna everything in the 'partition treaty'. Others said, more hopefully, that France was determined to support the Elector against any dismemberment of his inheritance – 'Chaos!' Frederick wrote. He was determined to take an ostentatiously legalistic position and he was unsurprised to receive from Vienna an equally legalistic-sounding statement by Kaunitz of the Habsburg claim.[3] His own position, he made clear, must be based on the constitution of the Empire.[4]

Letters were being exchanged urgently with every German court. Frederick had liked Joseph when they met but had thought him a young man in a hurry, rather as Frederick had been when he first came to the throne of Prussia – 'He has brains,' he said, 'and could go far. It's a pity he always takes the second step before the first!' And Frederick was determined not to act precipitately. To the Danish Queen Dowager, Juliana Maria, he quoted the Emperor Augustus – 'Hasten slowly.'[5] It was not always Frederick's way but on this occasion it was wise. He kept his communications open not only to the Elector Palatine, Karl Theodor, but to the latter's nephew and heir, Zweibrücken. The whole Empire, both Catholic and Protestant, he told Goltz in Paris, was outraged by Austrian actions. A large part of Bavaria was simply to be appropriated by Austria under an agreement the Elector Palatine had no right to make. Even Saxony – so often a feeble link – thought Vienna's pretensions fraudulent and suggested cooperation with Prussia.

Frederick planned to draw out any exchanges with Vienna as long as possible. He wrote to Zweibrücken urging him absolutely to reject the 'partition treaty' forced upon his uncle and to stand up for his rights; and he offered Prussian support.[6] He was rewarded by learning that Zweibrücken had done so and, significantly, had refused to accept from the Emperor the Order of the Golden Fleece[7] – a humiliation for Joseph. And Frederick also got possession of a letter from Karl Theodor to Zweibrücken in which he admitted having signed the treaty under Austrian compulsion. Zweibrücken, Frederick heard from Count Goertz – whom he had sent to Regensburg in Bavaria as a special envoy with a wide 'travelling' brief, making contacts as appropriate – was ready to 'throw himself into the arms of the King of Prussia';[8] and Frederick wrote to him with enthusiastic gratitude.[9] He also received with affectionate pleasure messages of support from the widow of the late Elector of Bavaria, Max Joseph.[10] He kept the Tsarina closely informed, and in February he made a formal protest to Austria, following one made by Zweibrücken to the Imperial Diet.[11]

Frederick was, he said, 'prepared to defend the laws and liberties of Germany'. He was gratified by the support he was getting. He was pleased that he had been able to appear as champion of the just claims of an ill-used heir, Zweibrücken, and of a bullied, hoodwinked claimant, Palatine, rather than as a principal acting ahead of all others as often in the past. He reckoned, however, that war was now inevitable. Austrian treatment of the Bavarian succession was an outrage. The Electorate had been betrayed by its ruler into the suzerainty of the Habsburgs. He told Finckenstein that he was ready for a cold response from Vienna to his memorandum and '*je prévois qu'il faudra bien employer l'épée*'.[12]

The 'cold response' from Vienna was received by Frederick at Potsdam on 23 February 1778. It was, he said, so badly reasoned that it could be refuted by any young student of law.[13] He reckoned that by now most of the princes of Germany were united behind the cause he was espousing. The stance to be taken by France must be important, and he sent to Goltz a copy of the Austrian note saying that he simply wished to know whether France intended to remain neutral, to back 'the Tyrant of Germany' (Joseph) or to play the honourable part of guarantor of the Peace of Westphalia.[14] He sweetened this message with some friendly albeit cautious wishes for France's success in her difficulties with Britain.

'Most' of the princes of Germany might be with Frederick and Zweibrücken, but he greatly hoped that on this occasion Saxon support might be secured before hostilities actually began. Frederick learned with some concern from his representative in Dresden, von Alvensleben, that the Elector of Saxony was declaring he would have to take the Austrian side if it came to war, despite the fact that his sister was married to Zweibrücken, a match Frederick had keenly promoted. Such reports, he said, 'made him blush with shame for Germany',[15] and he wrote bitterly to Prince Henry of what 'poor specimens, *pauvres espèces*', these princes of the Empire could be. Alvensleben, characteristically, simply received a sharp note saying how pleased the King would be if his dispatches were less prolix and verbose. He wanted, he said, to know where Austrian troops were and whither moving.[16] On 7 March Frederick wrote seventeen letters, half of them to his generals and wholly concerned with the organization and movement of troops. The winter was coming to an end and with the spring of 1778 a new campaigning season would begin. Reports from Vienna were of Austrian forces concentrating in Bohemia, Moravia and Galicia, establishing a cordon of observation round the south-eastern limits of the Prussian domains. Frederick accepted this calmly. He could not understand what the Austrians would hope to do in Galicia* but he was expecting war and ready for it. He wrote vigorously to St Petersburg about the weakness of the Elector Palatine, the bullying cupidity of Austria, and the hope which must be reposed in the Duke of Zweibrücken.[17]

Frederick understood that the Tsarina was friendly to his position. The attitude of France was, he said, weak and impenetrable, 'lethargy and honeyed words'.[18] They seemed '*pétrifiés*' by the Austrians. Frederick was, however, now receiving more favourable signs from Saxony, despite the earlier reported sentiments of the Elector. The Saxon remonstrance to Vienna, Frederick wrote, had not even received a reply, so arrogant was that court.[19] Frederick played on fears of Austria, offered his friendship and support, disclaimed ambitions; and was rewarded by a military convention between Prussia and Saxony, concerting measures in case of war; the convention, negotiated by Colonel von Zegelin, sent to Dresden for the purpose, was signed at the beginning of April.

The measures agreed with the Saxons[20] assumed having to deal with an Austrian army of 76,000 in Moravia between Olmütz and Königgrätz, a Croat light cavalry force at Gabel, in western Bohemia north of Niemes, and an army of 32,000 near Tetschen. If this was right, Frederick envisaged a largely Saxon advance past Leitmeritz which would lever the Croats out of Gabel and then operate towards Prague, prepared to besiege the city unless a major action against the Austrian army of Bohemia were fought on the way. The Prussian army of Upper Silesia would simultaneously operate from the north, threatening Vienna; the Saxons would operate under Prussian com-

---

* Southern Poland.

mand, and the right wing of the combined army, of which they would form part, would be under the orders of Prince Henry. The army of Upper Silesia would be under Frederick's direct control.

The enemy would thus be forced to look in two directions. The moment for a battle, if ever, would be when the Austrians had significantly weakened one of their armies to reinforce the other. The whole concept would be a two-pronged strategic advance. Whether the Russians would help remained to be seen.

In April Joseph moved his court and headquarters to Olmütz in Moravia.

Joseph – a novel and exhilarating experience – was about to take the field. So far the movements of both sides were characterized as precautionary – deployments to protect the 'just pretensions' of the Emperor, or of the Elector of Saxony, against possible hostile actions of others minded to disturb the peace. This was the customary verbiage of eighteenth-century warfare. In fact the Austrians had occupied parts of Bavaria in defiance of majority German opinion and Prussia, having enlisted Saxony, had decided to march against Austria. That was the military reality and everybody knew it. Frederick expected hostilities to open in mid-April. For the moment, and formally, there was peace, but he supposed that there would soon, under whatever pretext, be Austrian moves into Saxony, and into Silesia and Glatz. If not he would move himself.

Joseph, however, continued to attempt negotiation with Frederick. The Emperor was not facing as monolithic a body of sentiment as Frederick liked to suppose. Some princes – notably those of Hanover (in his guise as King of England) and of Hesse – were committed elsewhere, with troops beyond the Atlantic. The ecclesiastical rulers, prince-bishops, prince-archbishops, were by no means solid in opposition to Vienna (Frederick said, of course, that they had been either intimidated or corrupted).[21] The position of France remained equivocal. The Russians might again become involved against the Turks and were unlikely to welcome other commitments. Joseph did not believe his opponents held all the cards. He offered to recognize Frederick's chosen successors in the Margravates of Ansbach and Bayreuth in return for acceptance of the Austrian position over Bavaria.

Frederick's response was curt. The Emperor, like his predecessors, was answerable to Germany. Emperors had been deposed before now if they transgressed the laws of the Empire.[22] Frederick, as he had determined from the beginning, was taking his stand as champion of the Imperial constitution which, he affirmed, the Emperor was flouting by his transactions in Bavaria. His irreducible demand was for abandonment of Joseph's claims in that Electorate. In telling Solms in St Petersburg how matters stood, he said that he would probably have already had a hard fight with the Austrians before the Russians even believed a war had started – 'Look at the impertinent reply these b—s have sent me!' On 5 April he addressed his generals in Berlin, striking a near-nostalgic note: 'Most of us have served together from our earliest years and grown grey in the service of the fatherland.' Such reflections were true and moving, but not such as to arouse a white heat of patriotic and warlike fervour in his hearers.[23] On 11 April he moved to Glatz and set up his headquarters at Schönwalde, near Silberberg.

The opposing sides, still at peace, were grimacing at each other, with each anxious not to appear the aggressor. 'The aggressors,' Frederick declared vigorously on 13 April to Riedesel, in Vienna, 'are those who have usurped Bavaria!'[24] But the moves on both sides were cautious. A direct exchange[25] between Frederick and Joseph on 14 April, while as courteous as ever, exposed their differences without much equivocation. As to Bavaria Frederick would settle for nothing less than the *status quo ante* and he went so far as to say that Kaunitz, in his last memorandum, must have written in a fit of temper. Further mutually flattering exchanges a few days later changed nothing.[26]

Frederick, nevertheless, reckoned that there could be talk rather than battle until at least the end of May. He had stated his position, and time could help him by making the outrageous character of the Austrian demands more evident; they wanted a large part of Bavaria. He was, therefore, not displeased that a special Austrian envoy, Count Cobenzl, was to be sent to wait on him in Berlin. He told Finckenstein that he supposed nothing would come of this but if there were to be propositions which really satisfied the claims of Zweibrücken he would be prepared to listen.[27] Saxony, now an important ally, would need to be equally satisfied with anything which transpired. It is unlikely that Frederick expected any positive results from negotiation at this stage but he could not appear intransigent. Meanwhile the army was concentrating and he told the Princess of Orange, his dearest niece, that he and his Prussians were like actors preparing to play a new piece but the curtain was not yet up.[28]

There was occasional rebellion among the cast. Frederick was usually a master of detail, but on 12 May Herzberg, Finckenstein's colleague, wrote to Finckenstein that when he read Frederick's latest order about his exchanges with Joseph he could only conclude that Frederick had either failed to read, or had forgotten, the contents of Joseph's previous letter. The point related to the proposals for Ansbach and Bayreuth, but for so frank a criticism of the King to be voiced there must have been disquiet over Frederick's continuing grasp of business.[29] Some of the Austrian officials were forming the opinion – or said they were – that Prussian policy was not now well coordinated. Important men were not being informed about the line taken. This, if justified, reflected on the King.[30] The whole transaction was anyway unsatisfactory. Cobenzl, Austrian envoy with plenipotentiary powers, had gone to Berlin while Frederick – not one to delegate essential matters of peace and war – was at his headquarters at Schönwalde in Silesia. Communications took several days. It is hard to believe Frederick had any belief in this so-called negotiation, although he went along with it, considering propositions and producing 'counter-projects' of his own. These conceded nothing; and he made sure that St Petersburg and Paris were aware of them. He had, he said, spent five long months in a 'flux and reflux of uncertainties', but the spinning out of time was deliberate,[31] whether or not wise. The game had to be played but his mind must have already been on the campaign which would surely come; and lapses like the one noted by Herzberg indicate that that mind was not always what it once had been. Frederick was beginning to fail. He was sixty-six.

Intelligence reaching Frederick now led him to think that if hostilities actually began the Austrians proposed to stand on the defensive, at least initially.[32] The uncertainty as to whether or not war was coming was jading Frederick and his correspondence showed it. On all previous occasions his own decisions and actions had set the pace. Now, although he had welcomed a deferment of crisis and although he was as keen as ever not to appear an aggressor, his nerves were suffering. His letters, although usually as elegant and shrewd as ever, were sometimes repetitive, even rambling. He adverted often, however, to the 'insolent pride' of the house of Austria,[33] the 'unbridled ambition' of the Emperor. 'The court of Vienna doesn't want peace!' he said on 10 June 1778. 'They make vague proposals to us solely so that they can tell the French and Russians they've done all they can for peace!'[34] – there had been frequent exchanges by the medium of Cobenzl.

Frederick was irritated by the coolness of the support he was getting from St Petersburg, although it was to an extent explained by news of fresh Russo-Turkish clashes and of a Turkish invasion of the Crimea. He had expected little better than neutrality from Versailles, despite his reminders that the French were guarantors of the Peace of Westphalia, now being broken by the Austrians; the French had, however, refused actually to help Vienna. Frederick was now, without question, longing for the relief of tension which only military operations would bring. 'We are at the *dénouement*,' he told Finckenstein on 14 June[35] while waiting for Kaunitz's latest response. 'It will be as inadequate as all the others.'

There was a sense of unreality in the situation, nevertheless. In any development of crisis there has to be a certain change of perception for men to accept that argument, negotiation, is to be succeeded by actual armed force; and that the moment for this has arrived and cannot be avoided or postponed. In past wars Frederick had generally acted first, taken the initiative, presented his opponents with a *fait accompli* and then mastered developments. Now war was apparently to be undertaken from, as it were, a cold situation, a standing start. Frederick argued, and very comprehensively, that the cause was legitimate and good. But the conflagration of war needs a spark to be struck and despite the Austrians' (peaceful and unopposed) occupation of certain Bavarian territories there seemed no spark here. Frederick's brothers, Ferdinand and Henry, were both disturbed by the situation;[36] and Henry was further worried by the military and logistic difficulties he foresaw. Frederick tried to reassure him; unsuccessfully. Henry, who had believed for some time that the situation might be resolved by negotiation and territorial bargaining, remained critical.

Not only Frederick's brothers demurred. Herzberg, in Berlin, wrote a careful memorandum on 27 June. The Elector Palatine (unworthily, as Frederick angrily believed) had been able to come to terms with Vienna, however unjust the Austrian behaviour. Might Frederick, Herzberg asked, not enter another protest to the Imperial Diet? He could point out that Vienna had rejected all his reasonable proposals for peace. He could again present all the legal arguments and request a formal adjudication not by the Emperor – judge in his own cause – but by the Diet. This line of action could not fail to be applauded by France, Russia, Britain and most of the states of the Empire, whether Protestant or Catholic; and would be consistent with Frederick's obligations towards Saxony and towards Zweibrücken. It would be hard for Austria to oppose the idea of such an adjudication – at least without attracting universal obloquy. The difficulty, Herzberg acknowledged, would be to put military measures in reverse, and there would have been wasted expenditure; but it might be worth the sacrifice of 'a couple of millions', to avert the risks of war and secure such general support.[37]

Frederick's response was in two lines. 'Go for a walk and take your unworthy ideas with you! You were made to be a minister for cowardly creatures like the Elector of Bavaria. Not for me!' This was the mood of 'the army is ready'. The mood of December 1740. On 5 July Prussian troops crossed the Bohemian frontier.

Prussia and Saxony were at war with Austria. War was declared on 3 July 1778. Bavaria, formally, was neutral.

Frederick's plan was simple. The Austrians would be persuaded to abandon their pretensions in Bavaria by the well-tried expedient of a Prussian invasion of Bohemia and Moravia, supported by 20,000 Saxons. Bohemia is naturally defensible, with mountains, forest and rugged country marking the northern, north-western and north-eastern frontiers. The Prussian-Saxon forces would invade on a broad front so that the enemy would be kept on the wrong foot, threatened from several directions. Prince Henry commanded a western force, a right wing, operating from the Dresden area and directed on Prague. The main, or eastern force, the left wing, would be commanded by Frederick and would operate from Silesia and Glatz across the

Riesengebirge towards the Upper Elbe – little more than a stream at that point – around Königgrätz. This was consistent with his earlier convention with Saxony.

Frederick, starting from Glatz, crossed the frontier near Nachod in the old style, drums beating, bands playing; Nachod was a domain of Prince Piccolomini, the Austrian commander, and was always one of the main gates out of Silesia. On the same day, far to the west, Henry marched out of Saxony. There was little chance of strategic surprise. Not only had the preliminaries and the diplomatic exchanges been near-interminable but the Austrians had been conducting the Bohemian campaign against Frederick so often in the last three decades that matters were not unlike a well-rehearsed peacetime exercise. The two most skilled Austrian commanders, Loudon and Lacy, were in the field confronting, respectively, Henry and Frederick. Loudon was deployed on the Iser at Münchengrätz and warding the Saxon-Bohemian border, with his centre at Niemes. Lacy – in Frederick's stated view, the most able Austrian commander of his generation – was on the Upper Elbe where it runs from north to south and then turns west near Pardubitz. The two parts of the Austrian army, numbering more than Frederick's earlier estimates, exceeded in total the sum of the Prussians and Saxons. The latter, evenly divided between Frederick and Henry, amounted to about 160,000 men.

The Austrians, with Lacy and Loudon back-to-back although widely separated, had decided to stand on the defensive, as Frederick had forecast. Lacy had a strong position on the line of the Upper Elbe extending for about seven miles between Jaromiersch and Hohenelbe, near where the Upper Elbe flows from the hills, and this position he fortified with defensive works, mines and every device which could make assault difficult. In the west Loudon took up defensive north- and west-facing positions near the Saxon frontier.

The campaigns on the two fronts, west and east, were conducted in isolation from each other in operational terms. In the west Henry, always resourceful despite his reservations about the wisdom of the war, crossed the Bohemian border near Dresden, feinted as if moving by the main route from Plauen, west of the city; crossed the Elbe to the east bank at Pirna and marched by hill passes and minor roads via Rumburg, Tollenstein and Gabel, towards Niemes. 'So fair a plan,'

Frederick told him admiringly, 'has been inspired by a god!' and he said that he would model his own operations on it.[38] By this movement Henry manoeuvred Loudon into withdrawal towards the Iser, and Prague appeared his for the taking if he turned south. At this point, however, Henry decided that he must for a while assume the defensive.

In the east Frederick had assembled his army at Welsdorf, about four miles north of Jaromiersch, and taken stock of Lacy's position. It was disagreeably strong and the Austrian front had been extended by light troops and patrols to an overall length of nearly thirty miles. It would be hard to outflank it and equally hard to slip through it or storm it. Frederick attempted an operation on 16 August. Leaving Welsdorf early, he marched to his old battlefield at Soor and then made a large detour to the north to come at the river around Hohenelbe, where he would join the troops of Prince Karl Wilhelm Ferdinand of Brunswick, and where, with luck, Lacy would have less strength and be less strongly posted.

It did not work. The movement took too long through broken, wooded country and was actively harassed by the enemy's cavalry patrols. To bring up the Prussian artillery proved time-consuming, beyond what had been forecast. When Frederick and his army reached the designated battleground near Hohenelbe it was clear that Lacy had matched his move, side-stepping, and was in equivalent strength across the valley. There was little alternative to assuming, for a while, the defensive. Frederick rode out daily to see where there might be the chance of a coup – fruitlessly. He complained bitterly, as did Henry, at the difficulty of the country, narrow gorges, precipitous slopes, vile roads – a somewhat curious lamentation (echoed by Henry) considering that both knew the Silesian and Saxon borders, the Elbe, the Riesengebirge, pretty well.[39]

Frederick pressed Henry, who was at Lobositz, to exploit his earlier success; to advance at least to the Iser. Henry was unconvinced.[40] He thought the operation risky and the possible benefits questionable. He held Leitmeritz with its bridge and could thus operate on either bank of the Elbe. Like Frederick's eastern wing of the army, the western wing now stood on the defensive. Loudon, upset at having been out-manoeuvred by Henry, was preparing the Austrians to confront a new Prussian offensive on the Iser and Henry did not intend to comply.

Prague had been evacuated but he had no intention of marching deeper into Bohemia towards its capital.

Meanwhile Maria Theresa had decided to play a more personal part. The Empress-Queen was unhappy at the war. She feared for the safety of her son and like her distinguished opponent she had lived through enough death, destruction and despair. In mid-July she sent a personal envoy to Frederick under a safe-conduct, armed with a list of proposals for peace. Frederick, as ever, was effusive in his gratitude and esteem. He did not rebuff this opening of independent communication by the enemy. Separate 'negotiations' – conducted with ministers in Berlin – continued for some time but were ultimately broken off, somewhat to Frederick's relief, in mid-August. They had, he said, been marked by *'finesses et fausseté'*.[41]

The Emperor Joseph had now personally joined his troops. He had played a vigorous part in reanimating Loudon when that great soldier was depressed after his reverse at Henry's hands, and he had done a good deal to restore steadiness to the Austrian command, incidentally winning the soldiers' respect by his fearless demeanour and exposure to hardship. But there had been no major engagement. Neither side, whether western or eastern, could see much possibility of successful manoeuvre. Two – or more precisely four – great armies were confronting each other. Winter was approaching. Men and horses were getting hungry.

Logistics were beginning to dominate all. Frederick's main supply depot was at Nachod, a three-day turnround for replenishment transports,[42] and the supply train was inadequate for the requirement. Every letter from Henry was a complaint about supply and about the difficulties of the terrain, and he got little comfort from his brother. The Prince wrote on 29 August that he could survive until 10 September – no longer.[43] The soldiers were foraging in the countryside and, memorably, digging the unpopular potato so that the war became known as the Potato War. The weather was unusually harsh that year – it was already as cold in Berlin in August as normally at the end of October. There was wastage in the ranks from hunger, dysentery and desertion. Horses were suffering as severely as men, and foraging parties were being punished by the Austrian and Croat light cavalry. In September both the western and eastern wings of the Prusso-Saxon army began to withdraw – Henry by Leitmeritz with the Saxons moving through Zittau and Frederick by Schatzlar, some ten miles north of Trautenau, where he stayed several weeks. Frederick was not in a good mood. He had politely refused a request from the thirty-five-year-old Duke of Gloucester, brother of George III, to serve as a volunteer with the Prussian army, explaining that he could not give appropriate attention to such an attachment; the conditions would be disagreeable and it might be that France would take umbrage.[44]

His chief hope was that the Austrians would run out of money – 'The purses of great princes,' he had written in May, 'act as pulses of their boldness (*impertinence*) or their moderation,'[45] and he prayed that that of Maria Theresa was empty. He was hearing from deserters, and wanting to believe it, that Joseph, too, was in a black humour[46] and that the Empress-Queen was pressing her son towards peace.

In all these circumstances it was singularly courageous for Minister Herzberg, in Berlin, to address another memorandum to Frederick just as the withdrawal of the army was beginning. 'Sire, I hear that your second army is quitting Bohemia and that Your Majesty is obliged to withdraw to Silesia. Thus the campaign is lost – and what hope is there for the continuation of the war?' Herzberg then – more unwisely – gave a detailed assessment of military operations, based on troop count and other factors, admitting that he was neither a military man 'nor presumptuous!'[47] Frederick's reply was brisk but the heavens didn't fall. 'I don't disapprove of your motives in giving me your ideas but you will please me in future by confining yourself to political matters and leaving me to consider the military situation according to my own lights ... everyone should stick to his own métier.' He added that people like Herzberg understood nothing of these matters, were as ignorant as brutes. Military expeditions conceived by ministers were doomed, 'like those of the British in America', whose situation, he said, got worse every day.[48] But the rebuke was measured and did not seem to poison their dealings. Two things occur – that Frederick was persuaded by now that Herzberg was right, albeit for different reasons; and that the fear Frederick could undoubtedly inspire in subordinates was tempered by the sense that honesty would be respected.

The withdrawal had in some ways been disastrous. Henry had lost

3,000 baggage and artillery horses, difficult and expensive to replace. It was, he said, a result of poor quality and incompetence of the officers in charge of horses.[49] Frederick was appalled and said so, and his brother was deeply contrite. By October Henry was ill and the King was concerned about him. Henry had been openly unhappy about the war, but he had played his part in the western theatre with his usual ingenuity and skill; and Frederick had congratulated him with his customary generosity.

Snow fell heavily on 12 October and both armies, east and west, Prussian, Austrian, Saxon, were going into winter quarters. Frederick proposed to winter in Breslau, as so often in the past. The European powers were watching this inconclusive confrontation over the Bavarian succession without enthusiasm. There seemed to be a military stalemate, with neither side minded for anything like a decisive offensive. Both sides were negotiating for wider support without overwhelming success. France, despite being urged by Frederick to play a responsible part as a guarantor of the Peace of Westphalia, was clearly planning to remain carefully neutral. Britain was obsessed with her American losses and with France: she might, on behalf of Hanover, line up with the anti-Austrian German princes but certainly not effectively in military terms. Her navy was irrelevant to the immediate campaign and was anyway simultaneously committed in three directions – in watching the threat of French invasion, in protecting her possessions in the West Indies whence came a large proportion of her wealth, and in maintaining sea communications with an army in North America. She could and would do little effective.

The Russians, who had obligations towards Prussia, had certainly as yet offered no material support. Frederick knew that they were still anxious about the Turks which he understood, but after much negotiation he obtained a small something – an undertaking to make a 'declaration' to Austria, a declaration of support for Frederick and the German states opposing Austria. The Russians also proposed to move troops into Galicia – southern Poland, occupied by Austria after the partition – when Austrian troops moved out, as they planned to do. The possibility of a Russian physical presence might, Frederick thought, provide a helpful pressure point on Vienna. All this went distressingly slowly and, on the whole, disappointingly. Frederick, as often, complained of the extraordinary length of time it took for anything to happen in Russia – actual Russian troop movements, he said, could not fail to have a depressive effect on Austrian morale[50] although such was Russian equivocation that this might never come. When it did come – or was more seriously planned – in the winter of 1778, Frederick learned without enthusiasm that the Russians expected a great deal of logistic support from him, citing paragraphs of the 1772 agreement (for the text of which, shaken, he at once sent); while the eagerly-awaited 'declaration', designed to make Vienna tremble, was phrased in such feeble and 'honeyed' words that it could trouble nobody. Nevertheless Frederick said that he would gladly welcome Prince Repnin to Breslau during the winter to discuss and coordinate future measures.[51]

Frederick maintained an affectionate and often entertaining correspondence with the Grand Duchess, his niece in St Petersburg.[52] '*Si j'entretiens VAI* des sentiments de la haute estime,*' he wrote characteristically, '*elle dira cela n'est rien de nouveau, je la savais depuis longtemps.*' To his sister Ulrica in Sweden he wrote that, 'the campaign has not been brilliant! One must hope that the next will produce brighter opportunities!'[53]

The campaign had indeed not been brilliant. The poor appreciation of the difficulties of the terrain and the inadequate logistic provision were alike remarkable. The underestimate of how effectively the Austrians would be able to conduct a defensive (in the eastern theatre) was striking. There was no major battle – perhaps the one event which might have changed the course of the campaign but perhaps not – and one never appeared easy to provoke or force. The opposing forces were too evenly balanced for much likelihood of manoeuvre. Not until 1915 in Western Europe would a stalemate look so predictable. And nobody had the resources to endure a stalemate.

The political object had first seemed straightforward and defensible. Austria had attempted by unacceptable pressure to enlarge her domains and increase her influence; and Frederick, not unreasonably, had decided that a principled stand on behalf of the princes of the

---

* Votre Altesse Impériale.

German Empire in defence of the Imperial constitution coincided happily with the natural instinct of Prussia to oppose and curb Austria. Politically and diplomatically Prussia seemed to have a strong position.

What went wrong was the military dimension. He had planned the campaign carefully, but in Frederick's earlier campaigns, arguably less defensible in moral or political terms, he had taken the initiative. He had set the pace, and the pace had dictated events. In the war of Bavarian succession he did not. It was a deliberate decision. At the very beginning of the game he had decided to watch and wait and jockey others into positions he designed for them. It was only partially successful.

But undoubtedly what also went wrong was the human dimension. Frederick had lost much of his energy, zest and speed of mind, of that remarkable ability to seem to be everywhere and ahead of events, which had earlier so inspired the army. He was and seemed a great deal older, and how a major battle might have gone none can say. He had always commanded and governed very personally; now his ability to do so was in question.

Frederick spent the winter planning offensive operations for the next year and discussing them. To Henry he wrote on 1 November that he had 40,000 men in Upper Silesia and that its security should thus be assured.[54] There was skirmishing along the borders of Glatz, a few prisoners taken, some minor precautionary marches; but to most of Europe it seemed likely that the episode which had been dignified by the name of war, the war of Bavarian succession, would probably end without major military operations. It was a matter of deciding how to end it.

In November Frederick wrote a long 'justification',[55] a statement of the whole Bavarian succession question. Because Vienna had tried to introduce the succession to the 'Franconian margravates' – Ansbach and Bayreuth – into the business, Frederick needed, once again, to deal with that. Vienna had suggested that there was some equivalence: the Habsburgs might give up claims to Bavaria if Frederick gave up claims to Ansbach and Bayreuth. Frederick was unequivocal. This was to try to change the whole status of the issue. Claims to these margravates (both now also closely connected to him by marriage) were matters of the laws of inheritance, while Austrian occupation and proposed dismemberment of Bavaria was a violent usurpation and a different kind of question, from which Vienna wished to turn the eyes of the world by spurious legal quibbles in a different area. Frederick also affirmed that he had not the smallest intention of yielding in the matter of the Franconian margravates. There was no hint of compromise here, and he told Henry that the Austrians had no desire for serious peace negotiations.[56]

Henry thought that the distaste for war of Catherine and the wisdom of Maria Theresa, despite the fitful enthusiasms of the latter's son, would eventually work for peace. But – on 3 December – he also applied to Frederick for permission to retire. He felt his health unequal to the strains of campaign; and he reckoned his physical weakness was known to the army.[57]

Frederick did not acknowledge the personal request for a fortnight,[58] and then gave no response beyond hoping that his brother's health would recover with a period of rest (Henry was wintering at Dresden). He returned to the matter, however, a few days later, protesting (with truth) that commanders like Henry were hard to find. He hoped the Prince would defer his decision, at least for a little. In fact Frederick had already decided that the best replacement would be his nephew, Karl Wilhelm Ferdinand, Hereditary Prince of Brunswick,* and he sent him detailed instructions on 21 December.[59] Brunswick, Frederick's comrade in the abortive attempted operation near Hohenelbe in August, would command the army of Saxony, warding the Saxon-Bohemian border. He was married to Princess Augusta of Wales.

Prince Repnin had now arrived in Breslau with agreeable messages from Catherine, who nevertheless seemed to think, Frederick wrote acidly in the *Histoire*, that her envoy could descend as if from the Gods of Olympus to dictate laws to suffering humanity. The Austrian reaction to the Russian 'declaration' – disappointingly mild though the latter had been – was moderate in tone and Frederick, like Henry, was now getting news that Maria Theresa had re-established her ascendance over her son and was particularly minded for peace.[60] In December he told Brunswick that, to his astonishment, the Emperor Joseph had agreed to accept mediation. It had been suggested that

---

* 'Hereditary Prince' signified heir-apparent.

France and Russia should jointly act as mediators and at the end of December a plan was drafted for a treaty of peace. Maria Theresa and Frederick were the only sovereigns at war and a peace might be guaranteed by the King of France and the Tsarina, invited by the Electors Palatine and of Saxony, with the Duke of Zweibrücken represented.[61]

Frederick told Brunswick that the surest way to bring the Austrians to the peace table was always to attack them in Moravia and to carry war to the Danube. He was, nevertheless, pleased with the way matters were developing although he knew there would be plenty of horse-trading. Until very recently Austrian claims had, in his view, been pitched absurdly high. The military situation was a stalemate – he had not conquered Bohemia, nor changed the strategic balance by successful combat, but nor had Austria. Mediation was eminently desirable – and hard to get agreed since Russia, a suggested mediator, had a treaty with Prussia and to introduce the Tsarina as an arbitrator in internal German affairs was to create a precedent some found disturbing.

But Frederick was now in extraordinary favour with the German Diet. If the matter was handled adroitly both the King of Prussia and the Empress of all the Russias could be seen as asserting legality against the questionable pretensions of the Habsburgs. Peace 'preliminaries' were now being drafted. They seemed promising; they would, if translated into a treaty, give Bavaria intact to the heir of the late Elector, except for a small triangle of land where the rivers Inn, Salza and Danube meet, which would pass to the Emperor – an area which excluded the salt-mines of Reichenhall but included Braunau and Burghausen. Zweibrücken, recognized as a party to the treaty in his role of Elector-presumptive of the Palatinate, would thus inherit Bavaria. During the drafting sessions a formula, perfectly satisfactory to Frederick, was found for the ultimate inheritance of the 'Franconian margravates'* (Frederick had always supposed these would fall to Prussia in due course in any case). Another formula must be devised, Frederick insisted, to satisfy the concerns of Saxony, including some

---

* Ansbach and Bayreuth, for some time united, anyway, under one Margrave, Frederick's nephew.

indemnity; and Frederick said, loyally, that without this he could agree nothing. In the event this proved something of a sticking point, ultimately resolved by money; 4 million *écus*, payable by the Palatine. If all this could be given treaty form the war would have ended without great loss of life or destruction; and the pretensions of Austria would have been curtailed. Frederick would be seen as the champion of German legality, the prince of virtue.

Meanwhile, waiting for the next reaction from Vienna, he continued to plan vigorous military measures with Brunswick and to hope, nevertheless, for the realization of peace. He discouraged signs of euphoria about Austrian intentions which he discerned in St Petersburg – 'a little less credulity about Vienna in your quarter would be highly desirable!' he sharply told Solms.[62] He was referring to 'the next campaign' in his letters to Henry, and in a letter to the Queen Dowager of Denmark, '*Mon incomparable Reine*', he said that the Emperor was showing more passion for war than ever.[63] Frederick was receiving intelligence of a planned Austrian offensive in the new year towards either Glatz or Lower Silesia – an idea he reckoned he could pre-empt.[64] He had moved his headquarters to Silberberg and in some brisk little operations chased Austrian troops from the borders of Glatz. A source in Vienna had told him that the Austrians were longing for peace, and that the Emperor was drunk every afternoon;[65] Austria was also very, very short of money.

The Austrian reply to Frederick's latest messages – his reactions to the mediation proposals – was received in late February. It did not indicate further unexpected difficulties and proposed a venue for a peace negotiation. Austria, at the urging of Russia, seemed to be accepting all the French mediatory proposals which Frederick, subject to some detailed arguments, had found in essence satisfactory. Frederick told Catherine that so proud a court as that of Vienna had been defeated, not by battle but by a single word from her sacred lips! There were some vigorous Austrian skirmishes on the borders of Upper Silesia in March and an Austrian party led by several generals burned the town of Neu-stadt, destroying 240 houses,[66] but on specified days between 7 and 10 March an armistice was agreed on all fronts. On 11 March the negotiating parties assembled at Teschen, a small town on the borders of Silesia, about equidistant from Vienna and Breslau.

Frederick's diplomacy had been adroit and effective. He had not conquered in the field – indeed the Prussian performance had brought no decisive results and their manifest inability to deal with their logistic problems was unimpressive. But the existence of the Prussian army, its reputation and the reputation of its King, that King's clear readiness to fight if challenged, together with the generally acknowledged weakness of the Austrian claims on legal or moral grounds – these things determined events. And Frederick, unusually for one who was not a conqueror, emerged from the conflict with enhanced reputation. The negotiations at Teschen – drafting sessions, with the usual prolonged and suspicious arguments about wording here and there – were successful, a success remarkable in that Kaunitz, the principal originator of Austrian plans to invade and partition Bavaria, had achieved very little if anything of what he had hoped. Frederick's long conversation with Kaunitz some years previously had not softened his assessment of the Austrian's character – 'false and double-dealing', he called him, although always with a strain of admiration. There had been interruptions and setbacks but the peace treaty was ultimately agreed, and Frederick declared that it had been obtained not by sacrifice of allies or the plastering over (*plâtrée*) of disagreements, but in terms which conformed to the honour and dignity of Prussia.[67] It should, he wrote, lead to a *solid* peace.[68] There was no doubt that the peace reflected recognition that Prussia was dealing with Austria as an equal; and would continue to do so. The reign of Frederick had transformed Europe.

Ratification and signature followed in May 1779. The war of Bavarian succession, Frederick's last campaign, was over. It was Maria Theresa's birthday and in her honour Frederick ordered Prussian troops to evacuate certain agreed positions, earlier than stipulated, to mark the day. The Empress-Queen, his great opponent, understood and appreciated the gesture.

23

'Le Plus Grand Homme'

Frederick had taken the field and returned from it for the last time – the Peace of Teschen was signed on 13 May 1779. But the last enemy is death and Frederick's final campaign, like his greatest, lasted seven years.

He was tireless until the end in visiting every corner of Prussia. His tours of inspection then and later were legendary – and always marked by the King's personal contacts and interrogations of individuals – farmers, landowners, officials; most enjoyably veterans when he found them. On his tours of Prussia he was always particularly gracious to old soldiers, especially if they had been NCOs; and he retained a good memory for names. In the summer of '79: 'Who are you?' Frederick was touring in Brandenburg.

'Captain von Rathenow, Your Majesty.' Rathenow was an old officer from the wars.

'My God! *Dear* Rathenow! I thought you died years ago. Are you well?'

Rathenow, a local landowner, said that he was. Then: 'My God, Rathenow, you've become fat! Are you married? Is that your wife over there? Ask her to come here' – and as Frederick saluted the lady – 'Madam, in your husband I've met a good old friend. What was your maiden name? Ah yes, a daughter of the general?' And so forth. Frederick would move through Brandenburg as a ruler but also as the father of a huge, extended family.[1] Everywhere he peppered those he met with inquiries on the details of crops, sowings, prices, markets, economic conditions, problems.

But they were melancholy years, not least because Frederick's troubles in political terms often closely resembled those with which

596

his reign had started. Perhaps because these represented real and unsolved problems, perhaps because in certain directions he was too prejudiced by experience to see straight, perhaps because he was old, often in pain, without many friends, sadly embittered; but from whatever cause – and all of this contributed – he ended as he had begun, suspicious of much of the world.

And particularly, as originally, of Austria. By the start of 1780 Frederick thought that the Emperor Joseph was seeking to renege on obligations undertaken at Teschen.[2] His chief concern for his remaining years was to thwart Austrian attempts to get close to Russia, to Prussia's disadvantage. Vienna, he knew, would stop at nothing to disrupt his own relations with St Petersburg and replace it with an entente of their own making. He learned with displeasure of a carefully prepared meeting between the Tsarina and the Emperor in June 1780 at Mogilev in the Ukraine, a meeting at which Catherine had, it seemed, been favourably impressed by Joseph.[3] Frederick, wary of 'summits', expressed scepticism: 'I'm not surprised. When the Great of this world meet each other it's normal that first reports are full of praise and talk of splendid results. In my view nothing much will come of it and soon all that will remain will be a memory of the parties given!'[4] But he was not happy. Thereafter few weeks passed without his reference to 'Austrian intrigues'; to Joseph as 'the mortal enemy of our house';[5] to Austrian ambitions at someone else's expense. They wanted Bosnia, he wrote, to add to Austrian Croatia, although they might instead be bought off with money by Constantinople.[6] Everywhere he saw the hand of Kaunitz and the designs of Austria. It was as it had been in the 1740s.

Frederick was delighted that his nephew, Frederick William, the Prince of Prussia, was invited to St Petersburg in August 1780 – and stayed there until November. He hoped that personal contact between the two courts at princely level might be timely – he remembered the success of Prince Henry. His nephew was no Henry and he had little opinion of him, but Frederick William was the heir of Prussia and the King briefed him with care. 'The Tsarina's vain. Flatter her, but subtly. Show a sort of timidity, induced by your admiration. With the Grand Duke and Grand Duchess develop *intimate* affection, showing as much feeling for Russia as for Prussia.' And he told him to flatter Potemkin, who should be asked for the colonelcy of a regiment of Russian cavalry. Of the Russian ministers Panin was the most able (although this situation was already uncertain, to Frederick's concern, and Panin would soon appear at risk). Some others, particularly Repnin, should be complimented but Panin, at present, mattered most. The Prince should talk *peace*, and should show anxiety over what the Austrian Emperor might do after his mother's death – he might yet plunge Europe again into war.[7]

While the Prince was in St Petersburg Frederick wrote an affectionate family letter to him – 'Your children are well – I'm looking for a pony for your eldest boy so that he can learn to ride –'[8] instructing his Master of the Horse, Count Schwerin, very precisely on the matter. And Frederick William's visit seemed to go perfectly well, although there was little indication of warm personal relations emerging.

There were other concerns besides the ambitions of Austria – Frederick was glad that Russia had concluded an alliance with Holland. He was particularly fond of his niece Wilhelmina of Orange-Nassau, who had married the Stadtholder of Holland and was the stronger of the pair, taking on herself a good deal of diplomatic business, especially with her formidable uncle. He understood her often-voiced outrage at British actions at sea, consequences of the war with France and the war in America, which were bearing very hard on neutral nations whose ships were being stopped on the high seas and cargoes impounded in what Frederick called acts of piracy. The Dutch, as a maritime nation, were particularly injured and Frederick sympathized.

Frederick's resentments against Britain had never disappeared. 'If you want to know what principles are followed by the British Government, I'll tell you,' he wrote to the Princess at The Hague.[9] 'Stupid vanity; ignorance of the interests and strengths of other powers of Europe; pride in carrying, alone, "Neptune's trident"; mistrust and clumsiness in negotiations; ideas of establishing royal supremacy on the ruins of British liberty.' He described Stormont, Sackville and others among George III's ministers as having 'heads empty of brains'; and over the next two years he received news of British military disasters across the Atlantic with a good deal of complacency. And not only military disasters – he was fascinated to read of the Gordon Riots of June 1780, with London in the hands of the mob.

This prejudice of Frederick represented superficial irritation rather than a deep-seated principle of policy, but the irritation persisted and in the unceasing struggles between Britain and France he showed in his comments friendliness to France although he was watching with care the influence of the Austrian Marie-Antoinette. His feelings derived from anger at his treatment in the Seven Years War. They also reflected what he frequently referred to as British arrogance and insensitivity about how other nations might reason or react. He was pleased at a Russo-Dutch understanding because, he told his niece, it meant that '*Messieurs les Roast beeves*' would show greater respect to the Dutch flag, would treat the Dutch more as any power should treat its neighbours. He supposed, however, that the war was costing Britain dear and that she would soon find peace necessary. It would, of course, depend on how operations in America went; and soon they would go so badly that peace on American terms would become inevitable. 'I think a little humiliation, provided it's not excessive, will be to Britain's benefit,' he wrote after Cornwallis's capitulation with 6,000 men at Yorktown[10] on 19 October 1781. 'It will help diminish the insufferable arrogance with which they treat every other nation.' He had equivocated earlier when asked by agents of the American colonies to recognize them as France had done, but he knew that it would come shortly – and, in fact, one of Frederick's last acts of state in his reign would be to afford 'most favoured nation' status to the United States in September 1785.[11]

Nevertheless he wrote a friendly letter of advice to Clarendon, now in the government in London, whom he remembered with affection as Villiers, ambassador in Berlin. It was unfortunate that Frederick's feelings were not, at this time, sweetened by the influence and tact of an outstanding ambassador, as Mitchell had been. On the contrary, when the British envoy, Hugh Elliot, allegedly for medical reasons, travelled to Paris (despite the war), Frederick referred to him contemptuously as 'scatter-brained – it's odd the French let him in'. Elliot's real offence, however (apart from his earlier indiscretion), lay in an exchange of letters with Harris in St Petersburg which had been intercepted by the Prussian envoy and seemed to confirm Frederick's worst fears of British intrigues, aimed at disturbing his good relations with Russia.[12] It could no doubt be remarked that eavesdroppers seldom hear good of themselves, but Frederick was outraged by the 'insolent' remarks of one he referred to as an impertinent *clabaudeur* (brawler) and he ordered the postal authorities to intercept all Elliot's mail, hoping to find something which would tell against him with the authorities in Russia.[13] It was a bad period in Prusso-British relations.

Frederick, not unreasonably, presumed that Britain would do all in her power to pre-empt or disrupt an association of maritime powers which had been formed to protect neutrals and their shipping against the interventions of belligerents, in particular the British; an association with which the Russo-Dutch treaty was wholly consistent. The northern powers looked for protection to Russia. In the summer of 1780 there was a fire aboard a Russian ship at anchor at Kronstadt. British agency was suspected and a story was given currency that Harris had masterminded the outrage.[14] Frederick dismissed the idea – 'It's not credible. It's the work of some adventurer.' Nevertheless the *canard* was not unwelcome to him – Russian anger with Britain would not come amiss in present circumstances.[15] He was shown by von Thulemeier, his man at The Hague, an extract from a London newspaper in August 1780 ('as strong and coarse a piece as can be imagined') which referred to the Empress Catherine as 'a woman whose devilish temper put to death the father of her children, her husband, an Emperor anointed by God'. Frederick remarked that if that were read in Russia the Tsarina would remember it until the grave – 'I must share this thought with you!' he told von Thulemeier.[16] Von Thulemeier would know what to do.

Then, at the beginning of December 1780, Frederick referred to 'a new order of things'. The world had suddenly changed. He immediately and practically ordered a change of all codes,[17] new ciphers.* Maria Theresa was dead.

The great Empress-Queen had been Frederick's bitterest enemy but he respected her, probably more than any other contemporary. He admired her resolution, her strictness of personal morality, her

---

* This presumably implies some sort of word substitution code. The present author, no cryptologist, cannot understand further, but this was what Frederick instantly commanded.

implacability, her resilience. He was glad to have made contact with her son at Neisse and at Neustadt, although now he mistrusted him and was uneasy at what the succession might bring. 'I don't think there'll be war today or tomorrow,' he told Finckenstein, 'the Emperor will begin by reforming the internal economy.'[18] But he reckoned that Kaunitz's policy, a policy of ever-greater rapprochement with Russia and attempted isolation of Prussia, would be continued, and probably intensified. Austria's friendship with France appeared pretty firm – France was exhausted, was hoping for peace and respite from the long struggle with Britain at sea and in the New World; that struggle was having bad effects on international commerce. She would have no intentions, at present, of fresh continental involvement – alliance with Austria protected her against it. A difficulty impeding general peace was France's alliance with Spain, and Spain would not contemplate peace while Gibraltar remained in British hands.[19]

But it was on Austria's relations with Russia that Frederick's apprehensive eyes were fixed, as they always had been, and it was for this reason that Frederick devoted what seems a disproportionate amount of energy, time and worry to a certain family matter, one which had begun just before Maria Theresa's death. He had heard first in October 1780 of a project for a marriage between a prince of Tuscany – son of the Grand Duke and a nephew of Emperor Joseph – and a very young princess of Württemberg, Elizabeth Wilhelmina. The Tuscan prince was heir-presumptive to the Emperor (although the latter, twice a widower, might yet marry again); and the Württemberg princess was a sister of the young Grand Duchess of Russia, whose marriage Frederick had happily promoted. Her mother, a princess of Schwedt, was a sister-in-law of Frederick's brother Ferdinand who had married another Schwedt princess, and was also daughter of Frederick's sister, Sophia, who had married the Margrave of Schwedt. Frederick treasured the Württemberg girls as great-nieces. Elizabeth Wilhelmina's father, Frederick Eugen of Württemberg, unlike his brother, had been a general in the Prussian service, had performed what Frederick described as 'prodigies of valour' under Bevern in April 1757,[20] had taken command at Kunersdorf, and was a Protestant who had brought up his children accordingly. He was heir-presumptive to his eldest brother, the Duke, after a middle brother who in the event succeeded and reigned for only a short time. The reigning Duke Karl Eugen was a Catholic who had first married Frederick's niece, Wilhelmina's daughter. The marriage had ended in a separation and the Duke had settled down with a *maîtresse en titre*, Countess von Hohenheim, whom he ultimately married after the death of his wife in 1780. He had served against Prussia in the war.

Elizabeth Wilhelmina, exceptionally pretty, was only thirteen. She was her father's third daughter; she had another married sister, beside the Grand Duchess of Russia, and ten brothers. Nevertheless her marriage (if it took place) into the heart of the Habsburg establishment would surely cement the relationship of St Petersburg with Vienna alarmingly. It could mean that a future Emperor (the Prince of Tuscany) and a future Tsar (Paul) would be married to sisters. Princess Dorothea, the young girl's mother, was reckoned (at least by her uncle Frederick) to be ambitious and ruthless. She was said to be openly anticipating being mother-in-law of two Emperors, a prospect by which Frederick said she was clearly overwhelmed. He regarded the whole project as an Austrian intrigue and was determined to do what he could to frustrate it.

Frederick had particularly marked the Württemberg princess as a possible bride for the young Crown Prince of Denmark, an idea supported by Frederick's sister-in-law, friend and frequent correspondent, the Queen Dowager of Denmark, Juliana Maria; and at first it seemed this alternative idea might triumph. He was delighted to hear that the Russian Grand Duchess, the girl's sister, was hostile to the Tuscany match and had so informed her own (and thus the bride's) parents. Frederick was told that Russian ministers, notably including Panin, were opposed to a Habsburg marriage. But difficulties began to arise soon after Maria Theresa's death.

First, there was a report that Prince Frederick Eugen might never succeed to Württemberg, because the 'consort' of the reigning Duke was pregnant, after thirteen years of a childless union. Frustration of Frederick Eugen's hopes of succeeding might or might not work against the Habsburg marriage. Frederick thought the report fantasy. 'Although we no longer live in the age of miracles,' he wrote to Elizabeth Wilhelmina's eldest brother, Frederick, who was a major-general in the Prussian army, 'your uncle, the Duke, seems to want to return to it. This pregnancy is very remarkable'.[21]

It was also illusory. Although Frederick believed and wrote that the lady was in her forties, she was in fact under forty at the time. More important were reports of a strong prejudice in the Württemberg family against Frederick's idea of a Danish match; the young Danish prince's youth, character and face were all held against him. Panin, watching these matrimonial ideas closely from the Russian perspective but as a good friend of Frederick, suggested another idea. If the Danish prospect was so unpopular, might not the young princess instead be betrothed to the young son of the Prince of Prussia, the recent visitor to the Tsarina? It was true that the boy was not yet ten years old but arrangements might be made and surely the Prussian King's will would prevail in family matters?

Frederick was still set on the Danish marriage and his reaction to Panin was somewhat unctuous: 'To force my great-nephew into a political marriage repels me. She's three years older than him. Such unions are seldom happy – a Danish marriage would establish her well.'[22] But he came to believe that the Danish cause was lost, having no friends in either St Petersburg or Montbéliard* (the Württemberg residence), and he then turned again to Panin's idea. He was encouraged to hear that the Habsburg prospective bridegroom's mother (the Spanish Grand Duchess of Tuscany) was hostile to the Württemberg marriage because the girl was a Protestant.[23]

But Frederick, with every dispatch, began to get discouraging signs that this particular game was slipping through his fingers. There were indications that the Russians were again concerned about the Turkish threat, a concern which might impel them towards agreement with Vienna; and the immediate way to rebuild friendship with Vienna might be to promote a Habsburg–Württemberg marriage, in so far as it lay with Catherine. Frederick continued to believe in Catherine's good will towards himself, despite the self-evident efforts of Austria to disrupt it, but he was a realist. '*Quel imbroglio!*' he wrote in February 1781.[24] And it appeared that Catherine was now warming towards the marriage to a Habsburg of her daughter-in-law's sister.

---

* A largely Huguenot enclave which, for much of its history, was part of France, and had now been for some years under the rule of the Dukes of Württemberg.

Frederick was reduced to reliance on two remaining cards in his hand and he was inwardly too wise to presume much on their strength. First, he had now openly proposed the Prussian marriage for the young princess as a *pis aller*, and had obtained what he reckoned was a promise of support from her father, and from her uncle, the reigning Duke of Württemberg. The Württemberg word was pledged, Frederick said. His second card was what he called the '*jeune cour*' of Russia, the Grand Duke and Grand Duchess. He knew that their early reaction to the idea of the Habsburg marriage had been hostile and he had, he thought, established good relations with the young couple. He sent messages to them of renewed affection.

But in April 1781 this card, too, fell to pieces in his hand. He received a personal letter from the Russian Grand Duchess. She had been summoned by her mother-in-law, who had spoken of a Habsburg marriage for Elizabeth Wilhelmina, her sister, with enthusiasm. It was clear (she wrote) that the Tsarina was unaware of a counter-proposal for a Prussian marriage and it was also clear that, in her view, her mother-in-law would explode with fury at an idea so contrary to her own mind; and equal fury with her son and daughter-in-law if she suspected them of promoting it.[25] The Grand Duchess wrote to Frederick imploring him to write at once to the Württemberg parents, supporting the Tsarina's wishes, and to keep all else secret. It was a terrified letter.

Frederick told her that he could see no pretext under which the Tsarina could demand an end to a betrothal agreed, in his view, between the main parties, a betrothal to which the father of the prospective bride and her uncle-sovereign, the reigning Duke of Württemberg, had assented. The way to play the matter vis-à-vis Catherine, he wrote, would surely be to place all responsibility on the Duke, as head of the family. But Frederick knew that it was easier to write this than for a frightened young Grand Duchess to confront Catherine the Great. He got word to Catherine about the undertakings made to him in respect of his own great-nephew, 'promises made are indissoluble'; but he knew his hand was weak in the face of the Tsarina's determination, procured, he was certain, by the machinations of Vienna. The Emperor, he reckoned, had bullied or bought the Württembergs in spite of their engagements with himself. Despite his own protested reservations about disparities in age, he was dismissive when told (by the girl's father) of an 'invincible aversion' which his daughter had formed towards union with a boy three years younger than herself. Frederick was unimpressed by such argument. He replied coldly that he was astonished at the inconstancy of Prince Frederick Eugen. One letter from Russia had apparently been sufficient to make him revoke all his undertakings.[26]

Frederick knew well, and it made the reverse especially galling, that Joseph had been pressing the Tsarina hard to support the Habsburg marriage. He supposed there had been British bribery somewhere – the British were thought to be favouring improvement in Austro-Russian relations. He heard that Harris, in St Petersburg, had been allocated 150,000 roubles to do the business, and, 'I've done my best, I've pointed out the facts to the Tsarina as I see them and if it doesn't work English money will have done its work,' he told Finckenstein. 'I can't match it!'[27] To Frederick's credit he could more easily assume such intrigues by Harris than imagine him in his spare time acting as an incendiary of the Russian fleet!

Frederick had lost. The Russian *jeune cour* had proved broken reeds before the formidable will of the Tsarina. The Grand Duke and Duchess had set out on a grand tour of Europe in September 1781, a tour planned to last eighteen months which would take in Austria, Italy and other places in all of which Habsburg influence would be pervasive. Riedesel, from Vienna, suggested Frederick keep in touch with the young couple while on tour and continue his efforts to expose what he saw as Austrian intrigues and hostility.[28] Might he not, Riedesel suggested, send the Marchese Lucchesini to Italy with a letter to the Grand Duke Paul? Lucchesini was a recent arrival at Frederick's court, an agreeable young man from Lucca who some thought not unlike Algarotti, and was now advanced to be a gentleman of the chamber with a salary of 2,000 *écus* per annum, to the irritation of others at court. Frederick did not send Lucchesini, but he wrote personally to the touring Grand Duchess, telling her that if she found it possible to revisit Berlin one day he could explain much about the machinations of the Emperor and it would take no more than two minutes.[29]

Frederick conceded defeat. Goertz, envoy in St Petersburg, felt a failure and wished to resign his post, but Frederick told him that one could only keep quiet and shut one's eyes to the intrigues by which the Prussian game had been defeated; Goertz could no more resign at this point than a general could quit the battlefield when battle was going against him. Battles of that kind cannot be kept going beyond a certain point and Frederick was generally adept at seeing when the point had come. He was resilient.

A casualty of the battle was the elder Württemberg son, Prince Frederick, a major-general in the Prussian service with the colonelcy of a regiment. He realized that the King was furious with his family and felt betrayed by his parents' compliance with Russian and Austrian wishes; and he wrote to Frederick to say so, and to apply to resign, giving some rather over-elaborate reasons for the application. Frederick replied icily. He had heard that Prince Frederick had accepted some money from the Emperor 'to clear his debts', although he did not refer to this. 'There was no need for contrivances,' Frederick wrote. 'You could simply have said that your mother thinks you'll do better in the service of the Emperor than in that of Prussia. Your regiment has now been allocated to someone else, so if you ask permission to leave, regard the request as already granted.'[30]

Frederick believed his principal enemy in the whole affair had been Dorothea of Württemberg, the young princess's mother, and he did not forgive her. The Emperor Joseph had visited France in August 1781 and spent two nights with the Württembergs at Montbéliard *en route*. In Frederick's view Joseph had bought them, and Finckenstein agreed with him. The Württemberg marriage project and the Grand Duke's European tour were all part of the same Vienna plot, to bribe, intrigue and bring about a serious breach between Prussia and Russia.[31] As to relations between Austria and Russia, the central issue round which the entire dispute and much else had revolved, there were attempts to negotiate a treaty in that same summer. Frederick did not think that much harm would come of this from his point of view. He had begun to recover his equilibrium; he thought that Catherine was suffering illusions about Joseph but that they would be short-lived – 'in the long term the interests of Austria and Russia are irreconcilable'.[32]

This smacked of illusions of another sort, the sort which had led Frederick into unpreparedness of mind in 1755. However that might be, Austro-Russian negotiations were suspended in midsummer, and at the end of the year 1781 Frederick composed an exposé of Joseph's policies. His information, congenial to him, was that the Emperor was antagonizing the international community widely; including, particularly, the German community. Prince Henry, nevertheless, had visited Joseph at Spa in September and described the meeting to Frederick in friendly terms. Frederick was wholly unimpressed; and, consistent with his most gloomy predictions, Catherine had refused to renew her treaty with Prussia which was shortly due to expire.

Frederick was still alert, vigorous and suspicious despite frequent pain and ill health. He was showing little evidence of withdrawal from business and his rebukes to his ministers together with the alarmingly close control he kept of affairs were still as striking as ever. 'You push my patience to the limit with the cackhanded way you do your job,' he told Goltz, in Paris.[33] 'You lost your father too young, he could have trained you!' General Konrad von der Goltz had died when his son was still young, and the latter was made to feel his own immaturity. Frederick was still complaining sharply, including to von Maltzahn in London, about the inadequacy of information and the poverty of dispatches. Von Maltzahn was relieved in March 1781 by a former captain of one of Frederick's 'Free Battalions', Count Lusi. It was Lusi and Goltz who had the task of keeping Frederick informed on the complex negotiations for peace in America. There had been peri-odic ideas that he might act as mediator (although he thought the parties too obstinate to make success likely), and he was pleased by Lusi's dispatch of 23 July 1782 saying that George III 'is now persuaded that it is necessary to renounce his sovereignty over America'. Fred-erick, inevitably, saw the struggle largely in terms of its European effects and he reckoned France was a winner and Britain a loser, as he had predicted from almost the first day.

Peace treaties were signed early in 1783. Frederick thought economic factors had been decisive.[34] He immediately told Goltz to discuss with Franklin (American representative in Paris) possible trade arrange-ments between the United States and Prussia. He had initially and mistakenly thought it possible that the new Union might not hold together and that some states might, when peace came, revert to a near-colonial relationship with Britain. It did not happen and Frederick moved without unreasonable delay to take advantage of the new situation.

Finckenstein was still serving faithfully in Berlin, and his colleague, Count Ewald Friedrich von Herzberg, was now often a guest at Sans Souci, a rare privilege for a minister.* Frederick sometimes fired questions at Finckenstein about past events – dates of meetings, venues, statistics. Finckenstein's staff had to deal with factual questionnaires which could have only one significance. Frederick was writing.

He was not only writing about politics; in a treatise on German literature, published in 1780, he attacked what he called the half-barbarous nature of the German language: Frederick's disparagement of his mother-tongue and indifference to German literature was often a cause of resentment in Germany – and it continued although this was a period when the genius of Goethe was already in flower. But his mind, very naturally, reverted much of the time to his own story and to reflections on the condition of the Prussia which he would soon bequeath. He had already, in 1779, written an account of the previous five years, bringing up to date the account of his reign, his *Histoire de mon Temps*, incidentally describing the young Emperor, Joseph, and incorporating a sustained note of warning about the unchanging ambitions of Austria. In 1782 he wrote a separate treatise, another *Considérations sur l'état politique de l'Europe*, a *Final Testament* which reinforced the same theme. It was unashamedly pessimistic. Unless the rulers of Prussia were resolute and strong their state would disappear. Germany would then become a unitary state, like France, under Habsburg ascendancy. The sovereign princes of Germany would be no more. Some might be happy to see this; but for those minded otherwise – and there was no doubt where Prussia would rank – where would alternatives lie? Where would there be counter-balancing alliances? If France, as seemed likely, continued her close relationship with Austria, where would be the options? With England? Always, he wrote, an unreliable expedient. With the Ottoman Porte? Possible, but good for little except some minor military diversion. If the states of Germany were confronted by the combination of Austria (with

---

* Herzberg later became President of the Academy.

France *complaisant*) and Russia – and when he was writing that seemed the forecast – what recourse had the central European princes?

He answered his own conundrum. In unity. And the impetus towards some new attempt at German unity independent of the power of Austria was provided by the conduct of the Emperor.

Joseph, enthusiastic and high-minded, had shown from the hour of his succession a certain lack of realism, of a sense of the practicable. A notable instance of this was his decision to try to improve in every way – economically, socially, judicially – the situation in the Austrian Netherlands. The Austrian Netherlands had for many years been governed by Joseph's uncle, Frederick's old and distinguished opponent the Archduke Charles of Lorraine, as Imperial Governor. His rule had been wise, beneficent and popular. Joseph, however, decided that matters could be improved, and when Charles died, shortly before Maria Theresa, the Emperor appointed his own sister, the Archduchess Maria Christina, as Governor. She was intended to be the agent of change – change dictated by the Emperor.

First, and internally, there must be wider religious toleration, a favourite preoccupation of Joseph. Certain laws offended against the principle of this – the population, whether Flemish or Walloon, was staunchly Catholic and the existing prejudices reached back into the Wars of Religion. Second, there was the so-called 'Barrier Treaty' whereby some of the Scheldt towns were garrisoned by Dutch troops, so that the shipping on the Scheldt – and thus the commerce of Antwerp – was regulated (or impeded) by another power. Joseph made a 'declaration' to Holland about this state of affairs which he found outdated and indefensible. The Princess of Orange, Frederick's niece, asked her uncle what he thought.

Frederick's views were simple. The Emperor, he said, clearly reckoned the 'Barrier Treaty' had lasted long enough. The interested powers were Britain, Holland and France. Britain was at war with Holland, and had been since 1780 when, at Russian instigation, the Dutch had joined the so-called 'armed neutrality' of continental powers in resistance of British claims and actions at sea. The Dutch, therefore, could expect no support in that quarter. The young Queen of France had now produced a male heir, so that for France the influence of Vienna would at the moment be paramount. With Britain hostile and France in sympathy with Austria little could impede the ambitions of the Emperor. Frederick wrote that his niece must view matters realistically.[35]

But it was not only with the internal and commercial situation of the Austrian Netherlands that Joseph was concerned. He had another project, more disturbing to the states of Germany. He thought it might be possible to give up the Austrian Netherlands altogether, to make them an independent 'Kingdom of Burgundy' under the present Elector of Bavaria.* In return for this kingdom and kingly title, the Emperor would acquire Bavaria and the Palatinate, to be united, by agreement, with Austria. The arrangements of the Treaty of Teschen would be reversed.

The idea, in theory, was not wholly far-fetched. The Danubian duchies of Austria and Bavaria were geographically, strategically and culturally close. They were Catholic, German, east of the Rhine. The Austrian Netherlands were west of the Rhine and the Meuse, were not German and were remote in sentiment from most of Germany. It was, of course, true that they had been for centuries at the heart of the Habsburg domains; Emperor Charles V had ruled from Brussels. But since that time the Empire had taken a very different form, and in Joseph's eyes if this exchange could be managed it could produce a more rational European system. He acquired the support of the Tsarina. He hoped for the support of France: although for the British the creation of a small independent kingdom between Channel and Rhine would constitute an inevitable temptation to France.

The idea, in the form in which it was promoted, was doomed whatever the support from St Petersburg or Versailles. What was suggested was a radical transformation of the map of Europe, and one unilaterally conceived in the mind of the Emperor. The exclusion of the Austrian Netherlands from the Empire of which the German princes still felt themselves a part, the absorption of Bavaria and the Palatinate effectively into Austria – these things were too much to

---

* They had originally formed part of the Duchy of Burgundy when Philip, youngest son of the King of France and Duke of Burgundy, had married in the fourteenth century the heiress of the Count of Flanders. More recently Philip II of Spain had 'created' a revived 'Kingdom of Burgundy' for his daughter Isabella to govern jointly (and rather successfully) with her husband, Archduke Albert of Austria.

accept, especially after a recent war which had been settled on different principles. The princes of the Empire might not always have shown much spirit in defence of their constitution in the past, but Frederick had worked on them with some success in the case of the Bavarian succession and he did so again now. A *Fürstenbund* was formed in 1785 under Prussian leadership, a league of sovereigns, both Catholic and Protestant; there were ultimately fifteen. The league included Hanover, Saxony, three ecclesiastical Electors, Weimar, Gotha, Brunswick, Baden, Anhalt, Ansbach, Mecklenburg, and Hesse. The princes of the *Bund* agreed to cooperate in matters of common interest. Their agreement represented a massive and united rebellion against the unilateral attempts of the Emperor to upset the status quo.

In the event the status quo would anyway not last long. Soon the two halves of the Netherlands, north and south, would be merged into a new and short-lived kingdom of the Netherlands; and soon thereafter that, too, would implode and what had been the southern, Austrian, Habsburg, Netherlands would ultimately re-emerge as the kingdom of Belgium somewhat as envisaged by Joseph. For a while, however, change had been defeated. Frederick had previously taken the view that some equilibrium was necessary between Prussia and Austria if German liberties were to be maintained. He now believed that this could only be achieved by the German sovereigns acting in concert. Shortlived though it might be, the *Fürstenbund* had exemplified this.

The creation of the *Fürstenbund* would later be hailed as an example of Frederick's far-sighted vision of the Imperial Germany which came later. This is to rationalize *post facto* – the *Fürstenbund*, like most of Frederick's political moves, came from his reaction to immediate circumstances and pressures, to his perception of the current 'correlation of forces'. Nevertheless the German princes, acting together, had successfully resisted Vienna. It was Frederick's last victory, and it was the first occasion on which Prussia gave the lead to something like a united Germany.

'My old Buddenbrock has died,' Frederick wrote to his niece in November 1781 – Buddenbrock had commanded the right wing at Chotusitz. 'He might have waited, to travel with me.' For the next four years he was unsparing in his daily routine and in the parades and exercises through which he put the troops. He was no easier on his generals, however distinguished. When the regiments in Silesia were exercised under General Tauenzien, one-time defender of Breslau, Frederick found the whole performance deplorable. There would usually be a brief comment sent, but on this occasion it was: 'My dear Tauenzien, I mentioned my criticisms in Silesia, and will now repeat, in writing, that my army there has never been worse. If I made tailors and cobblers generals the regiments couldn't be in worse shape . . .' and the letter continued with a detailed and derogatory description of each command and of the conduct of the manoeuvres themselves. Frederick concluded, 'I don't want to lose Silesia through the incapacity of my generals,' and he ordered Tauenzien to exercise his whole command for four days, in the next year, before the King arrived for the annual exercise. He had ordered one general into arrest. The letter ended, 'Your affectionate King.'[36]

There were, therefore, flashes of the old Frederick, but few of the comrades from the heroic days were left. Frederick visited Ziethen (living at Wustenau near Fehrbellin) when he could, and in December 1785 Ziethen waited on him in Berlin, refusing a chair (he was eighty-six) until Frederick said that unless the old man sat down he, the King, would leave him. Ziethen died soon thereafter. 'He led the advance guard – always!' Frederick said. 'I followed.'[37] He himself drew up a chair for Ziethen, regretting that his visitor had had to climb the staircase. They had been very close – it was on Ziethen's shoulder that Frederick had wept with sorrow and some guilt on hearing of August Wilhelm's death in 1758.

In the summer of 1785, Frederick remained in the saddle at a review for several hours during an unexpectedly heavy rainstorm. He never fully recovered, and for much of 1786 he sat at Sans Souci, gouty, asthmatic, lame. He had envied Prince Henry, who travelled to Paris for the first time in 1784, visiting Goethe at Weimar, Gibbon at Lausanne. 'What a comedown,' Frederick remarked to him on his return, 'to exchange Paris for Potsdam, where you'll only find an old dotard who's sent part of his heavy luggage on ahead!'

The 'old dotard' of Sans Souci spent much of his day in his chair, on the terrace, but he never stopped working. His presence still brooded over Prussia, and he still showed personal consideration for those near him. 'Walk up and down,' he commanded a sentry on the terrace. 'You can't stand still all the time when I can sit down!'[38] In January 1786 he twice received the distinguished Frenchman Comte de Mirabeau. It was not a success. Mirabeau chided him for not doing more for German literature, a fair charge Frederick rebutted with spirit – Mirabeau was brilliant, but no diplomat. And Mirabeau, like other visitors, commented on the relief he said he found on all faces when the end came as it did in August – he had been sent again to cover the important period anticipated following a change of sovereign; Europe was waiting for Frederick's death. Mirabeau, however, was allegedly the originator of one aphorism which would be remembered often in future days. Prussia, he said, was not a state which possessed an army but an army which possessed a state.[39]

The personal physician of George II in Hanover, Dr Zimmermann, a Swiss, also visited Frederick at this time. Zimmermann, a distinguished philosopher, had known him for some years. Later he published in Leipzig an account of his dealings with the King which some thought unconvincing and egotistical – he had first become friendly with him in 1771. Frederick seems to have tolerated him and Zimmermann's reports of their conversations were read with interest. Zimmermann noted every change in the King's physical condition (like his father he had dropsy), how he was sleeping, how he was eating. He recorded verbatim Frederick's alleged words – and they ring true – in the last seventeen days of his life. The King was energetic as ever in discussing philosophy – 'Locke and Newton were the greatest thinkers: but the French understand how to express things better than the English.' Gossip: what did Zimmermann make of the Hanoverian royal family? The Duke of York was praised, to Zimmermann's pleasure (the Duke was to marry Frederick's great-niece, Frederica, five years later). Fellow-rulers – Frederick spoke often of the genius of Catherine the Great. Nearer home – 'Germany is a sort of Republic,' Frederick said, and referred with satisfaction to having re-established that (with the *Fürstenbund*).

Zimmermann was clearly enchanted, although the effect on a natural courtier, as he appears, of the daily conversation of so famous a patient was obviously great. He kept in touch with Lucchesini after

Frederick's death, and greatly liked him – and learned from him, for Lucchesini had been Frederick's most constant companion for his last six years. Zimmermann recorded (in his book) much that was second-hand to him; but his own account shows a very recognizable Frederick – shrewd, argumentative, inquiring, decisive; and with beautiful manners. Until the end. 'The Hanoverian doctor,' Frederick wrote to his sister Charlotte, 'has done what he could. The truth is he couldn't help me, the old must make way for the young.'[40]

Frederick rode for what turned out to be the last time on 4 July 1786. All Prussia knew that the King was approaching his end. But although many noted that Frederick's death seemed unlikely to bring actual grief, every observer, friendly or hostile, reckoned that something unique was passing. Young von der Marwitz, later a distinguished general, saw a crowd gathered in the Berlin Wilhelmstrasse. Frederick had just entered by a door there, visiting his sister Amelia. It was a silent crowd, but 'everyone there knew', the young man noted, 'that he had spent his life in their service'. His achievement had been to defend Prussia against the world and to leave it stronger and better ordered, more prosperous and more populous, more secure, more influential in Europe than had been conceivable at the beginning of his reign. For good or ill it was a lasting achievement.

'Cover the dog, he's shivering,' were some of Frederick's last words as he woke at midnight on 16 August 1786, at Sans Souci. The dog was indeed shivering; and at twenty minutes past two in the morning of 17 August the great King died. The clock in his music room stopped at that hour, and was never wound again. Despite his wish to be buried quietly in the garden of Sans Souci his heir, Frederick William, decreed a great state funeral; and Frederick was laid next to his own father in a small vault in the garrison church of Potsdam. The vicissitudes of two of Europe's most destructive wars changed much, however; and after temporary displacement to a Hohenzollern castle the body of Prussia's greatest king was restored to Sans Souci in 1991, over two centuries after he died.

Frederick has often been described as a mass of contradictions, an enigma. From the time of his death onwards there has been controversy about his merits and faults, his triumphs and failures. He has been eulogized and fiercely attacked. Every facet of his policy and attitudes – political, moral, military, literary – has been scrutinized and fought over as if he were still alive.[41] Certainly Frederick embodied a range of qualities, defects, tastes, talents, opinions, ambitions and prejudices which often appear inconsistent with each other; but this may be said of many if the whole lifespan is considered, and certainly of those with broad and varied responsibilities, acting on the public stage and vulnerable to the transient pressure of great events as well as to the adulation or envy of contemporaries. Frederick was not a completely integrated human being, with every thought and action harmonized and rational. He had more sides to his character than most men: but he was – like most men – a complex of human desires, instincts and faults. His reign was long and his character developed during it.

His greatness lay to some extent in his unusual combination of introspection and decisiveness; and, because he was so articulate and indefatigable a recorder, both can be examined. Whether as ruler, soldier, or man, Frederick ceaselessly inspected his own thinking and motives while simultaneously acting on the political and strategic stage of his time in a manner which was often dominant and always memorable. He deceived himself little, and his failures in the field of action seldom derived from weakness of will, or indecision, or confusion of mind.

If there were contradictions in Frederick they more often simply signify that at times his deeds failed to match his ideals. He often fell below his own painfully evolved standards of how a sovereign, a general, a wise human being, should react and behave; and this is to say little except that he was a man. Furthermore his 'contradictory' character was surely exaggerated by his prolixity as an author – writing so much there were bound to be contradictions; the idealism of youth and ambition had often to be tempered by the sour lessons of experience and expediency. Theory and practice did not always coincide. And his every act or characteristic can be and has often been described in opposing terms. To one commentator his diplomatic dexterity has been, to another, his ruthless dishonesty; to one his endearing modesty and friendliness, to another his insecure craving for approval. Nevertheless if, rather than the variety of his character, his actual policies and performance are examined, a certain consistency and harmony can be found whether in sovereign, general or man. And his common sense was almost always striking.

First the sovereign, the ruler. It is certainly true that he recognized, as the years passed, a fundamental incompatibility between the ideals of the Enlightenment which he had first admired and the harsh realities of the political world in which he needed to fight and survive. And there was always a conflict, never resolved, between his belief in the actual advantages of monarchical autocracy (in hands like his own) and his enduring belief – equally sincere – in the rights and dignity of man, the ideals of John Locke, admired in his youth, the ideals which inspired the American Constitution, so alien to his mind in terms of practical politics. But Frederick recognized the conflict. He had studied his responsibilities, both in theory and practice, from almost the first day he was allowed to read. He had a considerable knowledge of European history and personalities and the knowledge illumines his correspondence: he would have thought lack of such knowledge crass in anybody seeking to influence European events. And he had, when coming to the throne, already evolved principles to guide him as a ruler – aged twenty-eight; and evolved them largely with his own mind.

His governing principles were autocracy and toleration. Autocracy, he believed, meant efficiency and equity; efficiency because power of decision lay with one responsible man, the prince, who could decide and act with sufficient instancy and authority; equity, because only the prince could regulate, by the instrument of wise laws, the conduct of one class of men to another and prevent injustice. He recognized that men may be oppressed by cruel laws, but believed as a historic truth that the cruellest of situations is lawlessness. 'I have been given a piece of *anarchy* to reform,' he wrote in assuming governance of the Prussian 'portion' of partitioned Poland. And he hated it. But Frederick's autocracy did not mean belief in purely arbitrary and unprincipled power – totalitarian and without reference to a higher moral authority. On the contrary, his ideal had always been Plato's philosopher king, regulating through wise laws (to which he, too, was subject) the brutal and conflicting passions of the ruled. Still less had he any sort of concept of a mystical union between sovereign and people. His autocracy was principled but pragmatic.

And the second principle was toleration, especially in religious matters. Frederick, a sincere son of the Enlightenment, abominated the sort of tendentious 'certainties' which could lead followers of one creed to persecute those of another. He was sometimes regarded (and when it was convenient described himself) as the champion of the Protestant cause in Europe, but his treatment of his subjects, of all faiths, was equitable, his friendships were indiscriminate in religious terms and his breadth of mind was beyond question. He was generous to and about Jews and other minorities. He built the first Catholic cathedral in Berlin, St Hedwig's, since the Lutheran Reformation – begun in 1747 and discontinued for lack of finance, it was finally consecrated in November 1773 to the great satisfaction of the Holy See; and Frederick built a school for Catholic children next to it.

The belief in autocracy led him to concentrate authority, sometimes to an inefficient degree, in his own hands. And the belief in toleration could lead him to cynicism, not simply about religious institutions but about belief itself. Nevertheless these were the two guiding principles of the King of Prussia, and they easily coexisted within him.

Frederick's regard for efficiency, for the importance of a well-executed government built on irreproachable integrity, led him not to reject but to welcome and build on the considerable achievements of his predecessors. He modernized – sometimes too fast until prudence intervened – and was determined to get rid of such vestiges of feudalism as serfdom,* the tying of a man to the soil, which he reckoned were not only inefficient but barbarous although they could not be immediately reformed without agricultural dislocation. In government he inherited a good system and in places he improved it. His rule was inconceivable without the best bureaucratic machine in Europe, carefully recruited, properly trained, ferociously supervised and utterly loyal to the person of the sovereign; the defects of autocracy, even – perhaps particularly – when served by such a machine, are self-evident but Frederick could never have been convinced that any alternative was preferable. His rule was more consensual than sometimes appeared. He

---

* Serfdom was not instituted in the newly acquired or colonized border provinces but its abolition in Prussia aroused strong opposition from landowners, who complained that only through the continuity of labour it produced could they and their sons leave home to serve in the army. It was not finally abolished in all its forms until 1810.

had to work with, not against, the other elements in the state – the nobility, the officers of the army, the landowners, the commercial entrepreneurs. He was the master, but he knew that efficient leadership is different from driving. Autocracy, on Frederick's model, differs from despotism. Nevertheless the prompt and accurate discharge of the state's business, the honest and efficient management of the state's finances, the wise regulation and encouragement of the state's economy – these things were crucial to the happiness of the people. They were the duty of the King. And the duty of the King also lay in promoting not only the material welfare of his people but their education. Frederick, always mindful of his own youth, cared passionately about education. At the end of his reign, in September 1779, he dictated a famous ordinance about higher education – emphasis on the classics, logic and rhetoric – which, he knew, created the true riches of the state.

Because he liked detail Frederick interfered too much, on occasion, and his economic initiatives were not always successful. He believed that the Prussian economy needed state direction and, on occasion, support; and in the circumstances of his reign he was probably right, although he never lost touch with the traditional agrarian order. He was criticized for his temperamental addiction (as some saw it) to French ideas, and he did not always gain the trust of his own bureaucracy; although essentially conservative he was impatient, and too prone to ignore or despise existing machinery in favour of improvised and *ad hoc* methods. He often grumbled at the lack of imagination, the resistance to change, of his civil service, although its honesty – largely an achievement of Frederick William – was vital for him.

Yet Frederick, as ruler, was in unquestioned control of the Prussian state and it was for this, he believed, that he had been born. The example of Prussia in the stern integrity of its domestic governance became known throughout Europe and beyond; and Prussia's strength and system spread a certain increased sense of confidence and self-sufficiency throughout the German states – sometimes accompanied by resentment, certainly, but contagious and essentially salutary. It was Frederick's victories in the field which made Prussia one of the first states of Europe but it was Prussia's ability to survive and even prosper, despite her small size, indefensible frontiers, relative poverty and the odds against her, which created her reputation. Her population doubled during his reign, yet all knew that most of Europe had at times combined to destroy her and been worsted. Such was the King's achievement. And although there was collapse after Frederick's death, before the revolutionary onslaught of Napoleon, that collapse was soon succeeded by recovery so that Prussia shared in the honours of Leipzig and the fruits of victory at Paris in 1815. The recovery showed a resilience which owed much to the heritage of Frederick.

The situation of Prussia as a small land power confronted and surrounded by larger and more numerous nations meant that Frederick's policy was always being tested by the opposition, actual or impending, of superior force; and in his conduct of foreign policy he emphasized the need for realism. In an age of much self-deception and illusion he was supremely realistic. The ruler, he believed, is *responsible* and has no right to indulge idealistic fancies which may, in the world as it is, simply penalize his subjects. On the contrary he must bring to his task all his qualities, and in particular adroitness and an ability to transcend over-narrow definitions of good faith; and it is, of course, in this area that Frederick has been most criticized as hypocritical or dishonest, most attacked for exemplifying discord between profession and practice. Men have asked for two and a half centuries how the philosophic moralist could act as he sometimes did.

Frederick, consistent at least by his own lights, rejected this criticism. He accepted war as a legitimate instrument of policy provided the cause was just: and when military operations had achieved their object – or manifestly couldn't – a prince should seek peace. Frederick was indefatigable and sincere in trying for peace, whether by mediation or principled compromise, if the battlefield had not produced acceptable decision; but once the sword was drawn, whether enthusiastically or reluctantly, he did not believe in sheathing it without an honourable outcome. And he was not the last ruler to find that wars are easier to begin than to conclude.

Yet Frederick claimed never, or almost never, to have acted except within international conventions and the laws of the Empire, with legal right on his side. He admitted that it might be necessary on very rare occasions – perhaps twice in a lifetime, he said – to renege on a treaty for some absolutely dominant reason; there might be no other way to survive, or an ally might already have broken the agreement, or an ally might be in the process of deceiving. He recognized that there was a case to answer and in his writings he claimed to have answered it. But he also preached that a sovereign *owes it to his people* to be 'wiser than serpents'. He should not betray them by timidity or by excessive scrupulosity if the situation demands promptitude, boldness and decision. Machiavelli said that a wholly disinterested power among ambitious powers must in the end perish, and 'I'm obliged to confess,' Frederick remarked, 'that Machiavelli is right!'[42]

Frederick's prime concern, very naturally given the position of Prussia, was with the Empire. He initially mistrusted it as a mere cloak for the ambitions of Austria but he later promoted and even identified with it, as a means of resisting Austrian hegemony, as a 'republic of princes'. His underlying obsession was with Austria and the house of Habsburg and it was only in reaction to Austria that he developed ideas of German unity. In one sense he destroyed, by his opposition to the Empire as it then was, the old idea of a universal, God-ordained Reich, heritage and vision of Charlemagne. But this had long been fading and its time had passed. There was a new dawn just beyond the horizon, the nation state was rising, the French Revolution with its emphasis on popular nationalism was only three years away when Frederick died. A new sort of Reich, a German Empire, forged and led by Prussia, was certainly not an ambition of Frederick; but the ultimate work of Bismarck, after the Napoleonic experience and several decades of revolution had transformed Europe, was inconceivable without Frederick's achievements, although this would not be recognized until a century after his death. While he lived Austria was the principal enemy.

As to the other states of Europe outside the Empire, Frederick at the end of his life was at peace with all. He was always wary of Russia. He feared Austro-Russian rapprochement. He had been strongly marked by personal experience of what he described as the sheer ferocity, the numbers, the primitive nature of the Russians as enemies, as well as by the extent of their lands and the near-Oriental character of their rulers and institutions. Russia made a strong Prussia absolutely necessary for Europe; but it should be a strong Prussia on good terms with Russia and extending a helping hand to the east when required. When this policy failed, as it did in 1756, Prussia was in trouble; and a key to the success of this policy would always be Poland.

The Poles, in Frederick's unchanging view, were a difficult and unpredictable people, with few talents for government or organization, with strong passions and with an outdated political identity. The partition of Poland – another development for which Frederick has shared much criticism – was in his opinion a desirable step towards peace and stability in central Europe, tidying up a volatile strategic situation or filling a potential vacuum where the Russian, Austrian and Ottoman Empires met. It removed at least some causes of conflict. And it had the effect of checking, or at least bridling, Russian western expansion. It meant that to their west the Russians must perceive not a temptation, not an opportunity, not a threat, but a wall. The wall of Prussia.

Frederick had and showed deep affection for France, even when France was at war with him and even when his mistrust and irritation over particular French actions – or statesmen – were at their strongest. He despised the French royal family, so out of sympathy did they seem with his own ideals of the ruler – economical, self-sacrificing, hard-working, austere. He thought French domestic management deplorable and bound to lead to trouble before long, although he was always keen to learn about French experiments in state enterprises. He found French vainglory absurd, and said so. But he never lost his admiration and love for French artistic, literary and intellectual achievements. He adored the French language – its rationality, its precision, its music, its conciseness. France, from such viewpoints, was his spiritual home. The proceedings of the Berlin Academy of Sciences were conducted in French (Frederick never personally attended it) and for him nothing else would have been conceivable. War with France hurt him, as an unnatural situation. His feelings for France were human, emotional, and spoke more of Frederick as man than as ruler; but they were very strong.

Towards Britain Frederick, more often than not, felt intense irritation despite his close relationship with the royal family through a mother he loved, and despite his admiration for British commercial enterprise and skill. This irritation was at its greatest in the last period of his life, after the Seven Years War, when he had, in his view, been betrayed by his ally, Britain. His feelings were not entirely just and showed less than his usual realism but they were consistent. In the main he found British conduct arrogant, seemingly both ignorant and insensitive about the views, interests and likely reactions of other nations and thus, in his view, ultimately stupid. He thought the British, for instance, dimwitted not to perceive that their ideas for a northern alliance (Prussia, Russia, Britain) would be regarded as provocative not only by other Baltic nations but also and notably by France, a France now intimately connected with Austria. And when that sense of provocation developed into hostility, as it would, who on the continent would stand with Prussia? He thought the British looked at situations and possibilities with excessive insularity, and simplistically, and with too little sense of history. And he felt small sympathy over Britain's difficulties with her colonists in America, difficulties which he considered had been entirely provoked by British insensitivity and folly – and then addressed with insufficient forethought or strength.

But although Frederick has rightly been remembered as law-maker, administrator, just sovereign, assiduous diplomatist, he was named 'Great' by contemporaries largely because of his achievements at the head of his country's troops. Just as Napoleon, despite his extraordinary record in government, would have made in the end a negligible mark on history without the flight of the Grand Army's eagles to every corner of Europe and beyond, so Frederick as a historical figure is impossible to consider except against the blue and white background of the Prussian army.

As a soldier Frederick never neglected the political aims of a war. He admitted to an early desire for glory, to make a mark, to lay to rest for ever, perhaps, the contemptuous taunts of his father about his manhood, but he always knew that war is a political act, an instrument and extension of policy, justified by the hope of a better situation after a peace – he needed no Clausewitz to instruct him on that. And in this Frederick was, of course, a man of his time, a time of limited conflicts fought for finite aims. The era of national struggles involving the passions and ambitions of entire peoples, fought *à* *outrance* for total victory, lay in the future; a future Frederick would have regarded with horror and which would necessarily await a more democratic age and mood. Frederick experienced and sometimes inflicted the incidental savageries of war, the suffering, the slaughter, the destruction: and sometimes he seemed to anticipate the barbarities of a subsequent era, as when he bombarded (with questionable military utility) the beautiful city of Dresden.* But to continue a campaign until his enemies were utterly vanquished and had surrendered to him unconditionally he would have regarded as both impolitic and immoral.

But policy might dictate war, and if war was inevitable what mattered was to wage it efficiently; and that often meant striking first. Frederick's principles in warfare have sometimes been compared or contrasted with those of Napoleon. It has been said that Napoleon believed in the absolutely decisive battle, the battle of annihilation, the Cannae; and that, by contrast, Frederick practised a more attritional operational technique, exhausting the enemy (on the battlefield) with a series of widely separated attacks, keeping the enemy on the wrong foot, manoeuvring. That so comparatively few of Frederick's victories were decisive in the Napoleonic sense reflects not only technique but that Frederick fought for advantage rather than absolute victory; and was generally outnumbered. In fact each responded to the circumstances of any particular day, with best use of available resources and terrain, with a common sense and flexible reaction to the needs of the moment, rather than with any profound difference of theory. In all his directives Frederick recognized that unless it is deliberately resolved to avoid battle manoeuvre must have as its object successful combat. The idea of movement and manoeuvre bringing victory without fighting he would have regarded as laughable, probably assenting to a modern military lecturer who said that some exponents of the merits of manoeuvre seemed to think that if one moves round an enemy with sufficient velocity he will get dizzy and fall down. That was not Frederick − his great fights exemplified imaginative and well-coordinated manoeuvres but they ended with shock and killing. He

---

* He sometimes asked his envoy, von Borcke, 'for my own curiosity', how the rebuilding was going. His uneasiness was evident.[43]

knew it could not be otherwise. In the two Silesian wars and the Seven Years War, Frederick fought fifteen major battles, and twelve of them were victories – several resounding victories. He lost three, but recovered from them.

Operationally, in the planning of the actual battle, Frederick and Napoleon each observed much the same principles. Use deception where possible, mislead, surprise: massive use of all available artillery to soften opposition to the assault; concentration of strongest possible resources at the point of decision; assault towards an enemy's 'vitals', the centre of his strength; attack in depth, so that the impetus of the operation can be maintained after the initial phases; exploit victory tirelessly. There is plenty in the record of each of these great commanders to exemplify some or all of these principles, and little to show they did not both believe in them, although in exploitation of victory Frederick was always mindful of longer time and political factors. Unlike Napoleon he was not disposed to be a destroyer of existing systems, even when in arms against them. As to the fighting itself, the Napoleonic and the Frederician battles differed, where they did, less from difference of theory than from differences in circumstances, ground, relative force strengths and contemporary equipment, making detailed comparisons generally inapplicable.

Certainly Frederick eschewed deep strategic advances, seeming less ambitious than Napoleon when the map was laid out before him, but this, as often as not, was because his aim could be defined in less far-reaching terms, and thus to limit its scope was wise. And, like Napoleon after him, Frederick believed strongly in the power of the offensive. The offensive, he said to Prince Henry, 'always has a great advantage over the defensive in war'. When political factors dictated delay in launching an offensive, as in the start of the war of Bavarian succession, he chafed. He certainly did not believe in the offensive where tactical factors made its success unlikely – far from it: he often showed himself a cautious commander. But he knew that the defensive, the waiting on an enemy's will and initiative, on an enemy's choices – that this deprives a commander and an army of the benefits of choosing place, timing, and proportionate strength. He sometimes adopted the defensive, but it was as a *pis aller*. It has been said that Frederick was often constrained to the strategic defensive because of the unreliability of his troops if 'loosed' in major offensive operations. This is questionable; Frederick, who favoured the offensive, as his writings make very clear, adopted the defensive only in response to the overall situation, and generally wisely. He was, for much of his fighting life, facing a huge preponderance of enemies.

Frederick, like Napoleon, studied terrain with great care. He understood the salient features of central Europe like a master surveyor. And what both shared was the divine spark of leadership, the gift of communicating energy and inspiring confidence in tired, frightened, dispirited men. This derived much, probably most, from a record of victory – troops felt they were following a winner. It derived from personal example. Frederick, the Prussian soldiers knew, was always where the fight was hottest, was watching every shift, every twitch of the battle with the eye of a master, was asking no more of any man than he would hazard himself. With this went – in the case of both men – a remarkable speed of reaction. Frederick thought fast, decided fast, spoke and wrote fast. All bore witness to his extraordinary calm in moments of crisis. He was almost invariably ahead of the game, although there were terrible exceptions, like Hochkirch. He noted everything on the battlefield and remembered it – he had what others called a 'poet's eye' for the bizarre sights war can produce – but while noting he was also analysing, thinking. His records show it. And Frederick never allowed campaigns to prevent his reading, his historical musing, even his literary appreciation. All Europe was aware of the picture of the great Prussian King, moving his army with extraordinary rapidity and skill to counter here an Austrian, here a French, there a Russian invasion, yet devouring in his travelling carriage the works of Sallust, of Tacitus; or breaking his simple supper in camp to declaim from Racine, the tears pouring from his eyes.

As a soldier Frederick excelled above all in the organization and preparation of his army – and could do this, of course, as King, as one who controlled not only the bodies of the soldiers but the resources of the state. He devoted enormous attention to weaponry, to formation training, to tactical system, theory and experimentation. He also devoted much effort to his intelligence services, to his communications, to logistics, supplies, depots, horse purchase and horse management. The financing of campaigns, his war chest, was his first care. But Frederick also paid great attention to the human factor, to what would, in modern times, be called personnel selection, promotion, recruitment, welfare. Manpower would always be a problem for him, since Prussia was a small state and the army in war would greatly depend on non-Prussian intakes or compulsions – although at critical times his élite regiments were still maintained as almost entirely Prussian. Frederick, nevertheless, seldom had enough men to provide garrisons for country he had overrun. He could not effectively occupy territory.

On the whole, and in this unlike Napoleon, Frederick was modest. He made deplorable mistakes, and – like most commanders – was sometimes rescued from disaster not by his own decisions but by the skill and bravery of the troops themselves, as at Chotusitz. He knew that he had had much to learn in the early days, the Silesian wars. Sometimes he indulged in wishful thinking. On the whole, however, he saw his achievements in war and his own failures with commendable clarity, and he wrote them down.

But above all he was indomitable. The darkest days of the Seven Years War, Europe east and west mustered against him, British support a disappointment, much of Prussia in enemy hands, saw him at moments utterly cast down, lands gone, friends gone, reputation gone. He recovered. He was resilient. No enemy triumphed over him for long. All Europe knew it. And Napoleon, the newly commissioned young artillery officer, still only seventeen when Frederick died, studied him deeply and knew it well. After the French triumph over Prussia at Iena and Auerstadt, Napoleon visited a cowed and French-occupied Berlin and went to the garrison church at Potsdam on 24 October 1806, where Frederick lay sleeping in his tomb. The little Corsican Emperor, surrounded by his marshals, gazed silently for a little. Then – 'Hats off, *messieurs*! If *he* were alive we would not be here!'

As a man, too, Frederick has been described as a contradiction. This is surely not so. His letters and essays from his earliest days strike the reader with their consistency and coherence. His views evolved, like those of any man who begins writing in adolescence and continues, with huge prolixity, until dying at seventy-four; but he showed the same qualities, and, as some would say, defects at the end of life as at its beginning.

Frederick was courageous. He cared little for death – 'Old people *should* die!' he wrote in 1775, indifferent. He was also indifferent to conventional condemnation of suicide: 'One's not master of one's arrival in this world. At least one should be allowed to leave it when life's no longer supportable.'[44] He was a brave man on the battlefield and he was brave in his endurance of pain and bodily ailments. He suffered greatly from ill health and he subjected his body to more strain than most men. He frequently complained – his letters are full of his gout, his stomach disorders, his haemorrhoids, his asthma, his influenza. The complaints were justified, but the ills seldom interfered with the painstaking, unsparing, dedicated conduct of business.

Frederick was inherently pessimistic, although when actually engaged in operations of war he could be sanguine, hearty, confident even to excess. But he was inclined to cynicism and he was often gloomy about mankind. 'Solomon said all men are mad,' he once remarked, 'and experience proves him right.' His poor opinion of his fellow-men did not improve – his long reign moved from one fearful war to another, from one scene of carnage and misery to many more. He did not shrink from war but he claimed not to seek it. He defended the cases where he had seemed to initiate hostilities as essentially defensive moves. Prussia had had to act or see overwhelming force assembled against her, designed to be used; and do nothing. That was not the duty of a king.

Frederick was humane. 'Before all things,' he told his generals in 1778, 'I prescribe as your most sacred duty that in every situation you exercise humanity on unarmed enemies,' and by most accounts he was as good as his word.[45] He waged war almost unceasingly, its horrors appalled him and he spent much of his time trying to negotiate acceptable conclusions to hostilities; but they had to be acceptable. Within Prussia his own conduct of justice was almost invariably merciful and markedly more merciful than most of his fellow-sovereigns. He loved above all to do justice to the weak, to correct the mighty and proud. 'I think him too gentle,' the Earl Marischal told Jean Jacques Rousseau in 1765. 'He will not have anyone hanged!' – and Marischal himself was a notably kindly man. Frederick enjoyed the chances of doing individual acts of kindness, of helping an unfortunate, forgiving a miscreant, providing for the widow, the orphan. The times were or could be cruel. But the King of Prussia was not cruel.

In his personal relationships Frederick loved and was generous to many of his relatives, especially the young; and when he loved he loved whole-heartedly and with warmth. His letters in this mood are convincing and moving. He could certainly be unkind – and his attitude to his wife sadly repels. But he loved his friends and suffered when there were estrangements, bereavements. There remained in his latter days few of the friends from earlier times to whom he could open his heart but they made a great difference to him. They were often less generous to him in reminiscence than he to them, and he kept part of himself in reserve. His lack of pomposity and readiness to treat men alike was famous and endearing. A Dutchman, a salesman, visiting Sans Souci, was shown round by an old man he supposed was the gardener but who refused a tip: 'We're not allowed to accept, I'm afraid!' said the King of Prussia.[46]

As a man of letters and philosopher – the terms in which Frederick would have most wished to be assessed – he was a child of his time, of the Enlightenment. His verse was generally pedestrian. His prose, on the other hand – and especially the best of his letters – was elegant, fastidious and musical. Judgement of his mind – his philosophy – turns on the view taken of the Enlightenment itself, deriving as it did from scientific discovery, and from sceptical reaction against the passionate certainties and animosities of the Reformation and Counter-Reformation. Frederick could have been at home in no other age, and his views and sentiments never progressed from it. Perhaps there was not much further to go, without the sort of leaps of faith to which he was temperamentally allergic.

In his tastes, his love of learning, his artistic talents and predilections, Frederick was a sensitive and distinguished polymath. He was not an innovator – he was essentially conservative, whether in politics, in music, in literature, in his devotion to the great French dramatists, in architecture and the planning of gardens, in pictures. He preferred the classical forms he had first learned and loved as the *ne plus ultra* of beauty. He was scornful of the later generation of French playwrights like Beaumarchais: 'What a comedown from Molière!' He was, therefore, unenterprising in his appreciation, reactionary. His disdain of German literature was notorious and a matter of great criticism by his countrymen. To some his tastes, talents, ambitions have evinced crudeness[47] rather than subtlety, and it is perhaps true that he never wholly assimilated that French culture he so yearned for – perhaps the air of Brandenburg was unfriendly to it and he was doomed to remain an outsider, despite the yearning. Even in the preferred forms of the eighteenth century he was backward rather than forward looking. For Haydn, composing during his middle and later years, he showed no knowledge or reverence; and he must, in the same years, have been familiar with the superb work of the earlier Mozart but did not evince much admiration for it. Perhaps the spirit of Vienna, of Munich, of Salzburg, so vivid in such masters, was uncongenial to the severe classicism of Frederick of Prussia and to his northern temperament. Whatever the cause it must be reckoned as a sadness, a flaw.

It was, however, probably Frederick's personality that was the most memorable facet of the man. His energy, his integrity, his military reputation, his love of impartial justice, his taste, his talents, his learning – all these were legendary in his lifetime. All, however, were brought most vividly to life by his physical presence, his spontaneity, his wit. That his wit could be unfeeling nobody denied; but few visitors did not bear witness to the fascination and range of his conversation, to the sheer entertainment which Frederick could generate. Frederick loathed being bored, and could show it. He had and has continued to have plenty of hostile critics. With so many-sided a man, reigning for so long, fighting so many battles, writing so many books, it could hardly be otherwise. But he rides across the European eighteenth century indefatigable, a little hunched, coat creased and snuff-stained, now raising a spy-glass to that eye which missed nothing, now turning in the saddle with a remark in that musical, sardonic voice; the 'ts' mispronounced as 'ds'; with a quizzical stare from those beautiful, penetrating, alarming eyes. *Alter Fritz.*

Let Charles Joseph, Prince de Ligne, himself a distinguished military commander and veteran of many wars, have the last word. The Prince was twenty-three years younger than Frederick and had been in almost every particular in the opposite corner. He had fought against Frederick in many a battle, including Leuthen and Hochkirch. He was a staunch Catholic, a loyal prince of the Empire and devotee of Maria

Theresa, an unswerving adherent of the house of Habsburg, a personal friend of the Emperor Joseph, a shrewd and witty *habitué* of the courts of Europe, as well as being a cultivated scholar and author in his own right. He had, incidentally, come to believe that over the Silesian question Frederick had had right on his side. But as for the King himself – Frederick, said the Prince de Ligne, was *'le plus grand homme qui ait jamais existé!'*[48] The greatest man who has ever lived. Like most superlatives the judgement is subjective, unprovable and improbable;[49] but it gives some insight into the impression made on contemporaries by Frederick II, King of Prussia.

Notes

1. Education of a Prince

1 H. A. L. Fisher, *History of Europe*, Arnold, 1936.

2 Sir Charles Hanbury-Williams, quoted in C. P. Gooch, *Frederick the Great*, Alfred Knopf, New York, 1947.

3 Thomas Mann, *Frederick the Great and the Great Coalition*, 1914.

4 Harold Nicolson, *Age of Reason*, Constable, 1960.

5 Norwood Young, *The Life of Frederick the Great*, Constable, 1919.

6 T. B. Macaulay, *Critical and Historical Essays*, 1864.

7 Thomas Carlyle, *Life of Frederick II of Prussia*, Chapman & Hall, 1858.

8 Friedrich Nicolai, *Anekdoten von König Friedrich II von einigen Personen die um ihn waren*, Berlin, 1788.

9 Reinhold Koser, *Geschichte Friedrichs des Grossen*, Stuttgart, Berlin, 1921.

10 Thomas Mann, *Frederick the Great*.

11 *Briefe an Fredersdorff*, ed. Richter, Hermann Klemm, 1926. Numbered serially, henceforth *Fr.*

12 Dieudonné Thiebault, *Original Anecdotes of Frederick II, King of Prussia*, trans. London, 1805. Thiebault was appointed Professor of Literature and spent time very close to the King. He made factual errors and confused dates but the personal picture he gives is convincing.

13 'Effeminister Kerl' – the numerous letters bewteen Frederick and Frederick William are published in several collections including Gustav Mendelssohn Bartholdy, *Friedrich der Grosse in seinen Briefen und Erlassen mit biographischen Verbindungen*, Munich, 1912, and Ernest Siegfried Mittler, *Briefe an seinen Vater 1732–1739*, Berlin, 1838 – numbered serially. Some also appear in Frederick's *Œuvres posthumes* (see Note on Sources, page 651) or in the *Briefwechsel mit Voltaire* (see below) or in the *Politische Correspondenz* (see below) or are extracted from *Histoire de mon Temps* (see below).

14 The English marriage project and its effect on Frederick's fortunes is very fully discussed in Koser, *Geschichte*, in Georg Winter, *Friedrich der Grosse*, Hoffmann, Berlin, 1907, and in Ernest Lavisse, *The Youth of Frederick the Great*, Richard Bentley, 1891, as well as (very partially) in the *Memoirs of Wilhelmina, Margravine of Baireuth*, David Stott, London, 1887.

2. Remusberg

1 Quoted in Christopher Duffy, *Frederick the Great*, Routledge & Kegan Paul, 1985.

2 *Briefwechsel Friedrichs des Grossen mit von Grumbkow und Maupertius*, ed. R. Koser, Leipzig, 1898. Henceforth *BMG*.

3 ibid.

4 ibid., 40.

5 Hanbury-Williams, see Gooch, *Frederick the Great*.

6 Ritter von Zimmermann, *Uber Friedrich der Grossen und meine Unterredungen mit Ihm*, Leipzig, 1788.

7 Nicolai, *Anekdoten*.

8 *Dreissig Jahre am Hofe Friedrichs des Grossen*, diary of the Queen's Chamberlain, Ernst Ahasuerus Heinrich Lehndorff. Lehndorff (who was brother-in-law to Frederick's chief minister, von Podewils) was, however, himself consumed by a thinly disguised sentimental passion for Prince Henry, so his

account, describing Marwitz as malicious, mendacious and a fantasist, may be partial.

9 See Pierre Gaxotte, *Frederick the Great*, G. Ball & Sons, London, 1941, and Winter, *Friedrich der Grosse*.

10 Carlyle, *Life of Frederick II*.

11 Zimmermann, *Uber Friedrich der Grossen*.

12 *Letters and correspondence of James Harris, 1st Earl of Malmesbury*, London, 1844.

13 See Baron von Bielfeld, quoted in Koser, *Geschichte*. Bielfeld described Rheinsberg as 'contrived by the taste and genius of the Crown Prince with the talent of Knobelsdorff'.

14 *Mittler Collection*, 26. Miscellany of Frederick's letters numbered serially (Ernst Siegfried Mittler, Berlin, 1838). Frederick's letters to his father (see Chapter 1) were also published as a separate volume.

15 ibid., 156.

16 The letters between Frederick and Voltaire, numbered serially, throughout all volumes, were edited by Reinhold Koser and Hans Droysen, distinguished Frederician scholars, under the title *Briefwechsel mit Voltaire*. In this book they are shown by *BV*. This is *BV*, 1.

17 *BMG*, 90.

18 Nicholas Henderson, *Prince Eugen of Savoy*, Weidenfeld & Nicolson, 1964.

19 Duffy, *Frederick the Great*.

3. The Challenge

1 *First Political Testament*, 1752, ed. Gustav Volz, Reimer Hobbing, Berlin, 1920. Henceforth *PT I*.

2 *Testament Politique*, 1768, ed. Volz. Henceforth *PT II*.

3 See Chapter 1.

4 BV, 59.

5 *PT I*.

6 ibid.

7 BV, 49.

8 Thiebault, *Original Anecdotes*.

9 Nicolai, *Anekdoten*.

10 BV, 110.

11 Quoted by the Duc de Broglie, *Frederick the Great and Maria Theresa, from hitherto unpublished documents*, Sampson Low, London, 1883.

12 BV, 131.

13 ibid., 137.

14 Koser, *Geschichte*.

15 *Politische Correspondenz Friedrichs des Grossen*, edited by various hands and published by Alexander Duncker in Berlin in forty-six volumes. The *Politische Correspondenz* includes a large number of the letters to which Frederick's were responses, largely drawn from the Prussian State Archives. It contains almost 30,000 letters of Frederick's, numbered serially. Quotations will refer to *PC* and the serial number. The letters to Camas are *PC*, 42 and 44.

16 PC, 92.

17 Bartholdy, *Friedrich der Grosse*.

18 BV, 116.

19 BV, 155.

20 ibid., 162.

21 PC, 141.

22 Nicolai, *Anekdoten*.

23 PC, 119.

24 Carlyle, *Life of Frederick II*.

25 See Nicolson, *Age of Reason*. Frederick's initial invasion of Silesia has been prime and chief target of criticism, especially by writers friendly to Austria and to the concept of a united Austrian-led German nation; see, for instance, Anna Klopp, *König Friedrich von Preussen und die deutsche Nation*, Friedrich Hunterschen, 1860, and many others.

4. The Mollwitz Grey

1 PC, 199.

2 ibid.

3 ibid., 200.

4 ibid., 227.

5 BV, 142.

6 ibid., 163.

7 PC, 229.

8 ibid., 299.

9 ibid., 311.

10 ibid., 330.

11 Nicolai, *Anekdoten*.

12 ibid.

13 PC, 332.

14 ibid., 382.

15 ibid., 436.

16 ibid., 425.

17 ibid., 494.

18 BV, 193.

19 *PC*, 510.
20 De Broglie, *Frederick the Great.*
21 *PC*, 534.
22 ibid., 557.
23 ibid., 561.
24 ibid., 575.
25 ibid., 610.
26 ibid., 605.
27 ibid., 564.

5. 'A Most Imprudent Manoeuvre'

1 De Broglie, *Frederick the Great.*
2 *BV*, 200.
3 *PC*, 733.
4 ibid., 726.
5 ibid., 731.
6 ibid., 751.
7 ibid., 761.
8 ibid., 768/9.
9 *Histoire de mon Temps* – henceforth *HMT*. Frederick's *Histoire* was a work of thirty-three chapters with numerous appendices and reproductions of correspondence. It was begun by him immediately after the Silesian wars but then revised, and completed late in his reign, after the war of Bavarian succession. After extensive editorial changes it only appeared publicly in 1788; but a text carefully reconstructed from Frederick's originals, with some additions taken from his battlefield dispatches, was published in *Œuvres de Frédéric le Grand*, ed. J. D. E. Preuss, published by Decker in Berlin in 1846 – henceforth

Œuvres. The *Histoire* constitutes Vols. III–VII. Frederick naturally disclaimed prejudice in the work, and it is no doubt sometimes questionable in factual detail. It leaves a very individual mark – lucid, simple, elegant and carrying the reader on with the force and excitement of the narrative. All is told in the third person – *Le Roi.*
10 *PC*, 813.
11 ibid., 848.
12 ibid., 871.
13 ibid., 890.
14 ibid., 894.
15 *BV*, 206.
16 *PC*, 900.
17 ibid., 904.
18 *BV*, 213.
19 *PT II* – 'Infanterie'.
20 Quoted in von Bremen (see Chapter 8, note 39, below).
21 F. Hildebrandt, *Anekdoten und Charakterzeuge aus dem Leben Friedrichs des Grossen*, Halberstadt, 1829.
22 cf. Hildebrandt, *Anekdoten*, Winter, *Friedrich der Grosse*, Nicolai, *Anekdoten*, and many more.
23 *Particular Instructions of the King of Prussia to the Officers of his Army*, trans. T. Foster, published 1797.
24 Abbé Denina, *Essai sur la vie et règne de Frédéric II Roi de Prusse*, Jacques Decker, Berlin, 1788.
25 *PC*, 905.

6. A Patchwork of Enemies

1 *PT II.*
2 *PT I.*
3 *PC*, 961.
4 ibid., 967.
5 ibid., 968.
6 *BV*, 219.
7 ibid., 220.
8 ibid., 221.
9 ibid., 227.
10 ibid., 232.
11 ibid., 233.
12 Koser, *Geschichte.*
13 *PC*, 1146.
14 ibid., 1176.
15 ibid., 1202.
16 ibid., 1296.
17 *BV*, 245.
18 ibid., 246.
19 *PC*, 1208.
20 ibid., 1208, fn.
21 ibid., 1300.
22 ibid., 1336.
23 ibid., 1348.
24 ibid., 1341.
25 ibid., 1368.
26 ibid., 1419.
27 ibid., 1370.
28 For example, *PC*, 1390 to Kling-graeffen.
29 ibid., 1373.
30 ibid., 1403.
31 ibid., 1406.
32 ibid., 1443.
33 ibid., 1432.
34 ibid., 1436.
35 ibid.
36 ibid., 1537.
37 ibid., 1437.
38 ibid., 1451.
39 ibid., 1499.
40 ibid., 1454.
41 ibid., 1500.
42 ibid., 1501.
43 ibid., 1519.

7. The Taste of Victory

1 *PC*, 1584.
2 ibid., 1585.
3 ibid., 1596.
4 ibid., 1609.
5 ibid., 1614.
6 ibid., 1615.
7 ibid., 1635.
8 Nicolai, *Anekdoten.*
9 *PC*, 1625.
10 ibid., 1627.
11 ibid., 1657.
12 ibid., 1699.
13 ibid., 1676.
14 ibid., 1693.
15 ibid., 1731.
16 ibid., 1707.
17 ibid., 1826.
18 ibid., 1813.
19 *HMT*, Chapter 14.
20 *Die Kriege Friedrichs des Grossen*, Mittler & Son, Berlin, 1895. This compilation, in many volumes, was produced by the Historical Section of the German Great General Staff and gives the most detailed blow-by-blow account of all Frederick's campaigns and battles, together with superb battle maps and sketches. Henceforth *GGS*.

21 *PC*, 1890.

22 ibid., 1872.

23 ibid., 1874.

24 *BV*, 264.

25 *HMT*.

26 *PC*, 1867.

27 ibid., 1925.

8. The Military Philosopher

1 *PC*, 1982.

2 ibid., 1988.

3 ibid., 1961.

4 ibid., 1967.

5 ibid., 2002.

6 ibid., 2003.

7 ibid., 2008.

8 *Fr*, 2.

9 e.g. *Fr*, 30.

10 *Fr*, 5.

11 *Œuvres* – Book 26, Chapter 1.

12 *PC*, 2035.

13 ibid., 2041.

14 ibid., 2049.

15 ibid., 2098.

16 ibid., 2099.

17 ibid., 2126.

18 ibid., 2125.

19 ibid., 2229.

20 ibid., 2224.

21 ibid., 2228.

22 ibid., 2489.

23 ibid., 2979.

24 ibid., 3097.

25 ibid., 2276.

26 ibid., 2334.

27 ibid., 2345.

28 ibid., 2361.

29 The Emperor Charles VI had in 1734 borrowed, in London, £250,000 at 7 per cent mortgaged on his possessions in Silesia. When Frederick acquired Silesia he had acquired the repayment obligation (capital and interest), of which, in 1752, £45,000 was still due. Frederick had numerous counterbalancing complaints about the actions of British privateers and their seizure of Prussian ships and cargo on the pretext that they were carrying goods to France in time of war between France and Britain, in defiance of established international convention. The arguments, often acrimonious, lasted until the Convention of Westminster between Prussia and Britain in January 1756 which settled the matter by compromise. Frederick had at one point suggested arbitration, which Britain declined. Thirty-three ships (mostly sailing to or from Hamburg) had been affected. Frederick took great interest in the negotiation and in the often disputed interpretations of maritime law. See Sir Ernest Satow, *The Silesian Loan and Frederick the Great*, Clarendon Press, 1915.

30 *PC*, 3050.

31 Karl Schweitzer, *England, Prussia and the Seven Years War*, Edwin Mallen Press, 1989.

32 *PC*, 2978.

33 e.g. ibid., 3099.

34 ibid., 3217.

35 ibid., 3387.

36 ibid., 3762.

37 *Military Instructions from the King of Prussia to his Generals* and *Particular Instructions of the King of Prussia to the Officers of his Army*, trans. T. Foster, published 1797. The *Instructions* were republished in 1936 by the house of E. S. Mittler & Son, Berlin, and include sketches (facsimile) in Frederick's hand of various battle formations. Publication was to mark the 150th anniversary of Frederick's death and was ordered by Adolf Hitler, by then at the head of the German Reich and Wehrmacht.

38 *PT I.*

39 W. von Bremen, *Friedrich der Grosse*, in the series *Erzieher* (teacher) *des Preussischen Heeres*, B. Behr's Verlag, Berlin, 1905. Von Bremen's slender volume summarizes, very clearly and concisely, the core of Frederick's operational doctrine.

40 See Theodor Schieder, *Friedrich der Grosse*, Propylaen Verlag, 1983, for a discussion of this apparent ambivalence.

41 Von Bremen, *Friedrich der Grosse.*

42 Thiebault, *Original Anecdotes.*

9. Sworded Aesthete

1 *HMT*, Book IV, Chapter I.
2 Thiebault, *Original Anecdotes.*
3 *HMT.*
4 Hildebrandt, *Anekdoten.*
5 ibid.

6 Thiebault, *Original Anecdotes.*
7 See Walther Hubatsch, *Frederick the Great of Prussia*, Thames & Hudson, London, 1975, for an account of the system.
8 *PT I.*
9 For a late comment see Sir Andrew Mitchell (an admirer of Frederick but sceptical of some of the Helvetius schemes, characterized as 'wild'), *Memoirs of Sir Andrew Mitchell*, ed. Andrew Bisset, Chapman & Hall, 1850.
10 *PC*, 4331.
11 Thiebault, *Original Anecdotes.*
12 Nicolai, *Anekdoten.*
13 ibid.
14 ibid.
15 ibid.
16 ibid.
17 e.g. *PC*, 4816.
18 Nicolai, *Anekdoten.*
19 Quoted by Gooch, *Frederick the Great.*
20 *Fr*, various.
21 Mitchell, *Memoirs.*
22 *Memoirs of Henri de Catt*, trans. F. S. Flint, Constable, 1916. De Catt accepted the position of confidential secretary (*Vorleser*) in 1757 and joined Frederick at Breslau in March 1758 after the King's greatest victory.
23 Thiebault, *Original Anecdotes.*
24 Nicolai, *Anekdoten.*
25 *PC*, 5109.
26 ibid., 5071.
27 ibid., 5014.
28 Mitchell, *Memoirs.*
29 *PC*, 4234.

30 ibid., 5919.

31 ibid., 4675.

32 ibid., 4183.

33 ibid., 2160.

34 Carlyle, *Life of Frederick II.*

10. Penalties of Prominence

1 *BV*, 267.

2 ibid., 282.

3 ibid., 289.

4 ibid., 296.

5 ibid., 301.

6 *PC*, 4206.

7 *BV*, 315.

8 ibid., 323.

9 ibid., 366.

10 ibid., 378.

11 ibid., 389.

12 *BMG*, 2.

13 Thiebault, *Original Anecdotes.*

14 *BV*, 388.

15 ibid., 397.

16 *PC*, 5850.

17 ibid., 5958.

18 For instance in Stockholm, e.g. *PC*, 6619 – a libel allegedly drawing on the Tyrconnel papers. The Queen of Sweden, Frederick's sister Ulrica, had consulted the Prussian Ambassador who, on Frederick's instructions, advised her to ignore it. Voltaire also produced a *Private Life of the King of Prussia*, anonymously.

19 Voltaire's detailed comments on Frederick's drafts have in some cases been published as *Miscellanies* from the Prussian Royal Archives, notably by Mittler & Son in Berlin in 1878.

20 *Œuvres*, Vol. I.

21 *PC*, 3672.

22 ibid., 4241.

23 ibid., 4431.

24 ibid., 4664.

25 ibid., 4493.

26 ibid., 3583.

27 ibid., 5193.

28 ibid., 4982.

29 ibid., 2789.

30 ibid., 5119.

31 ibid., 4857.

32 ibid., 4829.

33 ibid., 5351.

34 ibid., 5508.

35 ibid., 4579.

36 ibid., 5519.

37 ibid., 5611.

38 ibid., 5702.

39 ibid., 5624.

40 e.g. ibid., 5662.

41 ibid., 5381.

42 ibid., 5240.

43 ibid., 5312.

44 ibid., 3382.

45 *PT I.*

46 *PC*, 3091.

47 ibid., 5315.

48 The dispute about what should be deduced from the *Rêveries politiques* was most famously initiated by Max Lehmann in *Frederick the Great and the Origins of the Seven Years War* in 1894. There was a natural and vigorous response from historians loyal to Frederick's reputation. An excellent commentary on this '*Historikerstreit*' is given in

Erika Bosbach, *Die Rêveries politiques in Friedrichs des Grossen Politischen Testament von 1752*, Bohlau Verlag, Köln, 1960.
49 *PC*, 5783, 5837.
50 ibid., 5908.
51 ibid., 6282.
52 ibid., 4698.
53 ibid., 5970.
54 ibid., 6005.
55 ibid., 6071.
56 ibid., 6274.
57 ibid., 6274.
58 e.g. ibid., 6129.
59 ibid., 6488.
60 ibid., 6496.
61 Nicolai, *Anekdoten*.
62 Von Bremen, *Friedrich der Grosse*.
63 *PC*, 5349.
64 ibid., 5923.
65 ibid., 2612.
66 ibid., 6069.
67 ibid., 6174.

11. Quadrille to Distant Gunfire

1 *PC*, 6478.
2 ibid., 6565.
3 ibid., 6570.
4 ibid., 6606.
5 ibid., 6616.
6 ibid., 6270.
7 ibid., 6720.
8 ibid., 6774.
9 ibid., 6781.
10 ibid., 6745.
11 ibid., 7090.
12 ibid., 6817.
13 De Catt, *Memoirs*.
14 *BMG*, 189.
15 *PC*, 6818.
16 ibid., 6904.
17 ibid., 6906.
18 ibid., 6966.
19 ibid., 7110.
20 Thiebault, *Original Anecdotes*.
21 *PC*, 6942.
22 ibid., 6996.
23 ibid., 6997.
24 ibid., 7015.
25 ibid., 7027.
26 ibid., 7034.
27 ibid., 7056.
28 ibid., 7077.
29 ibid., 7175.
30 Fisher, *History of Europe*.
31 *PC*, 7214.
32 ibid., 7236.
33 ibid., 7258.
34 ibid., 7274.
35 ibid., 7275.
36 ibid., 7255.
37 ibid., 7165.
38 ibid., 7355.
39 ibid., 7402.
40 Mitchell, *Memoirs*.
41 *PC*, 7493.
42 ibid., 7520.
43 ibid., 7621.
44 ibid., 7482.
45 ibid., 7585.
46 ibid., 7643.
47 ibid., 7597.
48 ibid., 7626.
49 ibid., 7622.
50 ibid., 7661.
51 ibid., 7657.

52 Mitchell, *Memoirs*.
53 *PC*, 7758.
54 ibid., 7774.
55 ibid., 7771.
56 ibid., 7795.
57 ibid., 7880.
58 ibid., 7853.
59 ibid., 7841.
60 ibid., 7914.
61 ibid., 7922.
62 ibid., 7930.
63 Max Lehmann, *Frederick the Great*. And see note 48 to Chapter 10 above.
64 *PC*, 7987.

12. Into Hostile Territory

1 *PC*, 7937.
2 ibid., 7938.
3 ibid., 7955.
4 ibid., 8013.
5 ibid., 8054.
6 ibid., 8088.
7 ibid., 8140.
8 ibid., 8088.
9 ibid., 8066.
10 ibid., 8075.
11 ibid., 8124.
12 ibid., 8144.
13 ibid., 8208.
14 ibid., 8146.
15 ibid., 8144.
16 ibid., 8390.
17 ibid., 8312.
18 ibid., 8376.
19 Margaret Goldsmith, *Frederick the Great*, Gollancz, 1929.
20 *PC*, 8175.
21 ibid., 8265.
22 ibid., 8251.
23 ibid., 8481.
24 ibid., 8504.
25 ibid., 8352, 8354, 8415, 8416.
26 See, for instance, ibid., 8617 *et al.*
27 ibid., 8414.
28 ibid., 8619.
29 ibid., 8416.
30 ibid., 8275.
31 ibid., 8529, 8656.
32 ibid., 8286.
33 ibid., 8580.
34 ibid., 8533.
35 ibid., 8529.
36 ibid., 8472.
37 ibid., 8582.
38 ibid., 8631.
39 ibid., 8641.
40 ibid., 8520.
41 Mitchell, *Memoirs*.
42 *PC*, 8793.
43 Rex Whitworth, *William Augustus, Duke of Cumberland*, Leo Cooper, 1992.
44 *PC*, 8751.
45 ibid., 8778.
46 ibid., 8825.
47 ibid., 8818.
48 ibid., 8843.
49 ibid., 8871.
50 ibid., 8846.
51 ibid., 8859.
52 ibid., 8885.
53 Hildebrandt, *Anekdoten*.
54 *PC*, 8908.
55 ibid., 8931.

13. Kolin and After

1 *PC*, 8967.
2 Mitchell, *Memoirs*.
3 *PC*, 9079.
4 ibid., 8998.
5 ibid., 9056.
6 Bartholdy, *Friedrich der Grosse*.
7 *PC*, 9108.
8 ibid., 9125.
9 ibid., 9137.
10 Mitchell, *Memoirs*.
11 *PC*, 9145.
12 ibid., 9155.
13 ibid., 9197.
14 ibid., 9206.
15 ibid., 9214.
16 ibid., 9220.
17 ibid., 9275.
18 ibid., 9291.
19 Lehndorff, *Dreissig Jahre*.
20 *PC*, 9246.
21 De Catt, *Memoirs*.
22 Chester Easum, *Prince Henry of Prussia*, Madison, 1942.
23 *PC*, 10093.
24 De Catt, *Memoirs*.
25 *PC*, 9299.
26 ibid., 9183.
27 ibid., 9272.
28 ibid., 9326.
29 ibid., 9356
30 *HMT*, Chapter 6. Frederick called the seventeen central chapters *Histoire de la guerre de Sept ans*.
31 Lehndorff, *Dreissig Jahre*.
32 *PC*, 9429.
33 ibid., 9388.
34 ibid., 9393.
35 e.g. ibid., 9411.
36 ibid., 9471.
37 ibid., 9474.
38 For analysis of losses see *GGS*, Vol. 5, 'Anlage'.
39 *PC*, 9488.
40 Hildebrandt, *Anekdoten*.
41 *PC*, 9509.
42 ibid., 9497.
43 ibid., 9498.
44 ibid., 9492.
45 ibid., 9496.
46 ibid., 9529.
47 *GGS*, Vol. 6.
48 Bartholdy, *Friedrich der Grosse*.
49 *PC*, 9559.
50 Nicolai, *Anekdoten*.
51 ibid.

14. A Loathsome Trade

1 *PC*, 9574.
2 ibid., 9588.
3 ibid., 9672.
4 ibid., 9599.
5 ibid., 9598.
6 ibid., 9893.
7 ibid., 9600.
8 Mitchell, *Memoirs*.
9 *PC*, 9661.
10 ibid., 9843.
11 ibid., 9679.
12 Mitchell, *Memoirs*.
13 *PC*, 9759.
14 ibid., 9720, 9757.
15 ibid., 9960.
16 ibid., 9909.
17 ibid., 9702.

18 ibid., 9665.
19 ibid., 9799.
20 ibid., 9726.
21 Mitchell, *Memoirs*.
22 *PC*, 9906.
23 De Catt, *Memoirs*.
24 *PC*, 10031.
25 G. B. Malleson, *Loudon*, Chapman & Hall, 1884.
26 Hildebrandt, *Anekdoten*.
27 Koser, *Geschichte*.
28 *PC*, 9834.
29 ibid., 9887.
30 ibid., 10199.
31 De Catt, *Memoirs*.
32 *PC*, 10232.
33 Hildebrandt, *Anekdoten*.
34 De Catt, *Memoirs*.
35 Mitchell, *Memoirs*.
36 *PC*, 10233.
37 *PT II*.
38 *PC*, 10264.
39 ibid., 10289.
40 De Catt, *Memoirs*.
41 ibid.
42 ibid.
43 *PC*, 10400.
44 De Catt, *Memoirs*.
45 Malleson, *Loudon*.
46 Mitchell, *Memoirs*.
47 De Catt, *Memoirs*. De Catt was deeply moved by Frederick's demeanour after Hochkirch.
48 *PC*, 10406.
49 ibid., 10424.
50 ibid., 10427.
51 ibid., 10442.
52 Abbé Denina, writing a concise account of Frederick's reign soon after the King's death and certainly acquainted with most of the anecdotes about him and a good many of the personalities, including Frederick himself, described the pills in the little gold box as Frederick's intended solution to possible *capture* rather than as an escape from despair. See Denina, *Essai*.

15. 'I Am Lost, Prittwitz!'

1 De Catt, *Memoirs*.
2 ibid.
3 *PC*, 10643.
4 ibid., 10835.
5 Mitchell, *Memoirs*.
6 *PC*, 10787/8.
7 Mitchell, *Memoirs*.
8 *PC*, 10759.
9 ibid., 10672.
10 De Catt, *Memoirs*.
11 *PC*, 10964.
12 ibid., 10665.
13 ibid., 11112.
14 ibid., 10695.
15 ibid., 10910.
16 ibid., 10712.
17 ibid., 10764.
18 ibid., 11157.
19 ibid., 11236.
20 ibid., 11227.
21 ibid., 11321.
22 ibid., 11335.
23 ibid., 11345.
24 Hildebrandt, *Anekdoten*.
25 *PC*, 11359.
26 ibid., 11393.
27 ibid., 11506.

28 ibid., 11396.
29 De Catt, *Memoirs*.
30 *PC*, 11545.
31 ibid., 11659.
32 Easum, *Prince Henry*. The murmurings grew louder as the year went on.
33 Mitchell, *Memoirs*.
34 *PC*, 11557.
35 ibid., 11535.
36 ibid., 11593.
37 Easum, *Prince Henry*.
38 Mitchell, *Memoirs*.
39 *PC*, 11617.
40 ibid., 11947.
41 Frederick's correspondence in the first months of 1760 is full of examples of these sentiments, expressed almost daily.
42 *PC*, 11944.
43 ibid., 11794.
44 ibid., 11558.
45 ibid., 11403.
46 De Catt, *Memoirs*.
47 *PC*, 11827.
48 Mitchell, *Memoirs*.
49 *PC*, 11909.
50 ibid., 12174, 12180.
51 ibid., 12209.

16. Confidence Restored

1 *PC*, 12070.
2 ibid., 12166.
3 ibid., 12170.
4 ibid., 12143.
5 ibid., 12082.
6 ibid., 12121.
7 *HMT*, Chapter 12.

8 *PC*, 12303.
9 ibid., 12310.
10 *HMT*, Chapter 12.
11 Mitchell, *Memoirs* (to Holdernesse, 16 August).
12 *PC*, 12321.
13 ibid., 12422.
14 ibid., 12453.
15 ibid., 12441.
16 ibid., 12458.
17 ibid., 12459.
18 ibid., 12490.
19 Quoted by Gooch, *Frederick the Great*.
20 *PC*, 12619, 13189.
21 ibid., 12474.
22 ibid., 12698.
23 ibid., 13189.
24 De Catt, *Memoirs*.
25 *PC*, 12491.
26 ibid., 12609.
27 ibid., 12580.
28 ibid., 12597.
29 ibid., 12687.
30 ibid., 12698.
31 ibid., 12693.
32 ibid., 12781.
33 ibid., 12822.
34 ibid., 12986.
35 ibid., 13018.
36 Mitchell, *Memoirs*.
37 *PC*, 12802.
38 ibid., 12835.
39 ibid., 12921.
40 ibid., 12973.
41 ibid., 12971.
42 ibid., 13142.
43 ibid., 13195.
44 Mitchell, *Memoirs*.
45 ibid., 13332.

46 ibid., 13368.
47 Fisher, *History of Europe.*

17. The Second Miracle

1 *PC*, 13415.
2 ibid., 13466.
3 ibid., 13543.
4 Easum, *Prince Henry.*
5 *PC*, 13657.
6 Schweitzer, *England, Prussia and the Seven Years War.* Details are also given by Schweizer, where the text of the Galitzin dispatch is discussed in a manner showing Bute in a less hostile light (from Frederick's viewpoint).
7 *PC*, 13449.
8 ibid., 13599.
9 ibid., 13492.
10 ibid., 13653.
11 Easum, *Prince Henry.*
12 *PC*, 13793.
13 ibid., 13853.
14 ibid., 13678.
15 ibid., 13732.
16 ibid., 13753.
17 ibid., 13447.
18 ibid., 13518.
19 ibid., 13735.
20 ibid., 13867.
21 ibid., 13868.
22 ibid., 13898.
23 ibid., 13892.
24 ibid., 14010.
25 ibid., 14019.
26 ibid., 14155.
27 ibid., 14120.
28 ibid., 14149.

29 Sir Richard Lodge, *Studies in Eighteenth Century Diplomacy*, John Murray, 1930.
30 *PC*, 14207.
31 ibid., 14246.
32 ibid., 14276.
33 ibid., 14408.
34 ibid., 14417.
35 ibid., 14464.
36 Nicolai, *Anekdoten.*
37 Thiebault, *Original Anecdotes.*

18. Family Circles

1 *PC*, 15234.
2 Hildebrandt, *Anekdoten.*
3 *PC*, 17350.
4 Schieder, *Friedrich der Grosse.*
5 Thiebault, *Original Anecdotes.*
6 ibid.
7 Lehndorff, *Dreissig Jahre.*
8 Robert Asprey, *Frederick the Great. The Magnificent Enigma*, Ticknor & Fields, New York, 1986.
9 *PC*, 14401.
10 ibid., 14559.
11 ibid., 15234.
12 ibid., 16865.
13 ibid., 17315. She was the daughter of August Wilhelm, and Frederick felt periodic uneasiness about his treatment, which some thought cruel, of that prince.
14 ibid., 16669.
15 Thiebault, *Original Anecdotes.*
16 De Catt, *Memoirs.*
17 *PC*, 15472.
18 ibid., 22397.
19 ibid., 16140.

20 ibid., 17058, 17078.
21 Thiebault, *Original Anecdotes*.
22 ibid.
23 *BV*, 451.
24 ibid., 654.
25 *PC*, 16864.
26 Hildebrandt, *Anekdoten*.
27 *PC*, 17516.
28 ibid., 17888.
29 Lehndorff, *Dreissig Jahre*.
30 Nicolai, *Anekdoten*.
31 Schieder, *Friedrich der Grosse*.
32 Thiebault, *Original Anecdotes*.
33 Quoted in T. C. W. Blanning, 'Frederick the Great and Enlightened Absolutism', in H. M. Scott (ed.), *Enlightened Absolutism*, Macmillan, 1990, also on Kant.
34 Nicolai, *Anekdoten*.
35 Thiebault, *Original Anecdotes*.
36 There are over 400 letters to Prince Henry in the *Œuvres* (Vol. 26) as well as many in the *Politische Correspondenz*. The entire correspondence absorbed fifty large volumes of the Prussian State Archive.
37 Thiebault, *Original Anecdotes*.
38 *PC*, 16591.
39 *PT II*.
40 De Catt, *Memoirs*.
41 Hildebrandt, *Anekdoten*.
42 *PC*, 17370.
43 Schieder, *Friedrich der Grosse*.
44 *PC*, 17669.
45 ibid., 17649.
46 ibid., 16432.
47 ibid., 17001.
48 ibid., 17067.
49 ibid., 15726.

50 Harris, *Letters*.
51 *PC*, 17079.
52 ibid., 17188, 17227, 17263.
53 ibid., 16713.
54 ibid., 15951.
55 ibid., 16370.
56 ibid., 16424.
57 ibid., 16584.
58 ibid., 16499.
59 Harris, *Letters*.
60 *PC*, 14665.
61 ibid., 14763.
62 ibid., 14808.
63 ibid., 15240.
64 ibid., 15541.
65 ibid., 15016.
66 ibid., 16195.
67 ibid., 14887.
68 ibid., 15430.
69 ibid., 15828.
70 ibid., 15554.
71 ibid., 15590.
72 ibid., 17114.

19. 'A Very Quarrelsome People'

1 *PC*, 17392.
2 ibid., 16481.
3 ibid., 16053.
4 ibid., 16835.
5 ibid., 17654.
6 ibid., 16815.
7 ibid., 16873.
8 ibid., 17394.
9 ibid., 17407, 17431.
10 ibid., 17453.
11 ibid., 17574.
12 ibid., 17573.

13 ibid., 18562, 18655.
14 Communication, 1st Lord Gladwyn.
15 *PC*, 17556.
16 ibid., 17558.
17 ibid., 17743.
18 ibid., 17786.
19 ibid., 17625.
20 ibid., 17685, 16686.
21 ibid., 15883.
22 ibid., 15668.
23 ibid., 15593.
24 ibid., 15658.
25 ibid., 16690.
26 Thiebault, *Original Anecdotes.*
27 *PC*, 16116.
28 ibid., 16149.
29 ibid., 16132.
30 ibid., 16143.
31 ibid., 16181.
32 ibid., 16622.
33 Thiebault, *Original Anecdotes.*
34 *PC*, 17586.
35 ibid., 17587.
36 Harris, *Letters.*
37 ibid., 17786, 17917.
38 ibid., 18216.
39 ibid., 18050.
40 ibid., 17931.
41 ibid., 17985.
42 ibid., 18003.
43 ibid., 17972.
44 ibid., 17949, 18023.
45 ibid., 17903.
46 ibid., 18036.
47 ibid., 18048.
48 ibid., 18072.
49 ibid., 18193.
50 ibid., 18016.
51 ibid., 18251.

52 ibid., 19004.
53 ibid., 18308.
54 ibid., 18351.
55 ibid., 18357.
56 ibid., 18360.
57 ibid., 18480.
58 ibid., 18388.
59 ibid., 18505.
60 ibid., 18532.
61 ibid., 19012.
62 ibid., 18498.
63 ibid., 18618.
64 ibid., 18674.
65 ibid., 18611.
66 ibid., 18626.
67 ibid., 18579.
68 ibid., 18874.
69 ibid., 18742.
70 ibid., 18858, 18722.
71 ibid., 18995.
72 ibid., 18961, 18982.
73 ibid., 19272.
74 ibid., 19209.
75 ibid., 19245.
76 ibid., 19208.
77 Nicolai, *Anekdoten.*
78 *PC*, 19259.
79 ibid., 19257, 19258.
80 *PC*, 19184.
81 ibid., 19323.
82 ibid., 19276.
83 ibid., 19420.

20. Cutting the Cake

1 *PC*, 19274.
2 ibid., 19568.
3 ibid., 19573.
4 ibid., 19437.

5 ibid., 19608.
6 ibid., 19416.
7 ibid., 19445.
8 ibid., 19615.
9 ibid., 19622.
10 ibid., 19612.
11 ibid., 19515.
12 ibid., 19683.
13 ibid., 19643.
14 ibid., 19670.
15 ibid., 19675.
16 ibid., 19687.
17 ibid., 19716.
18 ibid., 19340.
19 ibid., 19814.
20 ibid., 19851.
21 ibid., 19719.
22 ibid., 19869.
23 ibid., 19981.
24 ibid., 20025.
25 ibid., 20017.
26 ibid., 20099.
27 ibid., 20113.
28 ibid., 20151.
29 ibid., 20169.
30 ibid., 20208.
31 ibid., 20291.
32 ibid., 19399.
33 ibid., 20266.
34 ibid., 20551.
35 ibid., 20188, 20203.
36 ibid., 20217.
37 ibid., 20315.
38 ibid., 20341.
39 ibid., 20536.
40 ibid., 20373.
41 ibid., 20582.
42 ibid., 20591.
43 ibid., 20685.
44 ibid., 20632.

45 ibid., 19331.
46 ibid., 20358.
47 ibid., 19374.
48 ibid., 19716.
49 Harris, *Letters*.
50 *HMT*.
51 *PT II*.
52 *PC*, 21102.
53 ibid., 21528.

21. Relations with an Old Enemy

1 *PC*, 23415.
2 ibid., 24093.
3 ibid., 21988.
4 ibid., 23770.
5 ibid., 21848.
6 ibid., 24729, 24779, 24740.
7 ibid., 24818.
8 ibid., 24910, 24905, 24909.
9 ibid., 24973.
10 Harris, *Letters*.
11 Hildebrandt, *Anekdoten*.
12 Recorded at second hand by Dr Zimmermann: Ritter von Zimmermann, *Uber Friedrich der Grossen und meine Unterredungen mit Ihm*, Leipzig, 1788, and confirmed to him by Marchese Lucchesini.
13 *PC*, 22625.
14 ibid., 18040.
15 ibid., 22398.
16 ibid., 20566.
17 ibid., 20562.
18 ibid., 24700.
19 Lehndorff, *Dreissig Jahre*.
20 *PC*, 21585.
21 ibid., 23490.

22 ibid., 21852.
23 Harris, *Letters*.
24 Gräfin von Hohenthal, *Zeugin einer Zeitenwende*, Degener & Cie, 1997.
25 *PC*, 24120.
26 ibid., 22425.
27 ibid., 23696.
28 ibid., 23787.
29 ibid., 25252.
30 ibid., 25243.
31 ibid., 21468.
32 ibid., 23565.
33 ibid., 23602.
34 ibid., 24120.
35 ibid., 24708.
36 ibid., 24766.
37 ibid., 24335.
38 ibid., 24461.
39 ibid., 25323.
40 ibid., 24553.
41 ibid., 24612.
42 ibid., 25417.
43 ibid., 24786.
44 ibid., 25351.
45 ibid., 25824.
46 ibid., 25424.
47 ibid., 24381.
48 ibid., 25281.
49 ibid., 25545, 25547.
50 ibid., 25617.
51 Thiebault, *Original Anecdotes*.
52 Harris, *Letters*.
53 *PC*, 23735.
54 ibid., 23791.
55 ibid., 24176.
56 ibid., 24127.
57 ibid., 24922.
58 ibid., 24578.
59 ibid., 25008.
60 ibid., 25270.
61 ibid., 25106.
62 ibid., 25655.
63 ibid., 25423.
64 ibid., 17418.
65 ibid., 18349.
66 ibid., 17433, 17442.
67 ibid., 18626.
68 ibid., 17514.
69 ibid., 25013. Claude de Ruhlière.
70 ibid., 25832.
71 ibid., 25866.
72 *HMT*. Final section, Chapter I: *Mémoires de la guerre de 1778*. This section includes, as appendices, Frederick's exchanges with Joseph and Maria Theresa on the Bavarian succession.

22. The Last Campaign

1 *PC*, 25853.
2 ibid., 25900.
3 ibid., 25894.
4 ibid., 25896.
5 ibid., 25837.
6 The exchanges of this time are well summarized in H. Temperley, *Frederick the Great and Kaiser Joseph*, Duckworth, 1915.
7 *PC*, 25959.
8 ibid., 25931.
9 ibid., 25965.
10 ibid., 25966.
11 ibid., 25977.
12 ibid., 25982.
13 ibid., 26011.
14 ibid., 26019.
15 ibid., 26039.

16 ibid., 26674.

17 ibid., 26079.

18 ibid., 26090.

19 HMT, *Mémoires de la guerre de 1778.*

20 PC, 26123.

21 ibid., 26132.

22 ibid., 26234.

23 Bartholdy, *Friedrich der Grosse.*

24 PC, 26244.

25 ibid., 26252.

26 ibid., 26266, 26274.

27 ibid., 26297.

28 ibid., 26309.

29 ibid., 26350.

30 ibid., 26402.

31 ibid., 26398.

32 ibid., 26412.

33 ibid., 26430.

34 ibid., 26447.

35 ibid., 26464.

36 ibid., 26474, 26486.

37 ibid., 26515.

38 ibid., 26549.

39 ibid., 26640.

40 ibid., 26630.

41 ibid., 26629.

42 ibid., 26590.

43 ibid., 26649.

44 ibid., 26600.

45 ibid., 26404.

46 ibid., 26654.

47 ibid., 26661.

48 ibid., 26666.

49 ibid., 26713, 26727, 26732.

50 ibid., 26702.

51 ibid., 26782, 26789.

52 ibid., 26707 et al.

53 ibid., 25736.

54 ibid., 26801.

55 ibid., 26830.

56 ibid., 26847.

57 ibid., 26896.

58 ibid., 26929.

59 ibid., 26950.

60 ibid., 26958.

61 ibid., 26985.

62 ibid., 27021.

63 ibid., 27104.

64 ibid., 27120.

65 ibid., 27170.

66 ibid., 27207.

67 ibid., 27299.

68 ibid., 27319.

23. 'Le Plus Grand Homme'

1 Chief Bailiff Froome. Recorded in P. Paret (ed.), *Frederick the Great*, Macmillan, 1972.

2 PC, 27803.

3 ibid., 27898.

4 ibid., 28091.

5 ibid., 28326.

6 ibid., 28320.

7 ibid., 28128.

8 ibid., 28204/5.

9 ibid., 27811.

10 ibid., 29021.

11 For an extended account of Frederick's cautious dealings with the Americans in rebellion against the British crown and the text of his commercial treaty with the United States, see Friedrich Kapp, *Friedrich der Grosse und die Vereinigten Staaten von Amerika*, Quandt & Handel, Leipzig, 1871, and Marvin L. Brown, *American Independence*

through Prussian Eyes, Duke University Press, Durham, N. Carolina, 1959. Brown gives copious quotations from dispatches between Frederick and his ambassadors on the American negotiations.

12 *PC*, 28645.

13 ibid., 28580.

14 ibid., 28033.

15 ibid., 27958.

16 ibid., 28227.

17 ibid., 28367.

18 ibid., 28368.

19 ibid., 27572.

20 *HMT*, Chapter 6, 'The Seven Years War'.

21 *PC*, 28374.

22 ibid., 28351.

23 ibid., 28442.

24 ibid., 28542.

25 ibid., 28685.

26 ibid., 28729.

27 ibid., 28693.

28 ibid., 29220.

29 ibid., 29224.

30 ibid., 29208.

31 ibid., 29232.

32 ibid., 28814.

33 ibid., 28414.

34 Brown, *American Independence*.

35 *PC*, 29171.

36 Hildebrandt, *Anekdoten*.

37 ibid.

38 Nicolai, *Anekdoten*.

39 The remark was first made (see T. C. W. Blanning in Scott (ed.), *Enlightened Absolutism*) by Georg Heinrich von Berenhorst.

40 Bartholdy, *Friedrich der grosse*.

41 For example, Werner Hegemann, *Frederick the Great*, Constable, 1929. Hegemann, a hostile commentator, composed imaginary conversations drawing on contemporary chronicles with a perceptive, albeit controversial, analysis of Frederick's policies and apologia.

42 *PT I*.

43 *PC*, 18202.

44 ibid., 24978.

45 Carlyle, *Life of Frederick II*.

46 Hildebrandt, *Anekdoten*.

47 Lytton Strachey, *Books and Characters*, Constable, 1922.

48 Nicolai, *Anekdoten*.

49 And has been mocked for its exaggerated tone, even by Carlyle!

Note on Sources

The prime sources for the character and career of Frederick the Great are to be found in his own writings. Perhaps not until the time of Winston Churchill has a man at the heart of great events written so copiously and so elegantly about them. Frederick loved writing. He wrote books, essays, orations, histories. He wrote a great deal of verse – most of it hard to admire. He wrote memoirs – of his family, his kingdom, his campaigns, his reign. He wrote for the most part in very elegant and beautiful French, a language he loved. Relatively few compositions are in German, which he wrote with little style, grammatical skill, or relish. On a few occasions, for a specific reason, he wrote in Latin. He knew no English.

Above all he wrote letters – thousand upon thousand of letters. He wrote many letters almost every day and often to the same recipient several times on the same day; and since he wrote with great spontaneity and frequency his letters serve almost the purpose of a diary, a record of his daily actions, thoughts, fears, hopes. Frederick's letters have been collected in a number of publications and they – together with his other writings, although the latter, being more carefully composed, are often less revealing – are a prime source for this book.

The most comprehensive collected edition of Frederick's works, the *Œuvres*, was edited by J. D. E. Preuss and published by Decker, in Berlin, in 1846. It replaced and largely subsumed a number of earlier editions, of which one had been published as *Œuvres posthumes*, by Voss, in Berlin, in 1788. Preuss aimed to publish Frederick's works in their totality – historic, philosophic and military – as well as much of his verse, and to establish authentic texts; the *Œuvres* includes (in the first volume) Frederick's *History of the House of Brandenburg* and moves (in the second volume) to his own story, his *Histoire de mon Temps*, until the end of the Seven Years War. The third volume of the *Œuvres* takes the reader to the partition of Poland and the war of Bavarian succession (1778), including his correspondence on the subject with Maria Theresa. In an appendix to the third volume are given a number of Frederick's very eloquent funeral orations as well as separate essays on specific subjects – Charles XII of Sweden, German literature and much else. Included is also Frederick's foreword to an edition of Claude Fleury's *Ecclesiastical History* with a characteristic opening sentence:

The establishment of the Christian religion had, like all empires, weak beginnings. A Jew, from insignificant origins, whose birth is questionable, who mingles with the absurdities of ancient Hebrew prophets some sound moral precepts, who had miracles ascribed to him and who ended by being condemned to an ignominious death, is the hero of the Sect.

Preuss produced twenty-six volumes in all, of which the latter contain a great many letters to family, friends, fellow-sovereigns, as well as most of his verse. Also included in the *Œuvres* are Frederick's *General Principles of War* and his writings on political philosophy, sometimes published separately (as was his first complete book, the *Anti-Machiavel*). Also published separately have been the numerous Military Directives: *Particular Instructions of the King of Prussia to the Officers of his Army: Military Instructions from the King of Prussia to his Generals* (not published until after Frederick's death); as well as the *Political Testaments* (1752, 1768 and 1782), in some cases entitled '*Considérations sur l'esprit politique de l'Europe*' (a title he also gave to one of his earliest essays).

There is a great deal of understandable duplication. Separate from the Preuss volumes, however, are a number of important collections of letters (although individual letters may appear in the *Œuvres* as well). Notable collections are the exchanges with Voltaire (*Briefwechsel mit Voltaire*) edited by Koser and Droysen and published in 1908, and those with von Grumbkow, Minister to Frederick's father, and with Maupertuis, President of the Academy of Sciences, also edited by Koser and published in 1898.

But the greatest and most illuminating collection is the *Politische Correspondenz Friedrichs des Grossen*, consisting of about 30,000 letters, numbered serially. It was edited by various hands, notably by G. E. Volz, and published in forty-six volumes by Alexander Duncker over many years in the late nineteenth and early twentieth century. The *Politische Correspondenz* also gives – on frequent and invaluable occasions – the text of the paper or letters to which Frederick was responding, culled in most cases from the Prussian State Archive. It virtually serves as a diary and can be described as indispensable to an understanding of the King's mind and opinions.

Because he wrote mainly in French, Frederick's letters were, naturally, translated into German for publication and some are only accessible in that form. His own letters in German – notably to his father between 1732 and 1738 – were collected and published in Berlin in 1838 (Ernst, Siegried, Mittler). Many of these also appeared in the collections of Gustav Mendelssohn Bartholdy (Munich, 1912), although some of the latter can also be found in the original French in the collections edited by Koser, Droysen and others.

Biography is essentially orientated towards one person; almost by definition it lacks historical balance. It is not history in the broader sense. But no biography should rely excessively on autobiography, in whatever form and however intriguing, and the next sources for Frederick's character and personality can be found in the many contemporary reminiscences of those who spent time at his court or in his family, whether as relatives, employees, protégés or visitors. It is inevitable that anecdotes found their way from one chronicler to another, and the veracity of some has been assessed as a good deal higher than that of others. Implausible gossip has generally been quite easy to spot, even if not already discredited by expert historians; but Frederick was a man of whom everybody talked, and the fact of a story existing often says something about him even where detail may be suspect.

In addition to this primary material Frederick has been the subject of a very large number of critical biographical works, in many countries, inevitably reflecting the times in which the work was penned as well as the temperament and predispositions of the author. These differ greatly as to the picture painted, ranging from the scholarly and comprehensive four volumes by Reinhardt Koser to the famous, if controversial, eight volumes of Thomas Carlyle. Certainly the verdict on Frederick has not simply followed the nationality of the author – many of the more hostile and sceptical works are by German pens, especially when there is any partiality by the author towards Austria.

Many excellent books have specifically covered Frederick's military achievements; and an invaluable work in many volumes commissioned by the German General Staff (*Die Kriege Friedrichs des Grossen*) was published between 1890 and 1914. The General Staff volumes contain admirable maps as well as detailed orders of battle for both the Prussians and their enemies at every stage of the wars, with reflections on the fighting and the generalship, and copious statistics. More recently, and notably, there are the particularly expert books of Christopher Duffy.

I have listed in the following Bibliography most published works consulted, and I acknowledge my debt to authors, living or dead, who have helped me; a debt equally valid whether I have agreed with their conclusions or not.

Bibliography

Anderson, M. S., *The War of Austrian Succession*, Longman, 1995.

Andrews, Stuart, *Enlightened Despotism*, Longman, 1968.

Asprey, Robert, *Frederick the Great. The Magnificent Enigma*, Ticknor & Fields, 1986.

Bartholdy, Gustav Mendelssohn, *Der König*, Munich, 1912.

Bayreuth, Wilhelmina, Margravine of, *Memoirs*, translation, David Stott, 1887.

Berney, Arnold, *Friedrich der Grosse*, Mohr, Tubingen, 1934.

Bosbach, Erika, *Die Rêveries politiques in Friedrichs des Grossen Politischen Testament von 1752*, Bohlau Verlag, Köln, 1960.

Brackenbury, C. B., *Frederick the Great*, Chapman & Hall, 1884.

Bremen, W. von, *Friedrich der Grosse* (in series *Erzieher des Preussischen Heeres*), Behr, 1905.

Broglie, Duc de, *Frederick the Great and Maria Theresa*, translation, Sampson Low, 1883.

Brown, Marvin I., *American Independence through Prussian Eyes*, Duke University Press, 1959.

Carlyle, T., *Frederick the Great*, Chapman & Hall, 1858.

Catt, Henri de, *Memoirs*, trans. F. S. Flint, Constable, 1916.

Craig, G. A., *The Politics of the Prussian Army*, Clarendon Press, 1955.

Cuthill, Edith, *The Scottish Friend of Frederick the Great*, Stanley Paul, 1915.

Davies, Norman, *Europe, a History*, Pimlico, 1997.

Denina, Abbé, *Essai sur la vie et règne de Frédéric II Roi de Prusse*, Jacques Decker, Berlin, 1788.

Droysen, G., *Geschichte der Preussen Politik*, Veit & Co., Leipzig, 1886.

Dubois, Paul, *Frédéric le Grand*, Paris, 1903.

Duffy, C., *Frederick the Great. A Military Life*, Routledge & Kegan Paul, 1985.

——, *The Army of Frederick the Great*, David & Charles, 1974.

Easum, Chester, *Prince Henry of Prussia*, Madison, University of Wisconsin, 1942.

Fisher, H. A. L., *A History of Europe*, Edward Arnold, 1936.

Fraser, Flora, *The Unruly Queen*, Macmillan, 1996.

Fredersdorff, M. G., *Briefe Friedrichs des grossen an seinem vormaligen Kammerdiener Fredersdorff*, Hermann Klemm, 1926.

Gaxotte, Pierre, *Frederick the Great*, translation, G. Bell & Sons, 1941.

German General Staff, *Die Kriege Friedrichs des Grossen*, Mittler & Son, Berlin, 1890–1914.

Goldsmith, Margaret, *Frederick the Great*, Gollancz, 1929.

Gooch, G. P., *Frederick the Great*, Alfred Knopf, 1947.

Goodwin, A., 'The Prussian Nobility', in S. Andrews, *Enlightened Despotism*, Longman, 1968.

Grumbkow, Count, *Briefwechsel mit Grumbkow und Maupertuis*, ed. Hirzel and Koser, from Prussian State Archive, Leipzig, 1898.

Hanbury-Tenison, Richard, *The Hanburys of Monmouthshire*, National Library of Wales, 1995.

Hegemann, Werner, *Frederick the Great*, translation, Constable, 1929.

Henderson, Nicholas, *Prince Eugen of Savoy*, Weidenfeld & Nicolson, 1964.

Henderson, W. G., 'Enlightened Mercantilism in Prussia', in S. Andrews, *Enlightened Despotism*, Longman, 1968.

Herzberg, E. F. von, *Huit Dissertations*, Decker, Berlin, 1787.

Hildebrandt, G., *Anekdoten und Charakterzeuge aus dem Leben Friedrichs des Grossen*, Halberstadt, 1829.

Hintze, Otto, *Die Hohenzollern und ihr Werk*, Berlin, 1915.

Hohenthal, Countess von, *Zeugin einer Zeitenwende*, Degener, 1997.

Horn, D. B., *Frederick the Great and the Rise of Prussia*, English University Press, 1964.

Hubatsch, Walter, *Frederick the Great of Prussia*, translation, Thames & Hudson, 1975.

Hufton, Olwen, *Europe: Privilege and Protest*, Harvester Press, 1980.

Johnson, Hubert C., *Frederick the Great and His Officials*, Yale University Press, 1975.

Kaplan, H. N., 'The First Partition of Poland', in S. Andrews, *Enlightened Despotism*, Longman, 1968.

Kapp, Friedrich, *Friedrich der Grosse und die Vereinigten Staaten von Amerika*, Quandt & Handel, Leipzig, 1871.

Klopp, Anna, *König Friedrich von Preussen und die Deutsche Nation*, Friedrich Hunterschen, 1860.

Knopp, Werner, *In Remembrance of a King*, Bonn, 1986.

Koser, Reinhold, *Geschichte Friedrichs des Grossen*, Stuttgart/Berlin, 1921.

Kugler, Franz, *Geschichte Friedrichs des Grossen*, Weberschen, Leipzig, 1840.

Lavisse, Ernest, *The Youth of Frederick the Great*, translation, Richard Bentley, 1891.

Lehmann, Max, *Frederick the Great and the Origins of the Seven Years War*, 1894.

Lehndorff, Ernst Ahasuerus Heinrich, *Dreissig Jahre am Hofe Friedrichs des Grossen*, Gotha, 1910.

Lodge, Sir R., *Studies in Eighteenth Century Diplomacy*, John Murray, 1930.

Longman, F. W., *Frederick the Great and the Seven Years' War*, Longmans Green, 1881.

Macaulay, Thomas Babington, *Critical and Historical Essays*, 1864.

Macdonogh, Giles, *Frederick the Great*, Weidenfeld & Nicolson, 1999.

Malleson, G. B., *Loudon*, Chapman & Hall, 1884.

Malmesbury, 1st Earl of, *Letters* (ed. 3rd Earl), Richard Bentley, 1870.

——, *Diaries and Correspondence*, Richard Bentley, 1844.

Mann, Thomas, *Frederick and the Great Coalition*, 1914.

Mitchell, Sir Andrew, *Memoirs* (ed. Bisset), Chapman & Hall, 1850.

Mitford, Nancy, *Frederick the Great*, Hamish Hamilton, 1970.

Mittler, Ernst Siegfried, *Letters of Frederick the Great to his Father*, Miller, Berlin, 1838.

——, *Miscellaneen zur Geschichte Königs Friedrichs des Grossen* (from Prussian Royal Archives).

Nicolai, Friedrich, *Anekdoten von König Friedrich II von einigen Personen die um ihn waren*, Berlin, 1788.

Nicolson, Harold, *The Age of Reason*, Constable, 1960.

Palmer, Alan, *Frederick the Great*, Weidenfeld & Nicolson, 1974.

Paret, P. (ed.), *Frederick the Great*, Macmillan, 1972.

Preuss, J. D. E. (ed.), *Œuvres de Frédéric le Grand*, Decker, 1846.

Ranke, Leopold von, *Friedrich der Grosse*, Duncker & Humboldt, 1878.

Raumer, Frederick von, *Frederick II and His Times*, translation, Chas. Knight, 1837.

Reddaway, W. F., *Frederick the Great and the Rise of Prussia*, Putnam, 1904.

Ritter, Gerhard, *Frederick the Great – a Profile*, Eyre & Spottiswoode, 1968.

Satow, Sir Ernest, *The Silesian Loan and Frederick the Great*, Clarendon Press, 1915.

Schieder, Theodor, *Friedrich der Grosse*, Propylaen Verlag, 1983.

Schroeder, Paul, *The Transformation of European Politics, 1763–1848*, Clarendon Press, 1994.

Schweitzer, Karl, *England, Prussia and the Seven Years' War*, Edwin Mallen Press, 1989.

Scott, H. M. (ed.), *Enlightened Absolutism*, Macmillan, 1990.

Showalter, Denis, *The Wars of Frederick the Great*, Longman, 1995.

Simon, Edith, *The Making of Frederick the Great*, Cassell, 1963.

Sorel, A., 'The Eastern Question', in S. Andrews, *Enlightened Despotism*, Longman, 1968.

Strachey, Lytton, *Books and Characters*, Constable, 1922.

——, *Characters and Commentaries*, Chatto & Windus, 1933.

Temperley, A. W. V., *Frederick the Great and Kaiser Joseph*, Duckworth, 1915.

Thiebault, Dieudonné, *Original Anecdotes of Frederick the Great*, translation, London, 1805.

Treitschke, Heinrich von, *German History in the Nineteenth Century*, G. Allen & Unwin, 1915.

Veale, F. J. P., *Frederick the Great*, Hamish Hamilton, 1935.

Voltaire, François Arouet de, *Briefwechsel mit Voltaire*, ed. Kosen and Droysen, 1908.

Whitworth, Rex, *William Augustus, Duke of Cumberland*, Leo Cooper, 1992.

Wiegand, Wilhelm, *Friedrich der Grosse*, Velhagen, Klassing, 1909.

Winter, Georg, *Friedrich der Grosse*, Ernst Hofmann, 1907.

Wright, Constance, *A Royal Affinity*, Frederick Muller, 1967.

Young, Norwood, *The Life of Frederick the Great*, Constable, 1919.

Zimmermann, Ritter von, *Uber Friedrich der Grossen und meine Unterredungen mit Ihm*, Leipzig, 1788.

NOTE: The political correspondence, political testaments and Directives of Frederick II referred to in text notes and in the Note on Sources are not included in the above Bibliography.

Index

Figures in bold indicate maps.

Austria – *cont.*
  loses Silesia 469
  plans to partition Bavaria 569,
    581
  population 231
  Prince Henry on 570
  principle motive of 304
  resurgence of 108
  and Russia 13, 263, 264, 268,
    280, 302, 305–6, 333, 410–14,
    450, 452, 463, 505, 523, 601,
    606–9, 620
  and Russian expansion in the
    Balkans 541
  and Saxony 121, 150, 165, 170,
    288
  self-interested 74
  seriously diminished by the Seven
    Years War 469
  as southern, Catholic, Habsburg
    18
  threatened from all directions
    106
  a traditional ally of Britain 15,
    83, 96, 282, 292, 330, 448
  treasury 114
  treaty of alliance with Britain,
    Holland and Saxony (1745)
    174
  treaty with the Turks (1771) 534,
    568
  tries to target Silesia 380, 411,
    412
  unready for war 71, 96
  at war with Prussia and Saxony
    (1779) 584
  see also Habsburg, House of
Austrian army 132, 336, 404
  advances in Alsace 161, 163, 164
  advances on Berlin 419–20
  advances on Prussia 361

artillery 127, 182, 189, 320, 323,
  328, 352, 401, 402, 443, 533
  guns 438
assembles on the Hungarian
  eastern frontier (1771) 541,
  542, 543
in Bohemia 319, 357, 579, 580
border skirmishes in the War of
  the Bavarian Succession 594
cavalry 89, 91, 93, 94, 117, 178,
  188, 189, 323, 324, 345, 353,
  373, 374, 383, 385, 398, 399,
  401, 403, 404, 418, 434, 443,
  496, 533
  light 587
Charles Emmanuel assists 143
and Chotusitz 116, 117
cowed by the Prussian army 133
cuirassiers 444
ejected from Bavaria 115
enters Bavaria 109, 139, 574
F. on 396
infantry 93, 117, 188, 323, 344,
  352, 373, 399, 403, 418, 434,
  533
Kaiser Regiment 439
marches towards Silesia (May,
  1745) 177
mobilized 302
in Moravia 87, 88, 102, 114, 115,
  579
moves into Upper Silesia
  (December, 1744) 172
occupies Olmütz 115
and the 'Pragmatic Army' 142
reforms 320
retakes Linz 109
retreat towards Prague (1757)
  345
and Russian expansion in the
  Balkans 541

906

ML

7/01